# WITHDRAWN
# Acceptance and Mindfulness in Cognitive Behavior Therapy

## Understanding and Applying the New Therapies

Edited by
James D. Herbert
Evan M. Forman

WILEY

John Wiley & Sons, Inc.

This book is printed on acid-free paper. ∞

For general information on our other products and services please contact our Customer Care Department within the United States at (800) 762-2974, outside the United States at (317) 572-3993, or via fax (317) 572-4002.

Wiley also publishes its books in a variety of electronic formats. Some content that appears in print may not be available in electronic books. For more information about Wiley products, visit our Web site at www.wiley.com.

*Library of Congress Cataloging-in-Publication Data*

Acceptance and mindfulness in cognitive behavior therapy : understanding and applying the
new therapies / edited by James D. Herbert, Evan M. Forman.
    p. ; cm.
  Includes bibliographical references and index.
  ISBN 978-0-470-47441-9 (pbk. : alk. paper); ISBN 978-0-470-91246-1 (ebk); ISBN 978-0-470-91247-8 (ebk);
ISBN 978-0-470-91248-5 (ebk)
  1. Mindfulness-based cognitive therapy. 2. Acceptance and commitment therapy.
I. Herbert, James D., 1962- II. Forman, Evan M.
  [DNLM: 1. Cognitive Therapy--methods. WM 425.5.C6 A1694 2010]
RC489.M55A33 2010
616.89'1425--dc22

                                                                                    2010019064

Printed in the United States of America

10  9  8  7  6  5  4  3  2  1

*To Lynn, Aaron, Elliot, and Joel (JDH)*
*To Emma and Eli (EMF)*

# Contents

# Contributors

Anu Asnaani, MA
Department of Psychology
Boston University
Boston, MA

Aaron T. Beck, MD
Department of Psychiatry
University of Pennsylvania
Philadelphia, PA

Lisa A. Benson, MA
Department of Psychology
University of California at Los Angeles
Los Angeles, CA

Michael J. Bordieri, MA
Department of Psychology
University of Mississippi
Oxford, MS

Andrew Christensen, PhD
Department of Psychology
University of California at Los Angeles
Los Angeles, CA

Gerald C. Davison, PhD
Department of Psychology
University of Southern California
Los Angeles, CA

David J. A. Dozois, PhD
Department of Psychology
University of Western Ontario
London, Ontario
Canada

Samuel J. Dreeben, BA
Department of Psychological and
    Brain Sciences
University of Louisville
Louisville, KY

Jessica J. Flynn, MSc
Department of Psychology
Kent State University
Kent, OH

Maureen K. Flynn, MA
Department of Psychology
University of Mississippi
Oxford, MS

Evan M. Forman, PhD
Department of Psychology
Drexel University, Philadelphia, PA

David M. Fresco, PhD
Department of Psychology
Kent State University
Kent, OH

Marvin R. Goldfried, PhD
Department of Psychology
Stony Brook University
Stony Brook, NY

Julia A. Glombiewski, PhD
Fachbereich Psychologie und Psychotherapie
Philipps-Universität Marburg
Marburg
Germany

Emily A. P. Haigh, PhD
Department of Psychiatry
University of Pennsylvania
Philadelphia, PA

Steven C. Hayes, PhD
Department of Psychology
University of Nevada
Reno, NV

James D. Herbert, PhD
Department of Psychology
Drexel University
Philadelphia, PA

Stefan G. Hofmann, PhD
Department of Psychology
Boston University
Boston, MA

Jonathan Kanter, PhD
Department of Psychology
University of Wisconsin-Milwaukee
Milwaukee, WI

Robert L. Leahy, PhD
American Institute for Cognitive Therapy
New York, NY

Michael Levin, MA
Department of Psychology
University of Nevada
Reno, NV

Nadia N. Lucas, BA
Department of Psychology
University of Mississippi
Oxford, MS

Christopher R. Martell, PhD
Department of Psychiatry and Behavioral
   Sciences
University of Washington
Seattle, WA

Meghan M. McGinn, MA
Department of Psychology
University of California at Los Angeles
Los Angeles, CA

Douglas S. Mennin, PhD
Department of Psychology
Yale University
New Haven, CT

Clive J. Robins, PhD
Department of Psychiatry and Behavioral
   Sciences
Duke University
Durham, NC

M. Zachary Rosenthal, PhD
Department of Psychiatry and Behavioral
   Sciences
Duke University, Durham, NC

Paul Salmon, PhD
Department of Psychological and Brain
   Sciences
University of Louisville
Louisville, KY

Alice T. Sawyer, MA
Department of Psychology
Boston University
Boston, MA

Sandra E. Sephton, PhD
Department of Psychological and Brain
   Sciences
University of Louisville
Louisville, KY

Regan M. Slater, BA
Department of Psychology
University of Mississippi
Oxford, MS

Adrian Wells PhD
Professor of Clinical and Experimental
   Psychopathology
University of Manchester
Manchester
United Kingdom

Kelly G. Wilson, PhD
Department of Psychology
University of Mississippi
Oxford, MS

# Foreword

## ACCEPTANCE AND MINDFULNESS IN COGNITIVE BEHAVIOR THERAPY

It seems that the acceptance and mindfulness concept has suddenly become pervasive in clinical psychology and related fields. Judging from the barrage of flyers I receive each week, it seems that one can hardly buy a psychological book these days without the terms "mindfulness" or "acceptance" in its title. This is especially true of self-help and other psychology trade books.

But the concept is increasingly found also in serious scientific articles and in convention programs, including – and especially! – those of the Association for Behavioral and Cognitive Therapies, a 45-year old organization that eschewed cognitive constructs in its earliest years, defining the field solely in terms of classical and operant conditioning. This is the behavior therapy that I cut my teeth on in the early 1960s, though even back then there were signs that equating behavior therapy with "the conditioning therapies" was unproductively constraining and not reflective of what self-identified behavior therapists actually *did* or even how they *thought about* what they did.

When I was learning behavior therapy and assessment in graduate school from Lazarus, Bandura, and Mischel, there were three kinds of reactions from nonbehavioral colleagues to the sometimes hypomanic pronouncements of the advocates of this "new wave." The first was "You are treating symptoms, not the disorder/disease itself and therefore you are likely to do harm." Or second, "I don't believe your reports of efficacy and effectiveness." Or third, coming from those who believed that the new approach had some promise, "Well, I've been doing 'that' for some time, only using different language to talk about the effectiveness of my ministrations."

I will freely admit that my reactions to the acceptance/mindfulness trend in cognitive behavior therapy often fall into the third category. To be specific, I sometimes find myself believing that the acceptance/mindfulness rhetoric represents less a third wave or new paradigm than it does theoretical and procedural restatements of the thinking and practices of clinicians whose work spans many decades.

For example, Skinner wrote in the 1950s about countercontrol, a theme I myself developed in a 1973 Banff conference, to be greeted by (good-natured?) skepticism bordering on ridicule. And then there is the relaxation training pioneered by Jacobson in the 1920s and adapted by Wolpe and Lazarus decades later as an anti-anxiety "response" for desensitizing maladaptive fear; anyone familiar with teaching this form of self-soothing understands the need to encourage the patient to "go with" the process, accepting and not worrying about new bodily sensations and the wandering of attention. And finally, how different from one another is the tenet in acceptance-based CBT that one can behave differently while accepting inconsistent thoughts (such as "I can't do it"), from the classic Skinnerian focus on changing overt behavior with little, if any, theoretical or procedural attention being paid to internal thoughts and feelings?

What has tended to be neglected in the midst of partisan battles between those who do and those who not see value in the acceptance/mindfulness approaches is a reasoned, scientifically grounded discourse that would help researchers and clinicians alike sort through the various claims and counter-claims. I am pleased to say that this book, skillfully conceived and edited by James Herbert and Evan Forman, provides just such a sober and open-minded appraisal of a trend that has sometimes suffered both from too much hype by its proponents and too sweeping a rejection by some orthodox cognitive (behavior) therapists who sometimes seem more interested in preserving the status quo than endeavoring to advance evidence-based psychosocial therapy both conceptually and procedurally.

You can imagine my pleasure at learning of a book project dedicated to an appraisal of the mindfulness and acceptance trends in cognitive behavior therapy. I was especially cheered knowing that the book is edited by Herbert and Forman, scholars who have taken a serious look at promising developments within the tradition of CBT without getting carried away with them. They have assembled some of the best and most creative thinkers on the topic in this lively and engaging volume.

The book begins with an introductory chapter by Herbert and Forman that reviews the explosive increase in interest in the concepts of psychological acceptance and mindfulness within CBT. The editors nicely lay out various clinical and theoretical questions that these developments raise and the conflicts that they have provoked within the field. Although clearly sympathetic to these new developments, the editors are careful not to take sides in these debates, leaving the subsequent chapters to speak for themselves.

What follows are a series of chapters on the major contemporary models of CBT. Although traditional perspectives such as cognitive therapy are represented, the focus is primarily on the various novel acceptance-based models. These chapters are written by the leading experts on each model. Each chapter not only describes the model in question but focuses on how it addresses key questions, including the role of direct cognitive change strategies, the role of mindfulness and acceptance, and the scientific status of both its clinical outcomes and theoretical processes.

The second section of the book consists of three chapters that take a broader, more integrative perspective on the various issues raised by the earlier chapters. The first, by proponents of traditional cognitive therapy, addresses these developments from that perspective. The second, by proponents of acceptance-based therapy, likewise provides an analysis from that point of view. Finally, my friend and colleague Marv Goldfried sums up and analyzes the dialogue with insights as a pioneering cognitive behavior therapist that sees values in ideas and practices that go beyond even expanded definitions of CBT.

Is the mindfulness and acceptance trend just old wine in new bottles? If you believe this to be the case, consider that the container that wine sits in can affect the experience of the drink. There's a reason one wouldn't imbibe an Opus One red wine directly from the bottle.

*Gerald C. Davison, PhD*
University of Southern California

# PART I

# New Developments in the Behavior Therapy Tradition

## Perspectives on Mindfulness and Psychological Acceptance

# 1

## The Evolution of Cognitive Behavior Therapy

### The Rise of Psychological Acceptance and Mindfulness

JAMES D. HERBERT AND EVAN M. FORMAN

So it is too that in the eyes of the world it is dangerous to venture. And why? Because one may lose. But not to venture is shrewd. And yet, by not venturing, it is so dreadfully easy to lose that which it would be difficult to lose in even the most venturesome venture, and in any case never so easily, so completely as if it were nothing...one's self.

—Kierkegaard, *The Sickness Unto Death* (1849)

Cognitive behavior therapy (CBT) has now become the dominant force in psychotherapy in much of the world, including North America, the United Kingdom, much of Europe, and increasingly throughout Asia and Latin America. The rise of CBT is due to the confluence of several factors, primary among which is the increased focus on evidence-based practice and associated calls for accountability in the delivery of behavioral health services (Baker, McFall, & Shoham, 2009). Throughout its history, CBT has been committed to a scientific perspective to the study of psychopathology and its treatment. Hundreds of studies have evaluated various cognitive behavioral theories of psychopathology, and hundreds more have assessed the efficacy of CBT interventions. This scientific literature has placed CBT in a unique position to dominate the field of psychotherapy.

This extraordinary growth immediately raises the question: What exactly is CBT? Does the term refer to a specific model of psychopathology or psychotherapy? Or perhaps to a domain of treatment, either in terms of targeted processes or pathologies? In fact, the term CBT has become so broad as to defy clear definition. The Web site of the Association for Advancement of Behavioral and Cognitive Therapies, the premier multidisciplinary, international organization devoted to CBT, avoids a specific definition of the term, instead describing the organization's mission as "the advancement of a scientific approach to the understanding and amelioration of problems of the human condition." Various theories, principles, models, and techniques fall under the general rubric of CBT, and these approaches have been applied to the full range of human experience, from the assessment and treatment of severe psychopathology and profound developmental delays to primary prevention efforts to enhancing peak performance among athletes. CBT has become largely synonymous with empirically supported, evidence-based psychological theories and technologies aimed at improving the human condition (Wittchen & Gloster, 2009).

Despite this broad plurality, some features are common to the various CBT approaches. For example, CBT therapists tend to focus primarily on the present rather than the past, to emphasize parsimony in theoretical explanations, to use learning principles (including principles related to how we interpret the world and/or how we relate to our own experience), and to espouse epistemological empiricism. In fact, the term is perhaps most useful as a way of contrasting what CBT *is not* rather than what *it is*. For example, CBT does not encompass psychotherapies that focus primarily on the supposed curative properties of insight into intrapsychic conflicts rooted in historical developmental events, nor those that posit that a supportive therapeutic relationship alone is sufficient for fundamental change of difficult problems. Although this broad perspective on the discipline can be frustrating to scholars who seek clear categories to demarcate schools of psychotherapy, it has the advantage of fostering a dynamic exchange of perspectives within a broad marketplace of ideas.

Like all scientifically-based disciplines, CBT is not static, but continuously evolving. Established theories and technologies continuously and inevitably give rise to new developments. There is a general recognition that current technologies are imperfect, awaiting refinement or even radical new developments, and that even our best current theories are incomplete or even "wrong," although we do not yet know precisely how. This progressive, natural evolution is evident today in the dramatic rise of theories and associated assessment, treatment, and prevention technologies that highlight psychological acceptance and mindfulness. The past decade has witnessed a veritable explosion in interest in these concepts by CBT scholars and practitioners alike, and theoretical formulations and intervention techniques targeting mindfulness and acceptance figure prominently in several novel models of CBT. While building on the foundation of traditional approaches to CBT, these developments have taken the field in new, exciting, and sometimes surprising directions.

## ACCEPTANCE AND MINDFULNESS IN CONTEXT

These developments have not been without controversy, however. The most contentious issues center on the degree to which they are truly novel, and whether or not they add incremental value to more traditional CBT models. Although acknowledging their roots in earlier models, some proponents of acceptance-based approaches view them as paradigmatically distinct from earlier, established forms of CBT.

Hayes (2004) proposes that the history of CBT can be divided into three overlapping but distinct generations. The first generation, commencing with the groundbreaking work of Skinner (1953), Wolpe (1958), and Eysenck (1952), spanned the 1950s and into the 1960s, and developed largely in reaction to the perceived weaknesses of psychoanalytic theory and therapy. The approach was based on carefully delineated learning principles, many of which were developed and refined through experimental work with animals, and there were close connections between basic scientific developments derived from the laboratory and applied technologies. The focus was on behavior modification using techniques derived from classical and operant conditioning principles.

According to Hayes, the second generation, beginning in the late 1960s and continuing through the 1990s, highlighted the importance of language and cognition in the development and treatment of psychopathology. The emphasis shifted toward exploration of the ways in which one's interpretations of the world, and especially the interpretation of emotionally relevant situations, shapes experience. Groundbreaking developments included Ellis' (1962) rational emotive behavior therapy, and Beck and colleagues' cognitive therapy (CT; Beck, Rush, Shaw, & Emery, 1979). Although still committed to a scientific perspective, the focus of research shifted from the development and applied translation of basic psychological principles to clinical trials evaluating the efficacy of multicomponent treatment programs. Although the concept of psychological acceptance occasionally figured in cognitive models, especially with respect to anxiety disorders, it played a relatively minor and secondary role with respect to direct cognitive restructuring (Dozois & Beck, this volume).

According to Hayes' analysis, the third generation of CBT began in the 1990s and reflects the emphasis of psychological acceptance and mindfulness principles in CBT. Like second-generation perspectives, third-generation approaches acknowledge the importance of cognitive and verbal processes in theories of psychopathology and its treatment. Rather than striving to change one's distressing thoughts and feelings, however, third-generation approaches focus instead on cultivating an attitude of nonjudgmental acceptance of the full range of experience to enhance psychological well-being. In addition, while not abandoning clinical trials, the third generation of CBT has seen a renewed interest in the field's traditional emphasis on links between basic theoretical principles and applied technologies.

Many CBT scholars, especially those interested in mindfulness and acceptance-based approaches, find Hayes' historical description to be a useful heuristic (e.g., Eifert & Forsyth, 2005). Others, however, believe that this analysis overstates the distinctiveness of these new developments relative to established theories and technologies (Arch & Craske, 2008; Hofmann & Asmundson, in press, 2008; Leahy, 2008). While acknowledging the increased interest in, and possible clinical utility of, acceptance and mindfulness techniques, these critics believe that they are not fundamentally distinct from existing approaches, especially at the theoretical level. Some of these scholars prefer the metaphor of a branching tree, with new developments deriving from older ones (Hofmann, 2010), or a stream, growing ever stronger and picking up stones as it flows downhill (Martell, 2008), rather than the metaphor of evolving generations. Another metaphor, that of three "waves," has generated especially heated rhetoric, with manuscripts espousing a revolutionary "third wave" (Hayes, 2004) and others ridiculing the term and suggesting the newer approaches are "old hat" (Hofmann & Asmunsdon, 2008). Such debates may be useful to the extent that they highlight specific issues that merit clarification. However, they are unlikely to be resolved anytime soon.

It is important to keep in mind that Hayes' analysis is not intended to represent "truth," but rather is a historical narrative aimed at illuminating broad trends in the field. The ultimate fate of this analysis cannot be determined immediately, and must await the judgment of historians. It is unwise to place too much stock in demarcations of historical periods that include contemporary events. A certain temporal distance from the developments in question often affords a less biased perspective that is more likely to stand the test of time. Thus, heated arguments over the validity of a particular narrative that includes current developments are premature.

Despite differing perspectives on this issue, there are two general points of agreement. First, it is undeniable that the past decade has witnessed a rapid increase in interest, among scientists, scholars, and clinicians alike, in acceptance and mindfulness–based theories and clinical approaches. For example, although the first major publication on acceptance and commitment therapy (ACT) only occurred in 1999 (Hayes, Strosahl, & Wilson, 1999), by the beginning of 2010 the electronic psychological index *PsycInfo* listed over 363 scholarly papers with the keywords "acceptance and commitment therapy." Similarly, mindfulness-based cognitive therapy's first *PsycInfo* listing is in 2000, and a recent search produced 150 references. Similar growth in the professional literature has occurred with other acceptance-based models, such as dialectical behavior therapy (DBT) and mindfulness-based stress reduction (MBSR). Second, as noted above, the term CBT does not represent a specific theoretical or therapeutic model, but rather a broad family of theories and interventions that includes both traditional as well as acceptance-based models alike (Forman & Herbert, 2009). Although some scholars use the term CBT interchangeably with CT (e.g., Hofmann & Asmundson, 2008), most recognize that CBT encompasses a wide range of approaches. Thus, contrasting "CBT" with a specific therapeutic model such as CT, ACT, or DBT (Linehan, 1993) represents a category error, analogous to comparing "trees" with "oaks." Instead, meaningful comparisons require juxtaposing specific models within the broad CBT family.

## HISTORICAL ROOTS OF PSYCHOLOGICAL ACCEPTANCE AND MINDFULNESS

Although the concepts of psychological acceptance and mindfulness have increasingly captured the attention of psychologists in recent years, they have deep historical roots, both in psychology itself and more broadly in both Eastern and Western cultural traditions (Williams & Lynn, in press). Current conceptualizations of mindfulness tend to trace their origins to Buddhist traditions, which are themselves rooted in earlier Hindu beliefs and practices. A central tenant of Buddhism is that human suffering is the result of desiring "that which is not," that is, an attachment to specific material objects and states of mind that cannot always be present. As all things are transient, such attachment results in suffering. Contemplative meditative practices are undertaken to reduce this suffering and to achieve spiritual enlightenment. The impact of language in shaping perceptions is recognized, as is the tendency to confuse conceptual understanding with direct experience. Buddhist epistemology tends toward pragmatism, with the focus on spiritual enlightenment. Ethical concerns are also central to Buddhist traditions. Virtuous behavior, or *Śila*, is determined by the intentions behind actions rather than their outward appearances. These intentions drive one's *Karma*, or the force that determines happiness, spiritual enlightenment, and the process of reincarnation. Buddhism stresses the "Middle Way," or the importance of moderation between extremes of self-indulgence and self-deprivation. As discussed below, many of these Buddhist ideas are reflected to varying degrees in modern acceptance-based models of CBT (Kumar, 2002).

Although the concepts of psychological acceptance and mindfulness are typically traced to ancient Asian philosophies, it should be acknowledged that such concepts have also featured prominently in Western culture. Various Hellenic philosophies, such as Stoicism, stressed the virtue of fostering acceptance of distressing experiences (Williams & Lynn, in press). Later, monastic Christian practices renounced earthly attachments and stressed the acceptance of human suffering as a necessary condition of its amelioration.

Despite the increased interest in the concepts of psychological acceptance and mindfulness among psychologists over the past two decades, these notions have in fact figured in the psychological literature for over a century. Williams and Lynn (in press) trace the concept of acceptance across 20th-century psychology, beginning with the writings of Freud (1910/1965), who noted that clinging to past painful experiences precludes attention to real and immediate concerns. Subsequent psychoanalysts viewed acceptance of the self as a primary goal of psychoanalysis, setting the stage for self-acceptance to become a central theme in psychotherapy in subsequent decades. The 1940s saw the groundbreaking work of Carl Rogers (1940), who viewed self-acceptance as closely associated with mental health and as the primary target of psychotherapy. For Rogers, self-acceptance went beyond simple cultivation of self-esteem to include acceptance of the totality of one's experience. The decades of the 1950s and 1960s witnessed the beginning of the empirical study of psychological acceptance. Several studies documented the relationship between positive self-acceptance and acceptance of others, as well as negative correlations between self-acceptance and psychopathology (e.g., Berger, 1955). During the 1970s, relationships between self-acceptance and other concepts were explored, including locus of control (e.g., Chandler, 1976). In addition, scholars began discussing notions of acceptance beyond the domains of "self" and "other." The 1980s saw continued exploration of the association of various concepts with self-acceptance, as well as early developments of interventions targeting psychological acceptance, such as Morita therapy (Ishiyama, 1987).

The 1990s was a pivotal decade for research and theoretical developments related to psychological acceptance. Most noteworthy was the gradual shift in focus from self-acceptance to the acceptance of one's ongoing subjective experience, and especially distressing experience, often referred to as psychological or "experiential" acceptance. This shift reflected in part growing recognition of the problematic conceptual overlap of self-acceptance with self-esteem. Unlike self-esteem, and echoing Rogers' (1940) earlier work, experiential acceptance refers to accepting the totality of one's experience regardless of its emotional valence. In addition, a number of psychotherapy models based in the CBT tradition and that highlighted experiential acceptance as a key tool were initially developed during this period.

# CONTEMPORARY CONCEPTUALIZATIONS OF ACCEPTANCE, MINDFULNESS, AND RELATED CONSTRUCTS

The growth in interest in acceptance and mindfulness has been accompanied by a proliferation of interrelated concepts and terms, and consensus has yet to emerge as to their precise definitions and their relationships with one another. These terms include mindfulness, psychological (or experiential) acceptance (and its antonym experiential avoidance), metacognitive awareness, distancing, decentering, re-perceiving, defusion, willingness, nonattachment, nonjudgment, and distress tolerance. Some of these concepts (e.g., mindfulness, acceptance) are used within a number of distinct theories and therapy models, whereas others (e.g., defusion, metacognitive awareness) are limited to a specific theory. For more widely used terms such as mindfulness, there are theory-specific nuances in meaning that can only be fully appreciated by a thorough understanding of the respective models. Nevertheless, a general understanding of these terms and their overlapping meanings is possible even without delving into the subtleties of the various theories.

## Mindfulness

By far the most frequently cited definition of mindfulness was offered by Kabat-Zinn (1994), as "paying attention in a particular way: on purpose, in the present moment, and nonjudgmentally" (p. 4). This definition highlights the original Buddhist focus on "bare attention," or the nondiscursive attention to the ongoing stream of consciousness without evaluation or judgment. In an effort to achieve greater clarity and consensus on the concept, Bishop and colleagues held a series of meetings among experts in the field, and concluded on an operational definition that stressed sustained attention to present experience, and an attitude of openness and curiosity, along with nonjudgmental acceptance toward that experience. Indeed, most definitions of the concept include these two factors of heightened awareness of one's subjective experience and nonjudgmental acceptance of that experience. This led Herbert and Cardaciotto (2005) to suggest that mindfulness be conceptualized as comprised of two distinct factors: "(a) enhanced awareness of the full range of present experience, and (b) an attitude of nonjudgmental acceptance of that experience" (p. 198). Cardaciotto, Herbert, Forman, Moitra, and Farrow (2008) subsequently developed the Philadelphia Mindfulness Scale (PHLMS) to assess these two dimensions. They presented psychometric data supporting the distinctiveness of the two aspects of mindfulness. Other common mindfulness scales include additional factors. For example, the Kentucky Inventory of Mindfulness Skills (Baer, Smith, & Allen, 2004), the Five-Factor Mindfulness Scale (Baer, Smith, Hopkins, Krietemeyer, & Toney, 2006), and the Cognitive and Affective Mindfulness Scale-Revised (Feldman,

Hayes, Kumar, Greeson, & Laurenceau, 2007) each include four or five components, further deconstructing the concepts of awareness and acceptance.

There are two key unresolved issues in relation to mindfulness. The first concerns how many constituents or dimensions are necessary to best capture the construct, and how these dimensions relate to one another. One perspective is that mindfulness is best considered a unitary construct. Brown and Ryan (2003, 2004) argue that there is no need to distinguish the acceptance and awareness components of mindfulness, because the latter necessarily subsumes the former. There are both conceptual and empirical grounds to question this claim, however. First, one can easily imagine situations of heightened awareness that occur in the absence of a nonjudgmental, accepting attitude. Panic disorder, for example, appears involve a heightened awareness of physiological cues but without concurrent acceptance of one's experience (e.g., Ehlers & Breuer, 1992, 1996).

Even if one concedes that awareness and acceptance are best thought of as distinct constructs, consensus has yet to emerge on how they are related to one another. A popular view is that awareness is a prerequisite to acceptance (Linehan, 1994). This position is consistent with approaches that emphasize mindfulness meditation as a clinical tool (e.g., MBSR, MBCT [mindfulness-based cognitive therapy]). Even in ACT, moment-to-moment awareness is a key intervention target. However, it is not clear that enhanced awareness is necessary for enhanced acceptance, or even if it is generally beneficial. One can imagine situations in which awareness is attenuated, but when distressing experiences do intrude on consciousness they are accepted nonjudgmentally and without struggle. For example, Csikszentmihalyi (1990) describes the state of "flow," in which one becomes so highly absorbed in a valued activity that awareness of other stimuli, both internal and external, is reduced. In the case of ACT, the emphasis on enhanced awareness derives from the goal of fostering sensitivity to prevailing environmental contingencies rather than dominance of behavior by verbal rules. However, conscious awareness is not necessary in order for behavior to be responsive to ongoing environmental contexts, and in fact it is possible that, at least in some contexts, attempts to increase awareness may paradoxically reduce such sensitivity. In addition, there are empirical grounds to question the value of awareness. As mentioned, Cardaciotto et al. (2008) found that the two subscales of the PHLMS (measuring awareness and acceptance, respectively) were not correlated with one another, and evidenced distinct associations with other measures; subsequent data have confirmed these findings (Herbert et al., 2010). In these studies, psychological acceptance has emerged as strongly associated with psychopathology and changes in acceptance have predicted therapeutic gains, but this has not been the case with awareness. Moreover, under certain conditions, increased awareness of subjective experience has been found to be associated with increased anger and hostility (Ayduk, Mischel, & Downey, 2002), increased pain intensity (Miron, Duncan, & Bushnell, 1989; Roelofs, Peters, Patijn, Schouten, & Vlaeyen, 2004) and increased pain-related disability (McCracken, 1997).

As mentioned, some theorists have deconstructed mindfulness into as many as five separate factors. Whereas some empirical support exists for four- and five-factor structures, there is also evidence that these factors overlap problematically (Baer et al., 2006), calling into question their conceptual distinctiveness and clinical utility. Clearly, the relationship between the constituents of mindfulness awaits further theoretical and empirical work.

The second unresolved issue with respect to mindfulness is how best to incorporate attentional processes in the concept. Although attention and awareness may at first glance appear synonymous, there are, in fact, subtle but important distinctions between them. Attention implies an effortful focus on a restricted range of experience, increasing awareness to some stimuli while de-emphasizing or even avoiding others. In contrast, awareness, at least in the context of mindfulness, suggests a conscious perception of the totality of experience without attempts to focus exclusively on some stimuli at the expense of others. Many discussions of mindfulness conflate these two concepts, perhaps due to the association of mindfulness as a psychological construct with the practice of concentrative meditation, which aims to foster focused attention. Some authors suggest, however, that any effort to regulate attention is inconsistent with thoroughgoing acceptance of the full-range experience (Cardaciotto et al., 2008; Brown & Ryan, 2004). Moreover, repeated findings that the awareness dimension of mindfulness is less or even inversely related to health challenge our current conceptualization (e.g., Baer et al., 2006; Forman, Herbert, et al., 2007; Cardaciotto et al., 2008). Thus, there may be advantages in respecifying the awareness aspect of mindfulness, for instance, without reference to focused attention. Nevertheless, the relationship between acceptance, awareness, attention, and perhaps other possible constituents of the mindfulness concept await further consensus.

## Decentering and Defusion

According to Beck, achieving a certain distance from one's cognitions is the first step in cognitive restructuring. Beck views such distancing as necessary but not sufficient for cognitive restructuring (Dozois & Beck, this volume). Several acceptance-based therapies, MBCT and ACT most prominently, have further developed the construct and place increased emphasis on it as a therapeutic strategy in its own right. These approaches use the terms decentering and defusion to refer to the process of experiencing subjective events, and thoughts in particular, from a certain psychological distance as mere mental events, rather than as reflections on the world or the self (Fresco et al., 2007; Hayes et al., 1999). The socially anxious person contemplating initiating a conversation with a stranger may have anticipatory thoughts such as "I'm going to make a fool of myself." A decentered or defused perspective would entail noticing the thought as a string of words (or sounds), without judging one way or another its truth value. For example, instead of becoming distressed at the thought, the individual might instead think, "that's interesting; I see that I'm having the thought that I'll make a fool of myself." Additionally, there is emphasis on the recognition that one can disentangle the process of having a thought from one's behavior. Thus, the socially anxious person can approach and begin a conversation with a stranger while simultaneously having the thought "I shouldn't talk to him; I'll just end up humiliating myself."

Although distancing and defusion often connote a degree of nonjudgmental acceptance of experience, the terms reflect more the noticing of one's experience from a detached distance rather than acceptance of that experience. In CT, for example, one learns to see one's thoughts from a distance not in order to accept them, but for the purpose of examining their truth value or functional significance as the first step of cognitive restructuring.

## Metacognition

Closely associated with the concepts of mindfulness, distancing, and defusion is the notion of metacognition or metacognitive awareness. This term is used in modern CBT models derived from cognitive theories. At its most basic, metacognition refers to knowledge of one's own cognitive processes (Flavell, 1976). As used in the CBT literature, the term refers a detached awareness of one's cognitions, in which they are noticed but experienced merely as mental events rather than as reflections of reality. The concept of metacognition plays a central role in two contemporary models of CBT: Segal, Williams, and Teasdale's (2001) mindfulness-based cognitive therapy, and Wells's (2000, 2008) metacognitive therapy. Although these models differ in important ways, they share an emphasis on the cultivation of a detached awareness of one's cognitive processes, and interventions aimed at changing beliefs about the role of cognition with respect to emotion and behavior rather than interventions targeting specific thoughts themselves.

In a series of studies, Teasdale and colleagues explored the relationship between metacognitive awareness and depression using a procedure known as the Measure of Awareness and Coping in Autobiographical Memory (MACAM). The MACAM is an interviewer-based measure designed to assess one's reactions to mildly depressive situations, by coding the degree to which these are described from a more detached, mindful perspective. Teasdale et al. (2002) found that currently asymptomatic individuals with a history of depression had lower levels of metacognitive awareness relative to never-depressed controls, and that lower levels of metacognitive awareness predicted higher relapse in patients with major depressive disorder. Based on these findings, Segal, Williams, and Teasdale (2001) developed mindfulness-based cognitive therapy (MBCT) for depression to target metacognitive awareness. Several studies support the efficacy of MBCT for preventing depressive relapse (Bondolfi et al., in press; Kuyken et al., 2008; Ma & Teasdale, 2004; Teasdale et al., 2002; Teasdale, Segal, & Williams, 2003), and an emerging literature supports the approach as a treatment for current depression (e.g., Barnhofer et al., 2009).

Another novel cognitive approach is metacognitive theory (Wells & Matthews, 1994), and its associated intervention model, metacognitive therapy (Wells, 2000, 2008). According to metacognitive theory, most negative thoughts and emotions are transient experiences that need not be problematic. In some individuals, however, even relatively minor negative thoughts or feelings trigger a pattern of rumination and worry, which in turn interferes with the self-regulation of one's internal experience. Once triggered, this rumination leads to increased emotional arousal, which in turn heightens further rumination, in a vicious cycle. This process is thought to be driven by metacognitive factors, which refer to executive cognitive processes that monitor and control thinking. Metacognition is divided into positive metacognitive beliefs, which reflect the presumed benefits of sustained threat monitoring, worry, and thought suppression, and negative metacognitive beliefs, which reflect beliefs about the uncontrollability of experience and the danger of certain thoughts. Both positive and negative metacognitive beliefs are thought to contribute to the initiation and maintenance of rumination. Psychopathology is viewed as the result of biases in metacognitive beliefs, rather than as the result of specific negative thoughts. Metacognitive therapy was developed to correct these biased metacognitive beliefs in order to restore better control over cognitive processes. Importantly, metacognitive therapy holds that such change will not take place by directly questioning automatic thoughts, but rather requires modification of metacognitive beliefs that control cognition itself. This is accomplished by interventions such as postponing worry to a specific and limited time of day, behavioral experiments, attentional training, paradoxical rumination prescription, and promoting states of detached mindfulness (Wells et al., 2009).

## Psychological Acceptance

Finally, there are a group of terms that suggest an open, nonjudgmental perspective on the totality of one's experience, and in particular the ongoing stream of present-moment experience. Such a perspective is reflected in the terms psychological acceptance and experiential acceptance. Butler and Ciarrochi (2007) define acceptance as "a willingness to experience psychological events (thoughts, feelings, memories) without having to avoid them or let them unduly influence behavior" (p. 608). Writing from a behavior analytic perspective, Cordova (2001) defines acceptance as "allowing, tolerating, embracing, experiencing, or making contact with a source of stimulation that previously provoked escape, avoidance, or aggression" (p. 215). Cordova also emphasizes that movement from avoidance to acceptance involves a change in the *function* of behavior, i.e., from escape to engagement. Kollman, Brown, and Barlow (2009) define acceptance as "a willingness to fully experience internal events, such as thoughts, feelings, memories, and physiological reactions." Williams and Lynn (in press) offer the definition: "the capacity to remain available to present experience, without attempting to terminate the painful or prolong the pleasant" (p. 7). These definitions all point to the open, nonjudgmental embracing of the totality of experience, as distinct from the acceptance of external situations that may provoke distress. For example, a person with a phobia can accept sensations of anxiety prompted by a phobic situation without accepting the situation itself, or the idea that he or she cannot approach it. In addition, the Williams and Lynn description highlights the critical—but often overlooked—point that psychological acceptance refers not only to the willingness to experience distressing experiences, but also the willingness to abandon efforts to hold on too tightly to positive experiences.

Another key aspect of psychological acceptance within CBT is that it is viewed as a means to an end, rather than an end in and of itself. CBT models that emphasize the fostering of acceptance do so in the service of larger goals, typically involving concrete behavior change. The depressed woman who has thoughts of helplessness and hopelessness is encouraged to accept those thoughts as mere mental events while simultaneously engaging in goal-oriented behaviors such as getting out of bed and going to lunch with a friend. In this sense, modern psychological conceptualizations of acceptance differ from those situated within philosophical or religious traditions, in that the latter emphasize the importance of acceptance for its own sake rather than as a tool to foster movement toward other life goals (Herbert, Forman, & England, 2009).

The distinction between the traditional concept of acceptance derived from ancient traditions and the modern psychological version is exemplified in a recent study examining the construct validity of acceptance. Kollman, Brown, and Barlow (2009) examined psychological acceptance in relation to two similar constructs: *cognitive reappraisal*, defined as "a form of cognitive change that involves construing a potentially emotion-eliciting situation in a way that changes its emotional impact" (Gross & John, 2003, p. 349, as cited in Kollman et al., 2009, p. 206), and *perceived emotional control*, defined as "perceived behavioral or indirect control over internal events, or the extent to which people believe they can continue to act in valued directions and meet life challenges regardless of their internal experiences" (Kollman et al., 2009, p. 207). The results of the study were mixed; on the one hand, analyses supported the convergent and discriminant validity of acceptance relative to both of the other constructs. On the other hand, acceptance was not associated with other predicted constructs of worry, social interaction anxiety, and well-being, whereas both cognitive reappraisal and perceived emotional control were. However, examination of the specific items the authors used to define the three constructs reveals that their "acceptance" items refer to "pure" acceptance, without any link to goal-directed actions. This use of the term reflects the ancient perspective described above. In contrast, their "perceived emotional control" items do not, in fact, reflect the ability to control one's emotions as the name implies, but rather reflect the concept of psychological acceptance as it is commonly used in acceptance-based CBTs, that is, as the ability to engage in purposeful behavior without needing to alter one's distressing experiences. Examples of these items include "I can perform effectively while having negative thoughts; I am able to deal with challenges when I'm anxious; I can handle my work or school obligations when feeling negative emotions." Thus, despite the problematic way in which the scales were labeled, these results suggest, not surprisingly, that the ability to behave effectively while simultaneously embracing distressing thoughts and feelings is correlated with relevant psychological constructs more than "pure" acceptance detached from behavior. In keeping with their roots in the behavior therapy tradition, acceptance-based CBTs therefore seek to cultivate psychological acceptance as a way of fostering behavior change and improving the human condition.

## CHARACTERISTICS OF ACCEPTANCE-BASED MODELS OF CBT

The ideas that thoughts and beliefs lead directly to feelings and behavior, and that to change one's maladaptive behavior and subjective sense of well-being one must first change one's cognitions, are central themes of Western folk psychology. We encourage friends to "look on the bright side" of difficult situations in order to improve their distress. We seek to cultivate "positive attitudes" in our children in the belief that this will lead to better academic or athletic performance. Traditional cognitively oriented models of CBT (e.g., CT, stress inoculation training, and rational emotive behavior therapy) build on these culturally sanctioned ideas by describing causal effects of cognitions on affect and behavior, and by interventions targeting distorted, dysfunctional, or otherwise maladaptive cognitions.

In contrast, a central feature of acceptance-based CBT models is the decoupling of subjective experience from overt behavior. That is, cognitions and other subjective experiences are not viewed as necessarily causally linked to behavior, and one can learn to behave in ways that are inconsistent with what would normally be expected based on one's cognitive or affective state. The emphasis is on changing the *relationship* between cognitions and behavior rather than changing the *content* of the cognitions themselves. It should be noted that this characteristic of acceptance-based approaches is a matter of emphasis, and not of definition. As discussed further below, cognitively oriented approaches sometimes emphasize acceptance rather than change of distressing cognitions, and acceptance-based approaches sometimes permit direct efforts to modify one's experience. Nevertheless, the respective approaches clearly differ in the degree of emphasis they place on acceptance versus change of subjective experience in the service of larger goals.

Like all forms of CBT, the various acceptance-based models are all committed to quantitative, empirical evaluation of therapeutic procedures and their associated theories. This scientific emphasis sometimes surprises certain clinicians and patients alike, who are initially drawn to acceptance- and mindfulness-based approaches because of their perceived "new age," "alternative," or even "mystical" qualities, but who do not share the core scientific values characteristic of the field of CBT. As one example, we have personally witnessed the shock among a number of clinicians who had enthusiastically embraced ACT, upon learning that the approach is grounded in functional contextualism, a modern philosophy derived from Skinner's radical behaviorism. Although the term mindfulness in particular has recently become a buzzword of popular psychology, its use (as well as the use of similar terms) in the approaches described in this volume is distinguished by a firm grounding in scientific theory and research. Despite their differences, all of the approaches reviewed herein share a common commitment to science.

Another feature of most acceptance-based CBTs is their de-emphasis of the putative historical roots of problems. Historical narratives are viewed as constructions that may or may not be accurate, and even if accurate, their exploration is viewed as neither necessary nor sufficient for therapeutic gains. In fact, focusing on a historical narrative may serve to crystallize it as a central part of one's identity, thereby reducing one's flexibility to behave in different, more adaptive ways.

Although they share an emphasis on mindfulness and acceptance processes and a de-emphasis on direct cognitive or affective control strategies, the various acceptance-oriented models of CBT derive from different theoretical streams, resulting in differences in basic assumptions, theoretical terms, and assessment and intervention techniques. For example, mindfulness-based stress reduction (Kabat-Zinn, 1990, 2003) developed largely outside of the CBT tradition as an approach to assist patients with chronic medical conditions. In contrast, a number of approaches were derived from earlier, traditional streams of CBT, and CT in particular. These include mindfulness-based cognitive therapy (Segal et al., 2001), metacognitive therapy (Wells, 2000, 2008), panic control treatment (Barlow & Craske, 2006), exposure and ritual prevention (Foa et al., 2005; Kozak & Foa, 1997), various exposure-based interventions (e.g., Marks, 1981), cognitive processing therapy (Resick & Schnicke, 1992, 1996), schema therapy (Young, Klosko, & Weishaar, 2003), and emotional schema therapy (Leahy, 2002). Reflecting their roots in traditional CBT, a characteristic of these approaches is that they often blend cognitive change strategies characteristic of CT with mindfulness and acceptance principles and interventions. Still other approaches have roots in the behavior analytic tradition; these include functional analytic psychotherapy (Kohlenberg & Tsai, 1991), behavioral activation therapy (Martell, Addis, & Jacobson, 2001), relapse prevention (Marlatt, Barrett, & Daley, 1999; Marlatt & Gordon, 1985), integrative behavioral couple therapy (Christensen, Jacobson, & Babcock, 1995; Jacobson & Christensen, 1996), and ACT (Hayes, Strosahl, & Wilson, 1999). These approaches tend to de-emphasize direct cognitive or affective change strategies in favor of more thoroughgoing cultivation of psychological defusion and acceptance. Each of these approaches is unique, and some represent general models of psychotherapy whereas others focus on a particular population or condition.

The various acceptance-based CBTs have profited from a free exchange of techniques. For example, the practice of formal mindfulness meditation, which was originally popularized by Kabat-Zinn in MBSR, has been adopted by a number of other models, including DBT and MBCT. Even traditional cognitive therapists working within the tradition of Beck's CT acknowledge the value of techniques aimed at fostering mindfulness and acceptance (Dozois & Beck, this volume). Where controversy has developed between the various perspectives, it has focused on two themes. First, as discussed above, there is the issue of whether these developments represent mere extensions of earlier models or more radical departures from them. Second, there is discord over the causal status of cognitions. Approaches derived from traditional streams of CBT retain an emphasis on cognitive causation, although they focus more on beliefs about the role of thoughts (e.g., metacognition) rather than automatic thoughts per se. In contrast, approaches rooted in behavior analysis, while acknowledging the importance of language and cognition in understanding and treating psychopathology, view cognition itself as a form of behavior, and focus on contextual control of the relationship between cognition, emotion, and overt behavior.

From this perspective, cognitions can participate in causal chains, but are not granted full causal status with respect to other behaviors. This tension has sometimes resulted in each camp presenting data that they believe support their perspective and that refute the position of the opposing camp, only to be met with bewilderment when the other side remains unmoved. For example, proponents of behavioral activation point to the results of component control studies of CT, in which behavioral activation or exposure alone is compared to behavioral activation (or exposure) plus cognitive restructuring. The majority of these studies have failed to demonstrate incremental effects of cognitive restructuring strategies (Dimidjian et al., 2006; Gortner, Gollan, Dobson, & Jacobson, 1998; Hope, Heimberg, & Bruch, 1995; Jacobson et al., 1996; Zettle & Hayes, 1987; see Longmore & Worrell, 2007, for a review). Cognitive theorists retort that such studies do not bear on the issue of cognitive causation, because even putatively "behavioral" interventions like behavioral activation can, and almost certainly do, produce cognitive changes, which remain the presumed proximal causes of therapeutic gains (Hofmann, 2008; Hofmann & Asmundson, 2008). Similarly, proponents of ACT have accumulated a substantial body of research demonstrating that psychological acceptance mediates therapeutic gains, which they view as supporting their contextual theory of cognition (Hayes, Levin, Plumb, Boulanger, & Pistorello, in press). They are sometimes surprised when cognitive theorists are unimpressed, insisting that these measures of acceptance are simply proxies for belief changes.

What the parties to these debates may be failing to appreciate is that the various perspectives are deeply rooted in distinct philosophical traditions and corresponding theoretical principles, and that differences among these philosophies and theories cannot be directly resolved through data. Cognitively oriented theorists are able to explain virtually any imaginable results produced by behavior analysts as deriving from some form of cognitive change. A change in experiential acceptance, for example, can be conceptualized as reflecting a shift in beliefs (or metacognition) about the truth or dangerousness of a specific class of thoughts. Conversely, behavior-analytically oriented theorists can explain findings supporting cognitive mediation as reflecting changes in derived stimulus functions. Thus, it will be impossible to design a definitive empirical test that will pit the two perspectives against one another in order to resolve which is more accurate or useful.

This does not mean, however, that the two perspectives are equally valid, or that these issues are doomed to remain unresolved. Modern philosophers and historians of science note that competing theories (and even more so their philosophical underpinnings) cannot be directly resolved through data (Kuhn, 1970). Rather, the theory that ultimately prevails will be the one that makes risky predictions that are then confirmed by data, especially predictions that have both high precision and broad scope (Herbert & Forman, in press). In contrast to such progressive theories, regressive theories make few novel and risky predications, insulate core concepts from falsification, and are left to offer post hoc explanations for new findings. It is too early to tell how the cognitive and the behavior analytic perspectives will fare in this regard, although some early signs raise concerns about the cognitive perspective. For example, upon publication of a component control study of CT by Dimidjian and colleagues (2006) that found no incremental effects of cognitive restructuring over behavioral activation alone for depression, the listserv for the Academy of Cognitive Therapy (a leading organization of cognitive therapists) erupted with posts dismissive of the findings. These posts centered either on the idea that behavioral activation must necessarily have resulted in cognitive change, which in turn produced the reductions in depression, or focused on methodological limitations of the study. Yet it is doubtful that many champions of CT would have predicted the results a priori, and it seems clear that few would have honed in on perceived methodological weaknesses had the results turned out differently. Had the results demonstrated incremental effects of cognitive restructuring, the study would have been heralded as a breakthrough by cognitive therapists. The reaction to this landmark study would appear to represent an example of regressive, post hoc theorizing. Although all theories rely at times on post hoc hypotheses to explain away inconvenient results, overreliance on such tactics at the expense of theory development is a sign of a theory in retreat. Of course, this one example does not mean that the cognitive perspective is doomed. Rather, it points to the importance of theories evolving with data if they are to stay relevant; more critically, it illustrates the kinds of factors that ultimately resolve tensions between competing theories.

## UNRESOLVED ISSUES WITH REGARD TO COGNITIVE CHANGE STRATEGIES

A host of unresolved questions surround the use of cognitive change strategies such as cognitive disputation and restructuring. First, the expected pattern of evidence supporting cognitive change as a key mediator of CBT effectiveness has not materialized (Longmore & Worrell, 2007). For instance, in the majority of studies examining the question, changes in dysfunctional thoughts do not reliably predict improvements in outcome variables. Moreover, improvements in dysfunctional thinking tend to be equivalent whether someone is treated with CT or with a pharmaceutical agent. However, some cognitive therapists have pointed out that a set of studies supporting cognitive mediation do exist (Hofmann & Asmundson, 2008). Others have asserted that cognitive change in response to pharmaceuticals is to be expected, given that cognition is part of the psychobiological system (Beck, 1984). Still others assert that cognitive change can be a mediator of CT in one study and an outcome of pharmacotherapy in another (DeRubeis et al., 1990). Potentially even more challenging to CT is the fact that a number of component analysis trials have found that adding cognitive change components to behavioral treatments produces no benefit and in some cases may even reduce effectiveness (Forman & Herbert, 2009). A counterargument is that the experiences resulting from "behavioral" interventions (e.g., exposure and behavioral activation) are almost certain to produce cognitive change. However, even if it were demonstrated that cognitive change is an important mediator of improvement, these component analysis studies beg the question of whether cognitive change *interventions* are necessary or advisable. After all, it is quite possible that treatments without cognitive change strategies may be more efficient, easier for patients to understand, easier for therapists to master, and/or easier to disseminate.

In addition to these questions stemming from empirical findings, some intriguing issues exist regarding each treatment's theoretical stance with respect to cognitive change strategies. Traditional CBT approaches regard cognitive change strategies as the bread and butter of treatment. However, CT cautions against direct attempts to "control" thinking (Alford & Beck, 1997), and strategies such as thought stopping have been discredited and are not part of mainstream CT. It is also true that CT conceives of cognitive change quite broadly. For example, one of the most common reminders to patients in CT is "just because you had a thought does not make it true," which is closer to constructs like cognitive defusion than to a direct attempt to change the content of the thought. Similarly, although a staple CT strategy concerns helping patients question the accuracy of their thoughts, a secondary strategy revolves around challenging the *usefulness* of thoughts.

As described above, metacognitive approaches take an even more nuanced view on cognitive change strategies. These approaches hold that thoughts that occur in the moment and provoke affective and physiological reactions (i.e., automatic thoughts) are *not* amenable to direct modification efforts, whereas beliefs about these thoughts (i.e., metacogniton, such as about the usefulness of worry) are responsive to cognitive restructuring (Wells, 2008; Teasdale, Moore, et al., 2002). Yet little if any direct empirical evidence exists to support the assertion that cognitive change strategies are more effective with certain types of cognitions than others. (Data showing that metacognitive interventions that target second-order—but not first-order—cognitions produce benefit can only be regarded as indirect support.)

ACT for its part is openly skeptical about any direct cognitive change strategies out of concern that they would lead to further elaboration of and entanglement with problematic cognitions, will drain resources away from more valued pursuits, and, like other forms of experiential control, are likely to fail, especially when the "stakes" are highest (Ciarrochi & Robb, 2005; Hayes, 2005; Hayes et al., 1999). On the other hand, ACT's fundamental pragmatism allows for cognitive (and other) change strategies to the extent they are effective and do not come with undue costs.

Such theoretical suppositions again demand both further theoretical specification and evidence that is not (yet) forthcoming. Under what circumstances is it useful to attempt to restructure thoughts, and when is it not? For example, surely it would be unwise for a middle-aged man who suddenly experiences shortness of breath and chest pains simply to accept these sensations without efforts to evaluate whether they may be signs of acute heart disease. On the other hand, targeting acceptance may indeed be appropriate for the same individual if he has been medically cleared and experiences these sensations regularly. Although some guidelines have been suggested to clarify when acceptance strategies are indicated (e.g., Farmer & Chapman, 2008; Herbert et al., 2009), further work is needed in this area. Additionally, what empirical findings would (and currently do) support contentions that cognitive change strategies are often psychologically problematic? Thus, many questions related to the use of cognitive change strategies are unanswered.

A related set of questions surrounds the role of psychological interventions in facilitating behavioral change. Although we have good reason to believe that behavioral strategies such as behavioral activation and exposure are among the most potent interventions in the CBT arsenal, it is not clear how we can best help patients make the necessary behavior changes. Any experienced clinician recognizes that one cannot simply prescribe behavioral activation or exposure in the same way one can prescribe a medication. Much work remains to be done in developing the most effective means of targeting such processes, especially when doing so provokes highly distressing thoughts and feelings.

Another unresolved issue is the role that component analysis studies ought to play in helping to revise current intervention technologies. Borkovec and Sibrava (2005) make a strong case that additive component control designs should be the methodology of choice because of their powerful ability to reveal cause-effect relationships, and therefore the active ingredients of psychotherapy. As discussed above, extant component control trials raise the possibility that the cognitive change components of CT are not active ingredients and should be abandoned. A good argument could be made that similar designs should be applied to acceptance-based treatment packages. Results may well indicate that many or even all of the nonbehavioral aspects of these treatments are superfluous. For all of the methodological elegance of additive designs, however, their interpretation is often not clear. First, the most dramatic findings concern a null result (i.e., that treatment component A is equivalent in effectiveness to treatment components A plus B), but the interpretation of null results should not take place without sufficiently large sample sizes and specialized statistical analyses. Also, some treatment components may be effective in one context and but not others. For example, it is possible that cognitive change components that target metacognitions may substantially add to the effectiveness of behavioral interventions, whereas cognitive change components that target automatic, first-order cognitions may not. Also possible is that an initial dose of cognitive restructuring is highly effective at establishing that a belief or set of beliefs (e.g., catastrophic misinterpretations of panic symptoms) is distorted, but further restructuring interventions add nothing to the treatment (whereas perhaps behavioral and/or acceptance-based strategies do). These types of questions are not addressed by current component analyses. Finally, using component control studies to deconstruct established multicomponent packages is far less efficient than using additive designs to test the incremental effects of treatment components in earlier stages of treatment development.

## FUTURE DIRECTIONS

Regardless of exactly how one situates these new developments, there can be no doubt that the growth of interest in acceptance and mindfulness over the past two decades has dramatically altered the field of CBT, and currently represents a major focus of theoretical development, clinical innovation, scientific research, and dissemination efforts. The initial resistance to these concepts within the field has now faded. Instead, psychologists are increasingly focusing less on the degree to which these approaches represent paradigmatic breaks with prior models, and more on substantive theoretical and empirical issues.

Several challenges lie ahead. First, there has been a proliferation of interrelated theoretical terms and concepts, which contributes to confusion. Some of these (e.g., cognitive defusion) derive from specific theories and have specific meanings within that theory, but nevertheless overlap significantly with similar concepts derived from other theories. In other cases, there are concepts shared by more than one theory (e.g., metacognition), but that have different meanings within each. Finally, there are broad concepts such as "mindfulness" that are borrowed from prescientific traditions and consequently are used quite differently by various theorists. Although it is unrealistic to expect widespread consensus across theorists on the precise meaning of these terms any time soon, it is incumbent on scholars to be as clear and precise as possible with respect to terminology.

Second, there is a need for creative technological innovations. There appears to be value in ideas such as seeing one's experience from a psychological distance; fully embracing distressing thoughts, feelings, sensations, and memories; avoiding excessive attachment to one's personal narrative; and decoupling subjective experience from overt behavior. However, these ideas are all counterintuitive and difficult to realize. Although many creative strategies have been developed, there remains much room for innovation.

A related issue is the need for clinical innovations to be firmly tied to testable theories, which are themselves subjected to empirical evaluation. As the father of modern social psychology Kurt Lewin noted, "there is nothing so practical as a good theory" (Lewin, 1951, p. 169). The new acceptance and mindfulness-based models of CBT vary in the degree to which they grounded in well-developed theories. Although an absence of close ties between theory and technology does not necessarily preclude the value of a technological innovation, such developments are most likely to make a lasting contribution when linked to a viable underlying theory.

A fourth challenge is the need for more research, including clinical outcome trials, treatment process studies, additive component analysis trials, and related theoretical studies of psychopathology and intervention models. There has been an explosion of relatively small-scale studies over the past decade, and larger, more methodologically sophisticated studies are now clearly warranted. Studies addressing important questions such as how and when to use cognitive change strategies would be particularly welcome. Challenges in securing funding for such studies remain, however, perhaps owing to the lingering association of concepts such as mindfulness with nonscientific, "new age" beliefs and practices. On a related theme, even clinical scientists themselves sometimes become overly wedded to particular concepts, terms, and procedures. We should not assume that "mindfulness," for example, is a sacred concept that cannot be deconstructed scientifically, nor that fostering the various aspects of mindfulness will necessarily always be beneficial. We cannot assume that meditative practices are uniformly helpful. These are questions to be studied, rather than foregone conclusions.

A related issue is the importance of ensuring that all of these new developments remain firmly grounded in science. Mindfulness-based therapies have tended to attract two types of followers: scientifically oriented theorists, researchers, and clinicians working at the cutting edge of new developments in CBT on the one hand, and clinicians and laypeople who are ambivalent—and sometimes even hostile—to a scientific approach to psychotherapy on the other. The latter are often attracted to these approaches due to their perceived status as "alternative" and nontraditional. If these developments are to represent substantive contributions rather than passing fads, they must remain firmly grounded in science.

Finally, there is the important issue of dissemination. Proponents of various acceptance- and mindfulness-based models of CBT have tended to be very active in disseminating their work, both to professionals and to the public at large. These efforts have often proceeded before the scientific status of an intervention for a particular domain has been well established. This is not necessarily as much of a problem for professionals, who at least in principle have the background and skills to interpret the extant state of the literature on behalf of their patients. But dissemination efforts directly targeting the public raise more questions, and consensus has yet to emerge on the most appropriate stage in the treatment development and evaluation process for widespread public dissemination, such as through self-help books (Redding, Herbert, Forman, & Gaudiano, 2008). At a minimum, proponents of CBT, and in particular the newer acceptance-based models of CBT, have an obligation to provide a frank discussion of the scientific status of their particular approach in any dissemination project.

# REFERENCES

Alford, B. A., & Beck, A. T. (1997). *The integrative power of cognitive therapy*. New York: Guilford Press.

Arch, J. J., & Craske, M. G. (2008). Acceptance and commitment therapy and cognitive behavioral therapy for anxiety disorders: Different treatments, similar mechanisms? *Clinical Psychology: Science & Practice, 5*, 263–279.

Ayduk, O., Mischel, W., & Downey, G. (2002). Attentional mechanisms linking rejection to hostile reactivity: The role of "hot" versus "cool" focus. *Psychological Science, 13*, 443–448.

Baer, R. A., Smith, G. T., & Allen, K. B. (2004). Assessment of mindfulness by self-report: The Kentucky inventory of mindfulness skills. *Assessment, 11*, 191–206.

Baer, R. A., Smith, G. T., Hopkins, J., Krietemeyer, J., & Toney, L. (2006). Using self-report assessment methods to explore facets of mindfulness. *Assessment, 13*, 27–45.

Baker, T. B., McFall, R. M., & Shoham, V. (2009). Current status and future prospects of clinical psychology: Toward a scientifically principled approach to mental and behavioral health care. *Psychological Science in the Public Interest, 9*, 67–103.

Barlow, D. H., & Craske, M. G. (2006). *Mastery of your anxiety and panic: Therapists' guide* (4th ed.). New York, NY: Oxford University Press.

Barnhofer, T., Crane, C., Hargus, E., Amarasinghe, M., Winder, R., & Williams, J. M. G. (2009). Mindfulness-based cognitive therapy as a treatment for chronic depression: A preliminary study. *Behaviour Research and Therapy, 47*, 366–373.

Beck, A. T. (1984). Cognition and therapy. *Archives of General Psychiatry, 41*, 1112–1115.

Beck, A. T., Rush, A. J., Shaw, B. F., & Emery, G. (1979). *Cognitive therapy of depression*. New York, NY: Guilford Press.

Berger, E. M. (1955). Relationships among acceptance of self, acceptance of others, and MMPI scores. *Journal of Counseling Psychology, 2*, 279–284.

Bondolfi, G., Jermann, F., Vander Linden, M., Gex-Fabry, M., Bizzini, L, Weber Rouget, B.,...Bertschy, G. (in press). Depression relapse prophylaxis with mindfulness-based cognitive therapy: Replication and extension in the Swiss health care system. *Journal of Affective Disorders*.

Borkovec, T. D., & Sibrava, N. (2005). The use of placebo conditions in therapy outcome research and the pursuit of placebo mechanisms. *Journal of Clinical Psychology (Special Issue), 61*, 805–818.

Brown, K. W., & Ryan, R. M. (2003). The benefits of being present: Mindfulness and its role in psychological well-being. *Journal of Personality and Social Psychology, 84*, 822–848.

Brown, K. W., & Ryan, R. M. (2004). Perils and promise in defining and measuring mindfulness: Observations from experience. *Clinical Psychology: Science and Practice, 11*, 242–248.

Butler, J., & Ciarrochi, J. (2007). Psychological acceptance and quality of life in the elderly. *Quality of Life Research, 16*, 607–615.

Cardaciotto, L., Herbert, J. D., Forman, E. M., Moitra, E., & Farrow, V. (2008). The assessment of present-moment awareness and acceptance: The Philadelphia Mindfulness Scale. *Assessment, 15*, 204–223.

Chandler, T. A. (1976). A note on the relationship of internality-externality, self-acceptance, and self-ideal discrepancies. *Journal of Psychology: Interdisciplinary and Applied, 94*, 145–146.

Christensen, A., Jacobson, N. S., & Babcock, J. C. (1995). Integrative behavioral couple therapy. In N. S. Jacobson & A. S. Gurman (Eds.), *Clinical handbook of couples therapy* (pp. 31–64). New York, NY: Guilford Press.

Ciarrochi, J., & Robb, H. (2005). Letting a little nonverbal air into the room: Insights from acceptance and commitment therapy: Part 2: Applications. *Journal of Rational-Emotive & Cognitive Behavior Therapy, 23*, 107–130.

Cordova, J. V. (2001). Acceptance in behavior therapy: Understanding the process of change. *The Behavior Analyst, 24*, 213–226.

Csikszentmihalyi, M. (1990). *Flow: The psychology of optimal experience*. New York, NY: Harper & Row.

DeRubeis, R. J., Evans, M. D., Hollon, S. D., Garvey, M. J., Grove, W. M., & Tuason, V. B. (1990). How does cognitive therapy work? Cognitive change and symptom change in cognitive therapy and pharmacotherapy for depression. *Journal of Consulting & Clinical Psychology, 58*, 862–869.

Dimidjian, S., Hollon, S. D., Dobson, K. S., Schmaling, K. B., Kohlenberg, R J., Addis, M. E.,...Jacobson, N. S. (2006). Randomized trial of behavioral activation, cognitive therapy, and antidepressant medication in the acute treatment of adults with major depression. *Journal of Consulting & Clinical Psychology, 74*, 658–670.

Dozios, D. J. A., & Beck, A. T. (in press). Cognitive therapy. In J. D. Herbert & E. M. Forman (Eds.), *Acceptance and mindfulness in cognitive behavior therapy*. New York, NY: Wiley.

Ehlers, A., & Breuer, P. (1992). Increased cardiac awareness in panic disorder. *Journal of Abnormal Psychology, 101*, 371–382.

Ehlers, A., & Breuer, P. (1996). How good are patients with panic disorder at perceiving their heartbeats? *Biological Psychology, 42*, 165–182.

Eifert, G. H., & Forsyth, J. P. (2005). *Acceptance and commitment therapy for anxiety disorders: A practitioner's treatment guide to using mindfulness, acceptance, and values-based behavior change strategies*. Oakland, CA: New Harbinger.

Ellis, A. (1962). *Reason and emotion in psychotherapy*. New York, NY: Lyle Stewart.

Eysenck, H. (1952). The effects of psychotherapy: An evaluation. *Journal of Consulting Psychology, 16*, 319–324.

Farmer, R. F., & Chapman, A. L. (2008). *Behavioral interventions in cognitive behavior therapy: Practical guidance for putting theory into action* (Chapter 10). Washington, DC: American Psychological Association.

Feldman, G. C., Hayes, A. M., Kumar, S. M., Greeson, J. M., & Laurenceau, J. P. (2007). Mindfulness and emotion regulation: The development and initial validation of the cognitive and affective mindfulness scale—revised (CAMS-R). *Journal of Psychopathology and Behavioral Assessment, 29*, 177–190.

Flavell, J. H. (1976). Metacognitive aspects of problem solving. In L. B. Resnick (Ed.), *The nature of intelligence* (pp. 231–236). Hillsdale, NJ: Erlbaum.

Foa, E. B., Liebowitz, M. R., Kozak, M. J., Davies, S., Campeas, R., Franklin, M. E., . . . Tu, X. (2005). Randomized, placebo-controlled trial of exposure and ritual prevention, clomipramine, and their combination in the treatment of obsessive-compulsive disorder. *American Journal of Psychiatry, 162,* 151–161.

Forman, E. M., & Herbert, J. D. (2009). New directions in cognitive behavior therapy: Acceptance-based therapies. In W. O'Donohue & J. E. Fisher, (Eds.), *General principles and empirically supported techniques of cognitive behavior therapy* (pp. 102–114). Hoboken, NJ: Wiley.

Forman, E. M., Hebert, J. D., Moitra, E., Yeomans, P. D., & Geller, P. A. (2007). A randomized controlled effectiveness trial of acceptance and commitment therapy and cognitive therapy for anxiety and depression. *Behavior Modification, 31,* 772–799.

Fresco, D. M., Moore, M. T., van Dulmen, M. H. M., Segal, Z. V., Ma, H. S., Teasdale, J. D., & Williams, J. M. G. (2007). Initial psychometric properties of the experiences questionnaire: Validation of a self-report measure of decentering. *Behavior Therapy, 38,* 209–324.

Freud, S. (1965). *Five lectures on psycho-analysis* (J. Strachey, Trans.). New York, NY: W. W. Norton. (Original work published 1910)

Gortner, E. T., Gollan, J. K., Dobson, K. S., & Jacobson, N. S. (1998). Cognitive–behavioral treatment for depression: Relapse prevention. *Journal of Consulting and Clinical Psychology, 66,* 377–384.

Gross, J. J., & John, O. P. (2003). Individual differences in two emotion regulation processes: Implications for affect, relationships, and well-being. *Journal of Personality and Social Psychology, 85,* 348–362.

Hayes, S. C. (2004). Acceptance and commitment therapy, relational frame theory, and the third wave of behavioral and cognitive therapies. *Behavior Therapy, 35,* 639–665.

Hayes, S. C. (2005). Stability and change in cognitive behavior therapy: Considering the implications of ACT and RFT. *Journal of Rational-Emotive & Cognitive Behavior Therapy, 23,* 131–151.

Hayes, S. C., Levin, M., Plumb, J., Boulanger, J., & Pistorello, J. (in press). Acceptance and commitment therapy and contextual behavioral science: Examining the progress of a distinctive model of behavioral and cognitive therapy. *Behavior Therapy.*

Hayes, S. C., Luoma, J. B., Bond, F. W., Masuda, A., & Lillis, J. (2006). Acceptance and commitment therapy: Model, processes and outcomes. *Behaviour Research and Therapy, 44,* 1–25.

Hayes, S. C., Strosahl, K., & Wilson, K. G. (1999). *Acceptance and commitment therapy: An experiential approach to behavior change.* New York, NY: Guilford Press.

Herbert, J. D., & Cardaciotto, L. (2005). A mindfulness and acceptance-based perspective on social anxiety disorder. In S. Orsillo & L. Roemer (Eds.), *Acceptance and mindfulness-based approaches to anxiety: Conceptualization and treatment* (pp. 189–212). New York, NY: Springer.

Herbert, J. D., & Forman, E. M. (in press). Caution: The differences between CT and ACT may be larger (and smaller) than they appear. *Behavior Therapy.*

Herbert, J. D., Forman, E. M., & England, E. L. (2009). Psychological acceptance. In W. O'Donohue & J. E. Fisher, (Eds.), *General principles and empirically supported techniques of cognitive behavior therapy* (pp. 77–101). Hoboken, NJ: Wiley.

Herbert, J. D., Forman, E. M., Yuen E., Goetter, E., England, E., Massey, J., . . . Geboy, A. (2010, November). *Awareness, acceptance, defusion and psychopathology: Implications of recent data on the deconstruction of mindfulness.* Paper to be presented at the meeting of the Association for Behavioral and Cognitive Therapies, San Francisco, CA.

Hofmann, S. G. (2008). Common misconceptions about cognitive mediation of treatment change: A commentary to Longmore and Worrell. *Clinical Psychology Review, 28,* 67–70.

Hofmann, S. G. (2010, March). Cognitive therapy. In K. Salzinger (symposium chair), *Will the real behavior therapy please stand up?* Paper presented at the annual meeting of the Eastern Psychological Association, New York, NY.

Hofmann, S. G., & Amsundson, G. J. (in press). The science of cognitive behavioral therapy. *Behavior Therapy.*

Hofmann, S. G. & Asmundson, G. J. (2008). Acceptance and mindfulness-based therapy: New wave or old hat? *Clinical Psychology Review, 28,* 1–16.

Hope, D. A, Heimberg, R. G., & Bruch, M. A. (1995). Dismantling cognitive-behavioral group therapy for social phobia. *Behaviour Research and Therapy, 33,* 637–650.

Ishiyama, F. I. (1987). Use of Morita therapy in shyness counseling in the west: Promoting clients' self-acceptance and action taking. *Journal of Counseling & Development, 65,* 547–551.

Jacobson, N. S., & Christensen, A. (1996). *Integrative couple therapy: Promoting acceptance and change.* New York: Norton.

Jacobson, N. S., Dobson, K S., Truax, P. A., Addis, M. E., Koerner, K., Gollan, J. K., . . . Prince, S. E. (1996). A component analysis of cognitive-behavioral treatment for depression. *Journal of Consulting and Clinical Psychology, 64,* 295–304.

Kabat-Zinn, J. (1990). *Full catastrophe living: Using the wisdom of your body and mind to face stress, pain, and illness.* New York, NY: Delta.

Kabat-Zinn, J. (1994). *Wherever you go, there you are: Mindfulness meditation in everyday life.* New York, NY: Hyperion.

Kabat-Zinn, J. (2003) Mindfulness-based interventions in context: Past, present and future. *Clinical Psychology: Science and Practice, 10,* 144–156.

Kohlenberg, R., & Tsai, M. (1991). *Functional Analytic Psychotherapy.* New York, NY: Plenum.

Kollman, D. M., Brown, T. A., & Barlow, D. H. (2009). The construct validity of acceptance: A multitrait-multimethod investigation. *Behavior Therapy, 40,* 205–218.

Kozak, M. J., & Foa E. B. (1997). *Mastery of obsessive-compulsive disorder: A cognitive behavioral approach.* San Antonio, Texas: Graywind.

Kuhn, T. A. (1970). *The structure of scientific revolutions* (2nd ed.). Chicago, IL: University of Chicago Press.

Kumar, S. (2002). An introduction to Buddhism for the cognitive behavioral therapist. *Cognitive and Behavioral Practice, 9,* 40–43.

Kuyken, W., Byford, S., Taylor, R. S., Watkins, E., Holden, E., White, K., . . . Teasdale, J. D. (2008). Mindfulness-based cognitive therapy to prevent relapse in recurrent depression. *Journal of Consulting and Clinical Psychology, 76,* 966–978.

Lappalainen, R., Lehtonen, T., Skarp, E., Taubert, E., Ojanen, M., & Hayes, S. C. (2007). The impact of CBT and ACT models using psychology trainee therapists: A preliminary controlled effectiveness trial. *Behavior Modification, 31,* 488–511.

Leahy, R. L. (2002). A model of emotional schemas. *Cognitive and Behavioral Practice, 9,* 177–190.

Leahy, R. L. (2008, Winter). A closer look at ACT. *The Behavior Therapist,* 148–150.

Lewin, K. (1951). *Field theory in social science: Selected theoretical papers.* D. Cartwright (Ed.). New York, NY: Harper & Row.

Linehan, M. M. (1993). *Cognitive-behavioral treatment of borderline personality disorder.* New York: Guilford.

Linehan, M. M. (1994). Acceptance and change: The central dialectic in psychotherapy. In S. C. Hayes, N. S. Jacobson, V. M. Follette, & M. J. Dougher (Eds.), *Acceptance and change: Content and context in psychotherapy* (pp. 13–32). Reno, NV: Context Press.

Longmore, R. J., & Worrell, M. (2007). Do we need to challenge thoughts in cognitive behavior therapy? *Clinical Psychology Review, 27,* 173–187.

Ma, S. H., & Teasdale, J. D. (2004). Mindfulness-based cognitive therapy for depression: Replication and exploration of differential relapse prevention effects. *Journal of Consulting and Clinical Psychology, 72,* 31–40.

Marks, I. M. (1981). *Cure and care of neuroses: Theory and practice of behavioral psychotherapy.* New York, NY: Wiley.

Marlatt, G. A., & Gordon, J. R., (1985). *Relapse prevention: Maintenance strategies in the treatment of addictive behaviors.* New York, NY: Guilford Press.

Marlatt, G. A., Barrett, K., & Daley, D. C. (1999). Relapse prevention. In M. Galanter & H. D. Kleber (Eds.), *The American Psychiatric Press textbook of substance abuse treatment* (2nd ed.) (pp. 353–366). Arlington, VA: American Psychiatric Press.

Martell, C. R. (2008, July). *Twenty years of behavior therapy: Trends and counter-trends.* Address given at the annual convention of the British Association of Behavioural and Cognitive Psychotherapies, Edinburgh, Scotland.

Martell, C. R., Addis, M. E., & Jacobson, N. S. (2001). *Depression in context: Strategies for guided action.* New York, NY: W. W. Norton.

McCracken, L. M. (1997). "Attention" to pain in persons with chronic pain: A behavioral approach. *Behavior Therapy, 28,* 271–284.

Miron, D., Duncan, G. H., & Bushnell, M. C. (1989). Effects of attention on the intensity and unpleasantness of thermal pain. *Pain, 39,* 345–352.

Redding, R. E., Herbert, J. D., Forman, E. M., & Gaudiano, B. A. (2008). Popular self-help books for anxiety, depression and trauma: How scientifically grounded and useful are they? *Professional Psychology: Research and Practice, 39,* 537–545.

Resick, P. A., & Schnicke, M. K. (1992). Cognitive processing therapy for sexual assault survivors. *Journal of Consulting and Clinical Psychology, 60,* 748–756.

Resick, P. A., & Schnicke, M. K. (1996). *Cognitive processing therapy for rape victims: A treatment manual.* Newbury Park, CA: Sage.

Roelofs, J., Peters, M. L., Patijn, J., Schouten, E. G. W., & Vlaeyen, J. W. S. (2004). Electronic diary assessment of pain-related fear, attention to pain, and pain intensity in chronic low back pain patients. *Pain, 112,* 335–342.

Rogers, C. R. (1940). The processes of therapy. *Journal of Consulting Psychology, 4,* 161–164.

Segal, Z. V., Williams, J. M. G., & Teasdale, J. D. (2001). *Mindfulness-based cognitive therapy for depression: A new approach to preventing relapse.* New York, NY: Guilford Press.

Skinner, B. F. (1953). *Science and Human Behavior.* New York: Macmillan.

Teasdale, J. D., Moore, R. G., Hayhurst, H., Pope, M., Williams, S., & Segal, Z. V. (2002). Metacognitive awareness and prevention of relapse in depression: Empirical evidence. *Journal of Consulting and Clinical Psychology, 70,* 275–287.

Teasdale, J. D., Segal, Z. V., & Williams, J. M. G. (2003). Review of mindfulness-based cognitive therapy for depression: A new approach to preventing relapse. *Psychotherapy Research, 13,* 123–125.

Teasdale, J. D., Segal, Z. V., Williams, J. M. G., Ridgeway, V., Soulsby, J. M. & Lau, M. A. (2000). Prevention of relapse/recurrence in major depression by mindfulness-based cognitive therapy. *Journal of Consulting and Clinical Psychology, 68,* 615–623.

Wells, A. (2000). *Emotional disorders and metacognition: Innovative cognitive therapy.* Chichester, UK: Wiley.

Wells, A. (2008). *Metacognitive therapy: A practical guide.* New York, NY: Guilford Press.

Wells, A., Fisher, P., Myers, S., Wheatley, J., Patel, T., & Brewin, C.R. (2009). Metacognitive therapy in recurrent and persistent depression: A multiple-baseline study of a new treatment. *Cognitive Therapy and Research, 33,* 291–300.

Wells, A., & Matthews, G. (1994). *Attention and emotion: A clinical perspective.* Hove, UK: Erlbaum.

Williams, J. C., & Lynn, S. J. (in press). Acceptance: An historical and conceptual review. *Imagination, Cognition, and Personality.*

Wittchen, H. U., & Gloster, A. T. (2009). Developments in the treatment and diagnosis of anxiety disorders. *Psychiatric Clinics of North America, 32,* xiii–xix.

Wolpe, J. (1958). *Psychotherapy by reciprocal inhibition.* Stanford, CA: Stanford University Press.

Young, J. E., Klosko, J. S., & Weishaar, M. E. (2003). *Schema therapy: A practitioner's guide.* New York: Guilford.

Zettle, R. D., & Hayes, S. C. (1987). Component and process analysis of cognitive therapy. *Psychological Reports, 64,* 939–953.

# 2

## Cognitive Therapy

### DAVID J. A. DOZOIS AND AARON T. BECK

$M$ore than 45 years ago, Beck (1963, 1964) introduced his conceptual model of the role of cognition in depression and its treatment. Today, the main tenets of cognitive theory are well-supported by the empirical literature. Moreover, cognitive therapy (and generic cognitive-behavioral therapy) is one of the most actively researched psychotherapies (Butler, Chapman, Forman, & Beck, 2006), is consistently listed among the empirically supported therapies for a host of mental health problems and conditions (Chambless & Ollendick, 2001; DeRubeis & Crits-Christoph, 1998), and is believed to be as effective or superior to other dominant treatments, including antidepressant medication for depression (DeRubeis, Webb, Tang, & Beck, 2010).

This chapter describes cognitive theory and therapy with an emphasis on Beck's cognitive model. We begin by highlighting the main conceptual axioms of the cognitive model and its treatment techniques. Following this overview, we discuss the role that mindfulness- and acceptance-based strategies have played in the development of this model over time. As the reader will discern, our contention is that some notions of acceptance have, for some time, played a role (albeit a minor one relative to direct cognitive change strategies) in cognitive therapy (e.g., Beck, Emery, & Greenberg, 1985). Although mindfulness- and acceptance-based approaches may hold some philosophical assumptions that differ from that of traditional cognitive therapy, these newer forms of therapy are compatible with and complementary to cognitive therapy and represent logical extensions in its evolution (Hofmann, 2008a, Hofmann & Asmundson, 2008). In addition, we argue that achieving awareness and acceptance is only one step towards the crucial change that improves symptoms and well-being, namely cognitive change. The chapter concludes with a review of the empirical evidence of cognitive theory and therapy.

## THE COGNITIVE MODEL OF PSYCHOPATHOLOGY AND TREATMENT

### Cognitive Theory

The original formulation of the model underlying cognitive therapy has its roots in the philosophy of Immanuel Kant (1781/1929), who argued that the mind actively categorizes and organizes information to create representations of the external world. Kant also introduced the concept of schemas and stated that these cognitive templates or "spectacles" filter reality. This thinking was foundational to the development of the cognitive sciences and ultimately to the cognitive psychotherapies (Nevid, 2007). The conceptual foundation of cognitive therapy may also be attributed to the cognitive revolution that took place in psychology during the 1950s and 1960s (Beck, 2005). Particularly influential to cognitive theory were the writings of George Kelly (1955) and Albert Ellis (1962).

In the 1960s, Beck was interested in validating various psychoanalytic concepts to make them more accessible to the scientific community. He made depression the focus of his research. Rather than finding evidence supportive of the psychoanalytic formulation that depression was a result of anger turned inward, Beck instead documented themes of rejection, defeat, deprivation, and sensitivity to failure in the thoughts and dreams of depressed individuals. Beck also noticed that depressed mood was typically preceded by very rapid negative thoughts and that by helping people to become aware of these thoughts, test their validity, and modify unhelpful cognitions, their depression would improve (Beck, 1967, 1976). This research spawned the beginning developments of cognitive therapy (Beck, Rush, Shaw, & Emery, 1979).

Originally developed for the treatment of depression, cognitive therapy has now been applied successfully to a number of psychiatric conditions, including anxiety disorders (Beck et al., 1985), psychosis (Beck, Rector, Stolar, & Grant, 2008), personality disorders (Beck, Freeman, Davis, and Associates, 2004), substance abuse and dependence (Beck, Wright, Newman, & Liese, 1993), bipolar disorder (Basco & Rush, 2005), couples distress (Beck, 1988), and crisis management (Dattilio & Freeman, 1994). Throughout these developments, there has been a consistent emphasis on how unrealistic cognitive appraisals have a negative impact on one's emotions and behaviors.

According to Beck's model (Beck, 1963, 1964, 1967; Beck et al., 1985; Beck et al., 1979; Clark, Beck, & Alford, 1999) the cognitive appraisal of internal or external stimuli influences subsequent emotional states and behavioral repertoires. Specific cognitive models have been developed for various forms of psychopathology, but they typically rely on the basic framework originally proposed by Beck. At a general level, this framework posits a taxonomy of cognition, ranging from "deeper" cognitive structures to more surface-level cognitions (Dozois & Beck, 2008; Garratt, Ingram, Rand, & Sawalani, 2007). Specifically, three main levels of cognition are emphasized in this theory: (a) schemas; (b) information processing and intermediate beliefs (including dysfunctional rules, assumptions, and attitudes); and (c) automatic thoughts.

At the crux of the Beck's cognitive model is the construct of the schema. Schemas have been defined in many different ways, with some researchers emphasizing their content (e.g., core beliefs; Young, Klosko, & Weshaar, 2003) and others focusing on both their propositional and organizational properties (e.g., Dozois, 2007; Dozois et al., 2009; Ingram, Miranda, & Segal, 1998). The notion of a well-organized cognitive structure of stored information and memories that forms the basis of core beliefs about self has long been featured in the cognitive model. Kovacs and Beck (1978), for instance, defined schemas as cognitive structures of organized prior knowledge, abstracted from past experience, that influence the screening, coding, categorization, and assessment of incoming stimuli and the retrieval of stored information.

Schemas are adaptive in the sense that they allow individuals to process information in a highly efficient manner. However, there can also be a "hardening of the categories" (Kelly, 1963) such that assimilation dominates over accommodation (Piaget, 1947; 1950). As such, self-schemas may become negatively biased, maladaptive, rigid, and self-perpetuating.

According to Beck, maladaptive self-schemas develop during early childhood and become increasingly consolidated when subsequent experiences are assimilated (Beck et al., 1979; Kovacs & Beck, 1978). Poor early attachment experiences and other adverse events (e.g., childhood maltreatment) are some of the early predictors of the development of a negative or maladaptive belief system (Lumley & Harkness, 2009; Gibb, Abramson, & Alloy, 2004; Ingram, 2003). The activity of the schema, which may be quiescent for a number of years, is later activated by adverse circumstances (often resembling hardships in childhood, such as loss or rejection). The activated schemas may then bias which information is attended to and encoded and how information is retrieved and interpreted (Beck et al., 1979; Dozois & Beck, 2008).

Schemas have often been discussed in the literature as though they are synonymous with dysfunctional beliefs, underlying assumptions or even core beliefs. Theoretical revisions and empirical research have contributed to a clearer differentiation of these constructs (Beck, 1996; Dozois & Dobson, 2001b; Ingram et al., 1998; Teasdale, 1996). Ingram et al. (1998), for example, argued that the schema concept encompasses cognitive propositions (i.e., the actual content of information that is stored in memory; namely, core beliefs and assumptions) as well as the organization and structure of that information. The core beliefs that are organized within an individual's self-system are deep and absolutist statements (e.g., "I am unlovable," "I am incompetent," "I am worthless") that are often not directly articulated (Garratt et al., 2007).

Core beliefs that are organized within the self-schema influence the development of another level of thinking, namely processing biases and intermediate beliefs (Beck et al., 1979; Clark et al., 1999). This may be represented as attention, memory, or interpretational biases. For instance, individuals with anxiety disorders often believe that they are vulnerable and that the world is a dangerous place. Such individuals attend selectively to threat-pertinent information at the expense of information that is inconsistent with threat or information that suggests one has sufficient resources for dealing with it. An individual with tendencies toward aggression may attend to and encode information that is consistent with his or her pre-existing beliefs that others are malicious or that it is a "dog-eat-dog world." Situations in which negative events are ambiguous with regard to intent are often interpreted as being due to untoward intent (i.e., a hostile attribution bias; see Crick & Dodge, 1994). Someone vulnerable to depression, on the other hand, may have an underlying belief that he or she is unlovable. This belief may become especially powerful and reifying when negative life events occur that trigger this negative schema. Such an individual may then selectively attend to and recall information that is consistent with this negative view of self (e.g., paying attention to cues that are suggestive of being unlovable and minimizing information that is inconsistent with that belief).

Biased thinking may also be evident in faulty interpretations, "if-then" statements, and inaccurate causal attributions (Dozois & Beck, 2008). To illustrate, an individual may believe that making a mistake is equivalent to complete failure, or that his or her self-worth is contingent upon acceptance and approval from others. These dysfunctional attitudes may also be expressed as contractual contingencies (e.g., "*If* I fail at work, *then* I am a failure as a person;"see Kuiper & Olinger, 1986). Individuals adhering to such a belief may not experience emotional distress provided that they believe they are meeting their idiosyncratic criteria for self-worth (e.g., performing adequately at work). Yet adopting this rule will result in emotional distress when the contractual contingency is not met. Consequently, vulnerable individuals often generate personal rules and compensatory strategies (Young et al., 2003) for coping with negative core beliefs (e.g., "I must succeed in everything I do").

The activation of an individual's self-schema, and ensuing information processing biases, is also evident in more surface-level cognition, or what are referred to as automatic thoughts. Automatic thoughts pertain to the flow of positive and negative thoughts that run through an individual's mind each day and are not accompanied by direct conscious deliberation. Some researchers have argued that it is the relative balance of positive to negative automatic thoughts, rather than the absolute frequency of negative thoughts, that is functional or dysfunctional (e.g., Schwartz & Garamoni, 1986; for a review, see Clark et al., 1999). Automatic thoughts are often about oneself, the world, and the future—what Beck (1967) called the "cognitive triad." Although such thoughts are more superficial and proximal to a given situation than are other levels of cognition, they are functionally related to one's deeper beliefs and schemas and seem to arise associatively as different aspects of one's core belief system are activated.

Cognition is the primary focus of Beck's theory; however, this model does not simply state that cognitions *cause* emotions and behaviors. Instead, it is acknowledged that these variables are interrelated. Several related cognitive models have been advanced to characterize this interaction, and recent adaptations of Beck's model (e.g., the inclusion of modes) have taken into account the complex interplay among cognitive and affective systems (e.g., Beck, 1996, 2008; Teasdale & Barnard, 1993). The cognitive model maintains, however, that "the nature and function of information processing (i.e., the assignment of meaning) constitutes the key to understanding maladaptive behavior" (Alford & Beck, 1997, p. 11).

In addition to understanding cognition in psychopathology from the perspective of levels (from schematic structure to information processing to automatic thoughts), Beck's model also emphasizes content-specificity (Alford & Beck, 1997; Clark et al., 1999). That is, different patterns of cognition are purported to relate to specific clinical syndromes. Individuals who are depressed, for instance, are theorized to have core beliefs, dysfunctional attitudes, and automatic thoughts related to themes of personal loss, deprivation, and failure (Beck et al., 1979). In contrast, individuals with clinically significant anxiety tend to overestimate the probability of risk while simultaneously underestimating their resources for coping with potential threats. Their thoughts focus on themes of the self as vulnerable, the world as dangerous, and the future as potentially catastrophic (Beck et al., 1985). A person with paranoid personality disorder believes that others are malevolent, untrustworthy, abusive, and deceitful (Beck, Freeman, Davis, and Associates, 2004). On the other hand, an individual who experiences problems with substance abuse may have a set of core beliefs that emphasize the self as inept, weak, trapped, or helpless. Such individuals may also engage in permission-giving beliefs (e.g., "I will just use one more time, then I will stop") and hold particular beliefs about strategies for coping (e.g., "If I use, I can handle things better") and about the inability to resist urges (e.g., "Even if I stop using, the craving will continue indefinitely;" Ball, 2003).

## Cognitive Therapy

Although Beck's cognitive theory is top down (i.e., upon activation, the self-schema influences information processing which, in turn, impacts automatic thoughts), the model of treatment works primarily from the bottom up (i.e., from more proximal and surface-level cognitions to deeper cognitive structures). Cognitive therapy aims to help individuals shift their cognitive appraisals from ones that are unhealthy and maladaptive to ones that are more evidence-based and adaptive. There are three basic underlying principles: (a) cognition affects behavior and affect; (b) cognitive activity may be monitored and modified; and (c) by changing one's beliefs, one can exert desired changes in behavior and experience more satisfying emotional reactions (Dobson & Dozois, 2010). Although cognitive therapy uses various behavioral (and even, on occasion, acceptance) strategies, the focus is ultimately on altering beliefs. Patients learn how to treat thoughts as hypotheses rather than as facts. Framing a belief as a hypothesis provides an opportunity to test its validity, affords patients the ability to consider alternative explanations, and permits them to gain distance from a thought to allow for more objective scrutiny (DeRubeis et al., 2010).

Cognitive therapy is highly collaborative and involves designing specific learning experiences to help patients monitor their automatic thoughts; understand the relationships among cognition, affect, and behavior; examine the validity of automatic thoughts; develop more realistic and adaptive cognitions; and alter underlying beliefs, assumptions, and schemas (Dobson & Dozois, 2010). Although the specific techniques may vary contingent upon the disorder being treated, as well as the nature of the problem and the case formulation (Kuyken, Padesky, & Dudley, 2009), cognitive therapy includes the following primary components:

1. Establishing the therapy alliance
2. Behavioral change strategies

3.  Cognitive restructuring strategies
4.  Modification of core beliefs and schemas
5.  Prevention of relapse/recurrence

A detailed discussion of these change strategies is beyond the scope of this chapter, and interested readers may consult DeRubeis et al. (2010) and Dobson & Dobson (2009). An overview of these strategies is provided below.

The therapeutic relationship is a key component of all psychotherapies, including cognitive therapy. Many of the basic interpersonal variables advocated by Carl Rogers (1951), including warmth, accurate empathy, unconditional positive regard, and genuineness and trust, serve as an important foundation for cognitive and symptomatic change. As Beck et al. (1979) noted, however, we "believe that these characteristics in themselves are necessary but not sufficient to produce an optimum therapeutic effect" (p. 45). Dobson and Dobson (2009) summarize well the debate about nonspecific factors in psychotherapy by stating: "It is like a debate about whether it is the skeletal system, the nervous system, or the muscular system that permits humans to walk. Each of these factors is necessary but not sufficient. So it is in psychotherapy" (p. 225). Although the relative emphasis in the writings on cognitive therapy has been on the efficacy of various therapeutic strategies, this does not mean that relationship factors assume a secondary role. For instance, the Cognitive Therapy Scale (Young & Beck, 1980), which is used to assess competency in cognitive therapy, has numerous items that pertain directly to the establishment of the therapeutic alliance (Dobson & Dobson, 2009).

Behavioral strategies serve an important function in cognitive therapy. Although these methods may serve to alter one's reinforcement schedule (thereby increasing pleasure or mastery) or habituate to feared stimuli, the primary focus is on cognitive change. DeRubeis et al. (2010), for instance, describe the shifts in one's belief system that may take place with the use of self-monitoring. The thought that "I am always down; it never lets up" or "There is no point in getting out of bed" can be tested as hypotheses and by collecting data on one's activities and mood state. Similarly, behavioral exposure results in belief change (the reassignment of meaning) about the threatening nature of feared stimuli. Behavioral strategies are arguably the most powerful means to attain cognitive change in cognitive therapy (Wells, 1997).

Cognitive therapists also help patients to identify and test the validity of their cognitions. One important strategy for eliciting and evaluating negative automatic thoughts is the Daily Record of Dysfunctional Thoughts (DRDT), of which there are a number of variants (e.g., Beck et al., 1979; DeRubeis et al., 2010; Greenberger & Padesky, 1995). By requiring one to write down an activating event, the mediating thoughts, and the ensuing emotional response, the DRDT fosters more objectivity about and distance from one's thoughts. The evidence pertaining to a particular belief is then examined, using guided discovery and collaborative empiricism. Specifically, patients are asked a number of questions, including: "What is the evidence for or against this belief?" "What are the alternative ways to think about this situation?" "If my best friend or loved one knew that I had

**Table 2.1**   Common Cognitive Errors

| Title | Description |
|---|---|
| All-or-nothing thinking | Also called black-and-white or dichotomous thinking. Viewing a situation as having only two possible outcomes. |
| Catastrophization | Predicting future calamity; ignoring a possible positive future. |
| Fortune-telling | Predicting the future with limited evidence. |
| Mind-reading | Predicting or believing you know what other people think. |
| Disqualifying the positive | Not attending to, or giving due weight to, positive information. Similar to a negative "tunnel vision." |
| Magnification/ minimization | Magnifying negative information; minimizing positive information. |
| Selective abstraction | Also called *mental filter.* Focusing on one detail rather than on the large picture. |
| Overgeneralization | Drawing overstated conclusions based on one instance, or on a limited number of instances. |
| Misattribution | Making errors in the attribution of causes of various events. |
| Personalization | Thinking that you cause negative things, rather than examining other causes. |
| Emotional reasoning | Arguing that because something feels bad, it must be bad. |
| Labeling | Putting a general label on someone or something, rather than describing the behaviors or aspects of the thing. |

*Source:* All EAs. From *Evidence-Based Practice of Cognitive-Behavioral Therapy* (p. 129), by D. Dobson and K. S. Dobson. Copyright © 2009. Reprinted with permission from Guilford Press.

this thought, what would he or she say to me?" "What would it mean about me even if this particular thought was true?" (D. Dobson & Dobson, 2009; Greenberger & Padesky, 1995). From this analysis of the evidence, patients are then taught to generate alternative thoughts that incorporate the evidence and lead to a shift in their emotional experience. If a given thought is inconsistent with the weight of factual evidence that bears on the subject matter (e.g., "I am a failure"), the therapist helps the patient to alter and realign the thought so that it is evidence-based and, consequently, more adaptive and helpful.

There are a number of common cognitive "errors" or processing biases (see Table 2.1) that all of us experience at different times, particularly when affective arousal is high. Instructing patients about the types of processing biases that are typical for them may be beneficial, as it provides a convenient reminder about how their thinking may be unhelpful while promoting distance and objectivity. There may be times when a patient's thinking is not "distorted," but rather reflects the realities of given circumstances and hardships. In such instances, the emphasis is not on modifying cognition but on problem-solving, skill acquisition, and working out how best to approach the negative event or situation.

The next phase of therapy is predicated on the assumption that an individual's automatic thoughts and cognitive distortions are functionally related to deeper core beliefs and schemas. Often, it is the modification of these schemas that is believed to result in the most generalizable change and the greatest prevention of relapse (Dozois et al., 2009). With the use of the DRDT and other strategies (e.g., the downward arrow—this approach begins with an automatic thought; rather than testing the thought with evidence, a patient is encouraged to deepen his or her level of affect and explore the thought with questions such as "what it would it mean if this thought was true?", which typically helps to reveal deeper rules, beliefs, and assumptions), a number of themes emerge in therapy that provide clues as to the core beliefs that a given patient may hold. In therapy, the patient and therapist chip away at these "deeper" beliefs, using Socratic dialogue and guided discovery, role plays, behavioral experiments, and other change strategies (DeRubeis et al., 2010; D. Dobson & Dobson, 2009).

Finally, at the end of treatment, cognitive therapists focus on the prevention of relapse/recurrence. This includes, among other things, a gradual titration of sessions and spreading apart of their timing; reviewing the treatment strategies that were used and were most helpful; creating a plan for the future; discussing feelings about the termination of therapy; preparing for setbacks; identifying possible triggers of relapse (from the literature and the patient's unique background); and ensuring that the patient makes internal attributions for treatment change.

## MINDFULNESS- AND ACCEPTANCE-BASED STRATEGIES IN COGNITIVE THERAPY

Although mindfulness- and acceptance-based strategies have not played a major role in the development of Beck's cognitive model, there are vestiges of acceptance constructs in cognitive therapy. For example, cognitive therapists encourage patients to become scientists of their own thinking, thereby gaining a realistic appraisal of self, the world, and the future. Patients are taught to examine their predictions and interpretations to determine how an unrealistic appraisal may impact their emotional responses in a given situation. If, however, "there is good reason to be sad, angry, fearful, worried, and so forth, the [cognitive] therapist will not attempt to change these adaptive responses" (Hofmann & Asmundson, 2008, p. 7; also see Kovacs & Beck, 1978). Although different from the acceptance of internal experiences, another form of acceptance is toward problematic circumstances. In such cases, a therapist will help a patient to determine whether aspects of the problematic environment may be changed (problem-focused coping) and, if that is not possible, to accept these circumstances and engage more in emotion-focused coping (Lazarus & Folkman, 1984).

In the context of anxiety disorders, acceptance has played an important role in the cognitive model for some time. Beck et al. (1985), for example, developed a five-step AWARE strategy for dealing successfully with anxiety (see Table 2.2). AWARE emphasizes not simply tolerating or coping with one's anxiety but becoming mindful

**Table 2.2**   Coping with Anxiety Using AWARE

| A | Accept the anxiety | Agree to receive your anxiety. Welcome it. Decide to be with the experience rather than fighting it. Replace your rejection, anger, or hatred of anxiety with acceptance. If you resist the anxiety, you prolong the unpleasantness of it. |
|---|---|---|
| W | Watch your anxiety | Look at it without judgment—it is neither good nor bad. Don't look at it as an unwelcome guest. Instead, observe it and watch it fluctuate. Be one with your observing self and watch the peaks and valleys of your anxiety. Be detached. Remember, you are not your anxiety. Try to separate self from the experience and simply observe it. |
| A | Act with anxiety | Normalize the situation. Act "as if" you are not anxious. Function with it. Running from your anxiety may be helpful in the short-term, but it has long-term consequences. If you stick with it, your fear and anxiety will dissipate. |
| R | Repeat the steps | Continue to accept your anxiety, watch it, and act with it until it reaches a comfortable level. |
| E | Expect the best | What you fear the most rarely happens. Don't be surprised the next time you are anxious; instead, surprise yourself with how you handle it. As long as you are alive, you will have some anxiety. Don't buy into the idea that you have mastered anxiety for good. By expecting it in the future, you put yourself in a good position to be able to accept anxiety when it comes again. |

*Source:* From *Anxiety Disorders and Phobias: A Cognitive Perspective* (pp. 323–324), by A. T. Beck and G. Emery (with R. L. Greenberg), 1985, New York, NY: Basic Books.

of anxiety and embracing it. The idea is that resisting, fighting, avoiding, or suppressing anxiety only intensifies and prolongs it: "Paradoxically, by giving up the idea of control, the patient can be taught to control his [or her] anxiety. The therapist needs to sell the patient on the idea of accepting (not being resigned to) his [or her] anxiety" (p. 233). This emphasis reveals an important difference between cognitive therapy and acceptance-based approaches. The primary objective of promoting the acceptance of internal experiences in CT is to bring about cognitive change and symptom relief (e.g., a decrease in anxiety). Adopting an accepting stance is, paradoxically, one way to achieve such relief.

The idea that acceptance has the potential to bring about cognitive change is also a premise for exposure-based interventions in CT. Although the specific focus of exposure differs depending on the disorder being treated, the principle is the same—by facing anxiety-provoking stimuli, one's fears become extinguished (via habituation), new coping skills are developed, and significant cognitive change occurs. The change in threat-related cognitions occurs as new evidence is accumulated that is discrepant from one's beliefs, thereby providing an opportunity for new learning to take place. By inducing (and thereby accepting) bodily sensations in interoceptive exposure for panic disorder, for example, a patient not only habituates to these sensations; he or she learns that these sensations do not necessarily lead to a panic attack and that panic, although uncomfortable, is not dangerous. When this acceptance takes place, there is no longer a need to monitor bodily sensations (i.e., the appraisal of the sensations has shifted such that the internal sensations no longer carry threat meaning), and the escalation into panic does not occur (Clark, 1996). The same cognitive shift may occur for the other anxiety disorders. The treatment of post-traumatic stress disorder, for instance, typically involves confronting the trauma using imaginal exposure and cognitive reprocessing. Through exposure, patients learn that these images are indeed memories rather than on-going events and can make sense of them and integrate them with other aspects of their lives. A useful analogy is to "compare the trauma memory to a cupboard in which many things have been thrown in quickly and in a disorganized fashion, so it is impossible to fully close the door and things fall out at unpredictable times. Organizing the cupboard will mean looking at each of the things and putting them into their place. Once this is done, the door can be closed and remains shut" (Ehlers and Clark, 2000, pp. 336–337).

## Case Illustration

Sandra, a 30-year-old woman with a successful professional career, was referred for cognitive therapy. The chief complaints were major depression and post-traumatic stress disorder. The initial course of therapy began with behavioral activation (monitoring activity and introducing mastery and pleasure-oriented experiences) to reverse the downward spiral of avoidance and negative mood. Therapy then focused on monitoring, testing, and modifying negative automatic thoughts with the use of a DRDT. Sandra became adept at identifying negative thoughts, but found it difficult to evaluate the evidence, test the validity of her thoughts, or generate alternative and more helpful beliefs. With the help of her therapist, Sandra started to become more evidence-based in her thinking. Through the use of Socratic questioning, guided discovery, and other strategies (e.g., downward arrow), she was also able to identify some of her deeper, underlying core beliefs which pertained to incompetence ("I am a failure") and unlovability (e.g., "I am unlovable;" "I am defective"). Her belief about incompetence began to change, which resulted in some improvement in her mood. However, her beliefs about unlovability were heavily engrained and resistant to change.

Sandra grew up in a home that was devoid of emotional closeness. In addition, her family of origin taught her a depressotypic attributional style. From an early age, she learned to accept blame for negative events and deflect credit for positive ones. Against the backdrop of this history, Sandra was also a victim of sexual assault. In addition to the trauma of the assault itself, Sandra also attributed its cause ("I am evil"; "I deserved this"; "I made this happen") and consequence ("I am dirty"; "I am defective"; "I am broken") to herself. Therapy focused on imaginal exposure. Specifically, Sandra wrote a script outlining the details of what happened. She and her therapist worked to make this script even more detailed. Sandra was then asked to read this script aloud several times per day. She and her therapist also recorded this script, and her homework was to play it to herself repeatedly within the boundaries of time that they agreed upon. As a result of this exposure, and changes in her fear structure (e.g., coming to believe that it was a horrific memory but not something that was currently threatening), Sandra's intense fears and re-experiencing symptoms dissipated. However, she continued to believe that she was evil, dirty, and defective as a result of this assault. Moreover, she believed that she was the fundamental cause of this assault "because I am evil to the core" (a belief that was developed early in childhood and perpetuated through a lens of personalizing negative experiences and disqualifying positive ones). In addition to exposure, therapy emphasized cognitive reprocessing of the trauma, trying to make sense of her experience, altering her view of self, the world, and the future that shifted as a result of the trauma, and "reorganizing the cupboard" (Ehlers & Clark, 2000).

Sandra began to realize that she focused exclusively on negative events that, although incredibly painful, were isolated. She would see periodic mistakes and isolated negative events as "evidence" that she was evil and dirty. At the same time, she would ignore the mountain of evidence that was objectively more accurate and consistent and that suggested that she was competent, kind, caring, good, compassionate, and giving (characteristics that did not coincide with being dirty and evil). Sandra could recognize that she had a skewed view of herself that, although consistent with "old rules" taught in childhood, did not converge with the weight of the evidence about her character. She could grasp this concept in session, but found it difficult to hang on to, particularly when she experienced deep sadness or was fatigued physically or emotionally. She was encouraged to delicately balance an examination of the evidence with acceptance of her pain. Specifically, when she experienced intense sadness, she would examine her thoughts and test their validity. By doing this, she could recognize logically that she was not evil or dirty. However, she still *felt* evil and dirty. She was encouraged to accept this residual feeling (i.e., feeling ≠ fact) and to let it ride its course rather than trying to push it away or suppress it. Through a combination of cognitive change strategies and acceptance of pain, Sandra was able to shift her belief-system, break the ties in place between pain and responsibility that had made her pain self-defining, and grieve the pain itself.

## DISTINCTIONS AMONG COGNITIVE THERAPY AND OTHER CBT MODELS

Cognitive therapy is one of a number of cognitive-behavioral approaches that, at their core, attempt to change emotional distress and maladaptive behavior "by altering thoughts, interpretations, assumptions, and strategies of responding" (Kazdin, 1978, p. 337). The variety of approaches subsumed under the rubric of cognitive behavioral therapy fall into three major categories of therapies: (a) cognitive restructuring, (b) coping skills, and

(c) problem-solving. The commonalities and distinctions among these approaches have been reviewed elsewhere (e.g., Dobson & Dozois, 2010) and will not be reiterated here. Given the focus of this volume, we draw our attention to the distinctions among Beckian cognitive therapy and the acceptance- and mindfulness-based approaches.

Although cognitive therapy has acquired significant research support, it is not a panacea for all mental health problems, and the empirical literature suggests that there is room for improvement, particularly when the outcome is defined in terms of achieving "recovery" (e.g., Westen & Morrison, 2001). Our view is that the application of acceptance- and mindfulness-based strategies has the potential to improve standard cognitive therapy. Some empirical research is consistent with this view (e.g., Forman, Herbert, Moitra, Yeomans, & Geller, 2007), although, at present, none these newer approaches independently fulfill the criteria for empirically supported therapies (Öst, 2008).

As mentioned previously, acceptance strategies have been advocated within the context of cognitive therapy for anxiety (Beck et al., 1985; also see Table 2.2). Beck has also stated that the ability to separate or distance one's distress, pain, or anger from self-construal can result in the net effect of minimizing suffering (Dalai Lama & Beck, 2005). In addition to altering cognition, many of the strategies advanced by cognitive theory work to achieve distance from and perspective about one's predicament.

Though mindfulness- and acceptance-based strategies have not been emphasized in cognitive therapy relative to cognitive change interventions, their general approaches are not inconsistent with the cognitive model, and the approaches are, in many respects, more similar than distinct (Arch & Craske, 2008; Hofmann, 2008a; Hofmann & Asmundson, 2008). As Roemer and Orsillo (2009) pointed out, acceptance-based behavioral approaches to treatment are "part of the evolution of the CBT tradition, not something that exists outside of it" (p. 3). Congruent with this argument, we view these approaches as extensions or complementary components of cognitive therapy and not a "third wave" per se (see Hofmann, 2008a; Hofmann & Asmundson, 2008).

In our view, the recent focus on mindfulness- and acceptance-based approaches (e.g., Hayes, Follette, & Linehan, 2004; Hayes, Strosahl, & Wilson, 1999; Roemer & Orsillo, 2009; Segal, Williams, & Teasdale, 2002) and their addition to cognitive therapy is perhaps akin to other extensions of the model. To illustrate, Beck proposed that the early childhood environment was important in the development of core beliefs and self-schemas (e.g., Kovacs & Beck, 1978). However, Beck's writings did not focus on these early experiences. Rather, it was Jeffrey Young and his colleagues (e.g., Young et al., 2003; Young, Rygh, Weinberger, & Beck, 2008) who later expanded the cognitive model and added a more explicit focus on the developmental origins of early maladaptive schemas and their modification. Although such work represented an important extension of the cognitive model and contained new conceptual elements (e.g., schema compensation, schema maintenance) that advanced cognitive theory, it would not be considered a new "wave" of CBT. Such is our view of acceptance and mindfulness approaches.

Some of these approaches (e.g., dialectical behavior therapy; Linehan, 1993; mindfulness-based cognitive therapy; Segal et al., 2002; metacognitive therapy; Wells,

2002, 2008) have been well-integrated within the cognitive model (Roemer & Orsillo, 2009). Others (e.g., acceptance and commitment therapy [ACT]) appear to differ from mainstream cognitive therapy in their underlying philosophical assumptions (Hayes et al., 1999). For example, cognitive therapists generally adhere to the realist assumption—the idea that a "real world" exists that is independent of our perception of it and that it is possible to misinterpret or misperceive this reality (Dobson & Dozois, 2010). It is the interaction of the circumstances that a person finds him- or herself in coupled with idiosyncratic beliefs, assumptions, and schemas (the latter of which may distort thinking) that influence the appraisal of a specific situation or event (D. Dobson & Dobson, 2009). As such, cognitive therapy is typically oriented toward change strategies (e.g., helping someone become more evidence-based in his or her thinking). As noted previously, however, if one's appraisal is not inconsistent with the weight of the evidence, then other strategies (e.g., problem-solving, skill-building, or acceptance) are employed. In contrast, ACT is based on the philosophy of functional contextualism. ACT does not assume that the world is organized into discoverable parts but, rather, that it should be viewed within the context of its function. According to Hayes et al. (1999), cognitive therapy attempts to alter the form of private experience, whereas ACT attempts to alter the function: "The main way to weaken verbal relations effectively is to alter the content supporting the verbal processes, not by focusing on the verbal content" (p. 46). According to Hayes et al. (1999), viewing thoughts and feelings as the "problem" is itself part of the problem.

We contend that cognitive therapy actually attempts to modify both form and function, depending on the circumstances, and that a functional analysis of thought content and process is important. When thinking is colored more by the activation of core beliefs and schemas than by the evidence, cognitive therapists aim to help patients become scientists of their thinking to soften the "hardening of the categories" (Kelly, 1963), alter the filter of their cognitive "spectacles" (Kant, 1781/1929) and modify self-schemas, biased information processing, dysfunctional attitudes, and negative automatic thoughts. There are times when mindfulness- and acceptance-based strategies are used to facilitate such cognitive change.

Dual-system models have recently added to our understanding of cognition in psychopathology (e.g., Beevers, 2005; Farb et al., 2007; Ouimet, Gawronski & Dozois, 2009). These models, which have been adapted from the social-cognitive literature, assert that information processing is governed by two processes—one that operates in a relatively automatic fashion (associative-based processing) and one that is more cerebral and reflective (rule-based processing). Such processes correspond to neurological structures of the limbic system (e.g., the amygdala) and the prefrontal cortex, respectively. There are several instances in which the associative-based system is more likely to dominate processing—for example, when one's cognitive resources are low (e.g., due to cognitive load or fatigue) or when life stress disables reflective processing (Beevers, 2005). Cognitive therapy and mindfulness-/acceptance-based approaches may operate in a complementary manner, the former helping individuals to recognize, test, and modify negative self-referent thoughts and the latter to view such thoughts simply as mental events that occur and, at times, simply need to be accepted (Beevers, 2005).

We advocate for the use of acceptance-based strategies when one's reflective processing is disabled, when rule-based processing is engaged successfully (i.e., the individual has examined and aligned his or her thinking with the evidence) but the situation remains emotionally provocative, when the situation is not amenable to problem-solving (e.g., it is outside of one's control), and to counteract suppression and avoidance tendencies (Hofmann, 2008a; Hofmann & Asmundson, 2008; Williams, Teasdale, Segal, & Kabat-Zinn, 2007). However, we also contend that through acceptance there is cognitive change (e.g., via a metacognitive stance; see Alford & Beck, 1997; Segal et al., 2002; Wells, 2002) which we believe is fundamental to emotional well-being:

> One of the best-researched and most effective emotion regulation strategies is cognitive reappraisal... which is the core of CBT. Acceptance strategies intended to counteract suppression (experiential avoidance) are simply another tool in the arsenal of a CBT therapist to combat emotional disorders. (Hofmann & Asmundson, 2008, p. 13)

## THE NATURE AND VALUE OF COGNITIVE CHANGE STRATEGIES

The utility of directly testing and modifying thoughts has recently been questioned in the literature (e.g., Longmore & Worrell, 2007; but see Hofmann, 2008b). Part of this critique stems from depression treatment dismantling studies in which the data appear to indicate that behavioral activation performs equally well to interventions that focus on the modification of automatic thoughts or core beliefs (Dimidjian et al., 2006; Jacobson et al., 1996), and that there are no significant differences between these conditions in relapse rates at two-year follow-up (Dobson et al., 2008; Gortner, Gollan, Dobson, & Jacobson, 1998). Similar findings have been reported for the treatment of anxiety, where the addition of cognitive restructuring does not always add incrementally to exposure alone (see Longmore & Worrell, 2007, for a review). Behavioral activation has also been advocated as a stand-alone treatment for depression, and this approach has received some empirical support (e.g., Dimidjian et al., 2006). In some respects, these findings are not entirely surprising. Cognitive therapy has long advocated for the use of behavioral activation and behavioral experiments as a key strategy for altering patient beliefs (see Beck et al., 1979). Additional research is needed to determine when cognitive change can be implemented in more straightforward and cost-effective ways (e.g., behavioral activation) and when more direct cognitive interventions and deeper schema work may be indicated (Dozois et al., 2009).

Cognitive restructuring techniques are among the best researched and supported strategies for altering cognition. However, maladaptive cognitions may be modified in numerous ways, which include behavioral activation, in vivo and interoceptive exposure, and acceptance strategies. Our view is that each of these interventions results in cognitive change (although in some respects, this remains an empirical question). Moreover, some strategies may be superior to changing cognitions via thought records, Socratic dialogue, and guided discovery. An individual with panic disorder, for example, will benefit from knowing (intellectually) that his or her symptoms are not dangerous, but until these beliefs can be tested via in vivo and interoceptive exposure, experiential learning will not take place, and the belief may shift only partially. Such an integrated approach has long been advocated in cognitive therapy. By accepting anxiety, one also learns that it will not lead to harmful consequences (Beck et al., 1985) which involves a shift in belief. Thus, whether through direct cognitive restructuring, behavioral strategies, or acceptance, cognitive change may be the final common pathway for therapeutic improvement.

## EMPIRICAL EVIDENCE FOR THE COGNITIVE THEORY

The empirical literature has generally supported Beck's cognitive theory. Hundreds of studies from social, clinical, and cognitive psychology have shown that individuals filter information and respond to stimuli in a way that is consistent with their pre-existing attitudes, assumptions, expectations, and core beliefs (e.g., Olson, Roese, & Zanna, 1996; Tversky & Kahneman, 1974). Considerable advances have also been made to understand how cognitive processes (e.g., selective attention, memory) influence subsequent emotional responses (e.g., Beck & Clark, 1997; Clark et al., 1999; Mathews & MacLeod, 2002, 2005; Ouimet et al., 2009; Williams, Watts, MacLeod, & Mathews, 1997). Recent empirical work has also focused on the interactions among genetic, neurobiological, and cognitive factors (Beck, 2008; Beevers, Scott, C. McGeary, & McGeary, 2009).

Our review of the data pertaining to cognitive theories of psychopathology is necessarily selective (see Clark et al., 1999, for a comprehensive review of evidence for the cognitive model of depression) and focuses on Beck's notion that there are distinctive levels of cognition that work in synchrony to impact emotional and behavioral responses and that different emotional experiences or clinical disorders can be characterized by a unique set of core beliefs and automatic thoughts (i.e., content-specificity). The assumption that one can positively affect emotional well-being and behavioral patterns by restructuring maladaptive beliefs is also discussed within the context of the cognitive therapy outcome literature.

### Levels of Cognition

Based initially on clinical observations, Beck (1967) proposed a cognitive hierarchy comprised of schemas, intermediate beliefs (and information processing biases), and automatic thoughts. Research that has accumulated since Beck's original proposal continues to support the view that the self-system is best conceptualized in terms of different levels of cognitive analysis (e.g., Dozois, 2007; Dozois & Dobson, 2001a, 2001b; Ingram et al., 1998). For example, an increased frequency of negative automatic thoughts and dysfunctional attitudes commonly accompany depression and anxiety (e.g., Beck

& Perkins, 2001), and content-specific information-processing biases have been found in a number of disorders (for reviews, see Clark et al., 1999; Dobson & Dozois, 2004; Williams, Mathews, & MacLeod, 1996).

The extent to which cognitive factors are causally related to emotional problems has, however, been contested (e.g., Barnett & Gotlib, 1988; Coyne & Gotlib, 1983). A criticism of cognitive theory of depression, for example, is that the variables purported to have a causal influence on mood ebb and flow with the depressive experience. When individuals are depressed, they tend to show attention and memory biases and to demonstrate dysfunctional attitudes and negative automatic thoughts. Yet these information-processing biases seem to improve once depression remits (e.g., Dozois & Dobson, 2001a). In addition, information processing and negative thinking styles tend not to differentiate groups of previously depressed individuals and never-depressed controls (see Ingram et al., 1998, for review). Such findings are not consistent with the operations of what should be a stable schema.

It is important to bear in mind, however, that Beck's proposal was that the schema lies dormant until it is activated by stress. Indeed, studies that have activated the self-system by inducing a negative mood state (e.g., through the use of music, vignette, or autobiographical memory) have found differences between individuals with a history of depression and those who have never been depressed (e.g., Hedlund & Rude, 1995; Ingram, Bernet, & McLaughlin, 1994; Miranda, Gross, Persons, & Hahn, 1998; Miranda & Persons, 1988; Miranda, Persons, & Byers, 1990; Persons & Miranda, 1992; Segal, Gemar, & Williams, 1999; Soloman, Haaga, Brody, Kirk, & Friedman, 1998; Teasdale & Dent, 1987; for an excellent review, see Scher et al., 2005). Such studies have advanced the understanding of mood-congruent information-processing biases, and support the concept of stable cognitive structures that may become activated with changes in mood states.

Attentional biases have also been shown to be casually related to anxiety. MacLeod, Mathews and colleagues (MacLeod, Rutherford, Campbell, Ebsworthy, & Holker, 2002; Mathews & MacLeod, 2002; 2005), for example, tested the idea that transient information-processing biases can be induced in nonclinical participants and subsequently produce anxiety following a stressor. Research has also recently demonstrated that anxiety can be reduced by training individuals to shift their attention away from threatening stimuli (e.g., Amir, Beard, Burns, & Bomyea, 2009).

Longitudinal studies have also supported Beck's theory, demonstrating that the interaction of cognitive vulnerability (e.g., dysfunctional attitudes) and life stress predicts depression (e.g., Abela & D'Alessandro, 2002; Alloy et al., 2006; Hankin, Abramson, Miller, & Haeffel, 2004; Hankin, Fraley, & Abela, 2005; Joiner, Metalsky, Lew, & Klocek, 1999; Kwon & Oei, 1992; Lewinsohn, Joiner, & Rohde, 2001; but see Otto et al., 2007). Evans, Heron, Lewis, Araya and Wolke (2005) found that women who scored in the upper third on a measure of schematic content (a measure of interpersonal sensitivity) were three times more likely to experience depressive symptoms 14 weeks later than were women scoring in the bottom third. In a 2.5-year follow-up study, Alloy et al. (2006) found that cognitively high-risk participants were 3.5–6.8 times more likely than low risk participants to experience depression onset.

The concept of schema, although a central construct in Beck's theory, has historically been one of the most difficult to define and operationalize (Segal, 1988). Over the years, however, various assessment strategies have been developed to test this construct empirically. One of the earliest studies to examine self-referent processing was conducted by Rogers, Kuiper, and Kirker (1977) who documented that self-referent processing promotes a deeper level of encoding and yields a stronger and more elaborate memory trace than information that is not self-referent (see Symons & Johnson, 1997, for a review).

More recent research has provided evidence consistent with the idea of an organized self-schema in depression. Segal and his colleagues (Segal & Gemar, 1997; Segal, Gemar, Truchon, Guirguis, & Horowitz, 1995), for example, conducted an ingenious series of studies using a variation of the emotional Stroop task. After creating lists of ideographically-derived self-descriptive traits for each participant, these experimenters administered the modified Stroop task. Participants read the prime word (which varied in terms of its relatedness to the target adjective), named the color of the target, and then recalled the prime. Depressed individuals displayed longer reaction times for color-naming negative target words when the primes were self-descriptive than when they were not. This prime-target relatedness effect was not found for nondepressed individuals.

Other studies have used the Psychological Distance Scaling Task, which operationalizes self-schema assessment in terms of a computation of interstimulus distances among adjective stimuli having to do with self-representation. These studies reveal that negative information (particularly interpersonal in content) is well-consolidated in the self-schemas of individuals with anxiety and depressive disorders, whereas positive information is less well-organized in depression (Dozois & Dobson, 2001b; Dozois & Frewen, 2006; Lumley & Harkness, 2009). Negative self-structures in depression have also been shown to be stable across time, irrespective of symptom improvement (Dozois, 2007; Dozois & Dobson, 2001a).

## Content-Specificity

The content-specificity hypothesis states that each emotional experience and psychological disorder has a specific cognitive profile (Alford & Beck, 1997; Beck, 1976; Clark et al., 1999). In other words, it is an individual's specific appraisal of a particular event that dictates subsequence emotions. Anxiety, for example, is derived from evaluations of future threat or danger, sadness involves appraisals of loss, rejection, deprivation or failure, and anger results from an interpretation that one's misfortune is due to another's malicious intent. As such, different emotional experiences and clinical disorders can be distinguished on the basis of unique sets of core beliefs and automatic thoughts.

Research has generally supported the content-specificity hypothesis (Beck, Benedict, & Winkler, 2003; Beck, Brown, Steer, Eidelson, & Riskind, 1987; Beck, Wenzel, Riskind, Brown, & Steer, 2006; Clark, Beck, & Stewart, 1990; Hankin et al., 2004; Joiner et al., 1999; Ohrt, Sjödin, & Thorell, 1999; Schniering & Rapee, 2004; Westra & Kuiper, 1997; Woody, Taylor, McLean, & Koch, 1998). Westra and Kuiper (1997), for example, found that dysphoria was uniquely associated with adjectives pertaining to loss, failure, and hopelessness, whereas anxiety centered on themes of threat. These researchers also found content-specificity effects for selective attentional biases in dysphoria, anxiety, and bulimia using a visual probe detection task, and enhanced memory performance for domain-specific adjectives on an incidental recognition measure (but in dysphoric and bulimic groups only).

Joiner et al. (1999) found evidence for content-specificity in college students who were assessed before and after a midterm examination. Students who were high in dysfunctional attitudes and who scored lower than they had anticipated on their midterm showed increases in depressive symptoms. This relationship was mediated specifically by depressive (not anxious) cognitions.

Although some research has found only mixed support for the content-specificity hypothesis in anxiety and depression (Beck & Perkins, 2001), cognitive factors specific to each disorder appear to emerge when the unique symptom features of each disorder are examined (Clark, Steer, & Beck, 1994; Steer, Clark, Beck, & Ranieri, 1995). Beck, Benedict, and Winkler (2003), for instance, used the Mood and Anxiety Symptom Questionnaire (designed to distinguish depression- and anxiety-specific symptoms from general distress) and found that depression and anxiety were uniquely associated with their respective cognitions. As reviewed by Beck (2005), content-specificity has also been demonstrated in panic disorder, obsessive-compulsive disorder, eating disorders, body dysmorphic disorder, and the personality disorders.

# EMPIRICAL EVIDENCE FOR COGNITIVE THERAPY

## Treatment Outcome

The terms cognitive therapy and cognitive behavioral therapy (CBT) are often used interchangeably. Although cognitive therapy refers specifically to the Beckian approach, CBT is broader and is used to designate a set of techniques in which the cognitive therapy approach is used along with behavioral strategies (Beck, 2005; Dobson & Dozois, 2010).

Most empirical attention has been on cognitive therapy for major depressive disorder, with more than 75 clinical trials published since 1977 (see Butler et al., 2006). The data indicate that cognitive therapy is comparable to antidepressant medication for the acute treatment of depression, with both treatments producing results superior to placebo control conditions (see Hollon, Thase, & Markowitz, 2002). Recent studies have also demonstrated that cognitive therapy and pharmacotherapy are equally effective for severe depression (DeRubeis et al., 2005; Hollon et al., 2005; DeRubeis, Gelfand, Tang, & Simons, 1999). A particular benefit of cognitive therapy relative to antidepressant medication is that fewer patients (i.e., approximately half) relapse (Gloaguen, Cottraux, Cucherat, & Blackburn, 1998; but see Wampold, Minami, Baskin, & Tierney, 2002). The prophylactic effect of cognitive therapy was also recently demonstrated for severe depression (Hollon et al., 2005). However, Dimidjian et al. (2006) recently found that behavioral activation produced prophylactic effects similar to cognitive therapy.

Butler et al. (2006) reviewed meta-analyses of treatment outcome for cognitive behavioral therapies for a number of psychological disorders. A total of 15 methodologically rigorous meta-analyses were identified between 1967 to 2004, which incorporated 9,995 research participants in 332 studies. Large effect sizes were obtained for unipolar depression, generalized anxiety disorder, panic disorder, social anxiety, and childhood internalizing problems. Moderate effect sizes were found for couple distress, anger, childhood somatoform disorders, and chronic pain. Small effect sizes were obtained for sexual offenders. Cognitive behavioral therapy also showed promising results as an adjunct to mediation for schizophrenia (Beck et al., 2008; but see Lynch, Law, & McKenna, 2010).

Epp and Dobson (2010) recently reviewed the treatment outcome literature for cognitive behavioral therapy (including Beck's cognitive therapy and other cognitive and behavioral approaches) and summarized the meta-analytic data according to absolute efficacy (the extent to which cognitive behavioral therapy exhibits favorable outcome to no treatment, a wait list, or treatment as usual), efficacy relative to pharmacotherapy, and efficacy compared to other forms of psychotherapy (see Table 2.3; also see Dobson & Dobson, 2009). As demonstrated by Epp and Dobson (2010) and D. Dobson and Dobson (2009), cognitive therapy has garnered considerable supportive evidence. For some disorders (e.g., some anxiety disorders, bulimia nervosa), the evidence is strong enough to suggest that cognitive behavioral therapy should be considered the treatment of choice. Since publication of these reviews, a meta-analysis focusing on schizophrenia, severe depression, and bipolar disorder has not been as positive. Lynch et al. (2010) suggested that cognitive behavioral therapy is no more effective than nonspecific interventions for the treatment of schizophrenia and does not appear to reduce the risk of relapse (but see Kingdon, 2010).

### *Treatment Mechanisms/Processes*

Beck's approach seeks to have a positive impact on emotional well-being and behavior by restructuring idiosyncratic belief systems that have become distorted or out of sync with the evidence. Although researchers disagree on the specific change processes that take place over the course of successful cognitive therapy, it is generally agreed that they are cognitive in nature (for reviews, see DeRubeis et al., 2010; Garratt et al., 2007; Whisman, 1993).

A number of studies have examined changes in cognitive indices over the course of cognitive therapy. For example, research has demonstrated that CT for depression is associated with significant reductions in dysfunctional attitudes, attributional style, hopelessness, and cognitive bias (e.g., Beevers & Miller, 2005; DeRubeis et al. 1990; Jarrett, Vittengl, Doyle, & Clark, 2007; Oei & Sullivan, 1999; Rector, Bagby, Segal, Joffe, & Levitt, 2000; Westra, Dozois, & Boardman, 2002; Whisman, Miller, Norman, & Keitner, 1991). In

**Table 2.3**   Summary of Efficacy Findings by Disorder or Problem

| Disorder | Treatment | Absolute Efficacy | Efficacy Relative to Medications | Efficacy Relative to Other Psychotherapies |
|---|---|---|---|---|
| Unipolar depression | CBT | + | + | ≃ |
| Bipolar disorder* | CBT | + | | = |
| Specific phobia | Exposure and cognitive restructuring | ++ | + | + |
| Social phobia | Exposure and cognitive restructuring | ++ | ≃ | ≃ |
| Obsessive-compulsive disorder | Exposure and response prevention and cognitive restructuring | + | | + |
| Panic disorder | Exposure and cognitive restructuring | ++ | ≃ | + |
| Chronic post-traumatic stress disorder | Exposure and cognitive techniques | + | | = |
| Generalized anxiety disorder | CBT | + | + | + |
| Bulimia nervosa | CBT | + | + | + |
| Binge-eating disorder | CBT | + | | = |
| Anorexia nervosa | CBT | + | + | = |
| Schizophrenia* | CBT | + | | + |
| Marital distress | CBT | + | | ≃ |
| Anger & violent offending | CBT | + | | |
| Sexual offending | CBT | + | −** | + |
| Chronic pain | CBT | + | | ≃ |
| Borderline personality disorder | CBT | + | | ≃ |

*(continued)*

**Table 2.3** *(continued )*

| Disorder | Treatment | Absolute Efficacy | Efficacy Relative to Medications | Efficacy Relative to Other Psychotherapies |
|---|---|---|---|---|
| Substance-use disorders | CBT | + | | = |
| Somatoform disorders | CBT | + | + | + |
| Sleep difficulties | CBT | + | + | + |

*Note*: A blank space indicates insufficient or no evidence; − indicates negative evidence; + indicates positive evidence; = indicates approximate equivalence; ++ indicates treatment of choice, ~ indicates equivocal evidence, "CBT" indicates efficacy of specific components unknown; * indicates that CBT is typically used as an adjunct to medication in these disorders; ** indicates efficacy relative to physical treatments (i.e., surgical castration and hormonal treatments).

*Source:* From "The Evidence Base for Cognitive-Behavioral Therapy," by A. M. Epp and K. S. Dobson, 2010. In K. S. Dobson (Ed.), *Handbook of Cognitive-Behavioral Therapies* (3rd ed., pp. 39–73). New York, NY: Guilford Press. Reprinted with permission.

their review, Garratt et al. (2007) concluded that the research literature is generally consistent with the notion that cognitive therapy yields cognitive change that, in turn, predicts reductions in depressive symptomatology. Tang and DeRubeis (1999) also demonstrated that substantial reductions in depressive symptoms ("sudden gains") were preceded by significant cognitive shifts, such as when patients modified a maladaptive core belief. These findings have been replicated in subsequent studies (see DeRubeis et al., 2010, for review).

Research also suggests that shifts in threat-related cognitions and processing are associated with, and in some instances precede, improvement in cognitive behavioral therapy for anxiety. For example, a reduction in attentional biases toward threat have been found following cognitive behavioral therapy for generalized anxiety disorder (Mathews, Mogg, Kentish, & Eysenck, 1995), social anxiety disorder (Mattia, Heimberg, & Hope, 1993), and specific phobia (Lavy, van den Hout, & Arntz, 1993). Some studies have also demonstrated that changes in anxious cognitions predict symptom changes in cognitive behavioral therapy for panic disorder and social phobia (e.g., Hofmann et al., 2007), although not all evidence pertaining to cognitive mediation has been supportive (for reviews, see Arch & Craske, 2008 and Hofmann, 2008a). Longmore and Worrell (2007), for instance, argue that component analyses have often failed to support the idea that cognitive techniques add to treatment outcome. As Hoffman (2008a) points out, the failure to find that cognitive restructuring improves outcome over and above exposure-based strategies does not, however, preclude the possibility that these outcomes are mediated cognitively.

Most research that assesses cognitive mediation of symptom reduction has focused on the relative efficacy of cognitive therapy and antidepressant medication for depression. Some research has demonstrated that cognitive interventions are associated with greater reductions in dysfunctional attitudes related to need for social approval, hopelessness cognitions, low self-concept, and cognitive bias (e.g., Rush, Beck, Kovacs, Weissenburger, & Hollon, 1982; Whisman et al., 1991). However, these findings have also not been uniformly replicated (e.g., Simons, Garfield & Murphy, 1984; Moore & Blackburn, 1996). Indeed, shifts in cognitive content and processes are also associated with successful pharmacotherapy (e.g., Dozois et al., 2009).

As DeRubeis, Siegle, and Hollon (2008) have argued, however, antidepressants "seem to be symptom-suppressive rather than curative" (p. 789). For example, cognitive therapy and antidepressant medication may be equivalent in their modification of more surface-level cognitions (e.g., negative automatic thoughts and dysfunctional attitudes), but may differ in their ability to modify "deeper" cognitive structures. Segal, Gemar, and Williams (1999) administered the Dysfunctional Attitude Scale (DAS) to patients who had successfully completed either a trial of cognitive therapy or pharmacotherapy. The DAS was administered before and after a negative mood induction procedure, in which participants were to think about a time in their lives when they felt sad. While in a neutral mood state, there were no significant between-group differences on the DAS. Following the mood induction, however, those individuals successfully treated with antidepressants exhibited an increase in dysfunctional attitudes, an effect that was not evident in those treated with cognitive therapy (also see Segal & Gemar, 1997). Segal et al. (2006) further documented that this mood-reactivity predicted relapse 18 months later. Such findings indicate that cognitive therapy may differentially alter cognitive patterns associated with relapse.

More recently, Dozois et al. (2009) compared the combination of cognitive therapy and pharmacotherapy (CT+PT) to pharmacotherapy (PT) alone on depressive symptoms, surface-level cognitions (e.g., negative automatic thoughts) and the organization of self-representation (e.g., cognitive structures). Both groups showed significant and equivalent reductions in depressive symptoms, automatic thoughts, and dysfunctional attitudes. Individuals treated with CT+PT, however, demonstrated significantly greater cognitive organization (interconnectedness of adjective content) of positive interpersonal content and less well-connected negative interpersonal content than did individuals treated with medication alone. In addition, patients in the CT+PT group showed significant pre-post differences on positive and negative cognitive organization, an effect that was not evident in the antidepressant group. These findings suggest that cognitive therapy is able to modify cognitive structures that previous research has shown are stable into remission (Dozois, 2007; Dozois & Dobson, 2001a). Although these results are in need of replication, they do suggest that cognitive therapy alters conceptually deeper cognitive structures than does antidepressant medication. This deeper cognitive change may be one reason that cognitive therapy operates as a better prophylaxis against relapse than pharmacotherapy (cf. Gloaguen et al., 1998).

In addition to results of differential mood-reactivity and cognitive structure are neuroimaging data on changes in cognitive therapy (see DeRubeis et al., 2008; and Frewen, Dozois, & Lanius, 2008, for reviews). Goldapple et al. (2004), for instance, examined the neurobiological responses to cognitive therapy (in unmedicated depressed outpatients) and compared these findings to an independent sample of individuals treated with selective serotonin reuptake inhibitors (SSRIs). These researchers found different pre- vs. post-treatment changes in the metabolic activity (Positron Emission Tomography) of individuals treated with cognitive therapy compared to those treated with antidepressant medication. Goldapple et al. proposed that a top-down (cortical-limbic) therapeutic mechanism may have been active in cognitive therapy, whereas a bottom-up (limbic-cortical) mechanism may have active in anti-depressant treatment.

## CONCLUSION

Although the empirical literature has generally supported the main tenets of Beck's theory and therapy, the model has also been expanded and refined over time to incorporate new evidence from experimental cognitive science and the neurosciences (Alford & Beck, 1997; Beck, 1996; 2008; Clark et al., 1999). Much of this research has also initiated and fostered the growth of acceptance- and mindfulness-based approaches (e.g., Teasdale, Segal, & Williams, 1995). As discussed throughout this chapter, acceptance- and mindfulness-based strategies, although not historically emphasized in this theory, are not incompatible with this model. Indeed, such strategies have played a role in cognitive therapy for some time (e.g., Beck et al., 1985), although they have received far less empirical attention and are used less routinely than are direct cognitive change strategies. The primary focus of cognitive therapy is on cognitive change (ideally at the level of deeper cognitive structures), which we maintain is possible through direct cognitive restructuring, behavioral strategies (e.g., behavioral activation, exposure), and acceptance.

As noted earlier in this chapter, we consider acceptance and mindfulness strategies to be neither passing fads nor paradigmatic shifts ("third waves;" see Hofmann & Asmundson, 2008). Rather, our view is that these approaches represent an important component in the ongoing development and refinement of cognitive therapy, an extension that could quite possibly improve treatment outcome. Both explicit cognitive change strategies and acceptance strategies appear to relate positively to therapeutic change (e.g., Forman et al., 2007; Hayes, 2008). Research is needed to examine whether cognitive therapy and acceptance-based approaches produce their effects via similar or diverse mechanisms of change. Determining the extent to which these approaches may be optimally combined, establishing dose-response relationships, and ascertaining when and where to apply these strategies are also important directions for future research.

# REFERENCES

Abela, J. R., & D'Alessandro, D. U. (2002). Beck's cognitive theory of depression: A test of the diathesis-stress and causal mediation components. *British Journal of Clinical Psychology, 41,* 111–128.

Alford, B. A., & Beck, A. T. (1997). *The integrative power of cognitive therapy.* New York, NY: Guilford Press.

Alloy, L. B., Abramson, L. Y., Whitehouse, W. G., Hogan, M. E., Panzarella, C., & Rose, D. T. (2006). Prospective incidence of first onsets and recurrences of depression in individuals at high and low cognitive risk for depression. *Journal of Abnormal Psychology, 115,* 145–156.

Amir, N., Beard, C., Burns, M., & Bomyea, J. (2009). Attention modification program in individuals with generalized anxiety disorder. *Journal of Abnormal Psychology, 118,* 28–33.

Arch, J. J., & Craske, M. G. (2008). Acceptance and commitment therapy and cognitive behavioral therapy for anxiety disorders: Different treatments, similar mechanisms? *Clinical Psychology: Science and Practice, 15,* 263–279.

Ball, S. A. (2003). Cognitive-behavioral and schema-based models for the treatment of substance use disorders. In L. P. Riso, P. L. duToit, D. J. Stein, & J. (Eds.), *Cognitive schemas and core beliefs in psychological problems: A scientist-practitioner guide* (pp. 111–138). Washington, DC: American Psychological Association.

Barnett, P. A., & Gotlib, I. H. (1988). Psychosocial functioning and depression: Distinguishing among antecedents, concomitants, and consequences. *Psychological Bulletin, 104,* 97–126.

Basco, M. R., & Rush, A. J. (2005). *Cognitive-behavioral therapy for bipolar disorder* (2nd ed.). New York, NY: Guilford Press.

Beck, A. T. (1963). Thinking and depression: 1. Idiosyncratic content and cognitive distortions. *Archives of General Psychiatry, 9,* 324–333.

Beck, A. T. (1964). Thinking and depression: 2. Theory and therapy. *Archives of General Psychiatry, 10,* 561–571.

Beck, A. T. (1967). *Depression: Causes and treatment.* Philadelphia: University of Pennsylvania Press.

Beck, A. T. (1976). *Cognitive therapy and the emotional disorders.* New York, NY: International University Press.

Beck, A. T. (1988). *Love is never enough.* New York: Harper and Row.

Beck, A. T. (1996). Beyond belief: A theory of modes, personality, and psychopathology. In P. M. Salkovskis (Ed.), *Frontiers of cognitive therapy* (pp. 1–25). New York, NY: Guilford Press.

Beck, A. T. (2005). The current state of cognitive therapy: A 40-year retrospective. *Archives of General Psychiatry, 62,* 953–959.

Beck, A. T. (2008). The evolution of the cognitive model of depression and its neurobiological correlates. *American Journal of Psychiatry, 165,* 969–977.

Beck, A. T., Brown, G., Steer, R. A., Eidelson J. I., & Riskind, J. H. (1987). Differentiating anxiety and depression: A test of the cognitive content-specificity hypothesis. *Journal of Abnormal Psychology 96,* 179–183

Beck, A. T., & Clark, D. A. (1997). An information processing model of anxiety: Automatic and strategic processes. *Behaviour Research and Therapy , 35,* 49–58.

Beck, A. T., Emery, G., & Greenberg, R. L. (1985). *Anxiety disorders and phobias: A cognitive perspective.* New York, NY: Basic Books.

Beck, A. T., Freeman, A., Davis, D. D., & Associates (2004). Cognitive therapy of personality disorders (2nd ed.). New York, NY: Guilford Press.

Beck, A. T., Rector, N. A., Stolar, N., & Grant, P. (2008). *Schizophrenia: Cognitive theory, research, and therapy.* New York: Guilford.

Beck, A. T., Rush, A. J., Shaw, B. F., & Emery, G. (1979). *Cognitive therapy of depression.* New York: Guilford.

Beck, A. T., Wenzel, A., Riskind, J. H., Brown, G., & Steer, R. A. (2006). Specificity of hopelessness about resolving life problems: Another test of the cognitive model of depression. *Cognitive Therapy and Research, 30,* 773–781.

Beck, A. T., Wright, F. D., Newman, C. F., & Liese, B. S. (1993). *Cognitive therapy of substance abuse.* New York, NY: Guilford Press.

Beck, R., Benedict, B., & Winkler, A. (2003). Depression and anxiety: Integrating tripartite and cognitive content-specificity assessment models. *Journal of Psychopathology and Behavioral Assessment, 25,* 251–256.

Beck, R., & Perkins, T. S. (2001). Cognitive content-specificity for anxiety and depression: A meta-analysis. *Cognitive Therapy and Research, 25,* 651–663.

Beevers, C. G. (2005). Cognitive vulnerability to depression: A dual process model. *Clinical Psychology Review, 25,* 975–1002.

Beevers, C. G., & Miller, I. W. (2005). Unlinking negative cognition and symptoms of depression: Evidence of a specific treatment effect for cognitive therapy. *Journal of Consulting and Clinical Psychology. 73,* 68–77.

Beevers, C. G., Scott, W. D., McGeary, C., & McGeary, J. E. (2009). Negative cognitive response to a sad mood induction: Associations with polymorphisms of the serotonin transporter (5-HTTLPR) gene. *Cognition and Emotion, 23,* 726–738.

Butler, A. C., Chapman, J. E., Forman, E. M., & Beck, A. T. (2006). The empirical status of cognitive-behavioral therapy: A review of meta-analyses. *Clinical Psychology Review, 26,* 17–31.

Chambless, D. L., & Ollendick, T. H. (2001). Empirically supported psychological interventions: Controversies and evidence. *Annual Review of Psychology, 52,* 685–716.

Clark, D. A., Beck, A. T., & Alford, B. A. (1999). *Scientific foundations of cognitive theory and therapy of depression.* New York, NY: Wiley.

Clark, D. A., Beck, A. T., & Stewart, B. (1990). Cognitive specificity and positive-negative affectivity: Complementary or contradictory views on anxiety and depression? *Journal of Abnormal Psychology, 99,* 148–155.

Clark, D. A., Steer, R. A., & Beck, A. T. (1994). Common and specific dimensions of self-reported anxiety and depression: Implications for the cognitive and tripartite models. *Journal of Abnormal Psychology, 103,* 645–654.

Clark, D. M. (1996). Panic disorder: From theory to therapy. In P. M. Salkovskis (Ed.), *Frontiers of cognitive therapy* (pp. 318–344). New York, NY: Guilford Press.

Coyne, J. C., & Gotlib, I. H. (1983). The role of cognition in depression: A critical appraisal. *Psychological Bulletin, 94,* 472–505.

Crick, N. R., & Dodge, K. A. (1994). A review and reformulation of social information-processing mechanisms in children's social adjustment. *Psychological Bulletin, 115,* 73–101.

Dalai Lama, & Beck, A. T. (2005, June). A meeting of the minds: A discussion between his holiness the 14th Dalai Lama and Dr. Aaron Beck. International Congress of Cognitive Psychotherapy, Göteborg, Sweden.

Dattilio, F. M., & Freeman, A. (Eds.). (1994). *Cognitive-behavioral strategies in crisis intervention.* New York, NY: Guilford Press.

DeRubeis, R. J., & Crits-Christoph, P. (1998). Empirically supported individual and group psychological treatments for adult mental disorders. *Journal of Consulting and Clinical Psychology, 66,* 37–52.

DeRubeis, R. J., Evans, M. D., Hollon, S. D., Garvey, M. J., Grove, W. M., & Tuason, V. B. (1990). How does cognitive therapy work? Cognitive change and symptom change in cognitive therapy and pharmacotherapy for depression. *Journal of Consulting & Clinical Psychology, 58,* 862–869.

DeRubeis, R. J., Gelfand, L. A., Tang, T. Z., & Simons, A. (1999). Medications versus cognitive behavioral therapy for severely depressed outpatients: Mega-analysis of four randomized comparisons. *American Journal of Psychiatry, 156,* 1007–1013.

DeRubeis, R. J., Hollon, S. D., Amsterdam, J. D., Shelton, R. C., Young, P. R., Salomon, R. M.,...Gallop, R. (2005). Cognitive therapy vs medications in the treatment of moderate to severe depression. *Archives of General Psychiatry, 62,* 409–416.

DeRubeis, R. J., Siegle, G. J., & Hollon, S. D. (2008). Cognitive therapy versus medication for depression: Treatment outcomes and neural mechanisms. *Nature Reviews Neuroscience, 9,* 788–796.

DeRubeis, R. J., Webb, C. A., Tang, T. Z., & Beck, A. T. (2010). Cognitive therapy. In K. S. Dobson (Ed.), *Handbook of cognitive-behavioral therapies* (3rd ed., pp. 277–316). New York, NY: Guilford Press.

Dimidjian, S., Hollon, S. D., Dobson, K. S., Kohlenberg, R. J., Gallop, R., Markley, D. K., . . . Jacobson, N. S. (2006). Randomized trial of behavioral activation, cognitive therapy, and antidepressant medication in the acute treatment of adults with major depression. *Journal of Consulting and Clinical Psychology, 74,* 658–670.

Dobson, D., & Dobson, K. S. (2009). *Evidence-based practice of cognitive-behavioral therapy.* New York, NY: Guilford Press.

Dobson, K. S., & Dozois, D. J. A. (2004). Attentional biases in eating disorders: A meta-analytic review of Stroop performance. *Clinical Psychology Review, 23,* 1001–1022.

Dobson, K. S., & Dozois, D. J. A. (2010). Historical and philosophical bases of the cognitive-behavioral therapies. In K. S. Dobson (Ed.), *Handbook of cognitive-behavioral therapies* (3rd ed., pp. 3–38). New York, NY: Guilford Press.

Dobson, K. S., Hollon, S. D., Dimidjian, S., Schmaling, K. B., Kohlenberg, R. J., Gallop, R. J., . . . Jacobson, N. S. (2008). Randomized trial of behavioral activation, cognitive therapy, and antidepressant medication in the prevention of relapse and recurrence in major depression. *Journal of Consulting and Clinical Psychology, 76*(3), 468–477.

Dozois, D. J. A. (2007). Stability of negative self-structures: A longitudinal comparison of depressed, remitted, and nonpsychiatric controls. *Journal of Clinical Psychology, 63,* 319–338.

Dozois, D. J. A., & Beck, A. T. (2008). Cognitive schemas, beliefs and assumptions. In K. S. Dobson & D. J. A. Dozois (Eds.), *Risk factors in depression* (pp. 121–143). Oxford, England: Elsevier/Academic Press.

Dozois, D. J. A., Bieling, P. J., Patelis-Siotis, I., Hoar, L., Chudzik, S., McCabe, K., . . . Westra, H. A. (2009). Changes in self-schema structure in cognitive therapy for major depressive disorder. *Journal of Consulting and Clinical Psychology, 77,* 1078–1088.

Dozois, D. J. A., & Dobson, K. S. (2001a). A longitudinal investigation of information processing and cognitive organization in clinical depression: Stability of schematic interconnectedness. *Journal of Consulting and Clinical Psychology, 69,* 914–925.

Dozois, D. J. A., & Dobson, K. S. (2001b). Information processing and cognitive organization in unipolar depression: Specificity and comorbidity issues. *Journal of Abnormal Psychology, 110,* 236–246.

Dozois, D. J. A., & Frewen, P. A. (2006). Specificity of cognitive structure in depression and social phobia: A comparison of interpersonal and achievement content. *Journal of Affective Disorders, 90,* 101–109.

Ehlers, A., & Clark, D. M. (2000). A cognitive model of posttraumatic stress disorder. *Behaviour Research and Therapy, 38,* 319–345.

Ellis, A. (1962). *Reason and emotion in psychotherapy.* New York, NY: Lyle Stuart.

Epp, A., & Dobson, K. S. (2010). The evidence base for cognitive-behavioral therapy. In K. S. Dobson (Ed.), *Handbook of Cognitive-Behavioral Therapies* (3rd ed., 39–73). New York, NY: Guilford Press.

Evans, J., Heron, J., Lewis, G., Araya, R., & Wolke, D. (2005). Negative self-schemas and the onset of depression in women: A longitudinal study. *British Journal of Psychiatry, 186,* 302–307.

Farb, N. A. S., Segal, Z. V., Mayberg, H., Bean, J., McKeon, D., Fatima, Z., & Anderson, A. K. (2007). Attending to the present: Mindfulness meditation reveals neural modes of self-reference. *Social Cognitive and Affective Neuroscience, 2,* 313–322.

Forman, E. M., Herbert, J. D., Moitra, E., Yeomans, P. D., & Geller, P. A. (2007). A randomized controlled effectiveness trial of acceptance and commitment therapy and cognitive therapy for anxiety and depression. *Behavior Modification, 31,* 772–779.

Frewen, P. A., Dozois, D. J. A., & Lanius, R. A. (2008). Neuroimaging studies of psychological interventions for mood and anxiety disorders: Empirical and methodological review. *Clinical Psychology Review, 28,* 228–246.

Garratt, G., Ingram, R. E., Rand, K. L., & Sawalani, G. (2007). Cognitive processes in cognitive therapy: Evaluation of the mechanisms of change in the treatment of depression. *Clinical Psychology: Science and Practice, 14,* 224–239.

Gibb, B. E., Abramson, L. Y., & Alloy, L. B. (2004). Emotional maltreatment from parents, verbal victimization, and cognitive vulnerability to depression. *Cognitive Therapy and Research, 28,* 1–21.

Gloaguen, V., Cottraux, J., Cucherat, M., & Blackburn, I. (1998). A meta-analysis of the effects of cognitive therapy in depression. *Journal of Affective Disorders, 49,* 59–72.

Goldapple, K., Segal, Z., Garson, C., Lau, M., Bieling, P., Kennedy, S., & Mayberg, H. (2004). Modulation of cortical-limbic pathways in major depression: Treatment-specific effects of cognitive behavior therapy. *Archives of General Psychiatry, 61,* 34–41.

Gortner, E. T., Gollan, J. K., Dobson, K. S., & Jacobson, N. S. (1998). Cognitive-behavioral treatment for depression: Relapse prevention. *Journal of Consulting and Clinical Psychology, 66*(2), 377–384.

Greenberger, D., & Padesky, C.A. (1995). *Mind over mood: Change how you feel by changing the way you think.* New York, NY: Guilford Press.

Hankin, B. L., Abramson, L. Y., Miller, N., & Haeffel, G. J. (2004). Cognitive vulnerability-stress theories of depression: Examining affective specificity in the prediction of depression versus anxiety in three prospective studies. *Cognitive Therapy and Research, 28,* 309–345.

Hankin, B. L., Fraley, C., & Abela, J. R. Z. (2005). Daily depression and cognitions about stress: Evidence for a trait-like depressogenic cognitive style and the prediction of depressive symptoms in a prospective daily diary study. *Journal of Personality and Social Psychology, 88,* 673–685.

Hayes, S. C. (2008). Climbing our hills: A beginning conversation on the comparison of acceptance and commitment therapy and traditional cognitive behavioral therapy. *Clinical Psycholology: Science and Practice, 15,* 286–295.

Hayes, S. C., Follette, V. M., & Linehan, M. M. (Eds.). (2004). *Mindfulness and acceptance: Expanding the cognitive-behavioral tradition.* New York, NY: Guilford Press.

Hayes, S. C., Strosahl, K. D., & Wilson, K. G. (1999). *Acceptance and commitment therapy: An experiential approach to behavior change.* New York: Guilford.

Hedlund, S., & Rude, S. S. (1995). Evidence of latent depressive schemas in formerly depressed individuals. *Journal of Abnormal Psychology, 104,* 517–525.

Hofmann, S. G. (2008a). Acceptance and commitment therapy: New wave or Morita therapy? *Clinical Psychology: Science and Practice, 15,* 280–285.

Hofmann, S. G. (2008b). Common misconceptions about cognitive mediation of treatment change: A commentary to Longmore and Worrell (2007). *Clinical Psychology Review, 28,* 67–70.

Hofmann, S. G., & Asmundson, G. J. G. (2008). Acceptance and mindfulness-based therapy: New wave or old hat? *Clinical Psychology Review, 28,* 1–16.

Hofmann, S. G., Meuret, A. E., Rosenfield, D., Suvak, M. K., Barlow, D. H., Gorman, J. M., . . . Woods, S. W. (2007). Preliminary evidence for cognitive mediation during cognitive-behavioral therapy of panic disorder. *Journal of Consulting and Clinical Psychology, 75,* 374–379.

Hollon, S. D., DeRubeis, R. J., Shelton, R. C., Amsterdam, J. D., Salomon, R. M., O'Reardon, J. P., . . . Gallop, R. (2005). Prevention of relapse following cognitive therapy vs. medications in moderate to severe depression. *Archives of General Psychiatry, 62,* 417–422.

Hollon, S. D., Thase, M. E., & Markowitz, J. C. (2002). Treatment and prevention of depression. *Psychological Science, 39–77.*

Ingram, R.E. (2003). Origins of cognitive vulnerability to depression. *Cognitive Therapy & Research, 27,* 77–88.

Ingram, R. E., Bernet, C. Z., & McLaughlin, S. C. (1994). Attentional allocation processes in individuals at risk for depression. *Cognitive Therapy and Research, 18,* 317–332.

Ingram, R. E., Miranda, J., & Segal, Z. V. (1998). *Cognitive vulnerability to depression.* New York, NY: Guilford Press.

Jacobson, N. S., Dobson, K. S., Truax, P. A., Addis, M. E., Koerner, K., Gollan, J. K., . . . Prince, S. E. (1996). A component analysis of cognitive-behavioral treatment for depression. *Journal of Consulting and Clinical Psychology, 64,* 295–304.

Jarrett, R. B., Vittengl, J. R., Doyle, K., & Clark, L. A. (2007). Changes in cognitive content during and following cognitive therapy for recurrent depression: Substantial and enduring but not predictive of change in depressive symptoms. *Journal of Consulting and Clinical Psychology, 75,* 432–446.

Joiner, T. E., Jr., Metalsky, G.I., Lew, A., & Klocek, J. (1999). Testing the causal mediation component of Beck's theory of depression: Evidence for specific mediation. *Cognitive Therapy and Research, 23,* 401–412

Kant, I. (1929). *Critique of pure reason.* (N. K. Smith, Trans.). London, England: Macmillan. (Original work published 1781).

Kazdin, A. E. (1978). *History of behavior modification: Experimental foundations of contemporary research.* Baltimore, MD: University Park Press.

Kelly, G. (1955). *The psychology of personal constructs.* New York, NY: W. W. Norton.

Kelly, G. A. (1963). *A theory of personality.* New York: W. W. Norton.

Kingdon, D. (2010). Over-simplification and exclusion of non-conforming studies can demonstrate absence of effect: A lynching party? *Psychological Medicine, 40,* 25–27.

Kovacs, M., & Beck, A. T. (1978). Maladaptive cognitive structures in depression. *American Journal of Psychiatry, 135,* 525–533.

Kuiper, N. A., & Olinger, L. J. (1986). Dysfunctional attitudes and a self-worth contingency model of depression. In P. C. Kendall (Ed.), *Advances in cognitive-behavioral research and therapy* (Vol. 5, pp. 115–142). New York, NY: Academic.

Kuyken, W., Padesky, C. A., & Dudley, R. (2009). *Collaborative case conceptualization: Working effectively with clients in cognitive-behavioral therapy.* New York, NY: Guilford Press.

Kwon, S.-M., & Oei, T. P. S. (1992). Differential causal roles of dysfunctional attitudes and automatic thoughts in depression. *Cognitive Therapy and Research, 16,* 309–328.

Lavy, E., van den Hout, M., & Arntz, A. (1993). Attentional bias and spider phobia: Conceptual and clinical issues. *Behaviour Research and Therapy, 31,* 17–24.

Lazarus, R. S., & Folkman, S. (1984). *Stress, appraisal and coping.* New York, NY: Springer.

Lewinsohn, P. M., Joiner, T. E., & Rohde, P. (2001). Evaluation of cognitive diathesis-stress models in predicting major depressive disorder in adolescents. *Journal of Abnormal Psychology, 110,* 203–215.

Linehan, M. M. (1993). *Cognitive-behavioral treatment of borderline personality disorder.* New York, NY: Guilford Press.

Longmore, R. J., & Worrell, M. (2007). Do we need to challenge thoughts in cognitive behaviour therapy? *Clinical Psychology Review, 27,* 173–187.

Lumley, M. N., & Harkness, K. L. (2009). Childhood maltreatment and depressotypic cognitive organization. *Cognitive Therapy and Research, 33,* 511–522.

Lynch, D., Law, K. R., & McKenna, P. J. (2010). Cognitive behavioural therapy for major psychiatric disorder: Does it really work? A meta-analytical review of well-controlled trials. *Psychological Medicine, 40,* 9–24.

MacLeod, C., Rutherford, E., Campbell, L., Ebsworthy, G., & Holker, L. (2002). Selective attention and emotional vulnerability: Assessing the causal basis of their association through the experimental manipulation of attentional bias. *Journal of Abnormal Psychology, 111,* 107–123.

Mathews, A., & MacLeod, C. (2002). Induced processing biases have causal effects on anxiety. *Cognition & Emotion, 16, 3,* 331–354.

Mathews, A., & MacLeod, C. (2005). Cognitive vulnerability to emotional disorders. *Annual Review of Clinical Psychology, 1,* 167–195.

Mathews, A., Mogg, K., Kentish, J., & Eysenck, M. (1995). Effect of psychological treatment on cognitive bias in generalized anxiety disorder. *Behaviour Research and Therapy, 33,* 293–303.

Mattia, J. I., Heimberg, R. G., & Hope, D. A. (1993). The revised Stroop color-naming task in social phobics. *Behaviour Research and Therapy, 31,* 305–313.

Miranda, J., Gross, J. J., Persons, J. B., & Hahn, J. (1998). Mood matters: Negative mood induction activates dysfunctional attitudes in women vulnerable to depression. *Cognitive Therapy and Research, 22,* 363–376.

Miranda, J., & Persons, J. B. (1988). Dysfunctional attitudes are mood-state dependent. *Journal of Abnormal Psychology, 97,* 76–79.

Miranda, J., Persons, J. B., & Byers, C. N. (1990). Endorsement of dysfunctional beliefs depends on current mood state. *Journal of Abnormal Psychology, 99,* 237–241.

Moore, R. G., & Blackburn, I. M. (1996). The stability of sociotropy and autonomy in depressed patients undergoing treatment. *Cognitive Therapy and Research, 20,* 69–80.

Nevid, J. S. (2007). Kant, cognitive psychotherapy, and the hardening of the categories. *Psychology and Psychotherapy: Theory, Research and Practice, 80,* 605–615.

Oei, T. P. S., & Sullivan, L. M. (1999). Cognitive changes following recovery from depression in a group cognitive-behaviour therapy program. *Australian and New Zealand Journal of Psychiatry, 33,* 407–415.

Ohrt, T., Sjödin, I., & Thorell, L. (1999). Cognitive distortions in panic disorder and major depression: Specificity for depressed mood. *Nordic Journal of Psychiatry, 53,* 459–464.

Olson, J. M., Roese, N. J., & Zanna, M. P. (1996). Expectancies. In E. T. Higgins & A. W. Kruglanski (Eds.), *Social psychology: Handbook of basic principles* (pp. 211–238). New York, NY: Guilford Press.

Öst, L. (2008). Efficacy of the third wave of behavioral therapies: A systematic review and meta-analysis. *Behaviour Research and Therapy, 46,* 296–321.

Otto, M. W., Teachman, B. A., Cohen, L. S., Soares, C. N., Vitonis, A. F., & Harlow, B. L. (2007). Dysfunctional attitudes and episodes of major depression: Predictive validity and temporal stability in never-depressed, depressed, and recovered women. *Journal of Abnormal Psychology, 116,* 475–483.

Ouimet, A. J., Gawronski, B., & Dozois, D. J. A. (2009). Cognitive vulnerability to anxiety: A review and an integrative model. *Clinical Psychology Review, 29,* 259–270.

Persons, J. B., & Miranda, J. (1992). Cognitive theories of vulnerability to depression—Reconciling negative evidence. *Cognitive Therapy and Research, 16,* 485–502.

Piaget, J. (1950). *Psychology of intelligence* (M. Piercy and D. E. Berlyne, Trans.) New York, NY: Harcourt Brace. (Original work published in 1947).

Rector, N. A., Bagby, R. M., Segal, Z. V., Joffe, R. T., & Levitt, A. (2000). Self-criticism and dependency in depressed patients treated with cognitive therapy or pharmacotherapy. *Cognitive Therapy and Research, 24,* 571–584.

Roemer, L., & Orsillo, S. M. (2009). *Mindfulness- and acceptance-based behavioral therapies in practice.* New York, NY: Guilford Press.

Rogers, C. R. (1951). *Client-centered therapy.* Boston, MA: Houghton Mifflin.

Rogers, T. B., Kuiper, N. A., & Kirker, W. S. (1977). Self-reference and the encoding of personal information. *Journal of Personality and Social Psychology, 35,* 677–688.

Rush, A. J., Beck, A. T., Kovacs, M., Weissenburger, J., & Hollon, S. D. (1982). Comparison of the effects of cognitive therapy and pharmacotherapy on hopelessness and self-concept. *American Journal of Psychiatry, 139,* 862–866.

Scher, C. D., Ingram, R. E., & Segal, Z. V. (2005). Cognitive reactivity and vulnerability: Empirical evaluation of construct activation and cognitive diatheses in unipolar depression. *Clinical Psychology Review, 25,* 487–510.

Schniering, C. A., & Rapee, R. M. (2004). The relationship between automatic thoughts and negative emotions in children and adolescents: A test of the content-specificity hypothesis. *Journal of Abnormal Psycholology, 113,* 464–470.

Schwartz, R. M., & Garamoni, G. L. (1986). A structural model of positive and negative states of mind: Asymmetry in the internal dialogue. In P. C. Kendall (Ed.), *Advances in cognitive-behavioral research and therapy* (Vol. 5, pp. 1–62). New York, NY: Academic Press.

Segal, Z. V. (1988). Appraisal of the self-schema construct in cognitive models of depression. *Psychological Bulletin, 103,* 147–162.

Segal, Z. V., & Gemar, M. (1997). Changes in cognitive organization for negative self-referent material following cognitive behavior therapy for depression: A primed Stroop study. *Cognition and Emotion, 11,* 501–516.

Segal, Z. V., Gemar, M., Truchon, C., Guirguis, M., & Horowitz, L. M. (1995). A priming methodology for studying self-representation in major depressive disorder. *Journal of Abnormal Psychology, 104,* 205–213.

Segal, Z .V., Gemar, M., & Williams, S. (1999). Differential cognitive response to a mood challenge following successful cognitive therapy or pharmacotherapy for unipolar depression. *Journal of Abnormal Psychology, 108,* 3–10.

Segal, Z. V., Kennedy, S., Gemar, M., Hood, K., Pedersen, R., & Buis, T. (2006). Cognitive reactivity to sad mood provocation and the prediction of depressive relapse. *Archives of General Psychiatry, 63,* 749–755.

Segal, Z. V., Williams, J. M. G., & Teasdale, J. D. (2002). *Mindfulness-based cognitive therapy for depression: A new approach to preventing relapse.* New York: Guilford.

Simons, A. D., Garfield, S. L., & Murphy, G. E. (1984). The process of change in cognitive therapy and pharmacotherapy for depression: Changes in mood and cognition. *Archives of General Psychiatry, 41,* 45–51.

Solomon, A., Haaga, D. A. F., Brody, C., Kirk, L., & Friedman, D. G. (1998). Priming irrational beliefs in recovered-depressed people. *Journal of Abnormal Psychology, 107,* 440–449.

Steer, R. A., Clark, D. A., Beck, A. T., & Ranieri, W. F. (1995). Common and specific dimensions of self-reported anxiety and depression: A replication. *Journal of Abnormal Psychology, 104,* 542–545.

Symons, C. S., & Johnson, B. T. (1997). The self-reference effect in memory: A meta-analysis. *Psychological Bulletin, 121,* 371–394.

Tang, T. Z., & DeRubeis, R. J. (1999). Sudden gains and critical sessions in cognitive behavioral therapy for depression. *Journal of Consulting and Clinical Psychology, 67,* 894–904.

Teasdale, J. D. (1996). Clinically relevant theory: Integrating clinical insight with cognitive science. In P. M. Salkovskis (Ed.), *Frontiers of cognitive therapy* (pp. 26–47). New York, NY: Guilford Press.

Teasdale, J. D., & Barnard, P. J. (1993). *Affect, cognition, & change: Re-modeling depressive thought.* Hillsdale, NJ: Erlbaum.

Teasdale, J. D., & Dent, J. (1987). Cognitive vulnerability to depression: An investigation of two hypotheses. *British Journal of Clinical Psychology, 26,* 113–126.

Teasdale, J. D., Segal, Z. V., & Williams, J. M. G. (1995). How does cognitive therapy prevent depressive relapse and why should attentional control (mindfulness) training help? *Behaviour Research and Therapy, 33,* 25–39.

Tversky, M., & Kahneman, D. (1974). Judgment under uncertainty: Heuristics and biases. *Science, 185,* 1124–1131.

Wampold, B. E., Minami, T., Baskin. T. W., & Tierney, S. C. (2002). A meta-(re)analysis of the effects of cognitive therapy versus "other therapies" for depression. *Journal of Affective Disorders, 68,* 159–165.

Wells, A. (1997). *Cognitive therapy of anxiety disorders.* New York, NY: Wiley.

Wells, A. (2002). Worry, metacognition, and GAD: Nature, consequences, and treatment. *Journal of Cognitive Psychotherpy: An International Quarterly, 16,* 179–192.

Wells, A. (2008). Metacognitive therapy: Cognition applied to regulating emotion. *Behavioural and Cognitive Psychotherapy, 36,* 651–658.

Westen, D., & Morrison, K. (2001). A multidimensional meta-analysis of treatments for depression, panic, and generalized anxiety disorder: An empirical examination of the status of empirically supported therapies. *Journal of Consulting and Clinical Psychology, 69,* 875–899.

Westra, H. A., Dozois, D. J. A., & Boardman, C. (2002). Predictors of treatment change and engagement in cognitive-behavioural group therapy for depression. *Journal of Cognitive Psychotherapy: An International Quarterly, 16,* 227–241.

Westra, H. A., & Kuiper, N. A. (1997). Cognitive content specificity in selective attention across four domains of maladjustment. *Behavior Research and Therapy, 35,* 349–365.

Whisman, M. A. (1993). Mediators and moderators of change in cognitive therapy of depression. *Psychological Bulletin, 114,* 248–265.

Whisman, M. A., Miller, I. W., Norman, W. H., & Keitner, G. I. (1991). Cognitive therapy with depressed inpatients: Specific effects on dysfunctional cognitions. *Journal of Consulting and Clinical Psychology, 59,* 282–288.

Williams, J. M., Mathews, A., & MacLeod, C. (1996). The emotional Stroop task and psychopathology. *Psychological Bulletin, 120,* 3–24.

Williams, J. M. G., Watts, F. N., MacLeod, C., & Mathews, A. M. (1997). *Cognitive psychology and the emotional disorders* (2nd ed.). Chichester, West Sussex: Wiley.

Williams, M., Teasdale, J., Segal, Z., & Kabat-Zinn, J. (2007). *The mindful way through depression: Freeing yourself from chronic unhappiness.* New York, NY: Guilford Press.

Woody, S.R., Taylor, S., McLean, P.D., & Koch, W. J. (1998). Cognitive specificity in panic and depression: Implications for comorbidity. *Cognitive Therapy & Research, 22,* 427–443.

Young, J. E., & Beck, A. T. (1980). *Cognitive Therapy Scale rating manual.* Unpublished manuscript, University of Pennsylvania, Philadelphia.

Young, J. E., Klosko, J. S., & Weshaar, M. E. (2003). *Schema therapy: A practitioner's guide.* New York, NY: Guilford Press.

Young, J. E., Rygh, J. L., Weinberger, A. D., & Beck, A. T. (2008). Cognitive therapy for depression. In D. H. Barlow (Ed.), *Clinical handbook of psychological disorders: A step-by-step treatment manual* (4th ed., pp. 250–305). New York, NY: Guilford Press.

# 3

## Mindfulness-Based Cognitive Therapy

### DAVID M. FRESCO, JESSICA J. FLYNN, DOUGLAS S. MENNIN, AND EMILY A. P. HAIGH

According to the fourth revision of the *Diagnostic and Statistical Manual of Mental Disorders* (DSM-IV-TR, American Psychiatric Association [APA], 2000), Major Depressive Disorder (MDD) is a mood disorder characterized by one or more major depressive episodes (i.e., at least two weeks of depressed mood or loss of interest or pleasure in nearly all activities), accompanied by at least four additional symptoms such as changes in sleep, appetite or weight, and psychomotor activity; decreased energy; feelings of worthlessness or guilt; difficulty thinking, concentrating, or making decisions; or recurrent thoughts of death or suicidal ideation, plans, or attempts. MDD represents an enormous mental health challenge, with lifetime prevalence estimated at 17% (Kessler, Bergland, & Demler, 2005). Similarly, individuals who suffer from one depressive episode will, on average, experience four major depressive episodes of 20 weeks' duration over their lifetime.

According to a recently released World Health Organization study of 245,000 in sixty nations, MDD is more damaging to everyday health than chronic diseases such as angina, arthritis, asthma, and diabetes (Moussavi et al., 2007). MDD is estimated to cause the fourth-greatest burden of ill health of all diseases worldwide and will move into second place by 2020 (Murray & Lopez, 1998). Despite successful medication and psychotherapies, fewer than half of patients achieve remission (Casacalenda, Perry, & Looper, 2002), and relapse is more likely in individuals who do not fully recover (Jarrett et al., 2001; Thase, Entsuah, & Rudolph, 2001). For these reasons, both basic and treatment research efforts are homing in on the identification of vulnerability factors associated with the onset and maintenance of depression as well mechanisms that promote risk of relapse.

Meditation and other mental training exercises deriving from the 2,500-year Buddhist and Hindu traditions represent one potentially fruitful area of study that has the potential to expand contemporary models of depression as well as complement existing medication and psychotherapy treatments. The past 30 years have witnessed an increasing interest in meditation, yoga, and other mental training exercises that emanate from Hindu and Buddhist traditions. The use of these practices has dovetailed in recent years with the emergence of affective neuroscience, a subdiscipline within the fields of psychology, psychiatry, and neurology that examines the neural bases of mood and emotion. The union of these Eastern practices within the scrutiny of a Western scientific approach to investigation has lead to the development of novel and effective clinical interventions that aim to restore psychological functioning and reduce human suffering across a wide variety of illnesses (Ospina et al., 2008), while also offering a tantalizing glimpse into neural correlates of emotional processing (e.g., Cahn & Polich, 2006) and how factors (e.g., the presence of major depressive disorder, or a lifetime of monastic practice) result in signature patterns of activation within the brain (Davidson & Lutz, 2008). One practice that has been shown to have saliency to the study and treatment of MDD is mindfulness meditation. Kabat-Zinn (1995, p. 4), a contemporary theorist, practitioner, and teacher, describes mindfulness as a process of bringing a certain quality of attention to moment-by-moment experience by "paying attention in a particular way...on purpose...in the present-moment...non-judgmentally." The ability to cultivate a state of mindfulness is believed to arise with practice of Buddhist mental training exercises, such as meditation.

The objectives of this chapter are to provide a contemporary theoretical account of MDD as a bio-psychosocial condition that has been enriched by mindfulness and acceptance principles. In doing so, we create linkage to the traditional cognitive behavioral model, which, even early on, viewed MDD as arising from a failure to access metacognitive skills that promote healthy emotional processing. After reviewing evidence associating metacognitive awareness with depression, we posit that this emphasis on metacognition instead of cognitive content per se has created fertile ground to incorporate mindfulness principles into the etiology and treatment model. We conclude the chapter by reviewing findings from studies that include mindfulness-enriched treatments for MDD and other emotional disorders, and then frame issues facing our field given the promising start in incorporating mindfulness principles into our models.

## THE TRADITIONAL COGNITIVE BEHAVIORAL MODEL OF THE PSYCHOPATHOLOGY AND TREATMENT OF MAJOR DEPRESSIVE DISORDER

Cognitive diathesis-stress theories of depression (Abramson, Seligman, & Teasdale, 1978; Beck, 1967; 1976) have advanced our understanding of the etiology, maintenance, and treatment of the disorder in a number of ways. These theories posit that vulnerability to depression arises through early life experiences that lead one to develop a depressogenic view of the world. Specifically, the Reformulated Learned Helplessness Theory (Abramson et al., 1978) and Hopelessness Theory (Abramson et al., 1989) both conceptualize vulnerability to depression in terms of a depressogenic or pessimistic explanatory style (specifically, the tendency to view negative events as arising from stable, global, and internal causes). Similarly, Beck's (1967; 1976) theory of depression posits that vulnerability to depression is associated with dysfunctional attitudes and negative schema regarding the self, world, and future.

## Traditional Targets of Cognitive Therapy of Depression

Cognitive behavioral theories of depression have informed and influenced efforts to develop psychotherapies that include techniques to teach individuals how to identify and challenge pessimistic causal attributions for actual events (Seligman, 1980) or dysfunctional thoughts (Beck, Rush, Shaw, & Emery, 1979). Empirical findings consistently support the efficacy of cognitive therapy of depression (e.g., Hollon, Stewart, & Strunk, 2006). The specific mechanisms of change in cognitive therapy remain a topic of great interest in the field, and a detailed review is beyond the scope of the current chapter. Early in the canon of cognitive therapy, discussion focused on which facets of cognition were the most appropriate targets for change in cognitive therapy. Hollon and colleagues differentiate between two main kinds of cognitions: *cognitive structures* and *cognitive products* (Ingram & Hollon, 1986; Hollon & Garber, 1988; Hollon & Kriss, 1984; Kendall & Ingram, 1989). Cognitive structures represent "the way or manner in which information is represented in memory" (Ingram & Hollon, 1986, p. 263). Cognitive structures play an active role in the processing of information. Cognitive schemas (or schemata) represent a form of cognitive structure important to the cognitive theories and therapies for depression. In contrast, cognitive products represent directly accessible, conscious thoughts, such as self-statements, automatic thoughts, and causal attributions. Such products result from the processing of sensory input information through cognitive structures.

The distinction between cognitive structures and cognitive products is important with respect to cognitive therapy of depression. For example, theorists caution that targeting cognitive products will likely yield limited clinical utility, as such interventions amount to symptomatic treatments (Hollon & Kriss, 1984; Safran, Vallis, Segal, & Shaw, 1986). This issue has propelled treatment approaches that address cognitive structure. For example, Beck and colleagues (1979) state explicitly that changes in cognitive structures or core schemas represent critical change mechanisms in cognitive therapy. Similarly, Safran et al. (1986) assert that efforts at cognitive change should focus on core processes. Furthermore, Beck (1984) warned that depressed individuals would remain vulnerable for relapse when underlying cognitive structures were not targeted and changed. More recently, Hollon et al. (2005) found that patients treated with cognitive therapy who became unrealistically positive or optimistic in their thinking actually evidenced less durable treatment responses compared to patients who developed thinking that was seen as more realistic. Thus, throughout the history of cognitive therapy of depression, the discussion has, at times, centered on whether cognitive content change was sufficient to produce the therapeutic benefits or rather whether a more structural change in the relationship with cognitive material was the true mechanism of action. Clearly, the issue of cognitive change mechanisms has remained a topic of great interest (e.g., Jacobson et al., 1996; Tang & DeRubeis, 1999) and, more specifically, has provided opportunities to better elucidate the metacognitive nature of cognitive therapy.

## METACOGNITIVE APPROACHES TO EMOTIONAL PROCESSING

"Metacognition refers to one's knowledge concerning one's own cognitive processes or anything related to them" (Flavell, 1976, p. 232). In essence, metacognition represents a cognitive process that facilitates the making and transformation of meaning in our lives. Transforming meaning remains an important focus in many systems of psychotherapy particularly outside of traditional cognitive therapy (e.g., Brewin & Power, 1999; Greenberg, 2002). However, cognitive behavioral approaches, particularly in relation to fear and anxiety, have long discussed and studied emotional processing (e.g., Foa & Kozak, 1986; Rachman, 1980). A common thread tying together these approaches is an appreciation that the making and transformation of meaning is the result of the processing and integration of information, particularly emotionally laden information from multiple pathways. Specifically, investigators typically distinguish explicit higher-order conceptual processing involving primarily rule-based learning from more rapid, associational processing involving classically conditioned learning (e.g., Power & Dalgleish, 1997; Teasdale, 1999). These processing channels correspond closely to the higher and lower routes proposed by LeDoux (1996) in his neurobiological model of emotions. Similarly, Greenberg and Safran (1987) also stressed the importance of addressing multiple pathways to emotion within therapy. Thus, drawing from cognitive science approaches, these multilevel models of emotion processing stress the qualitative aspects of the information that are typically generated from higher and lower order emotional pathways and the manner in which they are retrieved (e.g., Leventhal & Scherer, 1987; Power & Dalgleish, 1997; Teasdale, 1999).

### Metacognitive Model of Depression

Although recent years have seen a growing emphasis on metacognitive factors in the etiology and treatment of depression (e.g., Teasdale, 1999), Beck's (1984) etiological and treatment model was inherently metacognitive in nature. For instance, Ingram and Hollon (1986, p. 272) stated that "cognitive therapy relies on helping individuals switch to a controlled, effortful mode of processing that is metacognitive in nature and focuses on depression-related cognition" and that "the long-term effectiveness of cognitive therapy may lie in teaching patients to initiate this process in the face of future stress." Barnard and Teasdale's multi-level theory of mind (1991; Teasdale, 1999) provides an explicit metacognitive framework for understanding the relationship between psychopathology and how individuals process their environment. According to Teasdale's theory, vulnerability to depression is associated with the degree to which an individual relies on a particular mode of mind to the exclusion of the other modes. Teasdale (1999) postulated that risk of recurrence and relapse to depression is related to the ease in which depressogenic, ruminative processing becomes reinstated, rather than the presence or absence of particular negative beliefs or assumptions.

## METACOGNITIVE PROCESSING AND DEPRESSION

### Interacting Cognitive Subsystems and Vulnerability to Depression

Barnard and Teasdale's (1991) multilevel theory of mind, the Interacting Cognitive Subsystems (ICS), identifies three modes of mind available to individuals for processing information. The *mindless emoting* mode is characterized by purely reactive, sensory-driven reactions without attention to "the bigger picture." The *conceptualizing-doing* mode is associated with processing that involves a focus on conceptual content and analyses, for example, going grocery shopping. Finally, the *mindful-experiencing* mode of mind refers to the recognition of thoughts, feelings, and internal and external sensations, which culminate in a synthesis of awareness. The ICS theory strives to account for the ways in which humans process information both cognitively and emotionally.

According to ICS theory, mental health is associated with the ability to disengage from a particular mode of mind or to flexibly switch among the modes of mind. Thus, an optimal state is one in which individuals can deftly switch between the three identified modes of mind based upon conditions in the environment. Still, each of these modes of mind has particular relevance to one's vulnerability to depression.

Within the ICS framework, the mindful experiencing/being mode is characterized by cognitive-affective inner exploration, use of present feelings as a guide for problem-solving and a nonevaluative awareness of present subjective-self-experience. In this mode, feelings, sensations, and thoughts are directly sensed as aspects of subjective experience, rather than being objects of conceptual thought. Of the three different processing configurations, the mindful experiencing/being mode is the only configuration conducive to emotional processing. Emotional processing involves integrating new elements within the existing schema to create new alternative patterns of schematic meanings. The mindful/experiencing mode of mind is thought to relate to emotional well-being (Teasdale. 1999).

In contrast, according to ICS theory, the mindless emoting and conceptualizing/doing modes of mind are theorized to confer vulnerability to depression (Teasdale, 1999). Individuals in a mindless emoting mode have a conscious experience characterized as being immersed in, and identified with, their affective reactions, with little self-awareness, internal exploration, or reflection. This mode can be contrasted with the awareness of subjective experiences characteristic of the mindful experiencing/being mode. One form of mindless emoting mode is *cognitive reactivity*, which is defined as a change in one or more cognitive indices in response to an emotion evocation challenge (Fresco, Segal, Buis, & Kennedy, 2007). Cognitive reactivity has been associated with psychological vulnerability and increased risk to depression (Segal, Gemar, & Williams, 1999; Segal et al., 2006).

Thus, Teasdale (1999) postulates that the risk of recurrence and relapse to depression is related to an individual's capacity to alternate between processing modes in a flexible manner depending on input from the environment. In this way, individuals who remain rigidly in a mindless emoting or conceptualized/doing mode are subject to increased risk for negative affect states. However, it is particularly problematic when individuals vacillate between conceptualizing/doing and mindless emoting processing modes. Although not rigidly bound to one mode of processing, a rapid switching between these modes leaves individuals vulnerable to what Teasdale (1999) refers to as a "depressive interlock," which involves a feedback loop of ruminative thinking about the self, about depression, and about its causes and consequences. Depressive interlock occurs when the mind becomes dominated by processing information with negative, depressive content. This type of thinking creates a negative feedback loop that is hypothesized to maintain depression and reinstate it at time of relapse and recurrence. Teasdale suggests that this pattern of thinking is similar to Nolen-Hoeksema's (1991) conceptualization of depressive rumination. Therefore, when considering Teasdale's ICS model, any treatment for depression should result both in more time spent in mindful-experiencing mode and the ability to more flexibly switch among modes of mind depending on the context of emotional processing.

## Metacognition and Vulnerability to Depression

### *Metacognitive Awareness*

A central component of the metacognitive model of depression is the construct of *metacognitive awareness*, which is broadly defined as the ability to experience negative thoughts/feelings as mental events instead of being synonymous with one's self (Teasdale & Barnard, 1993; Teasdale, Segal, & Williams, 1995). This broadened perspective on negative events is encoded in memory and consequently represents a more adaptive way to relate to negative thoughts when they arise. Individuals high in metacognitive awareness, compared to individuals low in metacognitive awareness, are better able to evade depression and its sequelae when disidentifying with negative thoughts and feelings that arise in the face of a stressful situation. In recent years, several correlates of metacognitive awareness have received attention in correlational, prospective, experimental, and treatment studies.

Teasdale and colleagues (2002) examined the relationship of reduced metacognitive awareness to depression vulnerability and the effects of cognitive therapy on metacognitive awareness in relation to depression relapse. The first study revealed that euthymic patients with a history of depression demonstrated significantly lower levels of metacognitive awareness compared with age- and gender-matched nondepressed controls. In the second study, Teasdale et al. (2002) demonstrated that lower levels of metacognitive awareness accessed five months before baseline assessment predicted earlier relapse in patients with major depression. This finding is consistent with the hypothesis that the ability to relate to depressive thoughts and feelings within a wider perspective reduces the likelihood of future relapse. These researchers also found that cognitive therapy increased accessibility to metacognitive sets with respect to negative thoughts and feelings compared with the comparison treatment. Differences between cognitive therapy and the comparison treatment were evidenced only on memories encoded during the treatment phase and not on prior memories, suggesting that changes in metacognitive awareness, as a result of cognitive therapy, reflected cognitive therapy's effects on the encoding of depressing experiences rather than artifactual effects of cognitive therapy on the way depressing experiences were described in recall. Thus, cognitive therapy is successful at increasing metacognitive awareness, and these metacognitive gains are associated with positive outcomes.

## *Decentering*

Another construct closely related to metacognitive awareness is *decentering*, which represents one's ability to observe thoughts and feelings as temporary, objective events in the mind, as opposed to reflections of the self that are necessarily true. From a decentered perspective, "... the reality of the moment is not absolute, immutable, or unalterable" (Safran & Segal, 1990, p. 117). For example, an individual engaged in decentering would say, "I am thinking that I feel depressed right now" instead of "I am depressed." Decentering is present-focused and involves taking a nonjudgmental and accepting stance regarding thoughts and feelings. Although the concept of decentering can be found in traditional cognitive therapy (e.g., Beck et al., 1979), Teasdale and colleagues (2002, p. 276) suggest that it was primarily seen as "a means to the end of changing thought content rather than, as ... the primary mechanism of therapeutic change." In other words, both Beck and Teasdale agree that cognitive therapy has always included decentering as a concept and a capacity that successfully treated depressed patients cultivate. However, a primary difference between cognitive therapy of depression as delivered by Beck and colleagues (1979) and Teasdale and colleagues (2002) is that for Beck, decentering is a capacity that allows an individual to make the important change in one's core beliefs, whereas for Teasdale, decentering is, in and of itself, the capacity that produces durable relief from depression.

In a recent study, Fresco, Moore, and colleagues (2007) introduced the Experiences Questionnaire (EQ), an 11-item self-report measure of decentering. In a series of three studies, the factor structure was demonstrated in both student patient samples. Further, decentering, as assessed by the EQ, demonstrated theoretically meaningful correlates with concurrent self-report depression symptoms in college students ($r = -.40$), concurrent self-report ($r = -.46$) and clinician assessed ($r = -.31$) depression symptoms in depressed patients, experiential avoidance ($r = -.49$; Hayes et al., 2004), expressive suppression ($r = -.31$; Gross & John, 2003), and cognitive reappraisal ($r = .25$; Gross & John, 2003).

Fresco, Segal, and colleagues (2007) examined the relationship between decentering and treatment response in a secondary analysis of Segal et al. (2006). Segal and colleagues (2006) demonstrated that cognitive reactivity in conjunction with an emotion evocation challenge predicted relapse in patients treated to remission through either antidepressant medication (ADM) or cognitive behavioral therapy (CBT) in an 18-month prospective study. Fresco, Segal et al. (2007) demonstrated that patients who achieved a positive treatment response following random assignment to CBT evidenced significantly greater gains in self-reported decentering compared to patients with a positive treatment response to ADM. Further, post-treatment levels of decentering in conjunction with low levels of cognitive reactivity were associated with the most durable treatment response. Thus, the ability to decenter is an important mechanism of change that can result from cognitive therapy for depression. However, Teasdale and colleagues (2002) posit that effective and durable treatment of MDD results from an increase in metacognitive capacities rather than the more traditional approach that cognitive-behavioral therapy has treatment effects by changing cognitive content.

## *Explanatory Style and Flexibility*

Explanatory flexibility in the assigning of causal explanations for negative events is a metacognitive extension of explanatory style, the cognitive diathesis at the heart of the reformulated learned helplessness theory of depression. Broadly construed, explanatory flexibility is the ability to view events with a balance of historical and contextual information (Fresco, Rytwinski, & Craighead, 2007). Like explanatory style, explanatory flexibility is assessed with the Attributional Style Questionnaire (ASQ; Peterson et al., 1982), a self-report measure in which respondents are presented with hypothetical negative events and asked to record the main cause of the event, as well as numeric ratings on the causal dimensions of internality, stability, and globality. Whereas explanatory style is scored as the sum or average of the attributional dimensions, with higher scores indicating a more depressogenic style, explanatory flexibility is computed as the intra-individual standard deviation on the ASQ dimensions of stability and globality for negative events. A small standard deviation is considered rigid responding, and a large standard deviation is interpreted as flexible responding.

To date, studies in several contexts have demonstrated a relationship between explanatory flexibility and depression. Fresco and colleagues have shown that explanatory style and explanatory flexibility were relatively uncorrelated with one another, and that lower explanatory flexibility scores were not simply proxies for extreme responding in terms of explanatory style (Moore & Fresco, 2007), that explanatory flexibility is associated with concurrent depression and anxiety symptoms (Fresco, Williams, & Nugent, 2006), and that levels of explanatory flexibility at baseline were associated with higher levels of subsequent depression symptoms in the face of negative life events (Fresco, Rytwinski, & Craighead, 2007). In addition, a series of studies has demonstrated that an emotion provocation can engender reactivity in explanatory flexibility for individuals deemed at risk for reactivity (Fresco, Heimberg, Abramowitz, & Bertram, 2006), and that this reactivity interacts with intervening negative life events to predict depression symptoms eight weeks and six months later (Moore & Fresco, 2009). Further, reactivity of explanatory flexibility in the direction of reduced flexibility was associated with reductions in parasympathetic tone during the mood priming challenge and inferior recovery of parasympathetic tone following the mood priming challenge (Fresco, Flynn, Clen, & Linardatos, 2009).

Two studies have examined the relationship of explanatory flexibility to depression in the context of acute treatment for major depressive disorder. Specifically, in a secondary analysis of the dismantling study of cognitive therapy of depression conducted by Jacobson and colleagues (1996), findings revealed that depressed individuals responding to behavioral activation evidenced greater gains in explanatory flexibility, whereas depressed patients who received a combination of behavioral activation plus disputation of negative automatic thoughts evidenced reductions in pessimistic explanatory style (i.e., less stable and global attributions for negative events) (Fresco, Schumm, & Dobson, 2009b). Furthermore, the combination of increased explanatory flexibility and reduced pessimistic explanatory style predicted better protection from relapse during the two-year follow-up period (Fresco et al., 2009b). Thus, the behavioral activation part of the treatment may have resulted in changes in cognitive structure (i.e., flexibility), whereas the disputation of negative thoughts may have influenced cognitive content change, both of which predicted better protection from relapse.

Fresco, Ciesla, Marcotte, and Jarrett (2009a) conducted secondary analysis of another recent randomized clinical trial examining the benefits of cognitive therapy of depression. In the initial study, Jarrett and colleagues (2001) treated patients with MDD in an open-label fashion with cognitive therapy (CT) for 20 sessions. Responders were then randomly assigned to 10 additional CT sessions delivered over an eight-month period (Continuation Phase CT) or to an assessment-only condition. Patients were then followed with no further study treatment for 16 additional months. Findings revealed that patients who received continuation CT evidenced reduced rates of recurrence and relapse compared to patients who received no additional CT. In the secondary analysis conducted by Fresco and colleagues (2009a), findings indicated that gains in explanatory flexibility during the acute, open-label phase of CT preceded and predicted drops in self-report and clinician-assessed depression symptoms. However, continuation phase CT was not associated with additional gains in explanatory flexibility. Similarly, explanatory flexibility was not associated with rates of recurrence and relapse in the follow-up phase of the study. Thus, gains in explanatory flexibility provided by behavioral approaches may result in reduced relapse and recurrence and hence more durable treatment effects.

## Extreme Responding

Another metacognitive factor associated with depression symptoms is rigidity in assigning causal explanations to hypothetical negative or positive events on the ASQ. Specifically, several studies have found that extreme responses on the ASQ are related to poor clinical outcomes for patients with depression (Beevers, Keitner, Ryan, & Miller, 2003; Peterson et al., 2007; Teasdale, Scott, Moore, Hayhurst, Pope, & Paykel, 2001). In one study by Teasdale and colleagues (2001), 158 patients with residual depression currently being treated with antidepressant medication were randomly assigned to receive drug continuation with clinical management either alone or with cognitive therapy (CT). Participants were asked to report attributions on the ASQ before and following the treatment. Extreme responding (i.e., either "totally disagree" or "totally agree"), but not the content of responding (i.e., response to specific items) predicted relapse. Beevers and colleagues (2003) found similar results, in that poor change in extreme responding predicted a shorter amount of time until depressive symptoms returned in individuals treated for asymptomatic or partially remitted depression. Support was also garnered for the relationship between extreme responding and depression by Petersen and colleagues (2007) who found that medication-only treatment for chronically depressed patients was associated with an increased frequency in extreme responding on the ASQ compared to no significant change in responding when treated with CBT. Moreover, extreme responding on the ASQ predicted a significantly higher likelihood of depressive remission in these patients. Thus, cognitive therapy seems to have an effect on by reducing the likelihood of extreme responding which in turn leads to less depressive symptoms.

## *Metacognition Summary*

Numerous studies conducted by several independent investigators are converging on the role that metacognitive factors play in the treatment of major depressive disorder. Two findings are especially relevant at this point. First, to prevent relapse, it seems important to heighten the capacity to approach emotionally evocative situations with metacognitive awareness. Second, this metacognitive awareness is reflected in several constructs that have demonstrated a relationship to depression: decentering, explanatory flexiblity, and extreme responding. Specifically, existing psychosocial treatments can be augmented by targeting these capacities to achieve acute and durable treatment gains. Many questions remain unanswered regarding metacognition and well-being. However, one important question that is being hotly pursued is whether metacognitive awareness can be cultivated more readily than with standard psychosocial treatments. Part of the answer to this question stems from the observation that these metacognitive skills bear a close resemblance to the capacities believed to arise from the practice of mental training exercises that derive from Buddhist and Hindu traditions. The conceptual similarities have led clinical scientists (e.g., Segal, Williams, & Teasdale, 2002) and affective neuroscientists (e.g., Lutz, Slagter, Dunne, & Davidson, 2008) to take notice of these mental training exercises. Concentrative practices, such as mindfulness meditation, involve focusing attention on a specific mental or sensory activity, such as repeated imagery, sensations, sounds, or mantras. Cultivating such a practice is believed to foster metacognitive awareness (Teasdale et al., 2002). We now turn to a review of efforts to infuse Buddhist mental training exercises into Western treatments for MDD.

# USING MINDFULNESS MEDITATION TO PROMOTE METACOGNITIVE AWARENESS

Barnard and Teasdale's (1991) multilevel theory of mind posits that the mindful experiencing/being mode is the most likely mode of mind to lead to lasting emotional changes, which in turn has implications for prevention of relapse in depression. Furthermore, cognitive therapy can promote the mindful experiencing/being mode of mind. Specifically, one facet of cognitive therapy involves helping individuals create and encode in memory alternative schematic models that will be triggered by the same patterns of information that normally trigger depressogenic schematic models. A second facet helps individuals learn skills to disengage from fluctuations between the conceptualizing/doing mode and the mindless emoting mode (i.e., depressive interlock) in order to function in the mindful experiencing/being/mode.

Although cognitive therapy can lead to the cultivation of these capacities, Teasdale (1999) suggests that individuals would likely benefit from learning "mind management" skills to prevent depressive interlock at times of potential relapse. In recent years, interventions composed of mindfulness exercises (e.g., transcendental meditation, Maharishi [1963]; mindfulness-based stress reduction, Kabat-Zinn [1990]; and mindfulness-based cognitive therapy, Segal, Williams & Teasdale [2002]) have emerged as viable supplements to standard Western medical and psychological practices. Mindfulness has been described as a nonjudgmental awareness of moment-by-moment experiences (Kabat-Zinn, 1990). Mindfulness is an active process whereby attention to the present moment is cultivated in a way that allows a full and meaningful experience of all aspects of that moment without avoiding, judging, or ruminating about certain features. In mindfulness-based stress reduction (MBSR; Kabat-Zinn, 1990), participants are encouraged to use mindfulness techniques to introduce simplicity to their lives by focusing on basic experiences such as breathing, bodily sensations, and the flow of thoughts through one's mind. Kabat-Zinn describes the following as the foundations of mindfulness: nonjudging of the moment and of oneself, patience, beginner's mind (i.e., an openness to seeing everything as a new experience), trust in oneself and one's feelings, nonstriving (not needing a purpose to do something), acceptance of the moment and oneself, and letting go (or nonattachment). When considering Teasdale's (1999) metacognitive model, these practices serve to diminish a detached, goal-oriented focus (conceptualizing/doing mode of mind) and a frame of mind in which emotions are all-encompassing and experienced without awareness (mindless emoting). In MBSR, techniques such as deep breathing, body scans, and mindful walking are used to cultivate a mindful-experiencing attitude, integrating all aspects of experience into a meaningful whole. These techniques were originally designed to lessen some mental and physical suffering associated with chronic pain.

Mindfulness-based cognitive therapy (MBCT) borrows techniques derived from MBSR while in conjunction teaching cognitive-behavioral interventions to specifically target vulnerability to depressive relapse. MBCT is an eight-week group program run with up to 12 recovered recurrently depressed patients. The goal of the program is for patients to develop an awareness of, and to respond more effectively to, negative thinking patterns such as avoiding unwanted thoughts, feelings, and bodily sensations (Ma & Teasdale, 2004). The mindfulness skills aim to help participants to accept these negative thought patterns and to respond in intentional and skillful ways to these patterns. In this way, MBCT cultivates a decentered relationship to negative thoughts and feelings in the service of moving from an "automatic pilot" mode to a "being" mode of emotional processing. The therapy begins by identifying the negative automatic thinking that is characteristic of those experiencing recurrent episodes of depression, and by introducing some basic mindfulness practices. In the second session, participants are encouraged to understand the reactions they have to experiences in life more generally, and to mindfulness experiences more specifically. Mindful awareness is fostered in the third session by teaching breathing techniques to focus attention on the present moment. In the fourth session, experiencing the moment without becoming attached, aversive, or bored is presented as a way to prevent relapse. Session five is used to promote acceptance of one's experience without holding on, and session six is used to describe thoughts as "merely thoughts." In the final sessions, participants are taught how to take care of themselves, to prepare for relapse, and to expand their mindfulness practice to everyday life. In a recent study examining the relationships among mindfulness training, metacognitive awareness, and depressive symptoms, Carmody, Baer, and colleagues (2009) found that mindfulness training led to enhanced mindfulness and decentering. More to the point, both factors significantly predicted a reduction in psychological symptoms, suggesting to the authors that mindfulness and decentering are highly related.

## Case Study

"Kendra" is a 40-year old woman who presented for treatment after many unsuccessful attempts to rid herself of depression using many different treatments. Although not currently depressed, an evaluation of Kendra's life indicated that she had experienced four previous episodes of major depression dating back to when she was 17 years old, which corresponded to the stresses of her senior year in high school, the divorce of her parents, and the breakup of her first serious romantic relationship. Prior to this episode, Kendra viewed herself as a generally happy person with a supportive family. Following this episode, Kendra described herself as scarred by the experience, and said that subsequent major depressive episodes seemed to occur in the face of less severe stressors. Thus, although Kendra has managed to remain free of depression for the past six months, she remains quite concerned that she is a "depressive episode waiting to happen." In fact, the initial evaluation revealed that Kendra was presently highly reactive to any feelings of sadness or depression and that just about any stress in her life could set off a full-blown depression. Given Kendra's risk of relapse, the therapist suggested that she participate in a study of MBCT that was being offered in a local clinic.

In the first week, Kendra was encouraged to identify her feelings and to stop automatically reacting to situations by undertaking some simple exercises designed to promote mindful awareness. One such exercise is slowly savoring and attending to a raisin. Another awareness exercise is a therapist-led body scan. Kendra was also given several mindfulness exercises to complete as homework. In the second session, the therapist identified common reactions to negative thoughts and described methods of disengaging from these reactions. These instructions included techniques such as a thought and feelings exercise and a pleasant events calendar. Mindfulness exercises, including the body scan and a 10-minute meditation, were used to demonstrate positive ways to disengage from negative thoughts. Kendra responded favorably to these exercises and seemed to more clearly understand why her negative thoughts contribute to her depression. The goal of the third week was to introduce some more time-intensive mindfulness techniques that teach the ability to maintain awareness in the moment. Kendra reported that she felt she had more skills to deal with her negative thoughts and that if she was able to continue the mindfulness exercises on her own they might have lasting effects on her life. In the fourth week, Kendra learned about cognitive reactivity and how certain negative automatic thoughts can allow life experiences to spiral into episodes of depression. She also learned additional practices in mindfulness techniques, such as a 40-minute sitting meditation. After this session, Kendra reported that she better understood the process of depression and how her ability to disengage her mind from her automatic thoughts would provide her with protection against depressive relapse. In the fifth and sixth weeks of the program, Kendra again learned new mindfulness exercises aimed at gaining acceptance of all experiences and learning that thoughts are merely thoughts and not facts (i.e., decentering). In the seventh week, Kendra designed a plan for what to do if she senses a future relapse. The last week was focused on tying together all of the lessons provided and linking the practices learned to everyday life. Kendra finished the program feeling as if she "had learned about why her depressions happen" and that she now had "ways to stop the depression from coming back." She also felt a strong sense of control over possible future relapse because of the action plan created in session seven.

Kendra returned to her therapist a year after the MBCT treatment ended, describing feelings of slight depression. She reluctantly reported that she was no longer using the mindfulness strategies on a regular basis. However, she resumed practicing these strategies, and after a few weeks of practicing some of the techniques she learned in MBCT, she began to feel better and stopped therapy. The Kendra vignette typifies the experience of a patient who has suffered numerous bouts of depression and lives in fear of that next episode, and who has participated in the growing number of randomized controlled trials and open trials of MBCT. These studies are reviewed in the following sections.

## MBCT FOR DEPRESSION TRIALS

### Prevention of MDD

Several recent randomized clinical trials attest to the benefits of MBCT in preventing relapse of MDD. Teasdale and colleagues (2000) compared the effect of MBCT and treatment as usual (TAU) on relapse rates in 145 recovered recurrently depressed patients with two or more previous episodes of major depressive disorder (MDD). The patients enrolled had not taken any depression medication for at least 12 weeks prior to the study and agreed to random assignment to MBCT or TAU. For patients with three or more previous episodes of MDD, MBCT led to significantly lower relapse rates over a one-year follow-up period than TAU, with rates being 40% for MBCT and 66% for TAU. No significant differences in relapse rates were found between MBCT and TAU for patients with a history of less than three episodes of MDD. Using the same study design, several additional studies have replicated the finding that MBCT protects patients with three or more MDD episodes against depression relapse. Teasdale, Segal, and Williams (2003) found that relapse rates were 66% and 37% for TAU and MBCT respectively, and Ma and Teasdale (2004) found relapse rates of 78% for TAU and 36% for MBCT. Bondolfi and colleagues (in press) set out to replicate these results in two samples of Swiss individuals who were currently in remission but had previously experienced more than three previous episodes of depression. Two randomized controlled trials compared MBCT+TAU to TAU-only during the 14-month follow-up period. Although there were similar relapse rates for both the MBCT+TAU and TAU-only, there were significantly more days to first relapse in the MBCT+TAU group (median = 204 days) compared to median of 69 days for the TAU-only group. Thus, even when examined cross-culturally, MBCT has effects on depressive relapse when compared to the typical treatment of choice.

MBCT may also have benefits above and beyond other traditional treatments for depression. For example, Kuyken and colleagues (2008) conducted a two-group randomized controlled trial to compare maintenance antidepressant medication (m-ADM) and MBCT with support for tapering or discontinuing ADM for recurrent depressive individuals. As predicted, relapse rates were significantly higher in the m-ADM condition (60%) than the MBCT condition (47%). Interestingly, MBCT was also more effective at reducing ADM use, as evidenced by a significantly higher average number of days of ADM use for the m-ADM group (411.4) than the MBCT group (266.46). Furthermore, an unpublished study by Dobson and Mohammadkhani (personal communication, November 1, 2009) revealed preliminary results that the effects of MBCT may be comparable to CBT, even in another culture. These researchers conducted a randomized controlled trial to compare MBCT to group CBT and TAU in an Iranian sample in Tehran, Iran. After 52 weeks of observation, including eight weeks of treatment, both CBT and MBCT had similar rates of protection against relapse (13.4% and 11.7%) compared to TAU (41.1%).

## Acute Treatment of MDD Trials

Mindfulness-based cognitive therapy was designed to reduce relapse in depression, but it is has also been shown to have positive effects on current depressive symptom relief above and beyond the effects of TAU. In a controlled clinical trial, Kingston, Dooley, Bates, Lawlor, & Malone, (2007) randomly assigned 19 recurrently depressed patients with three or more previous episodes of MDD and current residual symptoms to receive either MBCT or TAU. As predicted, there was a larger reduction in self-reported symptoms of depression for the group receiving MBCT than the group receiving TAU. These researchers also expected that MBCT would have larger effects on reducing rumination, but there were no significant differences in self-reported rumination between the conditions.

In a controlled pilot study, Barnhofer and colleagues (2009) found that MBCT plus TAU ($n$ = 14) was more effective at reducing symptoms of depression than TAU alone ($n$ = 14) for individuals with chronic-recurrent depression who had experienced at least three previous episodes. Symptoms were reduced from severe to mild in the MBCT group, whereas there was no significant change in the symptom levels of individuals in the TAU-only group.

Findings from several open trials indicate that MBCT is effective at reducing symptoms of depression in treatment-resistant populations. A study designed to examine the acceptability and effectiveness of MBCT revealed that in addition to being acceptable to patients, treatment with MBCT was successful at reducing symptoms of depression and anxiety (Finucane & Mercer, 2006). Eisendrath and colleagues (2008) found that MBCT reduced symptoms of depression for medication-refractory depressed patients. Similarly, Kenny and Williams (2007) found that MBCT led to lower levels of depressive symptoms in depressed individuals who had been resistant to both antidepressant medication and cognitive therapy previously. Finally, Williams and colleagues (2008) found that treatment with MBCT led to reduced symptoms of anxiety and depression for individuals with remitted bipolar depression with suicidal ideation or behavior. In summary, there is strong evidence that MBCT reduces rates of relapse for recovered, recurrently depressed individuals with three or more episodes of depression. Also, it seems that MBCT might have benefits for relieving depression symptoms as well as relapse when compared to other traditional treatments for depression.

## Process and Mechanism Trials

Various studies have examined possible mechanisms of the effects of MBCT on depressive relapse. Teasdale and colleagues (2002) found that low metacognitive awareness on the Measure of Awareness and Coping in Autobiographical Memory (MACAM), indicating inaccessibility of metacognitive sets, predicted relapse to depression in patients with residual depression. In this study, both cognitive therapy (CT) and MBCT led to increased metacognitive awareness. However, CT reduced relapse in residually depressed patients, and MBCT reduced relapse in recovered depressed patients. Thus, both CT and MBCT may have their effects on preventing depressive relapse by changing the cognitive structure, such as relationships to negative thoughts, rather than the cognitive content, such as negative beliefs. Raes, Dweulf, Van Heeringen, and Williams (2009) examined the relationship between MBCT and cognitive reactivity and found that levels of trait mindfulness, measured by self-report, were significantly negatively correlated with cognitive reactivity, even when controlling for symptoms of depression and prior history of depression. Furthermore, when comparing the effect of MBCT and wait-list control on cognitive reactivity in individuals signing up to take MBCT (with no exclusion criteria), MBCT significantly reduced cognitive reactivity, and this effect was mediated by an increase in mindfulness skills.

Other research has revealed that when comparing MBCT to TAU, MBCT leads to a smaller discrepancy between ratings of the ideal and actual self (Crane et al., 2008), and more adaptive memory encoding (Williams et al., 2008). Also, when comparing MBCT to a wait-list control, recovered depressed individuals with suicidal ideation and behavior treated with MBCT showed significantly less thought suppression after treatment (Hepburn et al., 2009).

Despite the evidence showing that gains in metacognitive awareness are associated with recovery and durability of treatment gains, the more traditional view is that the benefits of cognitive therapy are in helping individuals change the content of their negative thoughts and core beliefs. Thus, Teasdale and colleagues (2002) sought to distinguish these two possibilities by training patients in increased metacognitive awareness without any explicit attempt to change belief in negative thoughts or underlying dysfunctional attitudes. One hundred participants, currently in remission or recovery from major depression, were randomized to receive either treatment-as-usual (TAU) or MBCT. Results showed that MBCT patients, compared to those who received TAU, evidenced increases in metacognitive awareness as well as lower rates of relapse and recurrence of major depression. Although, traditional cognitive therapy was not included in this study, the findings do show that at least in the context of MBCT, gains in metacognitive awareness, and not change in cognitive content, were associated with reductions in relapse and recurrence of major depression.

## APPLICATIONS OF MINDFULNESS TO ANXIETY DISORDERS

Mindfulness techniques have recently been examined as treatments for anxiety disorders (e.g., Evans et al, 2008; Ree & Craigie, 2007). We review these approaches herein. In our review of this literature, we focus on therapies more closely derived from MBSR and MBCT. Other treatments, such as acceptance and commitment therapy (ACT; Hayes, Strosahl, & Wilson, 1999) and dialectical behavioral therapy (DBT; Linehan, 1993), contain mindfulness principles and involve various mindfulness techniques. However, other chapters in this volume more comprehensively address these treatments.

### Implementations of MBCT

Several studies have also recently reported the results of studies that have adapted MBCT to treat individuals with a particular anxiety disorder (e.g., generalized anxiety disorder [GAD] or social phobia) with mixed results. Evans and colleagues (2008) reported that

MBCT led to reductions in anxiety and depression symptoms in individuals with GAD. Craigie, Ree, Marsh, and Nathan (2008) also found that a nine-session adaptation of MBCT produced reductions in self-report measures of worry, and depression and anxiety symptoms. However, the magnitude of changes was inferior to the effect sizes reported in other CBT treatments for GAD (e.g. Borkovec et al., 2002; Dugas et al., 2003). A larger study by Kim and colleagues (2009) revealed that individuals with GAD and panic disorder (PD) receiving MBCT showed significantly more improvement on self-reported anxiety and depression symptoms compared to those receiving an anxiety disorder educational program. Bögels, Sijbers, and Voncken (2006) treated nine severely socially phobic patients by adding mindfulness training to task concentration training, which involves teaching patients to redirect attention toward the task they are completing and away from bodily symptoms (Bögels, Mulkens, & de Jong, 1997) and found that this combination of techniques was effective at reducing social anxiety in this group. Thus, overall, MBCT shows some promise as an acute treatment for anxiety disorders, but the state of the field is rather preliminary. To date, few studies have been conducted that incorporate random assignment to condition, with active comparisons, and with long-term follow-up to assess the durability of treatment gains. In the better controlled studies, the findings have not yet been as encouraging as the studies with MDD samples. However, newer efforts that infuse aspects of mindfulness, as opposed to directly porting these protocols from one disorder to the other, are showing promise.

### *Novel Treatments for GAD Informed by Mindfulness Techniques*

Two recent treatments for GAD (emotion regulation therapy, Mennin & Fresco, 2009; and acceptance-based behavioral therapy [ABBT], Roemer & Orsillo, 2008), are presently being developed and evaluated. To date, only ABBT has yet demonstrated efficacy in an open trial (Roemer & Orsillo, 2007) and an RCT (Roemer, Orsillo, & Salters-Pedneault, 2008). In their randomized controlled trial, Roemer, Orsillo, and colleagues demonstrated that ABBT evidenced significant reduction in GAD symptoms, significant increase in end-state functioning, and decreases in depressive symptoms in 15 individuals with GAD compared to 16 randomly assigned to a wait-list for delayed treatment (Roemer et al., 2008). Preliminary findings from these two GAD protocols are encouraging, but time will tell whether they produce effect sizes superior to existing protocols not infused with mindfulness and acceptance strategies.

## SUMMARY, LINGERING QUESTIONS, AND FUTURE DIRECTIONS

As evidenced by the work reviewed in this chapter, our understanding of the etiology and treatment of major depressive disorder in particular, and emotional disorders in general, has greatly benefited from an infusion from Buddhist and Hindu principles and mental training exercises. Traditional cognitive behavioral models of psychopathology and treatment propelled our understanding of emotional disorders in the latter decades of the 20th century. However, the incorporation of theoretical and practical elements such as mindfulness meditation, when studied in a principled and empirical manner, is likely to play a large and increasing role in taking us even further in our understanding of adaptive and maladaptive aspects of the human condition. Despite the promise that mindfulness-enriched treatments have in reducing suffering and providing durable treatment gains, several important questions remain. We conclude this chapter by framing some of these questions and, where available, providing suggested ways to pursue answers to them.

## How has Mindfulness Influenced Our Perspective About the Nature of Psychopathology?

Unquestionably, cognitive behavioral models of the etiology and treatment of emotional disorders represent a principled, evidence-based approach to the study and treatment of these disorders (Hollon et al., 2006). Nonetheless, debates about the centrality of cognitive change have persisted. This has largely been fueled by findings that putative cognitive mechanism measures demonstrate change following noncognitive treatments, including antidepressant medication (e.g., Fresco, Segal, et al., 2007, Imber et al. 1990, Simons, Garfield, & Murphy, 1984) or simply with remission (Hollon, Kendall, & Lumry, 1986). But, as this debate has continued, the field has seen important growth and expansion. This entire volume is a testament to that work. One important development has been the emergence of models of psychopathology and treatment that emphasize emotion and emotion regulation (e.g., Kring & Sloan, 2009). In much the way that the cognitive behavioral movement arose from animal and basic research on classical and instrumental conditioning, emotion regulation models also translate principles from basic research into theories and approaches to treating emotional disorders. In fact, during the ascendancy of cognitive-behavioral models, emotions were largely misunderstood or viewed as epiphenomena secondary to cognition (Mennin & Farach, 2007). However, perhaps fueled in part by growing interest in neuroscience, emotion is no longer the "*terra incognita*" of clinical science (Samoilov & Goldfried, 2000). Systems within the cognitive behavioral tradition, such as DBT (Linehan, 1993), ACT (Hayes et al., 1999), and MBCT (Segal et al., 2002) began to take notice of emotion, which in turn has fueled many additional approaches represented in this volume. Interestingly, these systems were the first to find common ground with mindfulness and other mental training exercises derived from Buddhism and Hinduism.

## How Has Mindfulness Changed the Way We Deliver Psychosocial Treatments?

One trend that is quite apparent within the cognitive behavioral tradition has been a de-emphasis on direct cognitive change strategies, particularly those targeting cognitive content. Rather, as noted above, promoting decentering or metacognitive awareness was always part of cognitive therapy (Beck et al., 1979), but, in recent years, it has gained in prominence as the putative mechanism that promotes both acute and durable treatment effects rather than simply as one means to promote cognitive change (Teasdale et al., 2002). To bring this point into perspective, one of us (DMF) recently asked Zindel Segal to describe how MBCT has changed his implementation of CT, to which he answered that when working on a thought record with patients, he is now much more interested in the left side of the thought record, which emphasizes the identification of negative automatic thoughts, rather than the right side of the record, which focuses on disputation and generation of rational responses. By focusing on the left side of the thought record, patients are better able to cultivate a decentered perspective on negative cognitive content (personal communication, October 26, 2007).

## Does One Need to Practice Mindfulness to Produce Lasting Protection Against Depression?

The clinical benefits of mindfulness meditation are compelling. Recent reviews of more than 400 meditation trials (Ospina et al., 2008) and a recent meta-analysis of mindfulness meditation trials (Hofmann et al., in press) attest to the benefits for a variety of psychiatric and medical conditions. Despite these positive findings, the degree to which sustained practice of mindfulness is necessary for the therapeutic benefits has yet to be determined. As noted above, acute treatments for depression such as cognitive therapy produce gains in metacognitive awareness, which is associated with acute treatment response as well as the durability of treatment gains (Fresco, Segal et al., 2007). This implementation of cognitive therapy lacks any explicit mindfulness practice. Thus, a simple answer to the question is no. Mindfulness practice is neither necessary nor sufficient to produce treatment benefits. However, a related question is whether initiating and maintaining a mindfulness practice is associated with more rapid acquisition of therapeutic benefits. This question has yet to be studied systematically or quantified in treatment studies. Although not a direct answer to this question, the most thorough statement on a related topic was recently offered by Carmody and Baer (2009) who reviewed available studies of MBSR and MBCT in terms of length of treatment, number of sessions, and duration of each session. Carmody and Baer found that the effect sizes of the studies they reviewed were not statistically related to the length of protocol, nor the amount of assigned out-of-session practice. The available studies did not provide actual practice time. They go on to call for empirical investigations that systematically vary the amount of session time and assigned practice time. However, there is a growing body of research in affective neuroscience showing differences in patterns of neural correlates among adept meditators (i.e., monks) with tens of thousands of hours of practice compared to novice meditators (e.g., Davidson & Lutz, 2008), as well as differences in previously naïve meditators following completion of a course in mindfulness (e.g., Farb et al., 2007).

## How Can We Create Synergy Between Clinical Science and Neuroscience to Advance the Study of Mindfulness While Also Reducing Human Suffering?

Interest in integrating mindfulness and other mental training exercises into our Western models of psychopathology and treatments has never been greater. The findings are promising, and we are providing relief from suffering for many people. However, mindfulness-enriched treatments are equally vulnerable to the challenges faced by traditional cognitive behavioral treatments to convincingly isolate the mechanisms that produce treatment gains (Corcoran, Farb, Anderson, & Segal, 2009). We may in fact be reaching the limit that self-report measures and clinician assessments can tell us about mindfulness (Davidson, 2010). Our colleagues in the affective sciences have been touching the elephant that is mindfulness in different and complementary ways; in doing so, they are providing provocative clues to the biological and neural bases that arise with practice of these mental training exercises.

An important next step is to begin evaluating mindfulness-related treatment efficacy within the context of biomarker change. First, we must begin to examine whether and how patients with emotional disorders differ from healthy controls on the biological indices in the context of cognitive and emotional provocation tasks used in the basic affective sciences. Second, and importantly, we must also investigate the ways that all of our efficacious treatments, whether or not they possess mindfulness elements, impact biological and neural systems that are, in turn, associated with relief from disorders such as major depression while producing durable treatment gains.

## CONCLUSION

In this chapter, we reviewed the evidence supporting both cognitive behavioral therapy and mindfulness-enriched treatments as effective therapies for depression, which leads us to several conclusions. First, increasing metacognitive ability (e.g., decentering) has always been part of traditional cognitive therapy of depression—although recent findings emphasize metacognitive capacities as the active ingredient in cognitive therapy. Second, the benefits of increasing metacognitive abilities can be realized without explicitly practicing mindfulness exercises. Third, given that cognitive content change is less important as compared to cultivating metacognitive ability for the prevention of relapse, developing treatments that explicitly foster this ability may be more effective and enduring than treatments that produce metacognitive awareness as a by-product.

On balance, the findings are promising and are stretching our theoretical conceptualizations, and in turn helping us to reduce human suffering. Despite these encouraging developments, many challenges lie ahead. The fields of clinical science and neuroscience are shedding light on many aspects of normative and disordered aspects of our emotional lives. In some respects, this work is occurring on parallel and nonintersecting tracks. However, the time is ripe to embark on programs of translational research that creatively integrate and synthesize basic and applied research findings. As theory and experimental research become more complex, however, it has become increasingly important for researchers to clarify and agree on terminology and units of analysis. Questions such as: What is mindfulness? How should we measure it? Can we reliably measure it in first person accounts? Third person accounts? Biological and neural correlates? And, importantly, how can our clinical approaches benefit from the research? The work reviewed in this chapter, and indeed in this volume, suggests some preliminary answers to these questions. However, the road ahead is likely to be challenging, exciting, and rewarding as we strive to answer these remaining questions.

# REFERENCES

Abramson, L. Y., Metalsky, G. I., Alloy, L. B. (1989). Hopelessness depression: A theory-based subtype of depression. *Psychological Review, 96,* 358–372.

Abramson, L. Y., Seligman, M. E., Teasdale, J. D. (1978). Learned helplessness in humans: Critique and reformulation. *Journal of Abnormal Psychology, 87,* 49–74.

American Psychiatric Association. (2000). *Diagnostic and statistical manual of mental disorders DSM-IV-TR* (4th ed., text revision). Washington, DC: Author.

Barnard, P. J. & Teasdale, J. D. (1991). Interacting cognitive subsystems: A Systemic approach to cognitive-affective interaction and change. *Cognition and Emotion, 5,* 1–39.

Barnhofer, T., Crane, C., Hargus, E., Amarasinghe, M., Winder, R., & Williams, J. M. G. (2009). Mindfulness-based cognitive therapy as a treatment for chronic depression: A preliminary study. *Behaviour Research and Therapy, 47,* 366–373.

Beck, A. T. (1967). *Depression: Clinical, experimental and theoretical aspects.* New York, NY: Harper & Row.

Beck, A. T. (1976). *Cognitive theory and the emotional disorders.* New York, NY: International Universities Press.

Beck, A. T. (1984). Cognition and therapy. *Archives of General Psychiatry, 41,* 1112–1114.

Beck, A. T., Rush, A. J., Shaw, B. F., & Emery, G. (1979). *Cognitive therapy of depression.* New York, NY: Guilford Press.

Beevers, C. G., Keitner, G. I., Ryan, C. E., & Miller, I. W. (2003). Cognitive predictors of symptom return following depression treatment. *Journal of Abnormal Psychology, 112,* 488–496.

Bögels, S. M., Mulkens, S., & de Jong, P. J. (1997). Task concentration training and fear of blushing. *Journal of Clinical Psychology and Psychotherapy, 4,* 251–258.

Bögels, S. M., Sijbers, G. F. V. M., & Voncken, M. (2006). Mindfulness and task concentration training for social phobia: A Pilot study. *Journal of Cognitive Psychotherapy, 20,* 33–44.

Bondolfi, G., Jermann, F., Vander Linden, M., Gex-Fabry, M., Bizzini, L, Weber Rouget, B., et al. (in press). Depression relapse prophylaxis with mindfulness-based cognitive therapy: Replication and extension in the Swiss health care system. *Journal of Affective Disorders.*

Borkovec, T. D., Newman, M. G., Pincus, A., & Lytle, R. (2002). A component analysis of cognitive-behavioral therapy for generalized anxiety disorder and the role of interpersonal problems. *Journal of Consulting and Clinical Psychology, 70,* 288–298.

Brewin, C. R., & Power, M. (1999). Integrating psychological therapies: Processes of meaning transformation. *British Journal of Medical Psychology, 72,* 143–157.

Cahn, B. R. & Polich, J. (2006). Meditation states and traits: EEG, ERP, and neuroimaging studies. *Psychological Bulletin, 132,* 180–211.

Carmody, J., & Baer, R. A. (2009). How long does a mindfulness-based stress reduction program need to be? A review of class contact hours and effect sizes for psychological distress. *Journal of Clinical Psychology, 65,* 627–638.

Carmody, J., Baer, R. A., Lykins, L. B., & Olendzki, N. (2009). An empirical study of the mechanisms of mindfulness in a mindfulness-based stress reduction program. *Journal of Clinical Psychology, 65,* 613–626.

Casacalenda, N., Perry, J. C., & Looper, K. (2002). Remission in major depressive disorder: A comparison of pharmacotherapy. *American Journal of Psychiatry, 159,* 1354–1360.

Corcoran, K. M., Farb, N., Anderson, A., & Segal, Z. V. (2009). Mindfulness and emotion regulation. In A. M. Kring & D. M. Sloan (Eds.), *Emotion regulation and psychopathology: A transdiagnostic approach to etiology and treatment* (pp. 339–355). New York, NY: Guilford Press.

Craigie, M. A., Rees, C. S., Marsh, A., & Nathan, P. (2008). Mindfulness-based cognitive therapy for generalized anxiety disorder: A preliminary evaluation. *Behavioural and Cognitive Psychotherapy, 36,* 553–568.

Crane, C., Barnhofer, T., Duggan, D. S., Hepburn, S., Fennell, M. V., & Williams, M. G. (2008). Mindfulness-based cognitive therapy and self-discrepancy in recovered depressed patients with a history of depression and suicidality. *Cognitive Therapy and Research, 32,* 1573–2819.

Davidson, R. J. (2010). Empirical explorations of mindfulness: Conceptual and methodological conundrums. *Emotion, 10,* 8–11.

Davidson, R. J. & Lutz, A. (2008). Buddha's brain: Neuroplasticity and meditation. *IEEE Signal Processing 25,* 171–174.

Dugas, M. J., Ladouceur, R., Leger, E., Freeston, M. H., Langolis, F., Provencher, M. D.,...Boisvert, J.-M. (2003). Group cognitive-behavioral therapy for generalized anxiety disorder: Treatment outcome and long-term follow-up. *Journal of Consulting and Clinical Psychology, 71,* 821–825.

Eisendrath, S. J., Delucchi, K., Bitner, R., Fenimore, P., Smit, M., & McLane, M. (2008). Mindfulness-based cognitive therapy for treatment-resistant depression: A pilot study. *Psychotherapy and Psychosomatics, 77,* 319–320.

Evans, S., Ferrando, S., Findler, M., Stowell, C., Smart, C., & Haglin, D. (2008). Mindfulness-based cognitive therapy for generalized anxiety disorder. *Journal of Anxiety Disorders, 22,* 716–721.

Farb, N. A. S., Segal, Z. V., Mayberg, H., Bean, J., McKeon, D., Fatima, Z., & Anderson, A. K. (2007). Attending to the present: Mindfulness meditation reveals distinct neural modes of self-reference. *Social Cognitive and Affective Neuroscience, 2,* 313–322.

Finucane, A., & Mercer, S. (2006). An exploratory mixed methods study of the acceptability and effectiveness of mindfulness-based cognitive therapy for patients with active depression and anxiety in primary care. *BMC Psychiatry, 6,* 1–14.

Flavell, J. H. (1976) Metacognitive aspects of problem solving. In L. B. Resnick (Ed.), *The nature of intelligence* (pp. 231–236). Hillsdale, NJ: Erlbaum.

Foa, E. B., & Kozak, M. J. (1986). Emotional processing of fear: Exposure to corrective information. *Psychological Bulletin, 99,* 20–35.

Fresco, D.M., Ciesla, J. A., Marcotte, M. K., & Jarrett, R. B. (2009a). *Relationship of explanatory flexibility to the recovery from major depression and the durability of treatment gains following treatment with cognitive therapy.* Manuscript submitted for review.

Fresco, D. M., Flynn, J. J., Clen, S., & Linardatos, E. (2009, November). *Reactivity of explanatory flexibility following an emotion evocation challenge: Relationship of concurrent levels of parasympathetic tone.* Paper presented at the annual meeting of the Association of Behavioral and Cognitive Therapies, New York, NY.

Fresco, D. M., Heimberg, R. G., Abramowitz, A., & Bertram, T. L. (2006). The effect of a negative mood priming challenge on dysfunctional attitudes, explanatory style, and explanatory flexibility. *British Journal of Clinical Psychology, 45,* 167–183.

Fresco, D. M., Moore, M. T., van Dulmen, M., Segal, Z. V., Teasdale, J. D., Ma, H., & Williams, J. M. G. (2007). Initial psychometric properties of the Experiences Questionnaire: Validation of a self-report measure of decentering. *Behavior Therapy, 38,* 284–302.

Fresco, D. M., Rytwinski, N. K., & Craighead, L. W. (2007). Explanatory flexibility and negative life events interact to predict depression symptoms. *Journal of Social and Clinical Psychology, 26,* 595–608.

Fresco, D. M., Schumm, J. A. & Dobson, K. S. (2009b). *Explanatory flexibility and explanatory style: Modality-specific mechanisms of change when comparing behavioral activation with and without cognitive interventions.* Manuscript under review.

Fresco, D. M., Segal, Z. V., Buis, T., & Kennedy, S. (2007). Relationship of post treatment decentering and cognitive reactivity to relapse of major depressive disorder. *Journal of Consulting and Clinical Psychology, 75,* 447–455.

Fresco, D. M., Williams, N. L, & Nugent, N. R. (2006). Flexibility and negative affect: Examining the associations of explanatory flexibility and coping flexibility to each other and to depression and anxiety. *Cognitive Therapy and Research, 30,* 201–210.

Greenberg, L. S. (2002). *Emotion-focused therapy: Coaching clients to work through their feelings.* Washington, DC: American Psychological Association.

Greenberg, L. S., & Safran, J. D. (1987). *Emotion in psychotherapy: Affect, cognition, and the process of change.* New York: Guilford Press.

Gross, J. J., & John, O. P. (2003). Individual differences in two emotion regulation processes: Implications for affect, relationships, and well-being. *Journal of Personality and Social Psychology, 85,* 348–362.

Hayes, S. C., Strosahl, K. D., & Wilson, K. G. (1999). *Acceptance and commitment therapy: An experiential approach to behavior change.* New York, NY: Guilford Press.

Hayes, S. C., Strosahl, K. D., Wilson, K. G., Bissett, R. T., Pistorello, J., Toarmino, D.,…McCurry, S. M. (2004). Measuring experiential avoidance: A preliminary test of a working model. *The Psychological Record, 54,* 553–578.

Hepburn, S. R., Crane, C., Barnhofer, T., Duggan, D. S., Fennell, M. J., & Williams, J. M. G. (2009). Mindfulness-based cognitive therapy may reduce thought suppression in previously suicidal participants: Findings from a preliminary study. *British Psychological Society, 48,* 209–215.

Hofmann, S. G., Sawyer, A. T., Witt, A. A., & Oh, D. (in press). The effect of mindfulness-based therapy on anxiety and depression: A meta-analytic review. *Journal of Consulting and Clinical Psychology.*

Hollon, S. D., DeRubeis, R. J., Shelton, R. C., Amsterdam, J. D., Salomon, R. M., O'Reardon, J. P., . . . Gallop, R. (2005). Prevention of relapse following cognitive therapy versus medications in moderate to severe depression. *Archives of General Psychiatry, 62,* 417–422.

Hollon, S. D., & Garber, J. (1988). Cognitive therapy. In L. Y. Abramson (Ed.), *Social cognition and clinical psychology: A synthesis* (pp. 204–253). New York, NY: Guilford Press.

Hollon, S. D., Kendall, P. C. & Lumry, A. (1986). Specificity of depressotypic cognitions in clinical depression. *Journal of Abnormal Psychology, 95,* 52–59.

Hollon, S. D., & Kriss, M. R. (1984). Cognitive factors in clinical research and practice. *Clinical Psychology Review, 4,* 35–76.

Hollon, S. D., Stewart, M. O. & Strunk, D. (2006). Cognitive behavior therapy has enduring effects in the treatment of depression and anxiety. *Annual Review of Psychology, 57,* 285–315.

Imber, S. D., Pilkonis, P. A., Sotsky, S. M., Elkin, I., Watkins, J. T., Collins, J. F.,…Glass, D. R. (1990). Mode-specific effects among three treatments for depression. *Journal of Consulting and Clinical Psychology, 58,* 352–359.

Ingram, R. E., & Hollon, S. D. (1986). Cognitive therapy for depression from an information processing perspective. In R. E. Ingram (Ed.) *Information processing approaches to clinical. Personality, psychopathology, and psychotherapy series* (pp. 259–281). San Diego, CA: Academic Press.

Jacobson, N. S., Dobson, K. S., Truax, P. A., Addis, M. E., Koerner, K., Gollan, J. K., Gortner, E., & Prince, S. E. (1996). A component analysis of cognitive-behavioral treatment for depression. *Journal of Consulting and Clinical Psychology, 64,* 295–304.

Jarrett, R. B., Kraft, D., Doyle, J., Foster, B. M., Eaves, G. G., & Silver, P. C. (2001). Preventing recurrent depression using cognitive therapy with and without a continuation phase: A randomized clinical trial. *Archives of General Psychiatry, 58,* 381–388.

Kabat-Zinn, J. (1990). *Full catastrophe living.* New York, NY: Delta Trade Paperbacks.

Kabat-Zinn, J. (1995). *Wherever you go there you are: Mindfulness and meditation in everyday life.* New York, NY: Hyperion.

Kendall, P. C., & Ingram, R. E. (1989). Cognitive-behavioral perspectives: Theory and research on depression and anxiety. In P. C. Kendall & D. Watson (Eds.), *Anxiety and depression: Distinctive and overlapping features.* New York, NY: Academic Press.

Kenny, M. A., & Williams, J. M. G. (2007). Treatment-resistant depressed patients show a good response to mindfulness-based cognitive therapy. *Behaviour Research and Therapy, 45,* 617–625.

Kessler, R., Bergland, P., & Demler, O., (2005). Lifetime prevalence and age-of-onset distributions of DSM-IV disorders in the National Comorbidity Survey Replication. *Archives of General Psychiatry, 62,* 593–602.

Kim, Y. W., Lee, S-H., Choi, T. K., Suh, S. Y., Kim, B., Kim, C. M.,...Yook, K. H. (2009). Effectiveness of mindfulness-based cognitive therapy as an adjuvant to pharmacotherapy in patients with panic disorder or generalized anxiety disorder. *Depression and Anxiety, 26,* 601–606.

Kingston, T., Dooley, B., Bates, A., Lawlor, E., & Malone, K. (2007). Mindfulness-based cognitive therapy for residual depressive symptoms. *Psychology and Psychotherapy: Theory, Research and Practice, 80,* 193–203.

Kring, A. M., & Sloan, D. M. (2009). *Emotion regulation and psychopathology: A transdiagnostic approach to etiology and treatment.* New York, NY: Guilford Press.

Kuyken, W., Byford, S., Taylor, R. S., Watkins, E., Holden, E., White, K.,...Teasdale, J. D. (2008). Mindfulness-based cognitive therapy to prevent relapse in recurrent depression. *Journal of Consulting and Clinical Psychology, 76,* 966–978.

LeDoux, J. (1996). *The emotional brain: The mysterious underpinnings of emotional life.* New York, NY: Simon & Schuster.

Leventhal, H., & Scherer, K. (1987). The relationship of emotion to cognition: A functional approach to a semantic controversy. *Cognition and Emotion, 1,* 3–28.

Linehan, M. M. (1993). *Cognitive-behavioral treatment of borderline personality disorder.* New York, NY: Guilford Press.

Lutz, A., Slagter, H. A., Dunne, J. D., & Davidson, R. J. (2008). Attention regulation and monitoring in meditation. *Trends in Cognitive Sciences, 12,* 163–169.

Ma, S. H. & Teasdale, J. D. (2004). Mindfulness-based cognitive therapy for depression: Replication and exploration of differential relapse prevention effects. *Journal of Consulting and Clinical Psychology, 72,* 31–40.

Maharishi, Y. (1963). *Transcendental meditation.* New York, NY: New American Library.

Mennin, D. & Farach, F. (2007). Emotion and evolving treatments for adult psychopathology. *Clinical Psychology, 14,* 329–352.

Mennin, D., & Fresco, D. M. (2009). Emotion regulation as an integrative framework for understanding and treating psychopathology. In A. M. Kring & D. M. Sloan (Eds.), *Emotion regulation and psychopathology: A transdiagnostic approach to etiology and treatment* (pp. 339–355). New York, NY: Guilford Press.

Moore, R. G., Hayhurst, H., & Teasdale, J. D. (1996). *Measure of awareness and coping in autobiographical memory: Instructions for administering and coding.* Unpublished manuscript, Department of Psychiatry, University of Cambridge.

Moore, M., & Fresco, D. M. (2007). Depressive realism and attributional style: Implications for individuals at risk for depression. *Behavior Therapy, 38,* 144–154.

Moore, M. T., & Fresco, D. M. (2009). *Prospective study of reactivity of explanatory flexibility following a laboratory emotion provocation task.* Manuscript submitted for publication.

Moussavi, S., Chatterji, S., Verdes, E., Tandon, A., Patel, V., & Ustun, B. (2007). Depression, chronic diseases, and decrements in health: Results from the World Health Surveys. *Lancet, 370,* 851–858.

Murray, C. J. L., & Lopez, A. D. (1998). *Health dimensions of sex and reproduction. Global burden of disease and injury series, volume III.* Boston, MA: Harvard, University Press.

Nolen-Hoeksema, S. (1991). Responses to depression and their effects on the duration of depressive episodes. *Journal of Abnormal Psychology, 100,* 569–582.

Ospina, M. B., Bond, K., Karkhaneh, M, Buscemi, N., Dryden, D. D., Barnes, V.,...Shannahoff-Khalsa, D. (2008). Clinical trials of meditation practices in health care: Characteristics and quality. *Journal of Alternative and Complementary Medicine, 14,* 1199–1213.

Peterson, T. J., Feldman, G., Harley, R., Fresco, D. M., Graves, L., Holmes, A.,...Segal, Z. V. (2007). Extreme response style in recurrent and chronically depressed patients: Change with antidepressant administration and stability during continuation treatment. *Journal of Consulting and Clinical Psychology, 75,* 145–153.

Peterson, C., Semmel, A., von Baeyer, C., Abramson, L. Y., Metalsky, G. I., & Seligman, M. E. P. (1982). The attributional style questionnaire. *Cognitive Therapy and Research, 6,* 287–299.

Power, M., & Dalgleish, T. (1997). *Cognition and emotion: From order to disorder.* Hove, UK: Psychology Press.

Rachman, S. J. (1980). Emotional processing. *Behaviour Research and Therapy, 18,* 51–60.

Raes, F., Dewulf, D., Van Heeringen, C., & Williams, J. M. G. (2009). Mindfulness and reduced cognitive reactivity to sad mood: Evidence from a correlational study and a non-randomized waiting list controlled study. *Behaviour Research and Therapy, 47,* 623–627.

Ree, M. J., & Craigie, M. A. (2007). Outcomes following mindfulness-based cognitive therapy in a heterogeneous sample of adult outpatients. *Behaviour Change, 24,* 70–86.

Roemer, L., & Orsillo, S. M. (2007). An open trial of an acceptance-based behavior therapy for generalized anxiety disorder. *Behavior Therapy, 38,* 72–85.

Roemer, L., & Orsillo, S. M. (2008). *Mindfulness- and acceptance-based behavioral therapies in practice.* New York, NY: Guilford Press.

Roemer, L., Orsillo, S. M., & Salters-Pedneault, K. (2008). Efficacy of an acceptance-based behavior therapy for generalized anxiety disorder: Evaluation in a randomized controlled trial. *Journal of Consulting and Clinical Psychology, 76,* 1083–1089.

Safran, J. D., & Segal, Z. V. (1990). *Interpersonal process in cognitive therapy.* New York, NY: Basic Books.

Safran, J. D., Vallis, T. M., Segal, Z. V., & Shaw, B. F. (1986). Assessment of core cognitive processes in cognitive therapy. *Cognitive Therapy and Research, 10,* 509–526.

Samoilov, A., & Goldfried, M. R. (2000). Role of emotion in cognitive-behavior therapy. *Clinical Psychology: Science and Practice, 7,* 373–385.

Segal, Z. V., Gemar, M., & Williams, J. M. G. (1999). Differential cognitive response to a mood challenge following successful cognitive therapy or pharmacotherapy for unipolar depression. *Journal of Abnormal Psychology, 108,* 3–10.

Segal, Z. V., Kennedy, S., Gemar, M., Hood, K., Pederson, R., & Buis, T. (2006). Cognitive reactivity to sad mood provocation and the prediction of depressive relapse. *Archives of General Psychiatry, 63,* 749–755.

Segal, Z. V., Williams, J. M. G., & Teasdale, J. D. (2002). *Mindfulness-based cognitive therapy for depression: A New approach to preventing relapse.* New York, NY: Guilford Press.

Seligman, M. E. P. (1980). A learned helplessness point of view. In L. Rehm (Ed.), *Behavior therapy for depression* (pp. 123–142). New York, NY: Academic Press.

Simons, A. D., Garfield, S. L., & Murphy, G. E. (1984). The process of change in cognitive therapy and pharmacotherapy for depression. *Archives of General Psychiatry, 41,* 45–51.

Tang, T. Z., & DeRubeis, R. J. (1999). Sudden gains and critical session in cognitive-behavioral therapy for depression. *Journal of Consulting and Clinical Psychology, 67,* 894–904.

Teasdale, J. D. (1999). Emotional processing, three modes of mind and the prevention of relapse in depression. *Behaviour Research and Therapy, 37*(Suppl. 1), S53–77.

Teasdale, J. D., & Barnard, P. J. (1993). *Affect, cognition and change: Remodeling depressive thought.* Hove, UK/Hillsdale, NJ: Erlbaum.

Teasdale, J. D., Moore, R. G., Hayhurst, H., Pope, M., Williams, S., & Segal, Z. V. (2002). Metacognitive awareness and prevention of relapse in depression: Empirical evidence. *Journal of Consulting and Clinical Psychology, 70,* 275–287.

Teasdale, J. D., Scott, J., Moore, R. G., Hayhurst, H., Pope, M., & Paykel, E. S. (2001). How does cognitive therapy prevent relapse in residual depression? Evidence from a controlled trial. *Journal of Consulting and Clinical Psychology, 69,* 347–357.

Teasdale, J. D., Segal, Z. V., & Williams, J. M. G. (1995). How does cognitive therapy prevent depressive relapse and why should attentional control (mindfulness) training help? *Behaviour Research and Therapy, 33*, 25–39.

Teasdale, J. D., Segal, Z. V., & Williams, J. M. G. (2003). Review of mindfulness-based cognitive therapy for depression: A new approach to preventing relapse. *Psychotherapy Research, 13*, 123–125.

Teasdale, J. D., Segal, Z. V., Williams, J. M. G., Ridgeway, V., Soulsby, J. M., & Lau, M. A. (2000). Prevention of relapse/recurrence in major depression by mindfulness-based cognitive therapy. *Journal of Consulting and Clinical Psychology, 68*, 615–623.

Thase, M. E., Entsuah, A. R., & Rudolph, R. L. (2001). Remission rates during treatment with velafaxine or selective serotonin reuptake inhibitors. *British Journal of Psychiatry, 178*, 234–241.

Williams, J. M. G., Alatiq, Y., Crane, C., Barnhofer, T., Fennell, M. J. V., Duggan, D. S., . . . Goodwin, G. M. (2008). Mindfulness-based cognitive therapy (MBCT) in bipolar disorder: Preliminary evaluation of immediate effects on between-episode functioning. *Journal of Affective Disorders, 107*, 275–279.

# 4

## Metacognitive Therapy

### ADRIAN WELLS

The metacognitive theory of psychological disorder (Wells & Matthews, 1994; Wells, 2009) is grounded on a basic principle: Negative thoughts and emotions are usually transient experiences. They persist and become psychological problems because the individual activates a specific pattern or style of thinking that is damaging for self-regulation and the elimination of these distressing experiences. This pattern is called the cognitive attentional syndrome (CAS), and it consists of worry, rumination, threat monitoring, and coping behaviors that interfere with self-regulation. Psychological disorder is the consequence of "mental perseveration"—that is, repeatedly returning to and thinking about a particular topic.

## THE CAS

Worry and rumination are central features of the CAS. They consist of chains of predominantly verbal thinking in which the individual contemplates past events (rumination) and future possible threats (worry). For most people, negative thoughts such as "I'm going to die" fade as the individual directs resources to other task-focused processing. However, for the depressed or anxious individual, these thoughts are met with sustained rumination concerning the reason for living or worry about how to avoid danger. In each case, sustained thinking is a means of finding answers to suffering (e.g., Nolen-Hoeksema, 2000; Wells & Davies, 1994; Wells & Carter, 2001). Unfortunately, the process achieves the obverse as it maintains intrusions and broadens the sense of threat (e.g., Wells & Papageorgiou, 1995).

A further important feature of the CAS is threat monitoring: maintaining attention on potential sources of danger to the self and significant others. This takes different forms. For example, it may comprise "information searches" in which the person looks for facts or data. An individual with generalized anxiety may scan the Internet looking for facts and figures on the prevalence of illness within their region. The person suffering from trauma after being robbed in the street may scan the environment for people who are acting suspiciously. The problem with threat monitoring is that it maintains the sense of threat and personal vulnerability, so that negative emotions persist or escalate. This strategy is a means of configuring cognition so that the individual is safer. However, as it relies to some extent on anticipating the worst, it is closely linked to the process of worrying and it undermines a sense of safety.

The behaviors adopted by psychologically vulnerable individuals tend to be over-used and of a type that fail to provide learning experiences that can modify erroneous ideas and improve control over perseveration. Many of the strategies are metacognitive in nature and involve suppression or avoidance of certain thoughts or the maintenance of thinking in the form of worry (Wells & Carter, 2009; Wells & Davies, 1994). For example, the person with obsessive-compulsive disorder and contamination fears washes his hands to remove fears (negative thoughts) about being contaminated with germs and hence avoid the distressing effects of worry that he may contaminate his family. Furthermore, in cases like this, worry about possible contamination and monitoring for it (part of the CAS) are thinking strategies that are used to avoid potential danger. The deleterious effect is that the individual repeatedly acts as if the negative thought is valid and important. This prevents the development of a more flexible relationship with thoughts and one that detaches them from extended thinking. It also prevents the individual developing more direct metacognitive control over worry and rumination, which is needed to adaptively regulate emotions and negative ideas in the future. Some behaviors such as avoidance prevent the individual from revising his more general knowledge of himself and the world. For example, the person with social phobia who avoids asking questions in a group continues to believe people would act as if he was unintelligent because he has no disconfirmatory evidence. However, as we shall see, this general knowledge is much less significant than more specific types of metacognitive knowledge concerning the importance and control of thoughts in the metacognitive account of disorder (e.g., Myers, Fisher, & Wells, 2009; Solem, Haland, Vogel, Hansen, & Wells, 2009).

I have described how psychological disorder is associated with the activation of a pattern of thinking, the CAS, that prolongs and deepens negative beliefs and emotions. The next question is: What causes the CAS?

## ORIGINS OF THE CAS

According to metacognitive theory, the CAS is moderated by environmental factors such as repeated threats that are difficult to bring under control, or uncertainty or ambiguity that lead to continuous processing. However, the continued execution of worry, rumination, threat monitoring, and thought suppression in particular is dependent on metacognition.

Metacognition in metacognitive therapy is viewed as a subset or "level" of cognition that monitors, controls, and appraises thinking, consistent with general metacognitive theory (Flavell, 1979). Sustained dysfunctional thinking is viewed as a product of meta-cognition. Effectively, psychological disorder is a consequence of biased metacognition. The theory proposes that two broad classes of metacognitive knowledge give rise to the CAS. These are positive metacognitive (PMC) beliefs and negative metacognitive

(NMC) beliefs (e.g., Cartwright-Hatton & Wells, 1997; Papageorgiou & Wells, 2001a; Wells & Cartwright-Hatton, 2004).

PMC beliefs concern the value of engaging in sustained thinking, threat monitoring, and thought suppression. Examples include:

- I must worry about what can go wrong in the future in order to be safe.
- If I analyze why I feel depressed, I'll find an answer to my depression.
- By anticipating the worst, I won't be taken by surprise.
- If I look out for danger, I can avoid being hurt in the future.
- If I focus on signs of rejection, I can do something before it is too late.
- Stopping my bad thoughts will keep me from losing control.
- I must fill all the gaps in my memory in order to know I'm not to blame.

PMC beliefs support the initiation and maintenance of the CAS in response to negative thoughts and emotions.

In contrast, NMC beliefs focus on the meaning, importance, and consequences of thoughts and mental experiences (e.g., urges, memories, impulses). Two important domains are beliefs about the uncontrollability of thinking styles of worry and rumination and beliefs about the meaning and danger of specific thoughts or mental events. These beliefs also contribute to persistence of the CAS. More specifically, believing that worrying is uncontrollable means that the person does not make consistent highly motivated efforts to interrupt worry or rumination once it is initiated. Furthermore, believing some thoughts are important or dangerous leads to monitoring for such thoughts and anticipating (worrying) about them (i.e., features of the CAS), leading in turn to more intrusions or perseveration. Some examples are as follows:

- I have no control over my worrying.
- Negative thoughts have the power to harm me.
- Thinking certain thoughts is dangerous.
- Some thoughts could change me as a person.
- Having an incomplete memory of what happened means I'm abnormal.
- Thinking black thoughts is an illness I cannot control.
- Thoughts can tempt fate.

There is some specificity in the content of PMC and NMC beliefs across different disorders. For instance, in the metacognitive model of obsessive compulsive disorder (Wells, 1997), positive beliefs concern the importance of controlling and suppressing obsessive thoughts and engaging in rituals. The negative beliefs concern themes of thought-object fusions (e.g., "my bad thoughts can contaminate objects"), thought-event fusion (e.g., "thinking of accidents will make them more likely to happen"), and thought-action fusion (e.g., "thinking of harming someone will make me do it").

In depression, the PMC beliefs concern the value of rumination as a means of finding solutions to symptoms of sadness. The NMC concern the uncontrollability of rumination. In generalized anxiety, the PMC focus on the usefulness of worry as a coping strategy and the NMC on the uncontrollability and dangerousness of worrying.

## COGNITIVE ARCHITECTURE, METACOGNITION, AND EMOTION

As I described above, psychological disorder is associated with a sense of loss of control of thinking. This is an important subjective experience from a theoretical perspective, because it may reflect different mechanisms underlying pathology. Control difficulties may be the result of reflexive or "automatic processes" or may result from the involvement of "top-down" metacognitive factors. The metacognitive model proposes that self-control difficulties are the result of metacognitive knowledge (top-down) and choice of thinking strategy rather than due to some lower-level automatic or reflexive process.

So far, I have discussed metacognitive knowledge as a set of propositional, verbally expressible beliefs. But the theory suggests that metacognitive knowledge is probably better represented as a set of plans or programs that control thinking. Because metacognition controls thinking, it must do so with reference to an internal guide or set of goals for a given cognitive enterprise. These plans can be thought of as part of the individual's skills for controlling thinking—what we might consider part of overall executive control.

Metacognition is reciprocally linked to emotion in the model. Emotion has a metacognitive function in that it biases access to and retrieval of knowledge and also selection of metacognitive plans for controlling cognition. If the plan giving rise to the CAS is selected, then emotion persists, as the executive does not down-regulate lower-level (subcortical) emotion networks. Instead, resources are allocated to sustained threat modes of processing.

In summary, the metacognitive therapy (MCT) theory of disorder is predominantly a top-down model that is not reliant on learning theory principles of conditioned responses between thoughts and emotion or between environment and emotion. Such explanations are grounded in the lower level of processing. The theory instead equates disorder with bias in the control of cognition by more volitional processes predominantly at the metacognitive level. Individuals maintain cognitive control even when knowledge or beliefs about control are erroneous. However, in some cases, the type of control executed requires shaping and training so that individuals can exercise the most appropriate and flexible control over thinking in a given situation.

## NATURE OF METACOGNITIVE THERAPY

Metacognitive therapy focuses on removing the CAS and promoting new ways of relating to thoughts. To achieve this goal, metacognitions controlling thinking must be modified.

Because metacognitive knowledge and beliefs are represented as plans or programs for thinking and also as propositional information, treatment aims both to build new metacognitive control skills (i.e., strengthen plans) and to change the nature of propositional information. These aims are often interconnected and overlap in the strategies used in treatment. For example, practicing the postponement of chains of worry enhances control skills and also modifies erroneous knowledge about loss of self-control. However, because there are different types of knowledge, individual strategies may not change each type universally. For example, whereas controlling worry may challenge beliefs about its uncontrollability, this will not modify beliefs about its potential danger. In fact, patients may misuse control as avoidance and fail to discover that worry is harmless. Thus, individual treatments are best guided by disorder-specific models that delineate the nature and relationship between the types of metacognitive knowledge that operate in each case. Disorder-specific metacognitive models have therefore been developed and tested to maximize treatment outcomes.

The first task of the therapist is drawing out the individual case-formulation based on the model. This is followed by socializing the patient to the model. Here the therapist aims to illuminate the presence of the CAS and to illustrate its effects through reviewing examples, questioning its consequences, and conducting socialization experiments.

For example, in the treatment of depression, the therapist asks about responses to fluctuations in mood/symptoms or negative thoughts and identifies the nature and duration of rumination and the metacognitive beliefs associated with it:

Therapist (T): What has your mood been like in the last week?

Patient (P): It's not been a good week, I've been feeling dreadful.

T: Was there a trigger for feeling like this?

P: I just woke up with a feeling of dread, and it's been like that for the past few days.

T: Okay, what was that feeling like? I mean, was it a thought or sensation in your body?

P: I had an argument with my husband, and I just woke up thinking I'll feel like this forever.

T: Was that the initial thought?

P: Yes.

T: Okay, when you had that thought, what did you then go on to think about?

P: I started to think I would never get over my depression, and how everyone seems better off than me. But I don't really have anything to be depressed about. There just seems to be nothing I can do to stop feeling like this.

T: That sounds like a long chain of thoughts that we call ruminating. How long did that go on?

P: All morning. I just stayed in bed and carried on going over things in my mind.

T: What happened to your feelings as you did that?

P: Well they just got worse, until I had to get up and take care of things.

T: Have you been ruminating since then?

P: Yes, much of the time.

T: If it makes you feel worse, would it be a good idea to reduce the activity?

P: Yes, but how? I'm not sure I can control it, it's part of my illness.

T: If you could control it, would you feel better?

P: Yes. It would probably help, but I need to find out why I'm like this in the first place.

T: Sounds like you have some beliefs that analyzing yourself will help you.

P: If I can find an answer, then I can do something about it.

T: How long have you been ruminating like this to try and find an answer?

P: For as long as I've been depressed; it must be more than four years.

T: Have you been able to find the answer yet?

P: No.

T: Maybe the answer is to stop ruminating. Shall we look at how you can start to do that?

P: But I have no control; it just seems to happen.

T: It's good you've said that, because one of the first things we should look at is your belief that you have no control, as that might get in the way of you practicing new ways of relating to your thoughts.

Following socialization, the next step in treatment is modifying beliefs about uncontrollability through a combination of verbal methods such as guided discovery and behavioral experiments. For example, the therapist can ask the patient to start and stop ruminating in the session. Similarly, the therapist can identify occasions when the patient successfully interrupted rumination and question whether the patient can increase the activity. If rumination can be increased, it should be possible to decrease it, too.

The concept of *detached mindfulness* and worry/rumination postponement is then introduced. Patients are instructed in acknowledging the presence of a negative thought and then disengaging any sustained worry, rumination, suppression, or coping response. In particular, the patient is instructed to postpone any worry or rumination until a specified 15-minute period later in the day. This period is designated as the "worry-time," but the therapist emphasizes that it is not mandatory to use this period—and, in fact, most patients decide it is not necessary when the time comes. A range of exercises and metaphors is used in MCT to facilitate knowledge and skills of detached mindfulness, although these do not involve the formal practice of meditation. Throughout this phase of treatment, the therapist monitors the frequency with which detached mindfulness and postponement is practiced and the proportion of negative thoughts to which it is applied.

To facilitate this process, it is often necessary to challenge negative beliefs about uncontrollability and positive beliefs about the need to worry or ruminate. In the treatment of some disorders, particularly depression, additional training procedures such as attention training (Wells, 1990, 2007) are used at each session to help patients acquire greater awareness of the control they have over thinking processes so that control is experienced as distinct from the occurrence of individual events. Attention training consists of focusing on different sounds often presented at a range of locations in space and shifting attention between them. The individual is asked to continue following the attention allocation instructions even in the presence and awareness of spontaneous internal events such as thoughts or feelings.

In treating individual disorders, specific domains of negative metacognitive beliefs are challenged, such as beliefs about the danger of worrying (in generalized anxiety) and beliefs about the meaning and power of thoughts to cause events (in obsessive-compulsive disorder). Positive metacognitive beliefs about the need to engage in worry, rumination, or other forms of perseverative activity are modified in treatment. One strategy is the strengthening of dissonance between positive and negative metacognitions. For instance, the therapist draws attention to the conflict that exists between the belief that worry is beneficial and the belief that it can lead to bodily damage or mental breakdown. Specific strategies, such as worry mismatch strategies, worry modulation experiments, and paradoxical rumination-prescription techniques, are also used where appropriate (see Wells, 2009). Worry mismatch is a technique in which a recent worry script is written out, with each step in the worry sequence summarized. The patient is then asked to describe the events that actually occurred in the situation; this forms a "reality script." The two scripts are compared, and the therapist helps the patient discover the substantial mismatch that exists between the two. The question is then posed: "If worry does not resemble reality, then what's the advantage of worrying?" The worry modulation experiment consists of asking a person to worry more on some days and ban or postpone worry on others, then to assess the effects on outcomes such as quality of work performance or number of mistakes made. In this way, the therapist can help the patient to see that worrying is not helpful and thereby challenges PMC beliefs.

Toward the end of treatment, relapse prevention is undertaken. It consists of reviewing residual metacognitive belief levels and formulating a therapy "blueprint"—a plan for how to respond to negative ideas and emotions in the future. The blueprint contrasts the "old plan," consisting of the CAS, with the new response style, consisting of factors such as low conceptual processing, refocusing on external safety signals, reversal of avoidance, and banning threat monitoring.

Progress in treatment in modifying key elements of the CAS and important metacognitions is continuously monitored with self-report scales. Some of these instruments are designed for specific disorders (e.g., the Generalized Anxiety Disorder Scale, Major Depressive Disorder Scale, and Obsessive-Compulsive Disorder Scale; Wells, 2008). Others are more generic, and have been subjected to formal psychometric evaluations (e.g., the Metacognitions Questionnaire 30; Wells & Cartwright-Hatton, 2004).

## HISTORICAL CONTEXT OF MCT

Metacognitive theory grew out of the recognition that existing cognitive behavior therapy (CBT) theories did not capture or represent the complexities of cognition in psychological disorder. In particular, they were based on a limited model of attention, in which disorder was equated with automatic biases, but ignored important aspects, such as the difficult-to-control extended and selective nature of thinking style. An early influence on the development of the theory was work on self-focused attention and self-consciousness. Elevated self-focused attention is associated with most forms of psychological disorder (e.g., Carver & Scheier, 1981; Ingram, 1990) and appears to be a marker for a possible pathological process, such as the CAS. Our early empirical attempts sought to test the association between self-focus and worry, and self-focus and cognitive failures and coping (Matthews & Wells, 1988; Wells, 1985; Wells & Matthews, 1994). This subsequently led to the development and evaluation of the effects of an attention training technique that aimed to reduce the CAS and increase awareness of metacognitive control skills (Wells, 1990).

In our initial description of the clinical implications of the theory we argued that treatment should develop techniques that enable patients to discontinue sustained processing and take a metacognitive perspective on thoughts. We called this state "detached mindfulness" (Wells & Matthews, 1994); since then, a range of strategies to facilitate this state have been developed (Wells, 2005b). This approach developed independently of other acceptance or mindfulness-based approaches to treatment. It draws on information processing theory concerning levels of control of attention (Shiffrin & Schneider, 1977) and metacognitive theory of cognition and memory (e.g., Nelson & Narrens, 1990), and develops, expands, and applies these constructs to thinking processes in clinical disorder.

In our early work, we also noted that schema theory (Beck, 1976) connects disorder with negative automatic thoughts and with beliefs about the self and world. But negative automatic thoughts represent a small subtype of thinking that does not capture the predominant style of thinking seen in psychological disorder, which has a more repetitive, brooding quality better captured by concepts of worry and rumination. It was not clear how schemas or irrational beliefs as posited by Beck (1976) or Ellis (1962) give rise to disorder. How would such declarative representations control processing? It is wholly possible for two individuals with the same beliefs to show different emotional and thinking responses. It seemed that answers to this type of question concerning mental control might lead to advances in the understanding and treatment of psychological disorder, and so, metacognition became a central focus of research and reasoning behind MCT.

## THE ROLE OF MINDFULNESS AND ACCEPTANCE

As commonly used, mindfulness and acceptance are more general concepts than the construct of detached mindfulness that we described above. We provided a specific and precise definition of detached mindfulness that implicates designated psychological processes. It is specifically a state of being aware of a spontaneous thought (mindfulness) and hence involves meta-awareness. Coupled with this is "detachment," which signifies two factors: (a) giving up any response to the thought (e.g., worry, rumination, coping), and (b) being aware of the thought as separate from the self, in which the individual becomes aware of being the observer of the thought. It should be noted that this does not encompass being aware of the "here and now," as in meditation-based mindfulness. Conversely, meditation-based mindfulness does not specifically implicate meta-awareness (i.e., awareness of thoughts). Another point of contrast is that pathways to mindfulness based on meditation practices involve using the breath as an anchor for awareness and approaching situations with a "beginner's mind of openness." From the perspective of metacognitive theory, it is difficult to reconcile these mind states with the complete suspension of conceptual processing.

Meditation-based mindfulness is defined as present moment nonjudgmental awareness. This seems rather vague. To begin with, we might ask: nonjudgemental awareness of what? In the early phases, mindfulness of the breath is often used as an anchor to bring attention back to the present moment. This means that focusing on breathing could be a distraction from worrying or ruminating, which might be a good thing, but it would not be a good thing if the person believes that worrying can lead to mental disorder or if it is used to control obsessional thoughts that the person believes could lead to harm. As this example illustrates, a theory linking meditation-based mindfulness practices to psychological mechanisms and how such practices might impact them differentially is required in order to develop effective new intervention techniques.

## CASE EXAMPLE

Disorder-specific metacognitive models have been developed that capture the dynamics of the CAS and metacognition (Wells, 2009). These models provide a basis for empirical testing of theory and are the grounding for individual case formulations in clinical practice. The MCT approach is illustrated here within the context of treating generalized anxiety disorder.

Jenny was a 32-year-old mother with a lifelong history of worrying and anxiety. She met criteria for generalized anxiety disorder with concurrent mood disturbance and obsessional personality features. She was seeking treatment for her constant anxiety and panic attacks, which began when she returned to work after the birth of her child. Jenny reported that she had undergone relaxation therapy and coping skills training for her anxiety in the recent past but had not found this beneficial. At assessment, she completed the Beck Anxiety Inventory (BAI: Beck, Epstein, Brown, & Steer, 1988), the Beck Depression Inventory (BDI; Beck, Steer, & Brown, 1996), and measures of metacognition, including the Generalized Anxiety Disorder Scale–Revised (GADS-R; Wells, 2009) and the Metacognitions Questionnaire (MCQ-30; Wells & Cartwright-Hatton, 2004). Jenny scored 23 on the BAI and 14 on the BDI, indicative of moderate anxiety and mild depressive symptoms. Her scores on the metacognition measures revealed a range of positive and negative metacognitive beliefs and unhelpful coping behaviors. The following negative metacognitive beliefs were prominent:

- My worrying is uncontrollable: 90%
- Worrying could harm me: 60%

- I could go crazy with worry: 40%
- If I worry too much, I could lose control: 40%

Her positive metacognitive beliefs were as follows:

- Worrying helps me cope: 90%
- If I worry, I'll be prepared: 70%
- Worrying helps me solve problems: 50%
- Worrying means I don't make mistakes: 80%

In the first treatment session, the therapist worked with Jenny to construct the case formulation by reviewing in detail the thoughts, emotions, and beliefs that were active in a recent and distressing worry episode. In the case formulation, Jenny experienced a negative thought designated as the trigger: "What if I haven't included everything in the work accounts?" This activated her positive metacognitive beliefs about the need to engage in sustained worry as a means of coping. Her sustained worrying led to contemplating a range of possible problems and solutions, leading to an initial increase in anxiety. As her anxiety increased, negative metacognitions were activated concerning the uncontrollability of worry and possible harm resulting from it. This gave rise to worry about worry (meta-worry) and a sudden increase in anxiety. Her coping behaviors included asking for reassurance from work colleagues, using alcohol to control anxiety, and a combination of thought control strategies of trying to suppress work-related thoughts and engaging in sustained negative thinking to try and stop herself from worrying (e.g., "I repeatedly tell myself to snap out of it or I will damage myself with stress").

The unique features of this treatment approach are evident in that it did not focus on the content of worry, which is prone to vary. It did not focus on modifying emotion or managing anxiety symptoms. The approach did not aim to identify more general beliefs about the self or world, but rather viewed these simply as the content or end product of worry and rumination. The approach instead focused on modifying *metacognitive* beliefs and helping Jenny develop more effective metacognitive control skills that enabled termination of the CAS (worry/rumination, threat monitoring and unhelpful coping) but not at the expense of failing to change metacognitive beliefs.

Treatment proceeded through a sequence starting with the therapist socializing Jenny to the metacognitive model. Here the therapist helped her to see how it is not the content of worry that was the problem but how she related to negative thoughts and the failure to regulate worry effectively. This was achieved by asking how much of a problem would exist if only positive beliefs about worry turned out to be true. The therapist also asked how much of a problem would remain if Jenny discovered that worry could be controlled. The therapist helped Jenny to see how using coping behaviors such as reassurance seeking was counterproductive. This transferred the control of her mind to someone else and prevented her discovering that she could control her own worry.

The next step in treatment consisted of challenging beliefs about the uncontrollability of worry in the context of a detached mindfulness and worry postponement experiment. Jenny was helped to see the difference between a spontaneous negative thought (trigger) and the subsequent thinking response. The therapist introduced the idea that she could learn to respond to such triggers in new ways that did not necessitate worry. Jenny was helped to experience detached mindfulness using a free association and "tiger task." Specifically, in the tiger task she was asked to create a mental image of a tiger and to watch the image from a distance, remaining aware of herself as the observer without influencing the tiger's behavior. After practicing this for a minute, the therapist asked her if she had influenced the tiger's behavior in any way. The aim was for her to see how the image has a life of its own, without the need to control, modify, or influence it in any way. Having achieved this, it was suggested that she adopt the same approach with a negative thought. In combination with this approach, the therapist introduced the concept of worry postponement. This consisted of acknowledging a negative thought and deciding to postpone sustained worry until a set period later in the day. This was introduced as an experiment to test her belief that worrying was uncontrollable. Subsequently in treatment, these experiments and strategies were revised and implemented to systematically weaken Jenny's belief that worry was uncontrollable. In particular, Jenny was asked to try an experiment in which she actively worried as much as possible in response to a negative thought in order to prove that she could not lose control. When her level of belief in uncontrollability of worry was at 0%, the therapist moved to the next phase of treatment.

The next phase of treatment, commencing on the fourth session, focused on modifying beliefs about the danger of worrying before challenging positive beliefs about the need to worry in order to cope. Verbal reattribution methods and behavioral experiments were used to challenge these metacognition domains. In the last two sessions, an increasing amount of time was devoted to relapse prevention work. In total, treatment lasted 10 sessions, which were held weekly for 40–60 minutes each. By the end of treatment, Jenny scored 3 on the BAI and a 1 on the BDI, and her metacognitive beliefs ranged from 10 to 0. She reported that worrying and anxiety were no longer a problem and that her sleep had improved.

## THE NATURE AND VALUE OF DIRECT COGNITIVE CHANGE STRATEGIES

As the case illustration demonstrates, MCT does not focus on modifying cognition, at least at the content level. It focuses instead on modifying cognitive processes and the control of cognition. There is no attempt in MCT to reality-test negative thoughts or general beliefs, or to evaluate and challenge the content of worry and rumination. For example, in treating depression, the traditional cognitive therapist will focus on reality-testing beliefs about the self as epitomized by questions such as "Where is your evidence that you are a failure?" and "Is there any counter-evidence that goes against this conclusion?" In contrast, the MCT therapist asks, "How much time are you spending analyzing and ruminating about being a failure?" and "What are the advantages of doing that?" and "Can you reduce that activity?" Thus, in MCT direct change strategies are important, but they are aimed at modifying metacognitive beliefs rather than the content of cognition. In addition, and of equal if not greater importance, the metacognitive therapist directly changes the person's metacognitive experience of thoughts. Change in this dimension may not occur in standard CBT, or it may be limited. This is because thoughts are treated as if they are important and must be evaluated for accuracy. In contrast, the MCT therapist assumes that thoughts per se do not matter; the person's response to them does. Part of the goal of MCT is to help patients discover that they can function better without worry, rumination and focusing on threat.

The focus on metacognition rather than cognition can be illustrated in the treatment of obsessive-compulsive disorder. Cognitive approaches have emphasized beliefs such as inflated responsibility (e.g. Salkovskis, 1985), perfectionism, and intolerance of uncertainty (OCCWG, 1997). But these are defined not in metacognitive terms but as more general self-beliefs and biases in interpretations. For example, these schema-based approaches state that obsessional individuals interpret situations as a sign they will be responsible for harm (e.g., "I have touched the dustbin so I could contaminate my children"). Whereas the concept of metacognitive appraisal (i.e. interpreting thoughts) is sometimes an inherent part of this model, it need not be, and even when it is the role of metacognition, it is not developed. Treatment focuses on reality-testing the responsibility belief rather than explicitly changing the metacognitive level. What is missing is the role of metacognitive beliefs and the types of unhelpful relationships that exist with thoughts in OCD as exemplified in the metacognitive model. The metacognitive therapist is not concerned with responsibility because this is the end product or content of subsequent rumination and worry. In contrast, the metacognitive therapist is concerned with modifying erroneous beliefs about the power, meaning, and importance of thoughts. In the example given above, the metacognitive therapist changes the patient's relationship with and beliefs about the thought: "I could contaminate my children" instead of questioning the probability or evidence that this will occur.

Modification strategies are effective when they change metacognition. In particular, modification strategies aim to change the negative metacognitions about the uncontrollability, danger, and importance of thoughts and the need to worry and ruminate. Metacognitive awareness is a feature that traditional CBT and MCT have in common. For instance, the use of thought diaries and identifying cognitive distortions in standard CBT are likely to enhance meta-awareness. However, there is nothing inherent in meta-awareness that unambiguously modifies positive and negative metacognitive beliefs or provides the patient with new ways of controlling cognition. It may begin to shift the patient to a metacognitive level of processing, but it does not provide the practice of appropriate control over the CAS, which is specified as a key requirement of treatment in MCT.

The metacognitive model differentiates between multiple components of metacognition and assigns specific functional roles to them in causing pathology. It therefore offers implications concerning the factors that must change in order for psychological treatments to be effective. If this approach is correct, then the outcomes of various forms of CBT should be dependent on metacognitive change.

There is a tradition in psychotherapy of assuming that self-awareness or insight is beneficial, and perhaps even sufficient, for psychological recovery. But the MCT approach implies that such insight is not sufficient for recovery. One type of self-awareness is metacognitive awareness, the ability to focus on one's own thoughts. However, as I alluded to earlier, metacognitive awareness is a factor that is elevated in some disorders, such as obsessive-compulsive disorder, generalized anxiety, and trauma-related anxiety, in which individuals are very aware of their intrusive thoughts, memories, and difficult-to-control worries. Metacognitive awareness may be excessive or inflexible and may constitute a form of threat-monitoring, as might be the case with an obsessive individual who monitors and tries to control blasphemous thoughts. Evidence shows that obsessive symptoms are associated with heightened cognitive self-consciousness, which is the tendency to focus on thoughts (Cartwright-Hatton & Wells, 1997; Janeck, Calamari, Rieman, & Heffelfinger, 2003). It is necessary to move beyond the view of meta-awareness as a singular beneficial variable. We need to begin to explore how the effects of this factor are dependent on the individuals' goals for processing and their knowledge or beliefs about cognition. The MCT approach assumes that although metacognitive awareness can be useful, it is not usually sufficient in producing therapeutic change. Treatment strategies are useful and important when they facilitate metacognitive control (e.g., attention flexibility), interrupt the CAS, and modify metacognitive beliefs.

The model predicts that the CAS and metacognition must change in order for psychological treatment to be effective. An implication is that all effective psychological treatments, including traditional CBT, are effective because they fortuitously modify the CAS and metacognition. However, the overall efficacy of treatment is likely to be improved if it directly and by design focuses on metacognitive modification.

## EMPIRICAL SUPPORT FOR MCT THEORY AND THERAPY

Substantial empirical support has accrued over the past 25 years for the metacognitive theory of psychological disorder. This section provides a brief overview of this data.

### Evidence That a Generic Thinking Style, the CAS, Is Linked to Disorder

Self-focused processing is seen as a marker for the CAS in the metacognitive model. There is a substantial literature on self-consciousness, the tendency to focus attention inward on aspects of the self (e.g., Ingram, 1990), which is consistently and positively related to a wide range of psychological disorder.

More specifically, dispositional self-focus is positively correlated with worry in test situations (Wells, 1985) and in exposure to stressful stimuli (Wells, 1991). Private and public self-consciousness also appear to contribute to individual differences in cognitive failures independently of anxiety (Matthews & Wells, 1988), supporting the view that the CAS may impair cognitive control processes. Elevated self-attention is also associated with less use of problem-focused coping in stressful situations (Wells and Matthews, 1994).

## *Worry and Rumination*

Research on the effects of worrying provide clear support that it has negative psychological consequences. In particular, periods of induced worry can lead to greater subsequent thought intrusions (Borkovec, Robinson, Pruzinsky, & DePree, 1983; York, Borkovec, Vasey, & Stern, 1987).

Two studies tested the impact of worry on intrusive images following exposure to a stressful stimulus. The MCT model proposes that worrying can interfere with appropriate metacognitive control over emotional processing. Intrusive images/memories are considered to be an index of failed emotional processing. Butler, Wells, and Dewick (1995) showed a gruesome film to participants and then separated them into five-minute mentation groups. One group was instructed to settle down, another to imagine the events in the film, and a third to worry about the film. Participants who worried reported more intrusive images related to the film over the next three days compared to the other groups. Wells and Papageorgiou (1995) replicated and extended this effect. Mellings and Alden (2000) examined post-event worrying or rumination in people high in social anxiety and found it predicted recall of negative self-relevant information, negative bias in self-judgments, and recall of anxiety sensations on a subsequent occasion involving anticipation of a social interaction.

A substantial literature demonstrates negative effects of rumination. Dysphoric rumination leads to prolonged and more severe periods of depression than distraction, and predicts future depressive episodes (see Lyubomirsky & Tkach, 2004, for a review). Rumination reduces problem solving in stressful situations (Nolen-Hoeksema & Morrow, 1991), impairs cognitive performance (e.g., Hertel, 1998), and reduces motivation to engage in pleasant activities (Lyubomirsky & Nolen-Hoeksema, 1993).

In a large, longitudinal study of more than 1,100 community adults, those who showed clinical depression and a ruminative style at initial assessment had more severe and longer-lasting depression one year later, were less likely to show remission, and were more likely to have anxiety (Nolen-Hoeksema, 2000). Nolen-Hoeksema, Parker, and Larrson (1994) studied 253 bereaved adults. They were interviewed one month after the death of their loved one and again six months later. Rumination at the first interview was significantly and positively associated with depression at six months, and this relationship remained significant when depression level at one month was statistically controlled.

## *Attentional Threat Monitoring*

One of the features of the CAS is an abnormality in selective attention consisting of excessive or biased focusing on personally relevant information. The presence of such a bias is supported by studies that have examined subjects' ability to process one aspect or channel of information while filtering out competing channels (Mathews & Macleod, 1985; Gotlib & Cane, 1987; Kaspi, McNally, & Amir, 1995).

The finding of such bias is consistent with the MCT approach if such effects can be linked to the individual's conscious strategies for controlling attention. Early work on bias viewed these processes as automatic rather than as part of the individual's strategy for regulating cognition (Willams, Watts, MacLeod, & Mathews, 1988). However, the theory on which metacognitive therapy is based views bias as primarily reflecting strategic processing serving the person's coping strategy.

Consistent with this view, in depressed individuals the prior presentation of self-referent material increases interference (Segal & Vella, 1990) as does a self-focus manipulation in nonclinical subjects (Richards & French, 1992). Richards, French, Johnson, Naparstek, and Williams (1992) found bias associated with trait-anxiety only in trials that were blocked by word type, suggesting bias may depend on expectancy of threat stimuli. Furthermore, priming effects on the emotional Stroop have been found over time spans associated with voluntary processing (Segal & Vella, 1990; Richards & French, 1992).

Matthews and Harley (1996) tested two possible models of bias on the emotional Stroop using connectionist modeling. They tested an automatic model analogous to hardwired sensitivity to threat or repeated exposure effects, and an alternative model consistent with the metacognitive theory of a continuation of monitoring for threat while performing other tasks. Only the latter model simulated impairment in color-naming emotional words.

## *Maladaptive Metacognitive-Focused Coping*

An important idea is that worry and rumination can be used as coping strategies and, at least in part, are reactions to dealing with negative thoughts. Indeed, the effects of worry measured as a metacognitive coping strategy are distinct from the effects of worry assessed as an anxiety symptom (Roussis & Wells, 2008).

Studies using the Thought Control Questionnaire (TCQ; Wells & Davies, 1994) have repeatedly demonstrated that the use of worry and punishment to cope with distressing thoughts is elevated in patient samples and is associated with worse psychological outcomes. Warda and Bryant (1998) compared accident survivors with and without acute stress disorder (ASD) and found that those with ASD used more worry and punishment. Worry and punishment is also elevated in patients suffering from obsessive compulsive disorder (Abramowitz et al., 2003; Amir et al., 1997), and these strategies predict lower levels of recovery from depression and PTSD (Reynolds & Wells, 1999).

Longitudinal studies have demonstrated that higher levels of TCQ worry measured soon after motor vehicle accidents predict the later development of post-traumatic stress symptoms, even when symptom level at first assessment is controlled (Holeva, Tarrier, & Wells, 2001). Similarly, Roussis and Wells (2008) showed that TCQ-worry was a positive predictor of trauma symptoms after stress exposure in students, and that this relationship was independent of a measure of worry assessed as an anxiety symptom.

There is a broader but nonetheless relevant literature on the effects of thought suppression. This area has shown that attempts not to think a target thought may have counterproductive effects of increasing the intrusion immediately or subsequently. Thus, trying to remove a thought from consciousness is not particularly effective and may be prone to backfire in some circumstances (e.g., Purdon, 1999).

## Metacognitive Beliefs

The Metacognitions Questionnaire (MCQ; Cartwright-Hatton & Wells, 1997; Wells & Cartwright-Hatton, 2004) has been widely used to test the metacognitive model. Beliefs about cognition emerge as reliable correlates of symptoms of emotional disorder. For example, Wells and Papageorgiou (1998) demonstrated metacognitive correlates of obsessive-compulsive symptoms and worry. Hermans, Martens, De Cort, Pieter, and Eelen (2003) compared individuals with OCD to nonanxious controls and found differences on several dimensions. Individuals with OCD held higher negative beliefs about uncontrollability and danger of mental events; they reported more beliefs about harm resulting from thoughts; they monitored their thoughts more; and they had lower confidence in their cognitive abilities.

Positive relationships between metacognition and hypochondriasis (Bouman & Meijer, 1999), problem drinking (Spada, Moneta, & Wells, 2007; Spada & Wells, 2005), psychosis (Lobban, Haddock, Kinderman, & Wells, 2002; Morrison & Wells, 2007), depression (Papageorgiou & Wells, 2001b, 2009), trauma symptoms (Bennett & Wells, 2010) and generalized anxiety (Wells, 2005) support the role of metacognitive beliefs across pathologies.

## The Causal Status of Metacognition

Rassin, Merckelbach, Muris, and Spaan (1999) manipulated metacognitive beliefs about thought suppression and tested the effects on intrusive thoughts and discomfort. Some participants were led to believe that an EEG apparatus could detect the thought "apple" and that, upon doing so, the apparatus would deliver an electric shock to another participant. Other participants were told that the apparatus could detect the thought, but no information about electric shocks was given. Those subjects led to believe the thoughts had significance showed greater discomfort, more internally directed anger, and greater efforts to avoid thinking the forbidden thought.

In prospective studies, Yilmaz, Gencoz, and Wells (2007a) showed that metacognitive beliefs measured at time 1 predicted the development of symptoms of anxiety and depression six months later, even after controlling for stressful life events. Papageorgiou and Wells (2009) administered the Inventory to Diagnose Depression (IDD) to college students on two occasions, 12 weeks apart. Negative beliefs about the uncontrollability and danger of depressive thinking (rumination) measured at time 1 were a significant predictor of depression at time 2 when level of depressive symptoms and rumination at time 1 were controlled. Myers, Fisher, and Wells (2009) examined the longitudinal relationship between metacognitive beliefs and obsessive-compulsive symptoms. Beliefs about the power and meaning of thoughts measured at time 1 were significant predictors of symptoms of obsessive-compulsive distress three months later. In this study, beliefs concerning perfectionism and responsibility did not independently contribute to distress. Using a different measure of metacognitive beliefs, Sica, Steketee, Ghisi, Chiri, and Franceschini (2007) found that beliefs about the uncontrollability and danger of thoughts predicted obsessive-compulsive symptoms over a three-month period.

Metacognitive thought control strategies have also been shown to prospectively predict PTSD symptoms. Roussis and Wells (2008) measured stress symptoms, thought control strategies, and worry in college students on two occasions separated by approximately three months. A greater tendency to endorse the use of worry to control thoughts at time 1 was positively associated with PTSD symptoms at time 2, when level of stress exposure, worry assessed as an anxiety symptom, and PTSD symptoms measured at time 1 were controlled. Holeva, Tarrier, and Wells (2001) examined the predictors of PTSD following motor-vehicle accidents. The use of worry to control thoughts positively predicted the subsequent development of PTSD four to six months later.

There are a large number of studies that have examined the effects of metacognitive regulation strategies. Attempted suppression of specific thoughts shows that suppression attempts are rarely entirely successful, and may increase the occurrence of target thoughts (e.g., Merckelbach, Muris, van den Hout, & de Jong, 1991; Purdon, 1999; Wegner et al., 1987). Thus, metacognitive control strategies may run the risk of contributing to greater intrusions or a sense of reduced mental control. However, further research is needed to investigate the effects of metacognitive appraisal and beliefs on suppression effects. There is some initial suggestion that suppression effects on behavior may be influenced by metacognitive knowledge (Reuven-Magril, Rosenmann, Libermann, & Dar, 2009).

## Metacognition Versus Cognition

Several studies have sought to test the relative contribution of cognition (e.g., general schemas/beliefs) and metacognition to symptoms of psychological disorder. Cross-sectional investigations have demonstrated that metacognition contributes to disorder above cognition, and in some cases cognition did not explain additional unique variance in symptoms. Wells and Carter (1999) showed that meta-worry (worry about worry), but not worry per se, was independently associated with both pathological worry and the problem level caused by worry. Nuevo, Montorio, and Borkovec (2004) extended the above study and found that meta-worry consistently emerged as a positive predictor of pathological worry and interference from worry. This relationship held when the content of worry, trait anxiety, and uncontrollability were statistically controlled. Wells and Carter (2001) showed that patients with generalized anxiety had significantly higher negative metacognitive beliefs than a mixed-anxiety comparison group, and these differences remained when the frequency of worry was statistically controlled.

Ruscio and Borkovec (2004) addressed an important question of whether the presence or absence of GAD could be attributed to differences in cognition or metacognition. Their groups showed similar experiences of worry but substantial differences in negative beliefs about worry, demonstrating that metacognition rather than cognition distinguished individuals with a worry disorder.

Specific studies have examined the relative contribution of cognition and metacognition to obsessive-compulsive symptoms. In these studies, metacognitive beliefs concerning the power and meaning of intrusive thoughts reliably emerged as significant correlates of symptoms, but cognitive belief domains, including themes of inflated responsibility and perfectionism, did not contribute above metacognition (Gwilliam, Wells, & Cartwright-Hatton, 2004; Myers, Fisher, & Wells, 2009; Myers & Wells, 2005).

Yilmaz, Grencoz, and Wells (2007b) tested the unique contribution of metacognition versus cognition to depression. Cognition was measured with the Dysfunctional Attitude Scale, and metacognition was assessed with two measures of beliefs about rumination. The metacognition measures explained variance in depression symptoms, but the DAS did not.

A study by Solem, Haland, Vogel, Hansen, and Wells (2009) examined change in cognition and metacognition in patients undergoing exposure and response prevention treatment for obsessive-compulsive disorder. This treatment was effective in relieving symptoms. An analysis of symptom improvement and recovery showed that change in metacognition was the only significant predictor of improvement and recovery, and change in cognition was not, when they were simultaneous predictors in a regression equation.

## EVIDENCE OF TREATMENT EFFECTS

Several studies have examined the impact of the full metacognitive therapy treatment program as well as individual treatment components or techniques.

### Attention Training

Early studies explored the effects of the Attention Training Technique (ATT). This technique aims to increase awareness of metacognitive control over processing, making attention more flexible so that individuals can exit the CAS cycle. In the first test of ATT, it was used to treat a patient with panic disorder and relaxation-induced anxiety (Wells, 1990). Using an alternating treatments design, the effects of ATT were contrasted with the effects of an autogenic exercise chosen to reverse the effects of ATT. The new technique was associated with a reduction of symptoms and eventual elimination of panic attacks, whereas in contrast autogenic relaxation increased symptoms. In this case, the final use of ATT was associated with an elimination of panic attacks that was stable across a 12-month follow-up. In a later case-replication series, Wells, White, and Carter (1997) tested the effects of ATT in two panic disorder cases and a case of social phobia. A true-reversal methodology was used in the social phobia case, in which an initial phase of ATT was followed by instructions to practice body-focused attention, after which the ATT was reintroduced. Body-focus was intended to reestablish the CAS (e.g., threat-monitoring) and by reversing hypothesised ATT mechanisms of action provided a means of ensuring that the ATT had an effect on its reintroduction. In the two panic cases, the ATT was associated with significant decreases in panic attacks and reduction in negative beliefs. In the social phobia case, ATT reduced anxiety and negative beliefs, whereas the body-focus instruction increased them.

Papageorgiou and Wells (1998) examined the effects of ATT in a hypochondriasis case series. All patients showed large reductions in worry, illness beliefs, and body-focused attention that persisted across follow-up. The technique has also been examined in cases of recurrent major depressive disorder (Papageorgiou & Wells, 2000). In this study, four consecutive cases were given five to eight sessions of ATT after three to five weeks of baseline monitoring. Each case showed marked improvements in anxiety and depression following introduction of treatment, and the gains were maintained at three-, six- and twelve-month follow-ups. Measures of rumination and metacognitions showed that the ATT was associated with substantial reductions in these variables. A randomized controlled trial of ATT in the treatment of hypochondriasis was conducted by Cavanagh and Franklin (2000). Patients were allocated to either six sessions of ATT or to a no-treatment condition. Whereas the control group showed no improvement in symptoms, the ATT group improved in a range of outcome measures. There were substantial improvements in level of health worry, disease conviction and behavioral measures at post treatment and at 18-month follow-up.

ATT has also been incorporated in a training package for depressed patients by Siegle, Ghinassi, and Thase (2007). These authors found that an attention plus treatment-as-usual condition was superior in improving depression and rumination than treatment as usual. These authors provided additional preliminary data that the attention manipulation was associated with pre to post-treatment changes in subcortical (amygdala) activity in response to positive and negative stimuli.

## MCT Treatment Studies

Several case series and trials of MCT across different disorders support the effectiveness of treatment. There have been case-series evaluations in depression (Wells, Fisher, et al., 2009), post-traumatic stress (Wells & Sembi, 2004) and obsessive-compulsive disorder (Fisher & Wells, 2008). In addition, group treatments of OCD (Rees & van Koesveld, 2008) and comparative evaluations against CBT in adolescents suffering from OCD (Simons, Schneider, & Herpert-Dahlmann, 2006) have been reported.

Uncontrolled trials of chronic PTSD (Wells, Welford, et al., 2008) and GAD (Wells & King, 2006) have also been published. The treatment effect sizes and standardized recovery rates in these studies suggest that MCT is highly effective.

Nordahl (2009) reported a randomized trial of effects of MCT compared with treatment as usual in treatment-resistant patients with mixed presentations of anxiety and depression. MCT emerged as an effective treatment that showed overall superiority to CBT.

Randomized trials of MCT for GAD (Wells et al., 2010) and PTSD (Colbear & Wells, 2009; Proctor et al., 2009) have demonstrated that MCT is superior to alternative treatments of applied relaxation in the case of GAD, and superior to wait-list or imaginal exposure in the treatment of PTSD. Standardized recovery rates across MCT studies of PTSD have returned rates of 78–90%. The recovery rates in GAD have been 80% based on trait-anxiety scores (Wells, et al., 2010).

These studies are promising, and suggest that MCT may be highly effective, producing recovery rates that might exceed those normally attributed to traditional CBT. The treatment gains are largely maintained over 6- or 12-month follow-ups. However, the sample sizes are small, follow-up is limited in length, and many of the trials have been conducted by leading proponents of MCT. Clearly, these limitations temper conclusions that can be currently drawn concerning treatment effects. However, an interesting feature of the treatment is its potential cost effectiveness, with treatment effects obtained within 12 sessions and in many instances recovery being achieved after as little as 8 hours/sessions of treatment.

## EVIDENCE OF TREATMENT MECHANISMS

Studies of treatment mechanism have examined the effects of manipulating attention, presenting mental sets that facilitate metacognitive change, and have explored metacognitive belief change as a predictor of treatment response.

In social phobia, the threat monitoring component of the CAS is marked by excessive self-focus on performance and embarrassing symptoms. Wells and Papageorgiou (2001) tested the effects of exposure on individuals with social phobia when it was presented under two conditions. One condition asked patients to shift to external attention focus (counteracting threat monitoring), while the other used a habituation rationale and asked patients to stay in the situation for the same planned period of time. The metacognitive condition involving attention refocusing was superior to the comparison condition in reducing anxiety and negative beliefs.

In a study of patients with obsessive-compulsive disorder, Fisher and Wells (2005) used a similar approach. They asked patients to listen to a loop tape of their obsessional thoughts under a habituation exposure condition or a condition that emphasized metacognitive change. The metacognitive condition was superior at reducing distress, urge to neutralize, and negative beliefs.

Two studies have evaluated metacognitive change as a predictor of treatment outcome. Solem, Halland, Vogel, Hansen, and Wells (2009) showed that change in metacognitive beliefs predicted improvement in symptoms in obsessive-compulsive patients receiving exposure therapy, but change in non-metacognitive dysfunctional beliefs (responsibility, perfectionism, etc.) did not. Spada, Caselli, and Wells (2009) found that metacognitive beliefs predicted drinking status across follow-up after a course of CBT in problem drinkers.

## FUTURE DIRECTIONS

Because MCT is based on an information processing model that specifies a cognitive architecture involving metacognitive and subcortical emotional processes, it should be possible to map these processes and linkages in the human brain. Developments in dynamic imaging techniques should be used to determine the neurological correlates of metacognitive techniques and measures. Moreover, the impact of strategies such as detached mindfulness and attention training should be explored. The model predicts that these techniques should increase executive control and be associated with reductions in activity in areas of the limbic system under exposure to threat or negative stimuli.

Of critical importance, future studies should aim to examine the effects of treatments, including conventional CBTs, on metacognition and on the role of metacognition as a mediator of treatment outcome. Because the MCT model is multidimensional, incorporating various features of metacognition, studies may seek to determine which components carry most treatment effects. Is it change in the content of metacognitive beliefs or the enhancement of metacognitive control as indexed by flexibility in attention, for example? The MCT approach provides a range of possibilities that go beyond concepts of simply enhancing metacognitive awareness or reality-testing the content of cognition.

The development of mindfulness and acceptance approaches in CBT has drawn greater attention to the multifaceted nature of aspects of cognition that are not always susceptible to reality testing. The use of meditation-based mindfulness has been one answer to the problem of high relapse following CBT for depression. But this is only one type of approach. Grafting new techniques onto existing treatments might provide a solution, but an alternative is to go for a complete rethinking of the fundamental therapeutic approach. MCT and some of the other approaches in this book attempt to do just that. They each ask different questions, and the one asked by MCT is specifically: "What is it that controls thinking?" If we agree that biased cognition is a cause of disorder, it is rather surprising that it has taken the field so long to address the questions of what gives rise to bias, and more importantly, what gives some but not all thoughts their continued salience.

Does the incorporation of mindfulness-based theory and strategies represent a paradigmatic change within the field of CBT? In my view it could, but as it currently stands it probably does not. This is because mindfulness approaches serve as an extension of CBT and have not forced a more fundamental change in the treatment. Furthermore, the goals of meditation-based mindfulness are far from fixed, which could threaten its progression. Sometimes it is viewed as an anxiety management technique, other times as a relapse prevention strategy, and others as a distraction from worrying. Without a coherent psychological framework for understanding the effects and for developing the use of mindfulness meditation, it can hardly be viewed as paradigmatic. In contrast, techniques such as ATT and detached mindfulness, as used in MCT, do not borrow from the meditation tradition; they have a specific theoretical origin grounded in modifying well-specified psychological mechanisms. However, they are still simply techniques used in MCT and do not in themselves constitute a paradigm change.

It is important to look beyond individual techniques at the empirical and theoretical basis of an approach to judge how well it explains pathology and gives rise to new forms of practice. As far as MCT is concerned, others shall judge its paradigmatic standing in the field. I would contend that it is radically different from the earlier content-based approaches in CBT and from the behavioral approaches, both of which have neglected metacognition, extended thinking, and intentions and goals in the person's selection of some thoughts over others.

# REFERENCES

Abramowitz, J. S., Whiteside, S., Kalsy, S. A., & Tolin, D. A. (2003). Thought control strategies in obsessive-compulsive disorder: A replication and extension. *Behaviour Research and Therapy, 41*, 529–54.

Amir, N., Cashman, L., & Foa, E. B. (1997). Strategies of thought control in obsessive-compulsive disorder. *Behaviour Research and Therapy, 35*, 775–777.

Beck, A. T. (1976). *Cognitive therapy and the emotional disorders.* New York, NY: International Universities Press.

Beck, A.T., Epstein, N., Brown, G., & Steer, R. A. (1988) An inventory for measuring depression. *Archives of General Psychiatry, 4*, 561–571.

Beck, A.T., Steer, R.A. & Brown, G. (1996). *Beck Depression Inventory-II.* San Antonio, TX: Psychological Corporation.

Bennett, H., & Wells A. (2010). Metacognition, memory disorganization, and rumination in posttraumatic stress symptoms. *Journal of Anxiety Disorders, 24*, 318–325.

Borkovec, T. D., Robinson, E., Pruzinsky, T., & DePree, J. A. (1983). Preliminary exploration of worry: Some characteristics and processes. *Behaviour Research and Therapy, 21*, 9–16.

Bouman, T. K., & Meijer, K. J. (1999). A preliminary study of worry and metacognitions in hypochondriasis. *Clinical Psychology and Psychotherapy, 6*, 96–102. Special Issue: Metacognition and Cognitive Behaviour Therapy. Chichester, UK: Wiley.

Butler, G., Wells, A., & Dewick, H. (1995). Differential effects of worry and imagery after exposure to a stressful stimulus: A pilot study. *Behavioural and Cognitive Psychotherapy, 23*, 45–56.

Cartwright-Hatton, S., & Wells, A. (1997). Beliefs about worry and intrusions: The meta-cognitions questionnaire and its correlates. *Journal of Anxiety Disorders, 11*, 279–296.

Carver, C. S., & Scheier, M. F. (1981). *Attention and self-regulation: A control theory approach to human behaviour.* Berlin, Germany: Springer-Verlag.

Cavanagh, M. J., & Franklin, J. (2000). Attention training and hypochondriasis: Preliminary results of a controlled treatment trial. Paper presented at the World Congress of Behavioral and Cognitive Therapies, Vancouver, Canada.

Colbear, J. & Wells, A. (2009). Randomised controlled trial of metacognitive therapy for post-traumatic stress disorder. Manuscript submitted for publication.

Ellis, A. (1962). *Reason and emotion in psychotherapy.* New York, NY: Lyle Stuart.

Fisher, P. L., & Wells, A. (2005). Experimental modification of beliefs in obsessive-compulsive disorder: A test of the metacognitive model. *Behaviour Research and Therapy*, *43*, 821–829.

Fisher, P. L., & Wells, A. (2008). Metacognitive therapy for obsessive-compulsive disorder: A case series. *Journal of Behavior Therapy and Experimental Psychiatry*, *39*, 117–132.

Flavell, J. H. (1979). Metacognition and metacognitive monitoring: A new area of cognitive-developmental inquiry. *American Psychologist*, *34*, 906–911.

Gotlib, I. H., & Cane, D. B. (1987). Construct accessibility and clinical depression: A longitudinal investigation. *Journal of Abnormal Psychology*, *96*, 199–204.

Gwilliam, P., Wells, A., & Cartwright-Hatton, S. (2004). Does meta-cognition or responsibility predict obsessive-compulsive symptoms: A test of the meta-cognitive model. *Clinical Psychology & Psychotherapy*, *11*, 137–144.

Hermans, D., Martens, K., De Cort, K., Pieters, G., & Eelen, P. (2003). Reality monitoring and metacognitive beliefs related to cognitive confidence in obsessive-compulsive disorder. *Behaviour Research and Therapy*, *41*, 383–401.

Holeva, V., Tarrier, N., & Wells, A. (2001). Prevalence and predictors of acute PTSD following road traffic accidents: Thought control strategies and social support. *Behavior Therapy*, *32*, 65–83.

Ingram, R. E. (1990). Self-focused attention in clinical disorders: Review and conceptual model. *Psychological Bulletin*, *107*, 156–176.

Janeck, A. S., Calamari, J. E., Riemann, B. C., & Heffelfinger, S. K. (2003). Too much thinking about thinking? Metacognitive differences in obsessive-compulsive disorder. *Journal of Anxiety Disorders*, *17*, 181–195.

Kaspi, S. P., McNally, R. J., & Amir, N. (1995). Cognitive processing of emotional information in posttraumatic stress disorder. *Cognitive Therapy and Research*, *19*, 433–444.

Lobban, F., Haddock, G., Kinderman, P., & Wells, A. (2002). The role of metacognitive beliefs in auditory hallucinations. *Personality and Individual Differences*, *32*, 1351–1363.

Lyubomirsky, S., & Nolen-Hoeksema, S. (1993). Self-perpetuating properties of dysphoric rumination. *Journal of Personality and Social Psychology*, *65*, 339–349.

Lyubomirsky, S., & Tkach, C. (2004). The consequences of dysphoric rumination. In C. Papageorgiou & A. Wells (Eds.), *Depressive rumination: Nature, theory and treatment* (pp. 21–41). Chichester, UK: Wiley.

Matthews, G., & Harley, T. A. (1996). Connectionist models of emotional distress and attentional bias. *Cognition and Emotion*, *10*, 561–600.

Mathews, A., & MacLeod, C. (1985). Selective processing of threat cues in anxiety states. *Behaviour Research and Therapy*, *23*, 563–569.

Matthews, G., & Wells, A. (1988). Relationships between anxiety, self-consciousness and cognitive failure. *Cognition and Emotion*, *2*, 123–132.

Matthews, G., & Wells, A. (1999). The cognitive science of attention and emotion. In T. Dalgleish & M. Power (Eds.), *Handbook of cognition and emotion* (pp. 171–192). New York, NY: Wiley.

Mellings, T. M. B., & Alden, L. E. (2000). Cognitive processes in social anxiety: The effects of self-focus, rumination and anticipatory processing. *Behaviour Research and Therapy*, *38*, 243–257.

Merckelbach, H., Muris, P., van den Hout, M., & de Jong, P. (1991). Rebound effects of thought suppression: Intrusion dependent? *Behavioural Psychotherapy*, *19*, 225–238.

Morrison, A. P., & Wells, A. (2007). Relationships between worry, psychotic experiences and emotional distress in patients with schizophrenia spectrum diagnoses and comparisons with anxious and non-patient groups. *Behaviour Research and Therapy*, *45*, 1539–1600.

Morrison, A. P., Wells, A., & Nothard, S. (2002). Cognitive and emotional predictors of predisposition to hallucinations in non-patients. *British Journal of Clinical Psychology*, *41*, 259–270.

Myers, S., Fisher, P. L., & Wells, A. (2009). An empirical test of the metacognitive model of obsessive-compulsive symptoms: Fusion beliefs, beliefs about rituals and stop signals. *Journal of Anxiety Disorders*, *23*, 436–442.

Myers, S., & Wells, A. (2005). Obsessive-compulsive symptoms: The contribution of metacognitions and responsibility. *Journal of Anxiety Disorders, 19*, 806–817.

Nelson, T. O., & Narens, L. (1990). Metamemory: A theoretical framework and some new findings. In G. H. Bower (Ed.), *The psychology of learning and motivation.* New York, NY: Academic Press, pp. 125–173.

Nolen-Hoeksema, S. (2000). The role of rumination in depressive disorders and mixed anxiety/depressive symptoms. *Journal of Abnormal Psychology, 109*, 504–511.

Nolen-Hoeksema, S., & Morrow, J. (1991). A prospective study of depression and posttraumatic stress symptoms after a natural disaster: The 1989 Loma Prieta earthquake. *Journal of Personality and Social Psychology, 61*, 115–121.

Nolen-Hoeksema, S., Parker, L. E., & Larson, J. (1994). Ruminative coping with depressed mood following loss. *Journal of Personality and Social Psychology, 67*, 92–104.

Nordahl, H. M. (2009). Effectiveness of brief metacognitive therapy versus cognitive-behavioral therapy in a general outpatient setting. *International Journal of Cognitive Therapy, 2*, 152–159.

Nuevo, R., Montorio, I., & Borkovec, T. D. (2004). A test of the role of metaworry in the prediction of worry severity in an elderly sample. *Journal of Behavior Therapy and Experimental Psychiatry, 35*, 209–218.

Obsessive Compulsive Cognitions Working Group—OCCWG. (1997). Cognitive assessment of obsessive-compulsive disorder. *Behaviour Research and Therapy, 35*, 667–681.

Papageorgiou, C., & Wells, A. (1998). Effects of attention training in hypochondriasis: An experimental case series. *Psychological Medicine, 28*, 193–200.

Papageorgiou, C., & Wells, A. (1999). Process and metacognitive dimensions of depressive and anxious thoughts and relationships with emotional intensity. *Clinical Psychology and Psychotherapy, 2*, 156–162.

Papageorgiou, C., & Wells, A. (2000). Treatment of recurrent major depression with attention training. *Cognitive and Behavioural Practice, 7*, 407–413.

Papageorgiou, C., & Wells, A. (2001a). Metacognitive beliefs about rumination in recurrent major depression. *Cognitive and Behavioral Practise, 8*, 160–164.

Papageorgiou, C., & Wells, A. (2001b). Positive beliefs about depressive rumination: Development and preliminary validation of a self-report scale. *Behavior Therapy, 32*, 13–26.

Papageorgiou, C., & Wells, A. (2003). An empirical test of a clinical metacognitive model of rumination and depression. *Cognitive Therapy and Research, 27*, 261–273.

Papageorgiou, C., & Wells, A. (2009). A prospective test of the metacognitive model of depression. *International Journal of Cognitive Therapy, 2*, 123–131.

Proctor, D., Walton, D. L., Lovell, K., & Wells, A. (2009). A randomised trial of metacognitive therapy versus exposure therapy for post-traumatic stress disorder. Manuscript submitted for publication.

Purdon, C. (1999). Thought suppression and psychopathology. *Behaviour Research and Therapy, 37*, 1029–1054.

Rassin, E., Merckelbach, H., Muris, P., & Spaan, V. (1999). Thought-action fusion as a causal factor in the development of intrusions. *Behaviour Research and Therapy, 37*, 231–237.

Rees, C. S., & van Koesveld, K. E. (2008). An open trial of group metacognitive therapy for obsessive-compulsive disorder. *Journal of Behavior Therapy and Experimental Psychiatry*, doi: 10.1016/j.jbtep.2007.11.004.

Reuven-Magril, O., Rosenman, M., Liberman, N., & Dar, R. (2009). Manipulating meta-cognitive beliefs about the difficulty to suppress scratching: Implications for obsessive-compulsive disorder. *International Journal of Cognitive Therapy, 2*, 143–151.

Reynolds, M., & Wells, A. (1999). The thought control questionnaire—Psychometric properties in a clinical sample, and relationships with PTSD and depression. *Psychological Medicine, 29*, 1089–1099.

Richards, A., & French, C. C. (1992). An anxiety-related bias in semantic activation when processing threat/neutral homographs. *Quarterly Journal of Experimental Psychology, 40*, 503–528.

Richards, A., French, C. C., Johnson, W., Naparstek, J., & Williams, J. (1992). Effects of mood manipulation and anxiety on performance of an emotional Stroop task. *British Journal of Psychology, 8*, 479–491.

Roussis, P., & Wells, A. (2006). Post-traumatic stress symptoms: Tests of relationships with thought control strategies and beliefs as predicted by the metacognitive model. *Personality and Individual Differences, 40*, 111–122

Roussis, P., & Wells, A. (2008). Psychological factors predicting stress symptoms: Metacognition, thought control and varieties of worry. *Anxiety, Stress and Coping, 21,* 213–225.

Ruscio, A. M., & Borkovec, T. D. (2004). Experience and appraisal of worry among high worriers with and without generalized anxiety disorder. *Behaviour Research and Therapy, 42,* 1469–1482.

Salkovskis, P. M. (1985). Obsessional-compulsive problems: A cognitive-behavioural analysis. *Behaviour Research and Therapy, 23,* 571–583.

Segal, Z. V., & Vella, D. D. (1990). Self-schema in major depression: Replication and extension of a priming methodology. *Cognitive Therapy and Research, 14,* 161–176.

Shiffrin, R. M., & Schneider, W. (1977). Controlled and automatic human information processing: II. Perceptual learning, automatic attending, and a general theory. *Psychological Review, 84,* 127–190.

Sica, C., Steketee, G., Ghisi, M., Chiri, L. R., & Franceschini, S. (2007). Metacognitive beliefs and strategies predict worry, obsessive-compulsive symptoms and coping styles: A preliminary prospective study on an Italian non-clinical sample. *Clinical Psychology and Psychotherapy, 14,* 258–268.

Siegle, G. J., Ghinassi, F., & Thase, M. E. (2007). Neurobehavioral therapies in the 21st century. Summary of an emerging field and an extended example of cognitive control training for depression. *Cognitive Therapy and Research, 31,* 235–262.

Simons, M., Schneider, S., & Herpertz-Dahlmann, B. (2006). Metacognnitive therapy versus exposure and response prevention for pediatric obsessive-compulsive disorder. *Psychotherapy and Psychosomatics, 75,* 257–264.

Solem, S., Haland, A. T., Vogel, P. A., Hansen, B., & Wells, A. (2009). Change in metacognitions predicts outcome in obsessive-compulsive disorder patients undergoing treatment with exposure and response prevention. *Behaviour Research and Therapy, 47,* 301–307.

Spada, M. M., Moneta, G. B., & Wells, A. (2007). The relative contribution of metacognitive beliefs and alcohol expectancies to drinking behaviour. *Alcohol and Alcoholism, 42,* 567–574.

Spada, M. M., & Wells, A. (2005). Metacognitions, emotion and alcohol use. *Clinical Psychology and Psychotherapy, 12,* 150–155.

Spada, M., Caselli, G., & Wells, A. (2009). Metacognitions as a predictor of drinking status and level of alcohol use following CBT in problem drinkers: A prospective study. *Behaviour Research and Therapy, 47,* 882–886.

Warda, G., & Bryant, R. A. (1998). Thought control strategies in acute stress disorder. *Behaviour Research and Therapy, 36,* 1171–1175.

Wegner, D. M., Schneider, D. J., Carter, S. R. III, & White, T. L. (1987). Paradoxical effects of thought suppression. *Journal of Personality and Social Psychology, 53,* 5–13.

Wells, A. (1985). Relationship between private self-consciousness and anxiety scores in threatening situations. *Psychological Reports, 57,* 1063–1066.

Wells, A. (1990) Panic disorder in association with relaxation induced anxiety: An attention training approach to treatment. *Behaviour Therapy, 21,* 273–280.

Wells, A. (1991). Effects of dispositional self-focus, appraisal, and attention instructions on responses to a threatening stimulus. *Anxiety Research, 3,* 291–301.

Wells, A. (1997). *Cognitive therapy of anxiety disorders: A practice manual and conceptual guide.* Chichester, UK: Wiley.

Wells, A. (2005a). The metacognitive model of GAD: Assessment of meta-worry and relationship with DSM-IV generalized anxiety disorder. *Cognitive Therapy and Research, 29,* 107–121.

Wells, A. (2005b). Detached mindfulness in cognitive therapy: A metacognitive analysis and ten techniques. *Journal of Rational-Emotive & Cognitive –Behavior Therapy, 23,* 337–355.

Wells, A. (2007). The attention training technique: Theory, effects and a metacognitive hypothesis on auditory hallucinations. *Cognitive and Behavioral Practice, 14,* 134–138.

Wells, A. (2009). *Metacognitive therapy for anxiety and depression.* New York, NY: Guilford Press.

Wells, A., & Carter C. (1999). Preliminary tests of a cognitive model of generalised anxiety disorder. *Behaviour Research and Therapy, 37,* 585–594.

Wells, A., & Carter, K. (2001). Further tests of a cognitive model of generalized anxiety disorder: Metacognitions and worry in GAD, panic disorder, social phobia, depression, and non-patients. *Behavior Therapy*, *32*, 85–102.

Wells, A., & Carter, K. (2009). Maladaptive thought control strategies in generalized anxiety disorder, major depressive disorder, and non-patient groups and relationships with trait anxiety. *International Journal of Cognitive Therapy*, *2*, 224–234.

Wells, A., & Cartwright-Hatton, S. (2004). A short form of the metacognitions questionnaire: Properties of the MCQ 30. *Behaviour Research and Therapy*, *42*, 385–396.

Wells, A., & Davies, M. (1994) The thought control questionnaire: A measure of individual differences in the control of unwanted thought. *Behaviour Research and Therapy*, *32*, 871–878.

Wells, A., Fisher, P. L., Myers, S., Wheatley, J., Patel, T., & Brewin, C. (2009). Metacognitive therapy in recurrent and persistent depression: A multiple-baseline study of a new treatment. *Cognitive Therapy and Research*, *33*, 291–300.

Wells, A., & King, P. (2006). Metacognitive therapy for generalized anxiety disorder: An open trial. *Journal of Behavior Therapy and Experimental Psychiatry*, *37*, 206–212.

Wells, A., & Matthews, G. (1994). *Attention and emotion: A clinical perspective*. Hove, UK: Erlbaum.

Wells, A., & Papageorgiou, C. (1995) Worry and the incubation of intrusive images following stress. *Behaviour Research and Therapy*, *33*, 579–583.

Wells, A., & Papageorgiou, C. (1998). Relationships between worry, obsessive-compulsive symptoms, and meta-cognitive beliefs. *Behaviour Research and Therapy*, *39*, 899–913.

Wells, A., & Papageorgiou, C. (2001). Brief cognitive therapy for social phobia: A case series. *Behaviour Research and Therapy*, *39*, 713–720.

Wells, A., & Sembi, S. (2004b). Metacognitive Therapy for PTSD: A preliminary investigation of a new brief treatment. *Journal of Behavior Therapy and Experimental Psychiatry*, *35*, 307–318.

Wells, A., Welford, M., Fraser, J., King, P., Mendel, E., Wisely, J., ... Rees, D. (2008). Chronic PTSD Treated with Metacognitive Therapy: An open trial. *Cognitive and Behavioral Practice*, *15*, 85–92.

Wells, A., Welford, M., King, P., Papageorgiou, C., Wisely, J., & Mendel, E. (2010). A pilot randomized trial of metacognitive therapy vs. applied relaxation in the treatment of adults with generalized anxiety disorder. *Behaviour Research and Therapy*, doi:10.1016/j.brat,2009.11.11013.

Wells, A., White, J., & Carter, K. (1997) Attention training: Effects on anxiety and beliefs in panic and social phobia. *Clinical Psychology and Psychotherapy*, *4*, 226–232.

Williams, J. M. G., Watts, F. N., MacLeod, C., & Mathews, A. (1988). *Cognitive psychology and emotional disorders*. Chichester, UK: Wiley.

Yilmaz, E. A., Gencoz, T., & Wells, A. (2007a). The causal role of metacognitions in the development of anxiety and depression: A prospective study. Paper presented at the World Congress of Cognitive and Behaviour Therapy, Barcelona, Spain, July 2007.

Yilmaz, E. A., Gencoz, T., & Wells, A. (2007b). The unique contribution of cognitions and metacognitions to depression. Paper presented at the World Congress of Cognitive and Behaviour Therapy, Barcelona, Spain, July 2007.

York, D., Borkovec, T. D., Vasey, M., & Stern, R. (1987). Effects of worry and somatic anxiety induction on thoughts, emotion and physiological activity. *Behaviour Research and Therapy*, *25*, 523–526.

# 5

## Emotional Schema Therapy

### A Bridge Over Troubled Waters

ROBERT L. LEAHY

## EMOTIONAL SCHEMA THERAPY

Almost everyone has experienced sadness, anxiety, anger, regret, jealousy, envy, and resentment. It is hard to imagine living a complete life without having feelings that are difficult or troubling. Just as we all may have bizarre, weird, or unwanted thoughts—but fail to become obsessive-compulsive—so also we may have a full range of emotions without having an "emotional" or "psychiatric" disorder. What leads some of us to become incapacitated by thoughts and emotions, while others appear capable of integrating these experiences into a more fulfilling life? *Emotional schema therapy* (EST) proposes that emotional disorders are often the result of the interpretations and evaluations of one's emotions and the strategies employed to cope with those emotions (Leahy, 2002, 2009b). I shall begin by discussing some contrasts and similarities between emotional schema therapy and two models to which it bears resemblance—the Beckian model of cognitive therapy and Wells' metacognitive therapy.

Traditional Beckian cognitive therapy places an emphasis on how individuals appraise situations and their ability to cope with them, bearing some resemblance to the appraisal model advanced by Lazarus. Specifically, in the Beckian model patients are encouraged to identify their spontaneous or "automatic" thoughts ("I will fail" or "I am a loser") and to examine the semantic nature, logical errors, and evidentiary basis of these thoughts. In addition, these automatic thoughts are then linked to conditional rules or underlying assumptions ("If I don't do perfectly well on an exam, then I am a failure"), where these conditional rules are, in turn, related to underlying schemas or core beliefs about self (defective, helpless, superior) and others (judgmental, unreliable, inferior). In the traditional Beckian model, emotions are viewed as the consequence of specific interpretations of reality, with little or no emphasis placed on interpretations of emotions themselves. The Beckian model recognizes that thoughts are not equivalent to reality, and the emphasis is on the content of these thoughts and how they may be submitted to evidentiary and logical evaluation.

Wells has advanced a metacognitive model that has implications for understanding the processes underlying a wide range of disorders (Wells, 2009). Rather than focus on the specific content of thoughts, Wells emphasizes the beliefs about the function and nature of thinking itself.

Metacognitive models of "thinking about thinking" have a long history in developmental psychology, from Piaget's (1932; 1967) description of decentering and non-egocentric thinking (Feffer, 1970) to Flavell's metacognitive description of role-taking and egocentrism in children and adolescents (Flavell, 2004). The initial emphasis on metacognitive or non-egocentric thinking was on the ability to understand informational deficits of others in relationship to the self and the ability to coordinate the perspectives or thinking of others in relationship to self or to each other. The interest in thinking about the nature of thinking was further advanced by Teasdale and his colleagues, identifying several levels of experience, including sensations/perceptions, propositional statements with content, and awareness of the "architecture" or structural organization of experience (Teasdale, 1999a; Teasdale, 1999b). Moreover, there has been considerable interest in "theory of mind," which has been a focus in terms of the growth of social cognition about other "mentalities," especially in young children, individuals with autism or Asperger's syndrome, and in nonhuman primates (Baron-Cohen, 1995; Bjorklund & Kipp, 2002; Fonagy & Target, 1996). The model advanced by Wells draws on prior contributions to understanding theory of mind, but the emphasis in his model is on how individuals comprehend the function and nature of their own thinking, and how to modify dysfunctional or "unhelpful" strategies and interpretations.

For example, consider how the cognitive approach advanced by a pure "earlier" Beckian (Beck, Emery, & Greenberg, 2005) would differ from more recent cognitive approaches, including metacognitive models, as applied to OCD. In the original Beckian approach, the therapist would examine the factual and logical content of the intrusive thoughts and consider the costs and benefits of ritualizing or neutralizing (Beck, et al., 2005). Thus, the earlier cognitive model stressed propositional statements, content of the thought, and the assumptions underlying the thought. For example, an intrusive thought ("I am contaminated") would be submitted to factual and logical evaluation—stressing the content or schematic nature of the thought. However, cognitive models have advanced considerably in the last 30 years to incorporate a wide range of perspectives on how thoughts and sensations are evaluated and which strategies are evoked to cope with these internal experiences. These newer models are considered part of the general cognitive therapy model, but place less emphasis on the schematic content of the thoughts.

The cognitive model of obsessive-compulsive disorder (OCD) has been elaborated by Salkovskis, Clark and others to examine the evaluations that one gives to these thoughts. Although some might argue that cognitive therapy only emphasizes the content of thinking, in fact Salkovskis, Clark, and their colleagues—all clearly "cognitive therapists"—have focused on the evaluations of intrusions, such as appraisals of personal responsibility, relevance, control, and other factors (Salkovskis, 1989; Salkovskis & Campbell, 1994; Wells, 2009).

The metacognitive approach to OCD illustrates the processes that lead from "intrusive thoughts" to ritualization, avoidance, and anxiety (Wells, 2009). Rather than focus on the schematic content of intrusive thoughts, the metacognitive approach proposes that evaluation and control of intrusive thoughts results in OCD and other psychological disorders (Salkovskis, 1989; Salkovskis & Campbell, 1994; Wells, 2009). Cognitive appraisals of thoughts, rather than the thoughts themselves, underpin OCD. Safety behaviors, thought-suppression strategies, self-monitoring, cognitive self-consciousness, and beliefs that thoughts are out of control are often the consequence of problematic appraisals. Psychological disorders are viewed as the result of the *response* to thoughts, sensations, and emotions that follow from problematic evaluations of the personal relevance of a thought, responsibility for suppressing, neutralizing, or acting on implications of a thought, thought-action fusion, intolerance of uncertainty, and perfectionistic standards (Purdon, Rowa, & Antony, 2005; Rachman, 1997; Wells, 2000; Wilson & Chambless, 1999). Indeed, one can argue that OCD reflects a specific disorder of "theory of mind"—that is, that the mind should be clear, pure, and free of unwanted thoughts and that the mind needs to be monitored and controlled. Ironically, this disorder of "theory of mind" suggests that the mind is a potentially dangerous place.

Similarly, the metacognitive model proposes that panic disorder is maintained by perfectionistic expectations of how emotions and sensations function, the need to monitor threat "from within," and the need to avoid situations that may provoke physiological arousal (Wells, 2009) Similar to Acceptance and Commitment Therapy (ACT; Hayes, Strosahl, & Wilson, 2003), metacognitive approaches to anxiety stress the role of avoidance and failed attempts at suppression. Metacognitive and cognitive models, however, provide detailed descriptions of these underlying "theories of mind" and propose specific behavioral experiments to test explicitly derived hypotheses about these propositions about mind and sensations. It is noteworthy that there appears to be convergence between these metacognitive and ACT approaches in the use of mindfulness-enhancing interventions and in utilizing the observing role toward thoughts and sensations as therapeutic interventions.

However, more traditional cognitive models of anxiety and depression (in contrast with the metacognitive emphasis described above) stress the schematic *content* of specific disorders. Thus, depression is characterized by content related to a negative view of self, experience, and the future; anger is related to humiliation and blocked goals; social anxiety to inadequacy and judgment by others; and obsessive-compulsive disorder to danger and responsibility. Metacognitive models, in contrast, stress the *process* of thinking and *strategies for control*—that is, "this is just another thought" offers a metacognitive detachment from a thought, while "when you use these safety behaviors you maintain your fear that things are really unsafe" indicates how specific coping strategies maintain the disorder. Traditional cognitive models, which use the Socratic technique to collect evidence to test the content of thoughts, are based on an assumption that thoughts are often biased and distorted. In contrast, metacognitive models stress that overutilization of thinking, worrying, rumination, and avoidance are the core problematic processes. Both ACT and metacognitive models share some common ground in focusing on the beliefs about *how* the mind functions rather than simply on the content of those beliefs.

Changing the function or implication of a thought and how one responds to the "occurrence" of a thought are common therapeutic strategies for both metacognitive and acceptance models (Hayes, Strosahl, & Wilson, 1999; Wells, 2009).

In this chapter, I outline an approach that is consistent with some aspects of traditional cognitive therapy, but also consistent with metacognitive and acceptance-based models. I refer to this as *emotional schema therapy* (EST) (Leahy, 2002; Leahy, 2007b; Leahy, 2009b). As indicated, traditional cognitive models of psychopathology have proposed that emotions may be exacerbated or evoked by cognitive content ("automatic thoughts") or that moods may be primed, evoking the latent cognitive schemas that perpetuate further emotional arousal (Beck, 1976; Miranda, Gross, Persons, & Hahn, 1998; Segal, et al., 2006). Thus, in traditional cognitive models, emotion either precedes, accompanies, or is a consequence of cognitive content. However, it is argued from the view of EST that emotions themselves may constitute an *object* of cognition— that is, they may also be viewed as *content to be evaluated*, controlled, or utilized by the individual (Leahy, 2002). This approach is derived from the field of "social cognition" (which is now often referred to as "theory of mind"), with its emphasis on "naïve psychology" models of intentionality, normalcy, social-comparison, and attribution processes (Eisenberg & Spinrad, 2004; Leahy, 2002, 2003b; Weiner, 1974). If one can argue that the metacognitive model stresses disorders of theory of mind, the emotional schema model stresses disorders of the theory of emotion and mind. Specific styles of self-reflective thinking and evaluations of one's own thoughts and feelings can lead to problematic appraisals and strategies of emotional regulation. These ideas serve as foundational theory for what I call "emotional schema therapy."

I have introduced the concept of "emotional schema" to suggest that people have a specific set of beliefs for processing, appraising, and reacting to their emotions. (This is different from the use of the term "emotion schema" by Greenberg, who views emotions as containing the cognitive content that may contribute to pathology, or Izard's concept of emotion schema, which refers to emotion-cognitive interactions; Greenberg & Paivio, 1997; Greenberg & Safran, 1987; Izard, 2009). I view emotional schemas as a set of interpretations and strategies—similar to the use of the term "schema" in Beck's cognitive model (Beck & Alford, 2008; Beck, Rush, Shaw, & Emery, 1979; Leahy, 2002). Although sharing some commonality with the idea of emotion-thought connections as described by Beck and Lazarus (Beck, 1976; A. Lazarus, 1984), emotional schema therapy focuses less on how emotions arise from thoughts and more on how the content of thoughts *about* emotions perpetuates unhelpful coping strategies. While acknowledging that emotions may be linked to cognitive content, behavioral, attentional, and memorial processes, EST emphasizes the theory of emotion implicit in the individual's response to his or her emotional experience. Moreover, the emotional schema model is predicated on the view that there are numerous potential schemas and strategies that are utilized in response to one's own emotions. Let us consider an example of these different schemas.

Ken is going through a breakup with his girlfriend, who text-messaged him that the relationship is over. Ken realizes that he is feeling angry, confused, sad, and anxious, and he discusses this with his friend, Dave. Fortunately, Dave validates the entire range of feeling that Ken is having, and adds that "relief" might be another possible feeling. In his discussion and expression of his feelings, Ken begins to realize that all his feelings make sense—even the ones that appear to contradict themselves (e.g., sad and relieved). He says he realizes that right now he will feel badly, but that these feelings will not last forever and he can still get things done even though he is feeling down. The relevant emotional schemas for Ken are that he can express his emotions and have them validated by others, his emotions are temporary and not overwhelming, his emotions make sense, he can tolerate conflicting feelings, and he does not avoid his emotions but acts in spite of them. Ken is not likely to be a candidate for therapy, because, even in the face of painful emotions, he accepts, tolerates, and integrates this experience into his life.

In contrast, Brian is having more difficulty with a similar breakup. Feeling ashamed of his feelings, overwhelmed, and confused by his emotions of anger, anxiety, sadness, and confusion, he decides to keep his feelings to himself. He cannot understand how he could have so many *different* feelings, as he ruminates to determine "once and for all" how he "really feels." This rumination leads to further avoidance and brooding on the past, a sense that he cannot escape from his feelings, and his reliance on alcohol to calm his unquiet mind. Brian illustrates a number of problematic emotional schemas: lack of expression and validation, belief that his feelings don't make sense, avoidance, rumination, reliance on alcohol to numb feelings, and a failure to accept the temporary, but difficult, feelings that he is experiencing. Rather than "process" his emotions, he gets stuck in them and relies on worry, rumination, avoidance, blaming, self-absorption, and substance abuse. This activates a vicious cycle of further dysregulation, resulting in more reliance on the failed strategies that he believes will provide him with safety from himself.

A schematic depicting emotional schemas is shown in Figure 5.1. Emotional schemas are evaluated with the Leahy Emotional Schema Scale (LESS), which assesses 14 dimensions (Leahy, 2002) of how one interprets, evaluates, controls, or responds to their own emotions. This schematic illustrates that awareness of an emotion, labeling emotions, and differentiating emotion are the first steps in coping with emotion. Indeed, current advances in neuroscience suggest that bringing emotion under conscious "top-down" control may activate the prefrontal cortex (PFC), thereby recruiting the ability to appraise, plan, and regulate emotion (Delgado, et al., 2004; Phelps, Delgado, Nearing, & LeDoux, 2004). At the next step, the individual pursues emotional avoidance (bingeing, purging, substance abuse, etc.) and/or appraises the emotion negatively. Appraisals include attribution (e.g., consensus, generalization, personal relevance, blaming), consequences of emotions, and evaluations of negativity (e.g., shame and guilt). Strategies of coping include avoidance, rumination, and worry, or acceptance, expression, and the seeking of validation. Thus, emotional schemas include behavioral, interpersonal, emotional, and cognitive appraisal responses.

Emotional schema therapy addresses the issue of "emotional reasoning" and "emotion heuristics" so often a part of anxious and depressive thinking, but also as a major

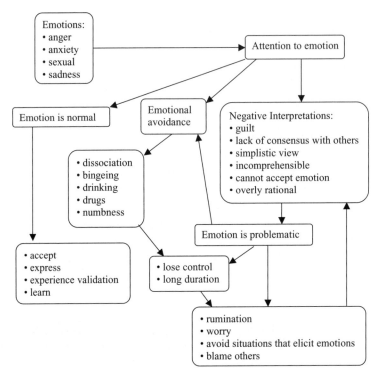

**Figure 5.1**  A Model of Emotional Schemas

component of thinking in nonclinical individuals (Kahneman & Frederick, 2005; Slovic, Finucane, Peters, & MacGregor, 2002). Anxious and depressed patients often predict events based on their current emotional state, very much as if their emotions are signs of external danger. Similar to "thought-action fusion," emotional reasoning and emotional heuristics are often implicit and seldom examined. By recognizing that emotions are mental events that are separate from external reality, the emotional schema therapist encourages a detached, mindful awareness of the emotion, while encouraging differentiation, labeling, and linking emotion to thoughts and variation across time and situations.

A core emotional schema is the belief that difficult emotions will last indefinitely and interfere with functioning. This is similar to the concept of "durability" or "affective forecasting," in which people in general tend to predict that pleasant or unpleasant emotions will last longer than they actually do (Gilbert, Pinel, Wilson, Blumberg, & Wheatley, 1998; Wilson, Wheatley, Meyers, Gilbert, & Axsom, 2000). The reason for this distortion in predicting the durability of emotion is unclear, but may reflect lack of consideration for coping strategies that will be employed for affect regulation, situational variants, or even nonconscious coping. This predictive bias appears to be more pronounced with anxious and depressed individuals and may account for the fear of experiential exposure. Reluctance to engage in exposure treatment is often a consequence of the belief that anxious arousal will last indefinitely and overwhelm the individual. Emotional schema therapy directly addresses the issue of affective forecasting by identifying this dimension, collecting information through behavioral experiments, and re-evaluating the schematic bias (Leahy, 2007b; Leahy, 2009a).

Other dimensions assessed include the belief that one's emotions are unique to the self, that there is no general consensus in how people would feel given the circumstance. Indeed, much reassurance-seeking is an attempt to normalize one's emotional responses by seeking validation that one's emotions make sense and are shared by others. Guilt and shame about emotion often is associated with increased anxiety or depression about emotional experience, further exacerbating an overfocus on emotion, rumination, and dispositional self-labeling. In the two examples above, Ken is able to normalize his emotion, partly by expressing these feelings and obtaining validation from his friend, and he is able to temporize the emotion as an adjustment response to a difficult, but temporary, experience. Consequently, he dwells less on the emotion, is less ruminative, and is able to act in spite of the emotion that he accepts for the time being. In contrast, Brian is "stuck" in his emotion, harbors these emotions privately due to feelings of shame and an overvaluation of autonomy, and is unable to continue until he "gets things sorted out." A key premise of emotional schema therapy is that it is not the emotion per se that is the problem, but the interpretations and strategies employed and the ability or willingness to act in spite of these feelings. EST shares a similar view of some aspects of this process with ACT and metacognitive therapy. A key difference, however, is in emphasizing the specific interpretations, theories, and strategies that are employed and how these confirm or disconfirm underlying theories of emotion regulation that are employed by the individual. For example, in emotional schema therapy, the emphasis is on clarifying and modifying the specific theory of one's emotion, using cognitive or Socratic evaluations, experiential tests, behavioral experiments, and other interventions to assist in normalizing, temporizing, linking emotion to values, and finding expression and validation. Wells' model stresses thinking, not emotion, and does not attempt to modify theory of emotion. All three models—ACT, metacognitive theory, and EST— are meta-experiential models, rather than simply focusing on the schematic content of appraisals of external stressors.

## COGNITIVE CHANGE STRATEGIES

The EST model stresses the following six themes:

1. Painful and difficult emotions are universal.
2. These emotions were evolved to warn of us of danger and tell us about our needs.
3. Underlying beliefs and strategies (schemas) about emotions determine the impact that an emotion has on the escalation or maintenance of itself or other emotions.

4. Problematic schemas include catastrophizing an emotion; thinking that one's emotions do not make sense; and viewing an emotion as permanent and out of control, shameful, unique to the self, and needing to be kept to the self.

5. Emotional control strategies, such as attempts to suppress, ignore, neutralize, or eliminate through substance abuse and binge eating, help confirm negative beliefs of emotions as intolerable experiences.

6. Expression and validation are helpful insofar as they normalize, universalize, improve understanding, differentiate various emotions, reduce guilt and shame, and help increase beliefs in the tolerability of emotional experience (Leahy, 2009b).

All of the foregoing are part of the psychoeducation and underlying philosophy of emotion guiding EST.

Emotional schema therapy assists the patient in the following: the identification and labeling of a variety of emotions; normalizing emotional experience, including painful and difficult emotions; linking emotions to personal needs and to interpersonal communication; identifying problematic beliefs and strategies (schemas) that the patient has for interpreting, judging, controlling, and acting on an emotion; collecting information, using experiential techniques, and setting up behavioral, interpersonal, and emotional "experiments" to develop more helpful responses to one's emotions (Leahy, 2002, 2003b, 2009a, 2009b).

The emotional schema therapist utilizes a number of cognitive, experiential, and behavioral interventions in order to test and modify dysfunctional emotional schemas and emotion control strategies. For example, consider the negative interpretations of emotion depicted in Figure 5.1. Guilt or shame over emotion may be addressed using standard cognitive therapy techniques. For example, the patient may equate having an emotion (anger) with being an angry, hostile, mean person. Standard cognitive therapy techniques, such as distinguishing between a thought and a behavior, can be used to challenge the view that emotions and behavior are equivalent. Other cognitive techniques can be used to examine positive, virtuous, or helpful behaviors that the person has engaged in to counter the view that one should be ashamed of an emotion. Normalizing the emotion, by examining how everyone has feelings of anger, can dissipate guilt and shame. The therapist can help the patient realize that choosing not to act on an angry or sexual feeling is actually a "moral choice" and that choices have more moral or ethical relevance when there is temptation to act otherwise. Guilty or shameful feelings about emotion may also be addressed by normalizing an emotion by establishing consensus that others share these feelings. Attribution interventions, derived from the "analysis of variance" model of Jones and Davis, help the patient examine the distinctiveness of an emotion ("you and others feel this way when you are responding to Sarah"), consensus ("almost everyone has these feelings at times"), and consistency ("you sometimes have these feelings but sometimes you don't") (Jones & Davis, 1965; Kelley, 1972; Weiner, 1986). Examining how emotions may co-vary with situation and time, while recognizing that others may often share the same emotional response, helps to reduce dispositional inferences about the self. Thus, if Carol knows that she is seldom jealous except when around Mark (low consistency) and that others would respond the same way toward Mark, given his behavior (high consensus and high distinctiveness), then Carol is less likely to make an inference that she is a "neurotic jealous person." Reducing negative dispositional inferences related to emotion can also help reduce the sense of shame or guilt and the belief that one will continue feeling this way no matter what the circumstances.

For example, in the case of Carol's jealousy, her feelings were elicited when Mark, her boyfriend, said he was having dinner with his flirtatious ex-girlfriend. Carol said she felt jealous, angry, and anxious, but added that she worried that she was "becoming that jealous girlfriend that men hate." She indicated that she worried that her jealousy would alienate Mark. Using an attribution analysis, she was able to recognize that she almost never expressed jealousy toward Mark in other situations and had seldom acted jealously with former partners. Moreover, when she collected consensus data from her friends they generally agreed that Mark was being insensitive and that her feelings were justified. We conceptualized her jealousy from an emotional schema model as "angry, agitated, worry" and examined how a multifaceted cognitive-behavioral model could be helpful. Specifically, we normalized jealousy as an ethologically valid and useful emotion that protected potential genetic investment, indicated that emotions and behaviors are different, used a mindful detachment of noticing and not judging the emotion, linked her jealousy to her higher values of commitment and honesty, and focused on relationship enhancement skills and diplomatic assertion, rather than reassurance seeking, pouting, or attacking (Leahy & Tirch, 2008).

A common belief about emotion that interferes with exposure therapy is that one's anxiety will last indefinitely and will eventually incapacitate the person. These emotional schemas lead the patient to "wait until I feel ready," relying on self-calming, reassurance, procrastination, avoidance, and other strategies to avoid experiential chaos. In some cases, the patient may argue that he is "too fragile" and, therefore, unable to engage in exposure until the self is "stronger" (Leahy, 2007a; Leahy, 2009a, 2009b). The therapist can help the patient examine the functional value of the belief that one is "too fragile." For example, one patient acknowledged that he evoked the "I am too fragile" belief prior to considering exposure and did not generally have this belief at other times. The consequence of the belief was that it decreased his likelihood to do exposure, thereby maintaining his belief in his fragility and limiting the enjoyment of his life. He recognized that he was highly invested in trying to convince his therapist that he was too fragile and that—indeed—he had succeeded with several other therapists in convincing them of this limitation. The therapist elicited specific predictions about the intensity and duration of his anxiety, should he do exposure, and the behavioral impact in terms of disability that this would have over the course of the day. His dire predictions were recorded, and he, in fact, did engage in the exposure and recognized over the next two days that he felt better. During the next session, his dire predictions were examined as functioning to preserve his avoidance and fragile-self beliefs, further reinforcing his belief that he needed to avoid. His other beliefs about emotional "readiness," pathologizing himself ("I must be psychotic"), reassurance seeking, and advertising his "sickness" to others in order to lower his and their expectations were also conceptualized as emotional schema strategies predicated on his view that avoidance was the best strategy. His emotional schemas were subsumed by a threat detection approach to life that he believed "kept him safe." Unfortunately, he had to acknowledge that he was both safe and sorry.

Avoidance of anxiety-provoking situations is usually based on faulty assessments of risk. For example, in the case above, the risk of contamination was exaggerated. However, the risk of maintaining OCD was minimized. I have found it useful to use a risk-risk paradigm, borrowing from the risk model advanced by Cass Sunstein (as applied to regulatory principles; Sunstein, 2005). According to the risk-risk model there is never a completely risk-free choice. Doing something or doing nothing both carry risks. Exposing oneself to "contamination" carries the small risk of getting sick, whereas not exposing oneself carries a higher risk of maintaining OCD. However, OCD patients overestimate risk of contamination by virtue of accessibility, emotion, and familiarity heuristics and maintain their beliefs that they cannot tolerate anxiety by avoiding and escaping. Unfortunately, "testing" the contamination of a substance generally cannot yield adequate data ("I might not get cancer for 10 years"), so the emphasis in emotional schema therapy is on tolerating anxiety.

We have found that the concept of "constructive discomfort" empowers patients to face their fears in a way that they believe that they are building "mental muscle" (Leahy, 2005c; Leahy, 2007a; Leahy, 2009a, 2009b). *Constructive discomfort* implies that tolerating and using discomfort in the service of important goals is a useful strategy in life. Indeed, the goal is "to do what you don't want to do that can help you get what you need to get." Similar to distress tolerance, willingness, and other empowering concepts from ACT and dialectical behavior therapy (DBT), constructive discomfort is a focus of EST.

Consider an OCD patient contemplating exposure to "contamination." Rather than focus on the content of the contamination (e.g., examining the evidence that there is real danger), the emotional schema therapist examines beliefs about the durability and overwhelming nature of experiencing anxiety. The focus is on the patient's theory about anxiety—and how to cope with it. Problematic coping strategies are identified (e.g., waiting to feel ready, seeking reassurance, pathologizing the self as fragile), and these strategies are identified as "confirmatory" processes that maintain the belief that anxiety cannot be tolerated (see Figure 5.2). These beliefs about tolerating anxiety are then examined and modified by examining the evidence about emotional schemas regarding durability, danger, and fragility and by setting up behavioral experiments to test the predictions elicited in the session (see Figure 5.3). The goal is not to prove that the stimulus is uncontaminated. The goal is to modify beliefs about emotions and problematic strategies of emotional control and avoidance.

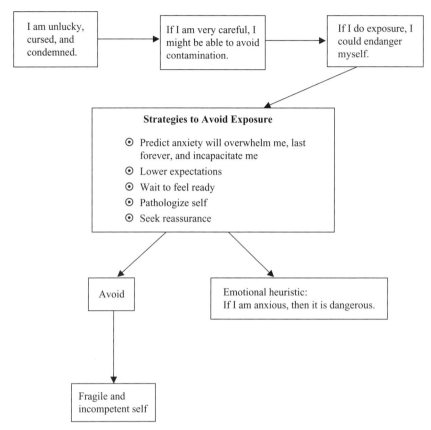

**Figure 5.2**   Emotional Schemas Maintaining Avoidance

## THE ROLE OF META-AWARENESS

Although conscious awareness is not an essential part of behavioral or emotional learning or change (Gray, 2004; LeDoux, 1996), the EST model nevertheless attempts to enhance conscious awareness and differentiation of emotion. This emphasis is because alexithymia (i.e., poor understanding and awareness of emotions) is often characteristic of individuals with anxiety, depression, and somatic problems (Grossarth-Maticek, Bastiaans, & Kanazir, 1985; Grossarth-Maticek, Kanazir, Schmidt, & Vetter, 1985; Honkalampi, Hintikka, Tanskanen, Lehtonen, & Viinamaki, 2000; Mennin, Heimberg, Turk, & Fresco, 2005; Mennin, Holaway, Fresco, Moore, & Heimberg, 2007; Spokas, Luterek, & Heimberg, 2009; Zahradnik, Stewart, Marshall, Schell, & Jaycox, 2009). The emotional schema therapist first assists the patient in identifying, labeling, and differentiating the range of possible emotions using emotion-focused therapy techniques (Greenberg, 2002). In addition to identifying existing emotions, the EST therapist also identifies problematic beliefs about emotion, such as the belief that one should always be rational, as well as beliefs about loss of control, duration, and shame. These beliefs are then examined using cognitive therapy

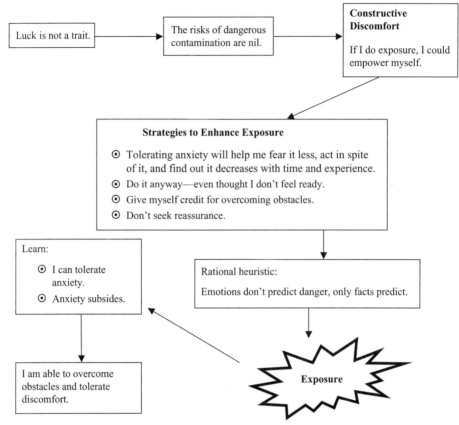

**Figure 5.3** Modified Emotional Schemas Enhancing Exposure

techniques such as examining the costs and benefits of the belief, examining the evidence for and against the belief, canvassing friends about their range of emotions, and using compassionate mind techniques to enhance self-acceptance and self-validation.

## EMOTIONAL SCHEMAS, COGNITIVE THERAPY, AND MINDFULNESS

Mindfulness is here defined as taking an observing stance in a nonjudgmental manner with open awareness in the present moment and with no attempt to control. One can argue that traditional cognitive therapy contains an initial step of mindful awareness, that is, noticing or observing that a thought is only a thought and acknowledging that thoughts come and go with time and situations. However, traditional cognitive therapy uses mindful awareness or detachment as techniques or experiences in therapy to address the content of the thought through logical, factual, and other persuasive techniques (Beck, Rector, Stolar, & Grant, 2009; Beck, et al., 1979; Leahy, 2003a). For example, stepping back and recognizing that one is having a thought—and that the thought is only a thought—may be considered a first mindful awareness of the thought. However, unlike the traditional mindfulness of breath exercise (or mindful awareness of a thought), the cognitive therapist examines the evaluations and factual nature of the thought, rather than "just allowing it to be." Thus, cognitive therapy is more proactive in modifying the believability of thoughts than is the case for the ACT therapist.

Emotional schema therapy includes mindfulness techniques, but focuses specifically on the schematic content of the beliefs *about emotions*. One might wonder if EST is similar to cognitive therapy in examining the content of thoughts or whether it is similar to MCT and ACT in stressing the experiential acceptance of emotion. Perhaps the most balanced answer is that EST does both. It would be incorrect to argue that EST involves disputation of emotions—since emotions are really a "given" of experience. However, EST does involve an appraisal of emotion—or, more specifically, it examines the kinds of appraisals that are made. One can also argue that the MCT model of Wells also involves an appraisal of thoughts in terms of responsibility and uncontrollability. These are clearly appraisals of function or implication, but not of the specific content contained in these thoughts.

There is debate as to what exactly constitutes so-called "third wave" approaches to cognitive behavior therapy. For example, should we include ACT, DBT, MBCT, and metacognitive therapy in this category, even if proponents of some of these approaches (e.g., Linehan and Wells) do not characterize their approaches as "third wave" (see Hofmann & Asmundson, 2008)? However, all of these foregoing approaches stress the focus on the *function* or *process* of thinking and experience, rather than the *schematic content* of thoughts. Although one can argue that cognitive therapy also evaluates the function of thinking (e.g., "What are the costs and benefits of this belief?"), most of the emphasis is on modifying beliefs and fostering problem-solving alternatives in coping. The emphasis in traditional cognitive therapy is generally on the schematic content of a thought—especially on its validity—borrowing from information processing models of attention, memory, and valuation of thinking (Beck & Alford, 2008). Emotional schema therapy combines elements of both "third wave" detached awareness and recognition of the process of thinking, while at the same time assessing the schematic content of *beliefs about emotion*. This is why I refer to them as emotional "schemas."

Emotional schema therapy is similar to Greenberg's emotion-focused therapy in its emphasis on emotional experience, expression, evaluation of primary and secondary emotions, viewing emotions related to needs and values, and the fact that emotions may also "contain" meanings (similar to Lazarus's "core relational themes"); (Greenberg & Paivio, 1997; Greenberg & Watson, 2005; Lazarus, 1999). However, EST is specifically meta-emotional (or metacognitive) in that it directly assesses *the beliefs about emotions* and how emotions function. Thus, the emphasis is not only on Rogerian processes of expression, validation, and unconditional positive regard, but also on the patient's implicit theories of emotion. This is similar to the approach taken by Gottman and his colleagues (Gottman, Katz, & Hooven, 1997). For example, the emotional schema therapist might examine the belief that painful emotions are an opportunity to develop deeper and more meaningful emotions, or the contrary belief that painful emotions are a sign of weakness and inferiority. The emotion-focused therapist utilizes expression and validation as central therapeutic techniques—as would the emotional schema therapist. However, EST views validation as a process that affects other cognitive (or schematic) *evaluations of emotion*. Thus, validation leads to a recognition that one's emotions are not unique, that expressing emotion need not lead to being overwhelmed, that there is generally less guilt and shame with validation, and that validation assists the patient in "making sense" of feelings. Thus, validation leads to changes in *beliefs* about emotion which can then lead to changes in the emotion itself (Leahy, 2005b).

Detached mindfulness, exposure, distress tolerance, and other experiential techniques are used in EST to test beliefs about one's own emotions—that is, they are subsumed, broadly speaking, as "cognitive therapy" interventions by virtue of positing hypotheses that are tested out against experience. Similar to the metacognitive model to which EST owes a great deal of influence, emotions are an "object" of thinking and experience and are distinguished from reality or from a *necessary* way in which the world is experienced. Thus, just as the metacognitive therapist assists the patient in recognizing, "this is just a thought," the emotional schema therapist assists in recognizing, "this is just a feeling that you are having for the present moment."

For example, mindful awareness of the emotion of jealousy entails recognizing that one has the feeling (as well as where one feels it, e.g., bodily sensations), acknowledging that the emotion may come and go over time and situations, and attempting to adopt a nonjudgmental stance toward the emotion, while accepting the feeling of jealousy as one of many emotions that may come and go. Imagery of an emotion as a series of ocean waves ebbing and flowing on a beach, while thinking "these feelings come and go," reflects the mindful awareness of the feeling. Detached observation, including descriptions, metaphors ("it feels like a dark cloud over my head"), and imagery enhance the acceptance of an emotion while relinquishing emotion suppression strategies. For example, the jealous patient could stand back, acknowledge her feelings, recognize that they come and go, notice where in her body she is feeling jealous, while noticing that observing and letting go of the emotion is followed by the reappearance of the feeling. As a result, the emotion becomes less frightening. In EST (similar to metacognitive therapy), mindful detachment helps test the belief that emotions are overwhelming and need to be suppressed (Wells, 2009). Specific cognitive content about emotion is identified: "What happens when you just stand back and observe?", "What happens when you don't suppress the emotion?" We use Rumi's poem *The Guest House* (1995) to illustrate that an emotion can be an unexpected guest that shows up, is welcomed, and treated with courtesy. However, specific cognitive tests are conducted about the duration, overwhelming quality of an emotion, and judgments about emotions.

Part of emotional schema therapy is to reduce the moralistic judgments that are often made about certain emotions. Indeed, popular beliefs that some emotions are dangerous or "bad" only add to the lack of acceptance, the guilt, and even the fear of an emotion. Emotional schema therapy takes the view that all emotions have had adaptive value in the history of the species and, therefore, are part of human nature. This includes disparaged emotions such as envy, jealousy, resentment, desires for revenge or hatred, and all varieties of sexual feelings. Similar to the metacognitive and cognitive models of intrusive thoughts (Clark, 2005; Purdon & Clark, 1993; Wells, 2009), the emotional schema therapist treats emotions as "mental events" that occur internally, sporadically, and involuntarily and that carry no immediate relevance to moral turpitude. Some patients say to themselves, "what's wrong with me that I feel this way?", resulting in feelings of shame and guilt and a tendency to ruminate. The emotional schema therapist can assist the patient in changing this evaluative thought to, "I notice that I have a lot of feelings that come and go, and this is one of those feelings that I have." Indeed, one can view emotions as originating in the amygdala, with little conscious control over the feelings that occur (LeDoux, 1996). Just as visual illusions operate out of conscious awareness and control, so also do emotions become activated without conscious will or choice (Gray, 2004). Moralistic concepts such as "wrong" or "guilty" are more relevant to willful choices that are consciously made—that is, choices involving action where alternatives are considered. If we view moral evaluation as appropriate (at times) only for free conscious choice unimpeded by duress, provocation, or diminished capacity, then one would not view "emotion" as a moral choice. Guilt and shame about an emotion is a "category error" in that a moral category is misapplied to a physiological or experiential phenomenon (Ryle, 1949). For example, it would make no sense to say that "You had a visual illusion because you are irresponsible" since visual illusions are not amenable to conscious choice. Emotional schema therapy helps the patient recognize that an emotion is not the same thing as a moral choice, thereby reducing the feelings of guilt over an emotion. For example, the married patient who fantasizes about a man other than her husband may be dissuaded from her guilt by recognizing that fantasies are common experiences and that feelings are not actions. Accepting that feelings and fantasies may come and go—and that they do not necessarily reflect anything pejorative about the person experiencing them—can help reduce the "anxiety about emotion" so often characteristic of patients with an active fantasy life. Moreover, helping the patient recognize that "temptation" is a necessary component for a true moral choice helps reduce the sense of "guilt" over having temptation, since there cannot be a meaningful moral decision without consideration of alternatives.

Emotional schema therapy shares with ACT a recognition of the role of values in clarifying what can incentivize choice in the face of hardship. The role of values, of course, is not new; it can be traced to ancient Greek and Roman philosophy, in which "values" were equated with "virtues"—that is, character habits such as courage, integrity, and self-control (as espoused by, e.g., Aristotle, Plato, Epictetus, Seneca, and Cicero). These virtues were often identified with the Stoic tradition, but they have continued for almost 2,000 years in Western philosophy and religion. Emotional schema therapy is not neutral about which values matter, but rather takes the position that classic virtues (as described by Aristotle) and values of compassion, kindness, and fairness (as described by Rawls) can inform the moral and ethical choices that the patient considers (Rawls, 2005). Aristotle viewed virtue as the qualities in a person that you would admire, and so the goal is to become a person that you would admire yourself. I have found it helpful to ask patients to attend to this simple question: "What are the personal qualities in someone who you would admire?" followed by, "How could you become a person who you would admire?"

Self-esteem is not based on popularity, achievement, power, wealth, or hedonism; it is based on the discrepancy between the qualities that you would admire and those that you recognize in yourself. The implicit social contract of fairness and justice is another way in which moral and ethical choices may be made. Specifically, how would you want to be treated if you did not know your actual or eventual status in society? This "veil of ignorance" model of ethical choice encourages consideration of fairness, compassion, kindness, and justice, rather than hedonistic or self-centered concerns of getting one's own way.

Thus, the patient who considers acting out a fantasy of infidelity can examine the choice in terms of the virtues of integrity and self-control and in terms of the implicit social contract of fairness and reciprocity underlying the primary relationship. The tension that underlies the choice helps clarify the commitment to these virtues and values and may clarify one's identity and the problems and strengths of the relationship. Thus, in EST, values are not arbitrary or neutral but are examined in the light of virtue and implicit social contracts of fairness and justice. Indeed, the concept of fairness has been extended by Nussbaum to recognize that compassion and protection of the very "weakest" (e.g., the disabled) may necessitate expanding the sense of social contract to focus more on kindness, compassion, and universal suffering rather than on effective contracts for determining justice (Nussbaum, 2005). It is far beyond the scope of this chapter to examine the implications of virtue, justice, compassion, and other moral sentiments, but it is worth emphasizing that emotions often have an evaluative and even moral component implied in their evaluations. Helping patients realize that values, virtues, and compassion can have emotional costs may help some tolerate—even grow—from the difficulties that arise in life.

Similarly, evaluations of emotions often imply that "feeling this way means I am crazy," a belief based on the assumption that "sanity" is characterized by purity of emotion. This is similar to the metacognitive process of evaluating intrusive thoughts as weird, disgusting, or crazy and the belief that unless these thoughts are suppressed or eliminated the person will lose control and go insane (Wells, 2002). The meta-emotional strategy in EST is to evaluate this "theory of emotion" by considering the following: "You have had these emotions many times, but you have not gone insane. How do you account for this?"; "Other people that you respect have these emotions but they are not insane. Why is that?" and "If you allowed yourself to accept the emotion rather than attempt to suppress it, what do you predict will happen?" Thought flooding can be used, in which the patient repeats over and over, "I notice that I have this feeling right now, and I accept this feeling at this moment." This usually results in an increase of anxiety followed by a decrease as the thought is repeated until it becomes boring (Freeston, et al., 1997). Attempts to suppress emotions (or thoughts) confirm the belief that emotions cannot be tolerated, similar to the confirmation of beliefs about suppressing intrusive thoughts. Acknowledging repeatedly that one has an emotion—by enhancing conscious acceptance—is a form of exposure to recognizing, accepting, and tolerating the emotion, and disconfirms the belief that an emotion must be eliminated lest the individual go insane.

## RESEARCH ON EMOTIONAL SCHEMAS

A number of studies support the view that emotional schemas are related to a variety of forms of psychopathology. Problematic emotional schemas are related to higher depression, anxiety, metacognitive factors of worry, experiential avoidance, marital discord, personality disorders, and diminished mindfulness (Leahy, 2002; Leahy & Napolitano, 2005; Leahy, Tirch, & Napolitano, 2009, Napolitano, Taitz, & Leahy, 2009, November-a; Napolitano, Taitz, & Leahy, 2009, November-b; Tirch, Leahy, & Silberstein, 2009). Even when anxiety is factored out, emotional schemas are related to problematic metacognitive processes underlying worry, suggesting that worry is a strategy of emotional avoidance based on negative interpretations of emotion (Leahy, 2005a). Thus, emotional schemas may "bridge the gap" between metacognitive and emotional avoidance models of worry (Borkovec, Alcaine, & Behar, 2004; Wells, 2004). Individuals reporting greater marital discord are more likely to endorse emotional schemas related to less expression and validation and greater blame—but also are less tolerance of conflicting feelings (Leahy & Kaplan, 2004). It may be that the ability to tolerate conflicting feelings toward one's partner is an emotional schema process that facilitates greater acceptance of the partner and greater willingness to work on the relationship.

Of particular interest is the relationship between emotional schemas and measures of experiential avoidance and mindfulness. In a recent study, the relationship between mindfulness and experiential avoidance was mediated by negative beliefs about emotions (Napolitano, et al., 2009, November-b). Finally, two preliminary studies indicate that training in mindfulness affects emotional schemas and that mindfulness decreases emotional avoidance by changing negative beliefs about emotions (Napolitano, et al., 2009, November-a).

Emotional schemas are also related to personality disorders. Patients scoring higher on borderline, avoidant, and dependent personality dimensions of the Millon Multiaxial Clinical Inventory endorse more negative emotional schemas, whereas patients scoring higher on narcissistic and histrionic personality dimensions have more positive emotional schemas (Leahy & Napolitano, 2005). These findings suggest that personality disorders may comprise different strategies of interpreting and coping with difficult emotions.

Although these foregoing studies offer support for the role of emotional schemas in processes underlying psychopathology, there is yet no evidence of the efficacy of EST per se or the mediating mechanisms involved. For example, it is not clear if emotional schema therapy is as effective as traditional cognitive or behavioral models, nor is there evidence as to which kinds of patients and problems would be particularly amenable. However, the empirical data thus far suggest that emotional schemas play a mediating role in a variety of pathological states and processes, and may therefore help bridge the apparent divide between the different "waves" in CBT. For example, the putative role of emotional schemas in mediating mindfulness, acceptance, experiential avoidance, and anxiety suggests that mindfulness and acceptance may affect how emotions are interpreted and, thereby, result in a reduction of anxiety. Similarly, modifying beliefs about emotions may obviate the reliance on worry as a strategy to avoid emotions, thereby modifying the metacognitive factors underlying the process of worry. It may be that the various theoretical approaches described in the current volume each contain an element of the important truth that pathological processes interact iteratively and simultaneously, and that no one model captures the entire "truth."

## FUTURE DIRECTIONS

One of the difficulties in predicting the future is being anchored in the present. It is unlikely that psychodynamic theorists in 1960 would have been able to predict accurately the cognitive revolution that gained momentum in the 1970s. And it is equally unlikely that cognitive theorists in the 1990s would have predicted the rise in popularity of ACT, DBT, or MBCT in recent years. While acknowledging the value of these contributions, a recent meta-analysis suggests that so-called "third wave" approaches have yet to establish efficacy equivalent to more established cognitive-behavioral interventions (Öst, 2008). Of course, science is continually advancing, and the much-needed research to meet the stringent criteria of "empirically supported studies" for these approaches may soon be available.

One trend that seems to be gaining some momentum is focused on transdiagnostic processes that appear to transcend specific categorical approaches to psychopathology (Barlow et al., 2004; Harvey, Watkins, Mansell, & Shafran, 2004). The newer cognitive models of psychopathology now focus both on the content of schematic processing and on the individual's evaluation of the process of thinking. For example, recent approaches to cognitive therapy for schizophrenia include both consideration of the content of delusional thinking (and how this content functions) and also on metacognitive awareness of the nature of intrusive thinking or delusions (Beck, et al., 2009). Similarly, the role of avoidance, and strategies and beliefs that contribute to avoidance, appears to have gained significance among cognitive therapists. The key question—perhaps from a cognitive perspective—is what is learned (or not learned) through avoidance? Indeed, extinction and exposure involve some "cognitive" mediation, insofar as they change expectancies. Perhaps current controversies pitting "experience" against "cognition" will turn out to be similar to the unnecessary dichotomization of emotion and thinking in the classic debates between Zajonc and Lazarus (Lazarus, 1982; Zajonc, 1984).

For some, the "chicken or egg" question may never be reconciled, although for others the either/or framing of the question is unnecessary. Indeed, the irony in resolving the "debate" between the primacy of one over the other approach may be resolved by invoking a much-maligned, but newly resurrected, concept that has gained respectability in neuroscience—namely, unconscious processing (Bargh, Gollwitzer, Lee-Chai, Trötschel, & Barndollar, 2001; Gray, 2004; Hassin, Uleman, & Bargh, 2005). Perception and categorization can occur outside the realm of conscious awareness and can have emotional impact. Thus, the dichotomy between thinking and feeling may be reconciled if we include nonconscious thinking—that is, nonconscious thinking may result in emotional responses.

Humans are arguably the only animal with the capacity for metacognitive awareness, perhaps accounting for the complexity of the pathology that emerges from their troublesome theories of mind and their reliance on worry as a coping strategy (Geary, 2005). However, research in neuroscience suggests that different areas and functions of the brain are activated when the individual employs different strategies for emotion regulation, in some cases relying primarily on the hippocampus and amygdala (Bottom-Up) while in other cases (Top-Down Processes) relying on the prefrontal cortex and related areas (Cahn & Polich, 2006; Lazar, et al., 2000; Quirk, 2007). Future research, utilizing neuroimagining technologies such as fMRI, may help clarify how mediating processes of acceptance, mindful awareness, cognitive restructuring, metacognitive processes, and emotional schemas are reflected in different (or similar) brain functions.

# REFERENCES

Bargh, J. A., Gollwitzer, P. M., Lee-Chai, A., Trötschel, R., & Barndollar, K. (2001). The automated will: Nonconscious activation and pursuit of behavioral goals. *Journal of Personality and Social Psychology, 81* (6), 1014–1027.

Barlow, D. H., Allen, L. B., & Choate, M. L. (2004). Toward a unified treatment for emotional disorders. *Behavior Therapy, 35,* 205–230

Baron-Cohen, S. (1995). *Mindblindness: An essay on autism and theory of mind.* Cambridge, MA: MIT Press.

Beck, A. T. (1976). *Cognitive therapy and the emotional disorders.* New York: International Universities Press.

Beck, A. T., & Alford, B. A. (2008). *Depression: Causes and treatment* (2nd ed.). Philadelphia: University of Pennsylvania Press.

Beck, A. T., Emery, G., & Greenberg, R. L. (2005). *Anxiety disorders and phobias: A cognitive perspective* (15th anniversary ed.). Cambridge, MA: Basic Books.

Beck, A. T., Rector, N. A., Stolar, N., & Grant, P. (2009). *Schizophrenia: Cognitive theory, research, and therapy.* New York, NY: Guilford Press.

Beck, A. T., Rush, A. J., Shaw, B. F., & Emery, G. (1979). *Cognitive therapy of depression.* New York: Guilford.

Bjorklund, D. F., & Kipp, K. (2002). Social cognition, inhibition, and theory of mind: The evolution of human intelligence. In R. J. Sternberg & J. C. Kaufman (Eds.), *The evolution of intelligence* (pp. 27–54). Mahwah, NJ: Erlbaum.

Borkovec, T. D., Alcaine, O. M., & Behar, E. (2004). Avoidance theory of worry and generalized anxiety disorder. In R. G. Heimberg, C. L. Turk & D. S. Mennin (Eds.), *Generalized anxiety disorder: Advances in research and practice* (pp. 77–108). New York, NY: Guilford Press.

Cahn, B. R., & Polich, J. (2006). Meditation states and traits: EEG, ERP, and neuroimaging studies. *Psychological Bulletin, 132*(2), 180–211.

Clark, D. A. (Ed.). (2005). *Intrusive thoughts in clinical disorders: Theory, research, and treatment.* New York, NY: Guilford Press.

Delgado, M. R., Trujillo, J. L., Holmes, B., Nearing, K. I., LeDoux, J. E., & Phelps, E. A. (2004). *Emotion regulation of conditioned fear: The contributions of reappraisal.* Paper presented at the 11th Annual Meeting of Cognitive Neuroscience Society, San Francisco, CA.

Feffer, M. H. (1970). A developmental analysis of interpersonal behavior. *Psychological Review, 77*(3), 197–214.

Flavell, J. H. (2004). Theory-of-mind development: Retrospect and prospect. *Merrill-Palmer Quarterly, 50*(3), 274–290.

Fonagy, P., & Target, M. (1996). Playing with reality: I. Theory of mind and the normal development of psychic reality. *International Journal of Psychoanalysis, 77 ( Pt 2)*, 217–233.

Freeston, M. H., Ladouceur, R., Gagnon, F., Thibodeau, N., Rhéaume, J., Letarte, H., et al. (1997). Cognitive-behavioral treatment of obsessive thoughts: A controlled study. *Journal of Consulting and Clinical Psychology, 65*(3), 405–413.

Geary, D. C. (2005). *The origin of mind: Evolution of brain, cognition, and general intelligence.* Washington, DC: American Psychological Association.

Gilbert, D. T., Pinel, E. C., Wilson, T. D., Blumberg, S. J., & Wheatley, T. P. (1998). Immune neglect: A source of durability bias in affective forecasting. *Journal of Personal Social Psychology, 75*(3), 617–638.

Gottman, J. M., Katz, L. F., & Hooven, C. (1997). *Meta-emotion: How families communicate emotionally.* Mahwah, NJ: Erlbaum.

Gray, J. A. (2004). *Consciousness: Creeping up on the hard problem.* Oxford, England; New York, NY: Oxford University Press.

Greenberg, L. S. (2002). *Emotion-focused therapy: Coaching clients to work through their feelings.* Washington, DC: American Psychological Association.

Greenberg, L. S., & Paivio, S. C. (1997). *Working with emotions in psychotherapy.* New York, NY: Guilford Press.

Greenberg, L. S., & Safran, J. D. (1987). *Emotion in psychotherapy: Affect, cognition, and the process of change.* New York, NY: Guilford Press.

Greenberg, L. S., & Watson, J. C. (2005). *Emotion-focused therapy for depression* (1st ed.). Washington, DC: American Psychological Association.

Grossarth-Maticek, R., Bastiaans, J., & Kanazir, D. T. (1985). Psychosocial factors as strong predictors of mortality from cancer, ischaemic heart disease and stroke: The Yugoslav prospective study. *Journal of Psychosomatic Research, 29*, 167–176.

Grossarth-Maticek, R., Kanazir, D. T., Schmidt, P., & Vetter, H. (1985). Psychosocial and organic variables as predictors of lung cancer, cardiac infarct and apoplexy: Some differential predictors. *Personality and Individual Differences, 6*, 313–321.

Harvey, A., Watkins, E., Mansell, W., & Shafran, R. (2004). *Cognitive behavioural processes across psychological disorders: A transdiagnostic approach to research and treatment.* Oxford, England: Oxford University Press.

Hassin, R. R., Uleman, J. S., & Bargh, J. A. (2005). *The new unconscious.* New York, NY: Oxford University Press.

Hayes, S. C., Strosahl, K. D., & Wilson, K. G. (1999). *Acceptance and commitment therapy: An experiential approach to behavior change.* New York, NY: Guilford Press.

Hayes, S. C., Strosahl, K. D., & Wilson, K. G. (2003). *Acceptance and commitment therapy: An experiential approach to behavior change.* New York: Guilford.

Hofmann, S. G., & Asmundson, G. J. G. (2008). Acceptance and mindfulness-based therapy: New wave or old hat? *Clinical Psychology Review, 28*(1), 1–16.

Honkalampi, K., Hintikka, J., Tanskanen, A., Lehtonen, J., & Viinamaki, H. (2000). Depression is strongly associated with alexithymia in the general population. *Journal of Psychosomatic Research, 48*(1), 99–104.

Izard, C. E. (2009). Emotion theory and research: Highlights, unanswered questions, and emerging issues. *Annu Rev Psychol, 60*, 1–25.

Jones, E. E., & Davis, K. E. (1965). From acts to dispositions: The attribution process in social psychology. In L. Berkowitz (Ed.), *Advances in experimental social psychology* (Vol. 2, pp. 219–266). New York, NY: Academic Press.

Kahneman, D., & Frederick, S. (2005). A model of heuristic judgment. In K. J. Holyoak & R. G. Morrison (Eds.), *The Cambridge handbook of thinking and reasoning* (pp. 267–293). New York, NY: Cambridge University Press.

Kelley, H. H. (1972). *Causal schemata and the attribution process.* Morristown, NJ: General Learning Press.

Lazar, S. W., Bush, G., Gollub, R. L., Fricchione, G. L., Khalsa, G., & Benson, H. (2000). Functional brain mapping of the relaxation response and meditation. *Neuroreport, 11*(7), 1581–1585.

Lazarus, A. (1984). *In the mind's eye.* New York, NY: Guilford Press.

Lazarus, R. S. (1982). Thoughts on the relations between emotion and cognition. *American Psychologist, 37,* 1019–1024.

Lazarus, R. S. (1999). *Stress and emotion: A new synthesis.* New York, NY: Springer.

Leahy, R. L. (2002). A model of emotional schemas. *Cognitive and Behavioral Practice, 9*(3), 177–190.

Leahy, R. L. (2003a). *Cognitive therapy techniques: A practitioner's guide.* New York, NY: Guilford Press.

Leahy, R. L. (2003b). Emotional schemas and resistance in cognitive therapy. In R. L. Leahy (Ed.), *Roadblocks in cognitive-behavioral therapy: Transforming challenges into opportunities for change* (pp. 91–115). New York, NY: Guilford Press.

Leahy, R. L. (2005a, November). *Integrating the meta-cognitive and meta-emotional models of worry.* Paper presented at the Association for the Advancement of Cognitive and Behavioral Therapy, Washington, DC.

Leahy, R. L. (2005b). A social-cognitive model of validation. In P. Gilbert (Ed.), *Compassion: Conceptualisations, research, and use in psychotherapy* (pp. 195–217). London, England: Routledge.

Leahy, R. L. (2005c). *The worry cure: Seven steps to stop worry from stopping you* (1st ed.). New York, NY: Harmony Books.

Leahy, R. L. (2007a). Emotional schemas and resistance to change in anxiety disorders. *Cognitive and Behavioral Practice, 14*(1), 36–45.

Leahy, R. L. (2007b). Emotional schemas and self-help: Homework compliance and obsessive-compulsive disorder. *Cognitive and Behavioral Practice, 14*(3), 297–302.

Leahy, R. L. (2009a). Emotional schemas in treatment-resistant anxiety. In D. Sookman & R. L. Leahy (Eds.), *Treatment resistant anxiety disorders: Resolving impasses to symptom remission* (pp. 135–160). New York, NY: Routledge.

Leahy, R. L. (2009b). Resistance: An emotional schema therapy approach. In G. Simos (Ed.), *Cognitive behavior therapy: A guide for the practicing clinician-Volume II* (pp. 187–204). London, England: Routledge.

Leahy, R. L., & Kaplan, D. (2004). *Emotional schemas and relationship adjustment.* Paper presented at the Association for the Advancement of Behavior Therapy, New Orleans, LA.

Leahy, R. L., & Napolitano, L. (2005, November 18–21). *What are the emotional schema predictors of personality disorders?* Paper presented at the Association for the Advancement of Behavior Therapy, Washington, DC.

Leahy, R. L., & Napolitano, L. A. (2005, November). *What are the emotional schema predictors of personality disorders?* Paper presented at the Association for the Advancement of Cognitive and Behavioral Therapy, Washington, DC.

Leahy, R. L., & Tirch, D. D. (2008). Cognitive behavioral therapy for jealousy. *International Journal of Cognitive Therapy, 1*(1), 18–32.

Leahy, R. L., Tirch, D. D., & Napolitano, L. A. (2009, November). *Meta-cognitive and meta-emotional processes affecting anxiety.* Paper presented at the Association for Behavioral and Cognitive Therapies, New York, NY.

LeDoux, J. E. (1996). *The emotional brain: The mysterious underpinnings of emotional life.* New York, NY: Simon and Schuster.

Mennin, D. S., Heimberg, R. G., Turk, C. L., & Fresco, D. M. (2005). Preliminary evidence for an emotion dysregulation model of generalized anxiety disorder. *Behaviour Research and Therapy, 43*(10), 1281–1310.

Mennin, D. S., Holaway, R. M., Fresco, D. M., Moore, M. T., & Heimberg, R. G. (2007). Delineating components of emotion and its dysregulation in anxiety and mood psychopathology. *Behavior Therapy, 38*(3), 284–302.

Miranda, J., Gross, J. J., Persons, J. B., & Hahn, J. (1998). Mood matters: Negative mood induction activates dysfunctional attitudes in women vulnerable to depression. *Cognitive Therapy & Research, 22*(4), 363–376.

Napolitano, L. A., Taitz, J., & Leahy, R. L. (2009, November-a). *Do changes in negative beliefs about emotions mediate the effects of mindfulness on experiential avoidance?* Paper presented at the Association for Behavioral and Cognitive Therapies, New York, NY.

Napolitano, L. A., Taitz, J., & Leahy, R. L. (2009, November-b). *Negative beliefs about emotions mediate the relationship between mindfulness and experiential avoidance: Two preliminary investigations.* Paper presented at the Association for Behavioral and Cognitive Therapies, New York, NY.

Nussbaum, M. (2005). *Frontiers of justice: Disability, nationality, species membership.* Cambridge, MA: Belknap Press.

Öst, L.-G. (2008). Efficacy of the third wave of behavioral therapies: A systematic review and meta-analysis. *Behaviour Research and Therapy, 46*(3), 296–321.

Phelps, E. A., Delgado, M. R., Nearing, K. I., & LeDoux, J. E. (2004). Extinction learning in humans: Role of the amygdala and vmPFC. *Neuron, 43*(6), 897–905.

Piaget, J. (1932). *The moral judgement of the child.* New York, NY: Harcourt, Brace Jovanovich.

Piaget, J. (1967). *Biology and knowledge.* Chicago, IL: University of Chicago Press.

Purdon, C., & Clark, D. A. (1993). Obsessive intrusive thoughts in nonclinical subjects: I. Content and relation with depressive, anxious and obsessional symptoms. *Behaviour Research & Therapy, 31*(8), 713–720.

Purdon, C., Rowa, K., & Antony, M. M. (2005). Thought suppression and its effects on thought frequency, appraisal and mood state in individuals with obsessive-compulsive disorder. *Behaviour Research and Therapy, 43*(1), 93–108.

Quirk, G. J. (2007). Prefrontal-amygdala interactions in the regulation of fear. In J. J. Gross (Ed.), *Handbook of emotion regulation* (pp. 27–46). New York, NY: Guilford Press.

Rachman, S. J. (1997). A cognitive theory of obsessions. *Behaviour Research and Therapy, 35,* 793–802.

Rawls, J. (2005). *A theory of justice* (Original ed.). Cambridge, MA: Belknap Press.

Rumi, & Barks, C. (1995). *The Essential Rumi.* San Francisco, CA: Harper.

Ryle, G. (1949). *The Concept of Mind.* Chicago, IL: University of Chicago Press.

Salkovskis, P. M. (1989). Cognitive-behavioural factors and the persistence of intrusive thoughts in obsessional problems. *Behaviour Research & Therapy, 27*(6), 677–682.

Salkovskis, P. M., & Campbell, P. (1994). Thought suppression induces intrusion in naturally occurring negative intrusive thoughts. *Behaviour Research & Therapy, 32*(1), 1–8.

Segal, Z. V., Kennedy, S., Gemar, M., Hood, K., Pedersen, R., & Buis, T. (2006). Cognitive reactivity to sad mood provocation and the prediction of depressive relapse. *Archives of General Psychiatry, 63*(7), 749–755.

Slovic, P., Finucane, M., Peters, E., & MacGregor, D. G. (2002). The affect heuristic. In T. Gilovich, D. Griffin & D. Kahneman (Eds.), *Heuristics and biases: The psychology of intuitive judgment.* (pp. 397–420). New York: Cambridge University Press.

Spokas, M., Luterek, J. A., & Heimberg, R. G. (2009). Social anxiety and emotional suppression: The mediating role of beliefs. *Journal of Behavior Therapy and Experimental Psychiatry, 40*(2), 283–291.

Sunstein, C. R. (2005). *Laws of fear: Beyond the precautionary principle.* Cambridge, UK: Cambridge University Press.

Teasdale, J. D. (1999a). Metacognition, mindfulness and the modification of mood disorders. *Clinical Psychology and Psychotherapy, 6,* 146–155.

Teasdale, J. D. (1999b). Multi-level theories of cognition-emotion relations. In T. Dalgleish & M. J. Power (Eds.), *Handbook of cognition and emotion.* (pp. 665–681). Chichester, England: Wiley.

Tirch, D. D., Leahy, R. L., & Silberstein, L. (2009, November). *Relationships among emotional-schemas, psychological flexibility, dispositional mindfulness, and emotion regulation.* Paper presented at the Association for Behavioral and Cognitive Therapies, New York, NY.

Weiner, B. (1974). Achievement motivation and attribution theory. Morristown, NJ: General Learning Press.

Weiner, B. (1986). *An attributional theory of motivation and emotion.* New York, NY: Springer-Verlag.

Wells, A. (2000). *Emotional disorders and metacognition: Innovative cognitive therapy.* New York, NY: Wiley.

Wells, A. (2002). Meta-cognitive beliefs in the maintenance of worry and generalized anxiety disorder. In R. G. Heimberg, C. L. Turk & D. S. Mennin (Eds.), *Generalized anxiety disorder: Advances in research and practice.* New York, NY: Guilford Press.

Wells, A. (2004). Meta-cognitive beliefs in the maintenance of worry and generalized anxiety disorder. In R. G. Heimberg, C. L. Turk & D. S. Mennin (Eds.), *Generalized anxiety disorder: Advances in research and practice.* New York, NY: Guilford Press.

Wells, A. (2009). *Metacognitive therapy for anxiety and depression.* New York, NY: Guilford Press.

Wilson, K. A., & Chambless, D. L. (1999). Inflated perceptions of responsibility and obsessive-compulsive symptoms. *Behaviour Research and Therapy, 37*(4), 325–335.

Wilson, T. D., Wheatley, T., Meyers, J. M., Gilbert, D. T., & Axsom, D. (2000). Focalism: A source of durability bias in affective forecasting. *Journal of Personal Social Psychology, 78*(5), 821–836.

Zahradnik, M., Stewart, S. H., Marshall, G. N., Schell, T. L., & Jaycox, L. H. (2009). Anxiety sensitivity and aspects of alexithymia are independently and uniquely associated with posttraumatic distress. *Journal of Traumatic Stress, 22*(2), 131–138.

Zajonc, R. B. (1984). On the primacy of affect. *American Psychologist, 39*(2), 117–123.

# 6

## Mindfulness-Based Stress Reduction

PAUL G. SALMON, SANDRA E. SEPHTON, AND SAMUEL J. DREEBEN

> The unquiet mind
> Can you be with this one breath,
> This moment, this now?
> —Paul Salmon

## HISTORICAL CONTEXT AND DESCRIPTION OF THE MODEL

### Mindfulness-Based Stress Reduction (MBSR)

This term denotes a time-limited, group-based behavioral medicine intervention initiated in 1979 by Jon Kabat-Zinn, who founded the Stress Reduction Clinic at the University of Massachusetts Medical Center in Worcester, Massachusetts. *Mindfulness* has been characterized by Kabat-Zinn (2003) as "...the awareness that emerges through paying attention on purpose, in the present moment, and non-judgmentally to the unfolding of experience moment by moment" (p. 145). "Present moment awareness" is fundamental to this definition, a point on which most definitions of mindfulness converge (Brown & Ryan, 2003). The foundation of MBSR rests on the simple but profound idea that much of our distress and suffering results from incessantly wanting things to be different from how they actually are. Wishing to be well; hoping for a cure; regretting past behavior that led to health problems; and trying somehow to recapture one's youth are all manifestations of this tendency.

### Clinical Applications of Mindfulness

The tradition of mindfulness is based in Buddhist meditation practices but has been widely applied in Western biomedical settings in the context of the *biopsychosocial* perspective advocated by Engel (1977). Epstein (1999) noted its compatibility with Western philosophical *pragmatism*, which emphasizes practical consequences of interactions between behavioral, emotional, and cognitive processes. MBSR programs have proliferated in recent years and are currently offered in several hundred domestic and foreign hospitals and clinics as part of a clear trend toward participatory health care (Salmon, Santorelli, Sephton, & Kabat-Zinn, 2009). Beginning with the publication of *Full Catastrophe*

*Living* and subsequent perspectives on mindfulness (Kabat-Zinn, 1990; Kabat-Zinn, 1994; Kabat-Zinn, 2005; Santorelli, 1999), public interest in mindfulness and MBSR increased substantially, aided by airing of the PBS series and accompanying book, *Healing and the Mind* by Bill Moyers (Moyers, 1993). The role of mindfulness in medical care and training continues to evolve as a promising preventive and treatment-oriented intervention in medicine (Ludwig & Kabat-Zinn, 2008), psychotherapy (Baer, 2006; Germer, Siegel, & Fulton, 2005; Roemer & Orsillo, 2008; Shapiro & Carlson, 2009) and recently the health/fitness area (Dutton, 2008; La Forge, 2005). Its influence extends to models of autonomy and self-regulation, including self-determination theory (Ryan & Deci, 2004). MBSR combined with Hayes and colleagues' relational frame theory (Hayes, Barnes-Holmes, & Roche, 2001), the conceptual framework of acceptance and commitment therapy or ACT (Hayes, Strosahl, & Wilson, 1999), and Linehan's (1993) mindfulness-centered dialectic behavior therapy (DBT) in the mid-1990s to initiate a powerful movement into the domain of cognitive behavior therapy (CBT), which until that time maintained primary allegiance to traditional Western cognitive and behavioral psychology. At present, mindfulness- and acceptance-based interventions significantly influence CBT (Hayes, Follette, & Linehan, 2004), especially evident in the work of Segal, Williams, and Teasdale (2002) with mindfulness-based cognitive therapy (MBCT).

## Center for Mindfulness

The Stress Reduction Clinic and flagship MBSR program are currently housed in the Center for Mindfulness in Medicine, Health Care, and Society (CFM) at the University of Massachusetts Medical Center. At the time of the original clinic's founding, however, complementary health-care programs were relatively rare, and for several years the MBSR program made do with makeshift facilities and faced professional skepticism. However, Kabat-Zinn's unique background—a Ph.D. in molecular biology with an abiding interest in Zen Buddhism—provided him with scientific credibility and a committed focus on the relief of human suffering as his life's work (Kabat-Zinn, 2005).

The MBSR clinic served as a referral conduit for medical patients throughout the hospital, referred by physicians, although in recent years self-referrals have comprised an increasing percentage of program participants (Salmon et al., 2009b). For some, life-threatening disease or trauma serves as a "wakeup call" leading to a heightened state of awareness and commitment to staying anchored in the present (Gallagher, 2009). For others, the motivation may be more benign. Whatever the root cause, participation in MBSR programs is typically motivated by a strong desire for *change*, to which the seemingly paradoxical response is one that advocates patience, self-trust, and *psychological acceptance*. As previously noted, wanting things to be different from how they currently are, prospective participants quickly learn, lies at the heart of suffering.

The CFM operates on the premise that "suffering" is a universal phenomenon, nowhere more obvious than in the heart of a major medical center, and has offered mindfulness-based complementary care in conjunction with the exemplary medical care patients receive. However, the concept of suffering from the perspective of MBSR is rather different from its common medical meaning, which tends to focus on physical pain. In the context of MBSR, suffering implies a sense of estrangement from oneself and present circumstances, or "... our fear of experiencing ourselves directly" (Epstein, 1995, p. 17). In keeping with its Buddhist origins, mindfulness provides a simple but powerful means of directing attention inward, providing a stable foundation for self-exploration and, eventually, eradication of suffering. In this sense, it serves as an antidote to the comparatively undisciplined but commonplace experience of "monkey mind," in which attention constantly shifts from place to place, forward and back in time, bringing to light an array of mental phenomena linked to various positive and negative psychological states having little to do with present-moment reality. Learning to recognize and respond by choice to such mental conditioning patterns is among the key benefits of mindfulness practice (Kristeller, 2003).

The MBSR program attracts participants for many different reasons. Some are facing medical challenges and seek relief from distress associated with such conditions, which often goes unaddressed or even is trivialized (R. S. Lazarus, 1984). Others are demoralized by the pace of modern life and the complexity of day-to-day events that are becoming increasingly challenging to manage. Still others have lost the sense of community that at one time bound people together, and are personally affected by a variety of social vulnerabilities, including widespread aggression, environmental alienation, and loss of moral and religious guideposts (Jason, 1997), and are looking for a stable point of orientation.

## The MBSR Program

The MBSR program is often referred to as "... a clinic in the form of a course" and was characterized by Brantley (2005) as a "psychoeducation approach" to clinical work. It is thus technically not psychotherapy, nor is it embedded in Western models of psychopathology or clinical diagnosis, in contrast to CBT. Rather, it is a form of complementary health care that evolved outside traditional models of psychotherapy, the central feature of which—mindfulness—has nonetheless been incorporated into a range of recent psychotherapeutic interventions. Having said this, we strongly endorse the view that the effectiveness of MBSR groups is enhanced by instructors who are not only well-grounded in the practice of mindfulness meditation, but who in addition have clinical training as psychotherapists or other helping professionals (Kocovski, Segal, & Battista, 2009; Teasdale, Segal, & Williams, 2003). It takes considerable skill to convey effectively the simple essence of mindfulness – nonjudgmental, present-moment awareness—to novice practitioners in ways that are not only comprehensible, but personally meaningful.

Clinical acumen is important in other ways as well—for example when determining whether or not MBSR is an appropriate intervention for a given individual, or when deciding how best it can be integrated with other forms of health care, including psychotherapy. It is our view that skillfully run MBSR groups embody the common factors of psychotherapy enumerated by J. D. Frank and Frank (1991), including (a) an effective working alliance with a helping person, (b) a healing setting, (c) a credible conceptual scheme and procedures for alleviating suffering, and (d) health restorative procedures involving active engagement of participants and instructors alike. It is notable that Frank and Frank's visionary work was broadly inclusive of socially sanctioned helping practices, cutting across professional, disciplinary, and even cultural boundaries for the purpose of highlighting near universal methods for addressing the widespread problem of *demoralization*, a correlate of *suffering*.

## Structure and Curriculum

As traditionally practiced, MBSR typically takes the form of a time-limited (eight-session) weekly group program of two to two and one-half hours' duration with a curriculum that approaches stress management by helping participants cultivate present-moment–focused attention in the face of challenging circumstances. The program employs a range of practices that effectively integrate elements of Buddhism with Western psychology, avoiding many of the pitfalls that can arise when meditation (or other) practices are culturally transplanted (Aronson, 2004). The body scan (inner-directed, body-focused attention), Hatha Yoga (gentle movement and stretching), and sitting meditation comprise three core mindfulness practices progressively incorporated into a daily home practice of between 45–60 minutes' duration. All three are recorded on CDs to provide home-based guidance. Each encourages mindful exploration of specific (though somewhat overlapping) facets of experience: somatosensory (body scan), kinesthetic (Hatha Yoga), and cognitive (sitting meditation).

Collectively referred to as *formal* mindfulness practices, the body scan, Hatha Yoga, and sitting meditation comprise the foundation of MBSR in terms of regular, daily practice. The program also emphasizes *informal* mindfulness practice, directed toward everyday real-world experiences such as eating, driving, talking, and working. Making these the center of attention is an effective way to integrate mindfulness into everyday life.

The MBSR program centers on key stress-related themes that integrate didactic and experiential elements. A preliminary interview (or group orientation session) functionally comprises the first session, providing participants with an overview of the program and encouraging their committed participation. The first of the eight actual program sessions introduces a theme of compassionate self-awareness and acceptance ("...no matter what your problems, there is more right with you than wrong with you"). Participants are invited to share their reasons for coming into the program, following which two core mindfulness practices (body scan, sitting meditation) are introduced and practiced. The session concludes with discussion of the first home practice assignment and a brief period of quiet sitting. Subsequent sessions begin with sitting meditation (which progressively increases in duration), followed by open discussion of weekly home practice and its effect(s) on present-moment awareness. The role of the instructor here is to encourage participants to focus on the "lived experience" of the practice, and to become aware of tendencies to become overly invested in striving for particular outcomes, such as relaxation or reduced stress.

Program sessions include informal didactic presentations illustrating various applications of mindfulness in stress management through topics including "Perception and Creative Responding"; "The Pleasure and Power of Being Present"; "Reacting vs. Responding to Stress"; and others. Materials in an accompanying workbook further amplify these themes via a practice log and self-reflection inventories. Yoga is first introduced in the third session, and subsequently becomes part of daily home practice. Traditionally, a Saturday mindfulness "retreat" is held between the sixth and seventh sessions, offering participants an opportunity for extended practice. By this point, home practice is becoming increasingly individualized, reflecting personal preferences for various combinations of sitting meditation, Yoga, and the body scan.

The eighth and final session provides closure for the entire program. Participants are encouraged to maintain their practice in a form that is personally meaningful, having now been exposed to a variety of both formal and informal practice techniques. Flexible utilization of multiple mindfulness resources effectively counters problems associated with unimodal techniques, such as inflexible implementation and inappropriate application (A. A. Lazarus, 1984). Such variety may also protect against "burnout" and early practice termination. Finally, some programs, such as the CFM, invite MBSR program graduates to attend subsequent weekend retreats as a means of periodically reinforcing their practice.

## Contextual Factors

A variety of contextual factors combine to provide a supportive atmosphere that, we believe, contributes to the high rates of program adherence reported by the CFM and, presumably, other MBSR program centers. Recently summarized by Salmon et al. (2009b, p. 275), these include: (a) a time-limited, group format of sufficient duration to foster lifestyle change; (b) an introspectively oriented educational approach; (c) multiple mindfulness practices to accommodate individual preferences and differences; (d) instructors with extensive personal meditation experience; (e) unifying experiential themes of suffering and wholeness; (f) integrative mind/body mindfulness practices; (g) diverse, heterogeneous participants; (h) extended meditation practice during a day-long, weekend retreat; and (i) a supportive learning context emphasizing sharing and active coping.

The MBSR program is multifaceted, interdisciplinary, and culturally inclusive. Its evolution reflects fairly recent social and cultural trends, which fostered a fruitful alliance between Buddhism and Western psychology that did not always exist. In the early 20th century, for example, meditation was viewed harshly and even with condemnation by Freud and his advocates. This was followed by gradually increasing tolerance, pragmatic acceptance, and widespread interest at both conceptual and applied levels as part of burgeoning interest in consciousness studies (Bankart, 2003). Currently, Buddhist-influenced teachings and practices are widely represented in clinical psychology, ranging from psychoanalytic (Epstein,

1995; Safran, 2003) to the range of cognitive behavioral perspectives represented in this book. However, MBSR teachers and practitioners alike can benefit from an appreciation of the historical and cultural contexts in which Buddhism has evolved (see, for example, Bankart, 1997; Bankart, Dockett, & Dudley-Grant, 2003).

## Embodied Practice

Both individually and collectively, MBSR practices contribute to the cultivation of mindfulness and implicitly convey the important idea that there is no one single or "right way" to accomplish this goal. At a broad level, mindfulness embodies characteristics that influence, but are nevertheless independent of, specific behaviors. Mindfulness provides a contextual setting that encompasses actions, thoughts, and feelings. A recent discussion of mindfulness by Brown, Ryan, and Creswell (2007) summarized these key elements as involving clear, nonconceptual awareness, a capacity for both sustained and flexible allocation of attention, being anchored in the present, and living in an engaged, nonjudgmental manner. The MBSR formal practices in particular provide a systematic means of embodying these characteristics in ways that resonate with personal inclinations and preferences.

The body scan, introduced in the first MBSR session, is an introspective practice in which attention is progressively directed from one body region to another, with instructions to simply pay attention to sensations as they arise. The practice, structured via a recorded narrative, serves several purposes. First, it initiates the process of turning attention inward and adopting an accepting attitude, a critical element of mindfulness. Second, it invites prolonged, quiet introspection by exposing the practitioner to the generally novel experience of maintaining a state of quiet, yet attentive, repose. Third, it provides a means of cultivating broad-based, intimate familiarity with the body, tracking in an even-handed manner through regions that may evoke painful, neutral, or positive sensations, or no sensations at all, along with judgmental appraisals (which ideally diminish over time). The body scan really has no direct parallel in Buddhist meditation as a formal practice, but it is nonetheless treated as an object worthy of mindful attention.

As employed in MBSR, the body scan provides a compelling vehicle for mindfulness practice. It fits nicely within the philosophy of somaesthetics, or "body consciousness" as discussed by Shusterman (2008), who describes mindful perception of physical sensations as a relatively advanced level of awareness fostering a degree of somatic sensitivity far below the level of external appearances. An important precursor to this perspective is that of Bakal (1999), who emphasized the importance of "somatic awareness" in health and wellness. He described it as a "commonplace inner experience" (p. 4) involving sensitivity to inner states, a hallmark of somatic relaxation and meditation practices. Somatic awareness is viewed by Bakal as a specific manifestation of mindfulness, a more global state of object-less awareness. His clinical approach mirrors that of MBSR, in terms of encouraging exploration of inner states with potential relevance to the full gamut of human emotional experience, including that of pain, distress, and suffering. We would only add that even if inner states are in fact "commonplace," they are seldom explored in a systematic manner with the sort of patience and openness advocated by MBSR practice.

Hatha Yoga, another key element of MBSR, has historical ties to Buddhism, but also developed as an independent philosophy and practice. One of several systems of Yoga, Hatha (literally *sun/moon*) Yoga shares a common purpose with MBSR, that of integrating mind and body (Salmon et al., 2009a). In the context of MBSR, Yoga provides a vehicle for mindfulness practice, experiencing the body in motion on a moment-by-moment basis. It was originally incorporated as a means of helping patients overcome *disuse atrophy*, physical deterioration associated with inactivity. An extensive research literature has evolved around Yoga, much of it, however, of inconsistent quality and limited applicability to Western health care, according to a review and critique by Innes et al. (2005). MBSR incorporates two Yoga sequences, neither of which is overly physically taxing, owing to its incorporation as a means of helping medical patients gently and mindfully transition from passive inactivity to adaptive movement. These sequences, comprised of standing, seated, and lying-down positions (*asanas*), have benefits of mobility in terms of balance, range of motion, strength, and flexibility when practiced regularly.

As recently noted elsewhere (Salmon, Lush, Jablonski, & Sephton, 2009a), few psychologists (or other health professionals) have extensive training in physical disciplines, including Yoga. Furthermore, psychotherapy has historically emphasized talk, not action. As a result, the mind/body integration achieved in MBSR has to date not been incorporated into clinical psychology practice, with a few exceptions (Williams, Teasdale, Segal, & Kabat-Zinn, 2007). This is unfortunate, because a substantial research literature supports the efficacy of physical activity in relief of depression, anxiety, and stress (Dunn, Trivedi, Kampert, Clark, & Chambliss, 2005; Martinsen, 2008; Smits and Otto, 2009). Until psychotherapy practice is expanded to incorporate movement-centered practices such as Yoga, it will not be able to take advantage of a significant source of symptomatic relief and adaptive functioning.

Sitting meditation is the third formal mindfulness practice in MBSR, and has received the most attention. It is appealing in its simplicity; after all, the instructions are simply to "just sit" and direct attention in a deliberate, sustained manner to various "objects of consciousness." In reality, "simple but not easy" is a more accurate characterization, as frequently repeated by MBSR teachers. When practiced effectively, sitting meditation integrates focused attention with minimal physical activity, traditionally a strange confluence of states for most Westerners. The primary purpose of sustained sitting in MBSR is to help practitioners cultivate a psychological "window" into inner states, a glimpse of which has previously been experienced via the Body Scan. Establishing a stable vantage point of this nature serves several adaptive purposes, not the least of which is intentionally directing attention inward. Cognitive behavior therapy routinely employs thought monitoring to elicit dysfunctional cognitions, but this is generally done with only limited instruction about how exactly to do this. In practice, sustained observation of inner physical or mental states can be very challenging, and MBSR is one of only a very few clinical practices that specifically teaches a means of doing so.

A second benefit of sitting meditation is that, over time, it can gradually foster a nonreactive stance toward thoughts and feeling states by virtue of nonreinforced exposure and habituation (Goleman, 1990). Coming to see thoughts as simply thoughts, rather than as stimuli linked to conditioned behavioral and emotional reactions, is a powerful introspective tool that effectively decouples the cognitive triad of thoughts, emotions, and behavior linked to psychological distress.

Mindfulness, cultivated via introspective methods that are fundamentally compatible with those of Western psychology, continues to influence current MBSR practices. For example, conscious awareness is emphasized in a variety of ways, through statements such as "being awake," "relaxed awareness," "paying attention," and "being fully conscious." Nonconscious states are likened to sleep, and imply a tendency to behave as if on autopilot, going through life in a rote, habitual manner. As noted by Brown and Ryan (2003), Kabat-Zinn (2003), and others, there is nothing inherently Buddhist about focused attention, and any tendency to treat mindfulness in a proprietary manner, associating it specifically with formal meditation practice for example, is unnecessarily restrictive.

The importance of sensory-mediated knowledge is emphasized in MBSR by encouraging participants to notice and pay attention to perceptual elements of experiential flow unencumbered by cognitive processing that acts as a filtering system. A fundamental and widely practiced sitting meditation begins with instructions to focus in turn on the breath, other internal sensations, environmental sounds, and finally thoughts (considered a sixth sense, in addition to hearing, vision, touch, taste, and smell). In addition to encouraging focus on sensory phenomena, this practice also illustrates our capacity for flexible attention allocation, a cognitive capacity characteristic of consciousness awareness.

## Mindfulness and the "Constructed World"

The premise that we live in a constructed "virtual world" of our own making is of fundamental importance in MBSR, as it is the case in Western constructivist perspectives such as those of Frank and Frank (1991), Meichenbaum (1977), and Mahoney (1991). Formal mindfulness techniques (body scan, sitting meditation, Hatha Yoga) are contextualized by statements such "everyone's experience will be different and unique," and a deemphasis on generic goals such as relaxation or insight. Instead, the importance of "just noticing" events in the moment-by-moment flow of experience is emphasized, without trying to make anything in particular happen. Nonjudgmental awareness is at the core of mindfulness practice, emphasizing clarity of perception and freedom from cognitive preconceptions. This psychological vantage point applies equally to informal practices, the intention being to develop a consistent, day-to-day perspective that extends beyond time set aside for structured meditation practice. It is embedded in a broader attitudinal framework described by Kabat-Zinn (1990) that we believe is of utmost importance. The components of this framework are: acceptance, "beginner's mind" (i.e., seeing things as if for the first time), letting go of preconceived, restrictive views, nonjudging, nonstriving, patience, and trust.

The inevitability of change figures prominently in MBSR, a reflection of its Buddhist heritage. However, the capacity to observe change is severely limited by the fact that much of our time is spent in incessant activity that does not provide a stable reference point. Encouraging "just sitting" is a simple way of quieting the body long enough so that that one's focus can shift to other objects of consciousness, including the mind. Moving around and doing things requires a certain amount of cognitive processing capacity that tends to narrow the scope of attention to instrumental concerns. Sitting quietly, on the other hand, produces an interesting and somewhat paradoxical state of relaxed awareness, which in turn reduces cognitive demands and frees the resultant capacity for other purposes.

Quiet, relaxed awareness provides an ideal vantage point from which to observe change processes that are otherwise typically obscured. Manifestations are everywhere. Observation of the breath reveals phasic change from breathing in to breathing out. Observation of inner states reveals both regular and intermittent interoceptive sensations signifying a myriad of changes in underlying physiological processes. Observation of sights and sounds reveals a constant but often subtle flow of energy states captured by sense organs that are themselves constantly changing. (For example, the capacity to observe coherent and apparently stable visual images derives from constant, nearly imperceptible eye movements that include both saccadic oscillations and broader scanning patterns). Observing thoughts, yet another capacity enhanced by quiet awareness, poses added challenges. It does not take much practice, however, to simply notice that thoughts change, and that they constantly come and go. This is a powerful insight, because it can illustrate that thoughts are separate from the thinker and have a seeming life of their own, much like other sense-based phenomena. It also becomes rapidly apparent that controlling thoughts is not a simple matter; one cannot just "shut off" thinking in the same way that one can eliminate external visual stimulation by sitting in darkness or eliminate sounds by wearing noise-canceling headphones!

## THE ROLE OF MINDFULNESS AND ACCEPTANCE STRATEGIES IN THE INTERVENTION MODEL

Mindfulness comprises the foundation of MBSR, and along with somewhat related but distinct pioneering work by Hayes, Strosahl, and Wilson (1999) and Linehan (1993), represents one of several convergent perspectives that have served as an important catalyst for more recent mindfulness- and acceptance-based psychotherapy models, such as mindfulness-based cognitive therapy (Segal, Williams, & Teasdale, 2002), mindfulness- and acceptance-based behavioral therapy (Roemer & Orsillo, 2009), and a range of other mindfulness-informed practices enumerated by Germer, Siegel, and Fulton (2005). As is often the case with catalytic agents of change, several of these mindfulness- and acceptance-based interventions developed largely outside traditional mainstream clinical practice, which for years was strongly rooted to traditional behavioral, cognitive-behavioral, and psychodynamic traditions. For example, both Kabat-Zinn and Linehan were personally steeped in Buddhist meditation practices, well outside the cultural traditions of Western psychotherapy, whereas Hayes' post-Skinnerian radical behaviorist perspective also diverged sharply from mainstream practices.

The MBSR program was originally conceived to help medical patients manage stress associated with medically challenging conditions, initially focusing on chronic pain. From firsthand experience with meditation, Kabat-Zinn was well aware that physical pain was an inevitable aspect of prolonged, relatively immobilized sitting. He reasoned that pain-related sensations provide an opportunity for mindfulness practice, which may eventually lead to an unbundling or deconstruction of the experience into elements consisting not only of bare sensations themselves, but also of associated thoughts and feelings with negative valences that drive a desire for things to change and the pain to dissipate. The latter phenomena, rather than the former, are believed to be at the root of suffering, which is fundamentally the desire for things to be different from how they are. Present-moment sensations characteristic of pain can thus be decoupled from cognitive and affective correlates of the experience that otherwise amplify the overall level of distress. Depressive and anxious thoughts and feelings, usually linked to past or future events, can lose their power when effectively bypassed in this manner. Although focusing in the present moment may bring up painful sensations, to some extent they can come to be experienced in an elemental manner (*bare attention*), unaccompanied by cognitive or affective phenomena, which evoked by past or future concerns, do not accurately reflect present-moment reality.

Practicing mindfulness seems paradoxical to many, at least at first glance. As noted above, it is often described as "simple but not easy." It invites opening to the experience of pain and other experiences we are inclined to avoid. Clinically, it proposes to relieve suffering, yet discourages striving to achieve this end. And although it advocates acceptance as a core attitude, MBSR outcome studies generally report significant changes in the lives of participants. To make sense out of such apparent paradoxes, practitioners need to have some overarching context, a meaning structure, within which to operate.

Brantley (2005) enumerated three radical themes at the heart of MBSR, each of which is intended to reinforce the program's significance in the Western biomedical context. The first is compassionate acceptance of oneself, regardless of adverse or challenging circumstances. This helps balance the traditional emphasis in Western medicine on diagnosing and eradicating disease. A second theme emphasizes the importance of *being*, rather than *doing*, as a way to counterbalance the medical model's action orientation. Third, participants are encouraged to give up preconceived ideas about what is right or wrong with them and adopt an attitude of "not knowing." Here, again, is a way of thoughtfully countering traditional Western medical thinking—in this instance, the near-total reliance on factual information and professional expertise.

These three themes are embedded in a broader context of MBSR that views medical conditions as but one of many stressors that are an inevitable part of life. All three are highly adaptive in this broader context. The emphasis on acceptance is but one of several attitudinal factors that emphasize psychological integrity and developing a capacity to openly and skillfully face challenging circumstances. Being rather than doing not only resonates with the theme of acceptance, but further articulates the importance of taking restorative time for reflection in the midst of personal conflict and turmoil. "Not knowing" is a way of encouraging skillful consideration of the many factors that come into play in the course of making informed decisions about one's life course. Being open to new ways of seeing things and being willing to change a predetermined course of action in the face of new evidence are both manifestations of this idea.

This perspective, now widely endorsed in contemporary psychotherapy, initially ran counter to prevailing behavioral and cognitive-behavioral strategies, which focused almost exclusively on techniques to change behavior patterns. How could so startling an emphasis on acceptance, "non-doing," and "not knowing" come to serve any useful function in the context of Western medical care, or even Western society for that matter? There are several plausible explanations. First, MBSR evolved at least in part as a response to the needs of patients who posed significant challenges to traditional medical practitioners, despite being recipients of first-rate, sophisticated medical care. It offered a form of complementary care that addressed psychological—as well as medical—needs of patients. It advocated a holistic view of healing and health to balance biomedical reductionism, with its emphasis on curing disease. Second, MBSR offered guidelines for living beyond the curative impact of medical care. Participants were encouraged to make lifestyle changes to help manage the inevitable stress of medical and other challenges of daily life. At the program's conclusion, for example, the "next session" is characterized as "the remainder of one's life." Third, the program mandated structured, day-to-day practices to help overcome behavioral passivity common in medical care settings. Expectations of daily practice were reinforced by the interesting phrase "You don't have to like it; you just have to *do* it!" The expectation was that participants who commit to the program would engage in a systematic process of behavior change whose benefits would only unfold over time, requiring a willingness to suspend final judgment as to its efficacy. Fourth, and perhaps most importantly, program participants were encouraged to take an active role in their overall state of health and wellness, a broad contextual framework that encompassed and extended beyond their particular medical condition.

## CLINICAL DESCRIPTION

George and Mary are a delightful couple in their mid- to late 60s who completed an eight-week MBSR program. George was diagnosed with Parkinson's disease several years earlier, and Mary reported what she described as "OCD-type" symptoms over the years. Both reported mild to moderate day-to-day stress in their lives, stemming from these and other sources. They were referred to the program by a neurology clinic to participate in an MBSR study, and were interested in knowing if participation in the MBSR program would further refine their coping skills. Both were exceptionally committed to the program, keeping detailed logs of time spent doing the body scan, Hatha Yoga, and sitting meditation, and completing a variety of weekly stress management home practice assignments.

The traditional eight-week MBSR program described earlier was employed with three replicated groups of dyads comprised of medical patients with Parkinson's disease and spouses or caregivers. Program sessions and home practice emphasized the body scan, Hatha Yoga (specifically adapted for this study), and sitting meditation. Eight weekly two-hour sessions were structured to include sitting meditation, weekly home practice reviews, didactic material, and extensive in-session coaching for the three formal mindfulness practices. Yoga poses were adjusted for individual needs. Intense discussions characterized most sessions. For example, the "caregiver" designation elicited critical commentary, for as pointed out by virtually all couples, caregiving involved a reciprocal commitment rather than being the unique responsibility of either individual. In fact, some caregivers were facing health challenges as daunting as Parkinson's disease, a fact that emphasized the inevitability of challenges to health and well-being.

Many couples, including Mary and George, practiced together, and in general found this to be a satisfying experience that strongly reinforced ongoing participation. Overarching concern with long-term progression of Parkinson's disease was evident periodically, though there was a tendency to downplay this by virtue of effective medication-based symptom management and frequent expressions of hope for a lasting cure. It was clear to everyone that, while the MBSR program was helpful in managing present-oriented stressors, it did not offer a cure.

By the program's end, Mary was less distressed about her OCD symptoms, which actually decreased significantly, along with her reported stress level. Both she and George reported coping with stress somewhat better than before. George reported being more aware of the importance of stress management in conjunction with his medical care to help manage the experience of Parkinson's disease. He also reported becoming more aware of his feelings and how they impact others. Mary cited "learning to live in the moment more often" as a lasting benefit of the program, along with learning to be more aware of how feelings and emotions can alter the perception of day-to-day circumstances. At the time of our last contact, both were continuing the mindfulness practice, using a combination of breath awareness, the body scan, and Yoga.

Mary and George's experience with the MBSR program is noteworthy in several respects. First, it illustrates the potential value of having a spouse or partner in the program, in terms of social support and an element of accountability. Second, a willingness to share personal experiences and feelings with each other and other group members brought depth and substance to weekly sessions, which included lively discussions of facing stressful life events. Third, as is true for many MBSR program participants, the apparent value of the program for Mary and George centered on developing awareness and living in the moment as effective means of facing stressful life circumstances, one day at a time. Acceptance of mindfulness as an ongoing process, rather than an anticipated goal, lies at the art of the practice (Kabat-Zinn, Massion, Herbert, and Rosenbaum, 1998).

## THEORETICALLY DISTINCT FEATURES OF MBSR

MBSR occupies a theoretical position that is distinct from CBT-based psychotherapy models by virtue of its emphasis on stress management and medical conditions, as opposed to treatment of specific psychological disorders. In an early paper, Kabat-Zinn et al. (1992) summarized contrasting features of MBSR and CBT as practiced at the time, providing a useful perspective from which to view subsequent evolutionary shifts in the latter. Identifying thoughts as "just thoughts" as opposed to "dysfunctional" is the first point of contrast, one that implies more of an emphasis on cognitive *processes* (MBSR) than *content* (CBT). Second, MBSR provides a framework for daily practice independent of emotional distress. Program instructors emphasize "living" as opposed to "coping" as a blueprint for lifestyle change. Third, heterogeneous group composition in MBSR contrasts markedly with the traditional psychotherapeutic focus on specific disorders. Fourth, controlled exposure to distressful stimuli—a mainstay of traditional CBT—is bypassed in favor of simply learning to attend openly to the contents of consciousness that arise without making any effort to evoke or otherwise control them. Finally, concentration and mindfulness are specifically cultivated as tools to explore inner experience, in contrast to the more externally oriented, data-gathering approach of CBT. It is interesting to note how the contrast between these perspectives has diminished dramatically in recent years, attesting to the influence of mindfulness and acceptance on contemporary formulations of CBT, beginning with mindfulness-based cognitive therapy (MBCT). Teasdale, et al. (1995) first proposed this integration of CBT and mindfulness (originally referred to as *attention control training*) to reduce depression relapse, then followed this with a supportive study (Teasdale, Segal, Williams, Ridgeway, Soulsby, & Lau, 2000) and subsequent replication (Ma & Teasdale, 2004). Mindfulness-based cognitive therapy makes extensive use of MBSR concepts and practices, grounded in nonjudgmental awareness and present-moment attention. Mindfulness is increasingly merging with CBT-oriented individualized psychotherapy for anxiety (Orsillo & Roemer, 2005), and other clinical conditions (Roemer & Orsillo, 2008; Didonna, 2009).

Underscoring this evolution is Barlow's commentary on Hayes, Follett, and Linehan's *Mindfulness and Acceptance* (2004) text, in which he states, "One of the most important treatment developments in recent years has been the theoretical and empirical elaboration of mindfulness and acceptance into evidence-based, cognitive-behavioral protocols" (Barlow, 2004). Hayes (2004) views this development as a third wave in the evolution of psychotherapy, by behavioral and cognitive formulations.

As originally formulated (Kabat-Zinn, 1990), MBSR is based on the transactional model of stress and coping (Lazarus & Folkman, 1984), consistent with its focus as a stress reduction program. According to this model, chronic stress (perceived inadequate resources to cope with challenging circumstances) unleashes a cascade of physiological and psychological reactions over time; if unchecked or left unaddressed, these reactions can eventually result in disregulation of key biological parameters (such as sleep, blood pressure, and autonomic activation), maladaptive coping (overwork, substance abuse), and eventual breakdown in the form of exhaustion, depression, and systemic disease (Everly & Lating, 2002). Mindfulness hypothetically breaks this cycle of stress reactivity and disregulation through the cultivation of conscious awareness to de-automate the process, thereby creating the opportunity for more deliberate, skillful responses in place of nonconscious, habitual reactions. Later in this chapter, we propose a variant of this model to provide a means of generating testable hypotheses concerning mechanisms by which MBSR may operate.

## NATURE AND VALUE OF DIRECT COGNITIVE CHANGE STRATEGIES

Both the terminology and the underlying logic of MBSR tend to be somewhat distinct from traditional CBT. For one thing, there is less emphasis on change in MBSR, particularly rapid, short-term change. A key element of MBSR practice is cultivating a capacity for sustained awareness of mental phenomena, predominantly in the context of sitting meditation, which occupies a significant amount of practice both within and outside program sessions. Sitting meditation is the quintessential means of "watching the mind" by quieting the body. It is fundamental to the "consciousness disciplines" described by Walsh (1980) that emphasize the challenges inherent in developing sensitive awareness to the nuances of inner life. Sitting quietly and directing attention systematically to various experiential elements (the breath, sensations, thoughts) is probably the most direct and powerful means of acquiring what in the context of CBT is termed "metacognitive awareness" or "distancing." There are important historical antecedents to this emphasis as well, predating the cognitive behavioral perspective. For example, Deikman (1982) described the "observing self" as a means to insight and understanding from a broad-based psychotherapeutic perspective. In the more narrowly psychotherapeutic context, Safran and Segal (1990) discussed "decentering" as a means of establishing and maintaining a grounded foundation for exploration of interpersonal relationships. From a more behavioral perspective, Goleman (1990) described sustained observation of thoughts and other internal events in a quiet setting with minimal physical activity as a way of "defusing" cognitive, affective, or somatic reactivity in a manner analogous to reciprocal inhibition or self-desensitization. These viewpoints, basically contemporaneous with the evolution of MBSR, suggest broad-based interest in refined self-observation as an agent of both acceptance and change.

## SIGNIFICANCE OF METACOGNITIVE AWARENESS, DISTANCING, OR COGNITIVE DEFUSION

*Metacognitive awareness, defusion,* and *decentering* are terms from the lexicon of psychotherapy, not MBSR. They reflect adaptations of the foundation of MBSR: sustained, nonjudgmental awareness in the field of consciousness. Individual practitioners of

MBSR are to a significant extent on their own in this regard, coming face-to-face with their inner experience despite the group practice format. However, it is in fact empowering to be with others while completely silent, a shared experience that is fundamental to the concept of *sangha*, a community of like-minded individuals. Ordinarily, group settings in psychotherapeutic contexts serve the purpose of *enhancing* interactions among members, but in the context of MBSR considerable time is devoted to shared silence and personal reflection. Although phrases such as "metacognitive awareness" and "cognitive distancing" are not really part of MBSR vernacular, they are fundamentally compatible with the practice. However, both terms may imply a sort of psychological detachment from one's experience that some might equate to emotionless objectivity. A more accurate way of characterizing the underlying idea in a way that is consistent with the concept of mindfulness from the perspective of MBSR is that there is a sense of clarity in the way with which one in engaged in the world that makes it possible to be aware of, rather than driven by, conditioned patterns of cognitive, emotional, and behavioral reactivity.

The group format of MBSR provides an ideal context for contemplative practice. Sitting quietly with a group of practitioners is an extraordinary experience, evoking a powerful sense of nonverbal engagement. This atmosphere is very difficult to recreate in the context of traditional one-on-one psychotherapy, because most of what transpires is verbally mediated and driven by pragmatic problem-solving agendas. Many therapists are unaccustomed to periods of silence, as are their patients, who in our society and culture are conditioned to expect authoritative assistance from helping professionals.

## COGNITIVE MODIFICATION STRATEGIES AND METACOGNITIVE AWARENESS

Fundamentally, MBSR does not actively teach cognitive modification strategies, at least not in the traditional sense of the term. The idea of modifying dysfunctional cognitions as a means of attaining metacognitive awareness would be considered foreign to MBSR-based practices for several reasons. First, there is really no particular effort made to modify cognitions, dysfunctional or otherwise. Rather, the intention of practice is enhanced *awareness* of cognitions and their patterns of occurrence, rather than their content or nature. Related to this, the idea of labeling cognitions as "dysfunctional" goes against the grain of the nonjudgmental attitude that one strives to cultivate in mindfulness practice.

Rather than using cognitive modification strategies to cultivate metacognitive awareness, the approach adopted in the MBSR program is to develop a capacity for sustained directed attention through formal meditation practice, initially focused on the breath, a tangible, phasic phenomenon immediately accessible as a focal point of attention. Subsequently, attention is systematically directed toward other physical sensations emanating from either internal (i.e., proprioceptive) or external sources as a way of further cultivating a capacity for flexibly allocated, sustained attention. Only after substantial practice observing tangible inner or outer sensations does one begin to use this acquired capacity to direct attention to thoughts and other objects of consciousness. Metacognitive awareness represents but one of several manifestations of this expanded awareness beginning with heightened sensitivity to sensory phenomena.

It is also worth pointing out that the concept of achievement or goal attainment— whether of metacognitive awareness or anything else—is de-emphasized in MBSR in favor of the slightly different concept of *intention*, which implies orienting oneself in a particular psychological direction without being excessively attached to any particular outcome.

## NECESSITY OF COGNITIVE CHANGE STRATEGIES

MBSR employs a balance of "acceptance" and "change" strategies, an idea that is explicitly developed by Linehan in dialectic behavior therapy (DBT). The concept of acceptance is clearly embodied in formal program elements, including the body scan, Hatha Yoga, and sitting meditation, because in each instance emphasis is on paying attention or noticing experiences as they emerge in awareness. In an interesting and somewhat paradoxical way, the emphasis on allowing things to simply "be as they are" may itself reflect change, in the form of a shift in perspective away from culturally goal-driven emphasis on achieving desirable and anticipated outcomes, such as relaxation, flexibility, or equanimity. By de-emphasizing pursuit of future goals, and focusing more on present-moment reality, there can be a palpable reduction in effortful striving that may ironically result in the attainment of what it is the individual has been seeking.

For example, people often practice Yoga with a goal of increasing flexibility. Making "becoming flexible" a goal engenders a sense of striving toward an outcome that is different from present-moment reality. Striving in turn tends to promote tension related to perception of the discrepancy between current and desired states, leading one to try harder to move into a particular pose. However, by giving up the promise of future flexibility and simply focusing on present-moment reality, the practitioner may also be able to physically "let go" and discover a state of physical release that was potentially always available, but obscured by effortful striving to attain that very state.

The word "change" is very interesting from the perspective of MBSR. In psychotherapy, we constantly talk about helping patients change and about facilitating change through therapeutic efforts, making "change" seem like a daunting, formidable task. Freud characterized the challenges inherent in changing as the "neurotic paradox": Why do people in the throes of neurotic misery seem incapable of changing? In reality, change is inevitable, a principle not only common in Buddhist philosophy but Western psychology as well: "Welcome or not, change is unavoidable. Life itself is change.... Each moment is different from every other. Nothing remains static for an instant, from a planetary to a molecular level" (Prochaska, Norcross, & DiClemente, 1994, p. 13).

## MINDFULNESS, MBSR, AND THE CONCEPT OF PSYCHOPATHOLOGY

We have already stated that MBSR is not really based on a theory of psychopathology, which lies more within the domain of traditional clinical diagnosis and psychotherapy. Historically, the roots of *mindfulness* in Buddhist philosophy place it outside the realm of the Western clinical practice, which is based on medically oriented diagnostic criteria for psychological disorders and corresponding specific interventions. Accordingly, mindfulness is not a dedicated technique, intended to relieve symptoms of depression, anxiety, or stress. Rather, it is widely described as a nonconceptual, observational process applicable to all aspects of life. For example, Gunaratana (1991) described mindfulness using three functional definitions: "(a) ... reminding us of what we are supposed to be doing; (b) seeing things as they really are; and (c) It sees the true nature of all phenomena" (p. 154). In Buddhist philosophy, mindfulness is but one of several means (*the eight-fold path*) leading to the eradication of suffering. The idea of "being mindful" is simply being open to the experience of everyday life, facing whatever comes along with minimal preconceptions or future expectations, as conveyed in Rumi's poem, *The Guest House*:

> This being human is a guest house
> Every morning a new arrival.
> A joy, a depression, a meanness,
> some momentary awareness comes
> as an unexpected visitor.
> Welcome and entertain them all ...
>
> —(Barks, 1994)

As originally conceived, the MBSR program did not place particular significance on medical or psychiatric diagnoses when evaluating referrals, other than excluding applicants with debilitating psychological conditions (psychosis, profound depression) that limited their capacity for engaged participation. The common thread drawing participants together was the shared experience of *suffering* for which they were seeking relief. There is an inviting correspondence between *suffering* as conceived of in Buddhist philosophy and the Western concept of *stress*. Both refer to a generalized, unpleasant state of being from which we seek relief, and both reflect a conviction that present circumstances are not how we expect them to be or wish they were. As previously noted, the effect of either prolonged stress or suffering can be to engender feelings of *demoralization*, the term used by J. D. Frank and Frank (1991) to characterize a global state of passivity and resignation. At the core of suffering is wanting things to somehow be different from the way we find them, whereas the essence of stress, as characterized by the influential transactional model of Lazarus and Folkman (1984), is feeling incapable of coping with circumstances as we find them. The sense of dissatisfaction common to both is striking and provides an inviting point of entry for cultivating *mindfulness*, with its emphasis on acceptance of present-moment reality. Focusing attention in this manner helps limit the scope of consciousness and limits the amount of cognitive "baggage"—ruminative, conjectural, often obsessive nonproductive thinking—that can easily segue into dystonic states of stress, anxiety, and depression, as noted by Borkovec (2002) and others. Paradoxically, positive changes seem especially likely to occur when one is able to give up the struggle of trying to change. This perspective lies at the core of recent empirically validated acceptance-based intervention models (Hayes, 2004; Linehan, 1993).

## TREATMENT OUTCOME STUDIES

Research on the effects of MBSR continues to grow rapidly, especially following the call by Bishop (2002) for greater conceptual and empirical development to supplant observational studies conducted during the early years of MBSR. Reviews of MBSR outcome studies include those by Salmon et al. (2004), meta-analyses by Baer (2003), Grossman, Niemann, Schmidt, and Walach (2004), Chiesa and Serretti (2009), Ledesma and Kumano (2009), and a theoretical and empirical review by Brown, Ryan, and Creswell (2007). Studies in these reviews were based on a wide range of target populations, including health care professionals, inner-city populations, prison populations, medical patients, psychiatric patients, and anxious patients, with males and non-whites somewhat underrepresented. Earlier studies focused on MBSR in its original context as a stress management program for various medical conditions, notable exceptions being studies by Kabat-Zinn and colleagues (1992), targeting anxiety and panic disorder, and Teasdale, Moore, Hayhurst, Pope, Williams, and Segal (2001), focusing on depression relapse. Overall, moderate effect sizes for MBSR on stress and related mental health measures were consistently reported: d=.54 (Grossman et al., 2004), d=.59 (Baer, 2003), and d=.48 (Ledesma & Kumano, 2009).

The consensus of these reviews is that MBSR shows promise as a clinical intervention, but more rigorous research methodology incorporating randomized control trials, larger sample sizes, long-term follow-up, and comparisons with other interventions is needed. Regarding the latter, randomized trials to date have employed primarily no-treatment, usual-treatment, or wait-list control groups. As a result, these studies are limited in their ability to account for primary MBSR effects due to lack of control for nonspecific factors (Baer, 2003; Chiesa & Serretti, 2009; Grossman et al., 2004). Given the distinctive "clinic within a course" format of MBSR, it is understandable why there are few suitable alternative interventions with which to compare it. However, Chiesa and Serretti (2009) did report one cohort-control study in which an MBSR course for mental health caregivers had a highly significant and beneficial effect on stress and well-being, compared to a didactic control condition matched for time commitment, instructor contact, and group delivery modality (Shapiro, Brown, & Biegel, 2007).

The broad range of medical and health conditions for which MBSR has been found to be helpful has led to debate as to the nature of its impact, which is clearly not disease-specific. This is clear enough, given that clinically (as opposed to research) based MBSR program groups are heterogeneous in composition. In fact, heterogeneity is a fundamental element of the program as originally conceived. The intended purpose is to emphasize the breadth of human suffering and resourcefulness of program participants, who are drawn from all walks of life, including medical patients and hospital personnel. Whatever the effect of participant heterogeneity on program outcome may be, it has not been evaluated in research to date, which has focused on MBSR for specific populations. Rapidly advancing research has produced strong evidence of MBSR benefits for diverse patient groups (Grossman et al., 2004), including chronic pain (Pradhan et al., 2007; Morone, Greco, and Weiner, 2008), and recurrent depression (Kuyken, et al., 2008).

Thus far, MBSR has yet to be the focus of deconstruction research, evaluating the relative contribution of program elements to the overall impact of the program as a whole. However, two key elements of MBSR—meditation and Yoga—have a long history of research-based application in the stress reduction literature (Benson, 1975; Lehrer & Carrington, 2002; Khalsa, 2004). It is noteworthy that the most recent revision of an authoritative, empirically based guide to clinical stress management now includes a section on Eastern meditation and therapeutic disciplines (Lerhrer, Woolfolk, & Sime, 2007).

The generally favorable convergence of MBSR research findings across a wide range of medical and related psychological conditions is certainly noteworthy, but at this juncture, as with any multicomponent intervention, it is difficult to determine what specific elements account for the program's effectiveness. In the hands of skilled practitioners, MBSR incorporates a range of beneficial factors common to most forms of psychotherapy (Hubble, Duncan, & Miller, 1999), including: (a) expectancy factors, (b) patient/extratherapeutic factors, (c) positive relationship factors, and (d) specific techniques. Although we stated earlier that MBSR is not, strictly speaking, a form of psychotherapy, it is certainly true that experienced instructors are psychologically sophisticated and bring a high level of expertise and sensitivity to their work. In this regard, one could make a fairly convincing case that MBSR shares features with psychotherapy that have proven effective in treating a wide range of symptoms of distress. As noted, individual studies assessing the impact of MBSR on anxiety and panic (Kabat-Zinn, 1992), as well as depression relapse (Teasdale, et al., 2001) attest to its flexibility in addressing psychological distress across different diagnostic categories.

Another perspective is to consider common aspects of psychopathology and then determine the degree to which they are addressed in MBSR intervention elements. Harvey, Watkins, Mansell, and Shafran (2004) provide a useful framework in this regard, referred to as a "transdiagnostic approach" to cognitive behavioral interventions. The foundation of the transdiagnostic model rests on evidence of high rates of co-morbidity across psychological diagnostic categories, and the comparative rarity of "pure" unitary diagnoses, which collectively suggest common underlying mechanisms across disorders. Of the five hypothesized common processes discussed by Harvey et al. (2004), *attention* is clearly the most relevant for MBSR, in terms of both self-focused and selective aspects. Baer (2007) notes that the widespread effects of mindfulness enhancing interventions may in part be due to their impact on attention control problems evident in a broad range of clinical conditions.

However, as Harvey et al. (2004) note, although attention is a key aspect of mindfulness and shows considerable promise as an outcome variable, empirical research is at only a very early stage. *Attention* is one of three key variables in the conceptual model of mindfulness (along with *attitude* and *intention*) proposed by Shapiro, Carlson, Astin, and Freedman (2006), who further subdivide it into several components amenable to empirical investigation. These include sustained attention (*vigilance*), being able to shift attention from one focal point to another, and the capacity to limit cognitive elaborations that tend to blossom once the seed of attention is focused (or "planted") on a specific object of awareness. Posner and Peterson (1990) underscore the adaptive significance of attention by noting the existence of both dedicated and network anatomical loci mediating specific functions amenable to experimental research. This working model has stimulated subsequent neurocognitive research on attentional networks with increasing clinical relevance (Raz & Buhle, 2006). A study by Jha, Krompinger, and Baime (2007) compared participants in two mindfulness programs with a non-meditation control group on laboratory measures of alerting, orienting, and conflict monitoring (task prioritizing) attention components. Participants in one group had no prior meditation experience and received the standard eight-week MBSR training program. Those in the second group were experienced meditators who participated in a one-month intensive mindfulness retreat. Control subjects neither had meditation experience nor received any training during the study. Retreat participants, adept at conflict monitoring to begin with, showed improved performance in alerting, compared to controls and MBSR participants. And the standard MBSR group enhanced both orienting and conflict monitoring performance.

With respect to MBSR as an intervention for diagnostically-specific clinical conditions, such as stress, anxiety, or depression, research is needed to establish its efficacy compared to other treatment modalities. According to a recent review by Lehrer and Woolfolk (2007), MBSR has yet to be compared to other stress management protocols such as relaxation training, biofeedback, non-MBSR meditation, or CBT-based protocols. Clearly the time has come to rectify this shortcoming in the research literature. For one thing, .it is important to avoid the indiscriminate application of the program with individuals or populations for whom it is not well suited (Kocovski, Segal, & Battista, 2009), such as those with severely debilitating psychological disorders (e.g., refractory depression, suicidality, untreated psychosis, etc.). For another, the importance of developing clinical "best practice" guidelines is a clear incentive to compare the efficacy of MBSR with other interventions for specific clinical groups.

We end this section with mention of burgeoning research on neurobiological functions, which is of particular relevance for MBSR because of its focus on stress management. Drawing on a wide array of measures, Treadway and Lazar (2009) provide a useful summary of these studies, which provide evidence of four significant clinical outcomes: (a) increased "in the moment" experience, (b) enhanced positive affect, (c) lower stress reactivity, and (d) cognitive vitality. In the future, it is anticipated that mindfulness research will increasingly incorporate the neurobiological assessment domain, along with ubiquitous self-report measures currently utilized.

## MINDFULNESS: MECHANISMS AND PROCESSES

Several authors have offered thoughtful conceptualizations of mechanisms by which mindfulness reduces stress (Kocovski, Segal, & Battista, 2009). Such models are helpful reference points in the current debate about whether or not mindfulness really represents a new intervention approach (Hofmann & Asmundson, 2008). Currently, metacognitive decentering—a capacity for observation of, and non-attachment to, ongoing cognitive activity—is the most prominent explanatory model (Hayes, Strosahl, and Wilson, 1999; Teasdale, 1999; Teasdale, Segal, & Williams, 1995). Shapiro, Carlson, Astin, and Freedman (2006) developed a metacognitive model hypothesizing that the beneficial effects of mindfulness result from reciprocal, ongoing interactions among (a) an established *intention* for engaging in the practice, (b) systematic *attention* to moment-by-moment experience, and (c) an attitudinal framework marked by acceptance and self-compassion. The effect of this is a perspective shift termed *reperceiving*, analogous to decentering, by which one's attachment to cognitive activity gradually diminishes. Reperceiving, in this model is further predicted to mediate changes in four mechanisms hypothesized to reduce psychological distress: self-regulation, values clarification, psychological flexibility, and openness to inner experience.

Recently, Carmody, Baer, Lykins, and Olendzki (2009) empirically tested Shapiro, Carlson, Astin, and Freedman's (2006) conceptual model using self-report measures from 309 participants in MBSR programs at the University of Massachusetts CFM. Subscales of the Five-Facet Mindfulness Questionnaire (Baer, Smith, Hopkins, Kreitemeier, & Toney, 2006) assessed mindfulness, attitude, and attention. Intention was determined by self-rated reasons for participating in the program at entry, and the Experiences Questionnaire (Fresco, Segal, Buis, & Kennedy, 2007) evaluated reperceiving/decentering. Mindfulness, reperceiving/decentering, and the four distress-reducing variables all showed positive changes pre- to post-treatment, along with reduced psychological distress. However, evidence for the predicted mediating role of reperceiving was weak, and of the four proposed change mechanisms, only psychological flexibility and values clarification significantly impacted distress.

A second way to conceptualize how mindfulness works, originally proposed by Kabat-Zinn (1990), is based on the transactional model of stress initially proposed by Lazarus and Folkman (1984). According to this model, mindfulness de-automates habitual patterns of stress reactivity by (a) increasing sensitivity to physiological activation cues and (b) enhancing stress appraisal processes. Both of these contribute to improved coping and can help reduce the negative effects of long-term, chronic stress by fostering a capacity to *respond*, rather than *react*, to potentially stressful events (Kabat-Zinn, 1990). In this model, potentially stressful events trigger an immediate ("primary") appraisal that is physiologically based, followed by a cognitively mediated ("secondary") assessment that balances the perception of threat or risk

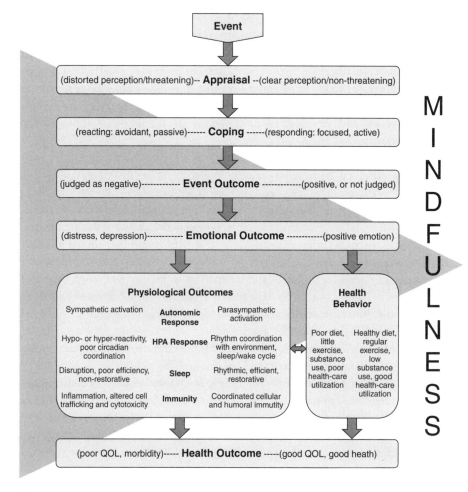

**Figure 6.1**   Stress-Reducing Aspects of MBSR: Adaptation of the Transactional Model of Stress and Coping (Lazarus & Folkman, 1984)

against perceived resources. In an empirically documented paper, Garland, Gaylord, and Park (2009) propose that mindfulness enhances the secondary appraisal process by fostering an openly receptive stance toward challenging circumstances.

An updated version of the transactional model that integrates elements of Lazarus and Folkman (1984), Kabat-Zinn (1990), and Garland, Gaylord, and Park (2009) has been developed by the present authors and is currently undergoing empirical testing (Figure 6.1). It illustrates how stress reactivity and coping patterns can be influenced by mindfulness, using constructs that lend themselves well to empirical testing. From this perspective, mindfulness functions by fostering heightened awareness of, and skillful responses to, potential stressors that otherwise elicit nonconscious, habitual reactions having adverse long-term consequences for health.

Referring to this figure, we hypothesize that mindfulness practice will promote movement from left to right on key components of the model; for example, from passive, avoidant, or reactive coping methods to active, focused, responsive management of difficult events. The model further proposes that the impact of mindfulness is especially relevant in present-moment circumstances that may have implications for future health-related outcomes. The capacity for accurate perception and appraisal, along with skillful responses to challenging circumstances of daily life, should reduce the incidence of habitual stress reactivity.

Although not depicted in the figure, we suggest that there are both direct and indirect effects of mindfulness on appraisal, coping, positive and negative mood, as well as on physiological stress responses. For example, simply focusing on the breath may result in a slower breathing rate and concomitant state of hypo-arousal (Salmon et al., 2004). In support of this, we recently observed reduced sympathetic activation during meditation (body scan) sessions, as well as over the course of MBSR training, among a cohort of fibromyalgia patients (Lush, Salmon, Floyd, Studts, Weissbecker, & Sephton, 2009). Activation-reducing qualities of both basic meditation techniques and Yoga have also been documented (Raub, 2002; Kristeller, 2007). Thus, formal mindfulness practices, done slowly and deliberately, may reduce physiological activation patterns associated with sympathetic nervous and/or HPA axis arousal.

Although both of these models offer promising directions for clinical research on MBSR, the task of identifying mechanisms that account for its impact is hampered by the rich, multicomponent nature of the program. So far, no studies have "deconstructed" the program in an attempt to isolate specific mechanisms of change. As an alternative to this approach, research efforts are beginning to focus on variables that permit assessment of dose/response effects, such as length of class sessions (Carmody & Baer, 2009) and individual meditation practice time (Carmody & Baer, 2008). These studies reported that formal meditation practice time correlated significantly with symptom improvement, and that home practice increased self-reported mindfulness, which mediated improved well-being and reduced depressive symptoms. Consistent with these results, a recent randomized study of "compassion" meditation by Pace, et al. (2009) reported that home practice time was associated with reduced distress and lower inflammatory response to laboratory stress. Although not all studies report reliable dose-response effects (Carlson, et al., 2003; Davidson, et al., 2003), evidence is beginning to accumulate suggesting that formal mindfulness practice is in fact a key aspect of the program's effectiveness, at least for some participants.

Recent research has focused on specific facets of mindfulness that, over time, will further contribute to an understanding of mechanisms that account for its effects. For example, Kabat-Zinn (1982) first proposed that mindfulness may reduce distress by fostering a capacity to differentiate organic and cognitive/interpretive aspects of pain, and to become less attached to the latter as a means of reducing suffering. Although the original focus of this principle was chronic pain, it has been widely applied to other distressing conditions, including depression (Segal, Williams, & Teasdale, 2002). A recent study of depressed individuals showed increased self-reported mindfulness after MBCT, which was associated with lower cognitive reactivity (activation of negative thinking patterns) in response to sad mood (Raes, Dewulf, Van Herringen, & Williams, 2009).

Mindfulness evidently impacts other capabilities as well, including processing ongoing events as if they are occurring for the first time (i.e., "beginner's mind"), rather than relying on previously conditioned, habitual reactions. A focus on the present moment rather than on rule-governed behavior (Hayes et al., 1999) can potentially "de-automate" such reaction patterns (Kabat-Zinn, 1990), and thereby increase response flexibility. This characteristic is consistent with Langer's research-based view of mindfulness as the capability to treat present circumstances as new and unique experiences that facilitate generating multiple alternative response options (Langer & Moldoveanu, 2000). Consistent with this perspective, a recent study by Levesque and Brown (2007) using the Mindfulness Acceptance and Awareness Scale (MAAS; Brown & Ryan, 2003), found that dispositional mindfulness moderates the negative impact of implicit (i.e., nonconscious, habitual) motivation on day-to-day behavioral autonomy.

Two recent laboratory studies examined this aspect of cognitive flexibility using the Stroop Test, an attention- and memory-intensive cognitive interference task in which subjects read color names printed in different colors (McLeod, 1991; Golden & Freshwater, 2003). Wenk-Sormaz (2005) compared a brief Zen-based breathing meditation session with a concentration task of comparable length in a randomized control study. Participants in the former condition demonstrated significantly reduced interference on the Stroop Test, indicating increased present-moment regulation of normally automated cognitive processes. A follow-up study revealed that a second group of meditation practitioners significantly increased the number of atypical responses on a category production task, further evidence of reduced automatic responding. Moore and Malinowski (2009) compared performance of mindfulness meditation practitioners and non-practitioners on the Stroop Test and reported similar results. Those in the meditation group scored significantly higher on the Kentucky Inventory of Mindfulness Skills (KIMS) and showed greater cognitive flexibility than nonpractitioners.

Overall, cognitive mechanisms appear to account for a significant proportion of beneficial effects attributed to mindfulness. Of these, decentering appears to be paramount, but as suggested above, information-processing aspects of cognition may be operative as well. Such mechanisms presumably underlie the beneficial effects of mindfulness on a range of clinically relevant variables documented in recent research, including self-focused attention and ruminative tendencies (Watkins & Teasdale, 2004), experiential avoidance (Arch and Craske, 2006; Hayes, 2004; Roemer & Orsillo, 2009), and perceived control (Astin, 1997; Kabat-Zinn, 1982).

## FUTURE DIRECTIONS

Several years ago, Dimidjian and Linehan (2003) articulated a systematic agenda for research on clinical mindfulness practice. Among the many questions for research they raised in this discussion, two in particular stand out, as relevant today as they were then: First, what is mindfulness? And second, how does mindfulness work? Concerning the nature of mindfulness, our current understanding of the concept is based largely on questionnaire measures intended to identify key characteristics and derive a widely agreed-upon operational definition, in keeping with traditional Western scientific practice. But as noted by Grossman (2008) and others, mindfulness is an elusive construct, one that is historically unfamiliar to Westerners. Rational science can only go so far in defining mindfulness—a state of being that is widely acknowledged to be largely preconceptual in nature. As recently noted by Shapiro (2009, p. 555), "…we must find ways of translating its nonconceptual, nondual, and paradoxical nature into a language that clinicians, scientists, and scholars can understand and agree on." Current reliance on verbally mediated self-assessment questionnaires limits sampling of mindfulness correlates to a single domain, and, according to Grossman, raises significant concerns about validity as well. We concur with his view that MBSR research should expand the range of outcome domains. This could include, for example, qualitative, interview-based assessments of novice and experienced practitioners. Detailed phenomenological investigations of the elusive "present moment" could be incorporated into mindfulness research, perhaps using the intriguing microanalytic interviewing technique developed by Stern (2004), in which a very brief (approximately five-second) "slice of life" is subjected to detailed exploration. The capacity of MBSR to systematically alter a range of physiological responses should be thoroughly investigated. Immune function, sleep patterns, and autonomic reactivity are examples of assessment domains that are practical to monitor. Current use of imaging technologies like fMRI to study cognitive and even social correlates of mindfulness is of course an especially promising avenue for research (Siegel, 2007; Stein et al., 2008).

The second question posed by Dimidjian and Linehan (2003) concerned the mechanism(s) by which mindfulness interventions operate. We have summarized contemporary responses to this question, and updated the original transactional model on which MBSR was based in this chapter. It is our hope that the current formulation will provide a useful framework for subsequent research. Nonetheless, it is important to remember that trying to uncover "mechanisms" is a characteristically Western approach to discovery that implies the existence of structures or processes that are amenable to empirical discernment and verification. Inherent limitations in this approach may delay true understanding of how mindfulness "works." Nevertheless, there are clear indications that we are further along in this process than was the case when Dimidjian and Linehan first proposed their research agenda.

## EMERGING TRENDS IN MINDFULNESS APPLICATIONS

There appears to be a clear historical and evolutionary progress leading to the incorporation of mindfulness and acceptance in CBT and other contemporary forms of psychotherapy. Hayes (2004) characterized acceptance/mindfulness interventions as a "third wave" of empirically oriented psychotherapy, evolving beyond earlier behavioral and cognitive behavioral intervention models. Several lines of influence and evidence appear to underlie this evolutionary development. First, psychotherapy increasingly focuses on inner experience, rather than merely on overt behavior. Cognitive behavior therapy's early emphasis on mental representations (schemas) and cognitive mediators of behavior and emotions launched this trend. However, its traditional reliance on an information processing, content-oriented focus frankly does not do justice to the richness and complexity of mental life, as noted by Teasdale and Barnard (1995).

Increased integration of MBSR-based and related contemplative practices into CBT will help expand the range of investigative tools available to patients and therapists alike. Second, current clinical practice standards are likely to influence the evolution of MBSR in terms of encouraging use of more dedicated pre- and post-program measures, and ensuring that new instructors are sufficiently skilled at recognizing and working effectively with psychologically challenging conditions that participants may bring to the table. Third, applications of MBSR will evolve beyond the current medical orientation to focus on negative psychological states, such as stress, anxiety, and depression, as well as the broader arenas of health promotion, wellness, and exercise science. New variants of the program, emphasizing health and wellness, will underscore the capability of the program to bring about healthy lifestyle changes that are independent of a medical or clinical context. Current program content related to physical activity (Yoga) and nutrition (mindful eating; see, for example, Kristeller, 1999) could be emphasized from the very outset of the program as a means of fostering healthy lifestyles. MBSR elements are likely to be incorporated into briefer, more flexible interventions. As noted recently by Carmody and Baer (2009), program session time is not significantly related to outcome effect size, suggesting that other elements, perhaps home practice time and quality, may be of greater importance. This opens up the intriguing possibility of developing individually tailored MBSR interventions that are less reliant on the traditional class-based group format.

We have little doubt that MBSR is a viable and vital clinical intervention. Despite its ancient Buddhist origins, it is still a relatively new addition to the Western repertoire of health management practices. Research on MBSR documentation has advanced from early descriptive to randomized controlled studies based on an increasingly diverse range of clinical populations. MBSR has had a substantial, catalytic impact on current CBT practices, along with early pioneering work by Hayes, Linehan, and others (e.g., Hayes, Jacobson, Follette, & Dougher, 1994). The program originated in a major Western medical center where it has flourished over the years, and MBSR practice has moved from the periphery into mainstream contemporary behavioral medical and psychotherapy. MBSR-based clinical research continues to be published at an accelerating pace, with favorable outcomes prevailing, even as the sophistication of research methodology increases.

The central focus of mindfulness—present-moment, nonjudgmental awareness—is simple and direct, having the potential to reach a broad and increasingly diversified range of people. Putting this message into practice in a meaningful way is not a simple undertaking, nor has it been particularly easy to convincingly demonstrate to the satis-faction of the Western scientific community that mindfulness has beneficial effects on stress management and health. But the persistence of the concept in Western medical care and now psychotherapy bodes well for its future. At the same time, it is worth not-ing, consistent with the Buddhist scheme of things, the importance—the inevitability, really—of *not-knowing*. Becoming overly attached to the idea that we can somehow "figure out" mindfulness is a recipe for egotistical frustration. In this regard, it would be well to keep in mind Rosch's (2007, p. 263) remark that "Acknowledging not knowing is what evokes the genuine humbleness prized by every healing and contemplative tradi-tion. It is also the basis of science."

# REFERENCES

Arch, J. J., & Craske, M. G. (2006). Mechanisms of mindfulness: Emotion regulation following a focused breathing induction. *Behavior Research and Therapy, 44*, 1849–1858.

Aronson, H. B. (2004) *Buddhist practice on Western ground: Reconciling Eastern ideals and Western psycho-therapy.* Boston, MA: Shambhala.

Astin, J. A. (1997). Stress reduction through mindfulness meditation. Effects on psychological symptomatol-ogy, sense of control, and spiritual experiences. *Psychotherapy and Psychosomatics, 66*, 97–106.

Baer, R. (2003). Mindfulness training as a clinical intervention: A conceptual and empirical review. *Clinical Psychology Science and Practice, 10*, 125–143.

Baer, R. (2006) *Mindfulness-based treatment approaches: Clinician's guide to evidence base and applications.* New York, NY: Elsevier.

Baer. R. (2007). Mindfulness, assessment, and transdiagnostic processes. *Psychological Inquiry, 18*(4), 238–271.

Baer, R. A., Smith, G. T., Hopkins, J., Kreitmeyer, J., & Toney, L. (2006) Using self-report assessment meth-ods to explore facets of mindfulness. *Assessment, 13*, 27–45.

Bakal, D. (1999) *Minding the body: Clinical uses of somatic awareness.* New York, NY: Guilford Press.

Bankart, C. P. (1997) *Talking cures: A history of Western and Eastern psychotherapies.* New York, NY: Brooks/Cole.

Bankart, C. P. (2003) Five manifestations of the Buddha in the West: A brief history. In K. H. Dockett, G. R. Dudley-Grant, & C. P. Bankart (Eds.), *Psychology and Buddhism: From individual to global community* (pp. 45–69). New York, NY: Kluwer Academic/Plenum.

Bankart, C. P., Dockett, K. H., & Dudley-Grant, G. R. (2003). On the path of the Buddha: A psychologists' guide to the history of Buddhism. In K. H. Dockett, G. R. Dudley-Grant, & C. P. Bankart (Eds.), *Psychol-ogy and Buddhism: From individual to global community* (pp. 13–44). New York, NY: Kluwer Academic/Plenum.

Barks, C. (1994) *Say I am you: Poetry interspersed with stories of Rumi and Shams.* Athens, Georgia: Maypop.

Barlow, D. (2004). Book jacket note, S. C. Hayes, V. M. Follegge, & M. M. Linehan (Eds.), *Mindfulness and acceptance: Expanding the cognitive-behavioral tradition.* New York, NY: Guilford Press.

Benson, H. (1975). *The relaxation response.* New York, NY: William Morrow.

Bishop, S. (2002). What do we really know about mindfulness-based stress reduction? *Psychosomatic Medicine, 64*, 71–84.

Borkovec, T. (2002) Life in the future versus life in the present. *Clinical Psychology Science and Practice, 9*, 75–80.

Brantley, J. (2005). Mindfulness-based stress reduction. In S. M. Orsillo and L. Roemer (Eds.), *Acceptance and mind-fulness-based approaches to anxiety: Conceptualization and treatment* (pp. 131–145). New York, NY: Springer.

Brown, K. W., & Ryan, R. M. (2003) The benefits of being present: Mindfulness and its role in psychological well-being. *Journal of Personality and Social Psychology, 84*(4), 822–848.

Brown, K. W., Ryan, R. M., & Creswell, J. D. (2007). Mindfulness: Theoretical foundations and evidence for its salutary effects. *Psychological Inquiry, 18*(4), 211–237.

Carlson, L. E., Speca, M., Patel, K. D., & Goodey, E. (2003). Mindfulness-based stress reduction in relation to quality of life, mood, symptoms of stress, and immune parameters in breast and prostate cancer outpatients. *Psychosomatic Medicine, 65,* 571–581.

Carmody, J., & Baer, R. A. (2008). Relationships between mindfulness practice and levels of mindfulness, medical and psychological symptoms and well-being in a mindfulness-based stress reduction program. *Journal of Behavioral Medicine, 331,* 23–33.

Carmody, J., & Baer, R. (2009). How long does a mindfulness-based stress reduction program need to be? A review of class contact hours and effect sizes for psychological distress. *Journal of Clinical Psychology, 65*(6), 627–638.

Carmody, J., Baer, R., Lykins, E. L., & Olendzki, N. (2009). An empirical study of the mechanisms of a mindfulness-based stress reduction program. *Journal of Clinical Psychology, 65*(6), 613–626.

Chiesa, A., & Serretti, A. (2009). Mindfulness-based stress reduction for stress management in healthy people: A review and meta-analysis. *Journal of Alternative and Complementary Medicine, 15,* 593–600.

Davidson, R. J., Kabat-Zinn, J., Shumacher, J., Rosenkranz, M., Muller, D., Santorelli, S. F., . . . Sheridan, J. F. (2003). Alterations in brain and immune function produced by mindfulness meditation. *Psychosomatic Medicine, 65,* 564–570.

Deikman, A. J. (1982). *The observing self: Mysticism and psychotherapy.* Boston, MA: Beacon Press.

Didonna, F. (2009). *Clinical handbook of mindfulness.* New York, NY: Springer.

Dimidjian, S., & Linehan, M. M. (2003). Defining an agenda for future research on the clinical application of mindfulness practice. *Clinical Psychology Science and Practice, 10,* 166–171.

Dunn, A. L., Trivedi, M. H., Kampert, J. B., Clark, C. G., & Chambliss, H. O. (2005). Exercise treatment for depression: Efficacy and dose response. *American Journal of Preventive Medicine, 28,* 1–8.

Dutton, G. R. (2008). The role of mindfulness in behavior change. *ACSM's Health and Fitness Journal, 12*(4), 7–12.

Engel, G. (1977). The need for a new medical model: A challenge for biomedicine. *Science, 196*(4286), 833–839.

Epstein, M. (1995). *Thoughts without a thinker: Psychotherapy from a Buddhist perspective.* New York, NY: Basic Books.

Epstein, R. (1999). Mindful practice. *Journal of the American Medical Association, 282*(9), 833–839.

Everly, G. S., & Lating, J. M. (2002). *A clinical guide to the treatment of the human stress response.* New York, NY: Springer.

Frank, J. D., & Frank, J. B. (1991). *Persuasion and healing: A comparative study of psychotherapy.* Baltimore, MD: Johns Hopkins University Press.

Fresco, D., Segal, Z., Buis, T., & Kennedy, S. (2007). Assessing attention control in goal pursuit: A component of dispositional self-regulation. *Journal of Personality Assessment, 86,* 306–317.

Gallagher, W. (2009). *Rapt: Attention and the focused life.* New York, NY: Penguin Press.

Garland, E., Gaylord, S., & Park, J. (2009) The role of mindfulness in positive reappraisal. *Explore (New York), 5*(1), 37–44.

Germer, C. K., Siegel, R. D., & Fulton, P. R. (2005). *Mindfulness and psychotherapy.* New York, NY: Guilford Press.

Golden, C. J., & Freshwater, S. M. (2003). *Stroop color and word test: A manual for clinical and experimental uses.* Wood Dale, IL: Stoelting.

Goleman, D. (1990). The psychology of meditation. In M. G. T. Kwee (Ed.), *Psychotherapy, meditation and health: A cognitive-behavioural perspective* (pp. 19–35). London: East-West Publications.

Grossman, P. (2008). On measuring mindfulness in psychosomatic and psychological research. *Journal of Psychosomatic Research, 64,* 405–408.

Grossman, P., Niemann, L., Schmidt, S., & Walach, H. (2004) Mindfulness-based stress reduction and health benefits: A meta-analysis. *Journal of Psychosomatic Research, 57,* 35–43.

Gunaratana, H. (1991). *Mindfulness in plain English.* Boston, MA: Wisdom Publications.

Harvey, A. G., Watkins, E., Mansell, W., & Shafran, R. (2004) *Cognitive behavioral processes across psychological disorders: A transdiagnostic approach to research and treatment.* New York, NY: Oxford University Press.

Hayes, S. C. (2004). Acceptance and commitment therapy and the new behavior therapies: Mindfulness, acceptance, and relationship. In S. C. Hayes, V. M. Follette, & M. M. Linehan (Eds.), *Mindfulness and acceptance: Expanding the cognitive-behavioral tradition* (pp. 1–29). New York, NY: Guilford Press.

Hayes, S. C., Barnes-Holmes, D., & Roche, B. (2001). *Relational frame theory: A post-Skinnerian account of human language and cognition.* New York, NY: Springer-Verlag.

Hayes, S. C., Follette, V. M., & Linehan, M. M. (2004) *Mindfulness and acceptance: Expanding the cognitive-behavioral tradition.* New York, NY: Guilford Press.

Hayes, S. C., Jacobson, N. S., Follette, V. M., & Dougher, M. J. (Eds.) (1994). *Acceptance and change: Content and context in psychotherapy.* Reno, NV: Context Press.

Hayes, S. C., Strosahl, K. D., & Wilson, K. G. (1999). *Acceptance and commitment therapy: An experiential approach to behavior change.* New York, NY: Guilford Press.

Hofmann, S. G., & Asmundson, G. J. (2008). Acceptance and mindfulness-based therapy: New wave or old hat? *Clinical Psychology Review 28*(1), 1–16.

Hubble, M. A., Duncan, B. L., & Miller, S. D. (Eds.) (1999). *The heart and soul of change: What works in therapy.* Washington, DC: American Psychological Association.

Innes, K. E., Bourguigon, C., & Taylor, G. (2005). Risk indices associated with the insulin resistance syndrome, cardiovascular disease, and possible protection with yoga: A systematic review. *Journal of the American Board of Family Practice, 18,* 491–519.

Jason, L. (1997). *Community building: Values for a sustainable future.* Westport, CT: Praeger.

Jha, A. P., Krompinger, J., & Baime, M. J. (2007). Mindfulness training modifies subsystems of attention. *Cognitive, Affective, and Behavioral Neuroscience, 7*(2), 109–119.

Kabat-Zinn, J. (1982). An outpatient program in behavioral medicine for chronic pain patients based on the practice of mindfulness meditation: Theoretical considerations and preliminary results. *General Hospital Psychiatry, 4,* 33–47.

Kabat-Zinn, J. (1990). *Full catastrophe living: Using the wisdom of your body and mind to face stress, pain, and illness.* New York, NY: Delta.

Kabat-Zinn, J. (1994). *Wherever you go, there you are: Mindfulness meditation in everyday life.* New York, NY: Hyperion.

Kabat-Zinn, J. (2003). Mindfulness-based interventions in context: Past, present and future. *Clinical Psychology: Science and Practice, 10,* 144–156.

Kabat-Zinn, J. (2005). *Coming to our senses: Healing ourselves and the world through mindfulness.* New York, NY: Hyperion.

Kabat-Zinn, J., Massion, A. O., Herbert, J. R., & Rosenbaum, E. (1998). Meditation. In J. C. Holland (Ed.), *Textbook of psycho-oncology,* (pp. 767–779). New York, NY: Oxford University Press.

Kabat-Zinn, J., Massion, A. O., Kristeller, J., Peterson, L. G., Fletcher, K. E., Pbert, L.,...Santorelli, S. F. (1992). Effectiveness of a meditation-based stress reduction program in the treatment of anxiety disorders. *American Journal of Psychiatry, 149*(7), 936–943.

Khalsa, S. B. (2004). Yoga as a therapeutic intervention: A bibliometric analysis of published research studies. *Indian Journal of Physiology and Pharmacology, 48*(3), 269–285.

Kocovski, N. L., Segal, Z. V., and Battista, S. R. (2009). Mindfulness and psychopathology: Problem formulation. In F. DiDonna (Ed.), *Clinical handbook of mindfulness,* (pp. 85–98). New York, NY: Springer.

Kristeller, J. (1999). An exploratory study of a meditation-based intervention for binge-eating disorder. *Journal of Health Psychology, 4*(3), 357–363.

Kristeller, J. (2003). Finding the Buddha/Finding the self: Seeing with the third eye. In S. R. Segal (Ed.), *Encountering Buddhism: Western psychology and Buddhist teachings* (pp. 109–130). Albany: State University of New York Press.

Kristeller, J. (2007). Mindfulness meditation. In P. M. Lehrer, R. L. Woolfolk, & W. E. Sime (Eds.), *Principles and practice of stress management*, 3rd ed. (pp. 393–427).

Kuyken, W., Byford, S., Taylor, R. S., Watkins, E., Holden, E., White, K.,...Teasdale, J. D. (2008). Mindfulness-based cognitive therapy to prevent relapse in recurrent depression. *Journal of Consulting and Clinical Psychology*, 76(6), 966–978.

La Forge, R. (2005). Aligning mind and body: Exploring the disciplines of mindful exercise. *ACSM's Health & Fitness Journal*, 9(5), 7–14.

Langer, E., & Moldoveanu, M. (2000). The construct of mindfulness. *Journal of Social Issues*, 56(1), 1–9.

Lazarus, A. A. (1984). Meditation: The problems of any unimodal technique. In D. H. Shapiro and R. N. Walsh (Eds.), *Meditation: Classic and contemporary perspectives* (pp. 691). New York, NY: Aldine.

Lazarus, R. S. (1984). The trivialization of distress. In J. C. Rosen and L. J. Solomon (Eds.), *Prevention in health psychology*. Lebanon, NH: University Press of New England.

Lazarus, R. S., & Folkman, S. (1984). *Stress, appraisal, and coping*. New York, NY: Springer.

Ledesma D., & Kumano H. (2009). Mindfulness-based stress reduction and cancer: a meta-analysis. *Psycho-Oncology*, 18, 571–579.

Lehrer, P. M., & Carrington, P. (2002). Progressive relaxation, autogenic training, and meditation. In D. Mos, A. McGrady, T. C. Davies, & I. Wickramasekera (Eds.), *Handbook of mind-body medicine for primary care*, (pp. 137–150). Thousand Oaks, CA: Sage.

Lehrer, P. M., & Woolfolk, R. W. (2007). Research on clinical issues in stress management. In P. M. Lehrer, R. W. Woolfolk, & W. E. Sime (Eds.), *Principles and practice of stress management*, 3rd ed. (pp. 703–721). New York, NY: Guilford Press.

Lehrer, P. M., Woolfolk, R. W., & Sime, W. E. (2007). *Principles and practice of stress management*, 3rd ed. New York, NY: Guilford Press.

Levesque, C., & Brown, K. W. (2007). Mindfulness as a moderator of the effect of implicit motivational self-concept on day-to-day behavioral motivation. *Motivation and Emotion*, 31, 284–299.

Linehan, M. (1993). *Cognitive-behavioral treatment of borderline personality disorder*. New York, NY: Guilford Press.

Ludwig, D. S., & Kabat-Zinn, J. (2008). Mindfulness in medicine. *Journal of the American Medical Association*, 300(11), 1350–1352.

Lush, E., Salmon, P., Floyd, A., Studts, J. L., Weissbecker, I., & Sephton, S. (2009). Mindfulness meditation for symptom reduction in fibromyalgia: Psychophysiological correlates. *Journal of Clinical Psychology in Medical Settings*, 16(2), 200–207.

Ma, S. H., & Teasdale, J. D. (2004). Mindfulness-based cognitive therapy for depression: Replication and exploration of differential relapse prevention effects. *Journal of Consulting and Clinical Psychology*, 72, 31–40.

Mahoney, M. (1991). *Human change processes*. New York, NY: Basic Books.

Martinsen, E. W. (2008). Physical activity in the prevention and treatment of anxiety and depression. *Nordic Journal of Psychiatry*, 62 (Suppl.) 47, 25–29.

McLeod, C. M. (1991). Half a century of research on the Stroop effect; An integrative review. *Psychological Bulletin*, 109(2), 163–203.

Meichenbaum, D. (1977) *Cognitive behavior modification: An integrated approach*. New York, NY: Plenum Press.

Moore, A., & Malinowski, P. (2009). Meditation, mindfulness, and cognitive flexibility. *Consciousness and Cognition*, 18, 176–186.

Morone, N. E., Greco, C. M., & Weiner, D. K. (2008). Mindfulness meditation for the treatment of chronic low back pain in older adults: A randomized controlled pilot study. *Pain*, 134(3), 310–319.

Moyers, B. (1993) *Healing and the mind*. New York, NY: Doubleday.

Orsillo, S. M., & Roemer, L. (Eds.) (2005). *Acceptance and mindfulness-based approaches to anxiety: New directions in conceptualization and treatment*. New York, NY: Springer.

Pace, T. W., Negi, L. T., Adame, D. D., Cole, S. P., Sivilli, T. I., Brown, T. D.,...Raison, C. L. (2009). Effect of compassion meditation on neuroendocrine, innate immune and behavioral responses to psychosocial stress. *Psychoneuroendocrinology*, 34(1), 87–98.

Posner, M. I., & Peterson, S. E. (1990). The attention system of the human brain. *Annual Review of Neuroscience, 13,* 25–42.

Pradhan, E. K., Baumgarten, M., Langenberg, P., Handwerger, B., Gilpin, A. K., Magyari, T.,... Berman, B. M. (2007). Effect of mindfulness-based stress reduction in rheumatoid arthritis patients. *Arthritis & Rheumatism 57*(7), 1134–1142.

Prochaska, J. O., Norcross, J. C., & DiClemente, C. C. (1994). *Changing for good: The revolutionary program that explains the six stages of change and teaches you how to free yourself from bad habits.* New York, NY: William Morrow.

Raes, F., Dewulf, D., Van Heeringen, C., & Williams, J. M. G. (2009). Mindfulness and reduced cognitive reactivity to sad mood: Evidence from a correlational study and a non-randomized waiting list controlled study. *Behavior Research and Therapy, 47,* 623–627.

Raub, J. A. (2002). Psychophysiologic effects of Hatha Yoga on musculoskeletal and cardiopulmonary function: A literature review. *Journal of Alternative and Complementary Medicine, 8,* 797–812.

Raz, A., & Buhle, J. (2006). Typologies of attentional networks. *Nature Reviews Neuroscience, 7,* 367–379.

Roemer, L., & Orsillo, S. M. (2008). *Mindfulness- and acceptance-based behavioral therapies.* New York, NY: Guilford Press.

Rosch, E. (2007). More than mindfulness: When you have a tiger by the tail, let it eat you. *Psychological Inquiry, 18,* 258–264.

Ryan, R. M., & Deci, E. L. (2004). Autonomy is no illusion: Self-determination theory and the empirical study of authenticity, awareness, and will. In J. Greenberg, S. L. Koole, & T. Pyszczynski (Eds.), *Handbook of experimental existential psychology* (pp. 449–479). New York, NY: Guilford Press.

Safran, J. D. (Ed.) (2003). *Psychoanalysis and Buddhism: An unfolding dialogue.* Boston, MA: Wisdom Publications.

Safran, J. D., and Segal, Z. V. (1990). *Interpersonal process in cognitive therapy.* New York: Basic Books.

Salmon, P., Sephton, S., Weissbecker, I., Hoover, K., Ulmer, C., & Studts, J. (2004). Mindfulness meditation in clinical practice. *Cognitive and Behavioral Practice, 11*(4), 434–446.

Salmon, P., Lush, E., Jablonski, M., & Sephton, S. (2009a). Yoga and mindfulness: Clinical aspects of an ancient mind/body practice. *Cognitive and Behavioral Practice, 16,* 59–72.

Salmon, P., Santorelli, S. F., Sephton, S. E., & Kabat-Zinn, J. (2009b). Intervention elements promoting adherence to mindfulness-based stress reduction (MBSR) programs in a clinical behavioral medicine setting. In S. A. Shumaker, J. K. Ockene, & K. A. Reikert (Eds.), *The handbook of health behavior change,* 3rd ed. (pp. 271–285). New York, NY: Springer.

Santorelli, S. (1999). *Heal thyself: Lessons on mindfulness in medicine.* New York, NY: Bell Tower.

Segal, S. V., Williams, J. M., & Teasdale, J. D. (2002) *Mindfulness-based cognitive therapy for depression.* New York, NY: Guilford Press.

Shapiro, S. (2009). The integration of mindfulness and psychology. *Journal of Clinical Psychology, 65*(6), 555–560.

Shapiro, S., Brown, K. W., & Biegel, G. (2007). Teaching self-care to caregivers: Effects of mindfulness-based stress reduction on the mental health of therapists in training. *Training and Education in Professional Psychology, 1,* 105–115.

Shapiro, S. L., & Carlson, L. E. (2009). *The art and science of mindfulness: Integrating mindfulness into psychology and the helping professions.* Washington, DC: American Psychological Association.

Shapiro, S. L., Carlson, L. E., Astin, J. A., & Freedman, B. (2006). Mechanisms of mindfulness. *Journal of Clinical Psychology, 62*(3), 373–386.

Shusterman, R. (2008). *Body consciousness: A philosophy of mindfulness and somaesthetics.* New York, NY: Cambridge University Press.

Siegel, D. J. (2007). *The mindful brain: Reflection and attunement in the cultivation of well-being.* New York, NY: W. W. Norton.

Smits, J. A. J., & Otto, M. (2009). *Exercise for mood and anxiety disorders: Therapist guide.* New York, NY: Oxford University Press.

Stein, D. J., Ives-Deliperi, V., & Thomas, K. G. F. (2008). Psychobiology of mindfulness. *CNS Spectrum,* *13*(9), 752–756.

Stern, D. N. (2004). *The present moment in psychotherapy and everyday life.* New York, NY: Norton.

Teasdale, J. D. (1999). Emotional processing, three modes of mind and the prevention of relapse in depression. *Behavior Research and Therapy, 37,* S53–S77.

Teasdale, J. D., & Barnard, P. J. (1995). *Affect, cognition, and change: Re-modelling depressive thought.* East Sussex, UK: Erlbaum.

Teasdale, J. D., Moore, R. G., Hayhurst, H., Pope, M., Williams, S., & Segal, Z. V. (2001). Metacognitive awareness and prevention of relapse in depression: Empirical evidence. *Journal of Consulting and Clinical Psychology, 68,* 615–623.

Teasdale, J. D., Segal, Z., & Williams, J. M. G. (1995). How does cognitive therapy prevent depressive relapse and why should attentional control (mindfulness) training help? *Behavior Research and Therapy, 33*(1), 25–39.

Teasdale, J. D., Segal, Z. V., & Williams, J. M. (2003). Mindfulness training and problem formulation. *Clinical Psychology: Science and Practice, 10,* 157–160.

Teasdale, J. D., Segal, Z. V., Williams, J. M. G., Ridgeway V. A., Soulsby, J. M., & Lau, M. A. (2000). Prevention of relapse/recurrence in major depression by mindfulness-based cognitive therapy. *Journal of Consulting and Clinical Psychology, 68*(4), 615–623.

Treadway, M. T., & Lazar, S. W. (2009). The neurobiology of mindfulness. In F. Didonna (Ed.), *Clinical handbook of mindfulness* (pp. 45–57). New York, NY: Springer.

Walsh, R. (1980). The consciousness disciplines and the behavioral sciences: Questions of comparison and assessment. *American Journal of Psychiatry, 137*(6), 663–673.

Watkins, E., & Teasdale, J. D. (2004). Adaptive and maladaptive self-focus in depression. *Journal of Affective Disorders, 82*(1), 1–8.

Wenk-Sormaz, H. (2005). Meditation can reduce habitual responding. *Alternative Therapies in Health and Medicine, 11,* 42–58.

Williams, M., Teasdale, J., Segal, Z., & Kabat-Zinn, J. (2007). *The mindful way through depression: Freeing yourself from chronic unhappiness.* New York, NY: Guilford Press.

# 7

## Dialectical Behavior Therapy

### CLIVE J. ROBINS AND M. ZACHARY ROSENTHAL

Dialectical behavior therapy (DBT) grew out of Marsha Linehan's attempts in the 1970s and 1980s to apply the standard behavior therapy of that time (e.g., Goldfried & Davison, 1976), which had already demonstrated efficacy with a range of disorders, to chronically suicidal individuals (Linehan, 1987). The assumption was that suicidal behaviors are usually attempts to escape a life perceived to be not worth living, and therefore these individuals needed to develop skills not only to better tolerate emotional distress, but also to create a life that they do view as worth living. Helping patients learn these skills involved direct skills training through instruction, modeling, rehearsal, and coaching, as well as use of principles of reinforcement and exposure. However, these patients with multiple suicide attempts tend to be sensitive to criticism and prone to emotion dysregulation, and a strong focus only on change strategies can lead them to feel that their level of distress is not understood, or even that they are being blamed for their problems. They may respond with anger at the therapist or withdraw from treatment. On the other hand, letting go of an emphasis on change can lead the patient to feel that the therapist is not taking his or her pain seriously, which in turn may generate hopelessness or anger. In either case, the patient may feel invalidated. Research by Swann and his colleagues (e.g., Swann, Stein-Seroussi, & Giesler, 1992) demonstrates that invalidation of an individual's basic self-constructs leads to increased emotional arousal, which in turn leads to cognitive dysregulation and impaired processing of new information. To help these patients, Linehan surmised that validation would have to play an important role in treatment.

Clinical and empirical observations led Linehan to develop a treatment program that focuses not only on helping patients to make changes in their behaviors and environment, but also communicates acceptance of their current state and their environment, and integrates acceptance and change through a dialectical process. As most of the chronically suicidal individuals treated with this approach turned out to meet diagnostic criteria for borderline personality disorder (BPD), the treatment manuals were developed for that disorder (Linehan, 1993a, 1993b).

The first randomized controlled trial (RCT) of DBT (Linehan, et al., 1991) examined its efficacy with outpatient women diagnosed with BPD and recent suicidal and other self-injurious behavior, and reported significantly better outcomes than treatment as usual on treatment retention, rates of suicide attempts, other self-injurious behavior, and hospitalization rates. Subsequent RCTs by other research groups in the United States (Koons et al., 2001) and in the Netherlands (Verheul et al., 2003) also reported efficacy for this population, and Linehan's group have even found it more effective than comparison treatment by BPD experts. Clinical implementation of outpatient DBT programs around the United States and in other parts of the world was stimulated particularly by the publication of Linehan's initial outcome study, and the treatment was subsequently adapted for suicidal adolescents (Miller, Rathus, & Linehan, 2007; Rathus & Miller, 2002), BPD inpatient programs (Barley et al., 1993; Bohus et al., 2004; Swenson, Sanderson, Dulit, & Linehan, 2001), day treatment programs (Simpson et al., 1998), and correctional facilities for adults (McCann, Ball, & Ivanoff, 2000) and adolescents (Trupin, Stewart, Beach, & Boesky, 2002).

Although developed as a treatment for chronically suicidal individuals, many of whom met diagnostic criteria for BPD, DBT has also been shown in two RCTs (Linehan et al., 1999; Linehan et al., 2002) to be effective in treating substance abuse among patients with BPD and co-occurring substance use disorders. The treatment model appears to have even wider applicability, beyond BPD, as there also have been RCTs demonstrating efficacy of DBT adaptations for binge eating disorder (Telch, Agras, & Linehan, 2001), bulimia nervosa (Safer, Telch, & Agras, 2001), depression in the elderly (Lynch, Morse, Mendelson, & Robins, 2003), and bipolar adolescents (Goldstein, Axelson, Birmaher, & Brent, 2007). An uncontrolled pilot study suggests that DBT skills training may have benefit for treatment of adults with attention deficit hyperactivity disorder (Hesslinger et al., 2002). Standard DBT focuses on the individual, but it also has been adapted and researched for couples in which one member is diagnosed with BPD (A. E. Fruzzetti & Fruzzetti, 2003) or in which there is domestic violence (Fruzzetti & Levensky, 2000). Many of these adaptations are described by their originators in a recent volume edited by Dimeff and Koerner (2007). It is likely that other population or context-specific implementations will continue to be developed and investigated. In this chapter, we primarily focus on standard DBT as a treatment for individuals diagnosed with BPD.

Core elements of DBT include (a) a biosocial theory of psychopathology; (b) treatment principles derived from learning theory, social psychology, and other areas of psychological science, as well as from dialectical philosophy; (c) a conceptual framework for stages of treatment and prioritization of treatment targets within each stage; (d) various treatment modes that each address different needs of the patient; and (e) several sets of acceptance strategies, change strategies, and dialectical treatment strategies. We provide an overview of these elements in the following sections.

# MODEL OF PSYCHOPATHOLOGY AND TREATMENT

## DBT Model of Psychopathology: Biosocial Theory

The nine DSM-IV criteria for BPD can be organized into five broad areas:

1. Emotion dysregulation (labile affect and undercontrol or overexpression of anger)
2. Relationship dysregulation (stormy, chaotic relationships and fears of abandonment)
3. Self-dysregulation (lack of sense of identity, emptiness)
4. Behavior dysregulation (suicidal and self-injurious behaviors and other impulsive behaviors)
5. Cognitive dysregulation (transient stress-related paranoia, dissociative, or quasi-psychotic symptoms)

Among these, the conceptualization in DBT is that emotion dysregulation has a central role. According to Linehan's model, the other behavior patterns summarized by the diagnostic label largely can be viewed as either reflecting action urges associated with intense emotions combined with a paucity of emotion regulation skills (e.g., aggressive or overly submissive interpersonal behaviors and cognitive dysregulation), or attempts to regulate emotions (e.g., self-injury, substance use, binging and purging), or the long-term effects of a history of dysregulated emotions and behaviors (e.g., unstable relationships and consequent fears of abandonment, and impaired sense of self). The development and maintenance of BPD criterion behaviors is conceptualized in DBT as resulting from a series of transactions between two components: biological dysfunction of the emotion regulation system and an invalidating environment.

### *Emotion Dysregulation*

DBT proposes that individuals with BPD are biologically vulnerable to experiencing emotions more readily and more intensely than the average person, and have difficulty modulating their intensity. BPD may involve a dysfunction of parts of the central nervous system involved in regulation of emotions. Twin studies suggest a genetic influence on emotion dysregulation specifically (Livesley, Jang, & Vernon, 1998) and on BPD in particular (Torgerson et al., 2000). Other causal factors might include events during fetal development and early life trauma, which can have enduring structural effects on the developing limbic system (Sapolsky, 1996). Linehan's model contends that emotional vulnerability among individuals with BPD is characterized by heightened emotional sensitivity, heightened reactivity, and a delayed recovery following emotional arousal.

### *Invalidating Environment*

In an invalidating environment, individuals' communications about their private experiences frequently are met with responses that suggest these experiences are invalid, faulty, or inappropriate, or that oversimplify the ease of solving problems. Communications of negative emotions may be ignored or punished by others, but extreme communications are taken more seriously. Consequently, the individual may come to self-invalidate; not learn to set appropriate goals; not learn how to accurately label, communicate about, or regulate emotions; and learn instead to inhibit emotional expression or respond to distress with extreme behaviors.

### *Dialectical Transaction of Emotion Dysregulation and Invalidation*

Over time, as the individual's behavior becomes more extreme in attempts to regulate emotion or to communicate distress, he or she increasingly experiences invalidation from the environment, including from the mental health system. His or her responses are likely to be puzzling to others, who may conclude that the person is faking his or her response in order to manipulate a situation, is being entirely unreasonable and "crazy," or is not trying hard enough to control his or her behavior. If this belief is communicated, explicitly or implicitly (invalidation), the sensitive individual is likely to feel even more emotionally vulnerable. Thus, in this transactional model, the individual and those in his or her interpersonal environment continuously influence one another. Over time, the individual comes to experience more pervasive emotion dysregulation, which impairs learning, including learning emotion regulation skills, and he or she comes to rely on emotion regulation strategies such as self-injury and substance use that can be effective in reducing immediate emotional intensity, that negatively reinforce the behavior, but that also have short-term or long-term negative consequences.

## DBT Treatment Model

The most fundamental dialectic observed and attended to in DBT is that of acceptance and change. Treatment strategies in DBT for helping patients to change draw primarily on standard behavioral and cognitive therapy procedures and on principles and findings from research on learning, emotions, social influence and persuasion, and other areas of psychology. Treatment strategies for helping the therapist to convey his or her acceptance of the patient draw primarily on client-centered and emotion-focused therapies. Treatment strategies to help the patient develop greater acceptance of self, of others, and of life in general draw primarily on Zen Buddhist principles and practice. A dialectical stance informs and sustains the balance and integration of acceptance and change strategies.

### *Stages of Treatment and Treatment Targets*

One of the challenges in working with patients with BPD is the sheer number of problems they often present with and the fact that the problem viewed as most urgent by the patient and/or therapist often changes from session to session. A loss of focus and continuity can easily result. DBT is guided by a conceptual model of four stages of treatment and of the prioritizing of problems within a treatment session, particularly in stage 1. The broad stages of treatment include:

1. From behavioral dyscontrol to control
2. From emotional inhibition toward experiencing
3. From problems in living to ordinary happiness and unhappiness
4. From a sense of incompleteness to a sense of freedom and joy

DBT individual therapy sessions are guided by establishing a clear list of therapy targets and arranging these in a hierarchical order of priority that depends on their severity and impact on long-term functioning, rather than only on a short-term sense of urgency. Specifically, in stage 1 treatment, which has been the primary focus of research to date, life-threatening and related behaviors as the highest priority targets, followed by therapy-interfering behaviors of patient or therapist, then quality-of-life interfering behaviors and circumstances, and finally skills development (most of which is addressed in separate skills training mode of the treatment). Prior to beginning treatment, DBT explicitly includes a pretreatment stage, in which therapist and patient reach agreements about the most important treatment targets and the treatment structure, among other things.

## *Treatment Modes*

Comprehensive treatment for patients with BPD needs to address four functions:

1. Help the patient develop new skills
2. Address motivational obstacles to skills use
3. Help the patient generalize what he or she learns to daily life
4. Keep therapists motivated and skilled

In standard outpatient DBT, these four functions are addressed primarily through four modes of treatment: group skills training, individual psychotherapy, telephone coaching, and a therapist consultation team meeting, respectively.

Linehan found that it was extremely difficult for the therapist to focus on long-term skills acquisition in individual therapy because of the need to respond simultaneously to current crises, dysregulated emotions, and recent instances of behavioral dyscontrol. Consequently, she separated these two treatment functions into distinct treatment modes. Skills are taught in four modules: mindfulness, distress tolerance, emotion regulation, and interpersonal effectiveness. In individual therapy, the therapist helps the patient use whatever skills he or she has and is learning to navigate crises more effectively and to reduce problem behaviors. Problems with motivation to use skills are addressed primarily in individual therapy.

Patients are instructed to call their individual therapist for skills coaching (within agreed parameters) when they are in crisis or having difficulty controlling urges to self-injure, drink alcohol, leave work, or other problem behavior. A consultation team that meets regularly is also a required component of DBT, and has the purpose of keeping therapists motivated and providing guidance in conducting the treatment.

## Treatment Strategies

There are four primary sets of DBT strategies, each set including both acceptance-oriented and change-oriented strategies. Core strategies in DBT are validation (acceptance) and problem solving (change). Dialectical strategies present or highlight extreme positions that tend to elicit their antithesis. Communication style strategies include a reciprocal style (acceptance) and an irreverent one (change). Case management strategies include (a) environmental intervention for the patient (acceptance of the current limited capability of the patient), (b) being a consultant to the patient (change in the patient's capability), and (c) making use of a consultation team (balancing both acceptance and change).

## Commitment Strategies

The initial task in treatment is to determine whether there is, or can be, an agreement between patient and therapist on the goals and methods of treatment and the primary targets that will be initially addressed. For patients with suicidal and self-injurious behaviors in particular, there may or may not be strong commitment to work on the behaviors and situations that the therapist views as most problematic, or even to stay alive long enough for treatment to have a chance to be helpful. DBT therefore also includes a set of strategies for eliciting commitment, based on principles supported in research in social psychology, marketing, and motivational interviewing. These include:

1. Evaluating the *pros and cons* of changing and of not changing
2. *Foot-in-the-door* strategies, in which eliciting agreement to a small request increases the probability of subsequent agreement to a larger one
3. *Door-in-the-face* approaches, in which refusal of a large request increases the probability of subsequent agreement to a smaller one
4. *Devil's advocate*, in which the therapist tries to strengthen a weak commitment by noting the difficulty of or obstacles to change
5. *Connecting the present commitment to previous commitments* the patient has made
6. *Highlighting the patient's freedom to choose* whether or not to commit, while acknowledging the consequences of the choice (e.g., the patient may continue to be hospitalized, the therapist can choose not to treat the patient)

## Problem-Solving Strategies

The first step in helping the patient to change a problem behavior is to conduct a behavioral analysis of a particular instance of it. The focus is typically on a recent occurrence of the target behavior, and the analysis attempts to highlight the variables that maintain the behavior through principles of learning. Antecedent consequences are elucidated, and hypotheses are generated and tested about ways to disrupt chains leading to and following problem behavior. A helpful behavioral analysis will point to one or more solutions, and these solutions will be examined for their utility until an optimal solution is evident. To facilitate behavior changes, the therapist uses standard cognitive behavior therapy procedures, which can be usefully classified into four groups

1. *Skills training*, if the patient does not know how to behave more skillfully
2. *Contingency management*, if the patient's maladaptive behavior is being reinforced, or adaptive behavior is being punished or not reinforced
3. *Exposure*, if conditioned emotional reactions to particular stimuli interfere with adaptive behavior
4. *Cognitive modification*, if the patient's beliefs, attitudes, and thoughts interfere with adaptive behavior

Because contingency management and exposure are standard CBT procedures, we do not discuss them further here, except to say that in DBT, therapists particularly attend to the potential reinforcing, extinguishing, or punishing functions of their own behaviors, and that in addition to formal exposures, DBT affords many opportunities for informal exposures (through elicitation of difficult emotions, by mindfulness practice, etc.). As described below, relative to some other CBT approaches, behavioral analyses tend to be conducted in greater detail in DBT.

## Behavioral Analysis

The goal of a behavioral analysis in DBT is to understand the sequence of vulnerability factors, prompting events, thoughts, feelings, action urges, and observable behaviors that led to an instance of a particular problem behavior, as well as the personal, interpersonal, and other consequences that followed it. The first step is to describe the problem behavior objectively, specifically, and nonjudgmentally. An example might be "Friday evening, between 11 and 11.30 P.M., scratched ankles repeatedly with fingernails, enough to draw blood but not requiring stitches." It is helpful next to identify a prompting environmental event. The patient may initially be unable to identify one and, for example, respond with "I always feel suicidal." One useful strategy is to identify the time at which the urge increased. Solutions directed at the prompting event include avoiding such events (stimulus control) or changing them. It is often helpful to identify vulnerability factors that made the prompting event more difficult for the patient to cope with, such as other recent stressors, moods, lack of sleep, or inadequate nutrition. Solutions may then include attempts to reduce such vulnerability factors.

The therapist and patient also identify links in the chain from the prompting event to the problem behavior, which may include thoughts about the event, emotional reactions, subsequent behaviors, and reactions to those behaviors by the patient and others. The greater the number of links identified, the greater the number of potential solutions. Patients may need repeated controlled exposure to the situation to allow their emotional responses to habituate, to change what they tell themselves about the situation, to use interpersonal skills, or to use distress tolerance skills to cope with urges to engage in the problem behavior. The therapist also inquires about consequences of the problem behavior, including changes in the patient's emotions, responses of other people, and environmental changes. This may identify reinforcers that the therapist may be able to remove, and negative consequences that the therapist can highlight.

## *Validation Strategies*

Validation, which is used in DBT to balance problem solving, simply means communicating to the patient that his or her responses make sense, are understood, or are in a sense reasonable. It is important only to validate that which is, in fact, valid. Validation does not mean saying positive things about the patient, certainly if they are not true. Some things always are valid and so always can be validated, such as emotional responses, which are by definition always understandable reactions to a perception or thought, even if the perception or thought itself is not valid. Other things clearly are invalid, such as a belief that all other drivers on the road intend to harm the patient. Many things, however, can be valid in some way but not valid in another. For example, self-injury may regulate a patient's emotions. The behavior, therefore, is valid in terms of a short-term consequence. It makes sense. On the other hand, the behavior probably has various negative consequences and is not effective in helping the patient reach his or her longer-term goals in life. Early in treatment, it may be helpful to validate self-injury in the sense of communicating that it is understandable. This may be unnecessary or undesirable later in treatment. Validation can occur at a number of levels. First, unbiased listening and observing communicates to the patient that he or she is important. Second, accurate reflection communicates to the patient that he or she has been understood. Third, articulating emotions, thoughts, and behavior patterns that the patient has not yet put into words, when accurate, may help the patient to feel deeply understood. Fourth, validation in terms of past learning history or biological dysfunction communicates that, even if a behavior currently is maladaptive, its occurrence nonetheless makes sense. Fifth, validation in terms of the present context or normative functioning lets the patient know that that is how most people would respond in that situation. Finally, radical genuineness on the part of the therapist, who does not treat the patient as overly fragile, validates the patient's capability.

# ROLE OF MINDFULNESS AND ACCEPTANCE STRATEGIES

The underlying dialectic in DBT is that of acceptance and change. As discussed earlier, one manifestation of this dialectic is in the therapist's use of both acceptance-oriented strategies, such as validation, and change-oriented behavioral and cognitive strategies. Here, acceptance refers to behaviors of the therapist that convey acceptance of the patient, reflected in a set of *therapist treatment strategies*. Acceptance *by* the patient also is central to DBT as a set of *patient target behaviors*. Patients with BPD typically have great difficulty tolerating difficult situations and associated emotional distress, and often are harshly judgmental and non-accepting of themselves and/or other people. The life circumstances of BPD patients often are painful and difficult or impossible to change, as they are at times for us all. We cannot change the past. Moreover, some aspects of our current situation may not be immediately changeable, or the costs of changing may be too high. Acceptance can be helpful because it reduces suffering that results from continually telling oneself that the situation should not be the way it nonetheless is. Lack of acceptance can even stand in the way of change. For example, strong self-blame and guilt over self-injury, substance abuse, or binge eating do not usually lead to positive change, and may even lead to further problem behaviors such as self-punishment. DBT therefore includes both specific therapist treatment strategies and a set of skills for both patients and therapists to learn and practice to help them develop greater acceptance of self, of others, and of life in general.

Many of these skills and treatment strategies have roots in Buddhist principles and mindfulness meditation practices (e.g., Aitken, 1982; Hahn, 1976), as described further in Robins (2002) and Robins, Schmidt, and Linehan (2004). Buddhist principles and practices that guide DBT therapists' attitudes and behaviors and are taught to patients include: being mindful of the current moment, seeing reality without delusion, accepting reality without judgment, letting go of attachments that cause suffering, and finding a middle way instead of extremes in thinking and action. Buddhist thought is also characterized by the humanistic assumption that everyone has an inherent capacity for wisdom, a principle referred to in DBT as "Wise Mind."

## Treatment Strategies Targeting Patient Acceptance

### *Validation as Modeling and Facilitation of Self-Validation*

As noted above, validation as a treatment strategy can serve a number of intended functions and can have a number of effects. Here, we focus on how validation can be used to target patients' acceptance of themselves and the world. That is, DBT features the use of therapist validation as a means to several ends. Because emotional functioning is highlighted as a primary area of dysfunction in Linehan's biosocial model, one intended function of therapist validation is to improve the DBT patient's ability to experience and express emotions skillfully. By repeatedly confirming what is seen by the therapist as valid (i.e., anything the client experiences or does that makes sense, is useful, or is simply legitimate), and disconfirming what is invalid (e.g., it is not literally true that "I am bad" just because I have that thought), the aim is to help shape up the patient's ability to discriminate valid from invalid behavior.

Much like an inspector examining a conveyor belt for items that have problems before they are boxed and shipped to customers, the therapist helps the patient learn to identify experiences and behavior as valid or invalid. Of course, there are times when a behavior is both valid from one perspective (i.e., it makes sense *why* a thought occurred) and invalid from another perspective (i.e., the thought may not be literally true). This process leads to many instances of therapist validation of patient in-session behavior that the patient typically experiences as invalid. By training the patient to become more facile at recognizing and distinguishing between affective states, for example, the therapist is promoting acceptance of affective experiences as they are experienced. Importantly, the therapist also actively helps patients learn to validate the reasons why it may make sense that they have invalidated themselves cognitively (e.g., "I will never have a good relationship"), without validating the content or literal and permanent truth of the invalidating thoughts.

In addition to explicit training of validation as a skill to be learned directly, the therapist uses self-validation as a way to model to the patient. Therapists model validation by explicitly identifying how, for themselves, there are types of antecedents that commonly give rise to certain kinds of internal experiences. Similarly, therapists model how to accept oneself by validating one's own thoughts, emotions, and actions as making sense, being effective, and so on. This is done in a manner that is sometimes playful, sometimes matter-of-fact, but always genuine and with the patient's need to develop this skill clearly being targeted.

### Experiential Exercises as a Means to Build Acceptance

Therapists in DBT frequently use experiential exercises with their patients as a way to promote acceptance. There are no specific experiential exercises, other than those described below as mindfulness practice, that are required in DBT. Instead, the therapist has a wide range of possible exercises that he or she may choose to use as needed during session. This organic use of experiential exercises allows the therapist and patient to transition during sessions, sometimes back and forth within the same session, from problem-solving, chain analyses, or explicit change-focused skill training to experiential practices intended to promote acceptance, cognitive defusion, or, most broadly, insight.

Experiential exercises can be used to promote acceptance of thoughts as only thoughts and not things that have to be literally true. Patients can learn not to "buy thoughts as literally true" through experientially practicing to observe the content of thoughts changing as the context for thinking changes. Such exercises can help clients learn to accept thoughts that *seem true* now to be experienced simply as thoughts, neither to be held as literally true nor refused as untrue. Another use of experiential exercises might be to learn that urges to behave do not always require acting on the urge. Learning not to respond to urges can be an important skill that helps promote acceptance of the urge *as simply an internal experience*, and not a command from a homunculus dictating a required action need necessarily occur. Again, there is no specific single exercise that is required. Therapists can choose to use an experiential exercise that they judge will work well with any given patient in any given moment. Moreover, experiential exercises are not conceptualized as better or worse than explicit behavioral skills training. Rather, when promoting acceptance, experiential exercises can be the yin to didactic or explicit skill training's yang.

## *Mindfulness Skills*

Mindfulness refers to being aware of one's experiences in a nonjudgmental, receptive manner and participating in activity based on that nonjudgmental awareness. Kabat-Zinn (2003), for example, described mindfulness as "the awareness that emerges through paying attention on purpose, in the present moment, and nonjudgmentally to the unfolding of experience, moment-by-moment" (p. 145). In an attempt to operationalize mindfulness for a research context, Bishop et al. (2004) proposed that mindfulness includes two components: *self-regulation of attention* and *orientation to experience*. Self-regulation of attention involves nonelaborative observation and awareness of events, thoughts, sensations, feelings, action urges, and so on, from moment to moment. It entails the abilities to sustain attention on an intended focus and to switch attention at will to a new intended focus. For example, one may practice sustaining attention to one's breath. When the attention wanders from the breath, the practitioner learns to notice what he or she is focusing on and then move attention back to the breath. The second dimension of mindfulness—orientation to experience—concerns the attitude held towards present-moment experience, specifically an attitude of openness and curiosity toward whatever experience arises in each moment, without imposing judgments on or reacting habitually to the experience. We all are mindful to varying degrees across situations and occasions, and there appear to be relatively stable individual differences in average levels of mindfulness that are significantly related to a variety of indices of well-being (e.g., Brown & Ryan, 2003). Mindful awareness often occurs without any particular intentional training or practice, and there may be a variety of methods for increasing mindfulness. However, many spiritual traditions and, more recently, some physical and mental health interventions, propose that meditation practices can increase the ability to be mindful. There is evidence that experienced meditators on average score higher on measures of mindfulness (e.g., Baer et al., 2008; Brown & Ryan, 2003, Lykins & Baer, 2009), and that participation in a mindfulness-based intervention leads to increased self-reported mindfulness (e.g., Carmody & Baer, 2008, Shapiro, Oman, Thoresen, Plante, & Flinders, 2008).

Teaching and encouraging regular practices based on mindfulness meditation is the primary content and focus of interventions such as mindfulness-based stress reduction (MBSR; Kabat-Zinn, 1982) and mindfulness-based cognitive therapy (MBCT; Segal, Williams, & Teasdale, 2002). In DBT, mindfulness is viewed as critical for therapists' in-session awareness and participation, and as the core set of skills to be learned by patients, but these elements are parts of a whole that includes use of many other therapist behaviors and development of many other patient skills. Mindfulness skills not only are taught as a free-standing skills module, but also are included in each of the other three skills modules, in which the relevance of mindfulness for daily life (sometimes referred to as informal mindfulness practice, in contrast to formal practice such as sitting meditation or body scan) becomes clear. Nonjudgmental awareness, acceptance, and nonavoidance of emotions, thoughts, and action urges are beneficial for emotion regulation. The ability to focus mindfully on a chosen object or activity can facilitate the effective use of distraction to tolerate distress and avoid engaging in maladaptive escape behaviors; awareness of goals in interpersonal interactions and the ability to not lose sight of them in the context of strong emotions are important skills for interpersonal effectiveness.

Mindfulness skills are taught in DBT because of their potential for clinically significant benefits that can include, among others, being less "scattered" and distractible, particularly at times of strong emotion; being more aware of and able to let go of rumination; being more aware of action urges before acting on them; and being able to experience life more fully and richly. Like other skills, mindfulness can be developed with intentional, deliberate practice. One common practice is to sit comfortably with eyes closed, focusing the mind on the inhalations and exhalations of the breath, and noticing the thoughts, images, sensations, and action urges that enter one's awareness, allowing them to come and go freely without judging, holding onto, or trying to suppress them. Other objects of focus may also be used, such as external objects, a particular idea or class of thoughts, or activities such as walking or eating. Some practices may result in physical and mental relaxation, which may allow one's "wise mind" to be more accessible. However, relaxation is not a primary goal of mindfulness practice. In fact, awareness during mindfulness practice may at times increase awareness of unpleasant experiences. These experiences are not to be avoided, nor are pleasant experiences to be directly sought in mindfulness practice. Among other things, this affords an opportunity to observe that sensations, thoughts, emotions, action urges, and so on, are not permanent, but come and go like the waves of an ocean, while the observing self remains present.

In DBT, in the Mindfulness Skills module, mindfulness is taught as a set of "what" skills (what to do) and a set of "how" skills (how to do it). The "what" skills are *observing* one's sense experiences, *describing* what one observes (e.g., "I am aware of an urge to move"), and *participating*, i.e., interacting with the world. Practice in observing and describing are helpful steps toward participating mindfully. The "how" skills are *one-mindfully*, focusing on one thing at a time with full awareness, *nonjudgmentally*, without labeling experiences or behaviors as good or bad, and *effectively*, behaving in ways that are consistent with one's important goals and values, rather than getting caught up in goals such as proving a point. Some of the practical issues involved in teaching mindfulness skills in DBT groups are discussed in Robins (2002).

Mindfulness skills also feature among the skills taught in each of the other three modules. In the Distress Tolerance Skills module, for example, skills for getting through a crisis include distraction, self-soothing activities, and reminding oneself of the pros and cons of tolerating distress versus not tolerating it. All of these skills require the person to maintain focused awareness and to experience reality without judgment. In addition, mindfulness of daily activities, such as walking or doing dishes, is taught as a tool for increasing acceptance of life, and skills group participants learn to observe willfulness when it arises and to turn their mind toward acceptance of reality and willingness to act effectively. In the Emotion Regulation Skills module, one strategy taught for regulating emotions is simply to be mindful of the current emotion, observing it come and go, without fighting it, but also without holding onto, or amplifying it. This can decrease its duration or intensity, because unless "fueled" by thoughts or other behaviors, emotional responses are naturally short-lived. Furthermore, it provides another opportunity to observe that difficult emotions can be tolerated and do not have to be avoided, nor does the individual need to judge him or herself for an emotion, thereby setting off a cascade of secondary emotions about the emotion. In the Interpersonal Skills module, mindfulness features as one of the component skills for making assertive requests and refusals, as summarized by the acronym DEAR MAN: Describe the situation, Express how you feel about it, Assert what you want, and Reinforce the other person, doing all this Mindfully, while Appearing confident, and with willingness to Negotiate.

## Acceptance and Mindfulness of the Therapist

To teach mindfulness skills effectively to patients, to promote acceptance, and particularly to address patients' questions, it is essential that therapists and skills trainers have experience with mindfulness practice and with practicing acceptance of reality as it is. Along with potential benefit in the life of the therapist in general, regular mindfulness practice can also help the therapist maintain direction throughout the challenging course of treatment that BPD patients present. Mindfulness in therapy includes observing and describing the patient's behavior in session and out of session in a nonjudgmental manner, which can be particularly difficult when one feels criticized or is afraid that the patient may attempt suicide. The ability to stay focused on tasks and in the present moment when the patient becomes tangential or overwhelmed is essential in helping the patient progress. Mindfulness practice can also help a therapist regulate his or her own emotions during sessions. Maintaining awareness of one's breath and of shifts in one's emotional state enables a therapist not to react but to act in a more planned manner. A fourth area in which mindfulness practice may benefit the therapist is in dealing with his or her judgments about his or her own competence. The therapist must remember that, just like the patient, he or she is doing the best that he or she can in that moment. It simply is what it is. If a different therapist behavior or intervention is likely to be more effective, the therapist can plan the appropriate change without judgment of the previous behavior. Finally, it is essential for the therapist to develop an attitude of nonattachment, striving to help the patient reach certain goals, yet at the same time not being attached to those outcomes. This can be critical for decreasing suffering on the part of the therapist when those goals are not yet achieved or when the patient seems to be less committed to, or works less diligently toward, those goals than the therapist. This does not mean that frustration, worry, sadness, and other possibly difficult experiences do not arise, only that it may be possible to allow them to be present without internal struggle and attempts to avoid them, and without one's mind being hijacked by internal verbal elaboration on the experience. Difficulty in dealing with difficult emotions that arise as a therapist, particularly in working with "difficult-to-treat" patients, may contribute toward a therapist becoming burned out with a given patient or with conducting therapy in general. Although we are not aware of any relevant empirical data, cultivation of a sense of acceptance, in general and particularly within the context of one's work as a clinician, may help reduce the risk of burnout.

## Case Illustration

In this prototypical case example, the patient, Kate, is a 33-year-old single woman with BPD, social anxiety, recurrent symptoms of major depression, chronic pain, and a history of sexual victimization. Kate has been in DBT for five months, and during this time she has learned to use mindfulness skills to increase awareness of present cognitions, sensations, subjective feeling states, and action urges.

Therapist (T): So, before we get started, let's do what we have done before to help begin our session in a skillful way. Let's do a mindfulness practice.

Patient (P): I don't want to do a mindfulness practice. I am so mad right now. I can't even stand it! (Patient puts head down and sighs loudly.) You are not going to believe what my mother said to me today! I could just scream.

T: Your mind may be telling you that you can't stand being mad right now, and that you might scream, and those thoughts may *seem* true. But here's the thing: you *can* stand it, without screaming, because you have been really mad before, in this room, and you have tolerated feeling mad without making things worse. Let me ask you a question: In your Wise Mind, what do you think will be the most *effective* thing we can do right now—a brief mindfulness practice, or you telling me about how mad you are at your mom?

P: I want to tell you what she said. It was horrible.... Awful.

T: I would like to hear about it. The question is this: will me hearing about it right now help you more than us doing a mindfulness practice?

P: Okay, I get it. Let's do mindfulness first.

T: What kind of brief practice helps you the most when you are mad, to keep you from doing things that you might later regret?

P: I liked the loving kindness practice we did last time. I don't know why, but it actually helped me calm down.

T: Do you want to be less mad right now?

P: Yes!

T: Okay, then let's do this practice. Begin by settling into your chair, breathing in and out deeply to get centered. Now...

(Therapist directs a standard loving kindness practice.)

T: Okay, now, are you feeling less mad?

P: Yes. I am still mad at her, but that practice, I don't know what it is, but it really helps.

T: Good. Notice that you are tolerating feeling mad, and using skills to bring your anger down. Good work so far! Okay. So it has been over three months since you thought about hurting yourself, and all of a sudden this week you cut yourself. Let's talk some about what happened.

P: Okay. (Patient puts head down and looks away.)

T: But before we do, can I just check in with you about your current emotions? What emotions are you feeling, if any, right now?

P: Um, I don't know. I...I'm sorry; it's just that I...I am so mad at my mom right now. I know that's not what you want to talk about, but you just wouldn't believe what she said to me this morning. We were getting into the car to come here, and that bitch had the nerve—I'm sorry to swear, I know that I do that too much—but you won't believe what she said. We're getting into the car, and that's *my* car you know; she doesn't have the right to be bossin' me around in *my* car, and she starts in on me...starts calling me lazy, an idiot, you name it...

T: Not exactly her finest moment as a mom.

P: You're damn right! And listen to this...

T (interrupts gently): I will, but first let me ask you a question. Are you feeling any other emotions besides anger?

P: No, I'm just pissed.

T: And I see why. I'd hate to be called those things too. I wonder though, if you stop and be mindful of your emotions, now, in this present moment, what other emotions are you experiencing?

P: I don't know. The only thing I feel is anger.

T: There is no question that you are feeling anger. The question is whether there is anything else you are feeling, not instead of, but in addition to anger? You cut yourself this week for the first time in a while. And I am wondering if you are feeling any emotions related to talking about hurting yourself?

P: I don't want to talk about what happened.

T: Okay, good job noticing that. Try and notice if there is an emotion you are feeling related to not wanting to talk about hurting yourself.

P: Guilt? Shame?

T: Which one?

P: Well, I feel guilty for what I did, because I cut myself on purpose, knowing my mom would see it.

T: Okay. So, now that you are aware that you are feeling guilt right now, what skill could you use to help change your guilt? Or would you rather work on accepting and tolerating the guilt using more mindfulness skills?

P: No, I don't think I want to do another mindfulness exercise. But I can tell you that I feel really guilty, and mad, about what happened.

T: Your anger is related to your urge to scream about your mom. Can you be mindful of any urges you are having right now, coming from feeling guilty?

P: Yes. Like I said, I don't want to talk about what happened.

T: So, as you stop and notice your urges, the urge is to avoid talking about cutting yourself?

P: I guess.

T: Okay. Would it be skillful for you to act with the guilty urge or to act opposite to it by talking about what happened?

P: I guess we should talk about what happened.

T: Okay.

# THEORETICAL AND TECHNICAL DISTINCTIONS FROM OTHER CBT MODELS

## Differences Between DBT and Traditional CBT Treatments

In this section, we highlight several features of DBT that may distinguish it from other cognitive behavioral therapies (CBTs). We recognize that there are many differences between DBT and each other specific treatment model within the family of CBT treatments. It is beyond the scope of this chapter to specify each distinction between DBT and every contemporary CBT. Accordingly, we emphasize below several key areas in which DBT may be distinguished from other CBT interventions. These include (a) structural elements of DBT, (b) a dialectical philosophical framework, and (c) the use of both cognitive change and acceptance-based interventions.

### *Structural Elements of DBT*

Due primarily to the nature of the clinical population for which DBT was developed, there are a number of structural elements to DBT that may be unique. Although other CBT-based treatments include both individual and group-based therapy, we are not aware of any other intervention within the umbrella of CBT that includes a required weekly consultation team for therapists designed to treat therapist burnout. Indeed, being on a consultation team in DBT is not the same experience as a conventional client/clinic staffing meeting. This is because therapists on the team are required to treat each other using DBT skills and principles, including such things as conducting chain analyses on each, balancing acceptance and change, using dialectics, practicing mindfulness, and so on. Therapists on DBT consultation teams attend to other therapists' behavior during the team, helping to moralize and motivate therapists to continue working in an optimal way with these difficult-to-treat BPD clients.

In addition to the therapist consultation team, ad hoc telephone consultation between client and therapist is a unique structural element of DBT. Although it is conventional for clients across many psychotherapies to call their therapist "in crisis," in DBT telephone calls are explicitly encouraged. Because individuals with BPD frequently experience crises, there is a prescribed structure and function for these calls. After some time in DBT, the structure and consistent process that accompanies telephone consultation calls frequently leads to clients calling with fewer crises, being more clearly targeted to a specific problem when they call, and shorter phone calls.

Another structural element unique to DBT is the use of a treatment hierarchy of targets. As described previously, this framework allows the therapist to make decisions about which of the many possible problems to target in any given moment of a session. By including "therapy-interfering behavior" as a class of possible targets for treatment, the therapist is able to flexibly shift from helping the client troubleshoot such "quality of life" problems as depression or anxiety to, for example, the desire to stop going to the skills training group, or to an unwillingness to practice skills learned in group.

Whereas some cognitive behavioral therapies prescribe and some proscribe teaching skills to clients, another arguably unique element of DBT is the use of both direct skill training and experiential learning. The goal in DBT is to enhance learning of key life skills in order to promote a life that is worth living. As such, therapists in DBT are required to have the agility to shift from teaching skills (e.g., rehearsing, role playing, shaping, differentially reinforcing, etc.) to facilitating meaningful experiential learning (e.g., practicing mindfulness, using a behavioral experiment, etc.), sometimes within the same session. Although other treatments in the CBT family use both direct skill training and experiential learning (e.g., MBCT), in DBT there is perhaps more attention paid than in other treatments to balancing these different methods of learning across time.

## Differences Between DBT and Other CBT Treatments for BPD

Two other CBT approaches have supportive evidence. Cognitive therapy (CT) has shown efficacy in reducing suicidal behaviors (Brown et al., 2005), and schema-focused therapy (SFT) has been found to improve several outcomes in patients with BPD (Giesen-Bloo et al., 2006). Like DBT, there is acknowledgment that environmental contexts, biological factors, behavioral skills deficits, dysfunctional cognitive content and styles, and emotional responses all transact with each other and may need to be addressed in therapy. However, CT and schema therapy more strongly emphasize and focus on cognitions such as dysfunctional attitudes, beliefs, and information processing styles (and particularly in the case of SFT their origins), whereas DBT more strongly emphasizes biological dysfunction of the emotion regulation system, behavioral skills deficits, reinforcement contingencies, and other environmental influences. Conceptually, DBT does not include the construct of schema, instead discussing patterns of cognitive behaviors (thoughts), and in general being a more behavioral and function process–oriented, and less cognitive and form/structure–oriented, model of treatment. Cognitive styles and patterns, though never ignored, are less a focus in Stage 1 than is typically true in cognitive therapy, in part because distorted cognition is viewed as often a result of intense emotions rather than their cause, so that it is more useful to focus on development of behavioral and other skills for regulating emotions. In addition, many BPD patients experience a focus on distorted cognition, particularly early in treatment, as invalidating, and therefore reject it and may reject treatment. By Stage 2, and particularly Stage 3, it is often far more useful to use standard CT approaches, none of which are necessarily incompatible with DBT if used in a context of dialectically balanced strategies.

## *Dialectical Philosophical Framework*

As described above, the core change strategies in DBT are built around both behavior therapy and cognitive therapy. Indeed, it is this core that places DBT squarely in the family of cognitive behavioral therapies. Because dialectics are woven throughout all elements of the treatment, however, the application of standard behavior therapy and cognitive therapy interventions takes a different form in DBT. We have outlined above how the fundamental dialectic underlying DBT is that of acceptance and change. With both acceptance and change having equal importance in the model, it is important to highlight how DBT may be compared to other acceptance-based models of psychotherapy. We contend that a primary way to distinguish DBT from other acceptance-based treatments is through the former's use of dialectics.

When considering the key role that dialectics have in DBT, both the theoretical framework and the technical delivery of DBT can be contrasted against other contemporary acceptance-based behavioral therapies, including acceptance and commitment therapy (ACT; Hayes, Strosahl, & Wilson, 1999) and mindfulness-based cognitive therapy (MBCT; Segal et al., 2002). With regard to theory, dialectics underlie both the ontological and epistemological perspective taken by the DBT therapist. Ontologically, the patient is seen holistically, more than the sum of his or her parts, with multilayered and interrelating influences on daily functioning. Epistemologically, the solution to any given problem is found through a dialectical process. For each position that is taken (i.e., thesis), a counter or different position is taken (i.e., anti-thesis), and this natural tension between two alternative positions is used to find a new position (i.e., synthesis). The synthesis may or may not be the exact middle position between two extremes. The optimal place between polarities in DBT, for any given moment, is that which yields the most effective solution. In the same way that the best trajectory to throw a ball to another person is based on the strength and direction of the wind, the DBT therapist and patient must together decide what the most effective synthesis may be for any given problem, in any given context.

This reliance on the dialectical process of change provides perhaps the clearest distinction between DBT and both ACT and MBCT. This is not to say that either ACT or MBCT may, at times, include a dialectical process of change. However, these treatments neither prescribe nor proscribe dialectics. In contrast, dialectics are explicitly prescribed throughout all main components of the treatment. In DBT, the dialectical process of arriving at a working synthesis is found during individual therapy, group skills training, telephone consultation, and the therapist consultation team. Without the theoretical model prescribing a ubiquitous dialectical process of change, DBT is, quite literally, not DBT.

With regard to the technical delivery of treatment, dialectics also differentiate DBT from other acceptance-based treatments. On the one hand, similar to DBT, therapists in both ACT and MBCT use mindfulness exercises in session to facilitate experiential learning. As in DBT, both ACT and MBCT use mindfulness-based experiential exercises to help patients learn to change the context, not the content, of internal experiences. For example, rather than restructure the form or frequency of intrusive thoughts, as is done in more conventional cognitive therapy, therapists using ACT or MBCT would help a patient learn through experiential exercises to let go of the literal truth of intrusive thoughts, thereby letting go of the struggle to find sufficient evidence to support or refute the truth of the intrusion. Instead, the patient is encouraged to respond with a chosen, intentional, and values-driven action, irrespective of the content of internal experiences. This form and function of technical delivery of experiential learning in ACT and MBCT may, at times, be very similar in DBT.

On the other hand, the influence of a dialectical philosophy in DBT creates, at times, both a different form and function of mindfulness during DBT sessions. For example, the DBT therapist might direct the patient to use mindfulness skills for a variety of reasons, and in a variety of ways, including (but not restricted) to: (a) beginning a session effectively, thereby reducing therapy-interfering behavior such as being easily distracted; (b) helping conduct in-session behavioral analyses more effectively; (c) blocking attempts to escape from negative emotions during the session; (d) reducing emotional arousal prior to rehearsing, role-playing, or conducting in vivo exposure exercises; or (e) ending a session, in order to increase the probability that the patient will not immediately leave the session and engage in unskillful behavior. The dialectical process of change allows the therapist the flexibility to use mindfulness for these and other functions at any point during session, even if done inconsistently or unpredictably. Moreover, it is not important that the patient *does* mindfulness in any specific form (i.e., sitting, breathing, walking, etc.), for any specific amount of time, or with any specific instructional content. What matters is that the dialectical process of change provides the context for mindfulness to be used in session, in an organic way that is contingent upon in-session behavior. Mindfulness is used as needed during DBT sessions, which means that it can be used spontaneously and unpredictably, planned and consistently, or anywhere between these extremes. Dialectics allow the therapist to move swiftly with intention from helping the patient use mindfulness in one form or another, for one function or another, both within and across sessions.

# THE DBT PERSPECTIVE ON DIRECT COGNITIVE CHANGE STRATEGIES

## Role of Metacognitive Awareness, Distancing, or Cognitive Defusion

Mindfulness practices from Buddhism and other traditions include an important role for the intentional observation, and sometimes description, of one's thought content and process, which creates some distance from the involvement in the thought itself, separation between the observer and the observed, and greater possibility for seeing things as they actually are. Thoughts are not taken as literally "true" and to be acted upon. In standard CT, the patient usually is asked to keep a daily record of thoughts when distressed or in other situations, which can create a similar psychological distance—or "decentering"—from thoughts. Not only does such decentering allow for the possibility of examining their validity, at times it may be beneficial simply to remember that thoughts are just thoughts and may turn out to be different from reality. DBT attempts to promote greater metacognitive awareness, distancing, or cognitive defusion through mindfulness and other experiential exercises, cognitive therapy self-monitoring strategies, and other means. Improved self-observation may be of benefit in a variety of ways, one of which is the opportunity to examine the validity or usefulness of thoughts. DBT utilizes such opportunities for direct evaluation of thoughts, as well as strategies targeting acceptance of thoughts.

## The Use of Both Change-Oriented and Acceptance-Oriented Cognitive Interventions

It may be useful to outline the general stance taken in DBT towards direct cognitive change strategies. Given the emphasis in DBT of dialectics, it may not be surprising that therapists use both acceptance and change interventions to help patients manage distressing cognitions. Therapists in DBT help patients learn to identify cognitive response tendencies that are likely to be elicited by particular functional classes of stimuli. People diagnosed with BPD often experience intense emotions that are accompanied by thoughts that are commonly conceptualized as distortions in most forms of CBT. Thus, DBT therapists help patients learn to recognize the types of dysfunctional cognitions (e.g., mindreading, catastrophic thinking, all-or-nothing thinking, etc.) that they tend to have following certain types of internal or external antecedent stimuli. Thoughts that occur in the context of behavioral dyscontrol (e.g., self-injurious behavior, drug use, etc.) are targeted as being important to learn to attend to, and to develop new skills in response to, in order to disrupt the causal chain of events preceding and following such behavioral dyscontrol. Thoughts that occur as urges, cravings, or desires, for example, are targeted for intervention.

In DBT, considerable attention is paid to identifying the contextual variables that influence the probability of the most distressing thoughts or those thoughts that are most likely to be associated with behavioral problems. However, in DBT there is no a priori conceptualization that cognition causes behavior, or that changing cognition is *required* in order to change behavior. In DBT, cognition is seen simply as a kind of internal experience, or unobservable behavior, that can be linked in a complex causal chain of experiences before and after problem behavior. There is no literal restructuring of cognition, on the one hand, as thoughts are unobservable behavior and cannot be demonstrably manipulated in a clear and causal manner. Yet, on the other hand, DBT therapists often try to help patients learn to recognize how certain ways of thinking may be more helpful than other ways of thinking. Together, the therapist and patient work over time to develop new ways of responding (either acceptance or change) to unpleasant internal experiences, with the goal of developing a flexible and context-sensitive manner of responding that is consistent with a life worth living to the patient.

But how does the DBT therapist know whether to be more change- or acceptance-focused in response to unpleasant internal experiences? Early on in DBT, the therapist orients and reorients the patient to acceptance and change interventions as possible solutions yielded from chain analyses of problem behavior. As the patient learns and attempts to generalize newly learned cognitive acceptance and change strategies, the therapist helps evaluate what works best, when, and why. Certain acceptance skills may help some problem behaviors, in some contexts, whereas other problems may be best met in some contexts by change-focused strategies. The therapist and patient work together to identify the most effective skills to use in response to distressing internal experiences.

The effectiveness of both change and acceptance skills is evaluated through a variety of means. For example, therapists use a self-monitoring sheet, or diary card, to examine which skills are being used, and which are associated with improvement. Behavioral experiments are done during session to evaluate how the patient's use of change or acceptance skills reduces distress associated with certain internal experiences. Chain analyses are used to identify which skills were used, and which worked, during the past week. Some patients have a harder time than others learning how to use certain change or acceptance skills in response to distressing internal experiences. As the therapist attempts to motivate the patient to use skills, this includes determining which skills are easiest to use, when, and how. Using shaping as a learning principle, the therapist may encourage the use of a somewhat limited set of skills initially, but over time, gradually adds a broader array of both acceptance and change skills. In addition, when discussing therapy homework for the week, the therapist might assess the degree to which the patient understands the cognitive strategy (change- or acceptance-based), prefers to use it, and sees the link between this response and the broader set of values and goals linked to a life worth living.

# DATA ON THEORETICAL MODEL AND TREATMENT APPROACH
## Biosocial Theory of BPD

Linehan's model of the development and maintenance of BPD (Linehan, 1993) has been the subject of much empirical investigation in recent years. A full review of these data is beyond the scope of this chapter. However, recent reviews of the empirical literature examining emotional sensitivity (Domes, Schulze, & Herpertz, 2009) and reactivity (Rosenthal, Chapman, Rosenthal, Kuo, & Linehan, 2008) are available. In summary, individuals with BPD tend to demonstrate a heightened sensitivity to negative facial expressions of emotion (Lynch et al., 2006). However, not all studies have found this pattern of results, with some studies demonstrating a negativity bias, but not necessarily heightened sensitivity per se, in facial affect recognition among individuals with BPD (Wagner & Linehan, 1999). The majority of studies to date investigating emotional sensitivity have done so using facial affect recognition tasks, in which either static images or morphing expressions of faces are presented. Such experimental tasks are valuable, as they can help advance an understanding of whether individuals with BPD can be characterized by either heightened speed, accuracy, or speed and accuracy when classifying facial affective expressions. That said, emotional sensitivity needs to be investigated using other methods beyond facial affective classification. Neuroimaging holds much promise as a methodology for studying emotional sensitivity in BPD. Indeed, one study reported that individuals with BPD displayed hyperreactive amygdala responses to emotionally expressive faces (Donegan et al., 2003). At this point the exact nature of emotional sensitivity in BPD remains unclear. Future studies in this area should examine emotional sensitivity using neurobehavioral measures of the frequency of emotional responses to emotionally evocative stimuli.

In addition, studies based on self-report data consistently indicate that individuals with BPD report having greater emotional dysfunction than controls, defined variably as affective intensity, reactivity, and/or lability (e.g., Gratz, Rosenthal, Tull, Lejuez, & Gunderson, in press; Koenigsberg et al., 2001). Data from laboratory behavioral or psychophysiological experiments has inconsistently supported Linehan's hypotheses about emotional vulnerability in BPD. Across studies using emotionally evocative stimuli, researchers have reported that individuals with BPD are hyporeactive (Herpertz et al., 1999), hyperreactive (Ebner-Priemer et al., 2005), or not significantly different from controls. In addition to parsimonious explanations for these mixed findings (e.g., measurement error, small sample sizes, or the model offering inadequate predictions), one possibility is that BPD is a disorder defined, in part, by discordant emotional reactivity across systems of emotion (i.e., subjective feelings, motoric behavior, and physiology).

That is, individuals with BPD may report being highly emotionally reactive, but this higher subjective experience of emotional reactivity may not be congruent with being more emotionally expressive motorically, or having a higher magnitude of sympathetic arousal.

Another possibility is that, rather than simply being more emotionally reactive, individuals with BPD may be deficient in their ability to down-regulate negative affect. This prediction is at the heart of Linehan's model, which states that BPD criterion behaviors occur in the context of extreme deficits in neurobehavioral systems that regulate emotion. Indeed, in one recent study (Kuo & Linehan, 2009), individuals with BPD were found to have a similar magnitude of sympathetic arousal in response to emotionally evocative stimuli, yet demonstrated significant deficits in respiratory sinus arrhythmia after becoming emotionally aroused. This study provides key evidence suggesting that BPD may not be a disorder of heightened physiologic arousal in general, but may be better characterized by an inability to calm oneself when emotionally aroused.

In contrast to the recent studies examining emotional dysfunction in BPD, fewer studies have shed light on the role of an invalidating environment in BPD. Although there have been fewer experimental investigations of invalidation in BPD, findings from extant studies provide partial support for the model. Studies have reported that various indices of invalidation, including early sexual and physical victimization, higher parental criticism, and emotional neglect, all are associated with BPD (see Fruzzetti, Shenk, & Hoffman, 2005, for a review). Such self-reports of these adverse experiences are in no way unique to BPD. For this aspect of Linehan's model to be more rigorously tested, future studies need to prospectively examine the relationship between invalidation of internal experiences and the development of emotional dysfunction over time in BPD.

## DBT Treatment Outcomes

DBT has now been empirically evaluated in at least ten randomized controlled trials (RCTs). Overall, the clinical outcome data support the efficacy of DBT as a treatment for women with BPD, warranting its designation as "empirically supported" by Division 12 (clinical psychology) of the American Psychological Association. Four randomized controlled trials (RCTs) have found DBT to have superior efficacy compared with treatment as usual for women with BPD and suicidal or other self-injurious behavior (Koons et al., 2001; Linehan et al., 1991; Linehan et al., 2006; Verheul et al., 2003), particularly in reducing the frequency and medical severity of suicide attempts, self-injurious behavior, frequency and total days duration of psychiatric hospitalizations, and patient anger, and also in increasing treatment compliance and social adjustment (Linehan, Tutek, Heard, & Armstrong, 1994). These changes appear to endure over at least a one-year follow-up period (Linehan, Armstrong, & Heard, 1993; van den Bosch et al., 2002). The results of the Linehan et al. (2006) study are particularly compelling, as the comparison group was treatment by clinicians nominated by their peers as experts in the treatment of BPD.

Standard DBT also has been adapted for several other populations and treatment settings. RCTs have supported the efficacy of adaptations of DBT for women with BPD in a community mental health clinic (Turner, 2000), women with BPD and substance abuse or dependence (Linehan et al., 1999; Linehan et al., 2002), women with binge eating disorder (Telch, Agras, & Linehan, 2001) and bulimia (Safer, Telch, & Agras, 2001), and for depressed elders (Lynch, Morse, Mendelson, & Robins, 2003). Controlled but nonrandomized studies also suggest that adaptations of DBT may have efficacy for BPD patients in longer-term inpatient settings (Barley et al., 1993; Bohus et al., 2004) and for suicidal adolescents (Rathus & Miller, 2002); for a review of DBT outcome research, see Robins & Chapman (2004).

## DBT Treatment Mechanisms

The precise mechanisms underlying the efficacy of DBT are unknown. Why DBT works when it does can be addressed from two related perspectives: (a) to what extent are particular treatment components responsible for its effects? and (b) what factors mediate the effects of treatment on changes in symptoms and functioning?

Questions regarding DBT treatment components can address the relative importance of the primary modes of treatment (individual therapy, skills training, telephone consultation, and therapist consultation team), as well as the use of specific treatment strategies or groups of strategies. To date, there have been no published reports of component analysis studies designed to identify which treatment modes are differentially associated with better outcomes. One such study currently being conducted by Linehan's group compares standard DBT, DBT individual therapy with an "activities" group but no skills training, and DBT group skills training with individual standardized case management but no individual therapy. The relative importance of specific treatment strategies, and specifically of change strategies, acceptance strategies, and the integration of the two in DBT has not yet been directly studied. However, there are some data that are consistent with the idea that inclusion of both sets of strategies may lead to better outcomes. Shearin and Linehan (1992) reported that sessions in which DBT therapists were rated by their patient both as controlling and as fostering autonomy (a dialectical stance) were more highly associated with subsequent reductions in parasuicidal behavior or ideation than sessions in which therapists were rated only as controlling (pure change) or as only fostering autonomy (pure acceptance). Also, in a small randomized trial comparing DBT to a validation-only intervention for opioid-dependent individuals with BPD, participants receiving DBT had significantly better substance use outcomes in the last four months of a twelve-month treatment (Linehan et al., 2002). This study suggests that, for these particular outpatients, the inclusion of both acceptance and change delivered in DBT may have helped reduce substance use better than an acceptance-only intervention. However, participants in the validation-only treatment dropped out significantly less than those in DBT, indicating that, perhaps, a purely acceptance-based approach may help retain these individuals in treatment longer. Although this study does not provide direct evidence for specific treatment mechanisms, the results help clarify the respective roles of acceptance and change in treatment for individuals with co-occurring BPD and substance use disorders.

No mediational tests of mechanisms thought to underlie treatment outcome in DBT have been published. However, mediational models of emotional functioning in BPD have been conducted using Linehan's model as a framework. For example, several studies have found that problems with regulating negative affect fully mediate the relationship between emotional vulnerability and both BPD features (Cheavens et al., 2005) and diagnostic symptoms (Rosenthal, Cheavens, Lejuez, & Lynch, 2005). In addition, putative mechanisms of DBT have been suggested, including increases in mindfulness (Lynch et al., 2006) and use of other skills taught in DBT, as targets for study in future treatment outcome studies.

In summary, there is little currently known about why DBT works. To help elucidate this issue, we now turn to the ways in which DBT can be more rigorously studied in the future, with an emphasis on the identification of underlying mechanisms of change both common across cognitive behavioral therapies and unique to DBT.

## FUTURE DIRECTIONS IN THE STUDY OF DBT

There are a number of critical issues that need to be addressed in future studies of DBT. As discussed above, of primary importance is the identification of common and unique mechanisms of change. With specific regard to acceptance-based interventions in general and mindfulness in particular, future studies should begin to examine whether changes in treatment outcomes over time are preceded by changes in either acceptance interventions or the acquisition and generalization of mindfulness skills. Importantly, it may be informative for future studies to investigate the role of acceptance in general and mindfulness skills specifically as potential mechanisms of change across the different modes of DBT. For example, it may be that the emphasis on mindfulness and acceptance during the consultation team helps therapists in DBT by mitigating against burnout and bolstering empathy and willingness to work with borderline patients. However, even if mindfulness and acceptance are found in future studies to be mechanisms of therapist outcomes, they may not underlie other treatment outcomes for patients. That is, there may be different mechanisms accounting for different treatment outcomes.

Another set of potential future research directions concerns the range of applicability of DBT. Standard DBT may be most likely to be useful for individuals who have pronounced difficulties in many of the areas addressed by the particular skills taught, particularly those who present with maladaptive behaviors that may function to reduce distress (poor distress tolerance skills), or who are strongly emotionally reactive (poor emotion regulation skills), and/or individuals who respond poorly or adversely to primarily change-oriented treatment. The range of applications for which the treatment has been found to be helpful in RCTs is broader than only BPD. Most are for problems that involve difficulties with emotion regulation and/or distress tolerance, in congruence with the specific skills taught and with the fact that emotions are a strong focus of the whole treatment. In our own clinical practice and others we know of, DBT skills training, even when implemented without DBT individual therapy, appears to be helpful in some cases for patients with other conditions involving emotion regulation, such as mood and anxiety disorders, as an adjunct to standard CBT individual treatments. However, no research has yet been conducted to test this clinical impression. At the level of skills, patients with a very wide range of psychopathology may benefit from practice of at least some subset of the skills. For example, interpersonal skills, such as assertiveness and emotion regulation skills, are common deficits among inpatients with primary mood, anxiety, and other disorders. Mindfulness skills that may improve attention and increase nonjudgmental awareness and reality acceptance also are likely to be useful for a broad range of patients. The focus in DBT on acceptance, mindfulness, dialectics, and validation, may also be useful additions to standard, change-oriented CBT for many patients, such that DBT may be viewed as a general model of treatment, only some parts of which may be necessary or helpful for some problems, more for others.

# REFERENCES

Aitken, R. (1982). *Taking the path of Zen.* San Francisco, CA: North Point Press.

Baer, R. A., Smith, G. T., Lykins, E., Button, D. Kreitemeyer, J., Sauer, S.,...Williams, J. M. G. (2008). Construct validity of the five facet mindfulness questionnaire in meditating and nonmeditating samples. *Assessment, 15,* 329–342.

Barley, W. D., Buie, S. E., Peterson, E. W., Hollingsworth, A. S., Griva, M., Hickerson, S. C.,...Bailey, B. J. (1993). The development of an inpatient cognitive-behavioral treatment program for borderline personality disorder. *Journal of Personality Disorders, 7,* 232–240.

Beck, A. T., Freeman, A., Pretzer, J., Davis, D. D., Fleming, B., Ottaviani, R., et al. (1990). *Cognitive therapy of personality disorders.* New York, NY: Guilford Press.

Bishop, S. R., Lau, M., Shapiro, S., Carlson, L., Anderson, N. D., Carmody, J.,...Devins, G. (2004). Mindfulness: A proposed operational definition. *Clinical Psychology: Science and Practice, 11,* 230–241.

Bohus, M., Haaf, B., Simms, T., Limberger, M. F., Schmal, C., & Unckel, C. (2004). Effectiveness of inpatient dialectical behavioral therapy for borderline personality disorder: A controlled trial. *Behaviour Research and Therapy, 42,* 487–499.

Brown, G. K., Ten Have, T., Henriques, G. R., Xie, S. X., Hollander, J. E., & Beck, A. T. (2005). Cognitive therapy for the prevention of suicide attempts: A randomized controlled trial. *JAMA: Journal of the American Medical Association, 294,* 563–570.

Brown, K. W., & Ryan, R. M. (2003). The benefits of being present: Mindfulness and its role in psychological well-being. *Journal of Personality and Social Psychology, 84,* 822–848.

Carmody, J., & Baer, R. (2008). Relationship between mindfulness practice and levels of mindfulness, medical and psychological symptoms and well-being in a mindfulness-based stress reduction program. *Journal of Behavioral Medicine, 31,* 23–33.

Cheavens, J. S., Rosenthal, M. Z., Daughters, S. D., Novak, J., Kosson, D., Lynch, T. R., & Lejeuz, C. (2005). An analogue investigation of the relationships among perceived parental criticism, negative affect, and borderline personality disorder features: The role of thought suppression. *Behavior Research and Therapy, 43,* 257–268.

Dimeff, L. A., & Koerner, K. (2007). Dialectical behavior therapy in clinical practice: Applications across disorders and settings. New York, NY: Guilford Press.

Domes, G., Schulze, L., & Herpertz, S. C. (2009). Emotion recognition in borderline personality disorder: A review of the literature. *Journal of Personality Disorders, 23,* 6–19.

Donegan, N. H., Sanislow, C. A., Blumberg, H. P., Fulbright, R. K., Lacadie, C., Skudlarski, P.,...Wexler, B. E. (2003). Amygdala hyperreactivity in borderline personality disorder: Implications for emotional dysregulation. *Biological Psychiatry, 54,* 1284–1293.

Ebner-Priemer, U. W., Badeck, S., Beckmann, C., Wagner, A., Feige, B., Weiss, I.,...Bohus, M. (2005). Affective dysregulation and dissociative experience in female patients with borderline personality disorder: A startle response study. *Journal of Psychiatric Research, 39,* 85–92.

Fruzzetti, A. E., & Fruzzetti, A. R. (2003). Partners with borderline personality disorder: Dialectical behavior therapy with couples. In D. K. Snyder & M. A. Whisman (Eds.), *Treating difficult couples: Managing emotional, behavioral, and health problems in couple therapy.* New York, NY: Guilford Press.

Fruzzetti, A. E., & Levensky, E. R. (2000). Dialectical behavior therapy for domestic violence: Rationale and procedures. *Cognitive and Behavioral Practice, 7,* 435–447.

Fruzzetti, A. E., Shenk, C., & Hoffman, P. (2005). Family interaction and the development of borderline personality disorder: A transactional model. *Development and Psychopathology, 17,* 1007–1030.

Giesen-Bloo, J., van Dyck, R., Spinhoven, P., van Tillburg, W., Dirkesen, C., van Asselt, T.,...Arntz, A. (2006). Outpatient psychotherapy for borderline personality disorder: Randomized controlled trial of schema-focused therapy vs. transference-focused psychotherapy. *Archives of General Psychiatry, 63,* 649–658.

Goldfried, M. R., & Davison, G. C. (1976). Clinical behavior therapy. New York, NY: Holt, Rinehart & Winston.

Goldstein, T. R., Axelson, D. A., Birmaher, B., & Brent, D. A. (2007). Dialectical behavior therapy for adolescents with bipolar disorder: A 1-year open trial. *Journal of the American Academy of Child and Adolescent Psychiatry, 46,* 820–830.

Gratz, K. L., Rosenthal, M. Z., Tull, M. T., Lejuez, C. W., & Gunderson, J. G. (in press). An experimental investigation of emotional reactivity and delayed emotional recovery in borderline personality disorder: The role of shame. *Comprehensive Psychiatry.*

Hahn, T. N. (1976). *The miracle of mindfulness: A manual on meditation.* Boston, MA: Beacon Press.

Hayes, S. C., Strosahl, K., & Wilson, K. G. (1999). *Acceptance and commitment therapy: An experiential approach to behavior change.* New York: Guilford Press.

Herpertz, S. C., Kunnert, H. J., Schwenger, U. B., Eng, M., & Sass, H. (1999). Affective responsiveness in borderline personality disorder: A psychophysiological approach. *American Journal of Psychiatry, 156,* 1550–1556.

Hesslinger, B., Tebartz van Elst, L., Nyberg, E., Dykierek, P., Richter, H., Berner, M., & Ebert, D. (2002). Psychotherapy of attention deficit hyperactivity disorder in adults: A pilot study using a structured skills training program. *European Archives of Psychiatry and Clinical Neuroscience, 252,* 117–184.

Kabat-Zinn, J. (1982). An outpatient program in behavioral medicine for chronic pain patients based on the practice of mindfulness meditation: Theoretical considerations and preliminary results. *General Hospital Psychiatry, 4,* 33–47.

Kabat-Zinn, J. (2003). Mindfulness-based interventions in context: Past, present, and future. *Clinical Psychology: Science and Practice, 10*(2), 144–156.

Koenigsberg, H. W., Harvey, P. D., Mitropoulou, V., Schmeidler, J., New, A. S., Goodman, M.,...Siever, L. J. (2001). Characterizing affective instability in borderline personality disorder. *American Journal of Psychiatry, 159,* 784–788.

Koons, C. R., Robins, C. J., Tweed, J. L., Lynch, T. R., Gonzales, A. M., Morse, J. Q.,...Bastian, L. A. (2001). Efficacy of dialectical behavior therapy in women veterans with borderline personality disorder. *Behavior Therapy, 32,* 371–390.

Kuo, J. R., & Linehan, M. M. (2009). Disentangling emotion processes in borderline personality disorder: physiological and self-reported assessment of biological vulnerability, baseline intensity, and reactivity to emotionally evocative stimuli. *Journal of Abnormal Psychology, 118,* 531–544.

Linehan, M. M. (1987). Dialectical behavioral therapy: A cognitive behavioral approach to parasuicide. *Journal of Personality Disorders, 1,* 328–333.

Linehan, M. M. (1993a). *Cognitive-behavioral treatment of borderline personality disorder.* New York, NY: Guilford Press.

Linehan, M. M. (1993b). *Skills training manual for treating borderline personality disorder.* New York, NY: Guilford Press.

Linehan, M. M., Armstrong, H. E., & Heard, H. L. (1993). Naturalistic follow-up of a behavioral treatment for chronically suicidal borderline patients. *Archives of General Psychiatry, 50,* 971–974.

Linehan, M. M., Armstrong, H. E., Suarez, A., Allmon, D., & Heard, H. L. (1991). Cognitive-behavioral treatment of chronically parasuicidal borderline patients. *Archives of General Psychiatry, 48,* 1060–1064.

Linehan, M. M., Comtois, K. A., Murray, A. M., Brown, M. Z., Gallop, R. J., Heard, H. L.,…Lindenboim, N. (2006). Two-year randomized controlled trial and follow-up of dialectical behavior therapy versus therapy by experts for suicidal behaviors and borderline personality disorder. *Archives of General Psychiatry, 63,* 757–766.

Linehan, M. M., Dimeff, L. A., Reynolds, S. K., Comtois, K. A., Shaw Welch, S., Heagerty, P., & Kivlahan, D. R. (2002). Dialectical behavior therapy versus comprehensive validation plus 12-step for the treatment of opioid dependent women meeting criteria for borderline personality disorder. *Drug and Alcohol Dependence, 67,* 13–26.

Linehan, M. M., Schmidt, H., Dimeff, L. A., Craft, J. C., Kanter, J., & Comtois, K. A. (1999). Dialectical behavior therapy for patients with borderline personality disorder and drug-dependence. *American Journal on Addiction, 8,* 279–292.

Linehan, M. M., Tutek, D., Heard, H. L., & Armstrong, H. E. (1994). Interpersonal outcome of cognitive-behavioral treatment for chronically suicidal borderline patients. *American Journal of Psychiatry, 51,* 1771–1776.

Livesley, W. J., Jang, K. L., & Vernon, P. A. (1998). Phenotypic and genetic structure of traits delineating personality disorder. *Archives of General Psychiatry, 55,* 941–948.

Lykins, E. L. B., & Baer, R. A. (2009). Psychological functioning in a sample of long-term practitioners of mindfulness meditation. *Journal of Cognitive Psychotherapy: An International Quarterly, 23,* 226–241.

Lynch, T. R., Chapman, A. L., Rosenthal, M. Z., Kuo, J. R., & Linehan, M. M. (2006). Mechanisms of change in dialectical behavior therapy: Theoretical and empirical observations. *Journal of Clinical Psychology, 62,* 459–480.

Lynch, T. R., Morse, J. Q., Mendelson, T., & Robins, C. J. (2003). Dialectical behavior therapy for depressed older adults: A randomized pilot study. *American Journal of Geriatric Psychiatry, 11,* 33–45.

McCann, R. A., Ball, E. M., & Ivanoff, A. (2000). DBT with an inpatient forensic population: The CMHIP forensic model. *Cognitive and Behavioral Practice, 7,* 447–456.

Rathus, J. H., & Miller, A. L. (2002). Dialectical behavior therapy adapted for suicidal adolescents. *Suicide and Life Threatening Behavior. 32,* 146–157.

Robins, C. J. (2002). Zen principles and mindfulness practice in dialectical behavior therapy. *Cognitive and Behavioral Practice, 9*(1), 50–57.

Robins, C. J., & Chapman, A. L. (2004). Dialectical behavior therapy: Current status, recent developments, and future directions. *Journal of Personality Disorders, 18,* 73–89.

Robins, C. J., Schmidt, H., & Linehan, M. M. (2004). Dialectical behavior therapy: Synthesizing radical acceptance with skillful means. In S. C. Hayes, V. M. Follette, & M. M. Linehan (Eds.), *Mindfulness and acceptance: Expanding the cognitive-behavioral tradition* (pp. 30–44). New York, NY: Guilford Press.

Rosenthal, M. Z., Cheavens, J. S., Lejuez, C. W., & Lynch, T. R. (2005). Thought suppression mediates the relationship between negative affect and borderline personality disorder symptoms. *Behaviour Research and Therapy, 43,* 1173–1185.

Rosenthal, M. Z., Gratz, K., Kosson, D. S., Lejuez, C. W., Cheavens, J. S., & Lynch, T.R. (2008). Borderline personality disorder and emotional functioning: A review of the research literature. *Clinical Psychology Review, 28,* 75–91.

Safer, D. L., Telch, C. F., & Agras, W. S. (2001). Dialectical behavior therapy for bulimia nervosa. *American Journal of Psychiatry, 158,* 632–634.

Sapolsky, R. M. (1996). Why stress is bad for your brain. *Science, 273,* 749–750.

Segal, Z. V., Williams, J. M. G., & Teasdale, J. D. (2002). *Mindfulness-based cognitive therapy for depression.* New York, NY: Guilford Press.

Shapiro, S. L., Oman, D., Thoresen, C. E., Plante, T. G., & Flinders, T. (2008). Cultivating mindfulness: Effects on well-being. *Journal of Clinical Psychology, 64*(7), 840–862.

Shearin, E. N., & Linehan, M. M. (1992). Patient-therapist ratings and relationship to progress in dialectical behavior therapy for borderline personality disorder. *Behavior Therapy, 23*, 730–741.

Simpson, E. B., Pistorello, J., Begin, A., Costello, E., Levinson, H., Mulberry, S.,...Stevens, M. (1998). Use of dialectical behavior therapy in a partial hospital program for women with borderline personality disorder. *Psychiatric Services, 49*, 669–673.

Swann, W. B., Jr., Stein-Seroussi, A., & Giesler, R. B. (1992). Why people self-verify. *Journal of Personality and Social Psychology, 62*, 392–401.

Swenson, C. R., Sanderson, C., Dulit, R. A., & Linehan, M. M. (2001). The application of dialectical behavior therapy for patients with borderline personality disorder on inpatient units. *Psychiatric Quarterly, 72*, 307–324.

Telch, C. F., Agras, W. S., & Linehan, M. M. (2001). Dialectical behavior therapy for binge eating disorder. *Journal of Consulting and Clinical Psychology, 69*, 1061–1065.

Torgerson, S., Lygren, S., Oien, P. A., Skre, I., Onstad, S., Edvardsen, J.,...Kringlen, E. (2000). A twin study of personality disorders. *Comprehensive Psychiatry, 41*, 416–425.

Trupin, E. W., Stewart, D. G., Beach, B., & Boesky, L. (2002). Effectiveness of dialectical behaviour therapy program for incarcerated female juvenile offenders. *Child & Adolescent Mental Health, 7*, 121–127.

Turner, R. M. (2000). Naturalistic evaluation of dialectical behavior therapy-oriented treatment for borderline personality disorder. *Cognitive and Behavioral Practice, 7*, 413–419.

van den Bosch, L. M. C., Verheul, R., Schippers, G. M., & van den Brink, W. (2002). Dialectical behavior therapy for borderline patients with and without substance use problems: Implementation and long term effects. *Addictive Behaviors, 27*, 911–923.

Verheul, R., van den Bosch, L. M. C., Koeter, M. W. J., de Ridder, M. A. J., Stijnen, T., & van den Brink, W. (2003). Dialectical behavior therapy for women with borderline personality disorder. *British Journal of Psychiatry, 182*, 135–140.

Wagner, A. W., & Linehan, M. M. (1999). Facial expression recognition ability among women with borderline personality disorder: Implications for emotion regulation? *Journal of Personality Disorders, 13*, 329–344.

# 8

---

# Behavioral Activation in the Context of "Third Wave" Therapies

CHRISTOPHER R. MARTELL AND JONATHAN W. KANTER

---

## DESCRIPTION OF THE MODEL OF PSYCHOPATHOLOGY AND TREATMENT

The model of psychopathology and treatment presented by behavioral activation (BA)[1] is based on a behavioral theory of depression and has its philosophical roots in *functional contextualism* as described by Hayes, Strosahl, & Wilson (1999). Functional contextualism, in turn, evolved from earlier writings of B. F. Skinner on *radical behaviorism* (e.g., Skinner, 1953). BA's direct lineage with this traditional behavioral theory results in several key assumptions about how psychopathology is conceptualized and about the nature of the treatment techniques that follow from this conceptualization. The assumptions are simple to lay out and undoubtedly familiar to most readers. They are (a) thoughts and feelings are seen as behaviors to be explained rather than as causes of behavior; (b) an analysis of causality is not complete until the historical and contextual determinants of behavior are identified—this analysis is known as *functional analysis*; and (c) treatment techniques should target those determinants. Thus, in this model, thoughts and feelings are not direct causes of behavior, but can be accounted for, at least in principle, by functional analysis (Moore, 1980).

The functional analyses upon which BA's model of depression are based were initially presented by Lewinsohn (1974) and Ferster (1973, 1974). Lewinsohn suggested that depressive thoughts, feelings, and behaviors result from decreases in response contingent positive reinforcement (Lewinsohn, 1974; Martell, Dimidjian, & Lewinsohn, 2009). When positive reinforcers are decreased, operant behaviors previously maintained by those reinforcers are extinguished, and respondent emotional states, such as feeling sad, down, blue, and so forth, are elicited. Simply put, when positive reinforcement

---

[1] There are several variants of BA. In this chapter, we largely focus on BA as described by Martell, Addis, and Jacobson (2001), because this variant of BA has received the most empirical support and the techniques included in it have the most relevance to a discussion of mindfulness and acceptance. However, other important variants of BA exist, notably those of Lejuez, D. R. Hopko, Lepage, Hopko, and McNeil (2001), and Kanter, Busch, and Rusch (2009).

is decreased, one's relevant behavior slows down or stops, and one feels bad (Kanter, Busch, & Rusch, 2009).

There can be multiple causes for such decreases in response-contingent positive reinforcement. In some cases, the environment does not provide sufficient reinforcers. For example, an individual may be raised in an impoverished environment that may include literal poverty or lack of familial or social support. There may be a sudden loss of reinforcement. Such is the case when there is a death of a loved one. The individual may lack the requisite skill to access possible reinforcers in the environment. This may be the case when an individual is extremely shy or socially anxious and does not develop adequate assertiveness or communication skills in order to develop his or her social network. As discussed by Ferster (1973), there may be increases in negative reinforcement or punishment, as is the case for individuals whose lives are filled with daily hassles and chronic stress. Decreases in positive reinforcement result because, even though stimuli that would serve contingently as positive reinforcers are potentially available, the individual is not able to contact such reinforcement because the repertoire is dominated by escape and avoidance behavior. In these situations, we have increases in escape and avoidance behavior, in all its guises, as well as decreases in positively reinforced behavior.

These examples comprise only a partial list of behavioral factors associated with decreased positive reinforcement that are relevant to depression (Kanter et al, 2009). For example, schedules of reinforcement play a role in performance frequency, and Ferster (1973) proposed that schedules requiring large amounts of activity to produce a relevant change in the environment are most susceptible to loss and may explain phenomena such as highly successful people who have worked hard to attain a particular goal and become depressed when they appear to be at the height of their success. Regardless of the specific historical and current contextual determinants involved, when positive reinforcers are lost, reduced, or chronically low, the behavioral model posits that the symptoms and experience of depression will result. Individual differences in this experience are accounted for by differences in the relevant historical and current contextual features.

The BA model of psychopathology is consistent with other biopsychosocial theories and can be integrated with them. The model does not deny that some individuals are more vulnerable to depression than others, and that heritable factors play an important role. The model also does not deny that cognitive factors and cognitive styles are important. Multiple factors over time all interact to influence how one reacts to life events. However, ultimately these factors are cast in terms of the behavioral model, in that heritable factors and cognitive factors may influence the degree to which environmental events are reinforcing or punishing, but these factors do not need to change in order to change behavior. Ferster (1974) stated that "the common denominator among depressed persons is the decreased frequency of many different kinds of positively reinforced activity" (p. 35). The focus on reinforcement as the primary factor in depression is pragmatic, not dogmatic, as the theory leads to a set of clearly articulated and effective treatment techniques designed to increase contact with positive reinforcement (Martell, Addis, & Jacobson, 2001; Martell, Dimidjian, & Herman-Dunn, 2010).

## THE ROLE OF MINDFULNESS AND ACCEPTANCE-BASED STRATEGIES IN THE DEVELOPMENT OF THE MODEL

BA has recently been characterized as one of several new treatments, including Acceptance and Commitment Therapy (ACT; Hayes et al., 1999), emphasizing mindfulness and acceptance techniques (Hayes, 2004). The current formulation of the BA model and treatment undeniably has been influenced by this current trend in behavior therapy. ACT, like BA, has its foundation in the philosophy of functional contextualism, and both treatments target constructive treatment goals (e.g., "living a good life") with clients rather than targeting eliminative goals (i.e., symptom reduction). However, ACT, unlike BA, specifically eschews talk of symptom reduction and directly works with clients to mindfully accept the experience of unpleasant psychological experiences. In BA, talk of symptom reduction is not seen as problematic, and therapists have no concerns with symptom reduction as a goal. However, achieving long-term symptom reduction in BA requires acceptance of unpleasant psychological experiences in the short term, as one activates and re-engages in life rather than avoiding it.

In BA, activation is the primary strategy, not mindfulness or acceptance. We define activation broadly, including to increase behaviors in which a depressed client has ceased to engage, to increase activities that bring a sense of mastery or give pleasure, to increase goal-directed activities that bring clients closer to desired outcomes in their lives, and to increase the level of client engagement in all of these activities. Thus, both mindfulness and acceptance are implicit in the BA model, flow directly from the traditional behavioral theory upon which BA is based, and are explicated as specific strategies when necessary. In this way, mindfulness and acceptance are central to BA (for a full comparison of ACT and BA, see Kanter, Baruch, & Gaynor, 2006).

Traditional behavioral theory has long held that behavior change (including change in thoughts and feelings) can be produced through manipulation of contextual factors, and that one does not need to change thoughts and feelings to produce behavior change (Hayes & Brownstein, 1986). Although early stimulus-response behaviorists (e.g., Watson, 1913) argued that thoughts and feelings had no place in a science of behavior, and although many applied behavior analysts working with autism, developmental disabilities, or in other severe behavior management settings may focus exclusively on overt behavior, BA takes thoughts and feelings seriously. Fundamental to BA is an acknowledgement that thoughts and feelings may be painful and influential, and by focusing on overt behavior change while acknowledging these private events, BA clearly requires acceptance of them. The focus of BA is in the here and now, and clients are encouraged to be mindful of the environment around them, particularly when they are prone to brood or ruminate over past events. Unlike other mindfulness and acceptance approaches, BA does not suggest that all clients must be taught specific acceptance and mindfulness strategies. Focusing directly on behavior change may be enough, and sometimes acceptance and mindfulness simply come along for the ride. By acting according to a goal rather than a mood, a client may accept some level of dysphoria and reduce fighting against feeling badly; by attending to the elements of a task as an alternative to depressive rumination, the client may become more "mindful" of the activity in which he or she is engaging.

This is seen clearly in BA's concept of acting "from the outside-in" (Martell, Addis, & Jacobson, 2001). BA therapists conceptualize depression for clients as having environmental events that have led to a "less rewarding life," which resulted in depressed mood and associated emotional and physiological reactions. In BA, it is assumed that people respond naturally to moods and feelings. Thus, moods and feelings exert some stimulus control over other behavior in BA, but, consistent with traditional behavioral theory, *ultimate* causal status is reserved for environmental factors. For example, an individual who feels lethargic and fatigued may stay in bed later in the mornings, or sleep excessively during days off from work. Someone who feels sad may watch a poignant movie that elicits tears. In BA, we describe these behaviors as "secondary problems," in that they are responses to depressed mood, but they keep a downward cycle of depression going, because the more one engages in behavior such as sleeping excessively when one is lethargic, or watching tear-jerkers when one is sad, the more fatigued or sad one becomes. Furthermore, these activities often function as escape and avoidance and do not have a positive impact on the initial environmental stressors—or at least those environmental situations that are subject to change. In some cases, these activities can even make life problems worse. Such would be the case when a depressed client begins showing up late to work, procrastinates beginning projects, and responds to moods of the moment.

Acting according to a mood or feeling is natural, and many clients, when asked what they think needs to change in therapy, will suggest that they need to change these moods and then they can change their behaviors ("If I just had more energy or felt better, I would be able to…"). We refer to this as "acting from the inside-out." The dilemma for depressed clients is that the inside-out impetus is to escape, avoid, or not act at all. Therefore, waiting to feel better before acting will only perpetuate the cycle. Instead, we ask clients to act "from the outside-in." In other words, we help the client describe activities in which the client must engage, or activities that the client has engaged in during times when feeling better, and incorporate those activities into the client's schedule. There is no guarantee that the client will feel better, but there is a possibility that over time, as activities change, the client's mood will follow in the direction of the action. Acceptance of negative emotion is inherent in this notion of acting from the "outside-in." Rather than demand that one feel better before re-engaging in life, BA asks clients to feel whatever it is they are feeling, and re-engage anyway. It is, indeed, counterintuitive for most clients, but is at the heart of behavioral activation.

A second way in which acceptance and mindfulness are implicated in BA is with techniques suggested for dealing with depressed clients' ruminative thinking. Passive, ruminative, thinking styles are often associated with depressed mood (Nolen-Hoeksema,

Morrow, & Fredrickson, 1993), and BA therapists intervene at the level of teaching clients about the process and consequences of their thinking. Rather than ask, "how else could you have thought about that?" the BA therapist may ask, "what else could you have been doing instead of ruminating or brooding?" Usually, rumination serves as an avoidance function and can be conceptualized in BA as just like other avoidance behaviors (this conceptualization of rumination as a form of avoidance has received some empirical support; see Kanter, Mulick, Busch, Berlin, & Martell, 2006). Essentially, when ruminating, a client can be "lost in thought" and this process results in decreased contact with moment-to-moment contingencies and the painful emotions these contingencies may elicit. Thus, rumination, like other forms of avoidance, works in the short term in temporarily reducing unpleasant emotional states but does nothing in the long term to solve the problems that caused those states.

BA acknowledges that the content of much of the rumination of depressed clients is negative and painful in itself, and the cognitive content biases targeted by cognitive therapy (CT) (Beck, Rush, Shaw, & Emery, 1979) are real phenomena that characterize depression. The literature establishing negative cognitive content in depression is undeniable, but BA does not endorse the underlying cognitive model used in CT to account for this negative content (Clark, Beck, & Alford, 1999). In fact, theoretical models of cognitive content are somewhat superfluous to BA, because clinically it focuses on the process of rumination as behavior, rather than the content of rumination. Nonetheless, behavioral models of cognitive content exist (i.e., Relational Frame Theory; Hayes, Barnes-Holmes, & Roche, 2001) and have been applied to BA's theory of depression to provide a full account (Kanter, Busch, Weeks, & Landes, 2008; Kanter et al., 2007). Essentially, through relational processes, cognitive content may acquire aversive eliciting functions and have transformative effects on the environment consistent with those functions. This in turn renders additional environmental features reinforcing or not reinforcing. For example, although inaccurate, a man may fully believe he is about to lose his job, and the psychological effects of this belief may be consistent with actually losing the job.

In BA, clients are taught to focus on the behavioral process of rumination, recognize rumination as avoidance, and, as an adaptive alternative to rumination, encouraged to fully participate in the moment-to-moment experience that life presents, staying in full contact with the sights, sounds, smells, and so forth of the experience without slipping into rumination. In this context, mindfulness techniques are explicitly taught in BA as an alternative to rumination. They are not taught as an overarching skill that all clients must acquire; rather, they are determined to be relevant on a case-by-case basis depending on individual functional analyses of the client's problems and behavior.

## BRIEF CASE DESCRIPTION

Gerald was a 34-year-old married man with no children. He and his wife had been married for three years. Gerald had a successful career in sales, but had a constant feeling of dread and anxiety about his work. He particularly did not enjoy making "cold calls" to solicit new customers and thus avoided making such calls. He also had a great deal of independence in his job and controlled his own schedule. Gerald had been depressed for eight months, apparently triggered by the death of his father, with whom Gerald had been very close. Gerald had one other episode of depression years earlier, when he first left home to attend college. Changes and loss of the primary support from his family, particularly his father, were triggers for depression. After his father's death, Gerald began to stay in bed and missed entire mornings of work. He would call existing clients, but increasingly avoided the cold calls. He came to therapy after having been encouraged by his wife to seek help when Gerald had reported to her that he felt like life was not worth living. However, he stated that he did not want to die, and denied any intent to kill himself. He did report an overwhelming desire to escape through sleep and said he wished he could "hibernate and not have to face the world." He had lost nearly all interest in sex, had lost ten pounds due to a decrease in appetite, and he was refusing to have further discussions with his wife about starting a family and having children. Interestingly, Gerald had shown very little emotion at the time of his father's death, apart from crying at the funeral as the casket was carried to the cemetery. His wife thought that he had "adjusted quickly" to his father's death, which had followed an extended period of illness. After several months, however, it became apparent that Gerald's grief had turned to depression.

Gerald's therapist presented a BA case conceptualization to him, emphasizing that his feelings of sadness, fatigue, anhedonia, and decreased appetite, were the result of life being "less rewarding" (Martell, Addis, & Jacobson, 2001). However, his avoidance of work, decreased eating, and avoidance of conversations with his wife about their future had become secondary problems. Gerald and his therapist began by getting a baseline of Gerald's activities using activity monitoring charts. It was noted that there was a pattern in his behavior whereby his mood was better on days when he spent more time at work, and also that he was more likely to spend more time at work on days when he went to work earlier in the morning. He would even stay at work later on those days and make one or two of the initial contacts he so dreaded; he reported in the activity charts that his mood was improved and he felt that he had made a significant accomplishment. He and his therapist began activation by developing a plan for him to go to work earlier. On average, he was making it to work by noon. The plan was to move the time that he got to work up by 30 minutes every two days, with an ultimate goal of getting to work by 9:00 A.M. every day. By accomplishing his goal to go to work earlier, and facing his dread of particular clients and call them anyway, Gerald was engaging in activities that are considered implicit acceptance procedures in BA. He needed to accept feeling badly and having a desire to avoid and procrastinate, and get to work and deal with his clients anyway. When he would ruminate about how much he hated work, he learned to utilize a new behavior of getting ready for work and focusing only on each step of his morning routine until he was out of the house and on his way to the office. This is an example of the sort of "attention to experience" exercise that is akin to mindfulness in BA.

Once Gerald had made it to work by 9 A.M. three out of five workdays, he and his therapist added an interpersonal goal. Although he did not feel that he was ready to talk with his wife about starting a family, and still felt overwhelmed at the possibility, he agreed to suggest to his wife that they spend 30 minutes to an hour simply talking each day after dinner. He and his therapist invited her to join them for one session and together they set ground rules for the discussion so that Gerald would be more likely to engage and not become avoidant as a reaction to feeling anxious or overwhelmed. Gerald's therapist monitored his depression using the Beck Depression Inventory – II (Beck & Steer, 1987), administered every two weeks. Over a 24-session course of treatment, Gerald's scores decreased from an initial score of 40 to a score of 9. He reported at the end of treatment that he still had days when he felt like staying in bed, but had acquired practice at following his schedule rather than his mood, and was better able to engage in the day despite his mood. He was satisfied with his treatment, and he and his wife had begun to consider the possibility of having a child in the near future.

## WAYS IN WHICH THE MODEL IS THEORETICALLY AND TECHNICALLY DISTINCT FROM OTHER CBT MODELS

BA uses no specific thought modification strategies, and the notion that the necessary function of behavior change is ultimately to change beliefs (Hollon, 2001) is not consistent with the BA model. The goal of BA is behavior change that will either help to improve clients' moods over time or help to improve their lives and allow them to better cope with changing moods. The desired result is a robust behavioral repertoire for contacting and maintaining contact with diverse and stable sources of positive reinforcement that are in keeping with the client's goals and values. The goal of any intervention in BA is not to change how the client perceives his or her life situation. When BA therapists attend to a client's ruminative, depressive thinking, they do so in order to assist the client in engaging in more productive behavior, whether that be private behavior such as problem-solving rather than brooding, or public behavior such as engaging in a pleasant conversation with a friend. The important factor is to help the client engage in the moment, in the hopes that this will bring the client into contact with potential outcomes that will positively reinforce antidepressant behavior.

We see this version of BA as one of a long list of successful applications of traditional behavioral theory, dating back to the early writings of Skinner and the development of early behavior modification strategies. Whereas BA has been described as a *third wave* behavior therapy (Hayes, 2004), there is nothing particularly distinct about the model, and one can understand it fully in *first wave* behavior therapy terms. That said, it is a new model of depression, integrating and expanding on previous work. Hopefully, it capitalizes on behaviorism's strengths—a pragmatic, simple theory with clearly articulated and effective treatment techniques—and is seen by our colleagues as exemplary and comprehensive compared to earlier models, even if not highly distinctive.

The BA theory of depression is clearly distinct from traditional cognitive models of depression, and these differences have been articulated throughout BA's history. However, while the theories are clearly distinct, we believe the key metric is empirically distinguishing BA's mechanisms of action. In this regard, the BA model cannot be held out as remarkably distinct from other CBT models, given that the current literature on treatment outcome using BA has limited reporting concerning mechanism of change in BA. For example, in the well-known component analysis study of cognitive therapy (CT) for depression (Jacobson et al., 1996) both BA and CT clients showed significant increases in the frequency and enjoyability of pleasant events (as per BA's model), and decreases in negative thinking and attributions of negative events to internal, stable, and global factors (as per CT's model). In fact, contrary to expectations, changes in attributional styles early in treatment predicted later changes in depression for BA clients, not CT clients, while changes in frequency of pleasant events predicted later changes in depression for CT clients, not BA clients. In a larger, randomized control trial comparing BA to CT and antidepressant medication (Dimidjian et al., 2006) that will be discussed below, similar measures that would inform understanding of the mechanisms of change were not reported.

One might conclude that the success of BA suggests that shifts in the content of cognition are unnecessary mechanisms of change. We are not, however, prepared to make this claim. It is noteworthy that studies of BA to date address only the efficacy of treatment, and not the mechanism of change underlying the treatment. The question is not whether or not cognitive change is an active, or perhaps even "the" active mechanism of change, but rather whether it is necessary to make efforts to directly change the content of cognition. As far back as 1984, Latimer and Sweet noted that the primary question at issue in reviews of the literature was whether therapies derived from cognitive theory were more effective than behavior therapy, rather than whether cognition was important or relevant. They concluded at that time that "the efficacy of cognitive therapy (excluding behavioral components) has not been demonstrated in clinical populations, and what evidence there is suggests that the "cognitive" procedural components of the cognitive therapies are less potent than established behavioral methods (Latimer & Sweet, 1984). Despite significantly more research devoted to the question of the incremental effects of cognitive procedures over behavioral ones, these conclusions remain valid today (Cuijpers, van Straten, & Warmerdam, 2007; Ekers, Richards, & Gilbody, 2008; Mazzucchelli, Kane, & Rees, 2009), and we would argue that the success of BA suggests that both purely behavioral approaches and cognitive approaches that focus on changing the content of thoughts have been shown to be successful in the treatment of depression.

Understanding the mechanism of change in our treatment is an important question that will help define treatment procedures in the future. Development of new measures to fully assess the hypothesized mediators and mechanisms of change in BA is clearly needed, and research in this area is in its infancy (reviewed by Manos, Kanter, & Busch, 2010). Two such measures, the Behavioral Activation for Depression Scale

(Kanter, Mulick, et al., 2006) and the Environmental Rewards Observation Scale (Armento & Hopko, 2007), have been developed and are in use, but it remains to be seen whether these measures will successfully identify key processes in treatment. More research in this area is needed, as is the parallel development of measures of therapist adherence and competence in BA, and research on the relations of adherence and competence to outcome.

One hypothesis to pursue that could clarify the current confusion regarding operative treatment processes is the possibility that BA's purported mechanism of action—client activation to contact positive reinforcement—will be shown to mediate relapse prevention rather than acute symptom reduction. Positive reinforcement, after all, may take some time to contact successfully.

Consider the following BA case, seen by the second author. The client was unemployed, depressed, had become hopeless about finding a job, and had given up job searching. The therapist provided an "outside-in" rationale, discussed with the client how avoidance of job searching had actually made the client feel worse and guaranteed that the client would never find a job, and successfully motivated the client to begin searching again. The client immediately started to feel better, even though the presumed reinforcer for the behavior—finding a job—had not occurred and would not occur for several months. During the intervening time when looking for a job, the client no longer met criteria for depression but also felt "close" to depression, and only after getting the job did the client feel confident the depression would not return. In this case, it is reasonable to hypothesize two possibilities regarding the immediate symptom change: (a) that approaching, rather than avoiding, searching for a job was reinforced, perhaps negatively through the reduction of worry, and (b) that an amelioration of hopelessness (Teasdale, 1985) was the mediator of immediate symptom change, and the contact with positive reinforcement was the mediator of relapse prevention. Thus a cognitive change may have occurred despite there having been no direct cognitive intervention, resulting in immediate symptom relief, but the key to relapse prevention was the increased activity that led to contact with reinforcement over time. In fact, Strunk, DeRubeis, Chiu and Alvarez (2007) found that clients who demonstrated having acquired BA skills during therapy were more likely to remain depression-free over a follow-up period after acute treatment with CT. Future research should explore these possible interactions of mediating effects rather than dogmatic explorations of mediators from one theory or the other.

It is certainly possible that cognitive changes of many types can result from BA. For example, although it is not seen as important to the mechanism of change in BA according to behavioral theory, other theorists could posit that metacognitive awareness, or "thinking about thinking," is quite relevant to BA. For example, BA therapists work with clients on the "process" of thinking rather than on the "content" of thinking (Martell, Addis, & Jacobson, 2001), and clients are taught to attend to experience rather than to ruminative thoughts, as discussed above. This change in stance from focusing on content to focusing on process can be seen as a metacognitive change, in that it requires clients to think differently about thinking. Likewise, cognitive processes defined in ACT, such as cognitive distancing (seeing that a thought is just a thought that can be observed) and cognitive defusion (seeing that thoughts do not control our emotions or behavior) (Hayes, Strosahl, & Wilson, 1999) may be seen as processes invoked by BA, specifically by BA's mindfulness and acceptance strategies. For example, clients are asked to act according to goals rather than moods, feelings, and thoughts such as "I can't face the world today." Clients act despite these thoughts, rather than identifying with the thought as a fact that controls behavior. BA, however, holds that it is more parsimonious (and potentially just as effective) to focus theoretical interpretations of BA on overt behavioral changes that can be more easily observed and that require less speculation.

## THE NATURE AND VALUE OF COGNITIVE CHANGE STRATEGIES

Research on treatment of depression is clear that cognitive changes occur over the course of successful treatment but is mixed with respect to establishing cognitive change as a mediator of treatment outcome (Kazdin, 2007; Longmore & Worrell, 2007). The mediators of change in depression in BA specifically are unknown, and cognitive and behavioral mediators are both viable candidates. What has become clear, however, is that standard CT techniques such as the use of Socratic questioning to evaluate thoughts and beliefs—which are not used in BA—are unnecessary for attaining decreases in depressive symptoms that are maintained over time. BA techniques alone appear to be quite powerful in producing these outcomes.

In initial trials of BA, the mandate against the use of cognitive interventions was necessary to distinguish BA from CT for research purposes. Carrying that mandate forward into typical practice settings would be an unnecessary artifact of a research methodology on clinical technique, although the empirical evidence that BA was efficacious without the use of cognitive techniques should strongly influence empirically based practitioners to refrain from peppering cognitive interventions throughout treatment. There are also pragmatic reasons to avoid cognitive restructuring in BA. Simply put, techniques aimed at changing cognitions might be confusing for clients in the context of a larger BA model that holds that behavior change can occur in the absence of cognitive change. Cognitive interventions would potentially dilute the power of the rationale for concrete and direct behavior change strategies. For this functional and pragmatic reason, not because of how BA needed to be conducted in clinical trials or because behaviorists must *a priori* reject any cognitive change intervention, we recommend that BA therapists not engage in explicit restructuring interventions.

Another reason for BA to exclude cognitive change strategies has to do with ease of dissemination and training in BA. It is assumed that BA is easier to train and implement than CT on the grounds that the theory and techniques are simpler, specifically with respect to activation versus restructuring techniques (Hollon, 2000). This is, of course, an assumption, and it is important for future research to address it. To the extent it is found to be the case that BA is easier to disseminate and implement and as effective as or more effective than CT, it would represent an important development in the treatment of depression with clear public health and policy significance.

Until such research clarifies these issues, BA certainly offers the practicing clinician some flexibility in the treatment of depressed clients. Therapists can use their own personal strengths without fear that they are withholding important aspects of therapy. For example, not all therapists are skilled at Socratic questioning, and there is now evidence that a more didactic, behavior-centered approach is as effective as CT. Some clients may be better candidates for a strictly behavioral approach, whereas others may be better suited to cognitive interventions. Although there have been few matching studies to guide therapists, behavioral assessment and functional analysis are tools that can be used with the individual case to direct treatment planning and suggest which techniques might be better suited for particular cases.

Therapists are encouraged to develop a good case conceptualization and may have compelling reasons to use standard CBT procedures for a particular case. Adding cognitive change strategies to BA, however, would suggest also incorporating the cognitive conceptualization and rationale of CT (Beck, Rush, Shaw & Emery, 1979), which has always included both behavioral and cognitive interventions. Therapists also may choose to use situational analyses and assess and modify a client's interpretations of discrete interpersonal situations, in which case the conceptualization, rationale, and procedures of Cognitive Behavioral Analysis System of Psychotherapy may be helpful (CBASP; McCullough, 2000).

## REVIEW OF DATA

### Theory of Psychopathology Associated With the Model

BA's theory of psychopathology is well supported, with data from a variety of sources suggesting that a wide range of environmental events and circumstances increase risk for and directly trigger depression (Kanter et al., 2007; Manos et al., 2010). Although much of this research did not explicitly invoke behavioral theory, it is consistent with the notion that losses of, reductions in, and chronically low levels of reinforcement are central to the onset of depression. Furthermore, it is clear that avoidance plays a central role in depression onset and maintenance, based on a large set of studies (Ottenbreit & Dobson, 2004).

Research explicitly attempting to measure reinforcement processes has been hampered by measurement issues (Manos et al., 2010). Early research using the pleasant events schedule (MacPhillamy & Lewinsohn, 1982) and related measures (Lewinsohn & Talkington, 1979; Youngren, 1978) largely produced results consistent with the theory, but not as strong or clear as hoped. More recent attempts to measure activation processes may be more promising (Armento & Hopko, 2007; Kanter, Mulick, Busch, Berlin, & Martell, 2006) but have yet to be explored in longitudinal research.

204 NEW DEVELOPMENTS IN THE BEHAVIOR THERAPY TRADITION

It is important to acknowledge that depression is a heterogeneous condition, and research clearly indicates that a variety of factors interact to produce depression (Gotlib & Hammen, 2002). BA makes no claims to have the only viable model of depression with empirical support. The available data are consistent with the BA model, however, and the model's strength is not that it uniquely accounts for all the data on psychopathology but that it is linked with clear and effective treatment techniques.

## Treatment Outcome

Empirical support for various versions of BA has been accumulating since the 1970s and is reviewed in three meta-analyses of BA (Cuijpers et al., 2007; Ekers, Kane, & Rees, 2008; Mazzucchelli et al., 2009). Ekers et al. (2008) analyzed 17 randomized trials of BA and found that BA is superior to no-treatment or minimal-treatment controls (12 comparisons), brief psychotherapy (3 comparisons), supportive therapy (2 comparisons) and cognitive behavioral therapy (12 comparisons). With an overlapping dataset, Cuijpers et al. (2007) found similar findings and also found 2 comparisons in which BA was superior to control at the 6- to 12-month follow-up, and several comparisons showing that adding cognitive techniques did not improve BA's effectiveness at the end of acute treatment or through follow-up. Mazzucchelli et al. (2009) reviewed 34 studies on several versions of BA and concluded that BA meets criteria as a "well-established," empirically supported intervention. An earlier review led DeRubeis and Crits-Christoph (1998) similarly to list BA as an empirically supported psychotherapy for depression.

To date, the largest treatment outcome study conducted on BA has been a randomized trial comparing BA, CT, antidepressant medication, and pill placebo for 240 depressed participants categorized by severity as having either mild depression or moderate-to-severe depression (Dimidjian et al., 2006). For the mildly depressed participants, no differences were found between conditions at the end of acute treatment. For the high severity subgroup, only BA and medication participants were significantly improved over placebo, while CT participants were not, and further analyses could not establish any differential effectiveness between BA and medication for the more severely depressed participants. Furthermore, the BA condition evidenced fewer dropouts compared to the medication condition. Survival analyses across a two-year follow-up period indicated that participants who were remitted at the end of acute treatment who had received prior CT or prior BA did as well as those who continued on medication across the follow-up period, and better than those who had remitted and were discontinued from medication (Dobson et al., 2008).

As discussed above, although research on outcomes in BA is quite strong, research on treatment mechanisms and processes in BA is limited in scope and methodology, and results are somewhat unclear. At this time, it is fair to say that BA is an empirically supported intervention, but the necessary and active components of BA have not yet been identified (for a review, see Kanter et al. in press), and BA's mechanism of action has neither been supported nor tested with precision.

## BRIEF OVERVIEW OF FUTURE DIRECTIONS

We believe that BA offers great promise as a simple, pragmatic approach that can be applied broadly. One area of current work is the development of BA protocols for problems beyond depression. Currently, versions of BA have been developed and evaluated for a variety of conditions and settings, including post-traumatic stress disorder (Jakupcak et al., 2006; Mulick & Naugle, 2004), co-morbid depression and obesity (Pagoto et al., 2008), depression in cancer patients (Hopko et al., 2008), inner city illicit drug use (Daughters et al., 2008), depressed college students (Gawrysiak & Hopko, 2009), depressed smokers (MacPherson et al., 2010), and depressed Latinos (Kanter, Santiago-Rivera, Rusch, Busch, & West, 2010). Ongoing grant-supported work on BA, not yet published, is also occurring with respect to complicated bereavement, atypical depression, depressive episodes in bipolar disorder, depressed adolescents, dementia patient caregivers, medical adherence, and depressed elderly African Americans. Because the BA emphasis on modifying avoidance behavior is relevant to the treatment of anxiety, and anxiety and depression are frequently co-morbid, BA techniques have been included as part of a unified treatment for depressive and anxiety disorders proposed by Barlow, Allen, and Choate (2004). BA encourages approach rather than avoidance and action in goal-directed rather than mood-directed ways. In many disorders, when a functional analysis identifies certain behaviors as avoidance behaviors, the techniques of BA may be helpful.

Over the past decade, a shift in behavioral and cognitive behavioral therapies has occurred, putting less emphasis on symptom change and greater emphasis on mindfulness and emotional acceptance (Hayes, Folette, & Linehan, 2005). BA has been a part of this shift. Clients undergoing BA are encouraged to be present through mindfulness, attentive to their ongoing experience, and to accept rather than fight negative emotions. Relative to other treatments representing these trends, BA maintains a consistent emphasis on behavior change and thus continues to follow traditional behavioral practices. However, compared to traditional behavioral interventions, BA is less concerned with clients feeling good and more concerned with clients engaging in good lives.

Some may suggest that the current trend of which BA is a part represents a paradigm shift of sorts. One factor to consider when evaluating this question is the fact that mindfulness and acceptance techniques have always been a part of the CBT tradition, just less emphasized than currently, and couched within a cognitive change model. For example, relaxation techniques have been key components of many CBT treatments for anxiety disorders. Beck and Emery (1986) proposed that anxious clients take an initial step of accepting their anxiety and proposed the acronym *AWARE*, in which clients Accept the anxiety, Watch their thoughts, Act constructively, Repeat the above, and Expect the best.

This treatment suggestion from 1986 is not radically different from modern treatment procedures used in BA. As another example, Arch and Craske (2008) note that defusion procedures (i.e., noticing that a thought is just a thought, rather than accepting that thought as a fact) have always been an initial component of cognitive restructuring procedures, in which a client first recognizes a thought as a hypothesis to be evaluated rather than as a fact.

Certainly a simple shift in emphasis on certain techniques over other techniques does not represent a paradigm shift. Such an argument was made by Latimer and Sweet (1984) with respect to the cognitive revolution. Based on Kuhn's (1970) suggestion that scientific revolutions occur when an incompatible new paradigm replaces, in whole or in part, an established paradigm, they argued that cognitive therapy was more "evolutionary" than "revolutionary." It may be that the current increase in emphasis on mindfulness and acceptance in cognitive behavioral therapies, at least in BA's case, also represents more of an evolution than a revolution. From our perspective, something larger than a shift in emphasis on certain techniques must occur, and such a theoretical shift has occurred in the past. For example, the cognitive revolution added new cognitive techniques and de-emphasized (but retained) behavioral techniques, which was part of the evolution. More importantly, however, a new theoretical model of cognition as essential to the study of psychopathology and change supplanted the earlier behavioral model, and this represented a true, perhaps revolutionary, shift.

Currently, most of the evidence behind and energy for such a true shift occurring with the third wave is with the ACT model, which has posited a break in underlying philosophy and a new theoretical model of psychopathology and change (Hayes, Levin, Plumb, Boulanger, & Pistorello, in press; Viladarga, Hayes, Levin & Muto, 2009). BA, in fact, is consistent with ACT's theoretical model of change but is also squarely situated in traditional behavioral theory. Thus BA, and perhaps some of the other treatments labeled as "third wave," represents more of a shift in emphasis, and a return to earlier behavioral models of change, rather than a new model. In BA, these newer ideas are linear extensions of behavioral models, and this represents a logical progression of science. Looking at the history of BA, although it well may be part of a new wave of behavior therapy, currently it seems more reasonable to see it as part of the modifications that occur during the normal progression of applied science. Martell (2008) suggested that the metaphor of a wave, washing away everything that has been before it, may be a less apt metaphor for the current shift in emphasis than that of a stream flowing downhill, picking up additional rocks and sticks along the way, growing progressively stronger and more powerful. In BA's case, it seems like the same stream.

While the ACT model certainly has accumulated considerable empirical support (Hayes, Luoma, Bond, Masuda, & Lillis, 2006), it is not clear to us if the new model proposed by ACT will take hold in the community. Paradigm shifts, after all, are not scientific matters per se (O'Donohue, Lilienfeld, & Fowler, 2007). In our opinion, this issue of paradigm shifts is best left to historians, and it is too early to tell. Paradigm shifts, to our knowledge, are to be assessed post hoc rather than claimed while the shift is occurring. Whether or not a paradigm shift is occurring, it is an exciting time to be a behavioral researcher and clinician, and—most importantly—with BA it is possible that true, meaningful steps have been taken to improve the efficiency, effectiveness, and durability of treatment for individuals suffering with clinical depression and related conditions.

# REFERENCES

Arch, J. J., & Craske, M. G. (2008). Acceptance and commitment therapy and cognitive behavioral therapy for anxiety disorders: Different treatments, similar mechanisms? *Clinical Psychology: Science & Practice, 5,* 263–279.

Armento, M. E. A., & Hopko, D. R. (2007). The environmental reward observation scale (EROS): Development, validity, and reliability. *Behavior Therapy, 38,* 107–119.

Barlow, D. H., Allen, L. B., & Choate, M. L. (2004). Toward a unified treatment for emotional disorders. *Behavior Therapy, 35,* 205–230.

Beck A. T., & Emery, G. (1986). *Cognitive therapy of anxiety.* New York, NY: Guilford Press.

Beck, A. T., Rush, A. J., Shaw, B. F., & Emery, G. (1979). *Cognitive therapy of depression.* New York: Guilford.

Beck, A. T., & Steer, R. A. (1987). *Beck depression inventory: Manual.* San Antonio, TX: The Psychological Corporation.

Clark, D. A., Beck, A. T., & Alford, B. A. (1999). *Scientific foundations of cognitive theory and therapy of depression.* New York: Wiley.

Cuijpers, P., van Straten, A., & Warmerdam, L. (2007). Behavioral activation treatments of depression: A meta-analysis. *Clinical Psychology Review, 27,* 318–326.

Daughters, S. B., Braun, A. R., Sargeant, M., Reynolds, E. R., Hopko, D., Blanco, C., & Lejuez, C. W. (2008). Effectiveness of a brief behavioral treatment for inner-city illicit drug users with elevated depressive symptoms: The life enhancement treatment for substance use (LET'S ACT). *Journal of Clinical Psychiatry, 69,* 122–129.

DeRubeis, R., & Crits-Christoph, P. (1998). Empirically supported individual and group psychological treatments for adult mental disorders. *Journal of Consulting and Clinical Psychology, 66,* 37–52.

Dimidjian, S., Hollon., S. D., Dobson, K. S., Schmaling, K. B., Kohlenberg, R. J., Addis, M. E., et al. (2006). Randomized trial of behavioral activation, cognitive therapy, and antidepressant medication in the acute treatment of adults with major depression. *Journal of Consulting and Clinical Psychology, 74,* 658–670.

Dobson, K. S., Hollon, S. D., Dimidjian, S., Schmaling, K. B., Kohlenberg, R. J., Gallop, R. J.,… Jacobson, N. S. (2008). Randomized trial of behavioral activation, cognitive therapy, and antidepressant medication in the prevention of relapse and recurrence in major depression. *Journal of Consulting and Clinical Psychology, 76,* 468–477.

Ekers, D., Richards, D., & Gilbody, S. (2008). A meta-analysis of randomized trials of behavioural treatments of depression. *Psychological Medicine, 38,* 611–623.

Ferster, C. B. (1973). A functional analysis of depression. *American Psychologist, 28,* 857–870.

Ferster, C. B. (1974). Behavioral approaches to depression. In R. J. Friedman & M. M. Katz (Eds.), *The psychology of depression: Contemporary* (pp. 29–45). Washington, DC: New Hemisphere Publishing.

Ferster, C. B. (1980). A functional analysis of behavior therapy. In, L. P. Rehm (Ed.), *Behavior therapy for depression: Present status and future directions* (pp. 18–196). New York, NY: Academic Press.

Gawrysiak, M., Nicholas, C., & Hopko, D. R. (2009). Behavioral activation for moderately depressed university students: Randomized controlled trial. *Journal of Counseling Psychology, 56,* 468–475.

Gotlib, I. H., & Hammen, C. L. (Eds.) (2002). *Handbook of depression.* New York, NY: Guilford Press.

Hayes, S. C. (2004). Acceptance and commitment therapy, relational frame theory, and the third wave of behavioral and cognitive therapies. *Behavior Therapy, 35(4)*, 639–665.

Hayes, S. C., Barnes-Holmes, D., & Roche, B. (2001). Relational frame theory: A post-Skinnerian account of human language and cognition. New York, NY: Kluwer Academic/Plenum.

Hayes, S. C., & Brownstein, A. J. (1986). Mentalism, behavior-behavior relations, and a behavior-analytic view of the purposes of science. *Behavior Analyst, 9*, 175–190.

Hayes, S. C., Levin, M., Plumb, J., Boulanger, J., & Pistorello, J. (in press). Acceptance and commitment therapy and contextual behavioral science: Examining the progress of a distinctive model of behavioral and cognitive therapy. *Behavior Therapy.*

Hayes, S. C., Folette, V. M., & Linehan, M. M., (Eds.), (2004). *Mindfulness, acceptance and relationship: The new behavior therapies.* New York, NY: Guilford Press.

Hayes, S. C., Luoma, J. B., Bond, F. W., Masuda, A., & Lillis, J. (2006). Acceptance and commitment therapy: Model, processes and outcomes. *Behaviour Research and Therapy, 44*, 1–25.

Hayes, S. C., Strosahl, K. D., & Wilson, K. G. (1999). *Acceptance and commitment therapy: An experiential approach to behavior change.* New York, NY: Guilford Press.

Hollon, S. D. (2000). Do cognitive change strategies matter in cognitive therapy? *Prevention & Treatment, 3*, Article 25.

Hollon, S. D. (2001). Behavioral activation treatment for depression: A commentary, *Clinical Psychology: Science and Practice, 8*, 271–274.

Hopko, D. R., Bell, J. L., Armento, M., Robertson, S., Mullane, C., Wolf, N., & Lejuez, C. W. (2008). Cognitive behavior therapy for depressed cancer patients in a medical care setting. *Behavior Therapy, 39*, 126–136.

Jacobson, N. S. Dobson, K. Truax, P. A., Addis, M. E., Koerner, K., Gollan, J. K.,...Prince, S. E. (1996). A component analysis of cognitive-behavioral treatment for depression. *Journal of Consulting and Clinical Psychology, 64*, 295–304.

Jakupcak, M., Roberts, L. J., Martell, C. Mulick, P., Michael, S., Reed, R.,...McFall, M. (2006). A pilot study of behavioral activation for veterans with posttraumatic stress disorder. *Journal of Traumatic Stress, 19*, 387–391.

Kanter, J. W., Baruch, D. E., & Gaynor, S. T. (2006). Acceptance and commitment therapy and behavioral activation for the treatment of depression: Description and comparison. *Behavior Analyst, 29*, 161–185.

Kanter, J. W., Busch, A. M., & Rusch, L. C. (2009). *Behavioral Activation: The CBT Distinctive Features Series.* East Sussex, England: Routledge Press.

Kanter, J. W., Busch, A. M., Weeks, C. E., & Landes, S. J. (2008). The nature of clinical depression: Symptoms, syndromes, and behavior analysis. *Behavior Analyst, 31*, 1–22.

Kanter, J. W., Landes, S. J., Busch, A. M., Rusch, L. C., Baruch, D. E., & Manos, R. C. (2007). A contemporary behavioral model of depression. In D. W. Woods & J. W. Kanter (Eds.), *Understanding behavior disorders: A contemporary behavioral perspective.* Oakland, CA: New Harbinger.

Kanter, J. W., Manos, R. C., Bowe, W. M., Baruch, D. E., Busch, A. M., & Rusch, L. C. (in press). What is behavioral activation? A review of the empirical literature. *Clinical Psychology Review.*

Kanter, J. W., Mulick, P. S., Busch, A. M., Berlin, K. S. & Martell, C. R. (2006). The behavioral activation for depression scale (BADS): Psychometric properties and factor structure. *Journal of Psychopathological and Behavioral Assessment, 29*, 191–202.

Kanter, J. W., Santiago-Rivera, A., Rusch, L. C., Busch, A. M., & West, P. (2010). Initial outcomes of a culturally adapted behavioral activation for Latinas diagnosed with depression at a community clinic. *Behavior Modification, 34*, 120–144.

Kazdin, A. E. (2007). Mediators and mechanisms of change in psychotherapy research. *Annual Review of Clinical Psychology, 3*, 1–27.

Kuhn, T. A. (1970). The structure of scientific revolutions (2nd ed.). Chicago, IL: University of Chicago Press.

Latimer, P. R., & Sweet, A. A., (1984). Cognitive versus behavioral procedures in cognitive-behavior therapy: A critical review of the evidence. *Journal of Behavior Therapy and Experimental Psychiatry, 15*, 9–22.

Lejuez, C. W., Hopko, D. R., LePage, J., Hopko, S. D., & McNeil, D. W. (2001). A brief behavioral activation treatment for depression. *Cognitive and Behavioral Practice, 8*, 164–175.

Lewinsohn, P. M. (1974). A behavioral approach to depression. In R. J. Friedman & M. M. Katz (Eds.), *The psychology of depression: Contemporary theory and research* (pp. 157–178). Washington, DC: Hemisphere Publishing.

Lewinsohn, P. M., & Talkington, J. (1979). Studies on the measurement of unpleasant events and relations with depression. *Applied Psychological Measurement, 3,* 83–101.

Longmore, R. J., & Worrell, M. (2007). Do we need to challenge thoughts in cognitive behavior therapy? *Clinical Psychology Review, 27,* 173–187.

MacPherson. L., Tull, M., Matusiewicz, A. K., Rodman, S., Strong, D. R., Kahler, C. W.,...Lejuez, C. W. (2010). Randomized controlled trial of behavioral activation smoking cessation treatment for smokers with elevated depressive symptoms. *Journal of Consulting and Clinical Psychology, 78,* 55–61.

MacPhillamy, D. J. & Lewinsohn, P. M. (1982). The pleasant events schedule: Studies on reliability, validity, and scale intercorrelation. *Journal of Consulting and Clinical Psychology, 50,* 363–380.

Manos, R. C., Kanter, J. W., & Busch, A. M. (2010). A critical review of assessment strategies to measure the behavioral activation model of depression. *Clinical Psychology Review, 30,* 547–561.

Martell, C. R. (2008, July). *Twenty years of behavior therapy: Trends and counter-trends.* Address given at the annual convention of the British Association of Behavioural and Cognitive Psychotherapies, Edinburgh, Scotland.

Martell, C. R., Addis, M. E., & Jacobson, N. S. (2001). *Depression in context: Strategies for guided action.* New York, NY: W. W. Norton.

Martell, C. R., Dimidjian, S., & Herman-Dunn, R. (2010). *Behavioral activation for depression: A clinician's guide.* New York, NY: Guilford Press.

Martell, C. R., Dimidjian, S., & Lewinsohn, P. M. (2009). Behavioral models of depression. In R. E. Ingram (Ed.), *The international encyclopedia of depression* (pp. 59–64). New York, NY: Springer.

Mazzucchelli, T., Kane, R., & Rees, C. (2009). Behavioral activation treatments for adults: A meta-analysis and review. *Clinical Psychology: Science and Practice, 16,* 383–411.

McCullough, J. P. (2000). *Treatment for chronic depression: Cognitive behavioral analysis system of psychotherapy.* New York: Guilford.

Moore, J. (1980). On behaviorism and private events. *Psychological Record, 30,* 459–475.

Mulick, P., & Naugle, A. (2004). Behavioral activation for comorbid PTSD and major depression: A case study. *Cognitive and Behavioral Practice, 11,* 378–387.

Nolen-Hoeksema, S., Morrow, J., & Fredrickson, B. L. (1993). Response styles and the duration of episodes of depressed mood. *Journal of Abnormal Psychology, 102,* 20–28.

O'Donohue, W. T., Lilienfeld, S. O., & Fowler, K. A. (2007). Science is an essential safeguard against human error. In S. O. Lilienfeld & W. T. O'Donohue (Eds.), *The great ideas of clinical science: 17 principles that every mental health professional should understand* (pp. 3–27). New York, NY: Routledge.

Ottenbreit, N. D., & Dobson, K. S. (2004). Avoidance and depression: The construction of the cognitive-behavioral avoidance scale. *Behaviour Research and Therapy, 42,* 293–313.

Pagoto, S. L, Bodenlos, J., Schneider, K., Olendzki, B., Spates, C. R., & Ma, Y. (2008). Initial investigation of behavioral activation treatment for comorbid major depressive disorder and obesity. *Psychotherapy: Theory, Research, and Practice, 45,* 410–415.

Skinner, B. F. (1953). *Science and human behavior.* New York, NY: Mcmillian.

Strunk, D. R., DeRubeis, R. J., Chiu, A. W., & Alvarez, J. (2007). Patient's competence in and performance of cognitive therapy skills: Relation to the reduction of relapse risk following treatment for depression. *Journal of Consulting and Clinical Psychology, 75,* 523–530.

Teasdale, J. D. (1985). Psychological treatments for depression: How do they work? *Behavior Research and Therapy, 23,* 157–165.

Viladarga, R., Hayes, S. C., Levin, M. E., & Muto, T. (2009). Creating a strategy for progress: A contextual behavioral science approach. *Behavior Analyst, 32,* 105–133

Watson, J. B. (1913). Psychology as the behaviorist views it. *Psychological Review, 20,* 158–177.

Youngren, M. A. (1978). The functional relationship of depression and problematic interpersonal behavior. *Dissertation Abstracts International, 39 (10-B),* 5096.

# 9

## Integrative Behavioral Couple Therapy

### An Acceptance-Based Approach to Improving Relationship Functioning

MEGHAN M. MCGINN, LISA A. BENSON, AND ANDREW CHRISTENSEN

Integrative behavioral couple therapy (IBCT) addresses couples' relational distress by fostering both acceptance and change of each partner's behaviors. Developed in the early 1990s by Neil Jacobson and Andrew Christensen, IBCT incorporates interventions characteristic of both the first and third "waves" of behavioral therapy (Christensen, Jacobson, & Babcock, 1995). While IBCT includes some techniques aimed directly at altering behaviors in one partner that are distressing to the other, it primarily attempts to enhance individuals' ability to empathize with their partners and respond in a more accepting way. Thus, whereas third wave individual therapies emphasize toleration and acceptance of one's own emotional experience (e.g., DBT, Linehan et al., 1991; ACT, Hayes, Strosahl, & Wilson, 1999), the challenge for participants in IBCT is to take the additional step of accepting the thoughts, feelings, and behaviors of another person. The rationale for this incorporation of acceptance-oriented technique into couple therapy is discussed at greater length below. It is worth noting here that acceptance may be an essential part of treating couple distress if only because many issues with which couples struggle are essentially unresolvable: a loud and emphatic style of arguing versus a quiet and retiring one, disagreement about whether to live in an urban or rural area, and many others. The treatment goal therefore may be not to eliminate the problem but to help the couple respond to it in a way that builds their intimacy rather than eroding it.

## MODEL OF COUPLE DISTRESS AND TREATMENT

IBCT is based on the notion that incompatibilities between partners are not a signal of a doomed relationship but rather a common characteristic of nearly all couples (Jacobson & Christensen, 1996). Some incompatibilities are innocuous; for example, if Mary has lively, flirtatious relationships with all her friends while Jim is content to stay by her side, both may be satisfied with this arrangement of their social life. Indeed, Mary's vivacity and Jim's stability may be what attracted them to each other. However, when incompatibilities match existing vulnerabilities in either or both partners, distress is more likely to result. If Jim has experienced sexual infidelity with two previous girlfriends, while Mary fears being controlled by a jealous man the way her mother was, they are more likely to experience conflicts around the issues of loyalty and independence.

The difference around which a couple has most of their difficulties is described as their "theme" in IBCT. The theme is seen as the driving force behind the couple's interactions, the content of their arguments being simply derivative of this theme. The primary theme for Jim and Mary is one of closeness and distance. Other common themes center on control and responsibility, conventionality versus unconventionality, and artistic, intuitive orientation versus reasoned, scientific orientation (Jacobson & Christensen, 1996).

The next step in the development of couple distress is "polarization" around the problem (Jacobson & Christensen, 1996). In this example, Mary was at first only mildly attentive to other men. When Jim anxiously began asking her to spend less time with their male friends, however, she became upset with what she perceived as attempts to control her behavior. She reacted by frequently making plans without Jim and refusing to tell him about her activities. The angrier he became with this behavior, and the more he attempted to punish her, the more of her life she hid from him, which then increased his distrust and suspicion. In this way, couples whose differences are initially quite small may become increasingly different as they react negatively to one another's behaviors (Jacobson & Christensen, 1996).

The interaction pattern for this example couple is a very common one we have termed "demand-withdraw" (Christensen, 1988; Heavey, Layne, & Christensen, 1993). Jim's position is that of the demander: He wants more of Mary's attention and affection, and he urges her to discuss with him how much he wants her to change her behavior. Mary, by contrast, wants more distance and freedom from Jim, and often sits silently through their "discussions" of the problem. Further polarization and repeated use of this interaction style eventually leads a to a "mutual trap," whereby the best way each partner can think of to handle the problem seems to never work and each feels "stuck" (Jacobson & Christensen, 1996). Here, Mary feels that the only way she can avoid arguments about whether she has been faithful is to hide all her feelings and experiences from Jim, while Jim cannot think of any way to stop Mary from looking for outside gratification except to show her how angry it makes him.

## OVERVIEW OF IBCT

Once the distressed couple presents for therapy, IBCT takes place in three stages: assessment, feedback, and treatment (Jacobson & Christensen, 1996). The therapist must first complete a thorough assessment of the couple's difficulties. The first session occurs with both partners present so that both can describe their perspectives on the presenting problem; this exchange also provides the therapist with an opportunity to observe the couple's interactional style. The therapist will also ask how the couple met, what attracted them to each other, and what their relationship is like when they have better days, in order to learn more about the couple's strengths.

Next, the therapist meets once with each partner separately, assuring them that what is discussed in these individual sessions will be kept confidential from the other partner if requested (Jacobson & Christensen, 1996). These sessions are an opportunity to obtain more information about how each partner views the couple's problem, how each partner's family history may be related to their current difficulties, how distressed each is, and how committed each is to the relationship. It is essential to ask in the individual setting whether any violence has occurred between the two and whether either has engaged in extramarital relationships. Guaranteeing confidentiality increases the probability that each individual will provide the therapist with accurate information to help determine the appropriateness of couple treatment. IBCT therapists do not accept for treatment couples in which there are moderate to severe levels of violence that could be injurious and/or couples in which one is not open with the other for fear of physical retaliation. These couples are referred to programs that target domestic violence. There is some evidence to suggest that certain subtypes of domestic violence perpetrators may be successfully treated in couple therapy (Stith, Rosen, McCollum, & Thompson, 2004); however, couple therapy that specifically targets violence is more appropriate for these couples than IBCT (e.g., Domestic Violence Focused Couple Treatment; Stith, McCollum, Rosen, Locke, & Goldberg, 2005). IBCT therapists will also not treat a couple in which either partner insists on continuing a secret affair, but will help the involved partner either tell the other partner of the affair or end the affair quietly and commit to therapy (see Atkins, Eldridge, Baucom, & Christensen, 2005). If the involved partner refuses to end the affair, the therapist will simply tell both partners that, unfortunately, the couple does not seem appropriate for couple therapy.

After completing these three assessment sessions, the therapist meets with both partners together to summarize and provide feedback. The first topic is the couple's current level of distress and commitment. Often, the couple will have completed measures of marital satisfaction and commitment so that the therapist can comment on how their scores compare to a normative sample. Then the therapist presents a formulation of the couple's presenting problem, which is essentially an individualized version of the theory of couple distress described above. It is important for the therapist to stop periodically to ask whether the couple agrees with this description and whether there is anything they would like to add. If the couple relates to the formulation, it can alter their understanding of the problem into one that is more interpersonal and less blaming. Importantly, the therapist also provides feedback about the couple's strengths, which can alleviate hopelessness. Finally, the therapist provides an overview of what IBCT treatment would be like. Once the couple has heard a formulation of their difficulties and an overview of how treatment would address those difficulties, the therapist gives them an opportunity to decide whether they would like to proceed with this treatment.

The treatment phase of IBCT is less formally structured than the assessment phase. The couple and therapist meet for approximately an hour each week. When the couple arrives for a session, they are invited to identify the most important positive and negative interactions they had in the past week and what they would most like to discuss in therapy. Typically, the events couples describe are related to the formulation (Jacobson & Christensen, 1996). For example, Mary and Jim might discuss an incident where she didn't tell him of lunch with a male co-worker.

Toward the beginning of therapy, the IBCT therapist emphasizes acceptance-focused interventions (Jacobson & Christensen, 1996). Encouraging acceptance can both produce behavioral change on its own and also facilitate the later use of direct change interventions. Specifically, the therapist promotes *empathic joining, unified detachment,* and *tolerance building.* To help partners join with one another when discussing a problem area, the therapist restates each person's position as a reasonable view with which the other partner could potentially sympathize and encourages both partners to express their emotions in a self-disclosing, vulnerable way (Christensen et al., 2004). For example, if Jim accuses Mary of not telling him about a lunch with a co-worker, the therapist might ask Jim about his feelings when Mary is away from him and he does not know what she is doing. The therapist might try to elicit his anxiety and fearful fantasies about her. It is more likely that Mary will be able to empathize with Jim's anxiety than be responsive to his accusations. While the therapist may need to take the role of eliciting each partner's unstated feelings early in therapy, as the two begin to treat each other more compassionately, they will be more likely to be more emotionally expressive on their own.

With respect to unified detachment, the goal of the therapist is to help the couple identify the usual course of their conflicts and find non-blaming ways of describing it. For example, a therapist might help Mary and Jim analyze the usual sequence of their conflicts, which often begin with Mary's cursory description of her day and Jim's accusatory questions about her activities but then lead to escalating questions and minimal responses until an open argument occurs. In addition to helping the couple articulate their "usual dance," the therapist may encourage them to find a metaphor or name for their pattern. Mary and Jim might find "cat and mouse game" or "district attorney and hostile witness scenario" as helpful ways to distance themselves emotionally from the pattern. By "objectively" describing the pattern of their conflictual interaction and by creating names and metaphors for these patterns, the IBCT therapist transforms the problem into an "it" that they can discuss, enabling them to reassert their underlying closeness and capacity for working together as a unit. Thus, both empathic joining and unified detachment use discussion of the couple's primary problem as a vehicle for building intimacy between them.

Tolerance-building interventions are also used, because often what is most destructive to the couple's relationship is not the original subject of their disagreement but how they react to one another when disagreeing (Christensen & Jacobson, 1996). If certain words or styles of arguing are particularly distressing to the other partner, it may be useful to provide a series of exposures to those behaviors and thus reduce their emotional impact. For example, Mary has likely become sensitive to Jim's questions about her activities, no matter how innocuous his questions (which, of course, are often not innocuous). Similarly, Jim has likely become sensitive about Mary's limited disclosure, even if it too is innocuous (which it sometimes is not). After Mary and Jim had progressed in therapy to the point where they were well aware of their interactional patterns and could discuss them, at least at times, with some degree of objectivity and compassion, the IBCT therapist might introduce a tolerance exercise. The therapist might ask the couple to role play an "end-of-the-workday-and-just-arrived-home scenario" where Jim asks questions and/or Mary provides limited disclosure. Such an exercise might lead to humorous distance on the part of both as they have difficulty getting into their roles. Or, if they assume their roles well, they may experience a smaller version of the emotional upset that they experience outside of the session. These emotional experiences can then be debriefed. Thus, the tolerance exercise provides an opportunity for both "unified detachment" (the humor of their failed attempt at role play) and "empathic joining" (an emotional debriefing of their experience in the session). These tolerance interventions can also be applied outside of the session. For example, a therapist might encourage Jim to pick a time during the week when he is not distressed or suspicious and start asking questions of Mary. The therapist gives this assignment in front of Mary, so that she can experience some doubt about the authenticity of Jim's questioning later that week. If the questioning does lead to reactions on her part, it gives a chance for Jim to experience Mary's sensitivity when he is more emotionally capable of empathizing with it. The couple is encouraged to discuss the assignment afterward. The entire process can lead partners to be more tolerant of this pattern of behavior, which is likely to rear its ugly head occasionally in their lives, no matter how successful therapy is.

Once a couple has developed a strong commitment to collaboration in addressing their problems through these acceptance-oriented techniques, the IBCT therapist can also introduce the behavior exchange, communication training, and problem-solving training typical of traditional behavioral couple therapy. Often the acceptance strategies above are sufficient for couples, but if not, these traditional strategies can be employed. For behavior exchange, both partners list specific behaviors that would please their partners, engage in these behaviors, and receive positive reinforcement from both the therapist and the other partner. In communication training, the therapist teaches the couple how to alternate listening and speaking, how to phrase their statements in a clear, emotion-focused way when speaking, and how to paraphrase how they understood the other person's message after listening. Problem-solving training involves teaching couples to define the problem before attempting to solve it, freely generate alternatives without evaluating them, and then identify the advantages and disadvantages of each alternative and select one to try. These strategies are used as needed if, for example, a couple needs to make an important decision together and appears to lack basic problem-solving skills.

IBCT therefore is "integrative" in the sense that it incorporates both acceptance- and change-oriented behavioral techniques according to a particular couple's needs. The primary task for the therapist in selecting and implementing interventions is ensuring that each is closely linked to the formulation and hence likely to make some alteration in the interactional pattern that has been most distressing to the couple.

# ACCEPTANCE-BASED STRATEGIES

To understand why acceptance can be so valuable for couples, it is helpful to consider the history of traditional behavioral couple (or marital) therapy (TBCT). Therapists have been using behavioral techniques to alter couple distress since the 1960s, but the first randomized clinical trial of a manualized behavioral couple therapy was conducted by Jacobson in 1977. This protocol (Jacobson & Margolin, 1979), which incorporates behavior exchange, communication training, and problem-solving training, has been shown to be more effective than any of its component behavioral interventions (Jacobson, 1984). Moreover, TBCT is as yet the only treatment for couple distress that meets criteria for an "efficacious and specific intervention" (Baucom, Shoham, Meuser, Daiuto, & Stickle, 1998, p. 58).

Unfortunately, it has become clear that there are limitations to TBCT's clinical utility. An analysis of four TBCT outcome studies (Jacobson et al., 1984) indicates that 54.7% of participating couples experienced reliable improvements in their marital satisfaction scores from pre- to post-treatment. However, only 35.3% of couples improved enough for their level of marital satisfaction to enter the nondistressed range (Jacobson et al., 1984). Also, many of these couples were unable to maintain their improvements through a follow-up period. Jacobson, Schmaling, and Holtzworth-Munroe (1987) found that 25% of TBCT couples experienced deteriorating marital satisfaction, and 9% divorced by the two-year follow-up, while Snyder, Wills, and Grady-Fletcher (1991) found that 38% of couples treated with TBCT divorced after four years. These results suggest that although TBCT can be helpful to couples, the changes are often short-lived or insufficient for true recovery from distress.

There are several types of couples for whom TBCT seems to be less beneficial. Couples who described themselves as less committed to the relationship gained less from therapy (Jacobson & Christensen, 1996). Also, couples benefited less if they were less emotionally engaged with each other; in particular, if they were no longer sexually intimate or if either partner tended to withdraw from conversations about the relationship (Jacobson & Christensen, 1996). Older couples were typically less successful in TBCT, with this limitation apparently specific to age rather than length of relationship (Jacobson & Christensen, 1996). Perhaps relatedly, couples with more traditional views about partners' roles in the family, especially with regard to housework, breadwinning, and caring for family members' emotional well-being, were less likely to improve in TBCT (Jacobson & Christensen, 1996). Also, couples benefited less from TBCT if they had widely divergent views of what they wanted from marriage, for instance, an emotionally supportive friendship versus a primarily instrumental partnership. As Jacobson and Christensen (1996) note, what couples from these categories have in common is a greater difficulty with flexibility, collaboration, and ultimately acceptance of their differences. It seems plausible that it is this lack of facility with mutual acceptance that made TBCT less successful for such couples.

Traditional behavioral couple therapy certainly acknowledges that a collaborative mindset is necessary for couples to engage in behavioral techniques. However, if a couple does not enter therapy willing to compromise and alter their own behavior in order to resolve their difficulties (which is quite common), the behavioral therapist must simply ask them to commit to trying collaborative techniques despite their feelings (Jacobson & Christensen, 1996). Unfortunately, even if a couple does attempt to simulate this collaborative mindset, the effects are unlikely to be enduring. Since B. F. Skinner (1966), behavior therapists have distinguished between rule-governed and contingency-shaped changes in behavior; the former kind of change occurs in response to specific imposed demands, while the latter proceeds more naturally from the person's response to the environment. TBCT's approach to establishing a collaborative mind-set is rule-governed, in that partners demonstrate it only in response to the therapist's request. When the rules are no longer so salient, it is not clear that the behavior will be maintained (Jacobson & Christensen, 1996). Moreover, an individual may feel little appreciation for his or her partner's efforts to engage in change techniques when it is clear that the partner does not truly wish to do so. If the collaborative behavior were prompted by the natural contingency of the partner feeling concern about the individual and wanting him or her to be happy, the individual is likely to find it more satisfying (Jacobson & Christensen, 1996).

When Jacobson and Christensen began to consider how to improve TBCT, therefore, one of their primary emphases was on helping partners accept and empathize with each other's needs in a naturally motivating way. Both had found in their clinical practice that conflict over change often masked feelings of hurt and pain (Jacobson & Christensen, 1996). Instead of focusing all their clinical attention on modifying the behavior of the "wrong-doer" in couple conflicts, an alternative option was to modify the "wronged" partner's response by introducing a new context from which he or she could respond. Implementing the acceptance techniques described above not only provided couples with specific strategies for managing their difficulties but also changed the patterns of their relationships in a way that altered their spontaneous responses to one another for the better.

Acceptance in the context of couple therapy differs from its role in individual therapy because it requires toleration of another person's experiences and behavior as well as one's own. It is important to note that this does not mean couples are expected to accept the status quo of their relationships (Jacobson & Christensen, 1996). Not only would this kind of acceptance be unlikely to alter relationship satisfaction, but it is likely to favor one partner's interests over the other's. It is typical in couple therapy for one individual (most often female) to have issues on which she is pressing for change while the other (most often male) enters therapy simply hoping she will stop being so distressed (Jacobson & Christensen, 1996). The IBCT therapist should not collude with the less demanding partner by promoting non-change.

Instead, acceptance in IBCT means letting go of the struggle to change in order to foster open, nondefensive expression and build greater intimacy around incompatibilities. Rather than being resigned to their inability to behave differently toward each other, partners who engage in acceptance techniques should come to feel that ceasing their efforts to change each other allows them to appreciate and care for each other more.

When this greater caring naturally alters the couple's emotional reactions to each other's behaviors, they often find they have less need for the actual behaviors to change. At the same time, somewhat paradoxically, the experience of feeling accepted by one's partner is often a significant motivator for behavior change, in that the pressure to change can be a major barrier to change (Jacobson & Christensen, 1996). For example, when Karen is constantly pushing her partner, Isabella, to be as organized and plan-oriented as she is, Isabella's resentment about her nagging may prevent her from taking action. If Karen instead begins to focus on how much she appreciates what Isabella's easygoing nature contributes to her life, thus eliminating that pressure, Isabella may find that she actually wants to start taking steps to achieve the goals that are meaningful to her or to both of them. However, behavior change is not considered the end goal or purpose of acceptance. In the beginning of therapy, this paradox is discussed with the couple to the extent that it is judged to facilitate a reduction in the pressure for change. When it occurs during treatment, behavior change is often highlighted and reinforced by the therapist, but treatment is still considered successful in the absence of actual changes in behavior if instead there are changes in the stimulus value of the behaviors and behavior change simply becomes less of a priority.

Given the extent of the evidence that TBCT is least helpful for those couples who find collaboration most difficult, a couple therapy that focuses on accepting one's partner's understandable reactions and relatable emotions offers a great deal of hope for renewed intimacy and true partnership. The emphasis on acceptance in IBCT is therefore essential for change, perhaps of a couple's behavioral patterns, but certainly of their lived experience of being in the relationship together.

# CASE EXAMPLE[1]

The following example illustrates IBCT case formulation and treatment. Carmella and Eduardo are a middle-aged married couple of Filipino descent who jointly operate a limousine company out of their home. They have been married for 20 years and have two teenage daughters. Carmella initiated their request for therapy, stating that the two were experiencing communication problems.

## Assessment and Feedback

During their three-session assessment period, the couple identified a number of seemingly disparate concerns in their relationship. Both expressed feelings of jealousy when the other spent time with members of the opposite sex, with Eduardo particularly expressing concern about a male family friend whom Carmella had known since childhood.

[1] The case example couple was seen by therapists Elizabeth Thompson, MA, and Joseph Trombello, MA, under the supervision of the third author. The names and demographic details were changed to protect the confidentiality of the couple.

Carmella complained that Eduardo was too uptight in his spending habits and that she and their children should be allowed some small indulgences. She also expressed concern that Eduardo did not have many interests outside of the family business, while she wanted to devote more time to her own interests and extended family relationships.

Both members of the couple described conflict surrounding sexual intimacy. Eduardo described that Carmella had made hurtful comments to him in the past regarding his sexual performance, while Carmella expressed that Eduardo's own embarrassment about his sexual performance and subsequent moodiness after sex make it a tense experience for both of them.

Carmella was further frustrated that her attempts to discuss issues in their relationship were met with silence or a change of topic. She felt she could never tell what was on his mind. Eduardo expressed resistance to these hot-topic conversations because they left him feeling attacked and taken for granted.

After their first joint assessment session, each partner was given three questionnaires to complete individually, the Outcome Questionnaire (OQ-45.2; Lambert, Hansen, et al., 1996), Dyadic Adjustment Scale (DAS; Spanier, 1976), and Conflict Tactics Scale (CTS; Straus, 1979). Scores on these measures revealed significant individual and dyadic distress (DAS = 78 and 73 for Carmella and Eduardo, respectively), and low levels of violence over the past year.

In the feedback session, the IBCT therapist presented his working conceptualization of the couple's relationship difficulties. The primary theme for the couple was formulated as a struggle over their differing needs for independence/autonomy. Carmella has a strong need for maintaining interests and relationships outside of her marriage, particularly given the amount of time the couple spends running their business together, while Eduardo is content to spend most of his time with Carmella and their children. This difference between them may have in fact drawn the couple to each other when they first met, as Carmella appreciated Eduardo's attention and care towards her while Carmella's individuality made her an engaging and interesting romantic partner for Eduardo. The difference became problematic over time, however, due to vulnerabilities in the partners that were exposed by their changing circumstances. Eduardo and Carmella moved closer to her family of origin and far away from Eduardo's family shortly after they were married, leaving Eduardo with no social ties outside of Carmella and little opportunity to make new friends when he spent most of his time starting up his business and family. Carmella is very close to her extended family members and is used to a lot of social activity, so she began she began to feel uncomfortable with spending such a large proportion of her time with Eduardo.

Carmella's need for autonomy comes out in any situation where Eduardo can be seen as exerting control, such as when he tries to cut down their spending or gets upset about whom she is spending time with. She reacts by demanding that Eduardo be less controlling and encouraging him to become more independent himself. Eduardo experiences this as very critical and, in turn, shuts down. Carmella experiences his withdrawal as secretive and avoidant of their problems. In addition, Eduardo feels threatened by Carmella's need for independence, but is in a bind because he worries his attempts to bring them closer (e.g., initiating physical intimacy) will be met with criticism. Through this demand/withdraw pattern, the couple has become more polarized in their positions and are now in a mutual trap, where both partners want closeness but feel powerless to achieve it while caught in this struggle over independence.

During feedback, the therapist also presented the couple with normative data regarding their level of distress and emphasized their strengths in their deep care for each other and their commitment to and pride in their family and business. The couple was asked for their feedback on the formulation and it was explained what future sessions would look like, after which they agreed to continue with therapy.

## Interventions

Based on the conceptualization, the primary interventions for Eduardo and Carmella were those that would break up their typical interaction pattern and encourage empathic joining and unified detachment from that pattern. Toward this end, the couple was asked to bring in issues that had come up during the week that had been successfully or unsuccessfully managed. The therapist worked with the couple to see their theme and interaction pattern in the event that they brought in and took specific steps towards altering the context. For instance, one week the couple discussed an argument they had over a birthday party for Carmella's niece that Eduardo did not attend because he preferred to stay home and relax on his day off. Carmella was furious when she returned and yelled at him for making her lie to her family about where he was. Eduardo, interpreting her response as a criticism of his less social personality, refused to discuss the issue. In session, the therapist worked to elicit softer expressions from Carmella, suggesting that she may have felt hurt that Eduardo did not attend the party. Carmella agreed that she was disappointed, and that she sometimes felt sad and embarrassed that Eduardo did not appear to have any interest in becoming closer to her family. In this altered context, Eduardo was able to respond empathically to Carmella, and disclosed his own feelings of anxiety in large social gatherings as well as his genuine preference at times to be alone. On several occasions, sexual incidents were discussed in therapy. These discussions were difficult for the couple; both of their anxieties about sexual contact were expressed, particularly Eduardo's distress when his sexual performance was not what he wanted and Carmella's anxiety that Eduardo would be angry and distant if he felt his own behavior in the sexual encounter was lacking. The therapist briefly suggested sensate focus exercises, but the couple was not interested in carrying through with them. Instead, the emotionally focused discussions themselves seemed to have an impact in lessening their sexual tensions. Over time they reported more relaxing and more fulfilling sexual encounters.

## Therapy Outcome

In the last few sessions of treatment, Carmella and Eduardo were having less negative within-session interactions and seemed to be bringing in fewer problematic events from the week for discussion. Eduardo displayed greater openness to expressing his feelings, and even suggested that they continue to set aside a weekly time to discuss issues together after therapy termination, while Carmella showed more receptivity to his comments. This observable improvement was confirmed by a brief satisfaction measure the couple completed each week, which showed consistent changes over the course of therapy, as well as by their post-treatment assessments in which both members of the couple's DAS scores where in the satisfied range.

## IBCT AND CBT

## IBCT and Behavioral Couple Therapies

IBCT shares common roots with other forms of behavioral couple therapy, including Traditional Behavior Couple Therapy (TBCT; Jacobson & Margolin, 1979) and Cognitive Behavioral Couple Therapy (CBCT; Baucom & Epstein, 1990), but is both theoretically and technically distinct from these therapies. As described earlier, IBCT represents a theoretical departure from TBCT in its emphasis on emotional acceptance and contingency-shaped rather than rule-governed behavioral change. Although IBCT, like TBCT, utilizes direct behavioral change interventions when appropriate, in practice these strategies are used less often than acceptance-building interventions, and when used, are administered in a more flexible and less rule-governed fashion. For example, communication training in IBCT would encourage partners to share their emotional reactions with one another, particularly softer emotions, but the therapist would not enforce formulaic "I statements" to express these emotional reactions.

CBCT also has roots in TBCT, but its development was dually influenced by TBCT and models of cognitive therapy (CT) for individual distress (Beck, 1970; Ellis, 1962). The cognitive model presumes that an individual's cognitions, emotions, and behaviors reciprocally impact one another, so that intervention aimed at one of these events (e.g., modifying dysfunctional cognitions) will lead to changes in the others (e.g., emotions and behaviors). CBCT is most dissimilar from IBCT in its use of direct cognitive modification strategies. CBCT assumes that individuals within a couple, in an attempt to make meaning out of relationship events, may engage in dysfunctional information processing. They may selectively attend to the negative behaviors of their partner, make maladaptive attributions about their partner's behavior, or hold unrealistic expectancies, assumptions, and standards about their partners and about romantic partners and relationships in general (Baucom & Epstein, 1990). In CBCT these types of cognitions are elicited and challenged during therapy, utilizing strategies similar to those used in individual CT (Baucom & Epstein, 1990). For instance, Sara may have the thought, "He doesn't care about me," in response to Tim coming home late without calling, which in turn influences her behavior to shout angrily at him when he gets home. One type of cognitive intervention would be to look at the evidence for and against Sara's thought, eliciting from the couple instances when Tim has demonstrated that he cares and/or alternative explanations for why Tim didn't call when he was late. In light of this evidence, Sara may come to modify her irrational thought (e.g., "There may be other reasons for Tim being late since he often demonstrates that he cares about me"), and she will be encouraged recall the modified thought when similar situations come up in the future.

From the IBCT perspective, this type of intervention is seen as problematic and unnecessary. By evaluating and modifying the content of Sara's thought, the therapist may actually exacerbate the extent to which Tim views Sara as "irrational" and thus blames her for their relationship difficulties. This is especially a risk when couples differ significantly in the way they process information and express emotion, as it can privilege the more "logical" partner at the expense of the "emotional" partner. Further, as many individuals enter couple therapy feeling invalidated by their partner, they may be more likely to experience these cognitive change strategies on the part of the therapist as invalidating as well. The IBCT therapist intervenes at the level of the couple's dysfunctional behavior pattern (e.g., through unified detachment) rather than the individual's dysfunctional thoughts, allowing the therapist to present a more complete and balanced view of the situation.

It is worth noting that couple therapy in any form is different from individual therapy in that private events (i.e., thoughts and emotions) from both individuals are elicited in therapy. By virtue of both partners sharing their experience, the absolute truth of any individual's thoughts may be "challenged" by the other partner. In the example described above, Tim may provide evidence for or against Sara's thought that he does not care when he describes his own interpretation of the event, which may or may not influence how much Sara believes this thought to be true. While this type of "reality testing" may occur in IBCT, it is not the primary goal of the therapy. Rather, IBCT highlights the *relative* truth of private events and uses this as a tool towards building intimacy. Before eliciting Tim's response in the situation described above, the IBCT therapist would likely highlight the sequence of events, (e.g., "when Tim didn't call it functioned to make you feel uncared for and you became angry by the time he got home") and validate the partner's experience, placing it within a broader context, (e.g., "the thought that Tim might not care for you must be very scary, especially given your experience as a child with your father being absent so much of the time"). The therapist, therefore, does not directly dispute whether or not Tim cares for Sara or label her thought as dysfunctional, but instead makes sense of her reaction and subsequent behavior so that Tim may hear it and respond less defensively. The therapist essentially presents the couple's experience as a dilemma. Sara and Tim are in a bind because Sara has an understandably strong reaction to the thought that Tim might not care about her, and at the same time, her behavior of shouting at him when he gets home functions to make Tim feel attacked and subsequently withdraw from conversation, leading to more distressed feelings from both members of the couple. This presentation validates the experience of both partners, while elucidating the antecedents and consequences of each partner's behavior.

More recently, CBCT therapists have broadened their repertoire of cognitive intervention strategies to include strategies that attend to macro-level patterns of behavior in couples and contextual factors such as prior relationships. CBCT therapists are also attending to emotional processes more than they had in the past, including interventions aimed at accessing and heightening emotional experience (Baucom, Epstein, & LaTillade, 2002). These recent enhancements, a reaction in part to criticisms of CBCT and its primary focus on cognitive strategies, make it more difficult to distinguish CBCT from other approaches, since it now includes so much under its umbrella. However, IBCT still differs from CBCT in its greater emphasis on a case formulation, its emphasis on contingency-shaped versus rule-governed behavior, and its de-emphasis on traditional cognitive strategies.

## IBCT and "Third Wave" Behavior Therapies

Although IBCT is not a direct adaptation of any particular model of individual therapy in the same way that CBCT came out of CBT for individuals, it shares several commonalities with acceptance-based behavioral therapies for individual distress. In IBCT, similar to Acceptance and Commitment Therapy (ACT) and Dialectical Behavior Therapy (DBT), there is an emphasis on the *function* of behaviors and internal events over their content and on *acceptance*, or the willingness to experience the world, one's self, and others as they are in the present moment. The DBT therapist, for instance, models acceptance through validating the patient's current behavior as an understandable attempt to solve a problem, while simultaneously helping the patient to understand both the function and consequences of his or her behavior. Likewise, the IBCT therapist validates each partner's current behaviors, thoughts, and emotions by describing these events as they function within a context that includes the personal histories and individual differences of both partners and the surrounding environment in which the partners co-exist. When the therapist is able to see each partner's behavior as an understandable reaction to the present context, it promotes the couple's acceptance of each other.

IBCT is also similar to ACT in that it is highly experiential. Couples have the experience of responding to new stimuli and may be reinforced by their partners for new ways of behaving within the session. For instance, a married couple may typically engage in a pattern in which the husband expresses anger and criticism towards his wife, resulting in the wife withdrawing from the conversation. In session, the therapist may elicit a "soft" disclosure from the husband, that is, the emotional experience behind his anger and criticism, such as his feelings of hurt or fear. The wife then experiences within the session the new stimulus of the husband's expression of softer emotions and may respond to this situation as she would naturally. If the wife stays in the conversation or offers support, the husband is reinforced for the new behavior of expressing a softer emotion. This occurs without the therapist prescribing any rule, such as "do not criticize" or "do not withdraw," that would structure the interaction and distance it from their normal experience of interacting. Rather, the couple experiences in the moment a new stimulus that naturally alters the context in which they respond.

## ROLE OF COGNITION IN IBCT

As described above, IBCT does not employ interventions aimed at directly modifying thoughts. Unlike some acceptance-based individual therapies, IBCT also does not employ strategies towards an explicit goal of achieving metacognitive awareness or cognitive defusion. Since the focus is on the couple, there is not the same emphasis on changing either individual's relationship with his or her own thoughts; thus, IBCT therapists do not directly attempt to detach couples from the content of their own thoughts or promote the experience of a thought as just a thought. However, the concept of unified detachment may operate through a similar mechanism, in that it is a technique aimed at distancing the partners, jointly, from their interaction pattern. The use of humor and/or metaphor and the descriptive rather than evaluative nature of unified detachment techniques distance the couple from whatever meaning they would normally make of their behaviors (e.g., blaming of the partner).

Further, IBCT therapists are interested in creating a shift in cognitive awareness from an individual awareness of one's own thoughts and emotions towards a dyadic awareness of both partners' thoughts and emotions, a kind of dyadic mindfulness. Through this process, individuals gain a more flexible and dialectical view of the situation, as they come to recognize that both their own experience and their partner's experience of the event contain elements of truth (i.e., both are understandable given the context). It is possible that a shift towards a dyadic awareness will also lead to metacognitive awareness if, by recognizing the validity of both partners' interpretations in a situation, the individual comes to experience his or her own interpretation of an event as just one of many possible interpretations. At this time, however, there is no research to support that IBCT indeed has this impact. The explicit purpose of moving towards a dyadic awareness in IBCT is to decrease blaming of the partner and thus, on some occasions, to be able to detach from the emotional turmoil (unified detachment) or, on other occasions, to experience empathic joining through expressions of these emotions.

## EMPIRICAL FINDINGS

### Theory of Couple Distress

Although the theory of relationship distress on which IBCT is based awaits full confirmation, there is empirical support for many of its components (see Christensen & Pasch, 1993). Of particular note is research on patterns of polarization, such as the common demand-withdraw pattern (Heavey, Layne, & Christensen, 1993). This pattern of interaction has been associated with relationship dissatisfaction across several different cultures (Christensen, Eldridge, Catla-Preta, Lim, & Santagata, 2006). Couples who are observed to display a strong wife-demand, husband-withdraw pattern tend to experience a decline in marital satisfaction over the next year (Heavey, Layne, & Christensen, 1993). This result suggests that engaging in this type of dysfunctional interaction pattern typically leads to further deterioration of the relationship in the way predicted by this theory.

## Treatment Outcome

What is arguably most important for a therapeutic approach is not the data support-ing its theory of distress but the outcome data attesting to its efficacy and effectiveness. There are two small clinical trials and one large multisite clinical trial that support the efficacy of IBCT. In an unpublished dissertation, Wimberly (1998) demonstrated that eight couples randomly assigned to a group format of IBCT were significantly more satisfied than nine wait-list couples at the end of therapy. In a small clinical trial of 21 couples, Jacobson, Christensen, Prince, Cordova, and Eldridge (2000) compared TBCT and IBCT; effect size data and clinical significance data favored IBCT. However, the most extensive data in support of the efficacy of IBCT comes from a large, two-site ran-domized clinical trial (Christensen et al., 2004) that enrolled seriously and chronically distressed couples as participants. One hundred thirty-four married couples in Seattle, Washington, and Los Angeles, California, participated in an average of 23 therapy ses-sions each over the course of approximately 36 weeks. Participants' mean ages were 41.6 years for wives and 43.5 years for husbands, mean length of marriage was 10 years, and the sample was approximately 80% Caucasian. Couples were excluded if either partner had a current diagnosis of schizophrenia, bipolar disorder, substance use or dependence, borderline personality disorder, schizotypal personality disorder, or anti-social personality disorder. Couples, in which the wife reported that the husband had engaged in dangerous levels of battering, also could not enter the study. To ensure that this was a significantly distressed sample that would provide a rigorous test of the treat-ment method, couples had to meet criteria for marital dissatisfaction on three separate measures over the course of three time points. Almost 100 couples who wanted couple therapy were excluded as not distressed enough; a follow-up indicated that half of these couples subsequently sought couple therapy in the community.

All study therapists were experienced community practitioners who delivered both TBCT and IBCT and received intense supervision in both (Christensen et al., 2004). Adherence coding indicated that TBCT and IBCT were distinguishable, and as practiced, IBCT therapists engaged in about three times as many acceptance-oriented interventions as TBCT therapists, while TBCT therapists had three times as many change-oriented interventions. Also, to ensure that the TBCT provided in this study was state-of-the-art, an outside consultant who co-wrote the original TBCT manual (Gayla Margolin of Jacobson & Margolin, 1976) provided competence ratings for selected TBCT sessions. The average rating was 52.1, which falls between "good" and "excellent." Participants' responses to measures of therapeutic bond and consumer satisfaction with therapy were also equivalent across treatment groups. These findings suggest that this trial was a fair comparison of the two treatments.

Multilevel modeling of how couples' self-reported marital satisfaction (DAS; the primary outcome measure) changed from pre-treatment to post-treatment indicated that couples improved significantly in therapy, with a fairly large effect size of $d = 0.86$ (Christensen et al., 2004). Trajectories for the treatment groups differed, however;

TBCT couples' satisfaction initially increased more quickly but then plateaued, while IBCT couples' satisfaction increased more steadily. Fully 71% of IBCT couples saw their satisfaction increase reliably or even reach a normative "recovered" level by the end of treatment, while only 59% of TBCT couples were in this clinical significance category.

The two-year follow-up to this study suggested that change in satisfaction after the end of treatment did not occur linearly (Christensen, Atkins, Baucom, & George, 2006). Instead, couples' trajectories followed a "hockey stick" pattern of decline in the weeks immediately following termination and then a reversal in which satisfaction again began to increase. Importantly, in the model that best fit these trajectories, the initial decline was significantly more rapid and more prolonged for TBCT couples than IBCT couples. However, by the two-year follow-up assessment, similar levels of clinically significant improvement were apparent for both treatments: 69% of IBCT couples and 60% of TBCT couples. Thus, about two-thirds of couples were reliably improved or recovered at the two-year follow-up assessment, a considerable number given the initial distress of this population (Christensen, Atkins et al., 2006).

## Predictors of Treatment Response

Common predictors of response to couple therapy include demographic variables, such as age and ethnicity; intrapersonal variables, such as personality and psychopathology; and interpersonal variables, such as communication style and commitment level. From a pool of possible predictors in each of these categories at pre-treatment, Atkins, Berns, and colleagues (2005) identified the best predictors of change in marital satisfaction from pre- to post-treatment in the Christensen, Atkins et al. clinical trial. Reporting a greater desire for closeness, better communication, and fewer steps taken toward divorce predicted a higher initial level of marital satisfaction. While husbands' and wives' initial satisfaction did not differ, husbands' improved more quickly and then slowed over time. Couples who have been married for more than 18 years also improved more quickly than couples with newer marriages. Unhappiness with one's sexual relationship was also an important predictor. Sexually unhappy couples in TBCT improve quickly in the beginning of treatment but then actually decreased in satisfaction toward the end of treatment, while sexually unhappy IBCT couples' satisfaction increased more steadily throughout treatment. Whereas interpersonal factors thus seem to be the most important predictors of marital satisfaction, they are strongest in predicting initial status, rather than rate of change. It is possible that this finding is due to behavioral couple therapy's success at helping all types of couples improve their satisfaction.

Baucom, Atkins, Simpson, and Christensen (2009) also identified the best pre-treatment predictors of a couple's clinical status at the two-year follow-up assessment in this clinical trial. Two particularly important predictors were encoded emotional arousal, measured as the fundamental frequency in a speaker's voice during interaction tasks, and power processes, specifically the extent to which a speaker's language was characterized by coercive ("hard") or collaborative ("soft") influence tactics during those tasks. Greater use of soft influence tactics was strongly associated with clinical improvement or recovery in IBCT couples only. Couples disinclined to use soft influence may have more difficulty with the task of empathic joining and therefore respond less well to IBCT (Baucom et al., 2009). Wives with higher encoded arousal were more likely to have deteriorated satisfaction in both treatment groups, although the effect was stronger for TBCT couples. Although high emotional arousal presents challenges for any therapist, IBCT's emphasis on emotion may have improved therapists' ability to help this kind of couple (Baucom et al., 2009). In combination, the results of these two studies suggest that although some characteristics like power processes and encoded arousal may indicate a preferred treatment, both treatments are able to meet the needs of most couples.

## Mechanisms of Change

Satisfaction may increase over the course of therapy for any number of factors, such as appropriate changes in the frequency of positive and negative behavior, changes in the acceptability of those behaviors, and communication between partners. Doss, Thom, Sevier, Atkins, and Christensen (2005) examined the frequency and acceptability of partners' desired behaviors as possible mechanism of change. Their results showed that TBCT led to greater changes in frequency of targeted behavior early in therapy, but IBCT led to greater changes in acceptance of targeted behavior both early and late in therapy. Importantly, change in behavioral frequency was strongly related to improvements in satisfaction early in therapy, while emotional acceptance was more strongly related to changes in satisfaction later in therapy.

Self-reported communication patterns also improved over the course of treatment (Doss et al., 2005). Both groups increased their incidence of mutually positive interactions, although the effect was significantly greater in TBCT. Also, both groups decreased their incidence of mutually negative interactions and demand-withdraw interactions. Each of these changes was associated with improvements in marital satisfaction for both husbands and wives. These results suggest that although TBCT's emphasis on behavioral changes produces results early in therapy, these changes may be neither as sustainable nor ultimately as beneficial to marital satisfaction as changes in behavior acceptability and communication style (Doss et al., 2005).

Cordova, Jacobson, and Christensen (1998) also examined communication as a potential mechanism of change but focused on observed communication behaviors during selected therapy sessions. IBCT and TBCT couples did not differ on detachment or soft emotion (such as fear or sadness) early in therapy, but IBCT couples displayed significantly more of each in the middle and late sessions. Across groups, increases in soft emotion and detachment, as well as decreases in problem behaviors, correlated with improvements in marital satisfaction. These results suggest that IBCT produces more significant changes than TBCT in couples' tendency to discuss problems in a non-blaming, empathy-inducing way, behaviors which are then associated with greater relationship satisfaction (Cordova et al., 1998).

## Specific Treatment Applications

An important subgroup of distressed couples is that group of couples in which at least one partner has participated in an affair. In the major clinical trial comparing IBCT and TBCT (Christensen et al., 2004), 19 couples are known to have been affected by one or more affairs. In 14 of these couples, the affair was disclosed before or during therapy; the remaining 5 did not disclose the affair to their partners or to the therapist (Atkins, Eldridge, Baucom, & Christensen, 2005), but the affair was discovered during follow-up. Disclosure couples began treatment significantly more distressed than non-affair couples, but their marital satisfaction improved at similar rates and their final treatment outcomes were indistinguishable from those of non-affair couples. In contrast, non-disclosure couples were even more distressed than disclosure couples and they ultimately experienced declines in marital satisfaction that are best characterized as treatment failures. These results suggest that it is possible to successfully treat couples who have experienced an affair using IBCT or TBCT, although individuals who refuse to disclose their affairs to their partners and continue the affair make a positive outcome much less likely (Atkins, Eldridge, et al., 2005).

Also, several authors have outlined ways to modify IBCT for couples in which one partner suffers from mental or physical illness. Specific versions of IBCT exist for major depression (Cordova & Gee, 2001; Koerner, Prince, & Jacobson, 1994), post-traumatic stress disorder (Erbes, Polusny, MacDermid, & Compton, 2008), and chronic pain (Cano & Leonard, 2006). However, at this time, the efficacy of these modifications has been demonstrated only through individual case studies.

These findings certainly are limited by their use of data from two small clinical trials and one large one. However, given the large sample size, use of multiple sites, and rigorous design of that large study, as well as the results of the previous smaller studies, it appears to be the case that IBCT is at least as efficacious as TBCT, which is known to be an efficacious and specific treatment for couple distress (Christensen et al., 2004). Furthermore, the results suggest several particular strengths of IBCT. IBCT seems to better protect couples against a typical decline in satisfaction after leaving therapy. IBCT is also more closely associated with the changes in communication style (e.g., using soft emotions) that are linked to improvements in marital satisfaction. For couples who begin treatment with the wife experiencing a great deal of emotional arousal, IBCT's emphasis on emotion appears to be particularly important. The evidence from this study therefore supports the value of IBCT's acceptance-based interventions in working with highly distressed couples.

## FUTURE DIRECTIONS

At present, with three clinical trials supporting its efficacy, we can say with confidence that IBCT is a viable treatment option for ameliorating marital distress and decreasing the likelihood of separation or divorce. In relation to other behavioral therapies, we know that IBCT appears to work as well as TBCT during the course of treatment and significantly better over the first two years of follow-up. IBCT and CBCT have not been directly compared in a randomized control trial. CBCT is also empirically supported and shown to be as effective as TBCT, and so, by extension, it is likely that a comparative trial of CBCT and IBCT would result in similar effect sizes for both therapies, with perhaps better follow-up for IBCT. However, at this point in the development of behavioral couple therapies there is general agreement in the field that it is not a particularly useful or interesting question simply to ask which full treatment package works better, considering that (a) most studies of this kind have failed to find between treatment differences in effectiveness, and (b) a study comparing full treatments does not allow us to answer the question of what components of treatment are driving the effects (Snyder, Castellani, & Whisman, 2006). Thus, many have suggested that future research should focus on the study of change processes rather than strictly on therapy outcome, including increased attention to client change processes, the private experiences of individuals (e.g., emotions, cognitions), and potential moderators of various change processes (Heatherington, Friedlander, & Greenberg, 2005). Both IBCT and CBCT have preliminary empirical evidence supporting their proposed change mechanisms. As described earlier, greater increases in the acceptability of target problem behaviors in IBCT were related to better treatment outcome (Doss et al., 2005), and couples in IBCT who showed increases in detachment over the course of therapy showed greater treatment gains (Cordova, Jacobson, & Christensen, 1998). Likewise, in support of CBCT mechanisms, those who received cognitive restructuring and emotional expressiveness training in addition to behavioral interventions showed significant changes in relationship-oriented cognitions over the course of therapy, whereas those receiving TBCT alone did not (Baucom, Seyers, & Sher, 1990). There has not been research to date assessing changes in acceptance in CBCT or cognitive change in IBCT, however, and we do not know if and when these are essential components of treatment. We are still a long way from identifying exactly *why* and *for whom* these treatments work.

One of the main barriers to comparative studies is that there is considerable overlap between treatments, particularly for behavioral therapies that share common roots, but also for non-behavioral couple therapies, such as emotion-focused couple therapy (EFT; Johnson & Greenberg, 1985) and insight-oriented couple therapy (IOCT; Synder & Willis, 1989). Indeed, Christensen (2010) has suggested that the best way for couple therapy research to proceed may be through implementing a unified protocol for couple therapy. The unified protocol consists of five key principles:

1. Provide a contextualized, dyadic, objective conceptualization of problems.
2. Modify emotion-driven dysfunctional and destructive interactional behavior.
3. Elicit avoided emotion-based private behavior.
4. Foster productive communication.
5. Emphasize strengths and encourage positive behavior (see Christensen, 2010, for full description).

From this framework, it is possible to ask questions about individual components across therapy orientations and determine the impact of each component alone or in combination with other components on relationship outcomes.

For example, it would be possible to examine the first principle in depth without introducing the other components. Since couples come into therapy with their own conceptualization of their difficulties, it would be possible to compare their pre-treatment conceptualizations with their conceptualization following assessment and feedback. We might ask what parts (if any) of the conceptualization presented by the therapist sticks with the couple, whether the degree or type of change in the partners' conceptualizations varies by theoretical orientation (e.g., cognitive vs. contextual) or by characteristics of the individuals or couples, whether the "new" conceptualization is maintained at a follow-up period, or whether the conceptualization alone has any impact on relationship distress compared to no treatment. There is already some evidence to support that an assessment-and-feedback-only intervention may be effective in boosting satisfaction, intimacy, acceptance, and attention to the relationship in "at-risk" couples (Cordova et al., 2005), suggesting that further examination of the conceptualization and feedback process is likely a fruitful direction for future research. This type of study has the advantage of being lower cost than a full clinical trial, and the more detailed analysis of a single component allows us to learn more about the client's experience, offering insight into what couples themselves experience as impactful.

A good example of existing work that includes a smaller-scale, in depth focus on the internal experience of treatment couples comes from the EFT literature. Greenberg and colleagues have examined change processes in terms of couple-identified "best" sessions, and found that these sessions are characterized by deeper emotional experiencing and more softening events (Greenberg, Ford, Alden, & Johnson, 1993). This methodology could be implemented in small samples across couple therapies to examine the fourth principal of eliciting emotion-based private behavior.

In addition to determining why couple therapies work, we are also interested in whether differences between couples and individuals may guide our use of intervention strategies. Here, again, it is likely to be less useful to compare full treatment packages than to examine specific elements of treatment. Individual psychopathology is one potential moderator of treatment that has been examined in a number of studies (Snyder, Castellani, & Whisman, 2006). In couples in which one or both members are depressed, for instance, it may be informative to examine contingency versus rule-governed strategies for fostering productive communication. From the individual therapy literature, it has been suggested by McCullough (2003) that individuals with chronic depression are characterized by a pre-operational cognitive style and therefore require experiential, contingency-shaped learning. We might predict that rule-based communication strategies will be less effective than contingency-based strategies in cases in which one member of the couple is chronically depressed, compared to couples characterized by single-episode or no depression. Focused research of this kind can more directly inform clinical application to any particular couple and increase the efficiency of treatment.

Implementation of the above recommendations may or may not contribute evidence to fuel the debate over the novelty, utility, and staying power of acceptance-based strategies over traditional cognitive change strategies. Both IBCT and CBCT have sought to address the limits of traditional behavioral couple therapy, and it remains an empirical question whether one has done so more effectively. The therapies represent two distinct trajectories from TBCT, with IBCT representing a movement towards a more contextualized approach, whereas CBCT has given more causal status to internal events, particularly with regards to cognitions. However, recent enhancements to CBCT that include greater attention to broad contextualized themes suggest that the two trajectories may be on course to intersect. The evidence gathered from research on change processes over the next several years will be critical in determining the future of acceptance-based couple interventions and may ultimately render the current debates irrelevant.

# REFERENCES

Atkins, D. C., Berns, S. B., George, W. H., Doss, B. D., Gattis, K., & Christensen, A. (2005). Prediction of response to treatment in a randomized clinical trial of marital therapy. *Journal of Consulting and Clinical Psychology, 73,* 893–903.

Atkins, D. C., Eldridge, K. A., Baucom, D. H., & Christensen, A. (2005). Infidelity and behavioral couple therapy: Optimism in the face of betrayal. *Journal of Consulting and Clinical Psychology, 73,* 144–150.

Baucom, B. R., Atkins, D. C., Simpson, L. E., & Christensen, A. (2009). Prediction of response to treatment in a randomized clinical trial of couple therapy: A 2-year follow-up. *Journal of Consulting and Clinical Psychology, 77,* 160–173.

Baucom, D. H., & Epstein, N. (1990). *Cognitive-behavioral marital therapy.* New York: Brunner/Mazel.

Baucom, D. H., Epstein, N., & LaTillade, J. J. (2002). Cognitive-behavioral couple therapy. In A. S. Gurman & N. S. Jacobson (Eds.), *Clinical handbook of couple therapy,* 3rd ed. (pp. 26–59). New York, NY: Guilford Press.

Baucom, D. H., Sayers, S. L., & Sher, T. G. (1990). Supplementing behavioral marital therapy with cognitive restructuring and emotional expressiveness training: An outcome investigation. *Journal of Consulting and Clinical Psychology, 58*(5), 636–645.

Baucom, D. H., Shoham, V., Meuser, K. T., Daiuto, A. D. & Stickle, T. R. (1998). Empirically supported couple and family interventions for marital distress and adult mental health problems. *Journal of Consulting and Clinical Psychology, 66,* 53–88.

Beck, A. T. (1970). Cognitive therapy: Nature in relation to behavior therapy. *Behavior Therapy, 1*(2), 184–200.

Cano, A., & Leonard, M. (2006). Integrative behavioral couple therapy for chronic pain: Promoting behavior change and emotional acceptance. *Journal of Clinical Psychology: In Session, 62,* 1409–1418.

Christensen, A. (1988). Dysfunctional interaction patterns in couples. In P. Noller & M. A. Fitzpatrick (Eds.), *Perspectives on marital interaction* (pp. 31–52). Clevedon, Avon, England: Multilingual Matters.

Christensen, A. (2010). A unified protocol for couple therapy. In K. Hahlweg, M. Grawe-Gerber, & D. H. Baucom (Eds.), *Enhancing couples: The shape of couple therapy to come* (pp 33–46). Göttingen: Hogrefe.

Christensen, A., Atkins, D. C., Berns, S. B., Wheeler, J., Baucom, D. H., & Simpson, L. (2004). Integrative versus traditional behavioral couple therapy for moderately and severely distressed couples. *Journal of Consulting and Clinical Psychology, 72,* 176–191.

Christensen, A., Atkins, D. C., Yi, J., Baucom, D. H., & George, W. H. (2006). Couple and individual adjustment for 2 years following a randomized clinical trial comparing traditional versus integrative behavioral couple therapy. *Journal of Consulting and Clinical Psychology, 74,* 1180–1191.

Christensen, A., Eldridge, K., Catta-Preta, A. B., Lim, V. R., & Santagata, R. (2006). Cross-cultural consistency of the demand/withdraw interaction in couples. *Journal of Marriage and the Family, 68*, 1029–1044.

Christensen, A., Jacobson, N. S., & Babcock, J. C. (1995). Integrative behavioral couple therapy. In N. S. Jacobson & A. S. Gurman (Eds.), *Clinical handbook of couples therapy* (pp. 31–64). New York, NY: Guilford Press.

Christensen, A., & Pasch, L. (1993). The sequence of marital conflict: An analysis of seven phases of marital conflict in distressed and nondistressed couples. *Clinical Psychology Review, 13*, 3–14.

Cordova, J. V., & Gee, C. B. (2001). Couples therapy for depression: Using healthy relationships to treat depression. In S. R. H. Beach (Ed.), *Marital and family processes in depression: A scientific foundation for clinical practice* (pp. 185–203). Washington, DC: American Psychological Association.

Cordova, J. V., Jacobson, N. S., & Christensen, A. (1998). Acceptance versus change interventions in behavioral couple therapy: Impact on couples' in-session communication. *Journal of Marital and Family Therapy, 24*, 437–455.

Cordova, J. V., Scott, R. L., Dorian, M., Mirgain, S., Yaeger, D., & Groot, A. (2005). The marriage checkup: An indicated preventive intervention for treatment-avoidant couples at risk for marital deterioration. *Behavior Therapy, 36*, 301–309.

Doss, B. D., Thum, Y. M., Sevier, M., Atkins, D. C., & Christensen, A. (2005). Improving relationships: Mechanisms of change in couple therapy. *Journal of Consulting and Clinical Psychology, 73*, 624–633.

Ellis, A. (1962). *Reason and emotion in psychotherapy*. Oxford, England: Lyle Stuart.

Erbes, C. R., Polusny, M. A., MacDermid, S., & Compton, J. S. (2008). Couple therapy with combat veterans and their partners. *Journal of Clinical Psychology: In Session, 64*, 972–983.

Greenberg, L. S., Ford, C. L., Alden, L. S., & Johnson, S. M. (1993). In-session change in emotionally focused therapy. *Journal of Consulting and Clinical Psychology, 61*(1), 78–84.

Hayes, S. C., Strosahl, K. D., & Wilson, K. G. (1999). *Acceptance and commitment therapy: An experiential approach to behavior change*. New York, NY: Guilford Press.

Heatherington, L., Friedlander, M. L., & Greenberg, L. (2005). Change process research in couple and family therapy: Methodological challenges and opportunities. *Journal of Family Psychology, 19*(1), 18–27.

Heavey, C. L., Layne, C., & Christensen, A. (1993). Gender and conflict structure in marital interaction: A replication and extension. *Journal of Consulting and Clinical Psychology, 61*, 16–27.

Jacobson, N. S. (1977). Problem solving and contingency contracting in the treatment of marital discord. *Journal of Consulting and Clinical Psychology, 45*, 92–100.

Jacobson, N. S. (1984). A component analysis of behavioral marital therapy: The relative effectiveness of behavior exchange and problem solving training. *Journal of Consulting and Clinical Psychology, 52*, 295–305.

Jacobson, N. S., & Christensen, A. (1996). *Acceptance and change in couple therapy: A therapist's guide to transforming relationships*. New York, NY: W. W. Norton.

Jacobson, N. S., Christensen, A., Prince, S. E., Cordova, J., & Eldridge, K. (2000). Integrative behavioral couple therapy: An acceptance-based, promising new treatment for couple discord. *Journal of Consulting and Clinical Psychology, 68*(2), 351–355.

Jacobson, N. S., Follette, W. C., Revenstorf, D., Baucom, D. H., Hahlweg, K., & Margolin, G. (1984). Variability in outcome and clinical significance of behavioral marital therapy: A reanalysis of outcome data. *Journal of Consulting and Clinical Psychology, 52*, 497–504.

Jacobson, N. S., & Margolin, G. (1979). *Marital therapy: Strategies based on social learning and behavior exchange principles*. New York, NY: Brunner/Mazel.

Jacobson, N. S., Schmaling, K. B., & Holtzworth-Munroe, A. (1987). Component analysis of behavioral marital therapy: 2-year follow-up and prediction of relapse. *Journal of Marital and Family Therapy, 13*, 187–195.

Johnson, S. M., & Greenberg, L. S. (1985). Emotionally focused couples therapy: An outcome study. *Journal of Marital and Family Therapy, 11*, 313–317.

Koerner, K., Prince, S., & Jacobson, N. S. (1994). Enhancing the treatment and prevention of depression in women: The role of integrative behavioral couple therapy. *Behavior Therapy, 25*, 373–390.

Lambert, M. J., Hansen, N. B., Umphress, V., Lunnen, K., Okiishi, J., Burlingame, G. M.,...Reisenger, C. W. (1996). *Administration and scoring manual for the OQ-45.2*. Stevenson, MD: American Professional Credentialing Services.

Linehan, M. M., Armstrong, H. E., Suarez, A., & Allmon, D. (1991). Cognitive-behavioral treatment of chronically parasuicidal borderline patients. *Archives of General Psychiatry, 48,* 1060–1064.

McCullough, J. P., Jr. (2003). Treatment for chronic depression using cognitive behavioral analysis system of psychotherapy (CBASP). *Journal of Clinical Psychology, 59*(8), 833–846.

Sevier, M., Eldridge, K., Jones, J., Doss, B. D., & Christensen, A. (2008). Observed communication and associations with satisfaction during traditional and integrative behavioral couple therapy. *Behavior Therapy, 39,* 137–150.

Skinner, B. F. (1966). *The behavior of organisms: An experimental analysis*. Englewood Cliffs, NJ: Prentice Hall.

Snyder, D. K., Castellani, A. M., & Whisman, M. A. (2006). Current status and future directions in couple therapy. *Annual Review of Psychology, 57,* 317–344.

Snyder, D. K., & Wills, R. M. (1989). Behavioral versus insight-oriented marital therapy: Effects on individual and interspousal functioning. *Journal of Consulting and Clinical Psychology, 57,* 39–44.

Snyder, D. K., Wills, R. M., & Grady-Fletcher, A. (1991). Long-term effectiveness of behavioral versus insight-oriented marital therapy: A 4-year follow-up study. *Journal of Consulting and Clinical Psychology, 59,* 138–141.

Spanier, G. B. (1976). Measuring dyadic adjustment: New scales for assessing the quality of marriage and similar dyads. *Journal of Marriage and the Family, 38,* 15–28.

Stith, S. M., McCollum, E. E., Rosen, K. H., Locke, L. D., & Goldberg, P. D. (2005). Domestic violence-focused couples treatment. In J. L. Lebow (Ed.), *Handbook of clinical family therapy* (pp. 406–430). Hoboken, NJ: Wiley.

Stith, S. M., Rosen, K. H., McCollum, E. E., & Thomsen, C. J. (2004) Treating intimate partner violence within intact couple relationships: Outcomes of multi-couple versus individual couple therapy. *Journal of Marital and Family Therapy, 30*(3), 305–318.

Straus, M. A. (1979). Measuring intrafamily conflict and violence: The conflict tactics scales (CT). *Journal of Marriage and the Family, 41,* 75–88.

Wimberly, J. D. (1998). An outcome study of integrative couples therapy delivered in a group format (Doctoral dissertation, University of Montana, 1997). *Dissertation Abstracts International: Section B: The Sciences & Engineering, 58*(12-B), 6832.

# 10

Understanding Acceptance and Commitment
Therapy in Context

## A History of Similarities and Differences With Other
Cognitive Behavior Therapies

KELLY G. WILSON, MICHAEL J. BORDIERI, MAUREEN K. FLYNN,
NADIA N. LUCAS, AND REGAN M. SLATER

Acceptance and Commitment Therapy or ACT (said as a word, not as letters) is a contemporary member of the general family of cognitive behavior therapies (CBTs). It is both similar to and different from CBTs that preceded it, just as those therapies are both similar to and different from the behavior therapies (BTs) that preceded them. The CBT movement is, and always has been, multifaceted and evolving. In fact, the name CBT is itself an evolution that arose when the near-ubiquitous attention to cognition among these therapies made CBT a more apt name for them than BT. Ocean waves are apt metaphors for describing the development of CBT, especially in that waves all arise from the same sea. Questions about distinction and discreetness invariably arise in the wake of any new therapy: Is there enough new stuff in it to merit mention, warrant a name, and mark a new chapter in the history of the discipline? As ever, those who believe ACT deserves these distinctions must make the case to their fellows. Ultimately, the community of scientists will decide.

### Similarities Among Various CBTs

The similarities among various models of CBT can be understood as having three primary sources.

First, there is a bond of shared values. What is currently the CBT movement started out as the BT movement, and relatively early on, it also included explicitly cognitive therapies (CTs). A common commitment to a robust empirical basis for clinical psychology united CT and BT, and it distinguished these psychotherapies from the numerous others that were far less interested in systematic data collection.

The second and third sources of similarity are sociological. For one thing, the current members of the CBT movement developed in close proximity to one another.

This proximity was facilitated by their commitment to a scientific perspective and by the fact that they were the minority within psychotherapy at their founding. Proximity has produced many shared concerns, language conventions, sensitivities, and methods.

For another, the intellectual lines within the CBT movement are mixed. Students at CBT-oriented programs, over time, hybridized the various intellectual lines in the CT and BT movements because they were often exposed to multiple faculty who promulgated them within departments and at conferences (e.g., Skinnerians, Hullians, social learning theorists).

## Differences Among CBTs

Although there were uniformities at the outset (the first source in the previous section), and sociological forces that facilitated them (the second and third sources in the previous section), there are now and always have been differences among the CBTs as well. The differences are clearest in the "purebred" therapies and more difficult to see among the "hybrids." Going back in time, prior to the rise of CT, we see differences among behavioral therapies that can be traced to the learning theory from which each therapy derived. Some early behavior therapists were better connected to the Pavlovian tradition, others to the Hullian, and still others to the Skinnerian behavior analytic tradition. Likewise, many modern behavior therapists mix once-distinct learning theories (as a result of the third source in the previous section).

Different still from the earlier learning theories that emerged from the animal learning tradition were social learning theories such as Bandura (1977). Concepts like self-efficacy, found in many social learning theories, place them in reasonable proximity to concepts put forward by Beck in his cognitive model. Early on in the development of cognitive therapy, Beck made clear both the similarities and differences between cognitive therapy and early versions of behavior therapy (see, for example, an excellent exposition in chapter 12 of Beck, 1976).

In describing his cognitive therapy, Beck (1976) suggests that he is not talking about a mere set of techniques that are different, but instead about (a) a system that specifies a model of psychopathology, (b) mechanisms of change, and (c) a set of techniques sufficiently tied to the model that new theoretically-consistent procedures could be generated easily (Beck, 1976). Examination of a long-lived psychotherapy text tells the story. Bergin and Garfield's *Handbook of Psychotherapy and Behavior Change* has no listing for cognitive therapy in its table of contents in the first edition (1971). In the second edition (1978) there is still no chapter on CT per se, but there is a chapter mentioning cognitive processes in psychotherapy. By the third edition (1986), and in all subsequent editions, there are specific chapters on cognitive therapy. Beck and others had made the case that there was something distinctive enough about CT to merit mention over and above behavior therapy.

Beck provides a prototype of the early "purebred" approach on the cognitive therapy side. Beck did not come from a behavioral laboratory and does not speak using the language of behaviorism that emerged from the basic psychology of learning labs. He did, however, have a clear commitment to empiricism. Cognitive therapy always contained some behavioral interventions in the form of behavioral experiments and was consequently a good fit for the then BT, now CBT, movement. In addition, Beck's assumption that cognition was a centrally important clinical concern was astute, ahead of its time, and resonated with many in the BT community.

ACT is a different sort of purebred. It emerges very directly from the behavior analytic wing of the behavior therapy movement. Other relatively clear members of this group include Functional Analytic Psychotherapy (Kohlenburg & Tsai, 1991) and Behavioral Activation (Martell, Addis, & Jacobson, 2001). Looking at the citation patterns among these more behavior analytic perspectives, one finds citations harkening back to B. F. Skinner and Charles Ferster (e.g., Hayes, Strosahl, & Wilson, 1999, cite Skinner, 1953, whereas Kohlenburg & Tsai, 1991, and Martell & colleagues cite Ferster, 1967). Beck was trained in psychoanalysis and behavior therapy, but generated his theory largely from clinical experiences. His theory emerged from what he saw as missing in the models in which he had been trained. Consider, for example, Beck's description of the discovery of automatic thoughts, which emerged directly from his sessions with patients. Because Beck was trained as a psychoanalyst, he routinely did free association work with clients. It was in this work that he discovered patterns of negative thinking (described in detail in Beck, 1976, pp. 29–35). Subsequently, Beck developed methods, improving on free association, to analyze and intervene upon these thought patterns. ACT differs in its developmental trajectory, because it makes its way not from the clinic practice to clinical theory, but instead from the basic behavior analytic laboratory to clinical theory (and back again).

## ACT IN THE CBT FAMILY

Given the description above, it is difficult to imagine that ACT would not have a significant resemblance to other CBTs. ACT started from the same intellectual genetics as many in the CBT movement and has grown and developed within the same community of researchers and practitioners. ACT's interest in cognition was certainly inspired in part by Beck, and some of the earliest ACT publications were attempts to understand, in behavioral terms, many of the issues raised by Beck, such as cognitive distancing (Zettle & Hayes, 1982). However, the development of ACT was also inspired by a growing recognition within the experimental analysis of behavior that rule-governed behavior had some special and interesting properties (Hayes, Zettle, & Rosenfarb, 1989; Zettle & Hayes, 1982). A central difference between Beck's model and the one proposed in ACT is precisely the role cognition plays in human functioning. Beck suggests:

The most important difference between cognitive and behavioral therapy lies in the concepts used to explain the dissolution of maladaptive responses....Most behavior therapists conceptualize the disorders of behavior...within a framework borrowed from the field of psychological learning theory....Since these concepts are derived mainly from experiments with animals, they focus on the observable behavior of the organism...this framework does not readily accommodate notions of internal psychological states such as thoughts, attitudes, and the like, which we commonly use to understand ourselves and other people.

(Beck, 1976, p. 322)

In many respects, ACT theorists agree with Beck. Behavior theory during the 1960s and 1970s was excessively reliant on animal models and, with some exceptions, did not take into account the complexities of human behavior connected to language and cognition. ACT shares a substantial concern with ACT about this omission. If one accepts the discrepancy between the importance of cognition and the emphasis provided it in early forms of behavior therapy, three options lie open. The first is to develop an entirely new theory. This was Beck's path, and it was also the approach taken by Ellis (1961). A second possibility is to add cognitive elements to existing behavioral techniques. Goldfried and Davison provide an example of early adopters of this strategy, and this was the path of the overwhelming majority within the behavior therapy movement (e.g., Goldfried & Davison, 1976). A third approach, one that was encouraged by added insights available from human conditioning research, is to continue the development of behavior theory such that it might more adequately answer the challenges posed by the cognitive critique of behavior therapy. This third approach has led to the development of ACT.

In addition to answering the cognitive critique, ACT has also sought to answer concerns about the place of meaning and purpose in CBT. Many from the humanistic and existential psychotherapies criticized behavioral approaches for their lack of attention to these areas—and to the humanists and existentialists, it likely seemed that the behavioral approaches' strong focus on data collection even precluded interest in these areas. Yalom, for example, suggests that "the basic tenets of existential therapy are such that empirical research methods are often inapplicable or inappropriate" (Yalom, 1980, p. 22).

ACT can be understood as a behavior analytic response to both the cognitive and existential critiques of traditional behavior therapy. ACT is the applied wing of a broader effort in contextual behavioral science with the aspiration of developing a science more adequate to the challenges of the human condition (Plumb, 2009). In what follows, we will outline the ACT model and its response to what we believe to be legitimate critiques of our tradition. This is not to express complete agreement with the critiques. Rather, it is to acknowledge that there is *something* within the critiques that bears addressing (cf. Forman & Herbert, 2009).

In an important sense, ACT is applied behavior analysis. ACT is both old and new. ACT is old in its strategy. Just like the earliest behavior therapists, we are attempting to apply basic behavioral principles to clinical problems. On the other hand, ACT is new because the theoretical framework and principles have been extended and because they are being applied to domains that have not been well explored empirically by behavior analysts.

ACT differs from traditional applied behavior analysis is two significant ways. First, the behavior analysis that is being applied is extended by its inclusion of an emerging analysis of complex human behavior found in relational frame theory (RFT), which we discuss briefly below (see Hayes, Barnes-Holmes, & Roche, 2001). Second, the application is being made to domains such as cognition, emotion, meaning, purpose, and values—among other areas—that have not historically been the center of interest in applied behavior analysis.

## THE ACT HEXAFLEX MODEL OF PSYCHOLOGICAL WELL-BEING

ACT is a process-oriented model, not a procedure-oriented model. Like Beck, we are interested in the specification of a model and change processes that are testable and capable of generating a wide variety of theoretically coherent procedures. ACT can be usefully understood as being composed of six core processes:

1. Contact with the present moment
2. Acceptance
3. Defusion
4. Self
5. Values
6. Commitment processes

These processes ought not be thought of as independent of one another. Rather, they are better conceptualized as different lenses through which we can view patterns of behavior (Wilson & DuFrene, 2009). Like facets in a gem, if we look into one, we will see all the others reflected. All six of these processes act together to promote the development of broader, more flexible patterns of activities, collectively referred to as psychological flexibility. The processes are described separately because we believe that doing so has scientific and clinical utility. To use one more metaphor, an exercise physiologist might examine the separate processes of speed, rhythm, and biomechanics in the context of running. Running is still a unitary act, but sometimes the physiologist will focus on a single aspect to help a runner perform better.

Traditional behavioral analyses have relied on a very specific language, using terms such as *discriminative stimuli*, *responses*, and *reinforcers*. Our concern is that this level of analysis is too molecular for a readily applied clinical model. ACT processes are clusters of broadly and readily applicable functional analyses. They all can be analyzed in the more specific molecular language of basic behavior analysis, and in fact such analyses are often undertaken by basic-behavioral science researchers. However, this basic language is too far abstracted from the phenomena with which clinicians typically work. Imagine a continuum of abstraction that has, at one end, a lay description of a particular psychological event. At the other end of the continuum, we might produce a description of the same event in terms of discriminative stimuli, operant responses, establishing operations, consequential operations, conditioned and unconditioned stimuli, and responses, with, perhaps, the interaction of streams of operant and respondent stimulus control. An ACT process account lies somewhere midway on this continuum. ACT process language is language with a purpose. The six-process model is cast in language intended to be amenable to clinical troubles and practice.

In the section that follows, each of the six core ACT processes is defined, and assessment and treatment implications for each process are discussed. In addition, some note is made of the ways in which the ACT model compares and contrasts with the currently dominant CBT model. The reader is left to decide whether the distinctions are adequate to merit notice.

## Present Moment Processes

### *Understanding and Assessing Present Moment Processes*

From an ACT perspective, many psychological difficulties can be understood, in part, as being caused by a failure of present moment processes. The issue being assessed by the ACT therapist is whether a client can bring flexible, focused attention to bear in the present moment. For the environment to shape individuals' behavior, the individuals must be psychologically present to the environment they inhabit. Common failures of present moment processes include worry and rumination, in which a client's engagement with the imagined future or remembered past interfere with his or her capacity to be shaped by ongoing contact with the environment. Worry and rumination are, of course, hallmark symptoms of a variety of mood and anxiety disorders. Other variants of failures of present moment processes include distractibility, in which attention is sensitive to events in the present moment but lacking in focus. This is often the case with ADHD-like presentations, but it is sometimes also seen among anxious and depressed clients in the form of problems with concentration and sometimes among clients with psychotic disorders who are distracted by hallucinations. Finally, some failures of present moment processes involve attentional focus but absent flexibility. Persons diagnosed with Asperger's Disorder, for example, may present in this manner—attention is highly focused on some particular object or event, but lacks flexibility. Assessment involves observation of these attentional processes as they occur naturally in the clinical conversation and also by directly focusing the client's attention and noting whether he or she is capable of doing so.

## Treating Present Moment Processes

Even though the presentations vary greatly in form, the treatment implications remain the same. An ACT therapist would expend some effort at shaping flexible, focused attention in the present moment. This could involve, for example, formal or informal mindfulness-like exercises or moment-by-moment noticing of emotion, bodily state, and cognition.

# Psychological Acceptance Processes

## Understanding and Assessing Acceptance Processes

Hayes and colleagues have described psychological acceptance components, and their reciprocal experiential avoidance, across a wide variety of psychological disorders (Hayes, Wilson, Gifford, Follette, & Strosahl, 1996). Acceptance processes identify a cluster of negative reinforcement contingencies that organize a person's behavior. To the extent that individuals work to reduce, eliminate, or postpone difficult experiences (e.g., thoughts, emotions, memories, and bodily states), they set the boundaries of the world they are permitted to inhabit. If memories of a childhood sexual abuse history are aversive and avoided, then contexts that elicit those memories will likewise be avoided. If they arise in the context of intimate relations, intimate relations may be avoided and impaired. If feeling stupid is to be avoided, then classrooms, tests, new jobs, and conversations with interesting and intelligent people may also be avoided. If feelings of anxiety are unacceptable, the person with panic attacks cannot go to the mall or ride on a bus. In ACT, the acceptance component of assessment involves the identification of avoided psychological content, such as painful emotions in anxiety disorders, negative thoughts in mood disorders, or urges to drink in alcoholism, as well as the patterns of behaviors that help the person avoid.

## Treating Acceptance Processes

Treating experiential avoidance involves acceptance-oriented interventions aimed at helping the client to open up psychologically to difficult experiences (Herbert, Forman, & England, 2009). Sensitively executed exposure strategies fit quite well in this domain. ACT does differ somewhat from most traditionally conceived exposure strategies, because exposure is tied explicitly to the pursuit of valued patterns of living, rather than to the reduction of anxiety and avoidance. Other interventions aimed at increasing acceptance and making contact with the consequences of nonacceptance involve metaphors, including some physical metaphors, Gestalt-like experiential exercises, and acceptance-oriented meditations, for example. Although psychological acceptance has been a theme within BT and CBT at least since Ellis (1961), it is sufficiently central to ACT that the word *acceptance* is in the name of the therapy model itself.

## Defusion Processes

### *Understanding and Assessing Defusion Processes*

Early in the development of the ACT model and the underlying conceptual framework of relational frame theory, the problematic impact of verbal rules was identified (Hayes, et al., 1989; Zettle & Hayes, 1982). For example, in an often-cited article by Shimoff, Catania, and Matthews (1981), participants were instructed to press a lever in order to earn points. Some participants were told nothing more than that, while others were instructed to press the lever very slowly in order to earn points. Participants given explicit instructions to press slowly began earning points right away. It took longer for the control participants to begin earning points, as their behavior was shaped gradually by their experience. Rapid presses produced no reinforcers, so participants' lever pressing gradually slowed down. Later in the experiment, the reinforcement delivery schedule was changed so that more rapid presses would earn more points. Most of the participants in the control condition, in which lever pressing was shaped by direct experience, began pressing more rapidly following the reinforcement schedule change. By contrast, more than half of the participants in the "press slowly" condition continued to press slowly for the entire 50-minute session, even though doing so was no longer the most efficient way to earn points. The remaining participants in the "press slowly" condition did eventually begin to press more rapidly, but transitioned to the higher rate more slowly than the participants who were shaped by experience. Something about the verbal specification of the contingencies seemed to generate insensitivity to directly experienced changing contingencies.

Stories about the world, including this very simple story about how to earn points, sometimes organize human behavior in ways that prevent behavior from being shaped by ongoing experience. This verbally structured world is parallel in some regards to ideas of schema and automatic thoughts in the cognitive therapy model, which arguably represents Beck's most central and influential insight. However, the ACT model takes a quite different view from cognitive therapy on the nature of the problem and its solution.

According to Beck, "cognitive therapy is best viewed as the application of the cognitive model of a particular disorder with the use of a variety of techniques designed to modify the dysfunctional beliefs and faulty information processing characteristic of each disorder" (1993, p. 194). Beck even distinguishes "method and mode of action" (Beck, 1976, p. 325). He asserts that even behavioral techniques "are effective *because* of the conceptual changes that are produced" (Beck, p. 331, emphasis added). Beck points quite directly at a testable meditational hypothesis more than 30 years ago; however, strong positive evidence for the claim has proven difficult to produce. In 1986, Hollon and Beck stated that "there is not, as yet, compelling evidence that cognitive therapy works, when it works, by virtue of changing beliefs and/or information processing, although that remains a very viable possibility" (Hollon & Beck, 1986, p. 451). As late as 2008, we find major cognitive therapists such as Dobson, Hollon, and colleagues suggesting that the mechanism of enduring good effects of cognitive therapy are "not well understood" (Dobson, et al., 2008, p. 475). Recent reviews have likewise noted the limited body of empirical support for the cognitive mediation of therapeutic changes in CBT (Longmore & Worrell, 2007). To emphasize, this is not calling into question the efficacy of cognitive therapy as a package. The evidence base for its outcome efficacy and durability of effects for depression is unparalleled. Rather, these discussions call into question both mechanisms (as suggested by CT's progenitors) and impact of some specific cognitive interventions (Dobson et al., 2008).

In ACT, the assessment of cognitive fusion involves the examination of the ways and extent to which verbal formulations of the world organize behavior and restrict freedom to pursue valued life directions. In some regards, this examination of the restrictions imposed by verbal formulation bears resemblance to some cognitive formulations. Treatment, however, often looks quite different, because the focus is on the function of these verbal formulations, rather than on their accuracy. Interventions are instead aimed at lessening the control exerted by the thoughts, so that the client can live fruitfully whether the thoughts are present or not. From an ACT perspective, this is essential. With some difficulties like anxiety or depression, we may see reductions in some negative cognitions. However, in other instances, such as schizophrenia or chronic pain, even successfully treated clients often experience persistent symptoms.

## *Treating Defusion Processes*

In ACT, there is no focus on changing the content of thought from invalid to valid or from irrational to rational. Instead, ACT is based on basic principles of behavior analysis, including those specified by Relational Frame Theory (RFT; Hayes, Barnes-Holmes, & Roche, 2001). RFT posits that the difficulty with verbal stimulus control is not so much that the content is inaccurate as it is that verbally established stimulus control often decreases behavioral flexibility. Sometimes content can be accurate and realistic, but not useful. A person with lifelong social anxiety may well be terrible at social interactions. The issue is not whether the thought (e.g. "I can't interact well with other people") is accurate, but whether allowing the thought to guide your behavior (e.g., staying at home) is useful. Beck was sensitive to whether thoughts were adaptive or not, however, he also targets thoughts on the basis of whether they are "realistic," "objective," "distorted," or "faulty." Although we may agree that clients' thoughts may have these qualities, we differ on the conditions necessary for clinical change. For example, CT would conceptualize exposure to social situations as a means to explore and ultimately correct cognitions with the assumption that more corrected cognitions will in turn lead to more functional behavior. In the ACT model, the emphasis is placed on functional behavior without regard for the accuracy of cognitive content. Defusion strategies are designed to facilitate values-consistent behavior *regardless* of change in cognitive content.

Both theory and evidence suggests that behavioral and emotional patterns can change even when the content of cognition does not. For example, in a trial of ACT with psychotic individuals (Bach & Hayes, 2002), a higher percentage of clients in the ACT condition reported psychotic symptoms than was found in the treatment-as-usual control condition, yet rehospitalization at four months was halved in the ACT condition.

The focus in ACT is altering the individual's relationship to his or her cognitions, rather than the content of cognition itself. Instead of asking the client to think of alternative, more rational cognitions, the ACT therapist might ask a client to repeat a distressing thought very rapidly, to imagine the thought on a leaf floating by in a stream, to interact with the thought as an imagined object in a Gestalt-like exercise, or to practice mindful awareness of the stream of thoughts, including the disturbing thoughts (Hayes, et al., 1999; Wilson & DuFrene, 2009).

## Self Processes

### *Understanding and Assessing Self Processes*

Self, from a behavioral perspective, is a class of behavior that emerges from repeated interactions with the social environment. *"Selfing"* would be a more technically accurate, if awkward, way of saying it. Everyone learns to answer questions from a particular perspective that is their own. This occurs through a history of being asked many questions: Are you sleepy? Are you hungry? What did you do before? What would you like to do later? Does that hurt? Does that taste bitter? We experience thousands of these questions from the moment we are born, and the answers all begin with "I." Eventually, "I'ing" or "selfing" from a particular unique perspective emerges as a repertoire of behavior (see Hayes, 1984; Skinner, 1953, 1974; Wilson & DuFrene, 2009).

According to the theory underlying ACT, perspective-taking underlies a sense of both self and of others. According to relational frame theory, the emergence of perspective-taking is part of a broader set of learning called *deictic frames* (McHugh, Barnes-Holmes, & Barnes-Holmes, 2009). Deictic frames are verbally constructed relationships that all involve perspective taking. For example, the referents of here and there, now and then, you and me, differ depending upon who is speaking and on the location of the speaker at the moment of speaking. The questioning environment is further enhanced by questions that add layers of complexity to perspective-taking. You are enjoying that ice cream now, but will you be hungry later? How do you think Jimmy felt when that happened? A rich questioning environment is thought to produce a rich and flexible repertoire of "self"ing or "I"ing. Or, said in a less technically accurate but language-friendly way, one develops a broad and flexible sense of self.

However, the shaping process can go awry. The most common difficulty is fusion with what ACT refers to as "self as content." Fusion with self as content involves excessive organization of behavior by verbal rules about self. A more common-sense way to think about this would be excessive attachment to particular thoughts about oneself or one's habitual roles. Persons with chronic psychological difficulties often become quite identified with their difficulties (e.g., "I am bipolar."). Fusion with self-as-diagnosis is often apparent in the difficulty with which a therapist is able to discuss any issue outside the presenting problem. Assessment of self processes in ACT consists of examining the client's flexibility in perspective-taking and making note of domains in which perspective taking is restricted.

## *Treating Self Processes*

In ACT, a number of interventions are designed to help a client make contact with a sense of self that is not experienced as identical with any particular content of consciousness. This goal might be thought of as cultivating a transcendent sense of self. It is not transcendent in any sort of mystical sense; instead, it is a sense of self as a movable perspective that transcends any particular content (see Hayes, 1984). Interventions such as the *observer exercise* (Hayes, et al., 1999) involve an eyes-closed exercise in which the client is asked to visualize his or her thoughts, emotions, bodily states, and roles at different points in his or her own history. We ask many questions that involve perspective-taking, especially focusing on noticing *that* the individual is taking different perspectives. Fusion with self-as-content, emotion, cognition, role, diagnoses, for example, is also targeted in the same way that fusion is addressed (see above). This is because some fusion is about the world, some is about the conceptualized future and a remembered past, and some is about the self (note similarities with Beck's cognitive triad; Beck, 1976). Fusion with self is not treated as qualitatively different from any other form of fusion. That is, the focus is not in veracity of content, rather it is on the narrowness and rigidity of the repertoire.

## Values Processes

### *Understanding and Assessing Values Processes*

Values have been talked about in a wide variety of ways in psychology, philosophy, and religion. Within the ACT model, "values are freely chosen, verbally constructed consequences of ongoing, dynamic, evolving patterns of activity, which establish predominant reinforcers for that activity that are intrinsic in engagement in the valued behavioral pattern itself" (Wilson & DuFrene, 2009, p. 66). This is not to say that this definition exhausts the meaning of values per se. Rather, this definition is a description of the use of the term *values* within the ACT model. The definition is technical and somewhat daunting; however, it can be unpacked in terms of four qualities in order to illustrate values work in ACT.

*First, values are freely chosen.* Clients often enter treatment with a list of "have-to"s. The "have-to"s may be parental, cultural, or subcultural mandates that tell the individual how he or she "should" be. Often there is a sense of urgency about what must change. In ACT, we are interested in some version of a question like, "If all of the 'have-to's in your life evaporated, and you could aim your life in a direction that would be really meaningful to you, what direction would you take?" It is not that we are fundamentally opposed to doing what has to be done; after all, life is full of responsibilities and obligations. But it is our sense that people often lose a sense of vital direction in their lives when they become thoroughly engrossed in psychological struggle because they *have to* be less anxious, less depressed, more assertive, more enthusiastic, and so on. Values work is aimed at freeing clients from the tyranny of *have to*.

*Second, values are verbally constructed.* That is, values work in ACT concerns itself with the client's active authoring of a valued direction in life. Clinical conversations about clients' "true" values or "core" values often are fraught with opportunities for second-guessing. "Are these really my values?" "Maybe I am just kidding myself." "What if I am wrong?" The problem with these conversations is that the answers appear to be fundamentally unknowable in any ultimate sense. The future is by definition unknowable. If we have to be sure first, we could easily wait a lifetime.

Rather than a conversation about discovering "true" values, ACT seeks to engage the client in the active construction of a valued pattern of living. One metaphor that can be used is the construction of a house. If we asked you to design a house in which you could live, you would make some decisions about size, the number of rooms, the way it would be furnished, and so on. If you built such a house, it would be odd indeed if we were to ask: "Is this your true house?" It is simply the house you have built. Similarly, we can ask clients to begin to verbally construct a values-house in different valued domains. What pattern would you construct?

*Third, values work involves ongoing, dynamic, evolving patterns of activity.* Values are not particular goals or particular acts—though living in accordance with one's values will naturally encompass many goals and acts. This quality can be seen clearly by looking at any substantial valued domain, such as being a husband. The pattern of activity that constitutes what it means to be a good husband in the first year of marriage is not the same as the pattern in year thirty. The pattern when one's spouse has been healthy is not the same as the pattern when the same spouse is diagnosed with cancer. These patterns change and grow over time. The same might be said for being a teacher, a father, or a friend.

*Fourth, values work in ACT involves a focus on reinforcers that are present in moment-by-moment engagement in the valued pattern itself.* These reinforcers are intrinsic to the pattern itself, as opposed to being focused on the outcomes that might accrue from the behavior. For example, good parenting increases the likeliness of good economic, social, and educational outcomes for our children. However, many, such as parents of children with terminal illness or profound disabilities, remain engaged in parenting even though these outcomes are guaranteed not to occur. Why? Because reading a story bedside, putting hand to fevered brow, sharing a meal, or just taking the time to talk are worthwhile parts of the pattern many call "good parenting," and the pattern can be chosen as worthwhile independent of any longer-term outcomes. In fact, if you look clinically at problems people have in parenting, they often involve excessive attachment to very specific, predetermined outcomes. Sometimes parents whose children *must* succeed in sports, academics, or socially, for example, end up alienating the children they aimed to nurture as they attempt to force these altogether virtuous ends.

Values assessment consists of examination of a client's capacity to actively construct patterns of living in different valued domains. Instruments such as the Valued Living

Questionnaire-II can be used to examine the extent to which people hold particular domains as values, one's level of activity within those domains, as well as a sense of obstructions to valued living in various domains (for a description of the VLQ-II and other ACT values assessment procedures, see Wilson, Sandoz, Flynn, Slater, & DuFrene, in press; and Wilson & Dufrene, 2009; see also Dahl, Plumb, Stewart, & Lundgren, 2009 for a broad coverage of this topic).

## *Treating Values Processes*

Values work in ACT can be deconstructed into two central components: values-centered mindfulness work and active values construction. When discussion of valued domains is highly constrained and the client shows much avoidance and/or has extremely inflexible descriptions of valued domains (i.e., values fusion and avoidance), the work takes on the look of defusion and acceptance interventions, in which the content is the valued domain. For example, in an exercise called "The Sweet Spot," the therapist asks the client to identify a sweet moment in some valued domain (see Wilson & DuFrene, 2009, with audio, and Wilson & Sandoz, 2008, for elaborated descriptions). The therapist leads the client in an extended mindfulness exercise in which the client dips down experientially into that moment, exploring in a slow, deliberate way the phenomenology of the moment—including visual, auditory, tactile, and emotional qualities of the moment. These exercises are aimed at bringing the individual into moment-by-moment contact with a valued domain of living and thereby, at least momentarily, disrupting values fusion and avoidance.

In the second component of values work, having created some flexibility around valued domains, the therapist might engage the client in a conversation that asks him or her to actively construct patterns of activity that would fit a given value. The emphasis in this work is less on "discovery" of values and more on the active authoring of a valued pattern of living. If inflexibility and avoidance re-emerge when working on values construction, the work shifts back to the more mindfulness-oriented values approach described in the previous paragraph.

## Commitment Processes

### *Understanding and Assessing Commitment Processes*

Commitment within the ACT model differs from values in that commitment involves specific engagement in a valued domain, rather than the generation of valued patterns of activity. A useful metaphor for understanding the meaning of commitment within ACT can be found in a simple breathing meditation. In a breathing meditation, the individual enters the meditation with the intention of bringing awareness to bear on his or her breath in a moment-by-moment way. Of course, what typically happens is that the meditator's attention drifts to aches and pains, to the cares of the day, and to an assortment of sensory, cognitive, and emotional content. The meditator's task in that moment is to notice the wandering of awareness and to return awareness gently to the breath. The heart of commitment in ACT is in that gentle return. The difference is that in a meditation, the individual returns to their breath. In ACT, and in living, commitment involves a return to a valued pattern of living.

Virtually all values of substance are values that we are likely at times to violate in both small and large ways. We value being parents, but find ourselves excessively impatient or preoccupied. We get busy with our lives, and valued areas are neglected. Many problems with commitment also emerge from avoidance and fusion. These can be assessed by asking clients about their level of committed action in a valued domain. Instruments such as the VLQ-II allow for systematic questions about level of action in valued areas, as well as satisfaction with those actions. When querying low levels of action, the therapist may find that questions about committed action generate rumination about past failures, worry about future failures, or outright refusal to discuss certain domains that are very painful. High functioning in committed action involves a fairly fluid ability to generate and act upon particular committed actions, large and small, that are consistent with one's chosen values.

### *Treating Commitment Processes*

Treatment of commitment processes can be as simple as values-directed behavioral activation if commitment fusion and avoidance are relatively low. Simple urging to engage in life-affirming action may be all the medicine some clients need. If fusion and avoidance are high, however, treatment should proceed in two steps in the same way that was discussed above with respect to values treatment. Initial commitment work should involve defusion and acceptance interventions, with particular committed acts as the content of the work. Experiential exercises can be used to ask a client to become present in a moment-by-moment fashion to particular committed acts in which they might like to engage, but feel inhibited about in some way. This work should explicitly take actual committed acts off the table. The client should be told that the therapist does not want him or her to do these acts for the time being, but just to take time to appreciate them in their richness. In addition, the work can be titrated by asking about the smallest possible committed act in a particular domain. As with values work of this sort, when we see avoidance and fusion lessen, the work can proceed to a collaborative conversation about particular acts the person could actually undertake. As with exposure work, pacing is critical. Re-emergence of avoidance and fusion should precipitate a slowing down of the work by the therapist and moving back into present moment–focused, acceptance and defusion-oriented work. When flexibility re-emerges, forward progress can resume.

## THE ROLE OF MINDFULNESS AND ACCEPTANCE-BASED STRATEGIES IN THE DEVELOPMENT OF ACT

The centrality of psychological acceptance is quite apparent within ACT, as acceptance is sufficiently vital to merit being identified in the name of the treatment. Three years before the publication of the first ACT text (Hayes et al., 1999), we published an article proposing experiential avoidance as a transdiagnostic functional dimension (Hayes et al.,

1996). The place of mindfulness in ACT is more complex. Unlike some other "third wave" CBTs, ACT does not come explicitly from a mindfulness tradition, as does for example mindfulness-based cognitive therapy (Segal, Williams, & Teasdale, 2001). Nor was there an early emphasis on concepts derived directly from the mindfulness traditions, as seen, for example, in dialectical behavior therapy (Linehan, 1993). However, understood at the level of process, there is considerable overlap between ACT and mindfulness.

Using Kabat-Zinn's definition as a starting point, we can see the way that mindfulness fits within the ACT model: "paying attention in a particular way: on purpose, in the present moment, nonjudgmentally" (1994, p. 4). Mindfulness, as it is understood in ACT, consists of four core ACT processes: (a) contact with the present moment, (b) acceptance, (c) defusion, and (d) self-as-context. At the heart of mindfulness is the bringing of attention to bear in the present moment. In ACT, we ask clients to notice thoughts and emotions in an ongoing way (present moment processes) with acceptance (acceptance processes). Regarding thoughts and emotions as what they are, arising within awareness, we are less likely to be caught by the content of consciousness and more likely to notice thought and emotion as ongoing processes (defusion processes). In addition, the act of observing with acceptance makes it more likely that our clients will notice the self that is distinct from the stream of events observed (self processes).

ACT has always contained elements that fit this process definition of mindfulness. However, it has been primarily in the past decade that the relationship between mindfulness and ACT has been more fully explored and exploited (e.g., Hayes & Plumb, 2007; Hayes & Wilson, 2003; and especially in Wilson & DuFrene, 2009). This has in part been the result of synergy among related contemporary models of CBT. Treatment developers within ACT are exploring mindfulness (e.g., Wilson & Dufrene, 2009) and ways that mindfulness measures might mediate outcomes in ACT; likewise, researchers within MBCT, such as Mark Williams, are exploring measures such as the acceptance and action questionnaire, used to measure psychological flexibility in ACT, within mindfulness-based treatment projects (M. Williams, personal communication, April, 2008). This intermixing of measures, approaches, and sensibilities is to be expected for the reasons described above with respect to the sociological relation of ACT to CBT. We help one another along, and shared intellectual space is especially common among some of the emergent CBTs. In the same way, CBTs of the 1980s are more similar to one another than they are to, say, the BTs of the early 1960s.

## CASE DESCRIPTION THAT HIGHLIGHTS TYPICAL AND UNIQUE FEATURES OF THE MODEL

Jane Thompson[1] is a 22-year-old European American female currently enrolled in college. She is the second of four children (two boys and two girls), and her parents

---

[1] This is a pseudonym. Identifying information in this case description has been altered to protect confidentiality.

divorced when she was 11. She presented with reports of difficulty concentrating due to thoughts that she cannot get out of her mind, problems differentiating her perceptions from reality, and inexplicable mood changes. She reports having difficulty with school as a result of her problems concentrating. She also reports having difficulty in her current romantic relationship due to frequent and sometimes dramatic mood changes.

Jane indicates that she also uses multiple substances, including marijuana, at least once per day. Jane reports a history of drug and alcohol use that started when she was in high school. She was admitted to an inpatient rehabilitation facility when she was a sophomore in high school and reports doing poorly in school as a result of drug use.

Jane also reports feeling uncertain about what she wants to do with her life. She indicates feeling conflicted between what her family wants her to do and what she wants to do. The following is an initial case conceptualization and possible treatment directions based on an intake interview.

## Present Moment Processes

Jane's deficits in present moment processes include inflexible, rapid speech. In session, Jane's speech was unresponsive to two types of present moment probes. When asked to slow her speech and bring attention to one particular difficulty, she continued to speak at the same rate and continued to jump from one topic to the next. Her self-reports were consistent with these in-session observations. She describes making a to-do list in her head, and then she says the thoughts about what she has to do or has already done persist throughout the day. She reports that these thoughts are popping up in her mind almost constantly and that this quality of attention is interfering with her functioning at school and in relationships. She reports that while making list in her head, she is missing out on her interactions.

*Treatment and assessment implications.* Treatment would include systematic work at slowing Jane's pace of speech and shaping flexible, focused attention. Initial impressions suggest such training will require multiple prompts for both pace and for remaining on one particular topic for increasing periods of time. The therapist should model a slow deliberate pace and a persistent return to particular topics in order to interrupt the current pattern of attention. Incorporating brief mindfulness exercises at the beginning of sessions and very brief exercises punctuated by transitions into more usual clinical dialogue should be used to build both flexibility and focus of attention.

## Acceptance Processes

Jane also exhibits deficits in psychological acceptance processes. Deficits in acceptance include avoidance strategies such as using drugs, which she reports using to "avoid mood changes" as well as to avoid seeing the world as "how it really is."

*Treatment and assessment implication.* An extensive drug history should be taken to examine the extent and duration of drug abuse as an avoidant strategy. Further assessment should include probing to see whether there are other areas in which her avoidant behaviors limit her ability to interact with the world or accomplish things she may want to do in the future. This process should involve generating particulars within the general avoided content (e.g., details about "mood changes" and "how it really is"). Acceptance cannot be fostered in the abstract; particular instances of avoided content must be identified so that acceptance work can be done. These particulars, if found to conflict with valued patterns of living, should be considered as targets for acceptance and defusion work. For example, Jane indicated that she often would use drugs when she felt overwhelmed by her schoolwork and family obligations. In-session acceptance might target "feeling overwhelmed" and provide a context where Jane could come in contact with "feeling overwhelmed" without engaging in avoidant behaviors.

## Defusion Processes

Jane has many fused beliefs about her drug use and about her life. These stories about why she uses drugs include the following: "Smoking marijuana helps with my relationships," "Drugs help me to have a better perspective on everything." She also has other fused beliefs about the world, including: "My parents don't get what I want to do," "I must go to and complete college because that is what my family wants," "I can't let my family down again," and "I need to know why my mood changes." Fusion was indicated by the inflexibility of these thoughts when probed in session. For example, probes aimed at taking different perspectives on predominant troubling thoughts led only to repetition of the thoughts and increasingly emphatic insistence on their veracity, even though the therapist never actually challenged the thoughts directly.

When identifying targets for defusion work, care must be taken to select thoughts that are related to Jane's presenting difficulties. It is most often the case that these thoughts will appear early in the therapeutic process, especially in response to questions about valued life directions or changes. For example, when Jane was asked if she would consider taking a break from drug use, she immediately countered with the statement "drugs help me to control my mood." This belief would be an appropriate target for defusion work, as it appears to support Jane's avoidant repertoire (i.e., drug use). Again, it is not the veracity of the statement that is of importance. Rather, it is the function of the statement, in this case as a reason why Jane could not consider stopping her drug use, that makes it an ideal target for defusion work.

*Treatment and assessment implications.* Further investigation of fused beliefs would include more in-depth probes about values related to family as well as assessing how much Jane believes these statements to be true. Treatment would include activities that help her to interact with the statements/beliefs differently and to help her to hold on less tightly to the beliefs as "true." Because fusion is very high, the work should focus on acceptance and mindfulness interventions, including very simple acceptance and mindfulness work around the values connected with these fused thoughts (e.g., family connections, being understood and appreciated by family and others).

## Self Processes

Jane has many fused beliefs about herself as well. These include, "I am how I want to be when I do drugs/smoke marijuana" and "I am a disappointment to my family because of my behavior in high school." As with fusion in general, in-session probes indicated great inflexibility in these thoughts about self. Other probes included requests to take different perspectives on herself, including a future perspective looking back. Jane was also asked to see and describe herself inside various life roles, as a sister, a student, and a daughter, among others. All of these probes resulted in repetition of fused beliefs about self, even when directly instructed to bring attention to other aspects of those roles.

*Treatment and assessment implications.* The assessment and treatment of self processes with respect to fused beliefs about the self would be similar in this case to those described for defusion. In addition, some exercises that incorporate being able to take multiple perspectives, such as imagining that your child/sister/other person had these thoughts and feelings, would also be incorporated. Work on mindfulness exercises described above would also facilitate more flexible interaction with self.

## Values

When asked what she would do if she could do anything, Jane indicated that she would go live in nature in a self-sustaining community. She indicated that living a more simple life that protects rather than harms the environment was important to her. She also stressed the value of living in a community where people are connected and work together. Given her beliefs about her family and her difficulties in this domain, it is likely that her family also figures prominently in her values. The ACT model assumes a certain intimacy between values and vulnerabilities. Thus, her heightened concerns about family suggest its importance to her as a value.

*Treatment and assessment implications.* A more formal assessment of values such as the VLQ-II would be appropriate to identify the relative importance of various valued domains as well as to determine which areas generate the highest levels of fusion and avoidance. Assessment would also involve probing for specific situations within domains that are important to Jane and asking her how some of the difficulty she is having in other processes (self-as-content, fusion, avoidance, and present moment deficits) is affecting her ability to live a life that would be in line with her values. Having made some progress in the areas of fusion and avoidance, work should begin at active re-authoring of domains of importance. Because of high levels of fusion and avoidance, we would anticipate considerable amounts of present-moment-focused defusion, and acceptance work would likely need to be repeated as the values work proceeded.

## Committed Action

Due to the severity of impairments in contact with the present moment, acceptance, defusion, and self-as-context, committed action work would likely not initially be emphasized with this client. The danger of moving too quickly into committed action is exemplified by the fact that probes asking about even very small particular acts that would be consistent with her values resulted in Jane's immediate return to discussion of fused thoughts about her failures and incapacities.

*Treatment and assessment implications.* As values work progresses, introduction of committed action should proceed. Initial work on committed action should be focused on acceptance and defusion, using committed action as the contents of that work. As flexibility emerged, Jane could be encouraged to choose increasingly larger patterns of committed acts. As with values work, we would anticipate the need to return with some frequency to acceptance and defusion work.

## DISTANCING, METACOGNITION, MINDFULNESS, AND DEFUSION: VARYING PERSPECTIVES ON COGNITION

The shift from BT to CBT marked an increase in interest in the role of cognition in psychological difficulties. As described above, ACT differs from traditional CBT in its lack of emphasis on direct change strategies; instead, ACT focuses on altering the client's relationship with difficult thoughts and emotions. A number of studies appear supportive of the possibility that clients can experience ecologically important life changes even when frequency and intensity of difficult emotion, cognition, and other painful content do not change.

Whereas the 1970s and 1980s saw an increased emphasis on cognition within the BT tradition, thereby transforming it to the CBT tradition, we are witnessing a different shift in emphasis in this domain among many emerging CBTs. Whether this shift will have the lasting effect on the field that the shift to cognition had will be revealed over time. At this point in time, however, although attention to cognition remains high, the focus has shifted to the individual's relationship to his or her cognitions. As has been emphasized throughout, there are commonalities and differences among related theoretical views regarding the role of cognition, including intervention, the purposes of intervention, and putative mechanism of change. To properly position ACT's approach to cognition, we must first provide a brief overview of contemporary theoretical accounts. As is frequently the case, we can see the seeds of the present shift in focus to earlier variants of CBT. Again, Beck provides inspiration and leadership with his concept of *distancing*.

## Distancing

Beck describes a technique he calls distancing, in which the client removes himself a step from disturbing thought and emotion by referring to himself in the third person:

> A patient can increase self-awareness by voluntarily choosing to distance himself from his anxiety. The patient can do this by referring to himself as or by his first name. In this exercise, the patient refers to himself as a separate entity through-out the day and comments on his anxiety from a distance: "Bill seems to be scared. His heart is beating. He seems to be concerned that others are thinking poorly of him. Bill is focusing on the impression he is making." By so distancing himself from his anxious response, the patient can gain a more objective picture of himself.
>
> (Beck, Emery, & Greenberg, 1985, p. 194)

Beck likewise speaks of psychological acceptance in the context of discussing distancing:

> "There's another fearful thought. I'll just count it and let it go." The patient is told to accept the thoughts rather than fight them. He observes his thoughts and lets them go.
>
> (Beck et al., 1985, p. 196)

However, Beck remains consistent at the level of presumed mechanism of action and the purpose of intervention. The proposed mechanism remains cognitive change:

> After the patient has learned to identify his faulty thinking, he learns how to cor-rect his distortions and how to restructure his thinking. Cognitive, behavioral, and affective strategies and techniques are used to help the patient learn more realistic and adaptive thinking.
>
> (Beck et al., 1985, p. 195)

One of the great virtues of Beck's theory, as he pointed out so eloquently in *Cognitive Therapy and the Emotional Disorders* (1976) is that the theory is testable. To date, we are not aware of any measures of distancing or ways of distancing that have been empirically demonstrated to be related to change in cognitive content and to ecologically relevant out-comes. Teasdale's Experiences Questionnaire has been described as a measure of decentering (EQ; Fresco et al., 2007). Some items in the EQ are decentering items that relate fairly clearly to Beck's concept of distancing: "I can actually see that I am not my thoughts." However, other items mix in concepts of acceptance: "I am better able to accept myself as I am." Whereas the former seem consistent with Beck's analysis, the latter appear more connected to Teasdale and colleagues, work in mindfulness-based cognitive therapy (MBCT).

## Metacognition

Wells describes metacognition as "stable knowledge or beliefs about one's cognitive system and knowledge about factors that affect the functioning of the system" (Wells, 1995, p. 302). When a client is experiencing cognition, it is often accompanied by positive or negative appraisal of those thoughts. For example, Wells's metacognitive model of generalized anxiety disorder parses worry into two types. Type 1 worry is worry about various difficulties, such as finances, health, or social outcomes. Type 2 worry, in contrast, is worry about worry. Moreover, type 2 cognitions are the primary intervention targets in the model (Wells, 1995). Wells makes a very similar argument with respect to the role metacognitions play in maintaining excessive rumination in depression, suggesting that cognitive change processes should target negative and positive beliefs about rumination instead of the content of rumination (Wells et al., 2009). The theory is quite consistent with Beck, in that it aims at altering faulty beliefs, but it provides a potentially important evolution in focusing on type 2 beliefs.

In metacognitive therapy (MCT), Wells, like Beck, suggests an acceptance strategy when he invites clients to actively increase worry. "Prescribing the symptom" is quite an old intervention (e.g., paradoxical intention in logotherapy; Frankl, 1959). However, Wells gives us something that has not been forthcoming in previous iterations: a testable mechanism of change. Wells proposes that, "cognitive therapy of GAD ought to focus on challenging meta-worry (Type 2 worry) with the aim of replacing meta-knowledge" (Wells, 1995, p. 311). The specific targets for change are negative catastrophic beliefs about worry *and* positive meta-beliefs about the usefulness of worry.

Wells and his colleagues are seeking empirical support for their model of metacognition as evidenced by the development of psychometric instruments (e.g., the Metacognition Questionnaire-30; Wells & Cartwright-Hatton, 2004), the analysis of the goodness of fit of their model in a clinical sample (Papageorgiou & Wells, 2003), and efficacy trials of MCT in disorders such as depression (Wells et al., 2009), generalized anxiety disorder (Wells & King, 2006), and obsessive-compulsive disorder (Fisher & Wells, 2007). The evidence thus far appears promising. However, formal meditational analyses are needed.

## Metacognitive Awareness and Mindfulness

Although there is some shared terminology between the metacognitive position espoused by Wells in MCT and the metacognitive position espoused by developers of MBCT, there are significant differences (see Wells et al., 2009, p. 293). The overlap in language systems results in part from the fact that both groups of researchers come at the phenomenon from a cognitive perspective. However, the MBCT approach developed by Teasdale and colleagues differs both at the level of intervention and at the level of putative mechanisms of action.

At the level of intervention, MBCT reduces the emphasis on cognitive challenge found in MCT and other mainstream CBTs. "The focus of MBCT is to teach individuals to become more aware of thoughts and feelings and to relate to them in a wider, decentered perspective as 'mental events' rather than as aspects of the self or as necessarily accurate reflections of reality" (Teasdale et al., 2000, p. 616). On the topic of mechanism of action, Teasdale and colleagues challenge the assumption that "reducing belief in depressive thoughts or dysfunctional assumptions (i.e., changes in thought content)" is responsible for change. Instead, they suggest that "shifts of cognitive mode, rather than being merely the means to the end of changing belief, may actually be the primary mechanism through which the relapse prevention effects of CT are achieved" (Teasdale et al., 2001, p. 354).

There is emerging support for the mechanism of change proposed in MBCT. Researchers have demonstrated that metacognitive awareness is a predictor of depression and susceptibility of relapse and that MBCT increased the availability of metacognitive sets (Teasdale et al., 2002). Additionally, MBCT has been shown to reduce overly general recall of autobiographical memory in patients treated for depression (Williams, Teasdale, Segal, & Soulsby, 2000) and to decrease categorical response styles in people suffering from depression (Teasdale et al., 2001). Furthermore, the changes in response style on measures of depression-related cognitions met the criterion for formal mediation, lending support of the mechanism by which MBCT generates clinical outcomes (Teasdale et al., 2001).

## Defusion

As described earlier, defusion is one of the six core processes in ACT. Defusion shares some features with all of the above, though conceptually it seems to have the most significant overlap with MBCT. Of course, the theoretical terms are different, because ACT and MBCT begin from very different theoretical origins, but the sensitivities about intervention and mechanisms of action overlap. First, MBCT teaches an accepting and open posture towards troubling cognition as a way to alter the patient's relationship to cognitive content. Second, both ACT and MBCT view that alteration in relationship to cognitive content as significant in its own right. When Beck and Wells discuss acceptance and openness to cognition, these processes are viewed as means to replacing inaccurate cognitive content. For Wells and colleagues, "the goal is not acceptance or greater awareness of the present moment but strengthening of executive control" (Wells et al., 2009, p. 293).

Another area of overlap between MBCT and ACT conceptualization is related to a subset of fusion we would refer to in ACT as fusion with self as content. According to MBCT, treatment is aimed at precipitating a shift in which "rather than simply *being* their emotions, or *identifying personally with negative thoughts and feelings*, patients relate to negative experiences as mental events in a wider context or field of awareness" (Teasdale, et al., 2002, p. 276, emphasis added). The patient's view of his or her negative thoughts shifts from a perspective of negative thoughts "as the 'reality by which I am condemned' to one in which they are experienced more as 'passing thoughts and feelings that may or may not have some truth in them'" (Teasdale et al., 2002, p. 276). Here we see overlap both in a lesser concern with veracity of thoughts than with the behavioral function of thoughts and with the lessening of identification of self with thoughts independent of veracity.

Defusion work does not ask the client to replace difficult cognitions with more rational or even with more workable thoughts. It is also not concerned with reducing or alleviating those difficult thoughts. ACT does not intervene directly to dispute or challenge either type 1 or type 2 cognitions. In fact, ACT takes the perspective that the frequency of distressing thoughts may not have to decrease at all. Rather, defusion is more like metacognitive awareness, in that it is concerned with increasing psychological flexibility when and if troubling thoughts occur, in order to allow the client to improve regardless of what thoughts arise. As previously suggested, this may be particularly important in domains in which distressing thoughts are likely to persist or recur. It is worth noting that MBCT has shown its best effects among individuals who have recurrent depressive episodes. Likewise, ACT has shown particularly robust effects in some areas, like chronic pain, diabetes, stress, and psychosis, for example, where recurrence or persistence of symptoms is a near certainty.

ACT researchers have been hard at work designing basic preparations and developing psychometric instruments to measure defusion as well as other core ACT processes. The empirical status of defusion as a process in ACT is discussed in the next section, in which evidence for ACT outcomes and processes is briefly examined.

## BRIEF REVIEW OF EVIDENCE ON THE ACT MODEL

Human suffering is ubiquitous. Over one quarter of individuals sampled in a major national survey of mental health met the criterion for a mental disorder within the past year (Kessler, Chiu, Demler, & Walters, 2005), and almost half of the individuals surveyed in a previous sampled reported suffering from a mental disorder at some point in their lifetime (Kessler et al., 1994). These data support the ACT assertion that human suffering is not an abnormal condition but instead an essential part of the human experience. ACT posits that natural language and cognitive processes, although adaptive in some domains, have a destructive potential in others. These basic language processes are the subject matter of RFT, which to date has generated more than 160 empirical studies providing broad support for this core underpinning of the ACT model of psychopathology.

The theoretical framework of the ACT treatment model has fostered a steady production of outcome research across a broad array of disorders and populations. There is growing evidence for the ACT model in treating clinical conditions such as mood disorders (Forman, Herbert, Moitra, Yeomans, & Geller, 2007; Zettle & Rains, 1989), substance abuse (Hayes, et al., 2004) and obsessive-compulsive disorder (Twohig, Hayes, & Masuda, 2006). Additional studies show support for the ACT model in the treatment of severe psychiatric problems such as psychoses, which have proven especially resistant to treatment (Bach & Hayes, 2002; Gaudiano & Herbert, 2006).

Findings have shown that ACT is also an effective intervention in nonclinical populations, which are often not targeted by traditional therapeutic models. Recent outcome research has demonstrated the efficacy of the ACT model in reducing stigma and burnout among substance abuse counselors (Hayes et al., 2004), helping parents of children with autism (Blackledge & Hayes, 2006), and reducing stress and increasing productivity in the workplace (Bond, Hayes, & Barnes-Holmes, 2006). Additionally, ACT has been employed as a health intervention to reduce seizure frequency in epilepsy (Lundgren, Dahl, Melin, & Kies, 2004), to help patients cope with chronic pain (Dahl, Wilson, & Nilsson, 2004; McCracken, Vowles, & Eccleston, 2005), as an aid in smoking cessation (Gifford et al., 2004), to improve diabetes management (Gregg, Callaghan, Hayes, & Glenn-Lawson, 2007), and to assist in weight loss (Forman, Butryn, Hoffman, & Herbert, 2009; Lillis, Hayes, Bunting, & Masuda, 2009; Tapper et al., 2009).

These studies referenced above are but a few of the ACT outcome studies published to date and are representative of the diverse range of disorders and populations studied by ACT researchers. The breadth of the research program is intentional. The ACT treatment development community, centered in the Association for Contextual Behavioral Science, is explicitly dedicated to the development of a broadly applicable model. Conducting treatment development in widely ranging contexts, with widely ranging difficulties, is central to the contextual behavioral science treatment development strategy (see Hayes in this volume).

A comprehensive review of outcomes and treatment comparisons of individual studies is well beyond the scope of this chapter. Instead, results from three recent meta-analyses of ACT interventions will be discussed to give readers a general impression of the current state of ACT outcome literature. Meta-analyses by both Hayes, Luoma, Bond, Masuda, and Lillis (2006) and Öst (2008) found moderate between-group effect sizes when ACT was compared to established treatments, and moderate to large effect sizes with respect to treatment-as-usual (TAU) and wait-list comparisons, in both cases favoring ACT.

Another recent meta-analysis provided a more conservative estimate of ACT's effectiveness, finding only moderate to small between-group effect sizes compared to TAU and wait-list conditions and equivalent outcomes when comparing ACT with established treatments (Powers, Zum Vörde Sive Vörding, & Emmelkamp, 2009). The fact that similar conclusions regarding efficacy are drawn by both ACT's leading proponents (Hayes and colleagues) and by strong critics such as Öst suggests that the outcome picture is promising. Although Öst has criticized the quality of ACT studies, this ought not be a surprise given the very different levels of funding for the ACT studies and CBT studies compared in the Öst meta-analysis and the relative exploratory nature of the treatments compared (Gaudiano, 2009a). For example, Öst's selected comparison CBT studies were all in the realm of anxiety and depression. These represent tests of the field's most developed treatments for our most studied disorders. By comparison, ACT trials were as diverse as medication refractory epilepsy, polysubstance-abusing drug addicts, and personality disorders. Öst's analysis is a comparison of ACT to more traditional models of CBT, but it is also a comparison on dimensions that have nothing to do with ACT and traditional CBT per se (e.g., funding levels, disorders treated, etc.; see Gaudiano, 2009a; Gaudiano, 2009b; & Öst, 2009 for an extended exchange on these methodological issues,).

Even given these limitations, meta-analyses demonstrate that ACT yields outcomes that are more effective than TAU, and at least equivalent with (and sometimes superior to) established CBT and CT treatments. For example, in a recent treatment study for anxiety and depression, the ACT and CT treatment conditions were both effective and produced equivalent outcomes (Forman, Herbert, Moitra, Yeomans, & Geller, 2007). Zettle and Rains (1989) also found that both ACT and CT were equally effective in reducing depressive symptoms. ACT has also shown superior results to established CBT treatments in several outcome studies. In a recent evaluation of ACT and CT for the treatment of eating pathology, the ACT treatment condition lead to a significantly greater reduction in eating pathology (Cohen's $d = 1.89$) compared to the CT treatment condition (Cohen's $d = .048$; Juarascio, Forman, & Herbert, in press). There is also preliminary evidence for the effectiveness of ACT with a recent studying demonstrating that ACT leads to more positive client changes than CBT when implemented by novice student therapists in a trainee clinic (Lappalainen et al., 2007).

A limitation of ACT in treatment comparison studies and meta-analyses is that many ACT treatment outcome measures are not as well established as measures of traditional outcomes, making ACT difficult to compare with established treatments. For example, Powers et al. (2009) selected group differences in pain intensity as the outcome measure when comparing an ACT intervention plus TAU to a TAU condition for their meta-analysis. There was not a significant difference between groups on this particular outcome measure. However, there was a major difference in terms of days of sick leave and medical utilization, with those in the ACT condition using ten times less sick leave and seven times less medical care than those in TAU (Dahl, Wilson, & Nilsson, 2004). Comparing traditional to contemporary approaches is never an easy process, and ACT researchers have expressed their concerns on a variety of methodological issues in these comparisons (Levin & Hayes, 2009; for an extended discussion of this point, see Gaudiano, 2009a, 2009b). However, it must be acknowledged that the ACT community needs to continue to strengthen the reliability and validity of its current and emerging process and outcome measures.

Of course, treatment outcomes are not everything. One of the encouraging recent developments within the CBT movement generally is a growing interest in examination of mechanisms of change (as seen above in discussion of cognitive mechanisms in ACT and other new CBTs), and especially in transdiagnostic dimensions (i.e., elements of psychotherapy models that remain constant across diagnostic specific variants of a model). The underlying theory of ACT suggests different processes of change relative to established CBTs. The question that must be answered is, does the treatment work according to the processes outlined in its theory?

Evidence supporting the notion that ACT works through six theorized processes is steadily accumulating, though measurement and demonstration of the importance of some processes lag behind others. Recent studies have demonstrated that acceptance and defusion mediated lower levels of tinnitus distress (Hesser, Westin, Hayes, & Andersson, 2009), psychological flexibility mediated work-related stress (Bond & Bunce, 2000), and acceptance of diabetes and changes in self-management behaviors mediated changes in blood glucose levels (Gregg, Callagan, Hayes, & Glenn-Lawson, 2007). Researchers are also beginning to go back and look at process of change on previously published data sets. For example, Zettle, Rains, and Hayes (in press) re-examined a treatment study comparing ACT and CT intervention for depression and found that defusion mediated changes in depressive symptoms in the ACT condition. In another recent reexamination, Gaudiano, Herbert, and Hayes (in press) found strong evidence of mediation in an ACT psychosis trial (Gaudiano & Herbert, 2006). These are just a few examples of mediation in the ACT literature (for a more in-depth review, see Hayes et al., 2006). Accounting for processes of change is a core component of the ACT development model and has become standard practice for ACT researchers to conduct meditational analyses in both basic and applied studies.

In addition to efforts documenting the mechanisms of change that are hypothesized to underlie ACT interventions, researchers have begun to conduct component analyses of core ACT processes to parse out the workings of different elements within the model. Using laboratory analogues of clinical conditions, researchers have compared ACT change processes (e.g., acceptance, defusion) to traditional CBT techniques (e.g., distraction). Component analyses of acceptance-based strategies suggest that they are more effective than control-based strategies in coping with intrusive thoughts (Marcks & Woods, 2007), tolerating pain in a cold-pressure task (Hayes et al., 1999; Masedo & Esteve, 2007), and coping with food cravings for individuals with a high susceptibility to cravings (Forman et al., 2007). Recent studies also support the use of defusion for coping with negative self-statements (Healy et al., 2008) and demonstrate the greater efficacy of defusion strategies compared to distraction or through control techniques (Masuda, Hayes, Sackett, & Twohig, 2004). These analogue studies, and others like them, provide empirical support for the underlying components of the ACT model and highlight the distinctive therapeutic processes that are thought to drive ACT outcomes. However, it is important to acknowledge that most ACT component studies to date have been analogue in nature. Future research is needed to demonstrate component control in clinical populations.

ACT enjoys a level of empirical support that reflects its emerging status (Hayes, Masuda, Bissett, Luoma, & Guerrero, 2004). ACT lacks the large RCT-outcomes evidence that some of the more established treatments within CBT enjoy. However, the ACT treatment development and research model appears to be on a different developmental trajectory from most mainstream CBTs. ACT researchers have sought support for the model on multiple levels from basic language processes to component analyses and meditational accounts to outcome studies, across a variety of populations and disorders. Thus far, this strategy has produced promising results.

## OVERVIEW OF FUTURE DIRECTIONS

As can be seen in the above review of ACT and of its relationship to alternative treatments both old and new, four major foci of future work seem apparent. First, as pilot data accumulate, ACT treatment outcome research should employ the most methodologically sound designs possible. Second, ACT researchers need to continue to develop reliable and valid measures of putative change processes. Third, the ACT treatment development community ought to continue its multipronged, iterative research program involving basic and applied research, small exploratory studies and larger well-controlled RCTs and experimental psychopathology studies that examine particular ACT components and processes. Finally, ACT treatment development researchers will need to pick up the burden of examining the relationship among some of the varied "third wave" CBTs, with an eye toward empirical tests of the different therapeutic models of intervention and change processes.

## REFERENCES

Bach, P., & Hayes, S. C. (2002). The use of acceptance and commitment therapy to prevent the rehospitalization of psychotic patients: A randomized controlled trial. *Journal of Consulting and Clinical Psychology, 70*, 1129–1139.

Bandura. A. (1977) *Social learning theory.* New York, NY: Prentice-Hall.

Beck, A. T. (1976). *Cognitive therapy and the emotional disorders.* New York, NY: International Universities Press.

Beck, A. T. (1993). Cognitive therapy: Past, present, and future. *Journal of Consulting and Clinical Psychology, 61*, 194–198.

Beck, A. T., Emery, G., & Greenberg, R. L. (1985). *Anxiety disorders and phobias: A cognitive perspective.* New York, NY: Basic Books.

Bergin, A. E., & Garfield, S. L. (Eds.). (1971). *Handbook of psychotherapy and behavior change.* New York, NY: Wiley.

Bergin, A. E., & Garfield, S. L. (Eds.). (1978). *Handbook of psychotherapy and behavior change* (2nd ed.). New York, NY: Wiley.

Bergin, A. E., & Garfield, S. L. (Eds.). (1986). *Handbook of psychotherapy and behavior change* (3rd ed.). New York, NY: Wiley.

Blackledge, J. T., & Hayes, S. C. (2006). Using acceptance and commitment training in the support of parents of children diagnosed with autism. *Child & Family Behavior Therapy, 28*, 1–18.

Bond, F. W., & Bunce, D. (2000). Mediators of change in emotion-focused and problem-focused worksite stress management interventions. *Journal of Occupational Health Psychology, 5*, 156–163.

Bond, F. W., Hayes, S. C., & Barnes-Holmes, D. (2006). Psychological flexibility, ACT, and organizational behaviour. *Journal of Organizational Behavior Management, 26*, 25–54.

Dahl, J. C., Plumb, J. C., Stewart, I., & Lundgren, T. (2009). *The art and science of valuing in psychotherapy.* Oakland, CA: New Harbinger.

Dahl, J., Wilson, K. G., & Nilsson, A. (2004). Acceptance and commitment therapy and the treatment of persons at risk for long-term disability resulting from stress and pain symptoms: A preliminary randomized trial. *Behavior Therapy, 35*, 785–802.

Dobson, K. S., Hollon, S. D., Dimidjian, S., Schmaling, K. B., Kohlenberg, R. J., Gallop, R. J., . . . Jacobson, N. S. (2008). Randomized trial of behavioral activation, cognitive therapy, and antidepressant medication in the prevention of relapse and recurrence in major depression. *Journal of Consulting and Clinical Psychology, 76*, 468–477.

Ellis, A. (1961). *A guide to rational living.* Englewood Cliffs, NJ: Prentice-Hall.

Ferster, C. B. (1967). Arbitrary and natural reinforcement. *Psychological Record, 17,* 341–347.

Fisher, P. L., & Wells, A. (2007). Metacognitive therapy for obsessive-compulsive disorder: A case series. *Journal of Behavior Therapy and Experimental Psychiatry, 39,* 117–132.

Forman, E. M., Butryn, M., Hoffman, K.L., & Herbert, J. D (2009). An open trial of an acceptance-based behavioral treatment for weight loss. *Cognitive and Behavioral Practice, 16,* 223–235.

Forman, E. M., & Herbert, J. D. (2009). New directions in cognitive behavior therapy: Acceptance-based therapies. In W. O'Donohue & J. E. Fisher, (Eds.), *General principles and empirically supported techniques of cognitive behavior therapy* (pp. 102–114). Hoboken, NJ: Wiley.

Forman, E. M., Herbert, J. D., Moitra, E., Yeomans, P. D., & Geller, P. A. (2007). A randomized controlled effectiveness trial of acceptance and commitment therapy and cognitive therapy for anxiety and depression. *Behavior Modification, 31,* 772–799.

Forman, E. M., Hoffman, K. L., McGrath, K. B., Herbert, J. D., Brandsma, L. L., & Lowe, M. R. (2007). A comparison of acceptance and control-based strategies with food cravings: An analog study. *Behaviour Research and Therapy, 45,* 2372–2386.

Frankl. V. E. (1959). *Man's search for meaning.* New York, NY: Washington Square Press.

Fresco, D. M., Moore, M. T., van Dulmen, M., Segal, Z. V., Teasdale, J. D., Ma, H., & Williams, J. M. G. (2007). Initial psychometric properties of the Experiences Questionnaire: Validation of a self-report measure of decentering. *Behavior Therapy, 38,* 234–246.

Gaudiano, B. A. (2009a). Öst's (2008) methodological comparison of clinical trials of acceptance and commitment therapy versus cognitive behavior therapy: Matching apples with oranges, *Behaviour Research and Therapy, 47,* 1066–1070.

Gaudiano, B. A. (2009b). Reinventing the wheel versus avoiding past mistakes when evaluating psychotherapy outcome research: Rejoinder to Öst. Unpublished manuscript. Retrieved from http://www.psychotherapybrownbag.com/psychotherapy_brown_bag_a/2010/01/the-empirical-status-of-acceptance-and-commitment-therapy-act-a-conversation-amongst-two-prominent-p.html

Gaudiano, B. A., & Herbert, J. D. (2006). Acute treatment of inpatients with psychotic symptoms using acceptance and commitment therapy: Pilot results. *Behaviour Research and Therapy, 44,* 415–437.

Gaudiano, B. A., Herbert, J. D., & Hayes, S. C. (in press). Is it the symptom or the relation to it? Investigating potential mediators of change in acceptance and commitment therapy for psychosis. *Behavior Therapy.*

Gifford, E. V., Kohlenberg, B. S., Hayes, S. C., Antonuccio, D. O., Piasecki, M. M., Rasmussen-Hall, M. L., & Palm, K. M. (2004). Acceptance-based treatment for smoking cessation. *Behavior Therapy, 35,* 689–705.

Goldfried, M. R., & Davison, G. C. (1976). *Clinical behavior therapy.* New York, NY: Holt, Rinehart, & Winston.

Gregg, J. A., Callaghan, G. M., Hayes, S. C., & Glenn-Lawson, J. L. (2007). Improving diabetes self-management through acceptance, mindfulness, and values: A randomized controlled trial. *Journal of Consulting and Clinical Psychology, 75,* 336–343.

Hayes, S. C. (1984). Making sense of spirituality. *Behaviorism, 12,* 99–110.

Hayes, S. C., Barnes-Holmes, D., & Roche, B. (Eds.). (2001). *Relational frame theory: A post-Skinnerian account of human language and cognition.* New York, NY: Plenum Press.

Hayes, S. C., Bissett, R., Korn, Z., Zettle, R. D., Rosenfard, I., Cooper, L., & Grudnt, A. (1999). The impact of acceptance versus control rationales on pain tolerance. *Psychological Record, 49,* 33–47.

Hayes, S. C., Bissett, R., Roget, N., Padilla, M., Kohlenberg, B. S., Fisher, G.,...Niccolls, R. (2004). The impact of acceptance and commitment training and multicultural training on the stigmatizing attitudes and professional burnout of substance abuse counselors. *Behavior Therapy, 35,* 821–835.

Hayes, S. C., Luoma, J. B., Bond, F. W., Masuda, A., & Lillis, J. (2006). Acceptance and commitment therapy: Model, processes, and outcomes. *Behaviour Research and Therapy, 44,* 1–25.

Hayes, S. C., Masuda, A., Bissett, R., Luoma, J., & Guerrero, L. F. (2004). DBT, FAP, and ACT: How empirically oriented are the new behavior therapy technologies? *Behavior Therapy, 35,* 35–54.

Hayes, S. C., & Plumb, J. C. (2007). Mindfulness from the bottom up: Providing an inductive framework for understanding mindfulness processes and their application to human suffering. *Psychological Inquiry, 18,* 242–248.

Hayes, S. C., Strosahl, K., & Wilson, K. G. (1999). *Acceptance and commitment therapy: An experiential approach to behavior change.* New York, NY: Guilford Press.

Hayes, S. C., & Wilson, K. G. (2003). Mindfulness: Method and process. *Clinical Psychology: Science and Practice, 10,* 161–165.

Hayes, S. C., Wilson, K. G., Gifford, E. V., Bissett, R., Piasecki, M., Batten, S. V.,...Gregg, J. (2004). A preliminary trial of twelve-step facilitation and acceptance and commitment therapy with polysubstance-abusing methadone-maintained opiate addicts. *Behavior Therapy, 35,* 667–688.

Hayes, S. C., Wilson, K. W., Gifford, E. V., Follette, V. M., & Strosahl, K. (1996). Experiential avoidance and behavioral disorders: A functional dimensional approach to diagnosis and treatment. *Journal of Consulting and Clinical Psychology, 64,* 1152–1168.

Hayes, S. C., Zettle, R. D., & Rosenfarb, I. (1989). Rule following. In S. C. Hayes (Ed.), *Rule-governed behavior: Cognition, contingencies, and instructional control* (pp. 191–220). New York, NY: Plenum.

Healy, H. A., Barnes-Holmes, Y., Barnes-Holmes, D., Keogh, C., Luciano, C., & Wilson, K. (2008). An experimental test of a cognitive defusion exercise: Coping with negative and positive self-statements. *Psychological Record, 58,* 623–640.

Herbert, J. D., Forman, E. M., & England, E. L. (2009). Psychological acceptance. In W. O'Donohue & J. E. Fisher (Eds.), *General principles and empirically supported techniques of cognitive behavior therapy* (pp. 77–101). Hoboken, NJ: Wiley.

Hesser, H., Westin, V., Hayes, S. C., & Andersson, G. (2009). Clients' in-session acceptance and cognitive defusion behaviors in acceptance-based treatment of tinnitus distress. *Behaviour Research and Therapy, 47,* 523–528.

Hollon, S. D., & Beck, A. T. (1986). *Cognitive and cognitive-behavioral therapies.* In S. L. Garfield & A. E. Bergin (Eds.), *Handbook of psychotherapy and behavior change* (3rd ed.) (pp. 443–482). New York, NY: Wiley.

Juarascio, A. S., Forman, E. M., & Herbert, J. D. (in press). Acceptance and commitment therapy versus cognitive therapy for the treatment of comorbid eating pathology. *Behavior Modification.*

Kabat-Zinn, J. (1994). *Wherever you go there you are: Mindfulness meditations in everyday life.* New York, NY: Hyperion.

Kessler, R. C., Chiu, W. T., Demler, O., & Walters, E. E. (2005). Prevalence, severity, and comorbidity of 12-month DSM-IV disorders in the national comorbidity survey replication. *Archives of General Psychiatry, 62,* 617–627.

Kessler, R. C., McGonagle, K. A., Zhao, S., Nelson, C. B., Hughes, M., Eshleman, S.,...Kendler, K. S. (1994). Lifetime and 12-month prevalence of DSM-III-R psychiatric disorders in the United States: Results from the national comorbidity survey. *Archives of General Psychiatry, 51,* 8–19.

Kohlenberg, R., & Tsai, M. (1991). *Functional analytic psychotherapy.* New York: Plenum Press.

Lappalainen, R., Lehtonen, T., Skarp, E., Taubert, E., Ojanen, M., & Hayes, S. C. (2007). The impact of CBT and ACT models using psychology trainee therapists: A preliminary controlled effectiveness trial. *Behavior Modification, 31,* 488–511.

Levin, M., & Hayes, S. C. (2009). Is acceptance and commitment therapy superior to established treatment comparisons? *Psychotherapy and Psychosomatic, 78,* 380.

Lillis, J., Hayes, S. C., Bunting, K., & Masuda, A. (2009). Teaching acceptance and mindfulness to improve the lives of the obese: A preliminary test of a theoretical model. *Annals of Behavior Medicine, 37,* 58–69

Linehan, M. M. (1993). *Cognitive-behavioral treatment of borderline personality disorder.* New York, NY: Guilford Press.

Longmore, R. J., & Worrell, M. (2007). Do we need to challenge thoughts in cognitive behavior therapy? *Clinical Psychology Review, 27,* 173–187.

Lundgren, T., Dahl, J., & Hayes, S. C. (2008). Evaluation of mediators of change in the treatment of epilepsy with acceptance and commitment therapy. *Journal of Behavior Medicine, 31,* 225–235.

Lundgren, T., Dahl, J., Melin, L., & Kies, B. (2004). Evaluation of acceptance and commitment therapy for drug refractory epilepsy: A randomized controlled trial in South Africa: A pilot study. *Epilepsia, 47,* 2173–2179.

Marcks, B. A., & Woods, D. W. (2007). Role of thought-related beliefs and coping strategies in the escalation of intrusive thoughts: An analog to obsessive-compulsive disorder. *Behaviour Research and Therapy, 45,* 2640–2651.

Martell, C. R., Addis, M. E., & Jacobson, N. S. (2001). *Depression in context: Strategies for guided action.* New York: W. W. Norton.

Masedo, A. I., & Esteve, M. R. (2007). Effects of suppression, acceptance and spontaneous coping on pain tolerance, pain intensity and distress. *Behaviour Research and Therapy, 45,* 199–209.

Masuda, A., Hayes, S. C., Sackett, C. F., & Twohig, M. P. (2004). Cognitive defusion and self-relevant negative thoughts: Examining the impact of a ninety year old technique. *Behaviour Research and Therapy, 42,* 477–485.

McCracken, L. M., Vowles, K. E., & Eccleston, C. (2005). Acceptance-based treatment for persons with complex, long standing chronic pain: A preliminary analysis of treatment outcome in comparison to a waiting phase. *Behaviour Research and Therapy, 43,* 1335–1346.

McHugh, L., Barnes-Holmes, Y., & Barnes-Holmes, D. (2009). Understanding and training perspective taking as relational responding. In R. A. Rehfeldt & Y. Barnes-Holmes (Eds.), *Derived relational responding: Application for learners with autism and other developmental disabilities* (pp. 281–300). Oakland, CA: New Harbinger.

Öst, L. (2008). Efficacy of the third wave of behavioral therapies: A systematic review and meta-analysis. *Behaviour Research and Therapy, 46,* 296–321.

Öst, L. (2009). Inventing the wheel once more or leaning from the history of psychotherapy research methodology: Reply to Gaudiano's comments on Öst's (2008) review. *Behaviour Research and Therapy, 49,* 1071–1073.

Papageorgiou, C., & Wells, A. (2003). An empirical test of a clinical metacognitive model of rumination and depression. *Cognitive Therapy and Research, 27,* 261–273.

Plumb, J. (2009, September 1). *Head, heart & hands: A motto for living and governing ACBS.* Retrieved September 30, 2009, from http://www.contextualpsychology.org/head_heart_hands_2009

Powers, M. B., Zum Vörde Sive Vörding, M. B., & Emmelkamp, P. M. (2009). Acceptance and commitment therapy: A meta-analytic review. *Psychotherapy and Psychosomatics, 78,* 73–80.

Segal, Z. V., Williams, J. M. G., & Teasdale, J. D. (2001). *Mindfulness-based cognitive therapy for depression: A new approach to preventing relapse.* New York, NY: Guilford Press.

Shimoff, E., Catania, A. C., & Matthews, B. A. (1981). Uninstructed human responding: Sensitivity of low-rate performance to schedule contingencies. *Journal of the Experimental Analysis of Behavior, 36,* 207–220.

Skinner, B. F. (1953). *Science and human behavior.* New York, NY: Free Press.

Skinner, B. F. (1974). *About behaviorism.* New York, NY: Alfred A. Knopf.

Tapper, K. Shaw, C., Ilsley, J., Hill, A. J., Bond, F. W., & Moore, L. (2009). Exploratory randomised controlled trial of a mindfulness-based weight loss intervention for women. *Appetite: Multidisciplinary Research on Eating and Drinking, 52,* 396–404.

Teasdale, J. D., Moore, R. G., Havhurst, H., Pope, M., Williams, S., & Segal, Z. V. (2002). Metacognitive awareness and prevention of relapse in depression: Empirical evidence. *Journal of Consulting and Clinical Psychology, 70,* 275–287.

Teasdale, J. D., Scott, J., Moore, R. G., Hayhurst, H., Pope, M., & Paykel, E. S. (2001). How does cognitive therapy prevent release in residual depression? Evidence from a controlled trial. *Journal of Consulting and Clinical Psychology, 69,* 347–357.

Teasdale, J. D., Segal, Z. V., Williams J. M. G., Ridgeway, V. A., Soulsby, J. M., & Lau, M. A. (2000). Prevention of relapse/recurrence in major depression by mindfulness-based cognitive therapy. *Journal of Consulting and Clinical Psychology, 68*, 615–623.

Twohig, M. P., Hayes, S. C., & Masuda, A. (2006). Increasing willingness to experience obsessions: Acceptance and commitment therapy as a treatment for obsessive-compulsive disorder. *Behavior Therapy, 37*, 3–13.

Wells, A. (1995). Metacognition and worry: A cognitive model of generalized anxiety disorder. *Behavioral and Cognitive Psychotherapy, 23*, 301–320.

Wells, A., & Cartwright-Hatton, S. (2004). A short form of the metacognitions questionnaire: Properties of the MCQ-30. *Behaviour Research and Therapy, 42*, 385–396.

Wells, A., Fisher, P., Myers, S., Wheatley, J., Patel, T., & Brewin, C. R. (2009). Metacognitive therapy in recurrent and persistent depression: A multiple-baseline study of a new treatment. *Cognitive Therapy and Research, 33*, 291–300.

Wells, A., & King, P. (2006). Metacognitive therapy for generalized anxiety disorder: An open trial. *Journal of Behavior Therapy and Experimental Psychiatry, 37*, 206–212.

Williams, J. M. G., Teasdale, J. D., Segal, Z. V., & Soulsby, J. (2000). Mindfulness-based cognitive therapy reduces overgeneral autobiographical memory in formerly depressed patients. *Journal of Abnormal Psychology, 109*, 150–155.

Wilson, K. G., & DuFrene, T. (2009). *Mindfulness for two: An acceptance and commitment therapy approach to mindfulness in psychotherapy.* Oakland, CA: New Harbinger.

Wilson, K. G., & Sandoz, E. K. (2008). Mindfulness, values, and the therapeutic relationship in acceptance and commitment therapy. In S. Hick & T. Bein (Eds.), Mindfulness and the therapeutic relationship (pp. 89–106). New York, NY: Guilford Press.

Wilson, K. G., Sandoz, E. K., Flynn, M. K., Slater, R., & DuFrene, T. (in press). Understanding, assessing, and treating values processes in mindfulness and acceptance-based therapies. To appear in R. Baer (Ed.), *Assessing mindfulness and acceptance: Illuminating the processes of change.* Oakland, CA: New Harbinger.

Yalom, I. D. (1980). *Existential psychotherapy.* New York, NY: Basic Books.

Zettle, R. D., & Hayes, S. C. (1982). Rule governed behavior: A potential theoretical framework for cognitive behavior therapy. In P. C. Kendall (Ed.), *Advances in cognitive behavioral research and therapy* (pp. 73–118). New York, NY: Academic.

Zettle, R. D., & Rains, J. C. (1989). Group cognitive and contextual therapies in treatment of depression. *Journal of Clinical Psychology, 45*, 438–445.

Zettle, R. D., Rains, J. C. & Hayes, S. C. (in press). Processes of change in acceptance and commitment therapy and cognitive therapy for depression: A mediational reanalysis of Zettle and Rains (1989). *Behavior Modification.*

# PART II
# Integration and Synthesis

# 11

Mindfulness and Acceptance

## The Perspective of Cognitive Therapy

STEFAN G. HOFMANN, JULIA A. GLOMBIEWSKI, ANU ASNAANI,
AND ALICE T. SAWYER

Cognitive behavioral therapy (CBT) refers to a family of interventions based on the premise that modifying maladaptive cognitions can improve emotional distress and behavioral problems. However, CBT is considerably more complex and cannot be reduced to this common principle or to any one particular CBT protocol. CBT has evolved into a scientific enterprise that incorporates a variety of treatment techniques. Mindfulness and acceptance-based interventions are two popular strategies that are fully compatible with CBT and have already been an integral part of many specific CBT protocols, including early formulations of the model. Because behavioral change strategies are important components of certain adaptations of this treatment, we use the term CBT rather than cognitive therapy.

This chapter will provide a critical review of the extensive CBT literature with the goal of clarifying the basic theoretical premises, the definition of the term *cognition,* and the use of mindfulness and acceptance strategies for contemporary CBT protocols. We begin our discussion with a brief review of CBT, its history, and the basic assumptions that define this family of interventions. We continue with a definition of the term *cognition* based on appraisal theories and information processing perspectives. We then examine the similarities and differences between mindfulness and acceptance-based interventions and traditional CBT. We conclude with suggestions for future research.

## HISTORICAL CONTEXT

The question of the relationship between mind and body is one of the great and still-unresolved challenges in philosophy and science. Cartesian dualism posits that soul (mind) and body are two distinct entities, with the mind being unique to humans, entirely immaterial, and linked to cognitions and consciousness, whereas the body is viewed as entirely material and comparable to a machine. Descartes further believed that, although emotions and sensations were caused by the body, consciousness of them was part of the soul (mind).

This mind-body problem has continued throughout the history of psychology. William James adopted a monistic and reductionistic perspective when he wrote in his *Principles of Psychology*:

> Taking all [...] facts together, the simple and radical conception dawns upon the mind that mental action may be uniformly and absolutely a function of brain-action, varying as the latter varies, and being to the brain-action as effect to cause. This conception is the "working hypothesis" which underlies all the 'physiological psychology' of recent years...
>
> (James, 1890; p. 6)

Similarly, Skinner adopted a monistic perspective and questioned the meaningfulness of the concept *cognition* and its uniqueness to humans. He argued in his book *Verbal Behavior* (Skinner, 1957) that any human behavior, including language and thought, is learned and shaped and maintained by the arrangement of past and present environmental contingencies.

Chomsky's (1959) critique of Skinner's book is often considered to be the initial spark that set off the cognitive revolution. Since then, the basic arguments from the cognitive and radical behaviorist perspectives have remained largely unchanged. Contemporary behaviorally-oriented authors still argue that mental processes should be seen simply as verbal behaviors, and that behaviors cannot cause other behaviors (Wilson, 1997). For example, it has been suggested that "cognition plays an important role in the regulation of other forms of behaviors (...), but it is not a causal role" (Wilson, Hayes, & Gifford, 1997, p. 56). In contrast, cognitive psychologists assume that emotions, affect, and behaviors can be directly caused by linguistically-based thought processes (Hauser, Chomsky, & Fitch, 2002).

## THE COGNITIVE CAUSALITY PREMISE

The basic premise of cognitive causality (i.e., the assumption that cognitions can cause emotions and behaviors) is certainly not new. The basic idea can be found in the teachings of Epictetus ("men are not moved by things but the view of them" from *The Enchiridion*), Marcus Aurelius ("If you are distressed by anything external, the pain is not due to the thing itself, but to your estimate of it; and this you have the power to revoke at any moment" from *Meditations*), and the writings of William Shakespeare ("there is nothing either good or bad, but thinking makes it so" from *Hamlet*).

Similarly, CBT is based on the premise that cognition is a meaningful construct that is distinct from behaviors and emotions. More importantly, CBT is based on the premise that maladaptive cognitions are mental processes that lead to emotional distress, and that correcting these maladaptive cognitions will in turn lead to improvements in emotional distress and maladaptive behaviors.

This perspective is consistent with other appraisal theories of emotions, which were one of the driving forces behind the cognitive revolution. These theories view an emotional response as the result of cognitive appraisal of events or situations (e.g., Beck, Emery, & Greenberg, 1985; Lazarus, 1982; Schachter & Singer, 1962). These approaches assume that cognitions are capable of producing emotions, and that emotions cannot occur without some kind of thought activity. At the same time, it is acknowledged that the functional relationships between cognition and emotion are interrelated. For example, in the case of anxiety, the process begins with a transaction that is appraised as harmful, threatening, or challenging (e.g., Beck et al., 1985). The appraisal and its attendant emotions influence the coping processes, which in turn change the person-environment relationship (e.g., Lazarus, 1982, 1991). The altered person-environment relationship is reappraised, and the reappraisal then leads to a change in emotion quality and intensity (Lazarus & Folkman, 1988). The influence of cognitions on emotions and behaviors provides humans with the ability to replace impulsive action, giving the person greater control over person-environment relationships and the capability of future planning. Rudiments of these capabilities are evident in animals, but humans develop a remarkable level of sophistication through their advanced cognitive development (e.g., Piaget, 1952).

The integral connection between cognitions, emotions, and behaviors has been recognized since the early formulations of CBT models. Ellis, for example, called his treatment approach *Rational Emotive Behavior Therapy* (Ellis, 2001) to emphasize the importance of behavioral and emotional/experiential aspects in cognitive therapy. Similarly, Beck (1991) distinguished among intellectual, experiential, and behavioral approaches, all of which he considers key aspects of therapy. As part of the intellectual approach, patients learn to identify their misconceptions, test the validity of their thoughts, and substitute these thoughts with more rational, objective ones. The experiential approach helps patients expose themselves to experiences in order to change these misconceptions. Finally, the behavioral approach encourages the development of specific behaviors that lead to more general changes in the way patients view themselves and the world. In sum, although based on the basic premise that changes in maladaptive cognitions can cause improvements of mental disorders, CBT recognizes the crucial importance of the behavioral and emotional/experiential aspects of psychological distress.

## THE ROLE OF COGNITION

### Definition

The term *cognition* can be defined in a variety of different ways, depending on the research and clinical paradigm that is adopted. We consider this to be a sign of the maturity of the construct and the underlying scientific models. Similar to terms in other scientific disciplines—such as the terms *gene* in biology and *gravity* in physics—the definition of the term *cognition* depends on the level of specificity and has changed as the models to explain cognitive processes have evolved. For example, the definition of the term *gene* at the level of the amino acids is different from what it is at the phenotype level. Similarly, different definitions of the term *cognition* are proposed by the information processing literature, appraisal theories, and, more recently, the affective and cognitive neuroscience literature.

Using an information processing perspective, Neisser (1967) defined cognitions as:

> ...all those processes, through which sensory input is transformed, reduced, processed, stored, called forth again and finally used.... [The concept of cognition] refers to these processes even when they take place without the existence of corresponding stimulation, as in the case of images and hallucinations. Concepts such as sensation, perception, image, retention, memory, problem solving, and thinking, along with many others, refer to hypothetical stages or aspects of cognition.... One can say that cognition participates in everything that a human being can do. (p. 19 )

Similarly, Beck (1991) wrote:

> Cognition as a singular noun refers to various processes in cognitive or information processing: perception, interpretation, recall. Each of the psychological systems (cognition, affection, and motivation) is interconnected so that changes in one system may produce changes in another system. (p. 371)

This definition, again, highlights the bidirectional nature of the relationship between emotions and cognitions (and behaviors); cognitions influence emotions, while changes in emotions can also lead to changes in cognitions.

With respect to cognitive therapy, cognitions were initially defined as dysfunctional patterns of thinking that were expressed as maladaptive beliefs and assumptions about the self, the world, and the future (Beck, 1963, 1964). These beliefs, or schemas, give rise to specific automatic cognitions, which are self-statements and thoughts that determine how a person may interpret a specific situation or event. Schemas involve information processing biases that act to maintain the beliefs through selective filtering of information. The result is a dysfunction that is uniquely associated with a bias in the initial stimulus registration phase of cognitive processing, such that attention is rapidly and automatically deployed toward threat-relevant and/or emotionally negative stimuli (Beck et al., 1985).

It should be noted that this early definition does not make a clear distinction between *cognitive content* and *cognitive process*. New treatment formulations place a greater emphasis on this distinction. In fact, the role of core beliefs and the maintaining processes are the central themes of the schema-focused approaches in CBT (e.g., Young, Klosko, & Weishaar, 2003). An example of a schema process is schema avoidance, which involves attempts to reduce awareness of the schema, thus allowing the person to escape the conflicts associated with the maladaptive schema content (see Young et al., 2003, for more details).

## Stages of Cognitive Processes

Early appraisal theorists have proposed a distinction between *schematic* and *conceptual* processing (Leventhal, 1984). In *schematic processing,* the evaluation occurs automatically and without complex cognitive activity. In *conceptual processing,* knowledge structures and appraisals shape emotions through conscious, deliberate, and abstract forms of reasoning. Other similar distinctions between cognitive processes can be found in the literature, assuming that cognitive activity can occur in a simple, rapid, automatic, and sub- or preconscious fashion, or in a more complex, slower, more deliberate, and multiple-process fashion.

The notion that there are different stages of cognitive processing has gained added support from the recent neuroscience literature. These studies suggest that at the initial stage, the precursor to conscious emotional experience operates outside of conscious awareness, whereas later stages involve conscious deliberations that operate more slowly, possibly reflected by the amygdala receiving sensory inputs from the thalamus both directly and by way of the cortex. For example, it has been shown that the central nucleus of the amygdala has extensive efferent connections to hypothalamic and brain stem structures modulating a wide range of autonomic and endocrine responses (Davis & Whalen, 2001). It is believed that the thalamo-amygdala projections are involved in the processing of the affective significance of sensory cues, whereas the cortico-amygdala projections are necessary to process complex stimuli (e.g., LeDoux, 1989). The subcortical neural pathway for emotional processing from the thalamus to the amygdala is assumed to permit the fast but crude processing of potential danger in the environment. The slower-acting cortico-amygdala projections may be seen as the neurophysiological analogue of appraisal and reappraisal of seemingly threatening, but actually harmless, situations or events (Lazarus & Smith, 1988).

These theoretical views suggest that cognitive activity involves both automatic (early) and deliberate (late) processes. The later processes may further be separated into primary and secondary appraisal (Lazarus, 1991). Primary appraisal evaluates *goal relevance, goal congruence or incongruence,* and *goal content* of an encounter (an event or situation). Goal relevance refers to the potential threat of the encounter. Goal congruence or incongruence concerns whether or not the encounter is appraised as being potentially harmful. Finally, goal content determines the quality of the emotion. For example, anxiety may be colored by feelings of shame and embarrassment if the person is not meeting the perceived social standards. In contrast to primary appraisal, secondary appraisal concerns the options and prospects for coping with the threatening encounter. Coping potential depends on whether, and in what way, the person can influence the person-environment relationship. The coping strategies can be problem-focused or emotion-focused.

Some forms of coping have a beneficial and calming effect on the emotional response, whereas other forms can further intensify the emotional response (e.g., Lazarus & Folkman, 1988). This is consistent with studies showing that attempts to suppress certain thoughts paradoxically increased the frequency of these thoughts during a post-suppression period in which participants were free to think about any topic (Wegner, Schneider, Carter, & White, 1987). Subsequent research has established links between this rebound effect as a laboratory phenomenon and clinical disorders. For example, thought suppression has been associated with increased electrodermal responses to emotional thoughts (Wegner & Zanakos, 1994), suggesting that it elevates sympathetic arousal.

More recent emotion theories conceive of suppression as a special type of emotion regulation strategy (Gross, 1998; 2002; Gross & John, 2003; Gross & Levenson, 1997). According to this model, emotion regulation strategies can be divided into antecedent-focused and response-focused strategies, depending on the time point during the emotion-generative process. Antecedent-focused emotion regulation strategies occur before the emotional response has been fully activated and include tactics such as situation modification, attention deployment, and cognitive reframing of a situation. Response-focused emotion regulation strategies, on the other hand, include attempts to alter the expression or experience of emotions after response tendencies have been initiated. These strategies include suppression and other experiential avoidance strategies. Results of empirical investigations have so far converged to suggest that antecedent-focused strategies are relatively effective methods of regulating emotion in the short term, whereas response-focused strategies tend to be counterproductive (Gross, 1998). Research suggests that cognitive reappraisal of the emotional stimuli is the most effective emotion regulation strategy because it alleviates subjective distress and increases tolerance of emotions without any detrimental effects (Gross, 1998; Hofmann, Heering, Sawyer, & Asnaani, 2009; Richards & Gross, 2000).

## Information Processing Perspective

Cognitive psychology and experimental psychology have offered psychologists rigorous methods to study cognitive processes, especially the very early stages of processing, in the research laboratory. These paradigms have led to influential information-processing models (e.g., Beck & Clark, 1997; Beck et al., 1985; Bower, 1981; Foa & Kozak, 1986; Williams, Watts, MacLeod, & Mathews, 1988), which were rooted in a mathematical theory of communication (Shannon, 1948; Shannon & Weaver, 1949). Foa and Kozak's (1986) model suggests that emotions are represented by information structures in memory and that anxiety arises when an information structure that is associated with escape or avoidance is activated. The model assumes that, as a result of repeated exposure to the feared stimulus in the absence of the feared consequence, the association between the propositions about threat and stimulus and/or the response element of a fear structure is weakened, leading to changes in the prediction of the feared consequences. This idea has recently been revisited, suggesting that exposure therapy is fundamentally a cognitive process that leads to changes in harm expectancy (Hofmann, 2008a). Consistent with this notion, and in line with Bower's (1981) network model, are results from the experimental psychopathology literature showing that anxiety is associated with cognitive biases favoring the processing of threat-related information (e.g., MacLeod & Mathews, 1991; McNally, 1996).

The information processing literature has further provided ample evidence to suggest that anxiety disorders differ from one another in how threatening information is processed (Amir, McNally, & Wiegartz, 1996; McNally, Foa, & Donnell, 1989; Mogg, Mathews, & Weinman, 1987; Rapee, McCallum, Melville, Ravenscroft, & Rodney, 1994; Vrana, Roodman, & Beckham, 1995; Wilhelm, McNally, Baer, & Florin, 1996). Therefore, disorder-specific information processing models have been formulated (e.g., Beck & Clark, 1997; Beck et al., 1985; Bower, 1981; Foa & Kozak, 1986; Heinrichs & Hofmann, 2001; Williams et al., 1988). Most of these studies have examined biases in attentional processes that occur at early information processing stages, and some studies have provided support for the assumption that individuals with anxiety disorders show hypervigilance toward threat that increases threat detection and can then lead to an exacerbation of anxiety (MacLeod, Rutherford, Campbell, Ebsworthy, & Holker, 2002; Mathews & MacLeod, 2002).

The dot-probe paradigm in anxiety disorders illustrates the level of methodological sophistication and scientific maturity in the study of anxiety cognitions. This paradigm measures the distribution of visual attention. As part of a typical dot-probe experiment, participants are asked to press one of two buttons to identify the location of a dot that follows one of two stimuli (words or pictures) presented on a computer screen. These stimuli typically vary in their emotional valence. The dot detection latencies determine whether visual attention has shifted toward or away from the threatening stimulus.

Early theorists hypothesized that anxious individuals are generally hypersensitive toward threatening information, which facilitates the processing of danger (Beck et al., 1985). Therefore, it was assumed that anxious individuals would show a bias towards threatening information. This idea has become known as the *hypervigilance hypothesis*. In contrast, other authors later argued in favor of an *avoidance hypothesis*, which states that anxious individuals tend to inhibit or even completely avoid deep processing of threatening information, leading to "cognitive avoidance" of threatening stimuli (Foa & Kozak, 1986; Mogg et al., 1987). These contradictory assumptions were later integrated into a two-stage model of information processing, which has become known as the *hypervigilance-avoidance hypothesis* (Amir, Foa, & Coles, 1998; Mogg, Bradley, Bono, &

Painter, 1997; Williams et al., 1988). This model suggests that anxious individuals who are hypervigilant to threatening information in the initial stage of its processing will avoid this information in a later stage. It should be noted, however, that the experimental support for this hypothesis has been mixed. In the case of social anxiety disorder, support for this hypothesis comes from studies using eye-tracking (e.g., Garner, Mogg, & Bradley, 2006), homographs (e.g., Amir et al., 1998), and the dot-probe paradigm with varying stimulus-onset asynchronies (e.g., Vassilopoulos, 2005). In contrast, other studies have failed to find clear evidence for a vigilant-avoidant attentional pattern (e.g., Heuer, Rinck, & Becker, 2007; Mansell, Clark, Ehlers, & Chen, 1999; Mogg, Philippot, & Bradley, 2004; Pineles & Mineka, 2005; Sposari & Rapee, 2007).

Nevertheless, more important for the cognitive model are recent studies showing that symptom improvement can be directly linked to changes in attentional biases (Mogg & Bradley, 1998). Initial evidence came from studies reporting a reduction in attention biases during the course of treatment in both uncontrolled (Mattia, Heimberg, & Hope, 1993) and waitlist-controlled studies (Mathews, Mogg, Kentish, & Eysenck, 1995). More importantly, recent research has shown that changes in cognitive biases at an early information processing stage can lead to later improvements in psychopathology (Amir, Beard, Burns, & Bomyea, 2009; Amir, Weber, Beard, Bomyea, & Taylor, 2008; MacLeod & Hagan, 1992; MacLeod et al., 2002). MacLeod and Hagan (1992) demonstrated that attention bias mediated affective responses to stressful real-life events. However, the only way to address definitively the question of causality is with experimental designs in which attention is manipulated (MacLeod et al., 2002). This issue was examined by two experimental studies manipulating attentional allocation directly through a process of attention modification (MacLeod et al., 2002). Using a dot-probe discrimination task, two words (one threat and one neutral word) were presented on a computer monitor. The words appeared for a brief interval (20 ms) followed by a visual probe. Participants were instructed to indicate the location of the probe. Conditions were designed to create a strong contingency between neutral or threat words and probe location (i.e., the probe replaced the threat word in the *attend negative* condition). The results showed that attention shifted according to condition, such that participants in the *attend negative* condition exhibited a tendency to orient toward the threat words, whereas participants in the *attend neutral* condition tended to orient toward neutral words. In addition, participants in the *attend negative* condition reported significantly greater negative mood in response to a stressful task than participants in the *attend neutral* condition, and also experienced higher levels of stress during an impossible anagram stressor.

Building on these studies, investigators recently modified the dot-probe paradigm such that participants were asked to detect a probe by identifying letters replacing one member of a pair of words. One of the words was threatening, the other word nonthreatening. Participants' attention was trained by including a contingency between the location of the probe and the nonthreat word. For the control group, the probe was equally likely to appear after the threat word and the nonthreat word. Participants in the training group showed change in attention bias and a decrease in anxiety as indicated by self-report and interviewer measures. This paradigm was successfully applied for treating generalized anxiety disorder (Amir et al., 2009) and public speaking anxiety (Amir et al., 2008). These studies suggest that maladaptive behaviors and subjective distress can be improved by modifying subconscious cognitive processes.

## THE FAMILY OF CBT APPROACHES

Since Beck's early formulation, a number of specific CBT protocols have been developed for various psychological problems. Although all CBT protocols have important similarities, CBT is not a single, specific treatment protocol. Rather, it refers to a family of interventions. Since Beck's CBT protocol for depression, CBT has undergone extensive scientific scrutiny through comparisons in randomized controlled trials, component analyses, and mediation analyses. The treatment has been shown to be effective for virtually all psychiatric disorders.

In the case of anxiety disorders, maladaptive cognitions are typically associated with future-oriented perceptions of danger or threat, including physical threat (e.g., fear of having a heart attack in the case of panic disorder) or psychological threat (e.g., fear of being embarrassed in the case of social anxiety disorder), focused upon a sense of uncontrollability of a situation or symptoms. For example, the contemporary CBT model of post-traumatic stress disorder assumes that dysfunctional cognitive processing of a past traumatic event is causally linked to the current emotional state associated with this event (Ehlers & Clark, 2000). As a result, the CBT techniques focus on the reappraisal of the memory of the trauma. In contrast, the CBT models of certain other mental disorders, such as health anxiety (Barsky & Klerman, 1983; Warwick & Salkovskis, 1990) and panic disorder (Clark, 1986) assume that it is the dysfunctional interpretation of harmless physical sensations rather than the dysfunctional processing of an identifiable event in the past that is associated with emotional distress and maladaptive behaviors. The maladaptive thoughts of individuals with social anxiety disorder are typically focused on interpersonal situations and are self-focused (e.g., Clark & Wells, 1995), whereas maladaptive cognitions related to obsessive-compulsive disorder and generalized anxiety disorder are primarily future-oriented or oriented toward the obsessional thinking (Salkovskis, 1985) or worrying process itself (e.g., Wells, 2000). The latter phenomenon is often referred to as *metacognition*.

Despite the differences in the cognitive conceptualizations of and approaches to treating mental disorders, all CBT treatment protocols are firmly rooted within the basic CBT approach, which assumes that maladaptive cognitions are causally linked to emotional distress, and that changing those cognitions results in improvement of emotional distress and maladaptive behaviors. Tailoring the treatment to the specific psychopathology by specifically modifying the CBT techniques greatly enhances the effect sizes for these disorders as compared to traditional CBT. Such tailored CBT approaches have been developed for post-traumatic stress disorder (e.g., Ehlers, Clark,

Hackmann, McManus, & Fennell, 2005), generalized anxiety disorder (Wells & King, 2006), social anxiety disorder (Clark et al., 2003), panic disorder (Clark et al., 1999), obsessive-compulsive disorder (Freestone et al., 1997), and health anxiety (Salkovskis, Warwick, & Deale, 2003), to name only a few.

Although CBT is effective for treating anxiety and other mental disorders (Butler, Chapman, Forman, & Beck, 2006; Hofmann & Smits, 2008), little is known about the underlying treatment mechanisms. In fact, relatively little direct empirical support exists for the basic premise of the CBT model, namely that cognitions play a causal role in treatment-related change. Furthermore, only scant evidence exists on the biological correlates of cognitions, cognitive biases, and cognitive mediation.

In a recent component analysis, Longmore and Worrell (2007) reviewed a selection of studies showing no significant difference between interventions with formal cognitive restructuring techniques and behavioral treatment modalities that do not include techniques to directly challenge cognitions. Based on this finding, the authors questioned the validity of the cognitive behavioral treatment model and argued that changes in symptoms are not mediated by changes in cognitions. However, as detailed in a commentary by Hofmann (2008a), a component analysis is insufficient to test cognitive mediation, because changes in cognitions can occur and mediate treatment change without explicit cognitive challenge procedures (Hofmann, 2008b). Instead, the appropriate procedure to study the mechanism of treatment change is by conducting cognitive mediation analyses. A number of studies provide clear support for cognitive mediation. For example, a recent laboratory study examining self-reported anxiety during anticipation of a public speech showed that negative self-focused cognitions fully mediated the effects of trait social anxiety on self-reported anxiety and heart rate variability during negative anticipation (Schulz, Alpers, & Hofmann, 2008). In addition, a number of studies provide support for the cognitive mediation model of treatment change in mental disorders, including panic disorder (Hofmann et al., 2007), social anxiety disorder (Hofmann, Moscovitch, Kim, & Taylor, 2004; Smits, Rosenfield, Telch, & McDonald, 2006), obsessive-compulsive disorder (Moore & Abramowitz, 2007), depression (Kaysen, Scher, Mastnak, & Reich, 2005; Tang, DeRubeis, Beberman, & Pham, 2005), and pain (Price, 2000). However, these studies provide only indirect evidence for cognitive mediation, and no study so far has conclusively demonstrated the presence of cognitive mediation using strict statistical tests.

One of the reasons for this relatively limited amount of evidence has to do with how to measure cognitions, especially in the context of the psychotherapy process. For example, questionnaires can only assess a limited range of cognitions or cognitive processes, and thought listing techniques or implicit measures are difficult to obtain. Furthermore, although the statistical procedures for mediation have been well defined since the seminal paper by Baron and Kenny (1986), analysis of mediation of treatment change is still in its infancy. In contrast to the Baron and Kenny (1986) criteria, which outline mediation tests for cross-sectional data, analyzing mediation of treatment change requires significantly more complex methodologies. Recently, for example, investigators have proposed criteria to study mediation of change using regression discontinuation and interrupted time series for single-group study designs (Doss & Atkins, 2006), structural equation modeling procedures for longitudinal tests (Cole & Maxwell, 2003), multilevel models (Kenny, Korchmaros, & Bolger, 2003), and linear regression models for randomized controlled trials (Kraemer, Wilson, Fairburn, & Agras, 2002). In sum, CBT has evolved since its early formulation. Recent adaptations to specific disorders are highly efficacious. Mediation analyses provide preliminary support for the validity of these CBT models. Nevertheless, more research is necessary. In particular, mediation studies are needed to identify the precise mechanism through which these treatments operate.

# MINDFULNESS

## Approach

Broadly defined, mindfulness is a process that leads to a mental state characterized by nonelaborative, nonjudgmental, present-centered awareness, in which each thought, sensation, and feeling is acknowledged and accepted as it is, while encouraging openness, curiosity, and acceptance (e.g., Bishop et al., 2004; Kabat-Zinn, 2003; Melbourne Academic Mindfulness Interest Group, 2006; Teasdale et al., 2000). Mindfulness-based therapy (MBT), which includes mindfulness-based cognitive therapy (MBCT; e.g., Segal, Williams, & Teasdale, 2002) and mindfulness-based stress reduction (MBSR; e.g., Kabat-Zinn, 1982), has become a very popular form of treatment in contemporary psychotherapy (e.g., Baer, 2003; Bishop, 2002; Hayes, 2004; Kabat-Zinn, 1994; Salmon, Lush, Jablonski, & Sephton, 2009). Bishop and colleagues (2004) distinguished two components of mindfulness, one that involves self-regulation of attention and one that involves an orientation toward the present moment characterized by curiosity, openness, and acceptance.

The basic premise underlying mindfulness practices is that experiencing the present moment nonjudgmentally and openly can effectively counter the effects of stressors, because excessive orientation toward the past or future when dealing with stressors can be related to feelings of depression and anxiety (e.g., Kabat-Zinn, 2003). This mental training is achieved through becoming skillful in the practice of mindfulness meditation, with the goal to become more aware of thoughts and feelings and to relate to them in a wider, decentered perspective as "mental events" rather than as aspects of the self or as necessarily accurate reflections of reality. It is further believed that, by teaching people to respond to stressful situations more reflectively rather than reflexively, mindfulness-based therapy can effectively counter experiential avoidance strategies, which are attempts to alter the intensity or frequency of unwanted internal experiences. These maladaptive strategies are believed to contribute to the maintenance of many, if not all, emotional disorders (Bishop et al., 2004). In addition, the slow and deep breathing involved in mindfulness meditation may alleviate bodily symptoms of distress by balancing sympathetic and parasympathetic responses (Kabat-Zinn, 2003). For example, in the case of Mindfulness-Based Stress Reduction (MBSR; Kabat-Zinn, 1982), the three key components are sitting meditation, Hatha Yoga, and body scan, which is a sustained mindfulness practice in which attention is sequentially directed throughout the body (Kabat-Zinn, 2003).

A number of meta-analytic reviews have been conducted to examine the efficacy of MBT (Baer, 2003; Grossman, Niemann, Schmidt, & Walach, 2004; Hofmann, Sawyer, Witt, & Oh, 2010; Ledesma & Kumano, 2009; Toneatto & Nguyen, 2007). The most recent meta-analysis on MBT was conducted by Hofmann and colleagues (2010). This study identified 39 studies totaling 1,140 participants receiving MBT for a range of conditions, including cancer, generalized anxiety disorder, depression, and other psychiatric or medical conditions. The results showed that MBT was moderately effective for improving anxiety and mood symptoms from pre- to post-treatment in the overall sample. In patients with anxiety and mood disorders, this intervention was associated with large effect sizes for improving anxiety and mood symptoms, respectively. The results suggest that MBT is a promising intervention for treating mood and anxiety problems in clinical populations, especially among patients with mood and anxiety disorders.

## Comparison to Traditional CBT

In addition to MBT, as defined earlier, mindfulness techniques have been integrated into various CBT protocols for acute emotional distress, including for the treatment of generalized anxiety disorder (Craigie, Rees, & Marsh, 2008; Evans, Ferrando, Findler, Stowell, Smart, & Haglin, 2008), panic disorder (Kabat-Zinn, Massion, Kristeller, & Peterson, 1992; Kim et al., 2009; Lee et al., 2007), social anxiety disorder (Bögels, Sijbers, & Voncken, 2006; Koszycki, Benger, Shlik, & Bradwejn, 2007) and depression (Barnhofer et al., 2009; Kingston, Dooley, Bates, Lawlor, & Malone, 2007; Ramel, Goldin, Carmona, & McQuaid, 2004; Williams et al., 2008) (for a review, see Baer, 2003; Bishop, 2002; Salmon, Lush, Jablonski, & Sephton, 2009; Segal et al., 2002).

A particularly popular and influential CBT treatment that integrates mindfulness-based techniques into its framework as a core component is dialectical behavior therapy (DBT; Linehan, Amstrong, Suarez, Allmon, & Heard, 1991). DBT is typically utilized in the treatment of borderline personality disorder, by taking a CBT approach that is based on a dialectical worldview. The term *dialectic* refers to the relationship between acceptance and change in order to enhance the patient's capabilities for affect regulation. Patients are encouraged to change their behaviors to emotional stimuli by concurrently accepting their suffering and histories with the aim of synthesizing change and acceptance (discussed in more detail below). DBT offers numerous mindfulness exercises in order to achieve this specific goal, which are traditionally taught in a weekly skills group (Linehan, 1993). Linehan (1993) describes mindfulness "what" skills (to observe, describe, and participate) and "how" skills (to do this nonjudgmentally, one-mindfully, and effectively). Apart from mindfulness exercises, DBT includes many cognitive and behavioral treatment procedures that are designed to change cognitions, behaviors, or emotions (Baer, 2003). DBT therefore unifies mindfulness-based strategies targeting psychological acceptance and traditional CBT procedures that directly target cognitions in order to change dysfunctional behavior.

Despite the close relationship between mindfulness-based CBT and more traditional forms of CBT, there appear to be subtle, yet potentially important differences. For example, Teasdale and colleagues (2000) wrote:

> Unlike CBT, there is little emphasis in MBCT on changing the content of thoughts; rather, the emphasis is on changing awareness of and relationship to thoughts. Aspects of CBT included in MBCT are primarily those designed to facilitate "decentered" views, such as "Thoughts are not facts" and "I am not my thoughts." The focus of MBCT is to teach individuals to become more aware of thoughts and feelings and to relate to them in a wider, decentered perspective as "mental events" rather than as aspects of the self or as necessarily accurate reflections of reality. (p. 616)

Related to *decentering* is the concept of *distancing* in traditional CBT. Distancing refers to the process of gaining an objective perspective toward thoughts and is regarded as a necessary step before the patient can successfully consider alternative explanations. Specifically, Beck (1970) wrote:

> Even after a patient has learned to identify his idiosyncratic ideas, he may have difficulty in examining these ideas objectively. The thought often has the same kind of salience as the perception of an external stimulus.... Distancing refers to the process of gaining objectivity towards these cognitions. (p. 189)

Patients are encouraged to "make distinctions between thought and external reality, between hypothesis and fact" (p. 189), and to realize that, "simply because he thinks something does not necessarily mean that it is true" (p. 190). Therefore, both distancing and decentering encourage patients to gain an observer-perspective of their thoughts. The difference between these two concepts is related to the underlying treatment model: Distancing is based on the notion that cognitions are beliefs about reality that may or may not be correct or adaptive, whereas decentering refers to the general detachment of thoughts from the self, regardless of whether or not these thoughts are an accurate perception of reality.

In sum, mindfulness-based strategies have been developed within a CBT framework. An important aspect of mindfulness trainings can be subsumed under the concept of *decentering*. Decentering is related to the CBT term *distancing* in that both require patients to become more aware of their thoughts, depersonalize them, and critically examine the reality of them. Whereas distancing is considered a necessary first step before attempting to challenge the validity of such thoughts, decentering is seen as a general process to encourage reflectivity over reactivity and reflexivity.

# ACCEPTANCE

## Approach

The theoretical basis of acceptance and commitment therapy (ACT) is relational frame theory (RFT; Hayes, Barnes-Holmes, & Roche, 2001), which is derived from a philosophical view known as functional contextualism (e.g., Gifford & Hayes, 1993; Pepper, 1942). This view attempts to offer a way to integrate cognition and language into a behavioral analytic framework. In essence, it is a reformulation of Skinnerian radical behaviorism to better account for human language and cognition (Hayes, Masuda, Bissett, Luoma, & Guerrero, 2004). Therefore, ACT is not an extension or modification of traditional CBT, because the premise of cognitive causality (i.e., the notion that cognitions can cause changes in emotions and behaviors) is rejected. A critical summary of ACT's critique toward CBT and a counter-critique have been provided elsewhere (Hofmann, 2008b; Hofmann & Asmundson, 2008, in press).

Despite these fundamental differences on the philosophical and theoretical level, there is a large degree of overlap between ACT and traditional CBT on the level of technique. An important goal of ACT is to discourage *experiential avoidance*, which is the unwillingness to experience negatively evaluated feelings, physical sensations, and thoughts (Hayes et al., 2004). To target experiential avoidance, ACT includes techniques that are intended to increase *psychological flexibility*, which is defined as "the ability to contact the present moment more fully as a conscious human being, and to change or persist in behavior when doing so serves valued ends" (Hayes, Luoma, Bond, Masuda, & Lillis, 2006, p. 7). The specific processes and techniques to reach this therapeutic goal include those aimed at fostering acceptance, cognitive defusion, being present, self as context, values, and committed action.

Acceptance strategies encourage patients to embrace unwanted thoughts and feelings—such as anxiety, pain, and guilt—as an alternative to experiential avoidance. The goal is to end the struggle with unwanted thoughts and feelings without attempting to change or eliminate them. The purpose of cognitive defusion is to change undesirable functions of thoughts and other private events (such as emotions). These strategies are intended to make the patient realize that any attempts to control private events are part of the problem, not the solution. Therefore, patients are encouraged not to act upon the thoughts and feelings, and ultimately to give up control. Patients are further encouraged to be in nonjudgmental, mindful contact with environmental events as they occur and to adopt a spiritual sense of self. Therapists further encourage patients to identify and commit to pursuing important life goals.

A recent review by Öst (2008) examined 13 randomized controlled trials (RCTs) of ACT and DBT, one of Cognitive Behavioral Analysis System of psychotherapy, and two of integrative behavioral couple therapy. The results showed that the RCTs used a significantly less stringent research methodology than comparable CBT trials. The mean effect size of the available studies was moderate for both ACT and DBT. None of these therapies fulfilled the criteria for empirically supported treatments as defined by the APA Division 12 Task Force. In a commentary, Gaudiano (2009) criticized Öst's (2008) review, arguing that the samples of the studies comparing ACT and traditional CBT were mismatched in terms of the populations being treated. Furthermore, the author argued that CBT received more grant support than ACT. Öst (2009) refuted these criticisms and argued that ACT should not be evaluated by more lenient criteria than already established therapies.

Another meta-analysis by Powers, Zum Vörde Sive Vörding, & Emmelkamp (2009) identified 18 RCTs ($n = 917$) testing the efficacy of ACT. The results showed an overall advantage of ACT compared to control conditions (effect size = 0.42). However, ACT was not significantly more effective than established treatments (effect size = 0.18, $p = 0.13$). Also, ACT was not superior to control conditions, suggesting that ACT is not more effective than established treatments.

## Comparison to Traditional CBT

CBT and ACT show many similarities on the level of technique; they both focus on increasing awareness of thoughts, feelings and physiological sensations, and seek to facilitate emotional expression. They use behavioral interventions, such as exposure exercises, problem solving techniques, role playing, modeling, and homework. They discourage patients from attempting to directly control thoughts or ruminate about the past. They emphasize clear articulation of goals, and they target improvements in quality of life, which include success in major life domains. The schema work in CBT is very similar to the value work in ACT.

However, there are substantial—and quite possibly irreconcilable—differences on the philosophical and theoretical levels between ACT and CBT with regards to the role of cognitions. ACT has been described as

> the applied extension of a 20 year long attempt to create a modern form of behavior analysis that could overcome this challenge by adding the principles needed to account for cognition from a functional contextual or behavior analytic point of view.
>
> (Hayes et al., 2006, p. 4)

In contrast to CBT, ACT does not adopt a tripartite model distinguishing between overt behaviors (actions), emotions (subjective experience), and cognitions (thought processes). Instead, ACT categorizes cognitions as a form of behavior, which is seen "as a term for all forms of psychological activity, both public and private, including cognition" (Hayes et al., 2006, p. 2).

Because cognitions are seen as a form of behavior, ACT focuses on identifying and modifying the *function*, rather than the *content*, of cognitions. Cognitive function is targeted in ACT by encouraging patients not to act on certain cognitions, but to accept them instead, without attempting to change their actual content.

The same acceptance approach is taught for unpleasant emotions. Emotional disorders, such as anxiety disorders and depression, may be viewed as the result of ineffective attempts to regulate undesirable emotions. Successful regulation of emotional states is an important human characteristic that facilitates social adjustment and overall well-being. Pursuing important life goals requires tolerance and management of a wide range of emotional states, including uncomfortable and distressing emotions. Effective psychological treatments for emotional disorders focus on promoting beneficial emotion regulation strategies and discourage the use of ineffective strategies.

As we described earlier (Hofmann & Asmundson, 2008), ACT appears to primarily counteract maladaptive *response-focused* emotion regulation strategies, whereas CBT promotes adaptive *antecedent-focused* emotion regulation strategies by encouraging cognitive reappraisal of the emotional triggers. The distinction between antecedent-focused and response-focused emotion regulation strategies is based on Gross's process model of emotions, which emphasizes the evaluation of external or internal emotional cues (Gross, 1998; 2002; Gross & John, 2003; Gross & Levenson, 1997). Once these cues have been processed, a set of experiential, physiological, and behavioral responses are activated and influenced by emotion regulation tendencies. The time point at which individuals engage in emotion regulation influences the efficacy of their regulatory efforts. As described above, antecedent-focused emotion regulation strategies occur before the emotional response has been fully activated and include tactics such as situation modification, attention deployment, and cognitive reframing of a situation. Response-focused emotion regulation strategies entail attempts to alter the expression or experience of emotions after response tendencies have been initiated and include suppression and other experiential avoidance strategies. Experimental studies and mediation analyses are needed to determine the most adaptive approaches for the particular emotional disorders.

## CONCLUSION AND FUTURE RESEARCH DIRECTIONS

Emotional disorders are associated with negatively valenced emotional responses, such as fear, sadness, anger, and heightened level of distress. The goal of CBT is not to eliminate or regulate these emotions in general. Instead, the goal is to foster the abilities of patients to provide for themselves more realistic and accurate appraisals of the situations they face. CBT techniques do not ask patients to think positively but rather employ strategies to regulate negative affectivity by using behavioral, experiential, and—of course—cognitive strategies.

As described above, the underlying core model of CBT is that cognitions profoundly and causally influence emotions and behaviors and, thereby, contribute to the maintenance of psychopathology. As we have discussed elsewhere (Hofmann & Asmundson, 2008), targeting the way one thinks about emotion-eliciting situations and experiences is different from approaches that attempt to regulate emotion through reduction of experiential avoidance (e.g., by embracing anxiety or pain). These latter strategies are characteristic of those employed by mindfulness-based techniques and acceptance and commitment therapy (ACT).

These strategies are not the least bit incompatible with a CBT approach on the level of technique, but there are some fundamental differences on the theoretical and philosophical level, especially between CBT and ACT. Furthermore, efficacy research so far has not clearly favored one treatment over the other. However, ACT, mindfulness-based strategies, and traditional CBT protocols do differ in the typical instructions patients receive to regulate negative emotions. Although the complete treatment packages cannot be easily tested against each other, it is certainly possible to examine specific therapeutic techniques under controlled laboratory conditions.

Some of our own recent research provides some direct evidence of the maladaptive use of certain emotion regulation strategies in patients with a wide range of emotional disorders (Campbell-Sills, Barlow, Brown, & Hofmann, 2006a). In this study, 60 patients who met diagnostic criteria for an anxiety or mood disorder and 30 individuals with no history of emotional disorders experienced an induction of a negative emotion by watching an emotional film. Spontaneous emotion appraisals and emotion regulation strategies were observed in both the clinical sample and the control sample. The patients in the clinical sample (panic disorder, generalized anxiety disorder, major depressive disorder, obsessive-compulsive disorder, and dysthymic disorder) reported significantly different emotional appraisals and emotion regulation strategies from those of nonclinical participants. Clinical participants reported greater anxiety focused on the occurrence of emotions, as well as less emotional clarity. They also endorsed more reliance on maladaptive emotion regulation strategies (e.g., suppression, rehearsal), rated their resulting emotions as less acceptable, and engaged in more emotion suppression. Higher levels of suppression were associated, in turn, with elevated heart rate during the emotion induction, as well as with inhibited recovery from skin conductance and finger temperature changes and subjective distress after the induction. These results are consistent with the notion that mood and anxiety disorders are associated with maladaptive emotion regulation strategies.

In another study (Campbell-Sills, Barlow, Brown, & Hofmann, 2006b), we instructed patients to engage in either emotion suppression activities or emotion acceptance activities during the emotion induction exercise. Suppression participants failed to recover from subjective distress after the induction, and manifested a different heart rate pattern compared to acceptance participants. Specifically, when patients were instructed to suppress their emotions, heart rate actually decreased from anticipation to termination of the film, while heart rate in the acceptance condition increased during this period. Thus, patients with emotional disorders endorsed more negative emotion appraisals and utilized counterproductive emotion regulation strategies compared to individuals without disorders. There was no evidence of differences among different diagnostic groups. Again, these results suggest that simple instructions to accept negative emotions can have a beneficial effect, whereas instructions to suppress emotions can have a detrimental effect in patients with emotional disorders.

In a third experiment (Hofmann et al., 2009), we directly compared the effects of the instructions to accept, suppress, or reappraise a social threat challenge. As expected, the suppression group showed a greater increase in heart rate than the reappraisal and acceptance groups, and the suppression group reported more anxiety than the reappraisal group. However, the acceptance and suppression groups did not differ in their subjective anxiety response. These results suggest that both reappraising and accepting anxiety are more effective for moderating the physiological arousal than suppressing anxiety. However, reappraising appears to be more effective for moderating the subjective feeling of anxiety than attempts to suppress or accept it. These data should be considered preliminary. However, we believe that they illustrate that it is possible to test scientifically even the most complex therapeutic techniques.

Another important source of data will come from treatment and treatment mediation studies. There is some preliminary evidence to suggest that ACT and CBT might work through different mechanisms of emotion regulation (Hayes et al., 2006). However, the evidence is too preliminary to draw any firm conclusions.

Future studies should examine the efficacy of enriched CBT approaches that include acceptance-based and other response-focused emotion regulation strategies. Specifically, future research may examine whether different adaptive emotion regulation strategies have an additive effect on outcome and whether outcome is maximized by tailoring emotion regulation strategies to an individual person or diagnosis. It has been shown that individuals differ in their habitual use of emotion regulation strategies (Gross & John, 2003; Hofmann & Kashdan, 2010), and that these individual differences are meaningfully associated with emotional experiences and psychosocial functioning. For example, individuals who habitually use reappraisal to regulate emotions experience more positive emotion and less negative emotion overall, have better interpersonal functioning, and report greater well-being. In contrast, individuals who habitually use suppression experience less positive emotion and greater negative emotion, have worse interpersonal functioning, and report lower well-being (Gross & John, 2003). It would be important to study to what extent the ability to flexibly apply different emotion regulation strategies to situational demands predict or mediate treatment outcome (Bonnanno, Papa, Lalande, Westphal, & Coifman, 2004). It is an exciting time for clinical psychologists.

## REFERENCES

Amir, N., Beard, C., Burns, M., & Bomyea (2009). Attention modification program in individuals with generalized anxiety disorder. *Journal of Abnormal Psychology, 118,* 26–35.

Amir, N., Foa, E. B., & Coles, M. E. (1998). Negative interpretation bias in social phobia. *Behaviour Research and Therapy, 36,* 945–957.

Amir, N., McNally, R. J., & Wiegartz, P. S. (1996). Implicit memory bias for threat in posttraumatic stress disorder. *Cognitive Therapy and Research, 20,* 625–635.

Amir, N., Weber, G., Beard, C., Bomyea, J., & Taylor, C. T. (2008). The effect of a single-session attention modification program on response to a public-speaking challenge in socially anxious individuals. *Journal of Abnormal Psychology, 117,* 860–868.

Baer, R. (2003). Mindfulness training as a clinical intervention: A conceptual and empirical review. *Clinical Psychology: Science and Practice, 10,* 125–143.

Barnhofer, T., Crane, C., Hargus, E., Amarasinghe, M., Winder, R., & Williams, J. M. G. (2009). Mindfulness-based cognitive therapy as a treatment for chronic depression: A preliminary study. *Behaviour Research and Therapy, 47,* 366–373.

Baron, R. M., & Kenny, D. A. (1986). The moderator-mediator variable distinction in social psychological research: Conceptual, strategic, and statistical considerations. *Journal of Personality and Social Psychology, 51,* 1173–1182.

Barsky, A. J., & Klerman, G. L. (1983). Hypochondriasis, bodily complaints, and somatic styles. *American Journal of Psychiatry, 140,* 273–283.

Beck, A. T. (1963). Thinking and depression: I. Idiosyncratic content and cognitive distortions. *Archives of General Psychiatry, 9,* 324–444.

Beck, A. T. (1964). Thinking and depression: II. Theory and therapy. *Archives of General Psychiatry, 10,* 561–571.

Beck, A. T. (1970). Cognitive therapy: Nature and relation to behavior therapy. *Behavior Therapy, 1*(2), 184–200.

Beck, A. T. (1991). Cognitive Therapy—A 30-year retrospective. *American Psychologist, 46*(4), 368–375.

Beck, A. T., & Clark, D. A. (1997). An information processing model of anxiety: Automatic and strategic processes. *Behaviour Research and Therapy, 35,* 49–58.

Beck, A. T., Emery, G., & Greenberg, R. C. (1985). *Anxiety disorders and phobias: A cognitive perspective.* New York, NY: Basic Books.

Bishop, M., Lau, S., Shapiro, L., Carlson, N. D., Anderson, J., Carmody Segal, Z. V., . . . Devins, G. (2004). Mindfulness: A proposed operational definition. *Clinical Psychology: Science and Practice, 11,* 230–241.

Bishop, S. R. (2002). What do we really know about mindfulness-based stress reduction? *Psychosomatic Medicine, 64,* 71–83.

Bögels, S. M., Sijbers, G. F. V. M., & Voncken, M. (2006). Mindfulness and task concentration training for social phobia: A pilot study. *Journal of Cognitive Psychotherapy, 20,* 33–44.

Bonnanno, G. A., Papa, A., Lalande, K., Westphal, M., & Coifman, K. (2004). The importance of being flexible: The ability to both enhance and suppress emotional expression predicts long-term adjustment. *Psychological Science, 15,* 482–487.

Bower, G. H. (1981). Mood and memory. *American Psychologist, 36,* 129–148.

Butler, A. C., Chapman, J. E., Forman, E. M., & Beck, A. T. (2006). The empirical status of cognitive-behavioral therapy: A review of meta-analyses. *Clinical Psychology Review, 26,* 17–31.

Campbell-Sills, L., Barlow, D. H., Brown, T. A., & Hofmann, S. (2006a). Acceptability and suppression of negative emotion in anxiety and mood disorders. *Emotion, 6,* 587–595.

Campbell-Sills, L., Barlow, D. H., Brown, T. A., & Hofmann, S. G. (2006b). Effects of suppression and acceptance on emotional responses in individuals with anxiety and mood disorders. *Behavior Research and Therapy, 44,* 1251–1263.

Chomsky, N. (1959). A review of B. F. Skinner's *Verbal behavior. Language, 35,* 26–58.

Clark, D. M. (1986). A cognitive approach to panic. *Behaviour Research and Therapy, 24,* 461–470.

Clark, D. M., Ehlers, A., McManus, F., Hackman, A., Fennell, M., Campbell, H., . . . Louis, B. (2003). Cognitive therapy versus fluoxetine in generalized social phobia: A randomized placebo-controlled trial. *Journal of Consulting and Clinical Psychology, 71,* 1058–1067.

Clark, D. M., Salkovskis, P. M., Hackman, A., Wells, A., Ludgate, J., & Gelder, M. (1999). Brief cognitive therapy for panic disorder: A randomized controlled trial. *Journal of Consulting and Clinical Psychology, 67,* 583–589.

Clark, D. M., & Wells, A. (1995). A cognitive model of social phobia. In R. G. Heimberg, M. R. Liebowitz, D. A. Hope, & F. R. Schneier (Eds.), *Social Phobia: Diagnosis, assessment and treatment* (pp. 69–93). New York: Guilford.

Cole, D. A., & Maxwell, S. E. (2003). Testing mediational models with longitudinal data: Questions and tips in the use of structural equation modeling. *Journal of Abnormal Psychology, 112,* 558–577.

Craigie, M. A., Rees, C. S., & Marsh, A. (2008). Mindfulness-based cognitive therapy for generalized anxiety disorder: A preliminary evaluation. *Behavioural and Cognitive Psychotherapy, 36,* 553–568.

Davis, M., & Whalen P. J. (2001). The amygdala: Vigilance and emotion. *Molecular Psychiatry, 6,* 13–34.

Doss, B. D., & Atkins, D. C. (2006). Investigating treatment mediators when simple random assignment to a control group is not possible. *Clinical Psychology: Science and Practice, 13,* 321–336.

Ehlers, A., & Clark, D. M. (2000). A cognitive model of posttraumatic stress disorder. *Behaviour Research and Therapy, 38,* 319–345.

Ehlers, A., Clark, D. M., Hackmann, A., McManus, F., & Fennell, M. (2005). Cognitive therapy for posttraumatic stress disorder: Development and evaluation. *Behaviour Research and Therapy, 43,* 413–431.

Ellis, A. (2001). *Overcoming destructive beliefs, feelings, and behaviors: New directions for rational emotive behavior therapy.* Amherst, NY: Prometheus Books.

Evans, S., Ferrando, S., Findler, M., Stowell, C., Smart, C., & Haglin, D. (2008). Mindfulness-based cognitive therapy for generalized anxiety disorder. *Journal of Anxiety Disorders, 22,* 716–721.

Foa, E. B., & Kozak, M. J. (1986). Emotional processing of fear: Exposure to corrective information. *Psychological Bulletin, 99,* 20–35.

Freeston, M. H., Ladouceur, R., Gagnon, F., Thibodeau, N., Rehaume, J., Letarte, H., & Bujold, A. (1997). Cognitive-behavioral treatment of obsessive thoughts: A controlled study. *Journal of Consulting and Clinical Psychology, 65,* 405–13.

Garner, M., Mogg, K., & Bradley, B. P. (2006). Orienting and maintenance of gaze to facial expressions in social anxiety. *Journal of Abnormal Psychology, 115,* 760–770.

Gaudiano, B. A. (2009). Öst's (2008) methodological comparison of clinical trials of acceptance and commitment therapy versus cognitive behaviors therapy: Matching apples with oranges? *Behaviour Research and Therapy, 47,* 1066–1070.

Gifford, E. V., & Hayes, S. C. (1993). Functional contextualism: A pragmatic philosophy for behavioral science. In: W. O'Donohue & R. Kitchener (Eds.), *Handbook of behaviorism.* San Diego, CA: Academic Press, Inc.

Gross, J. J. (1998). Antecedent- and response-focused emotion regulation: Divergent consequences for experience, expression, and physiology. *Journal of Personality and Social Psychology, 74,* 224–237.

Gross, J. J. (2002). Emotion regulation: Affective, cognitive, and social consequences. *Psychophysiology, 39,* 281–291.

Gross, J. J., & John, O. P. (2003). Individual differences in two emotion regulation processes: Implications for affect, relationships, and well-being. *Journal of Personality and Social Psychology, 85,* 348–362.

Gross, J. J., & Levenson, R. W. (1997). Hiding feelings: The acute effects of inhibiting negative and positive emotion. *Journal of Abnormal Psychology, 106,* 95–103.

Grossman, P., Niemann, L., Schmidt, S., & Walach, H. (2004). Mindfulness-based stress reduction and health benefits: A meta-analysis. *Journal of Psychosomatic Research, 57,* 35–43.

Hauser, M. D., Chomsky, N., & Fitch, W. T. (2002). The faculty of language: What is it, what has it, and how did it evolve? *Science, 298,* 1569–1578.

Hayes, S. C. (2004). Acceptance and commitment therapy, relational frame theory, and the third wave of behavior therapy. *Behavior Therapy, 35,* 639–665.

Hayes, S. C., Barnes-Holmes, D., & Roche, B. (Eds.) (2001). *Relational frame theory: A post-Skinnerian account of human language and cognition.* New York, NY: Kluwer Academic/Plenum.

Hayes, S. C., Luoma, J. B., Bond, F. W., Masuda, A., & Lillis, J. (2006). Acceptance and commitment therapy: Model, processes, and outcomes. *Behaviour Research and Therapy, 44,* 1–26.

Hayes, S. C., Masuda, A., Bissett, R., Luoma, J., & Guerrero, L. F. (2004). DBT, FAP and ACT: How empirically oriented are the new behavior therapy technologies? *Behavior Therapy, 35,* 35–54.

Heinrichs, N., & Hofmann, S. G. (2001). Information processing in social phobia: A critical review. *Clinical Psychology Review, 21,* 751–770.

Heuer, K., Rinck, M., & Becker, E. S. (2007). Avoidance of emotional facial expressions in social anxiety: The approach-avoidance task. *Behaviour Research and Therapy, 45,* 2990–3001.

Hofmann, S. G. (2008a). Cognitive processes during fear acquisition and extinction in animals and humans: Implications for exposure therapy of anxiety disorders. *Clinical Psychology Review, 28,* 200–211.

Hofmann, S. G. (2008b). ACT: New wave or Morita therapy? *Clinical Psychology: Science and Practice, 15,* 280–285.

Hofmann, S. G., & Asmundson, G. J. (2008). Acceptance and mindfulness-based therapy: New wave or old hat? *Clinical Psychology Review, 28,* 1–16.

Hofmann, S. G., & Asmundson, G. J. (in press). The science of cognitive behavioral therapy. *Behavior Therapy.*

Hofmann, S. G., Heering, S., Sawyer, A. T., & Asnaani, A. (2009). How to handle anxiety: The effects of reappraisal, acceptance, and suppression strategies on anxious arousal. *Behaviour Research and Therapy, 47,* 389–394.

Hofmann, S. G., & Kashdan, T. B. (2010). The affective style questionnaire: Development and psychometric properties. *Journal of Psychopathology and Behavioral Assessment, 32, 255–263.*

Hofmann, S. G., Meuret, A. E., Rosenfield, D., Suvak, M. K., Barlow, D. H., Gorman, J. M., . . . Woods, S. W. (2007). Preliminary evidence for cognitive mediation during cognitive behavioral therapy for panic disorder. *Journal of Consulting and Clinical Psychology, 75,* 374–379.

Hofmann, S. G., Moscovitch, D. A., Kim, H. J., & Taylor, A. N. (2004). Changes in self-perception during treatment of social phobia. *Journal of Consulting and Clinical Psychology, 72,* 588–596.

Hofmann, S. G., Sawyer, A. T., Witt, A., & Oh, D. (2010). The effect of mindfulness-based therapy on anxiety and depression: A meta-analytic review. *Journal of Consulting and Clinical Psychology, 78,* 169–183.

Hofmann, S. G., & Smits, J. A. J. (2008). Cognitive-behavioral therapy for adult anxiety disorders: A meta-analysis of randomized placebo-controlled trials. *Journal of Clinical Psychiatry, 69,* 621–632.

James, W. (1890). *Principles of psychology.* Cambridge, MA: Harvard University Press.

Kabat-Zinn, J. (1982). An outpatient program in behavioral medicine for chronic pain patients based on the practice of mindfulness meditation: Theoretical considerations and preliminary results. *General Hospital Psychiatry, 4,* 33–47.

Kabat-Zinn, J. (1994). *Wherever you go there you are.* New York, NY: Hyperion.

Kabat-Zinn, J. (2003). Mindfulness-based interventions in context: Past, present, and future. *Clinical Psychology: Science and Practice, 10,* 144–156.

Kabat-Zinn, J., Massion, A. O., Kristeller, J., & Peterson, L. G. (1992). Effectiveness of a meditation-based stress reduction program in the treatment of anxiety disorders. *American Journal of Psychiatry, 149,* 936–943.

Kaysen, D., Scher, C. D., Mastnak, J., & Reich, P. (2005). Cognitive mediation of childhood maltreatment and adult depression in recent crime victims. *Behavior Therapy, 36,* 235–244.

Kenny, D. A., Korchmaros, J. D., & Bolger, N. (2003). Lower level mediation in multilevel models. *Psychological Methods, 8,* 115–128.

Kim, Y. W., Lee, S. H., Choi, T. K., Suh, S. Y., Kim, B., Kim, C. M., . . . Yook, K. H. (2009). Effectiveness of mindfulness-based cognitive therapy as an adjuvant to pharmacotherapy in patients with panic disorder or generalized anxiety disorder. *Depression and Anxiety, 26,* 601–606.

Kingston, T., Dooley, B., Bates, A., Lawlor, E., & Malone, K. (2007). Mindfulness-based cognitive therapy for residual depressive symptoms. *Psychology and Psychotherapy: Theory, Research and Practice, 80,* 193–203.

Koszycki, D., Benger, M., Shlik, J., & Bradwejn, J. (2007). Randomized trial of a meditation-based stress reduction program and cognitive behavior therapy in generalized social anxiety disorder. *Behaviour Research and Therapy, 45*, 2518–2526.

Kraemer, H. C., Wilson, T., Fairburn, C. G., & Agras, W. S. (2002). Mediators and moderators of treatment effects in randomized clinical trials. *Archives of General Psychiatry, 59*, 877–883.

Lazarus, R. S. (1982). Thoughts on the relations between emotion and cognition. *American Psychologist, 37*, 1019–1024.

Lazarus, R. S. (1991). Progress on a cognitive-motivational-relational theory of emotion. *American Psychologist, 46*, 819–834.

Lazarus, R. S., & Folkman, S. (1988). Coping as a mediator of emotion. *Journal of Personality and Social Psychology, 54*, 466–475.

Lazarus, R. S., & Smith, C. A. (1988). Knowledge and appraisal in the cognition-emotion relationship. *Cognition and Emotion, 2*, 281–300.

Ledesma, D., & Kumano, H. (2009). Mindfulness-based stress reduction and cancer: A meta-analysis. *Psycho-Oncology. 18*, 571–579.

LeDoux, J. E. (1989). Cognitive-emotional interactions in the brain. *Cognition and Emotion, 3*, 267–289.

Lee, S. H., Ahn, S. C., Lee, Y. J., Choi, T. K., Yook, K. H., & Suh, S. Y. (2007). Effectiveness of a meditation-based stress management program as an adjunct to pharmacotherapy in patients with anxiety disorder. *Journal of Psychosomatic Research, 62*, 189–95.

Leventhal, H. (1984). A perceptual–motor theory of emotion. In K. R. Scherer & P. Ekman (Eds.), *Approaches to emotion* (pp. 271–291). Hillsdale, NJ: Erlbaum.

Linehan, M. M. (1993). *Skills training manual for treating borderline personality disorder.* New York, NY: Guilford Press.

Linehan, M. M., Amstrong, H. E., Suarez, A., Allmon, D., & Heard, H. L. (1991). Cognitive-behavioral treatment of chronically suicidal borderline patients. *Archives of General Psychiatry, 48*, 1060–1064.

Longmore, R. J., & Worrell, M. (2007). Do we need to challenge thoughts in cognitive behavioral therapy? *Clinical Psychology Review, 27*, 173–187.

MacLeod, C., & Hagan, R. (1992). Individual differences in the selective processing of threatening information, and emotional responses to a stressful life event. *Behavior Research and Therapy, 30*, 151–161.

MacLeod, C., & Mathews, A. (1991). Biased cognitive operations in anxiety: Accessibility of information or assignment or processing priorities? *Behaviour Research and Therapy, 29*, 599–610.

MacLeod, C., Rutherford, E., Campbell, L., Ebsworthy, G., & Holker, L. (2002). Selective attention and emotional vulnerability: Assessing the causal basis of their association through the experimental manipulation of attentional bias. *Journal of Abnormal Psychology, 111*, 107–123.

Mansell, W., Clark, D. M., Ehlers, A., & Chen, Y. P. (1999). Social anxiety and attention away from emotional faces. *Cognition and Emotion, 13*, 673–690.

Mathews, A., & MacLeod, C. (2002). Induced processing biases have causal effects on anxiety. *Cognition & Emotion, 16*, 331–354.

Mathews, A., Mogg, K., Kentish, J., & Eysenck, M. (1995). Effect of psychological treatment on cognitive bias in generalized anxiety disorder. *Behavior Research and Therapy, 33*, 293–303.

Mattia, J. I., Heimberg, R. G., & Hope, D. A. (1993). The revised Stroop color-naming task in social phobics. *Behavior Research and Therapy, 31*, 305–313.

McNally, R. J. (1996). Cognitive bias in the anxiety disorders. *Nebraska Symposium on Motivation, 43*, 211–250.

McNally, R. J., Foa, E. B., & Donnell, C. D. (1989). Memory bias for anxiety information in patients with panic disorder. *Cognition and Emotion, 3*, 27–44.

Melbourne Academic Mindfulness Interest Group (2006). Mindfulness-based psychotherapies: A review of conceptual foundations, empirical evidence and practical considerations. *Australian and New Zealand Journal of Psychiatry, 40*, 285–294.

Mogg, K., & Bradley, B. P. (1998). A cognitive-motivational analysis of anxiety. *Behavior Research and Therapy, 36,* 809–848.

Mogg, K., Bradley, B. P., Bono, J., & Painter, M. (1997). Time course of attentional bias for threat information in non-clinical anxiety. *Behaviour Research and Therapy, 35,* 297–303.

Mogg, K., Mathews, A., & Weinman, J. (1987). Memory bias in clinical anxiety. *Journal of Abnormal Psychology, 96,* 94–98.

Mogg, K., Philippot, P., & Bradley, B. P. (2004). Selective attention to angry faces in clinical social phobia. *Journal of Abnormal Psychology, 113,* 160–165.

Moore, E. L., & Abramowitz, J. S. (2007). The cognitive mediation of thought-control strategies. *Behaviour Research and Therapy 45,* 1949–1955.

Neisser, U. (1967). *Cognitive Psychology.* New York, NY: Holt, Rinehart & Winston.

Öst, L.-G. (2008). Efficacy of the third wave of behavioral therapies: A systematic review of meta-analysis. *Behaviour Research and Therapy, 46,* 296–321.

Öst, L.-G. (2009). Inventing the wheel once more or learning from the history of psychotherapy research methodology: Reply to Gaudiano's comments on Öst's (2008) review. *Behaviour Research and Therapy, 47,* 1071–1073.

Pepper, S. C. (1942). *World hypotheses: A study in evidence.* Berkeley: University of California Press.

Piaget, J. (1952). *The language and thought of the child.* London, England: Routledge and Kegan Paul.

Pineles, S. L., & Mineka, S. (2005). Attentional biases to internal and external sources of potential threat in social anxiety. *Journal of Abnormal Psychology, 114,* 314–8.

Powers, M. B., Zum Vörde Sive Vörding, M. B., & Emmelkamp, P. M. (2009). Acceptance and commitment therapy: A meta-analytic review. *Psychotherapy and Psychosomatics, 78,* 73–80.

Price, D. D. (2000). Psychological and neural mechanisms of the affective dimension of pain. *Science, 288,* 1769–1772.

Ramel, W., Goldin, P. R., Carmona, P. E., & McQuaid, J. R. (2004). The effects of mindfulness meditation on cognitive processes and affect in patients with past depression. *Cognitive Therapy and Research, 28,* 433–455.

Rapee, R. M., McCallum, S. L., Melville, L. F., Ravenscroft, H., & Rodney, J. M. (1994). Memory bias in social phobia. *Behaviour Research and Therapy, 32,* 89–99.

Richards, J. M., & Gross, J. J. (2000). Emotion regulation and memory: The cognitive costs of keeping one's cool. *Journal of Personality and Social Psychology, 79,* 410–424.

Salkovskis, P. M. (1985). Obsessional-compulsive problems: A cognitive-behavioral analysis. *Behaviour Research and Therapy, 23,* 571–583.

Salkovskis, P. M., Warwick, H. M., & Deale, A. C. (2003). Cognitive-behavioral treatment for severe and persistent health anxiety (hypochondriasis). *Brief Treatment and Crisis Intervention, 3,* 353–367.

Salmon, P., Lush, E., Jablonski, M., & Sephton, S. E. (2009). Yoga and mindfulness: Clinical aspects of an ancient mind/body practice. *Cognitive and Behavioral Practice, 16,* 59–72.

Schachter, S., & Singer, J. E. (1962). Cognitive, social, and physiological determinants of emotional state. *Psychological Review, 69,* 379–399.

Schulz, S. M., Alpers, G. W., & Hofmann, S. G. (2008). Negative self-focused cognitions mediate the effect of trait social anxiety on state anxiety. *Behaviour Research and Therapy, 48,* 438–449.

Segal, Z. V., Williams, J. M. G., & Teasdale, J. D. (2002). *Mindfulness-based cognitive therapy for depression: A new approach to preventing relapse.* New York, NY: Guilford Press.

Shannon, C. E. (1948). A mathematical theory of communication. *Bell System Technical Journal, 27,* 379–423.

Shannon, C. E., & Weaver, W. (1949). *A mathematical theory of communication.* Urbana: University of Illinois Press.

Skinner, B. F. (1957). *Verbal behavior.* New York, NY: Appleton-Century Crofts.

Smits, J. A. J., Rosenfield, D., Telch, M. J., & McDonald, R. (2006). Cognitive mechanisms of social anxiety reduction: An examination of specificity and temporality. *Journal of Consulting and Clinical Psychology, 74,* 1203–1212.

Sposari, J. A., & Rapee, R. M. (2007). Attentional bias toward facial stimuli under conditions of social threat in socially phobic and nonclinical participants. *Cognitive Therapy and Research, 31,* 23–37.

Tang, T. Z., DeRubeis, R. J., Beberman, R., & Pham, T. (2005). Cognitive changes, critical sessions, and sudden gains in cognitive-behavioral therapy for depression. *Journal of Consulting & Clinical Psychology, 73,* 168–172.

Teasdale, J. D., Segal, Z. V., Williams, J. M. G., Ridgeway, V. A., Soulsby, J. M., & Lau, M. A. (2000). Prevention of relapse/recurrence in major depression by mindfulness-based cognitive therapy. *Journal of Consulting and Clinical Psychology, 68,* 615–623.

Toneatto, T., & Nguyen, L. (2007). Does mindfulness meditation improve anxiety and mood symptoms? A review of the controlled research. *Revue Canadienne de Psychiatrie, 52,* 260–266.

Vassilopoulos, S. P. (2005). Social anxiety and the vigilance-avoidance pattern of attentional processing. *Behavioural and Cognitive Psychotherapy, 33,* 13–24.

Vrana, S. R., Roodman, A., & Beckham, J. C. (1995). Selective processing of trauma-relevant words in post-traumatic stress disorder. *Journal of Anxiety Disorders, 9,* 515–530.

Warwick, H. M. C., & Salkowskis, P. M. (1990). Hypochondriasis. *Behaviour Research and Therapy, 28,* 105–117.

Wegner, D. M., Schneider, D. J., Carter, S. R., & White, T. L. (1987). Paradoxical effects of thought suppression. *Journal of Personality and Social Psychology, 52,* 5–13.

Wegner, D. M., & Zanakos, S. (1994). Chronic thought suppression. *Journal of Personality, 62,* 615–640.

Wells, A. (2000). A cognitive model of generalized anxiety disorder. *Behavior Modification, 38,* 319–345.

Wells, A., & King, P. (2006). Metacognitive therapy for generalized anxiety disorder. *Journal of Behavior Therapy and Experimental Psychiatry, 37,* 206–212.

Wilhelm, S., McNally, R. J., Baer, L., & Florin, I. (1996). Directed forgetting in obsessive-compulsive disorder. *Behaviour Research and Therapy, 34,* 633–641.

Williams, J. M. G., Alatiq, Y., Crane, C., Barnhofer, T., Fennell, M. J. V., Duggan, D. S., . . . Goodwin, G. M. (2008). Mindfulness-based cognitive therapy (MBCT) in bipolar disorder: Preliminary evaluation of immediate effects on between-episode functioning. *Journal of Affective Disorders, 107,* 275–279.

Williams, J. M. G., Watts, F. N., MacLeod, C., & Mathews, A. (1988). *Cognitive psychology and emotional disorders.* Chichester, England: Wiley.

Wilson, K. G. (1997). Science and treatment development: Lessons from the history of behavior therapy. *Behavior Therapy, 28,* 547–561.

Wilson, K. G., Hayes, S. C., & Gifford, E. V. (1997). Cognition in behavior therapy: Agreements and differences. *Journal of Behavior Therapy and Experimental Psychiatry, 28,* 53-63.

Young, J., Klosko, J., & Weishaar, M. (2003). *Schema therapy: A practioners' guide.* New York, NY: Guilford Press.

# 12

## Mindfulness and Acceptance

### The Perspective of Acceptance and Commitment Therapy

MICHAEL LEVIN AND STEVEN C. HAYES

Science is inherently conservative. When claims are made that deviate from the mainstream, scientists are naturally skeptical. Any scientific field would quickly become chaotic if theories could be adopted or revised merely because claims were made. Even data from well-controlled studies can be insufficient without adequate replication and extensions.

Yet progressive science naturally entails and requires change. If a field is progressing, new discoveries are made, and old theories are found to be false. Though skepticism is a central feature of science, it is important to explore developments when they do occur, especially if they are unexpected or have broad implications. Failures to recognize new developments can significantly slow progress and may lead to worthwhile innovations being mislabeled, mischaracterized, or even passed over. By recognizing potentially important developments, challenges to existing theoretical models can be more thoroughly explored and new directions for research can be identified.

In recent years, there has been an increasing focus on the use of acceptance and mindfulness-based approaches within cognitive behavior therapy (CBT). Many of the treatments discussed in this book have incorporated such technologies, including mindfulness based stress reduction (MBSR; Kabat-Zinn, 1990), mindfulness-based cognitive therapy (MBCT; Segal, Williams, & Teasdale, 2002), acceptance and commitment therapy (ACT; Hayes, Strosahl, & Wilson, 1999), dialectical behavior therapy (DBT; Linehan, 1993), integrative behavioral couples therapy (IBCT; Jacobson & Christensen, 1996), and metacognitive therapy (Wells, 2008). Some of these approaches (along with many others that might be named) focus exclusively on the application of mindfulness and acceptance technologies, while others integrate them with additional behavior therapy or cognitive therapy components. With these newer treatments has come the question: Is this different from traditional CBT?

We have previously discussed these treatments as part of a larger, generation change of the core assumptions underlying CBT (Hayes, 2004). This claim has since been the subject of significant criticism (Arch & Craske, 2008; Hofmann & Asmundson, 2008; Leahy, 2008). The question of whether these treatments represent a change in CBT is important, but also poses certain challenges.

The process of determining whether a treatment approach is a significant development is relatively subjective compared to other scientific practices, especially in areas where terms are flexible. The ability for humans to form relations among events can easily lead to similarities being drawn between quite distinct approaches, or for trivial differences to be claimed. These natural language processes can lead the same scholar in the same year to conclude that ACT is the same as traditional CBT (Hofmann & Asmundson, 2008) and that ACT is the same as Morita Therapy (Hofmann, 2008). Logically this would entail that CBT is the same as Morita Therapy, a relatively obscure treatment developed in Japan that involves procedures such as sensory deprivation and intense physical exercise. But the problem is not the failure to see the conclusion. The problem is that natural language is too crude a tool to use for this scientific purpose.

A more objective and productive discussion of treatment differences may be possible by carefully comparing the theoretical models. A therapeutic approach typically includes a general model of psychopathology, intervention, and health. A theory is proposed regarding what contributes to the development, maintenance and exacerbation of various psychological problems, how to intervene, and the relevant processes of change in therapy. The goals of therapy and a conceptualization of health are explicitly or implicitly stated as a guide for treatment. Comparisons between treatments at this level bring a stronger orientation to important similarities and distinctions.

To determine whether acceptance- and mindfulness-based therapies are a significant development in CBT, we need to be able to define CBT. This is a surprisingly difficult task. There does not appear to be a consistent, agreed-upon definition within the field (Hayes, 2008; Mansell, 2008). The term CBT is sometimes used to describe CT specifically and at other times includes interventions that combine cognitive and behavioral components (Beck, 2005). As a whole, CBT includes a number of treatment packages, quite distinct in their specific technologies, suggesting it does not refer to a specific set of techniques or components. CBT also does not have a well-specified, universally agreed-upon model of psychopathology, intervention, or health. Theoretical models within CBT vary depending on the treatment developer and problem focus. CBT appears to be more a tradition than a model, theory, or approach. It is difficult to identify or to characterize developments within a loose and ill-defined collection of therapies.

Despite this eclecticism and confusion, there is a more general theoretical assumption that seems to underlie much of traditional CBT. Hofmann and Asmundson describe this assumption as "CBT is based on the notion that behavioral and emotional responses are strongly moderated and influenced by cognitions and the perception of events" (2008, p. 3). Similarly, in a recent large-scale meta-analysis of CBT outcome studies, Butler, Chapman, Forman, and Beck (2006) stated that "A defining feature of cognitive-behavioral therapy is the proposition that symptoms and dysfunctional behaviors are often cognitively mediated and, hence, improvement can be produced by modifying dysfunctional thinking and beliefs" (Butler et al., 2006, p. 19). This theoretical assumption seems to be central in the transition from behavior therapy to CBT (Hayes, 2004). Although a broad assumption does not represent a very precise theory, it does provide a representation of the traditional CBT model that can be compared to these newer therapies.

At this level of comparison, there are, in fact, significant differences between the theoretical models in traditional CBT and newer acceptance- and mindfulness-based therapies. Whether or not these treatments represent a progressive development, they do appear to have clear and important distinctions from the traditional CBT model at the level of core assumptions. We will begin by exploring these distinctions before addressing the issue of whether this is a new wave of treatments or merely an extension of traditional CBT.

## CHANGES IN THE MODEL OF PSYCHOPATHOLOGY

Treatments generally include an orientation toward a particular set of processes that are perceived to be relevant in the development and persistence of psychopathology. Behavior therapy began with the conceptualization of clinical problems using classical and operant learning principles. CBT built on this model with the claim that cognitive processes play an additional critical role. In this model, cognitive processes are generally given a causal status, mediating the relationship between events, both external and internal, and subsequent behavioral and emotional responses. The core conviction is that it is not the events themselves that produce a response, but rather one's perception and thoughts about them (Hofmann & Asmundson, 2008). Thus, psychopathology is largely attributed to biased cognitive processing of events and distortion of one's experience, due to the activation of particular dysfunctional beliefs and schemas, which produce the irrational and maladaptive cognitions characteristic of a specific disorder (Beck, 2005).

Acceptance and mindfulness-based therapies similarly recognize the importance of cognitions, as well as other private events such as emotions and sensations, in psychopathology. However, rather than necessarily placing a causal status on these experiences, most of these treatments take a more contextual or second-order approach. The relationship between behaviors, both private and overt, is understood in terms of the contexts in which they occur, including the person's approach to cognitive content. It is not so much the thoughts, feelings, and sensations themselves that are problematic, but rather one's relationship to these experiences.

For example, ACT uses the term *fusion* to describe contexts in which the literal, evaluative functions of language have dominant control over behavior. These contexts are often supported by the social verbal community, in which what one thinks and says is treated as literally true and guides subsequent actions. In these contexts, it appears as if thoughts cause behavior. A client who has the thought "I can't get out of bed" will not get out of bed. However, the functions of language are contextually controlled, and were the same client to experience the thought "I can't get out of bed" as just a thought, he or she might be more likely subsequently to get out of bed. Similarly, there are particular contexts in which one may respond to aversive emotions, thoughts, or sensations by attempting to suppress, avoid, or otherwise control their occurrence, a process ACT describes as experiential avoidance. In these cases it appears as if the emotion or sensation caused the avoidant response (i.e., leaving the room during a panic attack). However, the relationship is contextually controlled and can similarly be altered by establishing a context of acceptance in which one simply notices the aversive experience without trying to control it. Thus, the relationship between private events and overt behavior is viewed as contextually controlled rather than a priori defined through a specific causal pathway.

These models appear quite distinct in their general theory of psychopathology. The traditional CBT model suggests that cognitive processes play a central, causal role in psychopathology. The acceptance and mindfulness models tend to state that the relationship of cognitions, as well as other private events, to psychopathology is contextually controlled and how one relates to these experiences is much more important than the specific content.

## CHANGES IN THE MODEL OF THERAPEUTIC CHANGE

A central defining feature of any therapy is the proposed mechanism of change. Every treatment includes a theoretical model of what to target and how to target it in order to produce clinical gains. In addition to standard behavior therapy principles, CBT asserts the importance of targeting cognitive processes and that cognitive change is often necessary to effectively treat clinical problems. Thus, the therapist attempts to target clinical problems by helping clients to identify and modify relevant cognitive processes to be more accurate and rational through logical analysis and empirical tests (Beck, 2005; Hofmann & Asmundson, 2008).

Acceptance- and mindfulness-based therapies reduce the focus on directly altering cognitive processes or other private events. Instead, an explicit emphasis is placed on empowering clients to contact these private events in the present moment, considering them as distinct from who the clients are, without attempting to control their occurrence and turn attention to more important behavioral matters. This serves to establish an alternative way of relating to private events. Aversive feelings, thoughts, and sensations can be experienced without engaging in ineffective control strategies. Thoughts can be experienced as simply thoughts, and do not necessarily guide action. Essentially, these treatments seek to change the function of thoughts, feelings, and sensations. The form, frequency, or intensity of the experiences do not need to change and are treated as a much more secondary target than in traditional CBT.

It is important to note that there are some similarities in how traditional CBT and acceptance- and mindfulness-based therapies target cognitions. The process of identifying cognitions and treating them as hypotheses to be tested in CBT does overlap somewhat with acceptance and mindfulness processes such as decentering and defusion. In fact, comprehensive distancing, the therapy from which ACT was developed, was originally based in part on the notion that distancing was the active component of CT

(Zettle, 2005). However, the CBT model of intervention does not place an emphasis on this distancing process, focusing instead on changing the cognitive processes that are identified. Early component research showed that distancing in CT was not important to its effects and worked in a way distinct from ACT (Zettle & Rains, 1989).

In the modern era, distinct processes of change in acceptance- and mindfulness-based therapies are sometimes demonstrated through a desynchrony effect in which the typical covariations between private and overt behaviors are disrupted. For example, a randomized trial by Bach and Hayes (2002) tested a brief ACT intervention for psychosis. The study found that there was an increased report of hallucinations and delusions in the ACT condition compared to treatment as usual (TAU) at the four-month follow-up, but that the ACT condition had about 50% fewer rehospitalizations than TAU. In other words, the psychotic symptoms were still present, and in fact were being reported at a higher rate, but these symptoms were much less likely to lead to hospitalization. In addition, participants in the ACT condition reported significantly lower believability of their symptoms, suggesting that the desynchrony effect may have been due to a change in clients' relationship to their symptoms.

Another study by Vowles and colleagues (2007) randomly assigned participants with chronic lower back pain to a brief pain acceptance intervention, pain control intervention, or no intervention condition. The study found that participants in the acceptance intervention performed significantly better in a series of physical impairment tasks than participants with the other two conditions, but that there were no differences in self-reported pain. Thus, participants appeared to have persisted longer in these difficult tasks, despite experiencing an equivalent degree of pain. The traditional CBT model assumes a much more dependent relationship, in which symptoms such as hallucinations or pain intensity need to be reduced in order to achieve desired behavioral outcomes. Instead, these studies suggest that acceptance- and mindfulness-based therapies alter the function of private experiences to achieve clinical gains, even if the form of the private events does not change or even worsens.

In addition to the desynchrony effect, there is a growing body of process of change data from ACT outcome research that supports the theoretical model in acceptance- and mindfulness-based therapies. Studies have consistently demonstrated that interventions impact acceptance and mindfulness processes and that changes in these processes correlate with clinical gains (e.g., Bach & Hayes, 2002; Forman, Herbert, Moitra, Yeomans, & Geller, 2007). More importantly, formal meditational analyses have been conducted in at least 21 randomized trials (Hayes, 2009), consistently finding that the effect of ACT on clinical outcomes is mediated by changes in acceptance and mindfulness processes, including acceptance and psychological flexibility (e.g., Gifford et al., 2004; Gregg, Callaghan, Hayes, & Glenn-Lawson, 2007; Lappalainen et al., 2007; Lundgren, Dahl, & Hayes, 2008) and defusion (e.g., Gaudiano, Herbert, & Hayes, in press; Lundgren et al., 2008; Zettle & Hayes, 1986). This level of consistency in replicating mediational analysis is rare in psychology. Though temporal precedence of changes in the mediator before changes in the outcome is not always demonstrated, this criterion has been met in several studies (Gifford et al., 2004; Lundgren et al., 2008; Zettle & Hayes, 1986; as re-analyzed in

Hayes, Luoma, Bond, Masuda, & Lillis, 2006). These findings lend strong support to the theoretical model, which specifies that promoting acceptance and mindfulness in relation to one's internal experiences accounts for a significant proportion of treatment gains.

Outcome studies have also directly compared processes of change in ACT to traditional CBT. The first two published ACT outcome studies compared ACT to CT for depression (Zettle & Hayes, 1986; Zettle & Rains, 1989). Both data sets were recently re-analyzed using formal mediational analysis with the results indicating that reductions in the believability of negative self-relevant thoughts mediate outcomes in ACT, but not CT (Zettle & Hayes, 1986 re-analyzed in Hayes et al., 2006; Zettle & Rains, 1989, re-analyzed in Zettle, Rains, & Hayes, in press). Furthermore, reductions in the frequency of negative thoughts did not mediate ACT outcomes in either dataset, suggesting that the process of change is based on how clients' relate to their thoughts rather than the content or frequency of thoughts.

A randomized trial by Forman and colleagues (2007) compared ACT to CT for depression and anxiety. The correlation between changes in theoretical processes and changes in outcomes were compared between ACT and CT. The study found that changes in outcome correlated more in ACT than CT with changes in experiential avoidance and the acting with awareness and acceptance subscales of the Kentucky Inventory of Mindfulness Skills (KIMS; Baer, Smith & Allen, 2004). Another study by Lappalainen and colleagues (2007) found that ACT significantly reduced experiential avoidance compared to CBT at post, and that the level of experiential avoidance at post predicted outcomes at the six-month follow-up. The differences observed between ACT and CBT at the level of processes of change indicates that these are distinct treatment approaches that work through different mechanisms.

This focus on targeting the function of private events rather than their form is a substantial change from the traditional model of CBT. Cognitive processes do not need to change in a content sense to produce clinical gains. Rather the contexts that support the harmful functions of private events such as fusion and experiential avoidance are targeted. A client may still have negative thoughts about him- or herself, the world, and the future, but these thoughts are seen as just thoughts, rather than something that is literally true. Of course, this way of relating to one's private events can also be thought of as a cognition (or metacognition)—which is the sense in which most new CBT methods still involve cognition—but it is not in the same sense as the traditional CBT perspective, and it would distort the history of the field to ignore the difference. Whether this theoretical distinction actually reflects a difference in the processes of change in acceptance- and mindfulness-based treatments is an empirical matter. So far the data has been very supportive of this claim.

## CHANGES IN THE GOALS OF TREATMENT

Treatment models include an assumption, either implicitly or explicitly, of what constitutes psychological health, and corresponding goals of treatment. As a field, CBT has generally focused on the development of evidence-based treatments designed to target psychological symptoms as defined by specific syndromes. Though other targets may still be pursued in therapy, CBT largely focuses on first-order change strategies designed to reduce or eliminate problematic overt behaviors, thoughts, and emotions. In a recent article, Hofmann and Asmundson (2008) stated that "The goal in CBT is to reduce or eliminate psychological distress. This goal incorporates symptom reduction." (p. 7). Clinical gains thus appear to be generally defined as the alleviation of disorder-specific symptoms and psychological distress.

Acceptance- and mindfulness-based treatments tend to have a different perspective on treatment goals and the conceptualization of health. From this perspective, psychological distress in and of itself is not the problem. Rather, the problem is the particular functional relationships in which thoughts, feelings, and sensations interfere with effective life functioning and accomplishment of valued ends. Therapy seeks to develop broader, more effective behavioral repertoires, independent of whether or not psychological distress is present. Some treatments even specifically target clients' notion that psychological distress must first be eliminated prior to being able to engage in a valued life, as itself a focus of intervention.

This difference in treatment goals can be observed in reviews of third wave therapies by more traditional CBT researchers. For example, a meta-analysis of ACT by Powers, Zum Vörde Sive Vörding, and Emmelkamp (2009) used disorder-specific distress as the primary outcome across studies, placing measures such as quality of life and functioning as secondary. This approach indicates a significant distinction in treatment models and led to a misinterpretation of several studies. For example, in two chronic pain studies that were included, self-reported pain was treated as a primary outcome, while behavioral outcomes such as sick leave and physical functioning were considered secondary. The ACT model is thus flipped on its head, such that that alleviating psychological distress is key, while changes in life functioning and engagement are secondary.

## IS THIS NEW?

As a whole, acceptance- and mindfulness-based therapies differ significantly in their conceptualization of psychopathology, intervention, and health. The traditional emphasis on strategies designed to change the form, frequency, or intensity of private events has been replaced with a focus on their contexts and function. Rather than attempting to change the content of cognitions, treatment developers are increasingly focusing on changing how one relates to such cognitions and their subsequent impact on behavior. Instead of focusing on reducing psychological distress, these treatments focus on changing the relationship of psychological distress to overt behavior, empowering clients to engage in a valued life despite distressing experiences. This distinction in the processes of change has been consistently demonstrated empirically in outcomes studies. The traditional CBT model of identifying and changing irrational or maladaptive cognitive processes to eliminate psychological distress differs drastically from a model that seeks to alter the function of cognitions, emotions, and other private events in order to enhance broader, more effective behavioral repertoires.

There is the larger question, though, of whether these developments represent a new form of behavioral and cognitive therapy or reflect more of an extension of traditional CBT. The core assumptions underlying acceptance and mindfulness approaches are clearly not entirely new; they touch base with traditions that are thousands of years old. Even establishing that these assumptions are relatively new to CBT is difficult, because CBT itself is a rapidly moving target. In the past five years since the publication of a paper by Hayes (2004) describing third wave behavior therapies to the broader CBT community, the relationship between CBT and acceptance- and mindfulness-based therapies has changed significantly. Acceptance- and mindfulness-based approaches have become much more mainstream, and there appears to be relatively broad agreement that acceptance and mindfulness technologies can produce positive clinical gains, at least in some contexts. The outcome evidence consistently shows that acceptance- and mindfulness-based therapies produce a positive impact on a variety of psychological problems (Feigenbaum, 2007; Grossman, Niemann, Schmidt, & Walach, 2004; Hayes et al., 2006; Öst, 2008; Powers et al., 2009). Traditional CBT packages have begun incorporating or emphasizing these processes (e.g., Fairfax, 2008; Ong, Shapiro, & Manber, 2008). CBT researchers are even beginning to apply acceptance and mindfulness theoretical models to understand traditional cognitive technologies. For example, "Cognitive restructuring and cognitive defusion both aim to reduce avoidance and enhance exposure to previously avoided and suppressed internal experiences. Therefore, both may serve to reduce 'experiential avoidance'" (Arch & Craske, 2008, p. 267).

In many ways, it appears that CBT has already begun to absorb these new developments, incorporating them within the dominant paradigm. Researchers have attempted to account for the theoretical challenges posed by acceptance and mindfulness without significantly altering the traditional treatment model. For example, these processes have been re-interpreted as response-focused emotion regulation strategies (Hofmann & Asmundson, 2008) or as an extension of the traditional exposure paradigm (Arch & Craske, 2008). Ultimately, it seems likely that CBT can adopt many of these developments without drastically altering the approach.

This flexibility is in one sense positive, but it could also cost the field an opportunity to make a more drastic shift in the approach, not only to therapy, but to psychology as a science. When there are significant developments in a field, an opportunity arises to examine one's progress and scientific strategy. The developments in acceptance- and mindfulness-based therapies point to limitations in the current scientific strategy and a different approach we can take as a field. Although the theoretical and technological developments provided by acceptance- and mindfulness-based therapies are significant, the distinct and promising approach to scientific strategy they afford represents much more of the core of a new wave of behavior therapy and the potential for a radical paradigmatic shift within the field.

The scientific strategy of CBT largely reflects a Food and Drug Administration (FDA) model in which highly specified, manualized interventions are tested in randomized controlled trials (RCTs) for specific disorders. This approach emphasizes testing the efficacy of treatment packages over the theoretical model and a focus on syndromes over functionally defined clinical factors. This is due in part to a shift in the scientific strategy of behavior therapy that occurred with the development of CBT, in which theoretical models and interventions lost their connection to basic behavioral principles. This erosion of the traditional links between basic principles, theory, and technology that characterized the early behavior therapy movement and the focus on a FDA model of treatment testing may have reduced progressivity in the field. For example, improvements in effect sizes for psychotherapy have slowed (Wampold, 2001); there is limited knowledge of the processes of change and active components for CBT (Hayes, 2004; Longmore & Worrell, 2007); the syndromal approach characterized by the DSM has failed to yet identify diseases with distinct etiologies and methods of intervention (Kupfer, First, & Regier, 2002); and the adoption of CBT by practicing clinicians has been somewhat limited (Sanderson, 2002). Developments in acceptance- and mindfulness-based therapies suggest an alternative approach that may be more successful.

Some of the more recent acceptance- and mindfulness-based therapies have developed through a distinct scientific model. In particular, we will focus on the development strategy behind ACT, which we term *contextual behavioral science* (CBS; Hayes, Levin, Plumb, Boulanger, & Pistorello, in press). CBS is an inductive, principle-focused approach that developed out of clinical behavior analysis. It is based on the philosophical assumptions of functional contextualism (Hayes, 1993; Hayes, Hayes, & Reese, 1988). CBS involves multiple co-occurring research fronts that simultaneously emphasize basic research developing principles that are abstracted into theoretical models, which in turn inform treatment technologies that are tested through a diverse range of methodologies, including a particular emphasis on testing treatment components, processes of change, and effectiveness/dissemination. Detailed descriptions of CBS and its distinctions from other models of scientific development have been included in several recent publications (Hayes, 2008; Hayes et al., in press; Levin & Hayes, 2009; Vilardaga, Hayes, Levin, & Muto, 2008). In this chapter, particular features of CBS will be explored as alternatives that may serve to correct for limitations in the current scientific strategy of CBT and help guide a new wave of behavior therapy.

## MOVING FROM A TECHNOLOGY-FOCUSED MODEL TO A THEORY-FOCUSED MODEL OF TREATMENT TESTING

The FDA model of treatment development focuses on testing highly specified treatment technologies in RCTs. This methodology allows a researcher to control for the potential confounding variables that may threaten internal validity, enabling one to accurately determine whether a given treatment can produce clinical gains. Treatment packages can be carefully assessed and compared to inform decisions regarding treatment delivery and evidence-based guidelines.

However, this method alone does not provide any information regarding how such gains were made or the active components of the treatment (Borkovec & Castonguay, 1998). RCTs provide general information about treatment efficacy, but do little to inform the theoretical model. The focus is on testing the efficacy of the technology as an entire package, much more than on the utility of the treatment model, in specifying important treatment components and processes of change.

At first glance, this may make sense. A theory is only useful if it can translate into an effective treatment. Ultimately, we would want to know whether a given treatment can produce clinical improvements and whether it is more effective than other treatment options. The problems with emphasizing technology over theory testing arise over time, as can be seen by some of the current issues in CBT and clinical psychology more generally. These issues raise concerns regarding the progressivity of this model of science for clinical psychology.

The empirically supported treatments (ESTs) movement is a good example case. ESTs are defined solely by their outcome evidence, generally through RCTs (Chambless & Ollendick, 2001). The EST list thus represents a collection of evidence-based technologies, with no criteria based on theory. This emphasis on empirically validated technologies leads to conclusions such as eye-movement desensitization and reprocessing (EMDR) being listed as having strong research support, despite the fact that it appears to work through the same process as traditional exposure and is as effective with or without its only distinguishing feature, the additional eye movement training (Davidson & Parker, 2001). These criteria could allow countless therapies that target the same processes of change and include the same active treatment components to be listed as empirically supported due to technological distinctions of unknown importance (Herbert, 2003). The result could be an increasingly large and incoherent collection of therapies rather than an organized and progressive field.

The problems with a purely technological model can also be observed in looking at the current knowledge base in CBT. Several dismantling and component studies have raised the concern that the cognitive treatment component in CBT has no additive benefit above and beyond standard behavior therapy (Longmore & Worrell, 2007). CBT developed based on the notion that cognitive processes should be considered in addition to, or instead of, behavioral principles and that targeting maladaptive cognitions would lead to greater clinical outcomes. The inability to demonstrate the additive benefit of cognitive treatment components relatively consistently, and with adequate clinical significance, is a critical challenge to the CBT model. Yet, despite the fact that studies have suggested behavior therapy is as effective without cognitive therapy components for over a decade (e.g., Jacobson, Dobson, et al., 1996) the basic treatment model has not changed, and there has been no significant and conclusive rally by CBT researchers to disprove these findings empirically. This may be attributed in part to a model of science that emphasizes testing entire treatment packages over theoretically informed components. Whether particular components are inactive or do not conform with the theoretical model is considered secondary and is not crucial to the validity of the treatment approach.

In addition to questions regarding the active components of treatment, the processes of change in CBT are still unclear (Longmore & Worrell, 2007). This is concerning, given the vast number of well-controlled CBT outcome studies that have been conducted and the fact that there have been calls for process of change research in CBT for decades (Hollon, DeRubeis, & Evans, 1987). Again, this seems to reflect a narrow model of science in which theoretical models are largely untested—or, when they are tested, negative evidence is not accommodated.

There are CBT outcome studies that have demonstrated mediation of treatment outcomes through changes in targeted, disorder-specific cognitive processes (Hofmann, 2004; Hofmann et al., 2007; Smits, Powers, Cho, & Telch, 2004; Smits, Rosenfield, Telch, & McDonald, 2006). However, the measures used in these studies often only assess a very specific and relatively small part of the model, such as the estimated social cost of hypothetical negative events with social phobia (Hofmann, 2004) and fear of fear with panic disorder (Smits et al., 2004). Moreover, they fail to explain the much larger set of mediational failures (Longmore & Worrell, 2007). Testing small aspects of disorder-specific models provides some support to the importance of targeting cognitive processes, but does not adequately test the model. To adequately test the CBT model, the central processes of change need to be clearly stated and measured. Strong support for the model will require consistent mediational evidence.

Much the same kind of problem exists in the area of therapy components. There is by now quite a large set of data challenging the utility of cognitive therapy interventions in CBT (Longmore & Worrell, 2007). Hofmann and Asmundson (2008) have replied to these data with the claim that "a component analysis can neither support nor refute the CBT model because cognitions can change without explicitly targeting them" (pp. 9–10). This is true, of course, but it raises additional concerns. It fails to explain why the field should be interested in a theory that leads to components that do not add to outcomes, but only explains the operation of existing methods. It also could shift responsibility for testing theories from those who develop them to those who challenge them. On its arrival, traditional CBT claimed that its ideas were progressive. Component analyses test whether they are practically progressive. Consistency of mediation tests whether they are theoretically progressive. Both seem important, and both are the responsibility of advocates, not critics.

A focus on testing treatment packages, with little emphasis on testing theoretically derived processes of change and treatment components, has arguably slowed the progress of CBT as a field. The limitations in EST standards and difficulties in identifying the active treatment components and processes of change in CBT are indicative of this problem. Theory development and testing are central to a progressive science of psychology. Theories guide the development of new technologies and the application of technologies to new problems; they also provide a means to organize and refine treatment technologies. Focusing on empirically validating manualized treatments through RCTs does provide a high level of precision. The independent variables are clear, and one should be able to replicate the effects under the appropriate conditions. However, the scope is significantly limited. These findings do little to guide the application of treatment to new problems or to refine a treatment by enhancing its focus on active treatment components and processes of change. Instead, treatment developers are forced to guess which particular treatment components are active and would apply to a given problem. This can lead to increasingly large and heterogeneous treatment packages that are relatively imprecise in targeting the relevant processes for a given problem.

These problems and limitations suggest the need for an alternative, theory-oriented strategy for treatment testing. Some of the acceptance- and mindfulness-based therapies have taken this approach, focusing on testing theoretically derived treatment components and processes of change over a more exclusive focus on technology testing. This is generally done through the use of component studies and meditational analysis.

In this approach, treatment technologies and components are tightly linked to theoretical processes of change. Testing treatment components thus provides a test of the model in specifying important processes to be targeted. Often these studies use a micro component design in which a relatively brief intervention, linked to a particular set of processes of change, is tested in highly controlled conditions. This can be used to determine whether the component is psychologically active as well as to explore more precise theoretical questions. The ability to conduct micro component designs relatively quickly and at a low cost allows researchers to conduct component research early in treatment development. This avoids the reliance on expensive, multiyear dismantling studies that can generally only be conducted after multiple RCTs have been completed, at which point identifying inactive components would be much more problematic to treatment development. These dismantling studies are also necessary, but micro component studies can greatly increase our knowledge of treatment components and even processes of change.

There have been more than 40 micro component studies that have tested acceptance and mindfulness treatment components (Levin, Hildebrandt, Lillis & Hayes, under review). For example, studies have found that a brief acceptance-only intervention can increase behavioral persistence in difficult/distressing tasks (e.g., Levitt, Brown, Orsillo, & Barlow, 2004; Vowles et al., 2007) and increase willingness to engage in exposure (e.g., Eifert & Heffner, 2003) compared to nonintervention comparison conditions. Research has also found that brief mindfulness interventions can lead to increased persistence in difficult/distressing tasks (e.g., Hayes et al., 1999; Masedo & Esteve, 2007) and reduced distress during and after the task (e.g., Masedo & Esteve, 2007) compared to nonintervention controls. Studies have also tested the defusion or decentering component of mindfulness, finding that these interventions reduce believability and distress related to negative self-relevant thoughts (e.g., Masuda, Hayes, Sackett, & Twohig, 2004). Component studies such as these provide support for the theoretical model and suggest the benefits of including acceptance and mindfulness components in treatment packages.

A theory-oriented approach also includes a strong emphasis on examining processes of change and testing for mediation in outcome studies. Well-controlled clinical trials are essential in testing the treatment package. However, the success of the theoretical model is held to be just as important as, if not more important than, the efficacy of the technology. From this perspective, if the technology fails to impact the processes of change or clinical outcomes, then adaptations can be made and the model remains intact for the time being. If the technology is successful at impacting the outcome, but not through the specified processes of change—or if the technology impacts the processes of change but there is no change in outcome—then there is a significant problem for the theoretical model (Follette, 1995). In the first case, this would suggest that the intervention does not produce clinical gains through the theoretical processes of change. In the second case, the results would suggest that targeting the theoretical processes of change does not lead to clinical gains. If these results are not due to measurement problems or other methodological issues, the theoretical model of change is significantly challenged and must be adapted or even abandoned.

There is substantial research on the processes of change in acceptance- and mindfulness-based treatments, particularly with ACT. Researchers have stressed the importance of developing adequate measures of acceptance and mindfulness processes and including these measures in outcome studies. For example, virtually every published ACT outcome study has examined one or more process of change measures, with results consistently supporting the theoretical model. Because of the precision of the theory, these positive results focus on a relatively small number of processes.

The differences between traditional CBT and CBS are exemplified by recent reviews of the literature. For example, Öst (2008) conducted a meta-analysis of third wave behavior therapies, but focused entirely on RCT outcomes, ignoring process evidence and component research. Moving to more a theory-oriented model of treatment development could significantly improve our understanding of the processes of change and active components within treatments. This will serve to directly inform the application of treatment to new areas, the development of new technologies, and how to organize and refine treatment technologies. Focusing on testing and refining theoretical models can thus serve to significantly increase progress in clinical psychology.

## MOVING FROM A SYNDROMAL APPROACH TO A FUNCTIONAL APPROACH

The traditional CBT strategy focuses on developing and testing treatments for specific syndromes. For each disorder, a cognitive model is created and used to inform the development of a disorder-specific treatment. Treatments are then tested in RCTs using strict inclusion criteria.

This approach is based on the assumption that disorders will eventually lead to distinct disease entities with specific etiologies. However, this strategy has yet to be successful. The problems and concerns are best described by the planning committee for the DSM-V, who themselves appear skeptical of the potential success of this approach (Kupfer et al., 2002).

...the goal of validating these syndromes and discovering common etiologies has remained elusive. Despite many proposed candidates, not one laboratory marker has been found to be specific in identifying any of the DSM defined syndromes. (p. xviii)

Epidemiological and clinical studies have shown extremely high rates of comorbidities among disorders, undermining hypothesis that the syndromes represent distinct etiologies. Furthermore, epidemiological studies have shown a high degree of short term diagnostic instability for many disorders. With regard to treatment, lack of specificity is the rule rather than the exception. (p. xviii)

Many, if not most, conditions and symptoms represent a somewhat arbitrarily defined pathological excess of normal behaviors and cognitive processes. This problem has led to the criticism that the system pathologizes ordinary experiences of the human condition. (p. 2)

All these limitations in the current diagnostic paradigm suggest that research exclusively focused on refining the DSM-defined syndromes may never be successful in uncovering their underlying etiologies. For that to happen, an as yet unknown paradigm shift may need to occur. (p. xix)

Not only does this strategy seem unlikely to be successful, but it may have hindered progress. The DSM-V planning committee (Kupfer et al., 2002) states that the "reification of DSM-IV entities, to the point that they are considered to be equivalent to diseases, is more likely to obscure than to elucidate research findings" (p. xix), and "researchers' slavish adoption of DSM-IV definitions may have hindered research in the etiology of mental disorders" (p. xix).

The focus on being more and more precise in identifying and distinguishing specific symptom clusters appears to have developed at the cost of focusing on key functional variables that would be relevant for treatment. Distinctions often appear to be based more on topographical features, such as problem area and specific symptoms, rather than on functional relations that would guide treatment. This approach can be particularly problematic in combination with a technological model of treatment development in which specific treatment manuals are developed for each disorder, leading to an overwhelming number of treatments to develop, test, and disseminate.

An alternative is to approach clinical problems functionally. Instead of focusing on disorders, treatment targets are organized by clinically relevant functional variables. This involves considering the relation between antecedents, behaviors, and consequences, rather than categorizing problems based on their specific form. For example, a common functional variable in anxiety disorders is problematic behaviors maintained by avoidance of anxiety-provoking stimuli, which helps explain why exposure is such a key component of interventions across anxiety disorders.

This approach has been taken in some of the acceptance- and mindfulness-based treatments. Functional diagnostic dimensions that have been developed in the context of these treatments, such as experiential avoidance (Hayes, Wilson, Gifford, Follette, & Strosahl, 1996) and distress tolerance (Rodman, Daughters, & Lejuez, 2009), can be examined for their relevance across a range of topographically distinct problems. This provides a means of categorizing clinical problems in a way that directly informs treatment. If a treatment is found to be effective in targeting a particular functional diagnostic dimension, then it suggests the potential applicability of the treatment to wherever the functional dimension applies.

Acceptance- and mindfulness-based therapies have pursued this strategy by testing treatment across a range of topographically distinct yet functionally similar problems for which the treatment should apply. This provides a test of the scope of the theoretical model and helps to quickly identify the limits of the model and technology. When the treatment is ineffective for a given problem area, treatment developers can use these findings to further develop the technology and/or theoretical model. For example, the ACT model assumes that processes such as cognitive fusion and experiential avoidance may be relevant wherever language and cognition apply to human behavior. As a result, ACT has been tested and found to have a positive impact across a surprisingly vast range of areas, including depression, anxiety, psychosis, chronic pain, substance abuse, smoking, burnout, coping with chronic illness, obesity, self-stigma, prejudice, and adopting evidence-based treatments (Hayes et al., 2006; Hayes et al., in press).

CBT has similarly been successfully applied to a broad range of problem areas (Butler et al., 2006), but the lack of a clear set of change processes makes it harder to know what this generality means. The search for core common processes and transdiagnostic treatments may reflect the same concern.

There are significant limitations in anchoring evidence-based treatments to DSM syndromes. It is unclear whether these syndromes will ever lead to distinct disease entities (Kupfer et al., 2002). Meanwhile, the scope of the treatment is sacrificed to maintain a precise, yet functionally unimportant, target population. A functional diagnostic approach would provide an organizational system that directly informs treatment. Furthermore, this approach could help to increase the broad application of treatments to whatever areas are functionally relevant.

## MOVING FROM MANUALIZED TREATMENTS TO FLEXIBLE, PROCESS-ORIENTED TREATMENTS

The differences in scientific development strategies have implications in how treatments are disseminated and implemented. The traditional CBT approach has been to disseminate highly specified treatment manuals for specific disorders that have been adequately tested in RCTs. As researchers are unclear regarding which components are active and why, they are left with the option of having clinicians attempt to replicate what was done in the clinical trial as closely as possible. If changes are made, there would be no way to know whether the active components and processes were still included. This creates significant barriers to clinicians, particularly when one considers the vast number of disorder-specific manuals that would need to be learned in order to effectively treat the range of problem presentations encountered in clinical work. The low rate of adoption of ESTs by practicing clinicians (Sanderson, 2002) can be attributed in part to these problems.

Alternatively, a working knowledge of important functional diagnostic dimensions and the processes of change that effectively impact these variables can be used to develop a much more flexible intervention approach. Clinicians can learn to target important functional variables through any method that impacts the relevant processes of change. Though technologies are made available, these are presented as options and starting points in developing a clinicians' own repertoire of therapeutic techniques. This represents a shift from empirically supported therapies to empirically supported principles of change (Rosen & Davison, 2003).

This method has a number of potential advantages for dissemination and implementation (McHugh, Murray, & Barlow, 2009). The approach builds on the strengths of a clinician's existing repertoire in targeting the relevant process rather than requiring a specific technique to be learned. The number of treatments to be learned is also significantly reduced. Furthermore, treatment can be flexibly adapted with relative ease to specific circumstances.

ACT has attempted to pursue this strategy. Rather than a specific set of technologies, ACT reflects a model of treatment that combines acceptance and mindfulness processes with behavior change processes to promote flexible, values-consistent patterns of behavior. Therapists are encouraged to develop their own repertoire of techniques in order to promote these processes of change in their clients. Similarly, research has tested the ACT model across a range of treatment modalities, including group therapy (Zettle & Rains, 1989), workshops (Bond & Bunce, 2000), brief interventions (Bach & Hayes, 2002), and bibliotherapy (Lazzarone et al., 2007), as well as standard therapy formats (Wicksell, Melin, & Olsson, 2007). The flexible approach to treatment technologies and modalities afforded by a process-oriented treatment has served to enhance the ability to disseminate ACT and implement it in a variety of contexts.

## ENHANCING THE RELATIONSHIP OF BASIC AND APPLIED SCIENCE

Developing and testing flexible, process-oriented treatments that target functional diagnostic dimensions requires a well-elaborated and -tested theory. In particular, theoretical constructs are needed that are precise, have far-reaching scope, and that specify manipulable variables. Precision is necessary in order to maintain an organized and guided theoretical model. Without adequate scope, the theoretical model would not apply to a sufficient number of instances to be very useful. If precise and broadly applicable factors are identified, but do not specify manipulable variables, then they will provide little benefit to efforts at behavior change.

This is a significant challenge to achieve within the current CBT model of science. Theoretical models appear to be largely informed by applied research on psychopathology and intervention. Though these are important areas of research, it is unclear whether this strategy can produce constructs with sufficiently high precision and scope that will point to manipulable factors to target in treatment. For example, the cognitive theoretical model describes how the processing and construction of experiences is biased by dysfunctional beliefs and schemas, leading to irrational and maladaptive cognitions as well as other psychological symptoms (Beck, 2005). An emphasis on the biased processing of information through cognitive schemas provides broad scope, applying to just about anything a person experiences. Yet the precision of this model is less clear. Constructs such as beliefs, schemas, cognitive content, and processing are difficult to define precisely. These are not highly technical terms and instead refer to more lay definitions. Without a technical account of cognition that specifies what they are, how they develop, and how they change, it becomes difficult to know what to target and how to do so. Instead, intervention methods have to be developed from other sources, such as clinical experience and adapted technologies from other treatments. This can lead to a separation of theory from intervention technologies.

These difficulties can be traced back to a significant shift in scientific strategy that occurred with the transition from traditional behavior therapy to CBT. Originally, behavior therapy was united by the goal of applying operant and classical learning principles, developed in basic research, to the prediction and influence of human behavior. Findings from basic research were developed into precise yet generally applicable rules that could be directly applied to the prediction and influence of human behavior. These simple concepts could be used to unpack complex human behaviors, taking a bottom-up approach to treatment development. Researchers were able to translate these principles into successful interventions while simultaneously maintaining the close roots to a highly precise technical analysis. This led to the development of a variety of treatments, many of which remain as some of the most effective technologies in psychotherapy (e.g., contingency management, exposure). The problem was that this model did not include a strategy for what to do when the basic principles were insufficient, and basic behavioral researchers had not provided an adequate account of language and cognition.

This left treatment developers who saw the need to address cognition more thoroughly to rely on other sources. The information processing model from cognitive science replaced a foundation in basic behavioral science. Rather than a precise, technical analysis provided with basic behavioral principles, cognitive models were built on metaphors, such as the mind as a computer. The relevance of the cognitive model to psychopathology was initially based on systematic observations from clinical work, and later supported by applied empirical research (Beck, 2005). The structure and content of the intervention was based on experiences conducting psychoanalysis, as well as on features of behavior therapy (Beck, 2005). Thus, the notion that cognitive processes mediate psychological symptoms and that one could change irrational and dysfunctional cognitions through interventions such as logical analysis and hypothesis testing was not derived from basic research, but on systematic clinical observations, applied research on measurement development, and an information processing model. This represented a significant shift in scientific strategy, and one that seems to have remained to this day.

In a recent article, Hofmann and Asmundson (2008) disagreed with the claim that cognitive therapy is not directly linked to basic science. The authors provide several examples of how experimental psychopathology research and treatment outcome studies have served to inform treatment approaches. However, these types of methods are not equivalent to the highly controlled, basic laboratory studies that aim to develop technical analyses of high precision and scope that are linked directly to manipulable treatment factors. The authors also discussed neuroscience research that has attempted to model the impact of cognitive interventions on neural pathways as an example of basic science. Although neuroscience is a basic science and provides important information regarding the consistency of the model at the level of neurobiology, it does not substitute for a technical analysis of interventions at the level of analysis of psychology. Defining cognitive concepts and processes based on neurological pathways and activities will still not indicate manipulable contextual factors to be targeted in psychotherapy. Developing methods for altering the functions of the neocortex pose similar problems as targeting cognitive change.

Developers of ACT recognized the problems in the behavioral account of language and cognition and its importance to the prediction and influence of human behavior. However, the alternative of relying on clinically derived models and an information processing metaphor did not seem to be an adequate solution to the problem. Instead, Hayes and colleagues sought to develop an adequate basic behavioral account of language and cognition that could be used to build a form of CBT that maintained its tight link to basic principles. A unique approach was taken during this period in which applied researchers conducted much of the early basic research, which was only later adopted and continued by other basic researchers. Research began by studying rule-governed behavior (Hayes, 1989), later developing to research on derived stimulus relations, and ultimately producing Relational Frame Theory (RFT; Hayes, Barnes-Holmes & Roche, 2001). The research on rule-governed behavior and RFT directly informed the development of the ACT model of intervention and pathology, as well as specific assessment and intervention technologies (Barnes-Holmes, Barnes-Holmes, McHugh, & Hayes, 2004; Hayes et al., in press).

ACT and traditional CBT thus share a common interest in developing a model of psychopathology and intervention that adequately takes into account cognitive processes. Yet rather than relying on clinical and metaphorical computer or brain models, ACT developers attempted to address this issue while maintaining its behavioral roots. From a strictly clinical perspective, this approach was much slower than that taken by CBT. The first ACT outcome studies, then called comprehensive distancing, were tested in the early 1980s. The initial results seemed promising (Zettle & Hayes, 1986; Zettle & Rains, 1989), but the technical analysis of verbal behavior upon which it relied was still being developed. Thus, ACT developers took a 15-year hiatus from treatment testing to focus on developing the basic account of language and cognition and the theoretical model of treatment (Zettle, 2005).

Despite its sometimes slower rate of progress, maintaining a tight link to basic principles also provides substantial advantages in developing a theoretical model and associated intervention technology. The principles derived from a technical account of language and cognition can be used as building blocks for analyzing complex human behavior and developing theoretical models. Functional analysis of clinical problems can be conducted with these principles, orienting to important manipulable factors for intervention. Sets of these functional analyses begin to suggest common functional diagnostic dimensions and processes of change (e.g., experiential avoidance/acceptance, cognitive fusion/defusion), which can be abstracted into inductive theoretical models of intervention, psychopathology, and health. The tight link to basic principles and technical terms serves to maintain a precise, broadly applicable analysis that orients to manipulable factors. Thus, maintaining a tight link to a basic account of language and cognition, as well as other behavioral phenomena, can provide theoretical models that are highly effective in guiding the analysis and treatment of clinical problems.

## EXAMINING PHILOSOPHICAL ASSUMPTIONS

This chapter has highlighted a series of potential barriers to progress within the traditional CBT approach and has suggested several important features of CBS as an alternative strategy. Many of the distinctions between these two approaches are rooted in their unique assumptions regarding science. It is unclear whether a radical shift in scientific strategy is possible without a change, or at least examination, of the assumptions underlying these two distinct approaches.

Pre-analytic assumptions are a necessary part of science. Without assumptions such as the unit of analysis and criterion for defining "truth," there would be no way to conduct systematic research. These assumptions provide the foundation for a research program's approach to theory and methodology. Although these assumptions are necessary, researchers are not always aware of what their assumptions are. Explicating the philosophical assumptions of a research program can serve to identify inconsistencies in an approach and vitalize its theoretical models and research methods. This process is particularly important when significant shifts in scientific strategy are considered.

The philosophical assumptions of traditional CBT have not been clearly explicated beyond general references to ancient Stoic philosophy. However, researchers have pointed out the strong similarities between CBT and critical rationalism (Hofmann & Asmundson, 2008) and elemental realism (Hayes, Strosahl, & Wilson, in press). In these philosophical systems, truth is defined objectively. Theories are true in so far as they correspond with the world as it actually is. Knowledge is thus gained by attempting to falsify theories through hypothesis testing. These theories typically focus on developing models of human behavior that specify its discrete parts and forces, such as beliefs, schemas, emotional responses, and overt behavior. Developing accurate models that predict how these hypothetical constructs impact each other is assumed to lead to more effective interventions.

CBS is based on a distinct philosophy of science called functional contextualism (Hayes, 1993; S. C. Hayes, Hayes, & Reese, 1988). Functional contextualism differs from critical rationalism and elemental realism in that it is not concerned with ontological truth. Instead, truth is defined contextually with regards to the goals of the scientist. A pragmatic truth criterion of successful working in achieving the goals of the analysis is assumed. It is important that these goals be clearly stated to ensure agreement among scientists in a field. Within CBS, the prediction and influence of behavior is held as a unified goal.

The de-emphasis on ontological truth does not mean that functional contextualism denies reality. A world is assumed to really exist. However, any further partitioning of this one world is considered to be more a result of the behavior of the scientist than a reflection of an ontological truth. For example, the distinction of antecedents, behaviors, and consequences in behavior analysis is not an ontological claim, but rather a method of achieving prediction and influence. The "truth" of these partitions is defined only in the limited sense of their utility in predicting and influencing behavior.

The unit of analysis in functional contextualism is the organism interacting in and with a context. Rather than developing mechanistic models with discrete parts and forces, the behavior of the organism is considered as a dynamic interaction with context. Behavior is defined contextually and loses its meaning when studied independent of context. A consideration of both behavior and manipulable contextual factors within the unit of analysis reflects the goals of prediction and influence of behavior.

The philosophical assumptions of traditional CBT and CBS are fundamentally different. However, these differences cannot be resolved empirically. These assumptions are pre-analytic and are not testable hypotheses. Instead, they represent the assumptive base from which empirical tests can be made. Scientists can only explicate their assumptions, and there is little benefit from directly trying to disprove the assumptions of other research programs and fields. However, this does not mean that the assumptions of a research program cannot be brought into question. One can still evaluate whether the philosophical assumptions are likely to meet the goals of the program of research (Long, 2009).

The mission statement of the Association for Behavioral and Cognitive Therapies provides a concise description of these goals as "the advancement of a scientific approach to the understanding and amelioration of problems of the human condition." CBT and empirical clinical psychology as a field is generally united by this commitment. It is important to note that this is rooted in a pragmatic goal, the alleviation of "problems of the human condition." For many researchers, the adoption of a scientific approach is largely based on the assumption that it is the most effective strategy for ultimately solving these problems. The assumptions of traditional CBT can be questioned in terms of their capacity to meet this pragmatic goal.

The assumptive base of CBT narrows the focus of science to the prediction of behavior rather than prediction and *influence* (Biglan & Hayes, 1996). The emphasis is on developing and validating models that specify the relation between hypothetical constructs, such as how cognition mediates the relationship between events and subsequent behavioral and emotional responses. These models are tested by assessing their correspondence with reality through predictive tests. However, the ability to influence behavior is not central to the model and is more of an after-effect of developing accurate theories. There is no guarantee that manipulable contextual factors that would directly inform intervention are in such predictive models.

For example, suppose the claim is made that disordered thoughts lead to disordered emotions, and these in turn cause overt behavioral difficulties. From the perspective of functional contextualism, behaviors, cognitions, and emotions are all dependent variables of the organism. By definition, dependent variables cannot be directly manipulated by others. To change cognition, an independent variable is needed—in other words, something that can be manipulated. For example, CBT provides a number of strategies to change maladaptive cognitive processes, such as the Socratic method and hypothesis testing. These interventions represent independent variables in that they are environmental manipulations that can alter dependent variables. Yet, due to the emphasis on the predictive utility of models specifying the relationship of dependent variables to each other, these manipulable factors are rarely included in the theoretical accounts themselves. This contributes to the separation of intervention technology from theory. Treatment technologies are not directly informed by the theoretical model and instead are developed or adopted from other sources in the hopes that they will impact the relevant theoretical targets.

Another problem with theoretical models that focus on dependent variables is that they may prove to be inaccurate when contextual factors are considered. The relations between dependent variables may be different when the context in which they occur changes. For example, although negative self-relevant thoughts and avoidance of social situations may correlate, if an intervention targets negative-self relevant thoughts and thereby reduces their frequency this does not necessarily entail that social avoidance will change. In this case, it may be that negative thoughts no longer relate to social avoidance in the same way as predicted by the theory. Similarly, an acceptance and mindfulness intervention may target the relation of negative self-relevant thoughts to social avoidance rather than the content of the thoughts, potentially resulting in cases in which clients still have the same negative thoughts, but are much less avoidant of social situations. Considering how context interacts with these behavioral relations is important.

These limitations suggest that the philosophical assumptions underlying traditional CBT may limit its utility in achieving the pragmatic goal of alleviating human suffering. Alternatively, the assumptions of functional contextualism are rooted in the notion of developing a science that from its very core is based on meeting the pragmatic goals of science. The unit of analysis contains both behavior of the organism and manipulable contextual factors. Furthermore, the pragmatic goal of prediction and influence leads to a science that emphasizes functional accounts of human behavior that orient to methods of intervention. Many of the changes in scientific strategy proposed in this chapter developed out of this alternative model of science.

The criticism of elemental realism and critical rationalism is not that the assumptions are somehow wrong, but that the assumptions may not be the most effective in meeting the practical goals of clinical psychology. Functional contextualism introduces an alternative set of assumptions, which are designed specifically to meet the pragmatic goals of an applied science. This approach has been successfully applied in some of the acceptance- and mindfulness-based interventions, particularly ACT. Developing a more progressive science of clinical psychology thus may involve examining the philosophical assumptions of traditional psychological science and evaluating whether they are the most effective in meeting our goals as a field.

## CONCLUSION

An examination of the general theoretical model of pathology, intervention, and health for traditional CBT and acceptance- and mindfulness-based therapies leads to several clear distinctions between these approaches. Ultimately it is not important whether third-generation approaches are "new," as much as it is whether they are progressive. If the technologies being generated by the acceptance and mindfulness approaches are merely adopted and integrated into CBT, at best there will be an increase in treatment efficacy (though even that is not yet known), and there may be a shift toward certain research areas. Whatever benefits those changes provide will quickly be exhausted, however.

Similarly, although there is superficially the appearance of a political struggle between proponents of CBT and CBS, in fact science is not politics. If a political opponent is weakened, an adversary might win an election that otherwise would be lost. If a scientific "opponent" is weakened, the scientific support for an alternative is not increased one iota. Thus, the goal is not winning a fight—the goal is progress.

Over the long term, the importance of a book like this is to underline the need to rethink the scientific strategy being employed in applied science. Developments within acceptance- and mindfulness-based therapies point to limitations in the current model of applied science and provide an opportunity to make a more fundamental shift in our approach as a field to the challenges we face. Moving from a narrowly defined model of technology testing linked to specific disorders to a model of science that emphasizes theoretically derived processes of change and functional diagnostic dimensions that are rooted in a strong basic research program could have a profound impact on the progressivity of our science. That is a change that could yield benefits for decades to come.

# REFERENCES

Arch, J. J., & Craske, M. G. (2008). Acceptance and commitment therapy and cognitive behavioral therapy for anxiety disorders: Different treatments, similar mechanisms? *Clinical Psychology, Science and Practice, 15,* 263–279.

Bach, P., & Hayes, S. C. (2002). The use of acceptance and commitment therapy to prevent the rehospitalization of psychotic patients: A randomized controlled trial. *Journal of Consulting and Clinical Psychology, 70,* 1129–1139.

Baer, R. A., Smith, G. T., & Allen, K. B. (2004). Assessment of mindfulness by self-report: The Kentucky Inventory of Mindfulness Skills. *Assessment, 11,* 191–206.

Barnes-Holmes, Y., Barnes-Holmes, D., McHugh, L., & Hayes, S. C. (2004). Relational frame theory: Some implications for understanding and treating human psychopathology. *International Journal of Psychology and Psychological Therapy, 4*(2), 161–181.

Beck, A. T. (2005). The current state of cognitive therapy: A 40-year retrospective. *Archives of General Psychiatry, 62,* 953–959.

Biglan, A., & Hayes, S. C. (1996). Should the behavioral sciences become more pragmatic? The case for functional contextualism in research on human behavior. *Applied and Preventive Psychology: Current Scientific Perspectives, 5,* 47–57.

Bond, F. W., & Bunce, D. (2000). Mediators of change in emotion-focused and problem-focused worksite stress management interventions. *Journal of Occupational Health Psychology, 5,* 156–163.

Borkovec, T. D., & Castonguay, L. G. (1998). What is the scientific meaning of empirically supported therapy? *Journal of Consulting and Clinical Psychology, 66*(1), 136–142.

Butler, A. C., Chapman, J. E., Forman, E. M., & Beck, A. T. (2006). The empirical status of cognitive-behavioral therapy: A review of meta-analyses. *Clinical Psychology Review, 26,* 17–31.

Chambless, D. L., & Ollendick, T. H. (2001). Empirically supported psychological interventions: Controversies and evidence. *Annual Review of Psychology, 52,* 685–716.

Davidson, P. R., & Parker, C. H. (2001). Eye movement desensitization and reprocessing (EMDR): A meta-analysis. *Journal of Consulting and Clinical Psychology, 69,* 305–316.

Eifert, G. H., & Heffner, M. (2003). The effects of acceptance versus control contexts on avoidance of panic-related symptoms. *Journal of Behavior Therapy and Experimental Psychiatry, 34,* 293–312.

Fairfax, H. (2008). The use of mindfulness in obsessive compulsive disorder: Suggestions for its application and integration in existing treatment. *Clinical Psychology & Psychotherapy, 15*(1), 53–59.

Feigenbaum, J. (2007). Dialectical behavior therapy: An increasing evidence base. *Journal of Mental Health, 16*(1), 51–68.

Follette, W. C. (1995). Correcting methodological weaknesses in the knowledge base used to derive practice standards. In Hayes, S. C., Follette, V. M., Dawes, R. M., & Grady, K. E. (Eds.), *Scientific Standards of Psychological Practice: Issues and Recommendations* (pp. 229–247). Reno, NV: Context Press.

Forman, E. M., Herbert, J. D., Moitra, E., Yeomans, P. D., & Geller, P. A. (2007). A randomized controlled effectiveness trial of acceptance and commitment therapy and cognitive therapy for anxiety and depression. *Behavior Modification, 31*(6), 1–28.

Gaudiano, B. A., Herbert, J. D., & Hayes, S. C. (in press). Is it the symptom or the relation to it? Investigating potential mediators of change in acceptance and commitment therapy for psychosis. *Behavior Therapy.*

Gifford, E. V., Kohlenberg, B. S., Hayes, S. C., Antonuccio, D. O., Piasecki, M. M., Rasmussen-Hall, M. L., & Palm, K. M. (2004). Acceptance theory-based treatment for smoking cessation: An initial trial of acceptance and commitment therapy. *Behavior Therapy, 35,* 689–705.

Gregg, J. A., Callaghan, G. M., Hayes, S. C., & Glenn-Lawson, J. L. (2007). Improving diabetes self-management through acceptance, mindfulness, and values: A randomized controlled trial. *Journal of Consulting and Clinical Psychology, 75*(2), 336–343.

Grossman, P., Niemann, L., Schmidt, S., & Walach, H. (2004). Mindfulness-based stress reduction and health benefits: A meta-analysis. *Journal of Psychosomatic Research, 57,* 35–43.

Hayes, S. C. (1993). Analytic goals and the varieties of scientific contextualism. In S. C. Hayes, L. J. Hayes, H. W. Reese, & T. R. Sarbin (Eds.), *Varieties of scientific contextualism* (pp. 11–27). Reno, NV: Context Press.

Hayes, S. C. (Ed.). (1989). *Rule-governed behavior: Cognition, contingencies, and instructional control.* New York, NY: Plenum.

Hayes, S. C. (2004). Acceptance and commitment therapy, relational frame theory, and the third wave of behavior therapy. *Behavior Therapy, 35,* 639–665.

Hayes, S. C. (2008). Climbing our hills: A beginning conversation on the comparison of ACT and traditional CBT. *Clinical Psychology: Science and Practice, 5,* 286–295.

Hayes, S. C. (2009, August). *The way of the turtle: Creating clinical science from the bottom up.* Invited address presented at the meeting of the Japanese Psychological Association, Kyoto, Japan.

Hayes, S. C., Barnes-Holmes, D., & Roche, B. (2001). *Relational frame theory: A post-Skinnerian account of human language and cognition.* New York, NY: Kluwer Academic/Plenum.

Hayes, S.C., Bissett, R., Korn, Z., Zettle, R. D., Rosenfarb, I., Cooper, L., & Grundt, A. (1999). The impact of impact of CBT and ACT models using psychology trainee therapists: A preliminary acceptance versus control rationales on pain tolerance. *Psychological Record, 49,* 33–47.

Hayes, S. C., Hayes, L. J., & Reese, H. W. (1988). Finding the philosophical core: A review of Stephen C. Pepper's *World Hypotheses. Journal of the Experimental Analysis of Behavior, 50,* 97–111.

Hayes, S. C., Levin, M., Plumb, J., Boulanger, J., & Pistorello, J. (in press). Acceptance and commitment therapy and contextual behavioral science: Examining the progress of a distinctive model of behavioral and cognitive therapy. *Behavior Therapy*

Hayes, S. C., Luoma, J. B., Bond, F. W., Masuda, A., & Lillis, J. (2006). Acceptance and commitment therapy: Model, processes and outcomes. *Behavior Research and Therapy, 44,* 1–25.

Hayes, S. C., Strosahl, K. D., & Wilson, K. G. (1999). *Acceptance and commitment therapy: An experiential approach to behavior change.* New York, NY: Guilford Press.

Hayes, S. C., Strosahl, K. D., & Wilson, K. G. (in press). *Acceptance and commitment therapy: Developing a unified model of behavior change* (2nd ed.). New York: Guilford.

Hayes, S. C., Wilson, K. G., Gifford, E. V., Follette, V. M., & Strosahl, K. (1996). Experiential avoidance and behavioral disorders: A functional dimensional approach to diagnosis and treatment. *Journal of Consulting and Clinical Psychology, 64,* 1152–1168.

Herbert, J. D. (2003). The science and practice of empirically supported treatments. *Behavior Modification, 27,* 412–430.

Hofmann, S. G. (2004). Cognitive mediation of treatment change in social phobia. *Journal of Consulting and Clinical Psychology, 72,* 392–399.

Hofmann, S. G. (2008). Acceptance and commitment therapy: New wave or Morita therapy? *Clinical Psychology, Science and Practice, 15,* 280–285.

Hofmann, S. G., & Asmundson, G. J. G. (2008). Acceptance and mindfulness-based therapy: New wave or old hat? *Clinical Psychology Review, 28,* 1–16.

Hofmann, S. G., Meuret, A. E., Rosenfield, D., Suvak, M. K., Barlow, D. H., Gorman, J. M.,…Woods, S. W. (2007). Preliminary evidence for cognitive mediation during cognitive behavioral therapy for panic disorder. *Journal of Consulting and Clinical Psychology, 75,* 374–379.

Hollon, S. D., DeRubeis, R. J., & Evans, M. D. (1987). Causal mediation of change in treatment for depression: Discriminating between nonspecificity and noncausality. *Psychological Bulletin, 102*(1), 139–149.

Jacobson, N. S., & Christensen, A. (1996). *Integrative couple therapy: Promoting acceptance and change.* New York, NY: W. W. Norton.

Jacobson, N. S., Dobson, K. S., Truax, P. A., Addis, M. E., Koerner, K., Gollan, J. K., . . . Prince, S. E. (1996). A component analysis of cognitive-behavioral treatment for depression. *Journal of Consulting and Clinical Psychology, 64,* 295–304.

Kabat-Zinn, J. (1990). Full catastrophe living: Using the wisdom of your body and mind to face stress, pain and illness. New York, NY: Delacorte.

Kupfer, D. J., First, M. B., & Regier, D. A. (2002). *A research agenda for DSM V.* American Psychiatric Association.

Lappalainen, R., Lehtonen, T., Skarp, E., Taubert, E., Ojanen, M., & Hayes, S. C. (2007). The controlled effectiveness trial. *Behavior Modification. 31*(4), 488–511.

Lazzarone, T. R., Hayes, S. C., Louma, J., Kohlenberg, B., Pistorello, J., Lillis, J.,...Levin, M. (2007). The effectiveness of an acceptance and commitment therapy self–help manual: Get out of your mind and into your life. Paper presented at the meeting of the Association for Behavioral and Cognitive Therapies, Philadelphia, PA.

Leahy, R. L. (2008). A closer look at ACT. *Behavior Therapist, 31,* 148–150.

Levin, M., & Hayes, S. C. (2009). ACT, RFT, and contextual behavioral science. Chapter in J. T. Blackledge, J. Ciarrochi, & F. P. Deane (Eds.), *Acceptance and commitment therapy: Contemporary research and practice* (pp. 1–40). Sydney: Australian Academic Press

Levin, M,, Hildebrandt, M., Lillis, J. & Hayes, S. C. (under review). The impact of treatment components in acceptance and commitment therapy: A meta-analysis of micro-component studies.

Levitt, J. T., Brown, T. A., Orsillo, S. M., & Barlow, D. H. (2004). The effects of acceptance versus suppression of emotion on subjective and psychophysiological response to carbon dioxide challenge in patients with panic disorder. *Behavior Therapy, 35,* 747–766.

Linehan, M. M. (1993). *Cognitive-behavioral treatment of borderline personality disorder.* New York, NY: Guilford Press.

Long, D. M. (2009, May). History and philosophy of science. Paper presented at the 35th annual convention of the Association for Behavior Analysis International, Phoenix, AZ.

Longmore, R. J., & Worrell, M. (2007). Do we need to challenge thoughts in cognitive behavior therapy? *Clinical Psychology Review, 27,* 173–187.

Lundgren, T., Dahl, J., & Hayes, S. C. (2008). Evaluation of mediators of change in the treatment of epilepsy with acceptance and commitment therapy. *Journal of Behavioral Medicine., 31*(3), 225–235.

Mansell, W. (2008). The seven C's of CBT: A consideration of the future challenges for cognitive behaviour therapy. *Behavioural and Cognitive Psychotherapy, 36*(6), 641–649.

Masedo, A. I., & Esteve, M. R. (2007). Effects of suppression, acceptance and spontaneous coping on pain tolerance, pain intensity and distress. *Behaviour Research and Therapy, 45,* 199–209.

Masuda, A., Hayes, S. C., Sackett, C. F., & Twohig, M. P. (2004). Cognitive defusion and self-relevant negative thoughts: Examining the impact of a ninety year old technique. *Behaviour Research and Therapy, 42,* 477–485.

Masuda, A., Hayes, S.C., Twohig, M.P., Drossel, C., Lillis, J. & Washio, Y. (2009). A parametric study of cognitive defusion and the believability and discomfort of negative self-relevant thoughts. *Behavior Modification, 33,* 250–262.

McHugh, R. K., Murray, H. W., & Barlow, D. H. (2009). Balancing fidelity and adaptation in the dissemination of empirically-supported treatments: The promise of transdiagnostic interventions. *Behaviour Research and Therapy, 47*(11), 946–953.

Ong, J. C., Shapiro, S. L., & Manber, R. (2008). Combining mindfulness meditation with cognitive-behavior therapy for insomnia: A treatment-development study. *Behavior Therapy, 39*(2), 171–182.

Öst, L. G. (2008). Efficacy of the third wave of behavioral therapies: A systematic review and meta-analysis. *Behaviour Research and Therapy, 46*(3), 296–321.

Powers, M. B., Zum Vörde Sive Vörding, M. B., & Emmelkamp, P. M. G. (2009). Acceptance and commitment therapy: A meta-analytic review. *Psychotherapy and Psychosomatics, 78,* 73–80.

Rodman, S. A., Daughters, S. B., & Lejuez, C. W. (2009). Distress tolerance and rational-emotive behavior therapy: A new role for behavioral analogue tasks. *Journal of Rational-Emotive & Cognitive Behavior Therapy, 27*(2), 97–120.

Rosen, G. M., & Davison, G. C. (2003). Psychology should list empirically supported principles of change (ESPs) and not credential trademarked therapies or other treatment packages. *Behavior Modification, 27,* 300–312.

Sanderson, W. C. (2002). Are evidenced-based psychological interventions practiced by clinicians in the field? *Medscape Mental Health, 7*, 1–3.

Segal, Z. V., Williams, J. M. G., & Teasdale, J. D. (2002). *Mindfulness-based cognitive therapy for depression: A new approach to preventing relapse.* New York, NY: Guilford Press.

Smits, J. A., Powers, M. B., Cho, Y., & Telch, M. J. (2004). Mechanism of change in cognitive-behavioral treatment of panic disorder: Evidence for the fear of fear mediational hypothesis. *Journal of Consulting and Clinical Psychology, 72*, 646–652.

Smits, J. A. J., Rosenfield, D., Telch, M. J., & McDonald, R. (2006). Cognitive mechanisms of social anxiety reduction: An examination of specificity and temporality. *Journal of Consulting and Clinical Psychology, 74*, 1203–1212.

Vilardaga, R., Hayes, S. C., Levin, M., & Muto, T. (2009). Creating a strategy for progress: A contextual behavioral science approach. *Behavior Analyst.*

Vowles, K. E., McNeil, D. W., Gross, R. T., McDaniel, M. L., Mouse, A., Bates, M.,…McCall, C. (2007). Effects of pain acceptance and pain control strategies on physical impairment in individuals with chronic low back pain. *Behavior Therapy, 38*, 412–425.

Wampold, B. E. (2001). *The great psychotherapy debate: Models, methods, and findings.* Mahwah, NJ: Erlbaum.

Wells, A. (2008). *Metacognitive therapy for anxiety and depression.* New York: Guilford.

Wicksell, R. K., Melin, L., & Olsson, G. L. (2007). Exposure and acceptance in the rehabilitation of children and adolescents with chronic pain. *European Journal of Pain, 11*, 267–274.

Zettle, R. D. (2005). The evolution of a contextual approach to therapy: From comprehensive distancing to ACT. *International Journal of Behavioral Consultation and Therapy, 1*(2), 77–89.

Zettle, R. D., & Hayes, S. C. (1986). Dysfunctional control by client verbal behavior: The context of reason giving. *The Analysis of Verbal Behavior, 4*, 30–38.

Zettle, R. D., & Rains, J. C. (1989). Group cognitive and contextual therapies in treatment of depression. *Journal of Clinical Psychology, 45*, 438–445

Zettle, R. D., Rains, J. C., & Hayes, S. C. (in press). Processes of change in acceptance and commitment therapy and cognitive therapy for depression: A meditational reanalysis of Zettle and Rains (1989). *Behavior Modification.*

# 13

## Mindfulness and Acceptance in Cognitive Behavior Therapy

### What's New?

MARVIN R. GOLDFRIED

> God grant me the serenity
> to accept the things I cannot change;
> courage to change the things I can;
> and wisdom to know the difference.
>
> Living one day at a time;
> Enjoying one moment at a time.
>
> —Reinhold Niebuhr

Cognitive behavior therapy (CBT) has clearly come a long way since the 1970s, when cognitive constructs began to be introduced into behavior therapy. Most recently, notions such as mindfulness and acceptance have clearly broadened the scope of what we now call "cognitive behavior therapy." With this added complexity, there has also come controversy and confusion (see Herbert & Forman, in press). I consider it both an honor and a challenge to have been asked to comment on the current state of CBT.

Having arrived at Stony Brook as an assistant professor in 1964, I feel it is safe to say that behavior therapy, CBT, and I grew up together professionally. As a participant in, and observer of, the development of the field, I have my own perspective on where we now are in comparison to how we started. Although history has never been my strong suit, I am relying on long-term memory to inform me about where we have come from, along with my knowledge of what is going on clinically and empirically to comment on what is happening now and—far more risky—where I believe we need to go in the future.

To provide a context for the contributions to this volume, I begin with a brief history of CBT, followed by another contextual framework based on relevant observations coming from the sociology of science. I then comment on what is new in CBT, particularly as it relates to the role of cognition, behavior, and emotion. I follow this with a commentary on the growing movement to delineate empirically based principles of change that transcend varying intervention procedures, and end with some thoughts about where we go from here.

## A BRIEF HISTORY OF COGNITIVE BEHAVIOR THERAPY

Most of the early work on the development of behavior therapy occurred in both the United States and United Kingdom in the late 1950s. In response to their increasing dissatisfaction with the speculative nature of psychoanalysis, a number of more empirically minded therapists and researchers suggested that "modern learning theory" might serve as a firmer and more promising foundation on which to develop therapeutic interventions. During the 1960s, the very significant growth of what was to be called "behavior therapy" took place, which involved the extrapolation of research findings on classical and operant conditioning from the laboratory to the clinic. Clearly, the current, presumably new emphasis on "translational research" is really not all that new.

Initially, behavior therapists sought out the work on classical and operant conditioning in the development of their intervention procedures. However, it was also recognized by some that other research findings (e.g., on attitude change) might have relevance for clinical application and that, indeed, it was a mistake to consider behavior therapy as merely representing a new "school." In our book *Clinical Behavior Therapy*, Davison and I maintained that it would be more appropriate to view behavior therapy as

> reflecting a general orientation to clinical work that aligns itself philosophically with an experimental approach to the study of human behavior. The assumption basic to this particular orientation is that the problematic behavior seen within the clinical setting can best be understood in light of those principles derived from a wide variety of psychological experimentation, and that these principles have implications for behavior change within the clinical setting.
>
> (Goldfried & Davison, 1976, pp. 3–4)

Not surprisingly, the emergence of behavior therapy resulted in a major conflict between this new approach and more traditional psychoanalytic therapy. It was not unusual for behavior therapists to begin their articles, chapters, and books with comments on how psychoanalytic therapy would deal with a given problem, how this was misguided, and how behavior therapy provided a preferable alternative. For their part, psychoanalytic therapists argued that behavior therapy was not only naïve, but also Machiavellian in its premise. The fact that we used the language of methodological behaviorism (e.g., manipulation, control) no doubt contributed to this antagonism. In response to accusations that behavior therapy represented a form of control and brainwashing, many of us decided to place an emphasis on "self-control," so as to communicate the attempt to have clients serve as their own therapists (Goldfried & Merbaum, 1973; Thoresen & Mahoney, 1974). Because of the misunderstandings associated with this term, the approach was later described as one in which clients would be taught "coping skills" (Goldfried, 1980).

In the late 1960s, a number of behavior therapists began to entertain the idea that cognitive variables might play an important role in understanding and changing problematic behaviors. A very provocative article by Breger and McGaugh (1965), which appeared in the *Psychological Bulletin*, took behavior therapy to task for considering only operant and classical conditioning in understanding and changing human behavior. In essence, they were referring to the importance of the emerging area of cognitive psychology, which they maintained held important potential for psychotherapy interventions. Shortly thereafter, several faculty members at Stony Brook (including Davison, D'Zurilla, Valins, and myself) began to entertain the possibility of incorporating relevant cognitive variables into behavior therapy. We organized a symposium at the 1968 American Psychological Association convention entitled "Cognitive Process in Behavior Modification, " which was described as follows:

> The predominant conceptualization of the "Behavior Therapies" as conditioning techniques involving little or no cognitive influence on behavior change is questioned. It is suggested that current procedures should be modified and new procedures developed to capitalize upon the human organism's unique capacity for cognitive control.

Levin and Hayes (in press) are correct in their observation that the introduction of cognition into behavior therapy was based more on clinical need than available research data. Although there was relatively little work at the time being carried out in cognitive psychology, the contributions of Bandura (1969), Mischel (1968), and Peterson (1968) served as an important basis for justifying the introduction of cognition into behavior therapy.

Early attempts to integrate cognitive constructs into behavior therapy met with considerable resistance among some, particularly those whose work was based on operant conditioning. Nonetheless, an increasing number of behavior therapists who attempted to apply only classical and operant conditioning in therapeutic interventions with outpatient adults began to realize that cognitive methods of intervention were needed. As a result, such behavior therapists as Davison, Lazarus, Mahoney, Meichenbaum, and I formed a liaison with Beck and Ellis, who had developed interventions that were solely cognitive in nature. Those of us who were behavior therapists began to incorporate the contributions of both Beck and Ellis, who also made modifications in their cognitive approach to incorporate some behavioral constructs, such as Beck's use of behavioral activation (Beck, Rush, Shaw, & Emery, 1979). Over time, the number of behavior therapists who experienced the constraints of using only learning theory in their interventions increased, leading numerous others to incorporate cognitive interventions in their clinical work. Indeed, by the early 1980s, cognitive behavior therapy was the mainstream orientation of members of the Association for Advancement of Behavior Therapy (AABT).

In the mid-1980s, however, confusion began as to what exactly constituted "cognitive behavior therapy." In the National Institute for Mental Health (NIMH) collaborative study for the treatment of depression, which compared Beck's cognitive therapy with interpersonal therapy, the cognitive intervention was inaccurately described as "cognitive behavior therapy" (Elkin, Parloff, Hadley, & Autry, 1985). Although Beck was very clear that his approach should be considered "cognitive therapy" (Hollon & Beck, 1986), the cognitive therapy manual employed in the study (Beck, et al., 1979) was used to define "cognitive behavior therapy." As a consequence, much of what constituted essential CBT interventions of the 1970s and 1980s (e.g., behavior rehearsal, assertiveness training, modeling, reinforcement, relaxation training, desensitization, problem solving) had been eclipsed by cognitive therapy—in which the function of behavioral activation or experiments is to correct distorted cognitions. To this day, some (e.g., Levin & Hayes, in press) continue to use "cognitive behavior therapy" and "cognitive therapy" interchangeably.

The difference between cognitive behavior therapy and cognitive therapy may be illustrated in a therapy process analysis that compared Beck, Meichenbaum, and Strupp in their therapy with the case of Richard, who presented with depression following the breakup of his marriage (Goldsamt, Goldfried, A. Hayes, & Kerr, 1992). The process analysis revealed that all three therapists were comparable in their tendency to focus on the impact that other individuals may have made on Richard (e.g., "Richard, what did you think and how did you feel when your wife said that to you?"). There was a difference, however, between Meichenbaum's intervention with CBT and Beck's with cognitive therapy, in that the former focused much more on how Richard's behavior impacted on others (e.g., "What might you have done to make your wife angry at you?"). Interestingly enough, both Meichenbaum and Strupp—who was demonstrating relationally oriented psychodynamic therapy—were more comparable in this therapeutic focus. Thus, while both CBT and psychodynamic interventions were similar to cognitive therapy in exploring how Richard interpreted other people's behaviors, both additionally focused on the impact Richard made on others. A subsequent therapy process evaluation of cognitive therapy for depression similarly found this tendency to pay more attention to the impact that others made on clients than on how clients' behavior affected other individuals in their lives (Castonguay, Hayes, Goldfried, & DeRubeis, 1995).

The work of Jacobson, one of the early behavior therapists in the field, together with his colleagues, revisited the role that behavior therapy can play in the treatment of depression (Jacobson et al., 1996). In their initial work in this area, Jacobson and his colleagues found that the behavioral activation component of cognitive therapy, which encourages clients to schedule activities that they might enjoy and feel a sense of mastery with, was just as effective as an intervention that followed the complete cognitive therapy treatment manual. A later study by Dimidjian and her associates (Dimidjian et al., 2006) enhanced the behavioral activation intervention so as to incorporate more traditional behavior therapy procedures (e.g., use of behavioral skill training to increase the likelihood that clients will obtain what they want and need). In doing so, they found that what they called "behavioral activation"—which I prefer to think of as behavior therapy—was more effective than cognitive therapy in treating more severely depressed patients. These findings are consistent with the results of a study by Hayes, Castonguay, and Goldfried (1996), which indicated that cognitive therapy for depression had more of a positive impact when it focused on making actual behavioral changes in interpersonal relationships than on clients' perceptions of these relationships. A follow-up analysis of the Dimidjian and colleagues' dataset revealed that those patients who were not responsive to cognitive therapy were found to be more depressed, more impaired in their behavioral functioning, and exhibited relational problems (Coffman et al., 2007).

Some years ago, Davison and I described what we believed to be a more comprehensive functional analysis of depression, suggesting that depression can result from "*a perceived absence of any contingency between the person's own efforts and the reinforcing nature of the consequences that follow*" (Goldfried & Davison, 1976, p. 234). Within this conceptualization, the important maintaining variables may be *cognitive* ("perceived absence of any contingency"), *behavioral* ("person's own efforts"), and/or *environmental* ("consequences that follow"). Without denying genetic or biological predisposition, it was suggested that individuals may become depressed because they cognitively distort their inability to make an impact, because they lack the ability to do so, and/ or because they are in a life circumstance that does not yield to their efforts, however competent such efforts may be. Rather than devising an intervention based on a specific theoretical model that emphasized one maintaining variable over another, it would appear to make clinical sense to conduct an individualized case formulation, so as to highlight the variable or variables that may be playing the functional role.

In our eagerness to delve into the varying ways that cognition can have an impact on emotion and behavior, we as cognitive behavior therapists may have gotten too caught up in our emphasis on cognition. I fear that when we become actively involved in pursuit of a particular approach and try to convey its merits to others, it is all too easy to lose perspective. Indeed, I can well relate to that, as my emotional involvement in the attempt to introduce cognition into behavior therapy in the 1960s and 1970s prevented me from acknowledging the limitations of cognitive interventions. Indeed, the contributions by Levin and Hayes (in press), Martell and Kanter (in press), Linehan (as described in Robins & Rosenthal, in press) and K. G. Wilson, Bordieri, Flynn, Lucas, and Slater (in press) are similar, in that they can all be viewed as reminders of our behavioral roots, so as not to neglect the important role that learned behavior and functional analyses may have in the development and treatment of clinical problems.

The differing positions described in this volume and elsewhere reflect the different interpretations as to what constitutes "cognitive behavior therapy." However, the controversy goes beyond this, raising questions as to whether we are indeed experiencing a qualitatively new "wave" in the development of the field. What does acceptance and commitment therapy, for example, represent for those of us who call ourselves cognitive behavior therapists? Where do constructs such as mindfulness, acceptance, and metacognition—which are, after all, cognitive—fit into CBT? What about the place of behavioral activation? What is the role of emotion in bringing about change? I suspect that the ongoing debates on these questions may be rooted in a much larger issue, an issue that sociologists have documented as existing within scientific exploration more generally: namely, scientific competition.

# SOCIOLOGY OF SCIENCE

While we have been busy studying human behavior and the therapeutic change process, sociologists have been studying us. This is a specialty within sociology that focuses on the behavior of scientists, which I believe has relevance to the disagreements reflected in this volume.

In their work, sociologists of science have made the important distinction between the *core* of scientific knowledge and the *research frontier* (Cole, 1992). The core is defined as those findings within a given field about which there is a consensus among the research community, whereas the research frontier represents the cutting edge. Research by Cole (1992) on the grant review process has, interestingly enough, found that there is just as much disagreement among the natural sciences as there is among the social sciences at this cutting edge. Indeed, Cole suggests that whether a research grant proposal gets approved depends as much on the reviewer as on the merit of the application itself. However, the difference between psychotherapy research and practice and the natural sciences is that we do not have a core.

Part of the problem we have in obtaining a consensus may be traced to the fact that there is a long history of disagreement between researchers and practicing clinicians as to whose contributions are more important. Also relevant is that psychotherapy researchers and practitioners have the tendency to overlook past contributions in the field. For example, in an article describing how play therapy may be integrated into "cognitive-behavior therapy" for children, it was suggested that puppets could be used to model cognitive strategies and appropriate behaviors (Knell, 1998). The author refers to her contribution as "cognitive-behavioral play therapy," being the "offspring, and perhaps the newest and youngest" products of Beck's cognitive therapy. What she did not recognize was that this discovery was more than 50 years old. Chittenden (1942) described this very procedure in 1942, using doll play as a method for having children model cooperative behavior. Moreover, numerous other cognitive behavior therapists and theorists have described similar procedures as being an important foundation of behavior therapy (e.g., Bandura, 1969; Lazarus, 1960, Meichenbaum, 1977).

I have argued elsewhere that there are several factors that may prevent psychotherapy research and practice from forming a core, among which are theoretical differences, the importance of what is new, and the nature of the scientific social system itself (Goldfried, 2000). These variables are particularly relevant to the issues reflected in this volume.

## Theoretical Barriers

As noted by Herbert and Forman (in press), Kurt Lewin (1952) once suggested that "There is nothing more practical than a good theory" (p. 169). However, much depends on how one decides on whether the theory is "good" or not. Moreover, theories can be problematic because of the theoretician behind the theory. As noted by Boring (1964) in his discussion of the tenacity with which theoreticians will hold on to their theories, "A theory which has built up in the author's image of himself has become part of him. To abandon it would be suicidal, or at least an act of self-mutilation" (p. 682). The situation becomes even more complicated in an applied field such as psychotherapy, where social, political, and economic networks may continue to support the theory even after the limitations of the approach have been documented.

In his classic article "Are theories of learning necessary?" Skinner (1950) questioned the wisdom of building a research program around the attempt to support a particular theoretical position, maintaining:

> . . . that a theory generates research does not prove its value unless the research is valuable. Much useless experimentation results from theories, and much energy and skill are absorbed by them. Most theories are the eventually overthrown, and the greater part of the associated research is discarded. (p. 194)

Without mentioning any names, Skinner was referring to the competition that existed between Hull and Tolman, whose adversarial theoretical positions on the process of learning generated extensive research by each group—most of which has been forgotten with the demise of the theories and theorists.

Discussing the role of theory in science, Kuhn (1962) has argued that theories determine what questions will be asked and what will be viewed as a finding worth considering. In essence, our theories of therapy may be thought of as "theoretical schemas." By filling in the gaps, schemas may help us attend to issues that have not yet been observed or, because of their schematic nature, may lead to bias. Some years ago, Norman R. F. Maier (1960), referring to the bias existing in learning theory and research, developed what he called "Maier's law," which states that *"if the facts do not conform to the theory, they must be disposed of. . ."* (p. 208). This law was dramatically confirmed in a study by Mahoney (1976), who devised two versions of a manuscript that he sent to journal reviewers. The versions had identical Introduction and Methods sections, but different Results and Discussion. He found that when the results favored the reviewers' theoretical bias (radical behavioral), the manuscript was more likely to be accepted for publication than when they went counter to the reviewer's orientation. Moreover, when rejected for publication, the reviewers were more likely to find fault with the methodology than when the results were favorable.

## The Importance of What Is New

A typical association to "new" is "improved." To examine this association further, I once asked in group of graduate students to list as many associations as they could, within the course of one minute each, to the words "new" and "old." In reviewing their responses, the vast majority of associations with "new" were universally positive in nature, including such words as "good," "better," and "fresh." Not so with their associations to "old." Only half of the terms generated by "old" had positive connotations, such as "experienced," "established," and "wise." The remaining were clearly negative, including such terms as "boring," "decrepit," and "worn out." Indeed, Webster's *New Collegiate Dictionary* defines new as "of dissimilar origin and usually of superior quality," as in "introducing new blood." Very much in accord with the graduate students' associations, old is also defined "showing the effects of time or use" and "no longer in use: Discarded," as in "old rags."

Referring to the proliferation of therapy interventions, Kendall (2009) has recently commented on this issue, noting that the field is "easily seduced by 'new approaches,'" adding that these innovations "may be new in the labels used to describe them and new in the followers who are attracted to them, but are they new—genuinely different from existing approaches?" (p. 20).

As viewed within the broader context of scientific advancement, there is no question but that what is new is viewed as cutting-edge and important. With a field that has an agreed-upon core, it is indeed the research frontier that receives most of the attention. In the absence of an agreed-upon core, however, excessive focus on the cutting edge is unlikely to help the field progress in any meaningful way.

## The Norms of Science

When sociologists began writing about the behavior of scientists, their depiction was somewhat idealistic—if not naïve. For example, Merton (1942) originally described scientists as having the following four characteristics: (a) they were objective and used agreed-upon criteria in evaluating new knowledge; (b) the knowledge that they produced belonged to the entire scientific community; (c) their satisfaction rested solely with making contributions to the field; and (d) their judgments were based on logic and data, not on their personal beliefs. However, after several years of actually studying the behavior of researchers, Merton (1957) revised his original ideas. Indeed, his research found that there existed fierce competition within a given field, where debates existed over the priority of discovery, namely who got there first. His belief was that this competition not only reflected on the characteristics of the individual researchers, but also on the system in general, in that professional recognition typically goes to those who make discoveries. Indeed, one's career is advanced by making history, not knowing it.

Mitroff (1974), who studied the behavior of Apollo Moon scientists, revised Merton's four characteristics to more accurately reflect what actually goes on, namely: (a) the evaluation of any piece of research depends as much on the reputation of the researcher as well as any objective criteria; (b) rather than findings belonging to the entire scientific community, they are owned by the scientist who discovered them; (c) instead of knowledge for knowledge's sake, researchers are motivated to obtain findings that will be consistent with the beliefs of their reference group; and (d) researchers' personal beliefs are not set aside, and any skepticism that does exist is about the findings of others. Cole (1992), a student of Merton, reported on the social and political processes involved in research communities, suggesting that "scientists who are attuned to and adept at manipulating these...social processes will experience more career success than those who are not attuned or are less adept" (p. 181). All this was dramatically illustrated by Watson (1968), who offered an account in *The Double Helix* of the competitive side of scientists involved in the research on the DNA molecule. Researchers were people before they became researchers, and the extent that they continue to be people means that they will be influenced by all those forces to which humans are subjected.

## WHAT'S NEW IN COGNITIVE BEHAVIOR THERAPY?

Although behavior therapists used to compete with psychodynamic therapists, and cognitive behavior therapists used to clash with behavior therapists, we as cognitive behavior therapists seem to have reached a point where we are now arguing among ourselves. The work described above by sociologists of science provides a useful context within which to better understand such disagreements. With this context, we can now examine more closely the nature of the varying approaches appearing in this volume.

As suggested earlier, it is more appropriate to view behavior therapy and CBT as a generic label that includes numerous interventions. Our approach to therapy is based on the assumption that human behavior may be best understood in terms of both cognitive and behavioral variables, and that these may fruitfully be incorporated into therapeutic interventions. As Hofmann and colleagues (in press) have noted in considering cognitive behavioral interventions, sometimes the cognition appears before the behavior, but other times afterward. It can mediate how we feel, and it can negate the adequacy of what we do. Included among the cognitions addressed by cognitive-behavior therapists are:

- Acceptance of self and/or others
- Reattribution of another's motives
- Telling oneself a thought is just a thought
- Self-instructions for carrying out a task
- Attention redeployment
- Recognizing the impact others have on us
- Recognizing the impact one has on others
- Relabeling of internal sensations of anxiety
- Perception of being in control
- Being mindful of own's thoughts, emotions, and/or behaviors
- Re-evaluating a distorted belief

It is certainly possible to generate a still longer list of cognitions, as well as a comparably long list of relevant behaviors and emotions. The key question with regard to therapeutic utility is not to which school of thought specific cognitions, behaviors, or emotions belong, but rather the circumstances under which a focus on these variables may be useful in bringing about therapeutic change. As suggested earlier, the selection of those determinants in need of change depends on one's individualized case formulation—a point emphasized by Martell and Kanter (in press). Functional analysis in case formulation is still alive and well, and the focus of an intervention depends on the role being played by cognitions, behaviors, or emotions.

## The Role of Cognition

Most of the contributions described in this collection focus on cognitive interventions that directly attempt to change some aspect of the client's functioning. Various terms have been suggested for the way in which cognitive interventions work, such as "distancing," "decentering," "metacognition," "witnessing" and "reflective functioning." What they all seem to have in common is that they involve *self-observation.* Interestingly enough, Freud recognized the importance of having patients step back and view themselves in a descriptive, nonevaluative way. He referred to this as a function of the "observing ego," which aligns itself with the therapist's ability to observe the more maladaptive aspects of the patient's functioning. Sullivan similarly discussed the importance of self-observation when he described therapists as being "participant-observers," interacting with their patients but also observing the nature of the interaction. Much of what we do as therapists when we provide feedback to our clients about their thoughts, feelings, and actions, is in the hope that they will become better observers of their own behavior.

In one of the earliest books written on CBT, Meichenbaum (1977) characterized the role of self-observation as being at the core of cognitive-behavioral interventions:

> The first step in the change process is the client's becoming an observer of his own behavior. Through heightened awareness and deliberate attention, the client monitors, with increased sensitivity, his thoughts, feelings, physiological reactions, and/or interpersonal behaviors. As a result of the translation process that occurs in therapy, the client develops new cognitive structures (concepts) which permit him to view his symptoms differently. Attending to one's maladaptive behaviors takes on a different meaning—a meeting that contributes to a heightened vigilance or "raised consciousness." (p. 219)

In our own research on the process of change, we found that experienced cognitive behavior therapists placed more focus on the client's self-observations in portions of a session they deemed to be particularly therapeutic (Goldfried, Raue, & Castonguay, 1998). The same finding was obtained with interpersonally orientated psychodynamic therapists, who similarly focused on the client's self-observation (called "reflective functioning") during what they deemed to be the significant portion of the session.

The popularity of mindfulness in contemporary CBT is of considerable interest, especially since the practice of Buddhism clearly predates the practice of psychotherapy. And while it may be "in" as an intervention in CBT, it is not "new." For example, Shapiro (1978), in his book *Precision Nirvana,* as well as in his subsequent work in this area, described how Zen meditation may be used within behavior therapy as a technique to help clients self-regulate their anxiety. Similarly, Marlatt and Marques (1977) described how behavior therapists can make use of meditation to assist undergraduates in reducing their alcohol use. For an interesting account of the ongoing role of meditation in Marlatt's own life over the years—professional and personal—see his more recent account (Marlatt, 2006).

Meditation, as being aware and being in the moment, can serve the function of helping clients become more accepting of what they observe. A particularly important application of mindful meditation is with clients suffering from chronic depression, who are at risk of experiencing repeated episodes. Hofmann and colleagues (in press) cite the important contribution of Teasdale (1988), who suggested that becoming depressed about being depressed during these reoccurrences can serve to exacerbate their symptomotology. As described by Fresco and colleagues (in press), such individuals may benefit from changing how they construe a recurrence of depression when it occurs, as is the case with mindfulness-based cognitive therapy (Segal, Williams, & Teasdale, 2002). Salmon and Sephton (in press) advocate having clients engage in meditative practices to attain the ability to self-observe and accept. However, it should be recognized that not all clients may have the diligence required for the practice of meditation, and alternate methods of self-observation and acceptance may prove to be more practical—and just as effective—with some clients.

It is not surprising that it was in the 1970s—a time known for experimentation with "new age" practices—that the teachings of Buddhism gained considerable popularity in the United States. One particularly successful endeavor was developed by Werner Erhart (born John Rosenberg), called "Erhart Seminars Training" or *est* (Latin for "it is"). Involving two grueling weekend-long large-group seminars, the goal was to get "it." The presentations and exercises were based on the teachings of Buddhism, together with the work of such individuals as Dale Carnegie and Abraham Maslow. At the end of the second weary weekend, when participants—myself included—reflected on and complained about the emotional and physical ups and downs they experienced during the training, it was pointed out that these experiences and emotions were indeed a microcosm of their lives, and therefore we needed to accept "it." In addition to accepting what was, the other major lesson presented by est was that participants' lives would be better—both for themselves and in their relationships—if they lived up to their commitments.

Not only was *est* popular in general; it also caught the attention of some psychologists. In fact, two radical behaviorists—Baer and Stolz (1978)—argued that the training was not inconsistent with a behavioral orientation, and outlined what they viewed as the key aspects of *est*. Baer and Stolz characterized the notion of acceptance as follows:

> You can plan the future, but you cannot determine it. You will have to take it as it comes.... this is in no sense despair, but rather an amused recognition that very little goes as it was planned to go, or hoped for. (pp. 57–58)

They go on to add that "...loss of a loved one, defeat in competition, or unpredicted deprivations are accepted as natural events in a determined universe, rather than reasons for depression or despair" (p. 58). The learning that occurs in est, argued Baer and Stolz, was "...the establishment of a new repertoire, specifiable only as an increased awareness of their experience of shift in personal epistemology or context..." and "...more consistency in keeping agreements" (pp. 61–62).

The current focus on acceptance by different therapy approaches seems to serve different functions. With acceptance and commitment therapy (ACT), the goal is to defuse the negative emotional reaction clients may have to certain thoughts by recognizing that a thought is just a thought (Levin & Hayes, in press; Wilson et al., in press). The finding by Jacobson and his colleagues that behavioral couple therapy was not able to produce the needed change in the individuals gave rise to an approach that emphasized the need for each person in a relationship to accept the other as he or she is (McGinn, Benson, & Christensen, in press). And the use of acceptance in the context of dialectical behavior therapy serves the function of allowing the rejection-sensitive borderline patient to be more willing to consider the possibility of change (Robins & Rosenthal, in press).

I sometimes wonder whether cognitive behavior therapists' current interest in acceptance reflects the growing maturity of our orientation. In the early days of behavior therapy and cognitive behavior therapy, we approached the change process with a new optimism. We could do better than psychodynamic therapy, and we were going to prove it. And while there is no doubt that we have succeeded in ways not achieved by other orientations, we may be starting to recognize that we sometimes fall short of our hopes to bring about change. Because of biological and constitutional limitations, seriously adverse early learning experiences, the limitations of certain interventions to produce meaningful change in individuals, and what we simply do not know at this point in time, we need to accept the fact that change is not always possible.

## The Role of Behavior

Our emphasis on the importance of cognitive interventions—and our tendency to confuse cognitive therapy with CBT—may have caused us at times to underemphasize the very important role that behavior plays in the therapeutic change process. As a cognitive behavior therapist, I find it refreshing that renewed emphasis is being placed on behavioral interventions, as reflected in the work on behavioral activation, dialectical behavior therapy, and acceptance and commitment therapy.

For some cognitive behavior therapists, it might not be necessary to reintroduce behavioral interventions to what they do clinically, as these interventions never left. For them, the treatment of choice for anxiety disorders involves behavioral exposure—sometimes with and sometimes without the aid of relaxation or other interventions such as mindfulness training as a coping skill. This is certainly the case in the treatment of specific phobias and OCD. In numerous other clinical instances, clients lack the behavioral skills to cope with situations in their lives, be they intrapersonal or interpersonal in nature. Thus the anxiety that some individuals may experience in test-taking situations may be traced to the difficulty they have in learning the material. In such cases, the treatment of choice may involve teaching study skills. In interpersonal situations, individuals may be depressed because they do not get what they want, and may be unable to get what they want because they lack self-assertiveness skills. Under such circumstances, assertion training—which may also involve cognitive interventions—would be in order.

In short, the efficacy of behavioral interventions needs to be recognized in any comprehensive functional analysis of a clinical problem. As noted earlier, in my reading of the material on behavioral activation, I view this approach as very closely resembling original behavior therapy methods. It is perhaps unfortunate that the term *behavioral activation* is used, as it can easily be confused with the behavioral scheduling associated with cognitive therapy, when it actually involves much more, such as skill training.

## The Role of Emotion

Although G. T. Wilson (1982) emphasized the important role of emotion in the therapy change process several decades ago, relatively little emphasis has been placed on emotional variables within CBT. To be sure, emotion is taken into account in exposure for anxiety disorders, with the need to activate the arousal system in order to produce change. However, there is more to the role of emotion in the change process.

In contrast to CBT or cognitive therapy, our psychodynamic and experiential colleagues have long underscored the importance of emotional experiencing. In presenting a psychodynamic point of view, Strupp and Binder (1984) have suggested that what is usually described as "insight" actually refers to patients' "affective experiencing and cognitive understanding of the current maladaptive patterns of behavior that repeat childhood patterns of interpersonal conflict" (pp. 24–25). Greenberg and Safran (1987) have maintained that the lack of emotional awareness in interpersonal relationships can result in numerous problems between individuals, keeping people uninformed about some of the essential determinants of their behavior and the behavior of others. It should be noted that in the present volume, Leahy (in press) has strongly emphasized emotion-based interventions within a cognitive-behavioral framework, as opposed to what all too often involves a didactic, emotion-free intervention. Indeed, research by Castonguay and colleagues (Castonguay & Beutler, 2006) indicates that cognitive therapy for depression was more efficacious when therapists focused on clients' emotional experience.

Recent work in neuroscience has addressed the role of emotion, demonstrating that two different routes of emotional processing exist in the brain, with one involving the neurocortex and the other bypassing it (LeDoux, 1996). Thus, emotional reactions may not always involve cognitive mediation, and the way therapists deal with emotions may depend upon whether or not emotion is a conditioned reaction that is not a function of cognition. As noted by Fresco and colleagues (in press), the distinction made by Teasdale (1993) on the difference between propositional and implicational meaning is particularly relevant in this regard, with the former referring to denotative meaning and the latter to the more global, affective associations. Thus the propositional meaning of the term *springtime* is that it is a period of time between the winter and summer when trees and flowers begin to bloom. On the other hand, the implication meaning can carry with it such emotional reactions as rebirth, rejuvenation, and the feeling of well-being. Moreover, there may also be individualized emotional associations to springtime; someone who was subjected to traumatic loss in the spring may see the season as a very sad and stressful period.

The promising research that has been done on the clinical use of the two-chair technique by Greenberg and colleagues (e.g., Greenberg & Watson, 2006) can inform the way that emotion-focused interventions may be used within the context of CBT. If an individual is attempting to learn a more realistic way of putting certain unrealistic, emotionally laden cognitions into perspective, they can enact these two ways of thinking by espousing each while sitting in a different chair—each representing a different part of their thinking and feeling. Although practicing cognitive behavior therapists have used this procedure for several years, I know of no controlled clinical research that demonstrates the efficacy of this technique within a cognitive behavioral framework. Nonetheless, favorable clinical experiences reported by numerous colleagues—including Leahy (in press)—indicate that clients find this method to provide them with a sense of mindfulness regarding their distorted cognitions, and also to report meaning shifts in their perceptions of others and themselves. By having the client obtain a metacognitive awareness of distorted emotional meaning using this procedure, one comes close to what may be thought of as an in vivo intervention.

## STAGES OF THERAPY AND PRINCIPLES OF CHANGE

Given the diversity of procedures described in this volume, the question may be raised as to whether or not there are any points of agreement. I would suggest that they do reflect a core, and may usefully be understood within the context of more general stages of change and the principles that cut across different therapeutic approaches.

Therapy interventions, whether they consist of the interventions that fall into the general category of CBT or are based on other orientations, may be thought of as following four general stages. At the outset of therapy, patients typically present for therapy having problems in their lives, either not knowing why the problems exist, or having misconceptions as to their cause. Regardless of their understanding of these problems, it is typical that patients display an ineffectiveness or incompetence in dealing with the events with which they are confronted. At this initial point in the change process, they may be thought of as being in the stage of *unconscious incompetence*. As they begin therapy, interacting with a therapist who establishes an optimal alliance, clients become better aware of the factors—current and/or historical—that may have contributed to their incompetence. With this awareness, they move to the next stage of change, namely *conscious incompetence*. Using this understanding of the variables/determinants/dynamics that contribute to their incompetence, clients then begin to take deliberate steps to change their problematic thoughts, feelings, and behaviors—which brings them to the third phase of treatment, *conscious competence.* There then occurs an ongoing learning process (working through?), whereby new ways of thinking, feeling, and acting are attempted. In those instances in which we are successful therapeutically, new and more effective ways of functioning are learned and become less effortful and more automatic. Hence, the final phase of treatment is to reach the point of *unconscious competence.*

By focusing on this middle level of abstraction—somewhere between one's theoretical orientation and specific intervention techniques—it is also possible to examine more specific underlying principles that may be associated with the therapeutic change process. Responding to the growing interest in delineating principles of change (e.g., Rosen & Davison, 2003; Westen, Novotny, & Thompson-Brenner, 2004), Castonguay and Beutler (2006) have provided a comprehensive review of those research-based principles that operate across different approaches to therapy.

In a recent discussion of therapy change principles, I (Goldfried, 2009) suggested that the therapeutic change process involves the following commonalities:

1.  At the outset of treatment, it is important for the client to either arrive with or develop a *positive expectation* that therapy can help, and at least a minimal level of *motivation* to engage in the process.
2.  The appropriate expectation, motivation level, and active participation on the part of the client can be influenced by the nature of the *therapy alliance*, which involves a working agreement between therapist and client based on a good interpersonal bond, and agreement on the therapeutic goals and methods.
3.  A great deal of what we do in therapy—whether we consider ourselves cognitive behavior therapists or not—is to help clients to *become better aware* of those factors that contribute to their problems.
4.  With such an awareness, clients are ready to actively take steps to produce changes and have *corrective experiences* that can alter their thinking, feeling, and actions.
5.  Doing things differently and having corrective experiences further enhances their awareness of what does and does not currently work in their lives, which can produce still further real-life corrective experiences—along with still further awareness. It becomes a synergy between thoughts, emotions, and behaviors, which may be thought of as *ongoing reality testing.*

Like the four stages of change described above, these principles are still at a relatively high level of abstraction, and do not specify what the therapist actually needs to do in order to implement the principles. Thus, decisions need to be made as to the nature of the awareness that needs to be enhanced and the methods of doing so—which constitute the parameters of the more general principle. With respect to cognitive-affective interventions, depending upon the clinical formulation in any given case and what we know from the research literature, this may involve helping clients to reattribute the motives of a significant other, to re-evaluate a distorted belief, or simply to accept something that cannot be changed—all of which involve the goal of creating a shift in implicational meaning.

## WHERE DO WE GO FROM HERE?

As noted at the outset of this chapter, the conceptual and empirical foundations of behavior therapy were originally based on the dominant research that was present at that time, namely classical and operant conditioning. However, the broader view of behavior therapy and CBT is that they are neither schools nor waves, but rather evidence-based approaches to therapy. Although most of the evidence to date has pointed to the efficacy of either CBT or cognitive therapy, there nonetheless has been a growing body of research to indicate that interventions based on other orientations have empirical support, such as the process-experiential therapy by Greenberg and colleagues (e.g., Greenberg & Watson, 2006). Moreover, research on interpersonal issues has found that difficulties in close relationships are positively associated with depression (Davila & Steinberg, 2006), and that interpersonal therapy can be successful in treating eating disorders (G. T. Wilson, Wilfley, Agras, & Bryson, 2010). Also relevant is the finding that a behavioral intervention that places an emphasis on the importance of relational factors within therapy can produce clinical change (Kohlenberg & Tsai, 1991; Linehan, 1993; McCullough, 2000).

In short, although behavior therapy was originally based on learning research, had other research findings existed at the time—such as the findings we currently have available—our interventions probably would have looked very different, and indeed might not have even been called "behavior therapy." The availability of both basic and applied research findings from which we can now draw for clinical interventions additionally involve cognition, affect, interpersonal relationships, and neuroscience.

When the Association for Advancement of Behavior Therapy (AABT) changed its name to the Association for Behavioral and Cognitive Therapies (ABCT), it was clearly a step in the right direction. However, it may not have gone far enough. Interestingly enough, this very issue was raised more than 30 years ago by two prominent behavior therapists, Arnold Lazarus and Cyril Franks. In an article entitled "Has behavior therapy outlived its usefulness?" Lazarus (1977) commented on the broadening foundation and scope of behavior therapy at the time, particularly as it moved beyond classical and operant conditioning. In his article, he quoted a personal communication by Cyril Franks—one of the founders of AABT—who suggested: "Are we not at this stage in our development basically as an *Association for Advancement of the Scientific Study of Human Interaction*—in all its ramifications?" (in Lazarus, 1977, p. 550). Perhaps it is time to reaffirm our original identity as an organization and orientation that values empirically based interventions by changing the name of our organization to AEBT—the Association for Empirically Based Therapies.

One final point before closing: It is important to recognize that in the attempt to define how our particular approach is different from—if not better than—those of others, we inadvertently undermine the process of forming an agreed-upon core. Human behavior is far too complicated for us to champion a limited subset of variables within the general scope of CBT, and certainly not within the confines of any idiosyncratic theoretical orientation. The question is not *if,* but rather *when* certain variables and interventions are relevant. In short, if we are truly dedicated to advancing the field and helping those in distress, we need to put more of our efforts in knowing what, not who, is right.

# REFERENCES

Baer, D. M., & Stolz, S. B. (1978). A description of the Erhard seminars training (*est*) in terms of behavior analysis. *Behaviorism, 6,* 45–70.

Bandura, A. (1969). *Principles of behavior modification.* New York, NY: Holt, Rinehart, & Winston.

Beck, A. T., Rush, A. J., Shaw, B. F., & Emery, G. (1979). *Cognitive therapy of depression.* New York, NY: Guilford Press.

Boring, E. G. (1964). Cognitive dissonance: Its use in science. *Science, 145,* 680–685.

Breger, L., & McGaugh, J. L. (1965). Critique and reformulation of "learning-theory" approaches to psychotherapy and neurosis. *Psychological Bulletin, 63,* 338–358.

Castonguay, L. G., & Beutler, L. E., (Eds.). (2006). *Principles of therapeutic change that work.* New York, NY: Oxford University Press.

Castonguay, L. G., Goldfried, M. R., Wiser, S. L., Raue, P. J., & Hayes, A. M. (1996). Predicting the effect of cognitive therapy for depression: A study of unique and common factors. *Journal of Consulting and Clinical Psychology, 64,* 497–504.

Castonguay, L. G., Hayes, A. M., Goldfried, M. R., & DeRubeis, R. J. (1995). The focus of therapist interventions in cognitive therapy for depression. *Cognitive Therapy and Research, 19,* 485–503.

Chittenden, G. E. (1942). An experimental study in measuring and modifying assertive behavior in young children. *Monographs of the Society for Research in Child Development, 7* (1, Serial No. 31).

Coffman, S. J., Martell, C. R., Dimidjian, S., Gallop, R., & Hollon, S. D. (2007). Extreme nonresponse in cognitive therapy: Can behavioral activation succeed where cognitive therapy fails? *Journal of Consulting and Clinical Psychology, 75,* 531–541.

Cole, S. (1992). *Making science: Between nature and society.* Cambridge, MA: Harvard University Press.

Davila, J., & Steinberg, S. J. (2006). Depression and romantic dysfunction during adolescence. In T. E. Joiner, J. S. Brown, & J. Kistner (Eds.), *The interpersonal, cognitive, and social nature of depression* (pp. 23–41). Mahwah, NJ: Erlbaum.

Dimidjian, S., Hollon., S. D., Dobson, K. S., Schmaling, K. B., Kohlenberg, R. J., Addis, M. E.,... Jacobson, N. S. (2006). Randomized trial of behavioral activation, cognitive therapy, and antidepressant medication in the acute treatment of adults with major depression. *Journal of Consulting and Clinical Psychology, 74,* 658–670.

Dozois, D. J. A., & Beck, A. T. (in press). Cognitive therapy. In J. D. Herbert & E. M. Forman (Eds.), *Acceptance and mindfulness in cognitive behavior therapy.* Hoboken, NJ: Wiley.

Elkin, I., Parloff, M. B., Hadley, S. W., & Autry, J. H. (1985). NIMH treatment of depression collaborative research program: Background and research plan. *Archives of General Psychiatry, 42,* 305–316.

Fresco, D. M., Flynn, J. J., Mennin, D. S., Emily A. P., & Haigh, E. A. P. (in press). Mindfulness-based cognitive therapy. In J. Herbert and E. Forman (Eds.), *Acceptance and mindfulness in cognitive behavior therapy.* Hoboken, NJ: Wiley.

Goldfried, M. R. (1980). Psychotherapy as coping skills training. In M. J. Mahoney (Ed.) *Psychotherapy process: Current issues and future directions.* New York, NY: Plenum.

Goldfried, M. R. (2000). Consensus in psychotherapy research and practice: Where have all the findings gone? *Psychotherapy Research, 10,* 1–16.

Goldfried, M. R. (2009). Searching for therapy change principles: Are we there yet? *Applied and Preventative Psychology, 13,* 32–34.

Goldfried, M. R., & Davison, G. C. (1976). *Clinical behavior therapy.* New York, NY: Holt, Rinehart & Winston.

Goldfried, M. R., & Davison, G. C. (1994). *Clinical behavior therapy* (expanded ed.). New York, NY: Wiley-Interscience.

Goldfried, M. R., & Merbaum, M. (Eds.) (1973). *Behavior change through self-control.* New York, NY: Holt, Rinehart & Winston.

Goldfried, M. R., Raue, P. J., & Castonguay, L. G. (1998). The therapeutic focus in significant sessions of master therapists: A comparison of cognitive-behavioral and psychodynamic-interpersonal interventions. *Journal of Consulting and Clinical Psychology, 66,* 803–810.

Goldsamt, L. A., Goldfried, M. R., Hayes, A. M., & Kerr, S. (1992). Beck, Meichenbaum, and Strupp: A comparison of three therapies on the dimension of therapist feedback. *Psychotherapy: Theory, Research, Practice, Training, 29,* 167–176.

Greenberg, L. S., & Safran, J. D. (1987). *Emotion in psychotherapy: Affect, cognition, and the process of change.* New York: Guilford.

Greenberg, L. S., & Watson, J. C. (2006). *Emotion-focus therapy for depression.* Washington, DC: American Psychological Association.

Hayes, A. M., Castonguay, L. G., & Goldfried, M. R. (1996). The effectiveness of targeting the vulnerability factors of depression in cognitive therapy. *Journal of Consulting and Clinical Psychology, 64,* 623–627.

Herbert, J. D., & Forman, E. M. (in press). The evolution of cognitive behavior therapy: The rise of psychological acceptance and mindfulness. In J. D. Herbert & E. M. Forman (Eds.), *Acceptance and mindfulness in cognitive behavior therapy.* Hoboken, NJ: Wiley.

Hofmann, S. G., Glombiewski, J. A., Asnaani, A., & Sawyer, A. T. (in press). Mindfulness and acceptance: The perspective of cognitive therapy. In J. Herbert and E. Forman (Eds.). *Acceptance and mindfulness in cognitive behavior therapy.* Hoboken, NJ: Wiley.

Hollon, S. D., & Beck, A. T. (1986). Cognitive and cognitive-behavioral therapies. In S. L. Garfield & A. E. Bergin (Eds.), *Handbook of psychotherapy and behavior change* (3rd ed.) (pp. 443–482). New York, NY: Wiley.

Jacobson, N. S., Dobson, K., Truax, P. A., Addis, M. E., Koerner, K., Gollan, J. K.,... Prince, S. E. (1996). A component analysis of cognitive-behavioral treatment for depression. *Journal of Consulting and Clinical Psychology, 64,* 295–304.

Kendall, P. C. (2009). Principles of therapeutic change circa 2010. *Applied and Preventative Psychology, 13,* 19–21.

Knell, S. M. (1998). Cognitive-behavioral play therapy. *Journal of Clinical Child Psychology, 27,* 28–33.

Kohlenberg, R., & Tsai, M. (1991). *Functional analytic psychotherapy.* New York, NY: Plenum.

Kuhn, T. S. (1962). *The structure of scientific revolutions.* Chicago, IL: University of Chicago Press.

Lazarus, A. A. (1960). The elimination of children's phobias by deconditioning. In H. J. Eysenck (Ed.), *Behavior therapy and the neuroses* (pp. 114–122). New York, NY: Pergamon.

Lazarus, A. A. (1977). Has behavior therapy outlived its usefulness? *American Psychologist, 32,* 550–554.

Leahy, R. L. (in press). Emotional schema therapy: A bridge over troubled waters. In J. Herbert and E. Forman (Eds.), *Acceptance and mindfulness in cognitive behavior therapy.* Hoboken, NJ: Wiley.

LeDoux, J. E. (1996). *The emotional brain: The mysterious underpinnings of emotional life.* New York, NY: Simon and Schuster.

Levin, M., & Hayes. S. C. (in press) Mindfulness and acceptance: The perspective of acceptance and commitment therapy. In J. Herbert and E. Forman (Eds.), *Acceptance and mindfulness in cognitive behavior therapy,* Hoboken, NJ: Wiley.

Lewin, K. (1952). *Field theory in social science: Selected theoretical papers of Kurt Lewin.* London: Tavistock.

Linehan, M. M. (1993). *Cognitive-behavioral treatment of borderline personality disorder.* New York, NY: Guilford Press.

Mahoney, M. J. (1976). *Scientist as subject: The psychological imperative.* Cambridge, MA: Ballinger.

Maier, N. R. F. (1960). Maier's law. *American Psychologist, 15,* 208–212.

Marlatt, G. A. (2006). Mindfulness meditation: Reflections from a personal journey. *Current Psychology, 25,* 155–172.

Marlatt, G. A., & Marques, J. K. (1977). Meditation, self-control, and alcohol use. In R. B. Stuart (Ed.), *Behavioral self-management: Strategies, techniques, and outcomes* (pp. 117–153). New York, NY: Brunner-Mazel.

Martell, C. R., & Kanter, J. (in press). Behavioral activation in the context of "third wave" therapies. In J. Herbert and E. Forman (Eds.), *Acceptance and mindfulness in cognitive behavior therapy.* Hoboken, NJ: Wiley.

McCullough, J. P., Jr. (2000). *Treatment for chronic depression: Cognitive behavioral analysis system of psychotherapy.* New York, NY: Guilford Press.

McGinn, M. M., Benson, L. A., & Christensen, A. (in press). Integrative behavioral couple therapy: An acceptance-based approach to improving relationship functioning. In J. Herbert and E. Forman (Eds.), *Acceptance and mindfulness in cognitive behavior therapy.* Hoboken, NJ: Wiley.

Meichenbaum, D. (1977) *Cognitive behavior modification: An integrated approach.* New York: Plenum Press.

Merton, R. K. (1942). Science and technology in a democratic order. *Journal of Legal and Political Sociology, 1,* 115–126.

Merton, R. K. (1957). Priorities in scientific discovery: A chapter in the sociology of science. *American Sociological Review, 22,* 635–659.

Mischel, W. (1968). *Personality and assessment.* New York, NY: Wiley.

Mitroff, I. I. (1974). *The subjective side of science: A philosophical inquiry into the psychology of the Apollo moon scientists.* Amsterdam: Elsevier.

Peterson, D. R. (1968). *The clinical study of social behavior.* New York, NY: Appleton Century Crofts.

Robins, C. J., & Rosenthal, M. Z. (in press). Dialectical behavior therapy. In J. Herbert and E. Forman (Eds.), *Acceptance and mindfulness in cognitive behavior therapy.* Hoboken, NJ: Wiley.

Rosen, G. M., & Davison, G. C. (2003). Psychology should list empirically supported principles of change (ESPs) and not credential trademarked therapies or other treatment packages. *Behavior Modification, 27,* 300–312.

Segal, Z. V., Williams, J. M. G., & Teasdale, J. D. (2002). *Mindfulness-based cognitive therapy for depression: A new approach to preventing relapse.* New York, NY: Guilford Press.

Salmon, P. G., Sephton, S. E., & Dreeben, S. J. (in press). Mindfulness-based stress reduction. In J. Herbert and E. Forman (Eds.), *Acceptance and mindfulness in cognitive behavior therapy.* Hoboken, NJ: Wiley.

Shapiro, D. H., Jr. (1978). *Precision nirvana.* Englewood Cliffs, NJ: Prentice-Hall.

Skinner, B. F. (1950). Are theories of learning necessary? *Psychological Review, 57,* 193–216.

Strupp, H. H., & Binder, J. L. (1984). *Psychotherapy in a new key.* New York, NY: Basic Books.

Teasdale, J. D. (1988). Cognitive vulnerability to persistent depression. *Cognition and Emotion, 2,* 247–274.

Teasdale, J.D. (1993). Emotion and two kinds of meaning: Cognitive therapy and applied cognitive science. *Behaviour Research and Therapy, 31,* 339–354.

Thoresen, C. E., & Mahoney, M. J. (1974). *Behavioral self-control.* New York: Holt, Rinehart, and Winston.

Watson, J. (1968). *The double helix.* New York, NY: Mentor Books.

Wells, A. (in press). Metacognitive therapy. In J. Herbert and E. Forman (Eds.), *Acceptance and mindfulness in cognitive behavior therapy.* Hoboken, NJ: Wiley.

Westen, D., Novotny, C. M., & Thompson-Brenner, H. (2004). The empirical status of empirically supported psychotherapies: Assumptions, findings, and reporting in controlled clinical trials. *Psychological Bulletin, 130*, 631–663.

Wilson, G.T. (1982). Psychotherapy process and procedure: The behavioral mandate. *Behavior Therapy, 13*, 291–312.

Wilson, G. T.,Wilfley, D. E., Agras, S., & Bryson, S. W. (2010). Psychological treatments of binge eating disorder. *Archives of General Psychiatry, 67*, 94–101.

Wilson, K. G., Bordieri, M. J., Flynn, M. K., Lucas, N. N., & Slater, R. M. (in press). Understanding acceptance and commitment therapy in context: A history of similarities and differences with other cognitive behavior therapies. In J. Herbert and E. Forman (Eds.), *Acceptance and mindfulness in cognitive behavior therapy*. Hoboken, NJ: Wiley.

# Author Index

Moldoveanu, M., 155
Moneta, G. B., 98
Montorio, I., 99
Moore, A., 155
Moore, E. L., 276
Moore, J., 193
Moore, L., 256
Moore, M., 64
Moore, M. T., 10, 63, 65, 119, 252
Moore, R. G., 11, 18, 47, 62, 63, 64, 66, 71, 72, 75, 149, 150, 254
Morone, N. E., 150
Morrison, A. P., 98
Morrison, K., 37
Morrow, J., 196, 197
Morse, J. Q., 165, 186, 187
Moscovitch, D. A., 276
Mouse, A., 295, 302
Moussavi, S., 57
Moyers, B., 133
Mulberry, S., 165
Mulick, P., 205
Mulick, P. S., 197, 201, 203
Mulkens, S., 73
Mullane, C., 205
Muller, D., 154
Muris, P., 98, 99
Murphy, G. E., 47, 74
Murray, A. M., 186
Murray, C. J. L., 57
Murray, H. W., 306
Muto, T., 206, 299
Myers, S., 12, 84, 99, 100, 101, 253, 254

Naparstek, J., 97
Napolitano, L., 125
Napolitano, L. A., 125
Natens, L., 90
Nathan, P., 73
Naugle, A., 205
Nearing, K. I., 114
Negi, L. T., 154
Neisser, U., 270
Nelson, C. B., 255
Nelson, T. O., 90
Nevid, J. S., 27
Newman, C. F., 27
Newman, M. G., 73
Nguyen, L., 278
Niccolls, R., 255, 256
Nicholas, C., 205
Niemann, L., 149, 150, 278, 298
Nilsson, A., 256, 257
Nolen-Hoeksema, S., 62, 83, 96, 196, 197
Norcross, J. C., 147
Nordahl, H. M., 102
Norman, W. H., 44, 47
Novak, J., 188
Novotny, C. M., 331
Nuevo, R., 99

Nugent, N. R., 64
Nussbaum, M., 124
Nyberg, E., 165

O'Donohue, W. T., 206
O'Reardon, J. P., 43, 44, 59
Obsessive Compulsive Cognitions Working Group, 94
Oei, T. P. S., 41, 44
Oh, D., 75, 278
Ohrt, T., 42
Oien, P.A., 166
Ojanen, M., 257, 295, 296
Okiishi, J., 218
Olendzki, B., 205
Olendzki, N., 68, 152
Olinger, L. J., 29
Ollendick, T. H., 26, 300
Olson, J. M., 40
Olsson, G. L., 306
Oman, D., 174
Ong, J. C., 298
Onstad, S., 166
Orsillo, S. M., 37, 38, 75, 144, 302
Ospina, M. B., 58, 75
Öst, L., 37, 256, 257
Öst, L.-G., 126, 281, 298, 303
Ottenbreit, N. D., 203
Otto, M., 138
Otto, M. W., 41
Ouimet, A. J., 38, 40

Pace, T. W., 154
Padesky, C. A., 30, 31, 32
Padilla, M., 255, 256
Pagoto, S. L, 205
Painter, M., 273, 274
Paivio, S. C., 112, 121
Palm, K. M., 256
Panzarella, C., 41
Papa, A., 284
Papageorgiou, C., 83, 85, 90, 96, 98, 101, 102, 253
Park, J., 153
Parker, C. H., 300
Parker, L. E., 96
Parloff, M. B., 320
Pasch, L., 223
Patel, K. D., 154
Patel, T., 12, 101, 253, 254
Patel, V., 57
Patelis-Siotis, I., 27, 33, 39, 47
Patijn, J., 9
Paykel, E. S., 66, 254
Pbert, L., 144, 149
Pederson, R., 47, 62, 64, 112
Pepper, S. C., 280
Perkins, T. S., 40, 41, 43
Perry, J. C., 57
Persons, J. B., 41, 112

# Subject Index